# The Palgrave Handbook of Sound Design and Music in Screen Media

Liz Greene • Danijela Kulezic-Wilson
Editors

# The Palgrave Handbook of Sound Design and Music in Screen Media

Integrated Soundtracks

*Editors*
Liz Greene
Liverpool John Moores University
UK

Danijela Kulezic-Wilson
University College Cork
Ireland

ISBN 978-1-349-70380-7         ISBN 978-1-137-51680-0   (eBook)
DOI 10.1057/978-1-137-51680-0

Library of Congress Control Number: 2016959564

© The Editor(s) (if applicable) and The Author(s) 2016
The author(s) has/have asserted their right(s) to be identified as the author(s) of this work in accordance with the Copyright, Designs and Patents Act 1988.
This work is subject to copyright. All rights are solely and exclusively licensed by the Publisher, whether the whole or part of the material is concerned, specifically the rights of translation, reprinting, reuse of illustrations, recitation, broadcasting, reproduction on microfilms or in any other physical way, and transmission or information storage and retrieval, electronic adaptation, computer software, or by similar or dissimilar methodology now known or hereafter developed.
The use of general descriptive names, registered names, trademarks, service marks, etc. in this publication does not imply, even in the absence of a specific statement, that such names are exempt from the relevant protective laws and regulations and therefore free for general use.
The publisher, the authors and the editors are safe to assume that the advice and information in this book are believed to be true and accurate at the date of publication. Neither the publisher nor the authors or the editors give a warranty, express or implied, with respect to the material contained herein or for any errors or omissions that may have been made.

Cover image: © Olga Kuzmenko

Printed on acid-free paper

This Palgrave Macmillan imprint is published by Springer Nature
The registered company is Macmillan Publishers Ltd. London
The registered company address is: The Campus, 4 Crinan Street, London, N1 9XW, United Kingdom

# Acknowledgements

The editors would like to thank Kevin Donnelly, the series editor, for suggesting this project and Palgrave editors Chris Penfold, Harry Fanshawe and Lina Aboujieb for nurturing it from proposal to publication. We are grateful to our respective institutions, Dublin City University and University College Cork, for supporting this anthology throughout the process. We would also like to thank the Centre for Media Research at University of Ulster (Coleraine) for their initial support during our doctoral studies.

Liz Greene would like to thank her colleagues in the School of Communications, at Dublin City University and is grateful for financial support received through the Faculty of Humanities and Social Sciences Book Publication Scheme. On a personal note, thanks, above all, goes to Niamh, Dario and Marmaduke.

Danijela Kulezic-Wilson would like to thank University College Cork for assisting the realization of this project with sabbatical leave, the CACSSS Research Support Fund, the CACSSS Research Publication Fund and the Departmental Research Fund. She would also like to thank her colleagues from the Department of Music for their help and advice. The biggest thank you goes to her husband Ian for his unwavering support.

Most of all we would like to thank our contributors for their commitment and patience during the protracted process of putting this anthology together.

This book received financial support from the Faculty of Humanities and Social Sciences Book Publication Scheme at Dublin City University. It also received financial support from the College of Arts, Celtic Studies and Social Science Research Publication Fund, University College Cork.

# Contents

| | | |
|---|---|---|
| 1 | Introduction<br>*Liz Greene and Danijela Kulezic-Wilson* | 1 |
| Part I | Boundaries and Their Disintegration | 15 |
| 2 | From Noise: Blurring the Boundaries of the Soundtrack<br>*Liz Greene* | 17 |
| 3 | Interview 1: Sound Recording, Sound Design and Collaboration—An Interview with Ann Kroeber<br>*Liz Greene* | 33 |
| 4 | Organizing Sound: Labour Organizations and Power Struggles that Helped Define Music and Sound in Hollywood<br>*Gianluca Sergi* | 43 |
| 5 | Mixing as a Hyperorchestration Tool<br>*Sergi Casanelles* | 57 |
| 6 | Emotional Sound Effects and Metal Machine Music: Soundworlds in *Silent Hill* Games and Films<br>*K.J. Donnelly* | 73 |

## Part II  Presence, Immersion, Space — 89

**7** Towards 3-D Sound: Spatial Presence and the Space Vacuum — 91
*Miguel Mera*

**8** Inner and Outer Worlds in the Film *Gravity*:
A Multidisciplinary Approach — 113
*Gilbert Gabriel and David Sonnenschein*

**9** Intertwining Music and Sound in Film — 123
*Martine Huvenne*

**10** Interview 2: Reality and Representation—An Interview
with Dario Marianelli — 139
*Miguel Mera*

## Part III  Listening: Affect and Body — 151

**11** Sound Effects/Sound Affects: 'Meaningful' Noise
in the Cinema — 153
*James Wierzbicki*

**12** Listening to Violence: Point-of-Audition Sound, Aural
Interpellation, and the Rupture of Hearing — 169
*Tony Grajeda*

**13** Acoustic Disgust: Sound, Affect, and Cinematic Violence — 183
*Lisa Coulthard*

## Part IV  Time and Memory — 195

**14** Mad Sound and the Crystal-Image: The Soundtrack
of Rivette's *L'Amour fou* — 197
*Byron Almén and James Buhler*

**15** The Sonic Realm in *The Quatermass Experiment*: Medium
and Genre and Sound — 213
*Robynn J. Stilwell*

| 16 | Sound, Music and Memory in Jia Zhangke's 'Hometown Trilogy'<br>*Philippa Lovatt* | 229 |
|---|---|---|
| 17 | Vinyl Noise and Narrative in CD-Era Indiewood<br>*Ian Garwood* | 245 |
| 18 | Interview 3: Mixing Punk Rock, Classical, and New Sounds in Film Music—An Interview with Brian Reitzell<br>*Meghan Joyce Tozer* | 261 |

| Part V | Breaking Conventions | 271 |
|---|---|---|
| 19 | From Analogue to Digital: Synthesizers and Discourses of Film Sound in the 1980s<br>*Katherine Spring* | 273 |
| 20 | Unlearning Film School: The 'lo-fi' Soundtracks of Joe Swanberg<br>*Nessa Johnston* | 289 |
| 21 | The Janus Project: Cristobal Tapia de Veer's *Utopia*, Anempathetic Empathy and the Radicalization of Convention<br>*Annette Davison and Nicholas Reyland* | 305 |
| 22 | Interview 4: Building Bridges: Sound Design as Collaboration, as Style and as Music in *The Bridge*—An Interview with Carl Edström<br>*Annette Davison and Martin Parker* | 321 |

| Part VI | The Sound of Machines and Non-Humans | 329 |
|---|---|---|
| 23 | The Sound of an Android's Soul: Music, MIDI and Muzak in *Time Of Eve*<br>*Philip Brophy* | 331 |

24  The Sounds in the Machine: Hirokazu Tanaka's
    Cybernetic Soundscape for *Metroid*                             347
    *William Gibbons*

25  Redundancy and Information in Explanatory Voice-Ins
    and Voice-Offs                                                  361
    *Cormac Deane*

26  Interview 5: Under the Skin of Film Sound—An
    Interview with Johnnie Burn                                     377
    *John Hough*


Part VII   The Musicality of Soundtrack                             385

27  Electroacoustic Composition and the British Documentary
    Tradition                                                       387
    *Andy Birtwistle*

28  Renegotiating the Overture: The Use of Sound and Music
    in the Opening Sequences of *A Single Man* and *Shame*          403
    *Adam Melvin*

29  Interview 6: Orchestration, Collaboration,
    and the Integrated Soundtrack—An Interview
    with Matt Dunkley                                               421
    *Ian Sapiro*

30  Musically Conceived Sound Design, Musicalization of Speech
    and the Breakdown of Film Soundtrack Hierarchy                  429
    *Danijela Kulezic-Wilson*


Filmography                                                         445

Index                                                               453

# Notes on Contributors

**Byron Almén** is Associate Professor of Music Theory at the University of Texas at Austin. He is the author of *A Theory of Musical Narrative* and co-editor, with Edward Pearsall, of *Approaches to Meaning in Music*, both published by Indiana University Press. He is the co-author, with Stefan Kostka and Dorothy Payne, of the textbook *Tonal Harmony*.

**Andy Birtwistle** is Reader in Film and Sound at Canterbury Christ Church University, and is the author of *Cinesonica: Sounding Film and Video* (2010). In addition to research on film sound, he has published articles on artists' film and video, modernism and music, and Taiwan cinema. Andy is also a sound artist and filmmaker, and is currently the Director of the Centre for Practice Based Research in the Arts at Canterbury Christ Church University.

**Philip Brophy** writes on film, sound and music among other things. www.philipbrophy.com

**James Buhler** teaches at the University of Texas at Austin and has authored more than 20 articles on music, sound and film. He is co-author of *Hearing the Movies*, now in its second edition.

**Sergi Casanelles** is a composer for concert and film music. He has completed a PhD in Film Music Composition at NYU. His research is focused on studying the Hyperorchestra or how new technologies interact with music in film and how this interaction affects its aesthetics. He works as an Adjunct Professor at NYU Steinhardt, teaching Film Music Composition, History and Contemporary Technological approaches.

**Lisa Coulthard** is Associate Professor of Film Studies in the Department of Theatre and Film at the University of British Columbia. She has published widely on contemporary European and American cinemas, film violence and film sound. She holds a SSHRC Insight Grant for a study of cinematic sound and violence in the digital age and is currently completing a book on sound in the films of Quentin Tarantino.

**Annette Davison** is Senior Lecturer in Music at the Reid School of Music, University of Edinburgh. Recent publications explore music for television and short form promotional media. Her essays on the main title and end credit sequences for recent television drama serials can be found in *The Oxford Handbook of New Audiovisual Media* (2013), the journal *Music, Sound and the Moving Image* (2014) and on viewer behaviour in relation to these sequences in the Danish journal *SoundEffects* (2013).

**Cormac Deane** is Lecturer in Film and Media at the Institute of Art, Design and Technology, Dublin. His translation of Christian Metz's final work, *Impersonal Enunciation*, was published in February 2016. He is currently preparing a book-length media archaeology of the control room.

**K.J. Donnelly** is Reader in Film at the University of Southampton. He is author of *Magical Musical Tour* (2015*)*, *Occult Aesthetics* (2013), *British Film Music and Film Musicals* (2007), *The Spectre of Sound* (2005) and *Pop Music in British Cinema* (2001). He is also editor (with Phil Hayward) of *Tuning In: Music in Science Fiction Television* (2011), (with Will Gibbons and Neil Lerner) *Music in Video Games* (2014) and *Film Music: Critical Approaches* (2001).

**Gilbert Gabriel** is a professional musician Lecturer and Ivor Novello nominee whose compositions and songs have featured in TV, films and radio around the world. His film music credits include Hollywood films *Ferris Bueller's Day Off*, *Trains, Planes and Automobiles*, Diane Keaton's documentary *Heaven* as well as the worldwide hit *Life in a Northern Town* (The Dream Academy). He currently lectures on film soundtracks in England and Norway, and is External Examiner for Westminster University's Commercial Music Degree.

**Ian Garwood** is Senior Lecturer in Film and Television Studies at University of Glasgow. He has published extensively, in written and video essay form, on the relationship between sound, music and the moving image. He is the author of the book-length study, *The Pop Song in Film* (included in Close-Up 01 (2006)) and the monograph *The Sense of Film Narration* (2013).

**William Gibbons** is Associate Professor of Musicology and Associate Dean of the College of Fine Arts at Texas Christian University. He has published widely in the fields of musical multimedia and opera studies, including the monograph *Building the Operatic Museum: Eighteenth-Century Opera in Fin-de-siècle Paris* (2013) and the edited volume *Music in Video Games: Studying Play* (2014). His new book, *Unlimited Replays: The Art of Classical Music in Video Games*, is forthcoming.

**Tony Grajeda** is Associate Professor of Cultural Studies in the Department of English, University of Central Florida. He is co-editor of *Lowering the Boom: Critical Studies in Film Sound*, *Music, Sound, and Technology in America: A Documentary History of Early Phonograph, Cinema, and Radio*, and "The Future of Sound Studies," a special issue of *Music, Sound, and the Moving*

*Image*. His work on sound and culture has appeared in several anthologies, including *Hop on Pop*, *Ubiquitous Musics* and *Living Stereo*.

**Liz Greene** is Senior Lecturer in Filmmaking in the Liverpool Screen School, Liverpool John Moores University. Her research interests are in film sound, the audiovisual essay and documentary. She is on the editorial board of *The Soundtrack* journal and the International Advisory Board of *Alphaville*. She won an Irish Film and Television Academy Award for best sound in 2006 for *Pure Mule*. She continues to work in film sound and recently worked on *We Were There* (2014), *Breathe* (2015) and *Yakov Yanki Jack* (2015).

**John Hough** holds a BSc in Information Technology from the National University of Ireland at Galway and an MA in Postproduction with Sound Design from the University of York. He has previous experience working as a software developer, and is currently employed as Senior Technical Officer at the Department of Music, University College Cork. His current interests include production and postproduction sound for screen media, in particular the use of ambient sound design in film.

**Martine Huvenne** is Lecturer and researcher at the KASK & Conservatory, School of Arts Gent. Her research is focused on the auditory part of the creative process in the audiovisual arts. She obtained a PHD from UVA in 2012 with a dissertation on a phenomenological approach of sound in film. Huvenne is Curator of the Film Fest Gent annual Seminar on Music and Sound in Film. She also coordinates EPAS, a European postgraduate programme in Arts in Sound (www.epasound.org).

**Nessa Johnston** is Lecturer in Media, Film and Television at Edge Hill University, UK. Her research focuses on film sound production practice and soundtrack aesthetics in low-budget, American independent, experimental, alternative and cult films. She has had articles published in the journals *The Soundtrack*; *Music, Sound and the Moving Image*; *Popular Music*; *Alphaville*; and *The Velvet Light Trap*. She is also an Associate Editor of *The New Soundtrack*.

**Danijela Kulezic-Wilson** teaches film music, film sound and comparative arts at University College Cork. Her research interests include approaches to film that emphasize its inherent musical properties, the use of *musique concrète* and silence in film, the musicality of sound design and musical aspects of Beckett's plays. She is the author of *The Musicality of Narrative Film* (2015) and has published in journals such as *Music and the Moving Image*, *The New Soundtrack*, *Alphaville* and *Music, Sound and the Moving Image*.

**Philippa Lovatt** is Lecturer in Media and Communications at the University of Stirling. Her research focusses on the relationship between sound, space and embodiment with a particular focus on Asian cinema and experimental audiovisual work. She has published in *Screen*, *The New Soundtrack*, and *SoundEffects*, and is currently writing a monograph on Sound Design and the

Ethics of Listening in Global Cinema. She is an associate editor of *The New Soundtrack* and a founding member of the UK Sound Studies Network.

**Adam Melvin** is a composer and Lecturer in Popular and Contemporary music at Ulster University's School of Creative Arts & Technologies, Derry~Londonderry, Northern Ireland. A great deal of both his compositional and research practice is concerned with interrogating the relationship between music, sound, site and the visual arts, particularly moving image. He has received numerous international performances and broadcasts of his music while his research has been published in *The Soundtrack*.

**Miguel Mera** is an audiovisual composer and musicologist with a particular interest in the intersection between theory and practice. Miguel has created music for numerous film and television projects. He is widely published in music and moving image studies and his work includes Mychael Danna's *The Ice Storm: a film score guide*, *European Film Music*, *The Routledge Companion to Screen Music and Sound*, and many diverse chapters and articles. He is Reader and Head of Music at City University London.

**Martin Parker** Sound is at its best when you know what you're doing but you don't know what's going to happen. I explore this idea across my work in composition, improvisation and sonic art by experimenting with sound technologies, people and places. I teach a number of courses as Programme Director of the MSc Sound Design at the University of Edinburgh and am slowly developing a trilogy of pieces designed especially for performance in cinemas. More information at www.tinpark.com.

**Nicholas Reyland** is Senior Lecturer in Music and Film Studies at Keele University. A specialist in screen and Polish music, he is the author of *Zbigniew Preisner's 'Three Colors' Trilogy: A Film Score Guide* and co-editor (with Michael Klein) of *Music and Narrative since 1900*, among many other publications. He is also a member of the editorial boards of the journals *Music Analysis* and *Twentieth-Century Music*.

**Ian Sapiro** is Senior Research Fellow and Lecturer in Music at the University of Leeds, specialising in film music, musical theatre, orchestration and the overlaps between them. He is co-investigator on *The Professional Career and Output of Trevor Jones* research project, and author of *Ilan Eshkeri's* Stardust: *A Film Score Guide* (2013). His forthcoming publications include a monograph *Scoring the Score: the Role of the Orchestrator in the Contemporary Film Industry* and book chapters on film-score orchestration and musical-theatre adaptation.

**Gianluca Sergi** is an Associate Professor in film and screen industries at the University of Nottingham, where he is also the Director of the Institute for Screen Industries Research. He has published widely on the film industry, production cultures and film sound in particular, including *The Dolby Era: Film Sound in Contemporary Hollywood*.

**David Sonnenschein** is the author of *Sound Design: The Expressive Power of Music, Voice, and Sound Effects in Cinema,* the recipient of the Motion Picture Sound Editors Golden Reel, and a lecturer in Europe, Asia and South America. He produces online webinars at www.SoundDesignForPros.com. Sonnenschein began his career making educational films for the University of California and has produced/directed six feature films. Trained in classical music, he also practices sound healing with didgeridoo. He is currently developing music-language games for autistic children with his company iQsonics.com.

**Katherine Spring** is Associate Professor in the Department of English and Film Studies at Wilfrid Laurier University. Her research on the history of film sound and music has appeared in *Cinema Journal, Film History*, and *Music and the Moving Image*, and her book, *Saying It With Songs: Popular Music and the Coming of Sound to Hollywood Cinema*, was published in the Oxford Music/Media Series (2013).

**Robynn J. Stilwell** (Georgetown University) is a musicologist whose research interests centre on the meaning of music as cultural work. Publications include essays on Beethoven and cinematic violence, musical form in Jane Austen, rockabilly and 'white trash', figure skating, French film musicals, psychoanalytic film theory and its implications for music and for female subjects, and the boundaries between sound and music in the cinematic soundscape. Her current project is a historical study of audiovisual modality in television.

**Meghan Joyce Tozer** is a film music scholar whose work examines the ways in which screenwriter-directors integrate music throughout the creative process, as evidenced in their screenplays and collaborations with musician-composers. She recently earned an MM in Voice Performance and a PhD (ABD) in musicology from the University of California, Santa Barbara; her BA is in Music and English from Harvard University.

**James Wierzbicki** teaches musicology at the University of Sydney; along with exploring questions of modernity and the postmodern, his research focuses on twentieth-century music in general and film music in particular. His books include *Film Music: A History*, monographs on Elliott Carter and the electronic score for the 1956 film *Forbidden Planet*, and—most recently—*Music in the Age of Anxiety: American Music in The Fifties.*

# List of Figures

| | | |
|---|---|---|
| Fig. 5.1 | Different interpretations of a crescendo using the Piano Roll notation system from Apple Logic Pro X (Digital Audio Workstation) | 60 |
| Fig. 5.2 | Conceptual diagram for the hyperinstrument | 65 |
| Fig. 7.1 | *Gravity* (Alfonso Cuarón, 2013) opening sequence, 'The Hoover' (Logic Pro) | 105 |
| Fig. 7.2 | *Gravity* (Alfonso Cuarón, 2013) opening c. 37 seconds, surround vectorscope representation (5.1) (Izotope Insight Vectorscope) | 105 |
| Fig. 8.1 | Sound Spheres—David Sonnenschein (2011) | 117 |
| Fig. 8.2 | Dream States—Gilbert Gabriel (2013) | 119 |
| Fig. 15.1 | Futuristic and retrograde technology (*The Quatermass Experiment*, BBC, 1953). Left (a), Judith Carroon follows the rocket's orbits on a futuristic fiberoptic device; right (b), Quatermass and the technicians in mission control gather around a bulky stand microphone to follow the report from Tarooma Range, even though the sound appears to be coming from the small round speaker behind their heads | 219 |
| Fig. 15.2 | Quatermass and the Man from the Ministry (*The Quatermass Experiment*, BBC, 1953; *The Quatermass Xperiment*, Val Guest, 1955). In the television production (top left and right), the intercutting and body orientation suggests a semblance of face-to-face dialogue mediated by the telephone; the film (bottom) takes a more cinematic (and hostile) approach, with Quatermass and the man from the Ministry in the foreground, in the front and back seats, respectively, and other characters in the vehicle beside them | 221 |
| Fig. 24.1 | *Metroid* (Satoru Okada, 1986), 'Silence' (transcription by author) | 351 |
| Fig. 24.2 | *Metroid*, 'Tourian' (transcription by author) | 352 |
| Fig. 24.3 | Mother Brain in *Metroid* (Satoru Okada, 1986) | 355 |
| Fig. 24.4 | *Metroid*, 'Zebetite' (transcription by author) | 355 |
| Fig. 28.1 | George (Colin Firth) in *A Single Man* (Tom Ford, 2009) | 411 |
| Fig. 28.2 | Brandon (Michael Fassbender) in *Shame* (Steve McQueen, 2011) | 413 |

# LIST OF TABLE

Table 23.1  Music cues in *Time of Eve*  336

CHAPTER 1

# Introduction

*Liz Greene and Danijela Kulezic-Wilson*

The idea for this book has been a long time in gestation. We found ourselves conducting doctoral research at the same time, in the same institution (University of Ulster, Coleraine), and discovered a common interest in the totality of the soundtrack, although working in the separate disciplines of film music (Kulezic-Wilson) and film sound design (Greene). We shared many conversations exploring this terrain in some depth, which over time evolved into the idea of producing a co-edited book on sound design and music. This anthology expanded beyond our initial plans in terms of its length and the range of material under investigation to include a broader conceptualization of sound and music in screen media. This resulted in addressing areas of research that lay outside one or other of our areas of expertise, which we found to be both an advantage and a challenge. One of the clear advantages of having our previous training in different camps is that each of us was able to harness knowledge from our own area of research while posing questions about the others. The challenge was that we sometimes found we had different understandings of the same terms, or used and applied terminology differently. This nevertheless led to many fruitful conversations which allowed us to tease out the specific (inter) disciplinary issues of this volume which, we believe, is to its benefit.

The recent surge of scholarly activity addressing the habitual separation between audio and visual aspects of film in theory, pedagogy and practice may have alleviated the long-standing underrepresentation of sonic aspects of film in scholarship but it has also elucidated another division within the discipline, that between film sound and film music. While some scholarly conferences and symposia encourage the integration of these two sub-disciplines

L. Greene
Liverpool John Moores University, UK

D. Kulezic-Wilson
University College Cork, Ireland

in every possible way except in name, a number of recent monographs and edited publications about sound and music make it clear that the segregation still persists. One of the reasons for this, of course, is the same one that kept film music scholarship separated from the rest of film discourse for decades, namely the lack of musical education and possibly terminology which would give non-music specialists the confidence to address musical aspects of film. At the same time, a palpable resistance among some film music scholars to include sound in their field of research has exposed surprising signs of territorialism in a field which prides itself in being multidisciplinary. However, the fact that boundaries between scoring and sound design in contemporary cinema are becoming increasingly blurred has affected both film music and sound studies by expanding their range of topics and the scope of their analysis beyond those traditionally addressed. The use of *musique concrète* in sound design, the integration of speech and/or sound effects into film scores as well as musically conceived soundscapes—to mention only some examples of innovative techniques—demand new approaches to the study of the soundtrack which are prepared to consider the increasingly intertwined elements of silence, noise, speech, sound effects and music as an integrated whole.

This anthology does not attempt to offer a foundational theory for film sound or film music since the groundwork for both disciplines has been firmly laid already. One of the first significant publications to alert the field of film studies to the relevance of film sound and film music came in 1980 with a special edition of *Yale French Studies* on 'Cinema Sound' edited by Rick Altman. Since the mid-1980s when two seminal books appeared within two years—*Film Sound: Theory and Practice*[1] edited by Elisabeth Weis and John Belton (1985) and Claudia Gorbman's *Unheard Melodies: Narrative Film Music* (1987)—both disciplines have flourished remarkably, opening up numerous questions about the creation, function and perception of sound and music in film and setting out directions for further research in many significant monographs and edited collections, too numerous to be all listed here. The intention of this volume is rather to move the discussion forward by bringing these two fields together through the idea of an integrated soundtrack. The necessity to consider and communicate the functional interdependence of all elements of the soundtrack and the result of their joint accomplishment has already been addressed by some scholars in journal articles, historical volumes and monographs, including Michel Chion's highly influential *Audio-Vision* (1994); David Sonnenschein's practice-based exploration of music, voice and sound effects in *Sound Design* (2001); the meticulously exhaustive study of music and sound in film history *Hearing the Movies* by James Buhler, David Neumeyer and Rob Deemer (2010); and the most recent historical account of soundtrack development in *Sound: Dialogue, Music, and Effects* edited by Kathryn Kalinak (2015). In terms of advancing an interdisciplinary discussion that concerns various aspects of and a range of approaches to audiovisual media, notable steps were taken recently in two remarkable handbooks published by Oxford University Press—*New Audiovisual Aesthetics* (Richardson, Gorbman and

Vernallis, 2013) and *Sound and Image in Digital Media* (Vernallis, Herzog and Richardson, 2013). A number of specialized journals that appeared in recent years established their inclusive reputation by encouraging submissions in areas pertaining to all elements of film soundtrack, including *Music, Sound and the Moving Image* (2007–), *The Soundtrack* (2008–), *Music and the Moving Image* (2008–), *The New Soundtrack* (2010–), *Screen Sound Journal* (2010–) and *SoundEffects* (2011–).

A boundary-breaking ethos is also at the heart of this volume which has been conceived with the specific intention of bridging the existing gap between film sound and film music scholarship by bringing together distinguished scholars from both disciplines who are challenging the constraints of their subject areas by thinking about the soundtrack in its totality. This is also emphasized by the title of this anthology which, in comparison to other recent publications that address both sound and music, takes sound *design* and music as the subjects of its investigation. Francis Ford Coppola first used the term sound design in cinema to offer a screen credit for the creative work of Walter Murch on *Apocalypse Now* (Francis Ford Coppola, 1979), reflecting Murch's multifaceted involvement in the post-production of the film. Sound design evokes the idea of a 'holistic' approach to film and soundtrack and is considered here in that broadest sense from pre-production through production and into post-production, in contrast to narrower definitions which emerged later, referring mostly to the production of sound effects in post-production. The subtitle 'integrated soundtrack', on the other hand, refers for our purposes to practices, theories and histories, that consciously combine sound design and music into the overall concept and design of screen media. And while in some chapters the primary focus of investigation leans more towards either sound design or score for the purpose of in-depth discussion, each recognizes the functional interdependence of all sonic elements and that an effective soundtrack is the result of their joint achievement.

Another objective of this book is to look beyond the director as auteur and investigate the critical production of the screen media soundtrack with attention to sound and music personnel considering issues at stake below and above the line, exploring the whole process of producing an integrated soundtrack and outlining the distinct procedures involved in its creation. The collaborative media of filmmaking, animation, game design and television production are addressed not only in scholarly chapters but also through interviews with key practitioners that include sound recordists, sound designers, composers, orchestrators and music supervisors who honed their skills on films, TV programmes, video games, commercials and music videos.

While this anthology addresses historical events and circumstances that affected the evolution of the soundtrack either in terms of departmentalization or integration, most chapters focus on contemporary works, highlighting different practices from experimental, avant-garde and art house cinema to blockbuster films such as the enormously successful *Gravity* (Alfonso Cuarón, 2013), the subject of two chapters of this handbook. Many examples draw from art house cinema or independent filmmaking and many of these works come from Anglophone cinema. Chapters exploring aspects of French, Chinese and Japanese cinema broaden the focus of the works covered but it must be noted that there are whole regions, nations and continents that do not receive their deserved attention within this anthology. This is partly due to how the anthology evolved but also reflects the work being undertaken in the field, illuminating the need for further research into integrated approaches in non-Anglophone cinema.

On the other hand, the topics investigated in this anthology reflect accurately the concerns and interests of contemporary scholarship and not only that which deals with music and sound. The concepts of presence and immersion have been for some time on the list of 'hot' topics in film theory, posing questions about the relationship between corporeal and cognitive types of perception and response to cinema (see Elsaesser and Hagener, 2010), but also between different aesthetic and philosophical approaches to the ideas of cinematic form and storytelling (Jaffe, 2014). The enduring fascination with the dichotomy of body and mind—or the emphasis of one over the other—is apparent in this volume as well, epitomized in distinct sections discussing corporeal and affective aspects of cinema perception and representation on the one hand and more elusive issues of time and memory on the other. Amidst concerns about the nature of audiovisual spectatorship and representations of consciousness and time, history and memory, body, affect and violence, another theme looms large in this volume, that of boundary- and convention-breaking, inspiring innovative scholarship about the most current and relevant developments in both theory and practice. And while some chapters emphasize the historical or artistic and aesthetic contexts that enabled new practices to flourish, others focus on the unavoidable issue of technology. An ingredient of modern life which permeates every aspect of our existence and almost all our activities, technology is considered here not only as a catalyst of change and innovation but also as a mirror held up to humanity.

The content of this anthology could have been structured in a number of ways as there are many topical overlaps among the chapters. Its division into seven parts is to facilitate easier navigation, but the section headings—Boundaries and their Disintegration; Presence, Immersion, Space; Listening: Affect and Body; Time and Memory; Breaking Conventions; The Sound of Machines and Non-Humans; and The Musicality of Soundtrack—should by no means be perceived as boundaries and we certainly expect that they will not lessen the communication between chapters.

Boundaries and their disintegration is one of the running themes of this book and although only the title of Part I cites this topic directly, it is pertinent to many chapters, permeating the discussions about industry, labour, technology, aesthetics and audiovisual spectatorship. In Chapter 2, Liz Greene addresses the conceptual demarcations between noise, sound, sound effects, music and silence, commenting on the ambiguities in their definitions and the way their use in the audiovisual context emphasizes their shared qualities. Using primarily examples from Alan Splet's work on David Lynch's films, Greene demonstrates how the sounds—or noises—that 'we have learned to ignore', whether because they are perceived as silence or as a 'lack of sound', can have not only meaningful but also a highly effective role in sound design. Her point about the emotional impact of sound design that 'sounds like noise but acts like music' resonates with arguments from a number of other chapters and the increasing scholarly interest in dissipating boundaries between soundtrack elements and their functions. Greene's argument is complemented by her interview with Ann Kroeber in Chapter 3, which considers the collaborative roles of sound recording and sound design in screen media industries. Kroeber worked alongside her partner Alan Splet until his death in 1994 and has continued to work in film and video game sound. She discusses her work as a woman in a male-dominated field and stresses the positive developments in recent years in the film and game industries. The owner and curator of *Sound Mountain*, a sound effects library, Kroeber is also a specialist in animal recordings. In this interview, she talks about her approach to animal vocalization on *Duma* (Carroll Ballard, 2005), the musicality of animal sound and how through her sound design she was able to place the animal voices alongside the music track. She also discusses the production sound and music in *Blue Velvet* (David Lynch, 1986), her work on games and her collaborative approach to pedagogy.

The demarcations that Greene addresses in her chapter were in many ways defined by the organization of departmentalized labour in the Hollywood industry which affected the division between music and sound departments. As Gianluca Sergi reveals in Chapter 4, this division has its roots in the era when the introduction of synchronized sound started to threaten the jobs of musicians employed by the industry for live screen performances. The fierce fight to protect these jobs and the propaganda battle led by the American Federation of Musicians during their Music Defense League campaign, Sergi argues, eventually 'slammed the door on closer integration of music and sound in the cinema right at the very moment when sound departments were being established', with familiar consequences. The gradual disintegration of these boundaries many decades later and various forms of collaboration between sound and music departments can be attributed to several factors, including advancements in technology and the influence of changes in contemporary music, as discussed by Andy Birtwistle and Martine Huvenne in later sections in their respective chapters. The impact of the former in particular looms large in this volume, as many of our contributors address various forms of transformations and innovations in screen media resulting from the use of digital technology.

In Chapter 5 Sergi Casanelles argues that the extensive use of computer technology in sound and music (post)production creates a *hyperorchestra*—a virtual music ensemble which facilitates a music creation process that transcends the foundations of Western classical music based on the musical score. This virtual orchestra employs *hyperinstruments*—an array of traditionally recorded instruments, synthesized sounds or virtual instruments from sample libraries which are tailored to the needs of the audiovisual context by using sound processing and mixing. Casanelles contends that this manipulation of musical content produced by hyperinstruments in the process of hyperorchestration erases ontological differences between music and sound design, naturally encouraging integration of the soundtrack elements.

In Chapter 6 Kevin Donnelly also emphasizes the importance of technology in developing composers' taste for manipulating sound electronically, allowing the integration of recorded sound effects with music. His discussion about the interchangeable quality of musical and sound effects in an audiovisual context extends to the world of video games, focusing on the similarities and overlaps between the *Silent Hill* game and film franchises. Donnelly posits that using game soundtracks as a model for the *Silent Hill* film soundtracks resulted in the subversion of their classical roles, creating sound effects that have an emotional character and music that appears unemotional and mechanical, evocative of the role of traditional sound effects.

In Part II, with a focus on the listening space of the audience Miguel Mera, as well as Gilbert Gabriel and David Sonnenschein, suggest ways to interpret spatial boundaries in sonic terms, their chapters offering distinctly different analyses of *Gravity*. In Chapter 7 Mera considers *Gravity* alongside other films set in the vacuum of outer space in order to tease out the differences between *immersion* and *presence* with a focus on Dolby Atmos sound and how this new technology has had an impact on the audience's listening space. Mera makes a compelling argument for adopting the more experiential, psychologically correct term *presence* over the more commonly applied screen media term *immersion*, concluding that in *Gravity* 'the soundscape moves beyond a purely objective-internal perspective and encourages the audience to *become* Ryan Stone' (the protagonist played by Sandra Bullock).

In Chapter 8 Gilbert Gabriel and David Sonnenschein, on the other hand, focus solely on *Gravity* to offer their conceptual models of 'sound spheres' and 'dream states' to illustrate how sound design and music are deployed at various points throughout the film to represent the main character's physical and psychological diegetic world and the audience's listening position. Gabriel and Sonnenschein contend that the protagonist's subjective experience can be best illustrated through close analysis of the film text and readings of the soundtrack through examination of speech, sound design and music. They turn to the writings of Michel Chion and Theo Van Leeuwen in order to describe the aural and mental journey undertaken by Ryan Stone as she attempts to make her way back to earth.

In Chapter 9 Martine Huvenne offers different case studies with *Last Days* (Gus Van Sant, 2005) and *Atonement* (Joe Wright, 2007) in order to explore how we listen to film soundtracks. She adopts a phenomenological theoretical frame that outlines issues of demarcation between sound effects and music. In her examples she discusses the incorporation of sound effects and field recordings into the films' sound design and score such as the inclusion of Hildegard Westerkamp's previously produced sound composition in the sound design of Blake's (Michael Pitt) walk in the woods in *Last Days*, and the sound of Briony's (Saoirse Ronan) typewriting featured in Dario Marianelli's score in

*Atonement*. Huvenne proposes that the listening position of the audience is key to determining what is considered sound or music within a screen text. Continuing the discussion of Marianelli's score, Miguel Mera's illuminating interview with the composer in Chapter 10 explores the integration of sound and music in Joe Wright's films *Atonement*, *The Soloist* (2009), and *Anna Karenina* (2012). Marianelli outlines the opportunities and challenges in representing truth in fiction films and his desire to convey through music deeper layers of the protagonists' emotional characterization.

In Part III, this theme of listening continues with a focus on affect and the body. In Chapter 11 James Wierzbicki discusses numerous examples of sound effects in cinema with the goal of seeking out how sound operates as sound affect. He argues that sound effects often closely match what is seen on screen but if sound is 'treated in a way that makes it somehow stand apart from the film's norm, the ring or the bark or the clink can be something quite remarkable'—an affective sound can be created. Wierzbicki offers an historical overview of sound effects in film and details the implication that Dolby noise reduction had on how we listen in the cinema. He concludes with examples of how the treatment of sound through point of audition (Michel Chion's term, which is an aural equivalent to point of view) can affectively impact an audience.

In Chapter 12 Tony Grajeda also draws on Chion's concept of point of audition to illustrate how this can be a very effective way for the soundtrack to be more clearly heard. Using examples from *Saving Private Ryan* (Steven Spielberg, 1998), *Three Kings* (David O. Russell, 1999), *The Pianist* (Roman Polanski, 2002), *There Will Be Blood* (Paul Thomas Anderson, 2007), *Children of Men* (Alfonso Cuarón, 2006), and *Cop Land* (James Mangold, 1997), Grajeda posits that when a character on screen is in danger of losing their hearing, 'in such cinematic moments of extreme point-of-audition … subjectivity through sound is amplified through its near absence, when we are asked to experience a privileged perspective aurally as paradoxically a form of rupture'. Grajeda argues that this moment of hearing loss and trauma can provide the most significant aural close-up within the soundtrack, offering detail amidst absence.

Lisa Coulthard continues this investigation into listening to violence and affect in Chapter 13, exploring the ideas of acoustic disgust and sonic hapticity as a means to reconsider violence in screen media. She offers examples of sounds that are unlistenable due to their sonic properties and issues of proximity and intimacy. Drawing on research from over 100 scenes of violence in film and television, Coulthard's analysis surveys the type of sound heard within specific contexts, challenging ocularcentric conclusions. She contends that 'moist' sounds are the most disgusting for audiences as 'the already disturbing intimacy of the mouth in addition to the discomfiting defamiliarization of the ordinary (breath, mouth sounds, food sounds) combines with the audio close-up to create the "too close" and "too far" of violent disgust and excessive violence'.

The topics of time and memory permeate all the chapters in Part IV even though each chapter focuses on different aspects of temporality and its representation through sound. In Jacques Rivette's *L'amour fou* (1969), discussed by Byron Almén and James Buhler in Chapter 14, the narrative time-line is fractured, starting from 'the end' and then 'rewound' to take us through the story of the unravelling of a marriage, possibly through the prism of the protagonist's memory. Almén and Buhler's analysis draws on Deleuze's concept of the crystal image where the difference between the real object and its mirror image is indiscernible. While elucidating a complex series of representational reflections epitomized in different layers of narration and temporality, Almén and Buhler focus on the use of sound and music to show how the couple's crumbling relationship is reflected in an increasingly disjointed treatment of sound.

In Robynn Stilwell's and Philippa Lovatt's chapters time is considered in relation to acoustic spaces which can signify a particular place, genre, culture or social context. In Chapter 15 Stilwell looks at different versions of the *Quatermass Experiment* television serial (1953 and 2005) and the 1955 *The Quatermass Xperiment* film, using them as case studies for exploring generic tropes and aesthetic parameters of different media formats. Her analytical comparison of the original *Quatermass* series (BBC, 1953) with the 1955 film version and the 2005 television remake illuminate both the specificities and the cross-media influences between the soundscapes of the different versions—the influence of radio aesthetics in the original television production, the shift of emphasis from science fiction to horror in the 1955 Hammer film—offering a unique insight into how sonic identification of a medium or genre is shaped by historical context and available technology. In Chapter 16 Lovatt, on the other hand, explores the construction of social and cultural spaces through sound and music in Jia Zhangke's Hometown Trilogy set during the 1970s and 1980s in rural northern China, and how music communicates the relationship between memory and history. From traditional to revolutionary and propaganda songs of the early post-Mao period, through illegal Taiwanese pop music, the sounds of Bollywood emanating from the local cinema to the electronic rock music of the reform-era, music in Zhangke's films is used to communicate the passing of time and the characters' adjustment to social and cultural transformations following the end of the Cultural Revolution.

Lovatt also draws attention to how the introduction of tape recorders and cassettes challenged the constrictions imposed by the communist regime, allowing people to create their own listening spaces defined by their own musical choices. The format of music's representation is at the heart of Chapter 17 in which Ian Garwood explores the narrative significance of vinyl records in American Indie films of the 1990s and early 2000s which appeared at the time when the commercial market was dominated by the CD format, making vinyl 'a sign of subcultural distinction'. Garwood's lucid analysis of *The Royal Tenenbaums* (2001), *Pulp Fiction* (1994) and *Ghost World* (2001) demonstrates that the overt references to vinyl in these films and its aural signature marked by surface noise, scratches and crackles are not only symptoms of fetishizing a particular era or subculture but also have an expressive weight in terms of narrative commentary and characterization.

Curiously enough, Garwood's and Lovatt's chapters are the only ones in this anthology which are concerned with compilation scores of predominantly popular music, suggesting that the concept of an integrated soundtrack is possibly more readily associated with originally composed scores. Garwood's chapter, though, as well as Huvenne's chapter which deals with the rather unconventional compilation score in *Last Days*, addresses some of the finest examples of the practice that has become known as 'auteur music' owing to directors' hands-on approach to music which is treated as a 'key thematic element and a marker of authorial style' (Gorbman, 2007, p. 149). And while the idea of a *mélomane* director in full charge of the compilation scoring rings true in the cases of directors such as Wes Anderson, Quentin Tarantino and Gus Van Sant in his Death Trilogy phase, the last contribution in Part IV, Meghan Joyce Tozer's interview with Brian Reitzell in Chapter 18, reminds us that the role of a skilful music supervisor should not be underestimated either. A former punk drummer, music supervisor, composer and long-term collaborator of Sofia Coppola who worked as music supervisor on *The Virgin Suicides* (1999), *Lost in Translation* (2003), *Marie Antoinette* (2006), *The Bling Ring* (2013) and on the latter as composer as well, Reitzell disperses some myths about the know-it-all approach of director-*mélomanes* and offers valuable insight into his 'collage'-like approach to choosing pre-existing music for some of the most celebrated compilation scores of Indiewood.

Shifting boundaries and breaking moulds are among the defining characteristics of contemporary audiovisual culture which are frequently addressed in this anthology. Forces of transformation are often the product of a combination of different influences and, as argued in the first two chapters of Part V, issues of economy and technology often play important roles in provoking new approaches. In Chapter 19, which focuses on the adoption of digital synthesizers by film sound professionals in the early 1980s, Katherine Spring draws on the concept of 'transectorial innovation' introduced by Paul Thèberge (1997) in order to demonstrate how this process inspired some sound editors to adopt a new understanding of their job in musical terms, as 'sound composers'. Examining industry magazines from that period, Spring reveals the main concerns that surrounded this shift in practice which include questions about the role of human creativity in relation to computer technology, the authenticity of synthesized sound and how the new technologies stimulated the merging of the two previously distinct duties of music composition and sound editing. The availability of new technologies, however, does not always instigate more advanced or complex approaches to sound post-production, as demonstrated by Nessa Johnston's study of the American indie writer/director/actor Joe Swanberg in Chapter 20. Operating within micro-budgets with minimal crew and taking advantage of cheap digital technology which allows a simplified workflow of shooting and editing, Swanberg is one of the most prominent exponents of 'mumblecore' cinema—a movement renowned for its 'bad' sound. His remarkably extensive opus, which includes titles such as *Art History* (2011), *Silver Bullets* (2011), *The Zone* (2011) and *Drinking Buddies* (2013), is typical of production practices that take place beyond the fully professionalized industry sphere which, as Johnston argues, belong to the tradition of 'lo-fi' indie-sound aesthetics.

The questions of aesthetics explored in Chapter 21 by Annette Davison and Nick Reyland are not so much a matter of technology and economy but are rather concerned with the fundamental relationships between image and sound and their effect on shaping an audience's emotional responses. Using the example of Cristobal Tapia de Veer's music for the Channel 4 serial *Utopia*, Davison and Reyland argue that scoring strategies more usually associated with art house cinema have recently also infiltrated some high-quality television programmes. They theorize the term 'anempathetic empathy' in order to capture the show's unconventional relationship between narrative and de Veer's music which, empathetic and anempathetic by turns, challenges the audience's expectations and assumptions about the show's protagonists and their motives.

As Davison and Reyland's insightful analysis of *Utopia* also establishes, part of the film aesthetics that these high-end television dramas embrace includes the practice of combining some aspects of composition with sound design for narrative and affective purposes. This is just one of the topics addressed by the celebrated Swedish sound designer Carl Edström in Chapter 22, in an interview discussion recorded by Annette Davison and Martin Parker during his visit to the University of Edinburgh in February 2013. The main creative force behind the sound design of one of the big Nordic Noir hits, *The Bridge* (2010–), Edström in this interview discusses his working methods, the collaborative nature of the creative process and his work with the series' composer Johan Söderqvist.

Part VI investigates the sounds of machines and non-humans. In Chapter 23 Philip Brophy considers the use of MIDI music in Japanese animé, in Chapter 24 William Gibbons explores the production of sound design and music created on computers for video games, and in Chapter 25 Cormac Deane is concerned with issues of redundancy and language when the screen is a focal point in the film or television text. What all three chapters argue is the centrality of the machine for the aesthetic design of both soundtrack and narrative: Brophy through the characterization of the android; Gibbons with the looping mechanism of the computer to create both music and sound design for game sound; and Deane through the use of Automated Dialogue Replacement (ADR) and the looping of lines to tease out issues of repetition and redundancy.

Brophy's chapter uses *Time of Eve* (Yasuhiro Yoshiura, 2010) as a case study to ask questions about what is real, fake or possesses a soul in Japanese culture. Exploring the use of 'real' piano playing, MIDI performances, muzak aesthetics and the centrality of the android, Brophy argues in favour of the android, animé and MIDI, and makes connections between the machine and music that raises interesting ideas for music and sound scholarship as well as more broadly applicable philosophical questions.

Gibbons considers Hirokazu Tanaka's sound design and music score for the video game *Metroid* (1986), drawing connections between the earlier science fiction film *Forbidden Planet* (Fred M. Wilcox, 1956) and the machine environment of the game utilized to create the score and sound design. Gibbons' chapter successfully delineates the liminal space between sound effects and music, incorporating both processed and unprocessed sound, most of this composed sound coming from the computer that the game can be played on. What Gibbons' chapter does is highlight a different industrial practice in gaming that uses the computer as a point of origin not only for the production of the sound and music but also to reflect the sound of the machine itself in an aesthetic choice that allows the gamer to be thoroughly present in the machinic world.

Deane's chapter charts a more diverse terrain, centring instead on issues of redundancy on screen with a specific focus on the technoscientific. Discussing ADR, infant speech, the technoscientific and animal sounds, drawing from a broad range of examples, Deane makes connections between the redundant repeated image of data on the computer screen and an over-explication of what that data means through the vocalizations of characters within that world.

Concluding this section, John Hough's interview in Chapter 26 with Johnnie Burn, the sound designer on *Under the Skin* (Jonathan Glazer, 2013), also considers issues pertaining to the non-human, highlighting the innovative use of music and sound design in the formation of an alien/non-human character. Burn describes his working methodology with Glazer, his collaboration with the film's composer Mica Levi and discusses how he created both urban sounds through illicit recordings on Glasgow streets and the alien sounds of the *Female* (Scarlett Johansson) as key design elements of the soundscape.

Finally, Part VII of the anthology posits the musical approach to film as being one of the forces behind the integration of music and other soundtrack elements inspired by various types of musical practices from different eras, including traditional classical forms such as overture, electroacoustic music and popular music. As Andy Birtwistle argues in Chapter 27, this approach is not an invention of recent decades but was producing examples of intertwined sound design and music even in the early ages of sound cinema. Focusing on British documentary cinema, particularly the work of Basil Wright (*Song of Ceylon*, 1934) and Geoffrey Jones (*Snow*, 1963), Birtwistle explores ways in which these filmmakers and the composers they collaborated with—Walter Leigh and Daphne Oram respectively—approached recorded sound in a manner that prefigured and paralleled developments in avant-garde music after World War II. His term 'cinesonic transmigration' encapsulates the ethos of this approach in which sound effects, diegetic sounds and speech 'occupy some of the creative territory that has often been considered the exclusive preserve of music' while on the other hand electroacoustic compositional techniques are employed to produce musical forms that gravitate towards the territory of sound effects.

In his case studies of Tom Ford's *A Single Man* (2009) and Steve McQueen's *Shame* (2011) in Chapter 28, Adam Melvin argues that the logic of musical organization does not apply only to the film soundtrack but can also be considered in broader formal terms. He proposes a concept of the cinematic overture that extends beyond its conventional functions of establishing main musical themes and acting as a 'musical cushion' between the audience and the diegesis. Through a close analysis of the opening sequences of *A Single Man* and *Shame* Melvin shows how the integration of visual, musical and sonic material—both diegetic and non-diegetic—results in an audiovisual dynamic that adopts the sense of performative grandeur associated with traditional incarnations of the term.

Although the type of traditional musical score that Melvin addresses in his analysis is usually credited to a composer only, in the context of film practice the format in which the score appears on the soundtrack is often the result of close collaboration between a composer and an orchestrator as well as other members of the film's post-production team. Ian Sapiro's searching interview with film-score orchestrator Matt Dunkley in Chapter 29 illuminates key aspects of the orchestrator's role in the production of the soundtrack involving composer, director, music editor and recording/mix engineer. Talking about his collaborations with Clint Mansell on Darren Aronofsky's films *Black Swan* (2010) and *Noah* (2014) and with Craig Armstrong on Richard Curtis' *Love Actually* (2003) and Baz Luhrmann's *Moulin Rouge!* (2001) and *The Great Gatsby* (2013), Dunkley also provides insights into the impact of technology on the processes of orchestration and lesser known aspects of the orchestrator's job involving working with popular and other pre-existing music.

The idea of musicality that affects different aspects of film soundtrack addressed in Birtwistle's and Melvin's chapters also resonates with Danijela Kulezic-Wilson's exploration of the musical use of speech in contemporary cinematic landscape in Chapter 30. Drawing on the examples of Drake Doremus' *Breathe In* (2013), Harmony Korine's *Spring Breakers* (2012) and Shane Carruth's *Upstream Color* (2013), Kulezic-Wilson identifies the main strategies involved in the musicalization of speech, showing how the breakdown of classical soundtrack hierarchy stems from a more comprehensive sense of musicality affecting different aspects of film form. She contends that undermining the narrative sovereignty of the spoken word and endorsing the interchangeability of speech and music promote modes of perception which can change our expectations of narrative film and emphasize its musical and sensuous qualities.

With a broad scope of topics united around the idea of the integrated soundtrack this anthology reflects the concerns of interdisciplinary studies examining various facets of screen media, and points to areas in need of closer scholarly attention. We are delighted to be given this opportunity to offer such a range of scholarship and industry reflection on sound design and music and we look forward to seeing new developments in the study of the integrated soundtrack.

## Note

1. Weis and Belton's anthology includes a number of articles originally published in the special edition of *Yale French Studies* on 'Cinema Sound'.

## References

Altman, R. (ed) *Yale French Studies: Cinema/Sound* Special issue, Vol. 60.
Chion, M. (1994) *Audio-Vision: Sound on Screen*, ed/trans. C. Gorbman (New York: Columbia University Press).
Buhler, J., D. Neumeyer and R. Deemer (2010) *Hearing the Movies: Music and Sound in Film History* (New York: Oxford University Press).
Elsaesser, T. and M. Hagener (2010) *Film Theory: An Introduction through the Senses*. New York and London: Routledge.
Gorbman, C. (1987) *Unheard Melodies: Narrative Film Music* (London: BFI Publishing/Bloomington: Indiana University Press).
Gorbman, C. (2007) 'Auteur Music' in D. Goldmark, L. Kramer and R. Leppert (eds) *Beyond the Soundtrack: Representing Music in Cinema* (Berkeley and Los Angeles: University of California Press), 149–162.
Jaffe, I (2014) *Slow Movies: Countering the Cinema of Action* (London and New York: Wallflower Press).
Kalinak, K. (ed.) (2015) *Sound: Dialogue, Music, and Sound Effects* (New Brunswick, New Jersey: Rutgers University Press).
Richardson, J., C. Gorbman and C. Vernallis (eds) (2013) *The Oxford Handbook of New Audiovisual Aesthetics* (New York: Oxford University Press).
Sonnenschein, D. (2001) *Sound Design: The Expressive Power of music, Voice, and Sound effects in Cinema* (California: Michael Wiese Productions).
Thèberge, P. (1997) *Any Sound You Can Imagine: Making Music/Consuming Technology* (Hanover and London: Wesleyan University Press).
Vernallis, C., A. Herzog and J. Richardson (eds) (2013) *The Oxford Handbook of Sound and Image in Digital Media* (New York: Oxford University Press).
Weis, E. and J. Belton (eds) (1985) *Film Sound: Theory and Practice* (New York: Columbia University Press).

PART I

# Boundaries and Their Disintegration

CHAPTER 2

# From Noise: Blurring the Boundaries of the Soundtrack

*Liz Greene*

In 1980, Rick Altman edited the first significant collection of essays in a special edition on 'Cinema Sound' for *Yale French Studies*. It was a sizeable undertaking, and it quickly became an important resource for the study of film sound. In seeking a broader framework for such a study, Altman suggested a new way of approaching the discipline:

> We need to start, for once, not with the self-serving pronouncements of silent film directors and fans, but with the phenomenon of sound film itself, analysing its practices and possibilities rather than prescribing its supposed duties and drawbacks. (1980a, p. 15)

Analysing sounds' potential, both achieved and yet unrealized, opens up sound scholarship to the realities of sound theory, history and practice. Altman was keen to address the visual bias in film studies by directing attention to the soundtrack. Yet even here, one of the foundational theorists of film sound underplayed and even disregarded the value of sound effects in this early but important intervention in film sound studies. In his contribution 'Moving Lips: Cinema as Ventriloquism' he states:

> We see a door slam, we hear a door slam; the sound intensifies the sense of reality initially produced by the image, it anchors the visual reference to a slamming door in our auditory sense system, it precludes any distantiation which might possibly be produced by the sight of a slamming door unaccompanied by its familiar

L. Greene
Liverpool John Moores University, UK

© The Editor(s) (if applicable) and The Author(s) 2016
L. Greene, D. Kulezic-Wilson (eds.), *The Palgrave Handbook of Sound Design and Music in Screen Media*, DOI 10.1057/978-1-137-51680-0_2

sound—but all in all nothing entirely new is contributed by mimetic sound, whence the acknowledged lack of independence of the soundtrack. (1980b, p. 67)

Altman's lack of appreciation of the role of sound effects in the cinema is surprising when he has set a task of analysing all of sounds' possibilities. Indeed, the very example Altman gives is interesting in so far as a door slam can sound very different depending on various factors in film, for example, acoustics, material of the door, narrative, motivation, how it is mixed and other aesthetic choices. An illustrative example of a door being closed occurs in *The Godfather* (Francis Ford Coppola, 1972). The last dramatic sound of the film is heard when Michael (Al Pacino) has the door closed shut on his wife, Kay (Diane Keaton), excluding her from his business. Walter Murch, the post-production consultant on the film, went to great lengths to get the right sound of the door being closed. This sound had to convey the right set of emotions for the scene, encompassing the need to exclude, create a distance, and illustrate the breakdown of a marriage (Murch, 2000). This type of example does not just happen in prestigious films such as *The Godfather,* most films contain thousands of sound effects precisely because they do convey meaning, emotion and affect.

In the same edition of *Yale French Studies* Daniel Percheron and Marcia Butzel, in their article 'Sound in Cinema and its Relationship to Image and Diegesis', also miss the importance of both sound effects and music in their analysis when they argue that:

Sound effects and music are rarely conveyors of meaning. Sound effects, for the most part, are only added articulations of the image track, which they help to expand and make diegetic. The rather limited, vulgar, and phatic function of film music, and the programmatic, illustrative role to which, nine times out of ten, such music is assigned, is well known. Breaking away from these semantically impoverished types of sound, confronting and working with the image track, only the spoken word can constitute a highly significant system. (Percheron and Butzel, 1980, p. 23)

Percheron and Butzel are being reductive and, like Altman, they ignore the power of sound effects and music to create meaning in cinema. I draw attention to their arguments not for the purposes of highlighting individual instances of bias against sound effects/design or music in film studies, but rather to illustrate the distance travelled in academic scholarship into the study of sound and music in screen media. In the intervening 36 years (since this publication of this edition), a significant attention to the close analysis of sound effects has turned this previous bias into one of the most published areas of film sound studies. One pertinent example, Gianluca Sergi's comprehensive essay 'In Defence of Vulgarity' (2006) outlines the role, meaning and potential of sound effects in the cinema.

Since the sonic turn in film studies in the twenty-first century (Keeling and Kun, 2012, p. 3), an academic engagement with sound has meant a significant enquiry into industrial practices, including interviews with practitioners which has led to a narrowing of the gap between theory and practice through events such as conferences, workshops and symposia.[1] However, despite these important developments in sound and music studies, in the main, there is still a gap between how sound and music are designed, composed and produced, and how university departments teach film sound and music ensuring they remain separate entities with very few examples of integrated pedagogical approaches.

To address this gap, I am interested in unpicking the language used to discuss different aspects of the soundtrack and question the persistence of certain terminology, some of which can be seen as helpful and illuminating, but can also, in other cases, be regarded as unproductive and outdated. There is not only a demarcation in industrial practices, in who does what and how they are credited for that work, but there are also conceptual demarcations that have persisted, even in experimental practice. Quite often, the sound design team do not know what the composer is planning to bring to the mix and vice versa. This bottleneck in post-production has been well-documented (see Barnes, 2007, 2008; Thom, 1999), as key workers are operating in isolation and without full consultation throughout the creative process. I would like to argue that this separation is further compounded due to issues of language, definition, notation and consequently has a bearing on the prestige of the work produced.

## Alan Splet

This chapter will consider how an integrated approach can work, with the example of one key sound designer (and music editor) Alan Splet who is best known for his collaborative work with David Lynch. Splet began working in sound with Lynch on his short film *The Grandmother* (1970) and continued to work as a sound designer up until his premature death at the age of 54 in 1994. He won a Special Achievement Academy Award for his sound editing of *The Black Stallion* (Carroll Ballard, 1979) and forged productive collaborations with other filmmakers alongside Lynch and Ballard, with many memorable soundtracks for Peter Weir and Philip Kaufman, amongst others. This chapter will illustrate some of Splet's approaches across four of Lynch's feature films: *Eraserhead* (1977), *The Elephant Man* (1980), *Dune* (1984) and *Blue Velvet* (1986) and will also draw from Splet's broader filmography. I will be accessing the *Sound Mountain* effects library curated by Ann Kroeber, a sound designer and Splet's widow, in order to consider the work of a sound designer with close analysis of the sound effects stored in this archive. Splet is an exceptional sound designer to consider for these purposes. He held a privileged position within the film industry, which allowed him a protracted period of time in post-production to create the sound for the films he worked on. Therefore, I am not positing Splet as a typical example of a sound designer and music editor, but rather I would prefer to suggest he is a great example of what could be possible, and this is most clearly evident in his collaborations with Lynch.

Splet's design and creation of sound effects with Lynch have been regarded as noisy in much of the critical literature; in fact, the term noise is often used instead of sound design or sound effects when talking about their collaborations. It is important to investigate what is meant when academics and critics refer to this work in terms of noise, and also what is the resulting analysis from such a label. R. Murray Schafer states, 'Noise pollution results when man does not listen carefully. Noises are the sounds we have learned to ignore' (1977, p. 4). His assessment of noise pollution is pertinent for film sound and music studies, for he suggests that if we listen closely, noises cease and are replaced by meaningful sounds.

However, noise can be a useful term when there is further context provided within analysis. For example, Michel Chion uses the term noise to define a particular type of sound in Lynch's work. In relation to *Blue Velvet* he notes:

> Sound effects accompany the descent into the swarming insect world at the beginning of the film, as well as the sequence of shock-images in which Jeffrey relives his frightening discoveries. The rest of the time, however, Lynch creates a normal, peaceful atmosphere, undisturbed by noises from the beyond or winds from the interstices of this world. (2006, p. 84)

Here Chion is clearly explaining that the noises he is referring to are sound effects, and that these sounds are outside of the diegetic soundscape and are responsible for setting the mood. Discussing the earlier soundtrack of *Eraserhead*, Greg Hainge notes that, 'The noise permeating *Eraserhead* is an industrial drone which suggests that the viewer is inhabiting a machinic world, a world which is a production-line for sound' (2004, p. 138). He describes the quality of sound or noise produced—an industrial drone—and qualifies that the sound is being made to be consciously heard. Both Chion's and Hainge's examples are illuminating, but in another example, Kenneth C. Kaleta's use of noise is more problematic as it offers a loose reading of the sound of *The Elephant Man*:

> It is however in the noises and the absolute absence of any noises as soundtrack that Lynch is most distinctively present in *The Elephant Man*. As with the music, there is a network of appropriate, assimilated noises in the film. These noises are accompanied by their negation—absolute silence. And they operate in combination with dialogue and the visuals of a scene. Noises convey the film's theme; noises set the film's mood. (1993, p. 62)

Kaleta does offer some meaning to noise but never explains what these noises are or distinguishes between them. He falls back on this term without any reference to what this may mean sonically for an audience. The distinction between noise and the absence of noise in the soundtrack does not describe in enough detail what is actually heard in the soundtrack of *The Elephant Man*.

Kaleta is not alone here, there are evident limitations in the language and vocabulary utilized in film sound and music studies. Noise can offer a way of describing Lynch's soundscape, but within this critical writing on Lynch's films there is seldom any detailed analysis of what this noise is and what it might mean. These noisy sections of sound design are described mainly as spaces devoid of meaning and value. In film sound and music studies there can often be a shared understanding of many of these terms across disciplinary boundaries but at other times there are confusions in the use of terminology. There can also be different terms used by practitioners and theorists within film sound and music. With this in mind, I will turn initially to a discussion of noise, and then look to other terms such as sound, music and silence in order to unpick some of these areas and posit a way forward for sound and music scholarship.

## Noise

A productive point of departure for an analysis of noise is the taxonomy proposed in the Futurist manifesto *The Art of Noises*. In the manifesto Luigi Russolo suggests there are six families of noises and he defines them as follows:

1. Roars, Thunderings, Explosions, Hissing roars, Bangs, Booms
2. Whistling, Hissing, Puffing
3. Whispers, Murmurs, Mumbling, Muttering, Gurgling
4. Screeching, Creaking, Rustling, Humming, Crackling, Rubbing
5. Noises obtained by beating on metals, woods, skins, stones, pottery, etc.
6. Voices of animals and people, Shouts, Screams, Shrieks, Wails, Hoots, Howls, Death rattles, Sobs (Russolo, 2004, p. 13).

For Russolo these sounds were to be performed by a futurist orchestra to represent the noises of the environment. This list of noises is both emotive and evocative of the sounds that are dismissed in our soundscape. It is also a useful list in so far as Russolo drew no distinctions between voice, animal, machine or nature sounds or noises. For him the noise was the critical factor and not what created it.

Unlike the Futurists and their celebration of all types of noise, Douglas Kahn in *Noise, Water, Meat* takes an extract from James Joyce's *Ulysses* (1922) in order to draw a distinction between music and noise: 'Sea, wind, leaves, thunder, waters, cows lowing, the cattle market, cocks, hens don't crow, snakes hissss. There's music everywhere. Ruttledge's door: ee creaking. No, that's noise' (2001, p. 68). Kahn uses Joyce to assert that music is in the living organic sound whereas noise is in the man-made structure. In a move that chimes with the Futurists, Martin Shingler recognizes these distinctions but collapses them and highlights their affective function: 'Noise and music are powerfully evocative forms, operating on our imaginations and our emotions. They resonate with associations, triggering emotional responses in us that lie beyond words' (1998, p. 51). Shingler suggests there are commonalities in these two sonic entities. It is within these commonalities and the overlap between them that I will consider the noise or sound of Splet and Lynch.

Definitions of noise, sound, music and silence need to be (re)considered in order to highlight both the meaning and elusiveness in terminology. Throughout my analysis of film sound and music I shall be exploring the ambiguity of these terms as they pertain to particular sounds. It is imperative to delineate the differences in definitions and outline where the boundaries are blurred in sound and music terminology. Due to definitional confusion in the field of these seemingly basic terms, recourse to a non-specialist source is illuminating for this discussion. It is in the dictionary that the most basic conceptualizations of sound and music terminology are outlined and this highlights the limitations of language in the field.

In the *Oxford English Dictionary*, noise is defined in four ways:

1. *A sound, especially a loud or unpleasant or undesired one.*
2. *A series of loud sounds.*
3. *Irregular fluctuations accompanying a transmitted signal but not relevant to it.*
4. *Conventional remarks or speech-like sounds without actual words.*

Noise is the term most commonly associated with Lynch's first feature film, *Eraserhead*. In the film a complex relationship between synchronous and asynchronous sound exists due to the strange world Lynch creates. So much of the film operates from Henry's (Jack Nance) perspective. The sound of *Eraserhead* is wonderfully evocative illustrating the nature of the story; the world in which it is set; and the creative choices made by Splet in collaboration with Lynch. The industrial wasteland is visually shown in an early sequence, but it is the soundscape that continues this industrial bed of noisiness throughout the film, the noisy low-end rumbling hum continues and rarely ceases. The industrial warehouses are not seen again, but the soundtrack asynchronously provides the disturbing mood to the domestic settings of Henry's home life. The world sounds menacing to Henry; it is a horror film based in a surreal world. Much of this horror and suspense depends on the noisy low-end soundscape we are hearing.

The noise is loud and unpleasant and this is central to the design of both the soundtrack and the film world. Splet's sound design does contain often loud and/or unpleasant sounds but these sounds are desired within the film soundtrack as they make it to the final cut and mix. Therefore, Splet's sound design challenges the limitations of part of this definition.

The first two definitions in the dictionary then seem to apply here. However, the loudness referred to in the dictionary needs to be considered in a nuanced manner within the dynamic range of sound produced for a film. For example, in the opening sequence of *Blue Velvet* after Jeffrey's (Kyle Maclachlan) father, Mr. Beaumont (Jack Harvey), collapses on the ground in their idyllic garden, displaying a well-tended lawn with flowers and a white picket fence, the camera tracks through the grass in extreme close up. A very brief moment of silence is heard on the soundtrack (it was only on playing this sequence a number of times that I realized that a point of silence was achieved here). In order to make use of the dynamic range of sound (amplitude) Splet and Lynch create a moment of silence to immediately follow it up with a very loud and noisy soundtrack to hyper-synchronously represent the extreme close up of insects scurrying down into the earth. This was created through recording insects in a lab in Berkeley with a FRAP microphone in a glass beaker (see Greene, 2006). Noise is in opposition to the supersaturated primary colours present in the visual aesthetics of this opening sequence. Joanna Demers suggests, 'As beauty's opposite, noise reinforces the ideal of beauty' (2010, p. 93). In this opening sequence of *Blue Velvet*, the noise of the soundtrack and the colourful display of beauty in the visual image are entwined in an asynchronous embrace. The menacing sound and loudness of these insects further the tension created by Mr. Beaumont's dramatic collapse, and also allow for an aural metaphor to illustrate the digging down into the underbelly of middle America.

The third definition referring to signal interruptions at first correlates strongly with Jacques Atalli's position on noise when he states:

> A noise is a resonance that interferes with the audition of a message in the process of emission. A resonance is a set of simultaneous, pure sounds of determined frequency and differing intensity. Noise, then, does not exist in itself, but only in relation to the system within which it is inscribed: emitter, transmitter, and receiver. Information theory uses the concept of noise (or rather metonymy) in a more general way: noise is the term for a signal that interferes with the reception of a message by a receiver, even if the interfering signal itself has a meaning for that receiver. (1985, pp. 26–7)

Atalli develops his argument by outlining how noise can have meaning even if it is interfering with another signal. In Splet and Lynch's work, the noise or sound design is meant to convey meaning and mood within the film. The greatest strength in this application of noise lies in the ambiguity of this type of sound and in how this message is in turn read by audiences. If the audience does not believe that the director is trying to get them to feel something at a particular point in a film—that is, becoming aware of an attempt to over-manipulate them—they are more likely to trust the film's integrity. A piece of sound design that sounds like noise but acts like music—having an emotional impact—can carry an audience along without them being aware of it. The importance of Atalli's definition in outlining how noise creates meaning broadens the potential scope for the analysis of sound effects and noise.

The fourth entry in the dictionary offers a definition that implies the redundant nature of some sounds. This definition suggests that noises are not speech but speech-like. An interesting example of these speech-like sounds can be found in the *Sound Mountain* effects library. In *The Elephant Man* library, John Hurt as John Merrick can be heard breathing and slurping, making sounds and noises that are speech-like, but not actually speech. The very presence of this production sound in the *Sound Mountain* library highlights the importance of these sounds to the characterization of Merrick. Wearing a mask that creates a barrier between the performer and the audience, Hurt has the difficulty of not being able to fully utilize his facial expressions to illustrate the tortured character of Merrick. The importance of his voice and breathing becomes accentuated in order to create an empathetic character. There is meaning to be found in these noises, or as Atalli puts it, the 'interfering signal', as Joe Kember illustrates:

> The opening scenes of *The Elephant Man* thoroughly expose our difficulties in experiencing empathy for an inexpressive face. However, from the first close-up, and with progressively greater frequency and confidence, strategies of expression associated with the point-of-view shot, with Merrick's strangely musical and refined voice, and with the gradual emergence of his eyes, begin to penetrate the permeable membrane of the face, assuring intersubjective passage above and beyond the dynamics of attraction. (2004, p. 27)

Within the film, Merrick struggles for breath as a result of asthma, bronchitis, as well as having been born with a cleft palette, further compounding his difficulties in communication in this smog ridden environment. It is unusual that these breathing sounds are included with the sound effects reels—breathing sounds would usually be edited by the dialogue editor—but their presence here illustrates the importance of these elements to the development of Merrick's character, and for Splet's overall sound design. There is meaning to be found in these breathing and speech-like noises (Greene 2016c).

## Sound

When turning to the word sound, the dictionary offers more clinical and physical definitions:

1. *A sensation caused in the ear by the vibration of the surrounding air or other medium.*
2. *Vibrations causing this sensation.*
3. *What is or may be heard.*
4. *An idea or impression conveyed by words.*
5. *Mere words.*
6. *Any of a series of articulate utterances.*

Obviously, noise equally pertains to a definition about vibrations of the surrounding air. Also, the second and third definitions are relevant to both sound and noise, however, the fourth definition is different as it is more conceptual, allowing for ideas or an impression. This definition of sound is the first instance we have looked at that alludes to information or knowledge and it is critical to the differences between what has been perceived as sound and noise. Sound contains meaning or more specifically sound makes an impression or gives ideas and this is conveyed to us through words. In the definitions of noise explored earlier none include the capacity for knowledge or information. Noise is not privileged with this ability to create meaning, or noise, it could be inferred from the dictionary, lacks the meaning offered through words. An importance is placed in this definition on the ability of words to convey meaning. But then an immediate contradiction emerges with a fifth definition. Mere words may be nonsensical and act on us like noises, without specific meaning, but they can also contain an impression or an idea, in which case there is little difference between a word being perceived as either a sound or noise. Words or sound, it can be inferred, can also lack meaning. It is the context and the understanding and not the actual words—or the sounds of the words—that contain meaning. Therefore, these two definitions that state sound is something that contains ideas through words or mere words are not useful, or at least not for these purposes, but are rather illustrative of how false divisions are drawn between sound and noise. However, what is useful in unpicking these definitions is the underlying ability of sound to contain meaning and also lack meaning. Sound can then be considered a term that can encompass the totality of noise; all of the definitions discussed in relation to noise can be included in a discussion of sound, including issues of amplitude and meaning. This then allows for the possibility of replacing the term noise, or at least blurring the line between what is considered noise and sound.

The sixth definition raises further questions on this issue of meaning. The articulate utterances outlined here could refer to sounds created by words, but it is not necessarily so as utterance refers to the smallest units of speech and is not limited to words.[2] What is important in this definition is that sound is described as articulate—it is coherent, which again implies meaning. Articulate screams or shouts can contain sounds or units of speech but not necessarily specific words. Without a word in a scream or shout a meaning can still be present, but without meaning the scream or shout could be interpreted as noise. The meaning is therefore found in the context of the utterance and not the actual sounds or noises made.

An interesting example for this discussion on 'articulate utterances' occurred in the sound recording of *Blue Velvet*. Ann Kroeber, the production sound mixer, purposely recorded the distorting voice of Dorothy (Isabella Rossellini) as she breaks down in front of Jeffrey and Sandy (Laura Dern). The meaning is found in the noise of the distorted screaming voice. Rossellini's distorting vocalization offers an emotional and an affective layer of meaning to her 'hysterical' performance (see Greene, 2009, 2016b). The sounds of the actual words are unclear and are less relevant to conveying meaning; in fact, clarity of words could possibly take away from the affective experience of hearing this distorting recorded performance.

## Music

The definitions of music offered in the dictionary are both limited and limiting:

1. *The art of combining vocal or instrumental sounds (or both) to produce beauty of form, harmony, and expression of emotion.*
2. *The written or printed score of a musical composition.*
3. *Certain pleasant sounds e.g. birdsong, the sound of a stream, etc.*

Arguing against the need for music to contain harmony, John Cage stressed, 'The present methods of writing music, principally those which employ harmony and its reference to particular steps in the field of sound, will be inadequate for the composer who will be faced with the entire field of sound' (1961, p. 4). Taking Cage's lead, dismissing the need for music to produce beauty, form or harmony, as it has been by many twentieth- and twenty-first-century composers, musicians and theorists, this first definition is left with the combination of vocals or instruments to express emotion. However, this too has been undermined by avant-garde artists and *musique concréte* composers who use sounds found in everyday life to produce music. This is also precisely what a sound designer does on a film; indeed, there are often many similarities between *musique concréte* and sound design, and composers for film can equally include sound effects and design within their compositions. What is more interesting is the second definition, which I argue is critical to how music has been read and considered as a prestigious art form. It is this written score that gives music a prestige over other elements of the soundtrack. It is a text that can be studied, analysed and deciphered by scholars of music in a way that sound design and sound effects cannot be or have not been to date. However, it is important to note that not all music is written down. Traditional and folk music have shared this lack of prestige with sound due to this issue of notation. The prestigious nature of the written composition highlights the composer's creative work and deems it worthy of note at the outset of the film. Moreover, the written music is credited to a composer or composers, and in Hollywood film it is usually one composer who is given a front credit on the film as specified by the Directors Guild of America (DGA). The DGA refuses to allow a front credit for sound design. The one exception to this is the Coen brothers who refused to join the DGA unless their supervising sound effects editor Skip Lievsay was given a front credit. The DGA eventually relented (Lievsay, 2003).

If we can accept that music does not need to be beautiful, then the musicality of pleasant sounds should also be questioned. Why should the sounds of birds or a stream be more musical than say an air vent, a train, or the wind? And if these sounds can be considered music, as they have been since John Cage transformed our understanding of music in the second half of the twentieth century,[3] then are there really any differences between noise and music? Or noise, sound and music? As David Hendy suggests, 'one person's irritating din is another person's sweet music' (2013, p. 325).

I will consider a piece of sound design Splet created for *Dune* to give an example of the blurring boundaries between these terms and definitions. This atmospheric sound for *Dune* was later released as 'Space Travel with Changing Choral Textures' as part of *An Anthology of Noise and Electronic Music*.[4] A choral texture (as the title suggests) can be heard throughout this track. When analysing the waveform of this piece, and playing it in the Digital Audio Workstation (DAW) Pro Tools, I was reminded of David Hykes' composition 'Rainbow Voice' from *Dead Poets Society* (Peter Weir, 1989) as the choral textures are very similar in both pieces. This was another film that Splet created the sound design for. I would never have thought that these soundtracks were analogous, but when I imported the Hykes' composition to the Pro Tools session and ran the two together they perfectly harmonized and, visually, the waveforms were very similar in appearance. I could hear and see very little difference between the two pieces, Hykes' choral piece of music and Splet's ambient sound design that was later released on CD. That one is labelled music and the other sound design or sound effect or noise, is irrelevant to how they play in both films, both pieces have an affective impact on their audiences.

Peter Weir notes of Hykes' 'Rainbow Voice':

> So here we had a scene in which we needed a feeling that something awful was going to happen with Neil but you don't want the audience to just ... either jump to the conclusion ... you want ... to reinvigorate the cliché. So sound became terribly important there, music couldn't do a lot, and from memory I think I used ... David Hykes sound, that sort of strange kind of choral sound. (2007)

Weir does not consider this piece to be music in the traditional sense, instead he reads this as sound, although it is credited as music in the film, and Hykes is credited with its composition. However, this is a distinction he is sensitive to as for him, the lines are blurred between sound and music, just as they are for Lynch when he states, 'The borderline between sound effects and music is the most *beautiful* area' (Lynch in Rodley, 1997, p. 242, his emphasis). This is, indeed, the space where Splet's work comes into its own, whether he is creating sound design and sound effects to work with a music composition, or is working as a sound designer and music editor on Philip Kaufman's films—*The Unbearable Lightness of Being* (1988), *Henry and June* (1990) and *Rising Sun* (1993). When analysing the sound itself and its' graphical waveform it is arbitrary how sound and music are classified and/or defined.

What is possibly the trickiest area of the soundtrack to define is the moment when it is perceived to be silent. Again, the dictionary is definitive but not entirely precise.

## Silence

1. *Complete absence of sound*
2. *The fact or state of abstaining from speech*

This first definition is an interesting one; it is perhaps the most elusive and imprecise of all the definitions considered in this chapter as there has never been any examples of the complete absence of sound, either in the cinema or the known world. In a recent (2015) study, scientists in Hong Kong outlined that they are close to achieving silence but to date this has not yet been realized.[5] Instead, what we talk about, in screen media terms, is relative silence, which is determined in relation to sound that comes before or after silence. For example, in the illustration I gave above from the opening sequence of

*Blue Velvet*, silence is felt or perceived in relation to the dynamic range of other sounds, that is, the grass and insect sounds that precede and follow it. After Mr Beaumont has a heart attack, a moment of relative silence is achieved, and this silence can fittingly 'evoke the fear of the absence of life' (Sonnenschein, 2001, p. 125).

The composer Toru Takemitsu worked on *Rising Sun* alongside Splet. Takemitsu uses silence in his compositions for musical and conceptual purposes, and he proposed the following:

> The fear of silence is nothing new. Silence surrounds the dark world of death. Sometimes the silence of the vast universe hovers over us, enveloping us. There is the intense silence of birth, the quiet silence of one's return to earth. Hasn't art been the human creature's rebellion against silence? Poetry and music were born when man first uttered sound, resisting the silence. (Takemitsu in Cox and Warner, 2004, p. 4)

For Takemitsu silence is punctuated by sound. What is termed silence in screen media is rarely that; rather, the soundtrack contains certain low level ambient or atmospheric (atmos) sounds. As Shingler notes of silence in a related medium, radio:

> What we take for silence is often a subtle and virtually unnoticeable range of atmospheric sounds which are essentially a background to prominent or significant sounds. The silence of a church, a field, a forest, the sea, a living room, a mountain top or a cave all sound different and, therefore, they all sound. We may not consciously perceive it but we still hear it. This kind of silence, which broadcasters usually refer to as 'atmos', is perhaps the most subtle noise we ever hear on the radio. (1998, p. 55)

Silence can have great emotive and narrative ramifications in the cinema. It is one method used by sound designers to create ambiguity in film. These silent or atmos tracks offer the filmgoer the opportunity to hear the environment in which the film is set. It is rare in Hollywood film for the sound to get to a point of silence or relative silence for a protracted period of time. However, Splet's work does on a number of films, in particular in *The Black Stallion*, *Never Cry Wolf* (Carroll Ballard, 1983), *Dead Poets Society* and *The Unbearable Lightness of Being*.

The second definition of silence brings us back to the centrality of the spoken word. Human voices making speech sounds are the clearest indicator of a sound presence. Our collective attention is drawn to speech and we focus on this as a primary indicator of meaning. The absence of speech or speech-like sounds can be more readily perceived of as silence. Sara Maitland in *A Book of Silence* expresses it thus:

> For me personally the exact meaning of silence has grown and shifted as I practice it more, but it remains fairly literal: it is words and speech particularly that break

up silence. In addition I find human noises less silent than natural phenomena like wind and water. However, as time passes I increasingly realise there is an interior dimension to silence, a sort of stillness of heart and mind which is not a void but a rich space. (2008, p. 25)

Having spent a year in silence and isolation in rural Scotland, Maitland draws clear distinctions between human sound and environmental sounds. Perhaps that is why silence can be best perceived, as Shingler suggests, as atmos; the very power of sound design and sound effect is in our inability to perceive it as sound in the first place (see Greene, 2016a).

Due to the ambiguous nature of silence and noise they can appear to be very similar, close allies in fact, rather than, as is commonly perceived, being at opposing ends of the sound spectrum. Paul Hegarty asks, 'Is noise subjective? Could we not instead say that noise has to do with the subject: that which occurs as/at the limit of the subject; that which signals an immanence outside of the subject/object divide' (2001). Hegarty is asking similar philosophical and spiritual questions about noise that Maitland is seeking out in silence. Antonio Porchia suggests, 'A thing, until it is everything, is noise, and once it is everything it is silence' (2003, p. 24). In the liminal spaces of the soundtrack, in particular, in the use of silence and noise, the spirit can be evoked.

## Conclusion

This chapter problematizes the definitions of noise, sound, music[6] and silence as discrete elements within the soundtrack and illustrates the shared qualities all of these terms have for screen media. The blurring of lines between these is evident when considering Splet's contribution to film. His work crosses over all of these definitions and he succeeded in creating highly effective tracks that have subtly and overtly impacted on audiences, due to the ambiguity of his sound design and music editing.

Splet's work within the films discussed above is illustrative of the potential for a more integrated approach to the soundtrack. What facilitated Splet's creative contribution was the fact that many of the films had an extensive period of time for production and post-production sound. For example, it took seven years to complete *Eraserhead*, Splet worked on *Never Cry Wolf* for three years, and on *Blue Velvet* he was employed to gather sound effects as the production shoot was still underway. Splet was in a fortunate position to be consulted at the pre-production stage on many of his projects.

With the development of digital technologies—the dovetailing of technology for both sound and music—and the shrinking of budgets, the industry has witnessed a significant change in production and post-production scheduling. Very few sound designers have the time that Splet enjoyed for creating sound effects on independent art house films. Now it is generally only blockbuster films that have the budget to allow a sound designer work early on in the production phase. Consider the work here of Ben Burtt who was employed on

*Wall:E* (Andrew Stanton, 2008) at the pre-production stage to create both the voices and the sound worlds for the story. One possible upside of this change in workflow is that as budgets become squeezed, we may begin to witness fresh opportunities for sound and music to be worked on or collaborated on at the earliest stages, at least on micro-budget and blockbuster films.

Assessing the limitations of terminology within the dictionary may suggest to the reader that they should look elsewhere for more useful definitions. But I would prefer to suggest that it is these very limitations as outlined in the dictionary that are still resonant in film sound and music scholarship and which can offer some insight into the continued division(s) in our field(s). I am not suggesting that film sound and music scholars or practitioners are looking to these definitions for inspiration or insight in their daily research processes, but rather that there are some elements of these definitions that we have not considered, or challenged in our writings to date. Taking a close look at these definitions drawn from everyday usage illustrates the ambiguities in all of these terms. As Hendy argues, 'Instead of worrying about the usual boundaries between noise and music, or cacophony and silence, or speech and song, we need to discover the virtues of breaking them down' (2013, p. ix). It is in highlighting and knowing these definitions that allows them to be confronted. Altman's ambitious call to study film sound by 'analysing its practices and possibilities rather than prescribing its supposed duties and drawbacks' (1980a, p. 15) can be aided by naming what it is we are describing, and allowing false boundaries to be left behind in a search for a more meaningful engagement with the integrated soundtrack. This process allows for an exposure of such terms, illustrating the limits of terminology and the possibilities of all areas of the soundtrack. When it is difficult to pin down exactly what we are hearing, the soundtrack opens up the most creative space for listening. It is in these liminal spaces of the soundtrack that we are offered a way to affectively connect with the characters on screen. That does not mean that we do not attempt to define what we are hearing, but rather we need to work that bit harder to pin down how film sound and music are operating (on us).

## Notes

1. Such events include *The School of Sound* symposium, which has been held bi-annually in London since 1998; the *Sounding Out* conference was first held at the University of Staffordshire in 2002 and then moved to the University of Nottingham in 2004; in 2006 and 2008 it was held at the University of Sunderland. Another key event since 2006 is the annual conference of *Music and the Moving Image* at New York University, Steinhardt.
2. For more on oral utterance, see Ong (1982).
3. See Cage (1961).
4. Splet, A. (2006) 'Space Travel with changing choral textures' *An Anthology of Noise and Electronic Music*, Vol. 2, published by Sub Rosa.
5. For more information on this research into 'silence', see Malara (2015).

6. It is outside of the scope of this chapter to discuss Splet's contribution to music, but it is important to note that he edited the music for three Philip Kaufman films: *The Unbearable Lightness of Being*, *Henry and June* and *Rising Sun*. For more on this work, see Greene (2011).

## References

Altman, R. (1980a) 'Introduction', *Yale French Studies: Cinema/Sound* Special issue, Vol. 60, 3–15.
Altman, R. (1980b) 'Moving Lips: Cinema as Ventriloquism', *Yale French Studies: Cinema/Sound* Special issue, Vol. 60, 67–79.
Atalli, J. (1985) *Noise: The Political Economy of Music* (Minneapolis: University of Minnesota Press).
Barnes, R. (2007) 'Barton Fink: Atmospheric Sounds of the Creative Mind
Sound Practices of the Coen Brothers', *Offscreen*, Vol. 11, No. 8–9, http://offscreen.com/view/barnes_bartonfink, date accessed 17 February 2014.
Barnes, R. (2008) 'The sound of Coen comedy: music, dialogue and sound effects in Raising Arizona', *The Soundtrack*, Vol. 1, No. 1, 15–28.
Cage, J. (1961) *Silence: Lectures and Writings* (Hanover: Wesleyan University Press).
Chion, M. (2006) *David Lynch*, trans. Robert Julian, second edition (London: BFI Publishing).
Concise Oxford English Dictionary (1995) ninth edition, (Gloucestershire: Clarendon Press)
Cox, C. and D. Warner (eds) (2004) 'Introduction' in *Audio Culture: Readings in Modern Music* (New York and London: Continuum), 5–6.
Demers, J. (2010) *Listening through the Noise: The Aesthetics of Experimental Electronic Music* (Oxford: Oxford University Press).
Greene, L. (2006) 'Designing Asynchronous Sound for Film' in K. Rockett and J. Hill (eds) *National Cinemas and World Cinema: Studies in Irish Film 3* (Dublin: Four Courts Press), 134–140.
Greene, L. (2009) 'Speaking, Singing, Screaming: Controlling the Female Voice in American Cinema', *The Soundtrack Journal*, Vol. 2, No.1, 63–76.
Greene, L. (2011) '*The Unbearable Lightness of Being*: Alan Splet and Dual Role of Editing Sound and Music', *Music and the Moving Image*, Vol. 4, No. 3, 1–13.
Greene, L. (2016a) 'Silence', *SEQUENCE: Serial Studies in Media, Film and Music*, Vol. 5. No. 1, http://reframe.sussex.ac.uk/sequence5/
Greene, L. (2016b) 'Sound Recording, Sound Design and Collaboration: An interview with Ann Kroeber' in L. Greene and D. Kulezic-Wilson (eds) *The Palgrave Handbook of Sound Design and Music: Integrated Soundtracks* (Basingstoke: Palgrave Macmillan), 33–42.
Liz Greene (2016c) 'The Labour of Breath: Performing and Designing Breath in Cinema', *Music, Sound and the Moving Image*, Fall.
Hainge, G. (2004) 'Weird or Loopy? Specular Spaces, Feedback and Artifice in Lost Highway's Aesthetics of Sensation' in E. Sheen and A. Davison (eds) *The Cinema of David Lynch: American Dreams, Nightmare Visions* (London: Wallflower), 136–150.
Hegarty, P. (2001) 'Full With Noise: Theory and Japanese Noise Music', *Ctheory.net*, http://www.ctheory.net/articles.aspx?id=314, date accessed 16 September 2015.

Hendy, D. (2013) *Noise: A Human History of Sound and Listening* (London: Profile Books).

Kahn, D. (2001) *Noise, Water, Meat: A History of Sound In The Arts* (Massachusetts: MIT Press).

Kaleta, K. (1993) *David Lynch* (New York: Twayne Publishers).

Keeling, K. and J. Kun (eds) (2012) *Sound Clash: Listening to American Studies* (Baltimore: Johns Hopkins University Press).

Kember, J. (2004) 'David Lynch and the Mug Shot: Facework in *The Elephant Man* and *The Straight Story*' in E. Sheen and A. Davison (eds) *The Cinema of David Lynch: American Dreams, Nightmare Visions* (London: Wallflower), 19–34.

Lievsay, S. (2003) 'Presented paper' at *The School of Sound* London, 23rd–26th April.

Maitland, S. (2008) *A Book of Silence* (London: Granta Books).

Malara, M. (2015) 'Scientists discover path to silence with perfect sound absorption', *United Press International (UPI)*, http://www.upi.com/Science_News/2015/09/12/Scientists-discover-path-to-silence-with-perfect-sound-absorption/5751442059892/, date accessed 16 September 2015.

Murch, W. (2000) 'Stretching Sound to Help the Mind See', *New York Times*, http://www.nytimes.com/2000/10/01/arts/01MURC.html?pagewanted=all, date accessed 15 December 2015.

Ong, W. (1982) *Orality and Literacy: The Technologizing of the Word* (London & New York: Routledge).

Percheron, D. and M. Butzel (1980) 'Sound in Cinema and its Relationship to Image and Diegesis', *Yale French Studies: Cinema/Sound* Special issue, Vol. 60, 16–23.

Porchia, A. (2003) *Voices,* trans. W. S. Merwin, (Port Townsend: Copper Canyon Press).

Rodley, C. (1997) *Lynch on Lynch* (London: Faber & Faber).

Russolo, L. (2004) 'The Art of Noises: Futurist Manifesto', in C. Cox and D. Warner (eds) 'Introduction' in *Audio Culture: Readings in Modern Music* (New York and London: Continuum), 10–14.

Schafer, M. (1977/94) *The Soundscape: The Tuning of The World* (New York: Knopf).

Sergi, G. (2006) 'In Defence of Vulgarity', *Scope an Online journal of Film and TV Studies* (Sound Special Issue) Issue 5: Articles (June), http://www.scope.nottingham.ac.uk/article.php?issue=5&id=129, date accessed 21 November 2007.

Shingler, M. and C. Wieringa (1998) *On Air: Methods and Meanings of Radio* (London and New York: Arnold Publishers).

Sonnenschein, D. (2001) *Sound Design: The Expressive Power of music, Voice, and Sound effects in Cinema* (California: Michael Wiese Productions).

Thom, R. (1999) 'Designing a Movie for Sound', http://www.filmsound.org/articles/designing_for_sound.htm, date accessed 12 March 2014.

Weir, P. (2007) Director Interview on DVD during Ann Kroeber's lecture, *The School of Sound*, London, 18–21 April 2007.

CHAPTER 3

# Interview 1: Sound Recording, Sound Design and Collaboration—An Interview with Ann Kroeber

*Liz Greene*

Ann Kroeber is a sound designer, sound effects recordist and sound effects editor, and has been recording sound in the film industry since 1979, when she started working on *The Black Stallion* (Carroll Ballard, 1979), which won a Special Achievement Academy Award for Sound. She was the production sound mixer on *Blue Velvet* (David Lynch, 1986) and the sound designer on *Duma* (Carroll Ballard, 2005) and has more than 35 sound credits to her name. She continues to provide sounds for films and video games and is the curator and owner of *Sound Mountain,* a sound effects library service which is the home of her and her late partner, Alan Splet's sound recordings. In October 2015, she was interviewed by Liz Greene over Skype.

LG: Has an integration of sound and music been considered in the roles you have performed in sound recording and sound design? Were you thinking about the role that sound would play and music would play in different films that you worked on?

AK: Yes, I have been very fortunate with the films I have worked on. Especially with Alan [Splet], there was a real consideration of sound and music and it was very different from old Hollywood where the tradition is that the composer is king and he goes off to a foreign land, or a big concert hall and records his music and we don't hear it until the final mix. That is just awful. On the very first film I worked with Alan that actually happened and we were very, very fortunate [because the originally recorded music did not end up in the final mix]. It would

L. Greene
Liverpool John Moores University, UK

have been a disaster for the movie, for all our sound effects would have been crushed by the music and yet the music was beautiful in itself, but it was just so inappropriate for that movie.

**LG:** That was *The Black Stallion* (Carroll Ballard, 1979)?

**AK:** *The Black Stallion*, yes.

**LG:** So how did you get sound to still play a dominant role? Alan won an Oscar for that film.

**AK:** What happened was, when we realized that the music was going to kill our sound effects, we were given a little more time, and we came up with a way that by taking some of the themes of the music, and taking the layers of instrumentation out and having it very simple, that that could work for us. And we used that, and had a few musicians come in and improvise to the sound effects, we had already finished the sound effects tracks, and we played that for them and they could hear it in [their] headphones and then they played their instruments. Very few instruments went with that, it was delightful, it worked so well. The sound won a Special Achievement Award for Sound Editing [Academy Awards].

**LG:** Who organized for the musicians to come in?

**AK:** That was Richard Beggs actually, he got some musicians and he helped record that, kind of orchestrated it. They were very talented and very savvy and it was a delight. It was so much fun to watch and see how it was going.

**LG:** That is quite amazing in terms of today's schedules where everything has to be locked off by a certain point, and then you get to the mix and you have to deal with the problems that are at the mix. But you were given extra time to sort it out, how did that happen? I am intrigued by the fact that yourself and Alan quite often got so much time on the things you worked on?

**AK:** Well, back when, it was different when it was analogue. Everything is speeded up now with digital. They think you can do it much quicker. You still need to think of the artistry. With this [*The Black Stallion*] we only got two extra weeks so it wasn't a huge amount of time to work out the music. That time was going to be spent for music editing; they were going to edit the score but it ended up being this creative process.

**LG:** When the director, Carroll Ballard, found out that you were faced with that situation, music and sound were not integrating well together, what was his response to the music and the sound?

**AK:** Oh, he was really devastated and he was told there was nothing that could be done. We figured out a way to convince Francis [Ford Coppola, Producer of the film] that it wasn't in the best interest of his dad [Carmine Coppola, Composer of the film]; it really wasn't showing him in the best light. So he listened to it and he agreed to go ahead and let us try to come up with something that would work for everyone. I think it was actually very good for Carmine; Carmine's music did get to be shown in a much better way. It's really unfortunate that even some big pictures now are still done that way. Where an established composer will come in and the sound crew has no idea what the music is going to be. I went to a lecture with

E.J. Holowicki, a sound designer at Skywalker, and one of the first things he said was, 'Being a sound person, you have got to prepare yourself that your favorite sounds will probably never be heard in the movie'. (Laughing) It was so sad.

LG: Would you normally have contact with music people beforehand? Or, is it nearly always the case that music comes very late in the game and you are trying to scrabble for space in the soundtrack?

AK: Well it just depends, for *Duma* (2005), for example, a film I did the sound design for, which is another Carroll Ballard movie, I actually got to have the musicians listen to our sound effects first. We had African musicians that did the composition. Again, it was a well-known composer that had done the music for us. Carroll doesn't care who does it, it just didn't work, it wasn't appropriate for that movie. So, they heard our sound effects and vice versa, it was kind of a collaboration going back and forth. We got the music early and quite a bit earlier than the mix, so I was able to adjust sounds so that it would go with this music. It makes such a difference. Going through the jungle, through trees and forest, it was really special to hear what music was being played; to be able to make the birds and creatures sing to the music was wonderful.

LG: In terms of the musicality of sound and how sound can be used musically, can you talk a little bit about what you have worked on and how you consider those terms? I have heard you talking before about animals and the musicality of their voices.

AK: I think that animals have incredible voices; some of them can sound like primitive jazz singers. I did a recording once at a big cat preserve in the Mojave Desert and they had a collection of tigers, leopards and all kinds of big cats. They got to run around and hang out in a pretty big range. There is a thing that the cats do but they won't do it around humans where they do this chuffing sound. It sounds like a chorus and they call back and forth to each other at night. It is a beautiful sound, .in this group chuffing: 'dhro cho wo whu'.

I did this thing where I made friends with a tiger. He used to come over and just talk into my microphone once he got used to me; you know he figured out what I was doing, I explained it to him. He was just very cool about that. He had this big range he used to run around, he would come running right over to the fence and he would kind of chat: 'Grrr rrgh' into my microphone. I wanted to record them so I put the microphone and faced it towards Caesar's compound, the tigers' compound, and the leopards were in the background and I thought maybe I could catch them. Caesar walked right up to the microphone, he was like a jazz singer doing this solo to the chorus of leopards. It made me cry when I heard it, it was so beautiful. That is just one example, there is so much, you go out into nature and the quiet of night, you can hear the creatures singing back and forth to each other. I get the feeling it is more than just very specific mating things that they are doing. It is like the basis of our music is in nature. You can hear it. We are tied in with it much more than we realize it, with creatures. We have taken that music and evolved it. That is my experience. Wind and waves and all kinds of things that give you a feeling, a mood and emotion. There are so many kinds of winds that you could put into a film that really create a musicality and also give you an emotional feeling. There is a lot of tone in it, it is really remarkable when you stop and listen.

LG: When you were recording the tiger, was that for *Duma* or for something else?

AK: That was for a children's [video] game, *Kinectimals* (2010), it was being made in Cambridge, England. I just captured it, I was actually going for cubs and that is what I recorded for the game. I just wanted to do that to have for myself after I had finished work. On the last night I just set it up to see if I could capture it; I wanted to hear what this chuffing sound sounded like, it was wonderful.

LG: In *Duma*, when you were doing the sound design and you were working so much with animal sounds and placing animal sounds, did you have to consider, and I know you just mentioned there the exchange of music and sound effects with the composer and the African musicians, but did you try to do things musically or do you think in those terms? Do you think in terms of, this is sound or this is music, or are you working somewhere in between those things? How does it work for you?

AK: When I was recording, I recorded the cheetah. I was mainly interested in the expressive vocals of the cheetah. I was interested in the cheetah having a personality and capturing its different moods in sounds. Cheetahs have a very musical kind of sound; they have a bird-like tweeting that people don't really think would come out of a cheetah. In terms of music, I am really trying to get the emotional quality, having the music and the cheetah work together later.

LG: I was wondering could you give some examples of whether music was removed so that sound could play a leading role in a film or sound was removed in order for music to play a leading role? Do you have experience of that?

AK: Yes, *The Mosquito Coast* (Peter Weir, 1986) was a really good example of that. This was a kind of thing where the music and sound were done very separately. It was a big movie, it had a very big budget with famous actors, Harrison Ford and Helen Mirren were starring in it and River Phoenix. Maurice Jarre was the composer, a wonderful composer, but unfortunately he did not hear anything that we were doing and we didn't hear anything that he was doing. It was a classic Hollywood situation. We were working up in Berkeley, he did his work down in LA and we came together in the mix. What happened was, Alan did some really evocative jungle sounds and it was such a mood. There was one scene that was kind of mysterious and you don't know really what is happening. It is just a feeling and there is a boat on the river coming up and it is dark outside. Alan did the sound effects and they had a real musical quality to them. The insects were singing and gave you this real feeling of mood. When we got to the mix, Maurice Jarre had composed a whole feeling thing to it and the two were just not going to work together. Peter Weir just decided to completely go with the sound effects; it gave everything that he really wanted it to capture. It didn't need music there. It usually doesn't happen like that. Peter is very sensitive to sound. After the film was done, we went to a screening in LA and Maurice Jarre came up to us and he said to Alan: 'Are you a composer? You are a composer aren't you?' And Alan kind of looked at him like, 'Oh I'm sorry' and he [Jarre] laughed and said: 'I want to work with you from now on because I won't have to do so much work'. (Laughing)

LG: Have you ever had the opposite situation where the director said, 'No, I think I will go with the music', and you think that was the correct decision? That you pulled back from all the sound that was created because music was the right way to go. Because I am sure you have loads of examples of where you were maybe frustrated that the sound did not get to play its part but were the times when you thought, yes, absolutely, the music is so much more correct here for this scene?

AK: That's a really good question. In David's [Lynch] movies, David uses music as humour or romance, and sound effects are used for the fear and the scary bits or the emotional moody bits. So David uses many, many low tones and they have a musical quality too. He just loves that kind of stuff. I was working on a scene in *Blue Velvet* (David Lynch, 1986) and I remember originally we had all of these sound effects of gunshots—there was a battle outside. I cut all of this sound for gun shots and David decided to go with music, he used 'Love Letters Straight From Your Heart' and it was so ironic, so we just had a little tiny bit of gunfire you hear every now and then which worked with the music. It was just so much more appropriate, it was really great, it just changed the whole mood of that scene from a scary realistic gun battle to have this silly David humour that was sort of surreal and not so frightening.

LG: Speaking of David Lynch and Alan's collaboration with him for a moment, what do you think was unique about their relationship that led to such a fruitful collaboration?

AK: David first met Alan when David was a student. He [David] came to this production company that Alan's boss, Bob Collum, worked at and Bob would supply sounds for David or do some recording for his short films. Bob was busy and could not do it and he had Alan do it instead. David was initially very upset. They started working together, and it completely changed the way David did his soundtrack. The movie was called *The Grandmother* (1970), it is a student film. It was almost all sound effects, I think there is hardly any dialogue in the film, it is all done with sound effects. They just had a blast and they went off recording and the stuff they came up with is really something. It was always that way, they had an incredible understanding of each other and what each of them can do. Alan had a really good understanding of David's sensibility.

LG: Do you think that is one of the strengths that Alan had, that he was able to play to different directors' tastes?

**AK:** Yes, he was able to get out of his own ego to be able to hear and understand what the director wanted. Yes, I think that was definitely his strength. I am going to tell you a story about Carroll Ballard. When we were working on *Never Cry Wolf* (1983) Carroll was very critical, he has a way of being very, very, specific about what he wants and he can be difficult if you are sensitive to that sort of thing. Alan had worked for a week on getting the sound of wolves chewing on a carcass and he wanted to get the crunch right. He went and recorded up in a wolf preserve, a couple of hours from where we lived. He got a real carcass, to get the sound of the wolves chewing he used half of a cow's carcass. He came back, and Alan cut it in the film and Carroll listened to it and said, 'Nah, sounds like a bunch of dogs chewing on kibble'. All the work that had gone into that! You know, we listened to it and laughed because if you didn't know what had gone into it, that they actually were real wolves—that is exactly what it sounded like. Carroll was so right. So we ended up using all sorts of different kinds of things to create the aural image of wolves chewing on a carcass. It worked, it worked much better! It then became our joke when we were working on projects, if something wasn't working, we'd go, 'Nah, it sounds like a bunch of dogs chewing on kibble'. That was a really good thing, a lot of people would take it very personally and get really upset and not be able to move forward with it, with Carroll's criticism. The thing I always appreciated about Carroll was his taste, I think he has got really good taste and he has extremely good sound sense so when he is critical, it is to make it better and really listen, try to clue in to what his sensibilities are.

**LG:** So what would be different about Carroll to, say, Peter Weir or David Lynch? Would they be critical in different ways? Or were any of them uncritical? I'm curious to know how the sound was negotiated with all the different directors that you worked with.

**AK:** They have different styles. Peter has a different sensibility, a different way of communicating with people, it's maybe just a little easier. One time David's office called me up, David wanted a collection of 'dreamy winds' for a movie he was working on, *Lost Highway* (1997). So I got together these winds and I was thinking, 'dreamy winds' to me is kind of like sweet dreams, it has lovely high tones in it. I gathered together some samples in my library and described to David on the phone what I had found. All I heard on the other end was silence, a complete silence and all of a sudden this bell went off in my head, 'Oh my god, what am I thinking, I am talking to David Lynch for crying out loud! Dreamy means low and lower, it means nightmare dreams!' So I got together low and lower winds and tones and he was happy, it was perfect, that's what he needed.

**LG:** Did David work closest with Alan in terms of directors physically doing work? I know David now takes credit as sound designer on the films that he works on, but would he be the one cutting material with Alan or was Alan doing it all himself?

**AK:** David never physically edited sound when we worked with him and doesn't now, as far as I know.

LG: In terms of the human voice, I am thinking here of *Blue Velvet* and the production sound recording you did for that, I am wondering how you thought about music and sound design in relation to it? Or, was it just a matter of getting the dialogue as clean as possible?

AK: No, actually, when I was recording, I did the production sound mix on *Blue Velvet*, and when I was there, David listened to the recording as he was directing, so he had a headphone jack as well to hear the sound, which was fantastic on so many levels because people would be really respectful of sound because David cared about it. What happened was sometimes David would ask me to play music and only he and I would be able to hear it through the headphones so he would direct his movie to go with particular music, the style of music, and then he would have Angelo [Badalamenti] compose something similar to that style. For example, one time he had me play Shostakovich while Kyle [MacLachlan] was walking down the street at night. It just had this kind of mood that was perfect for him, for that movie. I did a thing with Isabella Rossellini's voice when she was whispering and screaming where I rode the gain, it was a little bit unconventional riding the gain right to the edge. You can do this with analogue, you can't do it now with digital, but there is this certain area of analogue that is just at the very edge before it breaks up and it sounds more like something between break up and the normal sound. It gave her voice an extra level of hysteria, almost a musical kind of quality to it.

LG: Did you listen to any of the music that David was listening to when you were recording?

AK: Oh absolutely, absolutely.

LG: And were you trying to mix levels with that in mind or were you listening to it and putting it to one side and getting on with the recording on set?

AK: No, I was mixing to the music.

LG: Was that a tricky thing to do?

AK: No, it was really fun to do. It was really great. I also would get ambiences to go with the music. As I record sound effects, I recorded a lot more than most dialogue recordists record because I thought, 'Why not get it now, we've got it. They can use it or not but this is a really lovely ambience'. The night crickets or moody feeling outside it would just work so well. I could mix with different microphones around and mix with the music.

LG: Are there any barriers to women working in sound? Or are there unique qualities that gender brings to different sound roles? Could you talk about the positive and negative aspects of being a woman working in sound?

AK: Especially in the early days, I think it was difficult because I was attractive and that was an incredible hindrance because people wouldn't take me seriously. And I was Alan's wife and I was dismissed in a way. We were like two kids in a sandbox and we worked really closely together. Alan was kind of shy and kept what he was doing a little to himself. I knew what he was doing and I had a lot of input in what he was doing and I think he respected me a lot. But for my colleagues,

I was his wife. After he died, I had hoped to take over the movie we were working on. We had started working on *The English Patient* (Anthony Minghella, 1996); I was hoping to continue with Alan's vision. Walter Murch took it over and wanted to do something completely different and wanted no trace of Alan or me in it. It was hard.

It is so much easier in Europe. I went to Scandinavia several years ago to give a talk, in Copenhagen. It was a combination of professionals and students who came and I was stunned by the audience, I asked people what they did and there were maybe nine or more directors there, major directors that were listening to a sound person, a woman talk about sound effects. And composers came, I was so honoured to have that audience and to speak about the collaboration of music and sound effects and how a director can be involved and express what she or he thinks and cares about. It just makes a movie so much richer. They really get it over there.

I just went and saw a movie I was involved in long distance called *Idealisten* (Christina Rosendahl, 2015) involving Peter Albrechtsen, a Danish sound designer. He has done a number of [Dolby] Atmos pictures, which few people here even know what that is. We have one Atmos theatre in San Francisco and they have three in Copenhagen. The way that the music was mixed in that film, it was so great with the sound effects, it was a beautiful job. The director, a woman, said that the music was composed before the movie was made and she directed that movie to music in different places and to Peter's sounds; it was such a collaboration, you can really hear it. I feel honoured to be able to help out however I can, suggesting sounds and coming up with ideas with them.

I mentioned sound folks in Scandinavia being more receptive to music and sound effects dancing together. Also I'd like to mention two prominent sound designers in the UK, Paul Davis and Eilam Hoffman. I worked with Eilam on the Cambridge children's [video] game I told you about. He was extremely encouraging and helpful about the sounds I provided and my recording for them. He is now a major sound designer for motion pictures. He did sound design editing for *Gravity* (Alfonso Cuarón, 2013), for example. He is also very interested in working with music in his movies.

LG: In terms of different roles and working as a woman in sound, was production sound easier or harder than sound effects recording?

AK: You know what, I was the production recordist on *Blue Velvet*, it was such a quirk that a woman got to do that; I think I may have been one of the first women who got to do that. I helped David out, he was recording auditions and looking at possibilities with actresses, they were shooting little sample scenes for people who were trying out for the Isabella [Dorothy Vallens] role. I just went and recorded it for him, he had a really fine cameraman and David really liked my recordings, he was really pleased with it and he asked me if I would do the production sound for *Blue Velvet*. I got this guy who had done a lot of boom operating to help me with it and I think he really thought he was going to be able to take over, 'You know Ann is Alan's wife, whatever!' and he was really going to be in charge. I kind of let him the first day and I didn't like where the mics were being placed, it just wasn't what I wanted, and I became very adamant about what I wanted and where the mics were going to go. It was really a problem because he was so balky with me, he used to bad-mouth me with the rest of the crew. It was hard. I just worked and put my head down and tried to get the best sound that I could. David heard it and he knew that it was working, so that was what mattered, he was listening to all of it while he was directing. It sounded good to him. When we got back to San Francisco to the studio, there was a guy who is very famous now, who has got a couple of Oscars under his belt for sound, and he was working with us at the time as a sound effects editor and he came into Alan's studio and I just happened to be standing there and he burst in and he goes, 'Alan, who was that guy that did the sound on this movie? Oh my god, how did he manage to record Kyle and Laura talking in a moving convertible and get such clean dialogue? How did he manage to perfectly record in one take whispering and screaming? I can't believe this sound, I think it is the best recording I've ever heard of production sound'. Alan kind of blushed and looked at me and all of a sudden a light went on and he realized that I had done it, that I had been the recordist. His face got so weird and he just ran out of the room. He did not say anything else, he was just like, 'Oh, okay, sorry'. He just went out. It wasn't like, 'My god, Ann, that was really incredible', or, 'good on you'. It was just like he wanted to take it back, because how could I have done something like that. The place that I was in, in that world, was less than.

**LG**: Do you think you had a harder time of it because you were Alan's wife?

**AK**: It was even harder because I was his wife. They assumed that I was doing things because I was his wife, thinking that I was hired without knowing what I was doing. I am really grateful that there is more understanding now and new directors are becoming more savvy about sound and the role that it plays and how important it is. Again, I had the experience when I was in Denmark, I was working with a sound designer who was doing an Atmos picture; it was a children's film but it was quite a big budget. He asked me would I help him with the dragon sounds. I supplied him with different possibilities and came up with ideas with him. Liz, I cannot tell you how honoured and delighted I was to work with this guy because I was taken so seriously and respected so much. It was a delightful collaboration and the director came in several times and he got involved with the collaboration, he was also just so respectful and appreciative. Women, we, I don't want to speak too generally, but, there is a tendency sometimes, we have a different way of approaching creativity which could be useful to the whole thing. It works together when there is collaboration and we are able to leave our egos at the door and really be involved together.

Another thing I'd like to say about being a sound woman working today, games guys seem much less gender conscious and I actually get treated with a lot of respect by them. For example, I was asked in December [2014] to speak at Dice Audio to the guys creating the sound for the new *Star Wars* game. I was so honoured that they would be interested in what an old lady had to say and delighted they wanted me to come out for drinks with them afterward. I also meet up with a group of game sound guys here for drinks once a month. I am so much older than they are and the first time I was really sceptical that they would even possibly be okay with my joining them. I can't tell you what a warm reception I got and how much fun I have hanging with them. We share all kinds of helpful info with each other.

I'll tell you this story also about students, I think it is important. I taught a class, it was a master class, in Stockholm, at the Stockholm Academy of Dramatic Arts. The students are very talented—the sound students were very impressive. They were preparing a final film that other students in the school had made. There were composers at the school doing music and they were all working together. There was a director, Ninja Thyberg, who had gotten a Cannes Film Festival student prize before she had even graduated for another film she had made. When I first looked at her film I was coming up with ideas with the students of what they might be able to do for sound and we were all talking together about it. The composer was there as well and I kind of felt like there wasn't a whole lot of sound effects possibilities in there. The music was beautiful, it worked really well with the film, and the dialogue worked so well. I thought the sound needed just the odd crickets in the background, just some ambience, but nothing too 'designy'. One time during that week someone said that the director really loved David Lynch and she wanted to meet me as she heard I had worked with David. So she came in and I asked her, 'What do you like about David's sound?' And she said, 'Oh, I don't know, I just like it'. She was a little hard to talk to at first and in her own world. I said to her, 'I have a lot of respect for you, you are a really good director, but I have to tell you, you are still a student and something that would be really helpful to learn is how to communicate to your sound people what you like and why you like it. This would be a really good example and I would love you to think some more about what you appreciate about David's sound.' She sat there and she thought about it and she said: 'Actually, I like that low tone and how it works. You know we could use that in the film maybe'. This light bulb went on and I thought, yes, we really could. Then the students started coming up with ideas and it was the most beautiful collaboration I have ever experienced when creating a soundtrack. Everybody had ideas and they played off of each other, the director did, and I did, I got so many ideas of how it could sound Lynchian. It was her film, it really wouldn't sound Lynchian, like a David Lynch track, it was her thing. It was her interpretation of Lynch and what she heard in his tracks is very different to what I would have guessed. But once I learned and she communicated that, then it was great for us, and the composer loved it. It was really, really helpful. If we could do that more when making movies, it would be fantastic.

CHAPTER 4

# Organizing Sound: Labour Organizations and Power Struggles that Helped Define Music and Sound in Hollywood

*Gianluca Sergi*

INTRODUCTION

Relationships between film composers and sound workers (designers, supervising sound editors, re-recording mixers) periodically show signs of underlying strains in this key relationship for a film's soundtrack. Consider for instance these two examples:

> People ask me how much collaboration there usually is between the composer and the sound designer. There is almost never any collaboration between the composer and the sound designer, or between the composer and the supervising sound editor. And that's a shame. (Randy Thom, n.d.)

> Scoring for films also requires playing musical chairs with dialog and sound effects. Rather than coexisting in the same sonic space as those elements, the composer must dance with and around these elements so the score won't be cut or pushed into deep background. No matter how careful a composer is, the recording engineer must be able to navigate within the vagaries of the Dolby matrix system. Like a car that understeers, he must steer sounds in a unique manner to avoid collisions. (Robert Hershon, 1997, p.10)

In 2011, the live musical *Priscilla, Queen of the Desert* opened in Broadway's Palace Theatre, New York. The production, based on the 1994 film, *The Adventures of Priscilla, Queen of the Desert* (Stephan Elliott), had already played successfully in different territories and cities: Australia, New Zealand,

G. Sergi
University of Nottingham, UK

© The Editor(s) (if applicable) and The Author(s) 2016
L. Greene, D. Kulezic-Wilson (eds.), *The Palgrave Handbook of Sound Design and Music in Screen Media*, DOI 10.1057/978-1-137-51680-0_4

in London's West End and in Toronto. During this time, the show had enjoyed an uneventful ride, good attendance and prestigious awards, including a Tony and an Olivier. Unbeknownst to all involved, the production was about to become the latest cause célèbre in a long-running debate that has characterized relations between musicians and recorded sound for nearly a century now. When *Priscilla, Queen of the Desert* reached Broadway, producers from the show asked the local representatives for the American Federation of Musicians (AFM hereon), Local 802, to exempt the show from the mandatory minimums for live performers in the orchestra (currently at 18 or 19, depending on the size of the theatre). The exemption, a special allowance included in the 2003 renegotiation of mandatory minimums between the AFM and The Broadway League (the national trade association for the Broadway industry), allows show producers to ask for a reduced number of live performers to be employed on artistic grounds. In the case of *Priscilla*, this request was based on the fact that the musical's use of disco music requires more of a pre-recorded, synthesized type of sound than the more orchestral nature of live music traditionally experienced on Broadway. More specifically, they requested the show use an orchestra of nine live performers playing, partly, against a pre-recorded music track (Healey, 2011).

The two sides could not agree and, after a neutral moderator adjudicated in favour of *Priscilla* and against the AFM, the show opened as planned on 20 March 2011. In response, the AFM escalated the confrontation by choosing to go to arbitration.[1] This rather unusual exacerbation of relations was partly in response to what the AFM saw as a dangerous overriding of musicians' rights as producers try to save money on their live productions by replacing live musicians with pre-recorded music. In its bid to thwart *Priscilla*, the AFM launched the 'Save Live Music Campaign' (though the campaign originated from the 'Council for Living Music', the latter was created by the AFM's Local 802 in the 1980s), commissioned a national survey on theatre-goers attitudes towards live versus pre-recorded music in musicals, canvassed other music professionals for support and launched a major website.[2]

In many ways this reaction may seem uncharacteristic: in previous years, the AFM had indeed granted the minimums exception to a number of Broadway shows and negotiations in 2003 to renew the contractual agreement between the AFM and theatre owners (The Broadway League) regulating issues including wages and musicians' minimum requirements for live theatre performances. Though fractious at times, the negotiations had not led to confrontation between the AFM and The Broadway League, until *Priscilla* that is. Arguments about the special nature of *Priscilla*'s omission of the entire live string section, the main reason put forward by the AFM in explaining their strong position with regard to shows, are not sufficient to explain the reaction and public campaign.

Indeed, far from being 'an exception', this dispute, its particular acrimonious nature and the very public stance taken by the AFM are but the latest incarnation of one of the most divisive debates in the sound arts, namely that of live music versus 'canned' music and recorded sound, dating back to the 1920s and the introduction of recorded music to the stage, as this chapter will go on to highlight. It is very fitting that this latest controversy should befall a production based on a film: the live versus canned music debate (though, as we shall see in this article, the word 'debate' hardly does justice to the strength and virulence of sentiments that characterized the debate in the cinema) was at the core of labour relations and cultural conversations around the introduction of synchronized sound to the movies in the late 1920s.[3]

It is the aim of this chapter to look back at the very origin of this debate at an industrial level, with particular attention to the extent to which it helped define the demarcation between film sound and film music and prevented the development of a more integrated relationship between the two departments, as the introductory quotes by Thom and Hershon illustrate.[4]

## Framing the Time: A Crucible of Change

The 1920s was a crucial period of change in the film industry. Most studios were either formed (Warner, MGM and Columbia all saw their beginnings in early 1920s) or came to maturity in that decade (particularly in the form of acquisitions of exhibition chains) and the notion of a 'studio' began to emerge in common parlance, with *Variety* coining the term 'majors' in 1924. It was also a period of intense production in Hollywood, with over 800 films produced every year, feeding a 100 million strong audience attending over 25,000 theatres in the USA alone. The latter continued to expand and ever more elaborate picture palaces were built across the USA with major urban centres in particular, the future beneficiaries of early sound installations, bringing in the lion's share of the takings.[5]

Unsurprisingly, this exponential growth in the industry was paralleled by a corresponding rise in the number of workers in the industry:

> When the market for feature films emerged after World War I, the demand for labor in Hollywood escalated dramatically. In 1921 there were over six thousand production workers. By 1928 moviemaking ranked as one of the most important industries in the city, and the number of production workers had grown to more than ten thousand. (Laslett, 2012, p. 84)

At this time, representation and organization proper was still in its infancy in the movie industry: only stage crafts were fully organized, mostly as a consequence of the existence of the International Alliance of Theatrical Stage Employees (IATSE), also known as IA. IATSE came to dominate below-the-line labour relations in Hollywood, which made the move to Southern California from the East coast in 1918 when it opened Local 33 in recognition of the growing relevance of Hollywood as a place of employment in entertainment.[6]

However, as financial returns and audiences grew, so did the realization amongst an increasing number of departments that their services were lucrative, in demand and in need of representation and protection. On 29 November 1926, studios (represented by the Motion Picture Producers and Distributors of America, known as the MPPDA, that would eventually evolve into today's MPAA) and the filmmakers unions (represented principally by the IA) signed the first studio basic agreement, the document that would pave the way for the actual contractual negotiations on wages and working conditions that have been the foundation of labour relations in the industry ever since (Scott, 2005, p. 31). Most departments, however, would neither seek nor achieve official 'guild' status until the mid-1930s when the introduction of the National Industrial Recovery Act (NIRA) in 1933 (in response to the great depression that followed the 1929 stock market crash) granted collective bargaining to labour movements thus fuelling a dramatic increase in representation and unionization across the USA.

As sound conversion had not yet fully begun, sound technicians were left out of the 1926 agreement:

> [Sound technicians] had not been included in the 1926 Studio Basic Agreement because they had not yet become a factor in the studio labor picture. In the period 1926–1933 both the IA and the IBEW sought to organize the sound men. The former was the more successful, but it could not obtain recognition for the craft in the major studios until the international presidents of the two organisations settled the jurisdictional issue. (Perry & Perry, 1963, p. 328)

Indeed, the nature of these early disputes were more jurisdictional than departmental: they were not so much about the need to protect the interests of any one category of workers; rather, they were the manifestation of the move out west (from New York mostly) of existing unions (as in the case of the IA) and the ensuing power struggle over who would control the studio territory when it came to labour.[7]

Within this context of shifting labour representation, the 'place' in the production process that sound artists occupied in the 1920s was itself unclear: at a time when Hollywood was hard at work establishing the style, genres, and related production processes to which the industry would become so well accustomed to for decades, the question of whether sound belonged to any one particular existing department in the industry or was an entirely new one was far from settled. Did film sound belong to the sonic arts (and might therefore be represented by the AFM)? Was it primarily a production process or would sound, like editing, become part of this post-production process? The question was important beyond issues of representation; studios themselves showed considerable confusion as to the manner in which they should ensure that their next generation of talent understood the role of sound in the cinema and the rules and methods in which they would need to train and professionalize. Writers, as a group, to name one noticeable example, were asked to attend courses about the properties of sound, both electric and physical.[8] The lack of a firm location in the production process and industrial structure meant in many ways that nobody truly 'owned' cinema sound in the run up to the swift change that would see Hollywood go from silent to sound at the end of the decade.

Studios found this a relatively comfortable position to be in, especially as it allowed them to turn a blind eye with regard to remuneration and music copyright. By the time the American Society of Composers, Authors and Publishers (ASCAP) and other similar organizations woke up to the fact that 'canned music' in the cinema was likely to be a popular success in the wake of hits like *Don Juan* (Alan Crosland, 1926), studios were more than happy to compensate musicians at a fraction of what it would have cost them to license the music or commission original music.[9] It is no accident that it should be ASCAP to take up the early fight with the studios. Composers and musicians were the only category of people working in the cinema that enjoyed organized support and representation. Unlike the (still very young) movie industry, the music industry had developed its own professional and labour organization relatively quickly after the introduction of the phonograph in 1877.

The most important of the professional organizations in this field was undoubtedly the AFM: formed in 1896 as an evolution from the National League of Musicians, it built very quickly a large member base. Its areas of influence were in fields as diverse as musical, opera, theatre and live/recorded music. Cinema was primarily of interest to the AFM not so much in terms of composers (the rise of the composer was to follow the introduction of synchronized sound in the late 1920s) but of musicians. Live music was performed in many theatres, particularly so in first-run theatres in larger urban areas and the arrival of synchronized sound to the cinema raised the spectre of layoffs and the death of live orchestras setting the scene for the development of what was to come.

Although sound was present from the inception of cinema as musical accompaniment, commentary on the on-screen action by narrators standing by the side of the screen in movie theatres, or early sound effects troupes similar to those operating in the theatre, the arrival of synchronized sound is still regarded as one of the pivotal moments in the medium's history.[10] Much has been written about the concerns and legitimate doubts that some filmmakers and actors expressed about the potentially disruptive nature of the coming of sound to film. To mention but a few: silent actors had to use their voice, directors had to learn to frame for sound, writers needed to write extensive dialogue that was to be performed not just read from intertitle cards, cinematographers were saddled with heavier and less flexible cameras, production designers needed to accommodate the need for microphone placement and so on.

The arrival of sound resembled more that of a long wave, moving slowly but surely towards the shore rather than one quick and sudden catastrophic jolt to industry structures. The emergence of Fox's Movietone and Warner's Vitaphone systems had introduced US audiences to recorded sound in the cinema from the mid-1920s and, by and large, had proven successful with audiences and studios alike. However, the emergence of these systems was seen at that time not necessarily as a precursor to the inescapable arrival of feature films employing synchronized sound (e.g. pre-recorded music, speech and effects to be played back in synch with the image) but primarily as an amusing and intriguing opportunity to maximize theatrical attraction as shorts played before the main feature film (itself now hardening into the 'long format' we are used to today). It was against this background of uncertainty mixed with hope and fear that seasoned industry leaders like D. W. Griffith could infamously be tempted to proclaim that: 'Talkies are a novelty. Sound will never last' (D.W. Griffith as quoted in Oderman, 2000, p. 191). This uncertainty became the ground for much debate within the industry in the months approaching and following the arrival of *The Jazz Singer* (Alan Crosland, 1927) and it goes a long way in explaining the somewhat conflicting views expressed by comments such as Griffith's at a time when studios were investing millions to convert to sound. Most importantly for this study, this mix of uncertainty about jobs at a time of great financial strains worldwide and the understandable concerns about the arrival of sound goes a long way in explaining the highly combustible nature of labour relations both amongst filmmakers and between studios and filmmakers' organizations.

## THE END IS NIGH: CANNED SOUND IS COMING!

While it is virtually impossible to pinpoint precisely the origin of the dispute around recorded sound in the movies (in many ways the dispute goes back to the introduction of recorded sound, its later use in radio and, more relevantly, in the theatre), there is plenty of evidence to suggest that the introduction in the mid-1920s of recorded vaudeville acts to be shown in movie theatres provided both the touch paper and the match to ignite it. This was not just a matter of jobs shifting from the realm of live performance to recorded music; for exhibitors in particular, this was an issue that touched upon the nature of programming, personal taste and the role of live musicians in helping exhibitors maintain a close and direct (live!) relationship between their movie theatre and the neighbouring community that patronized it, something that the AFM would draw directly from during their Music Defense League (MDL) campaign:

> Before the advent of synchronized sound, movie going was far from a standardized experience. Exhibitors resisted uniformity, often tailoring films, live acts, and music to local tastes. In particular, musicians viewed themselves as artists crafting a unique performance and a personal relationship with the audience. Live music, in short, allowed the audience a 'margin of participation' and provided an unpredictability rooted in specific local or cultural conditions. (Fones-Wolf, 1994, p. 4)

Here the issue of standardization is clearly presented in negative terms which coupled with the real threat of job losses amongst live performers, provided fertile ground for the debate on recorded sound that was soon to follow. The other side of the argument was also well represented though: studios without an exhibition chain (Warner being the most obvious example at the time) and smaller independents struggled to compete with the larger chains and the studios that owned them as the latter could parade the biggest vaudeville stars live on the proscenia of New York, Los Angeles and the other key urban areas at a time when, as noted earlier, cinemas in urban areas provided three quarters of all box office.

As Maggie Valentine notes:

> Sound films permitted not only Warner Bros., which owned neither a distribution chain nor a chain of first-run theatres, but also independent theatre owners such as Gumbiner to compete with the downtown movie palaces that could afford live prologues and big-time vaudeville acts. 'Canned vaudeville' meant that Warner Bros. could capture more impressive performers on film than the other theatres could get live. (Valentine, 1996, p. 37)

The combustive nature of this mixture of growing popularity of movies (particularly in urban areas), growth of studios, increasingly competing for patrons with ever more elaborate programmes, and the changing patterns of employment and labour representation was not going unnoticed amongst those who would ultimately be impacted on most dramatically: filmmakers themselves. Sensing the urgency to facilitate debate around the live versus canned contention and the introduction of synchronized sound to movies more widely, industry publications provided a platform for debate, with new publications emerging as a direct consequence.

On 15 August 1928, the first issue of *Sound Waves* was published in Hollywood, California.[11] Under the banner 'Heralding the Epoch of Science in Pictures', the first main title of the publication read 'Musician's Union Hits Synchronized Pictures!'. In actual fact, the extremely big type headline was the title of a letter to the editor from H.P. Moore, the then secretary of Local 47, Hollywood's branch of the AFM. The letter, published on the first page, clearly spelled out the terms of the fight:

> Now we have no desire to sail under false colors, so we readily admit that our peculiar interest in opposing such a substitution is that it might cost some of us jobs. (...) Looking a little further into the future, we foresee that the quality of our national music will be seriously affected if 'canned music' displaced other forms and reduced the musicians' opportunities of employment. (Moore, 1928, pp. 1 & 4)

While acknowledging that the fight was primarily centred around jobs, the letter clearly revealed the AFM's strategy of attempting to weave inextricably in the mind of the general public the arrival of recorded sound (in the guise of canned music) with the demise of quality music. In other words, the AFM clearly aimed at shifting the debate from an employment matter to one of social relevance for the wider public, in doing this implicitly acknowledging that a mere direct appeal to the public to shun recorded music, and those who used it, would likely never work in view of the latter's evident popular appeal amongst audiences, as the huge success of early sound films had demonstrated. To look for a counter-argument, one needed only look across the same page where a statement from French actress, significantly titled 'Mlle. Ana Xanthia answers Union statement', argues the exact opposite point:

> One is not mechanizing an art in recording talking motion pictures (...) Rather, Science is creating, for the first time, a new art and because of this means a new field of development for a true American music is opened. (...) Art is ever sacrifice and advancement cannot be halted by those who would place material above cultural gain. (Xanthia, 1928, p. 1)

Thus, the battle lines were clearly drawn in the earliest days of the arrival of recorded music and sound to the movies. The AFM were at great pains in demonstrating, without saying so too openly, that the talkies brought with them the risk of the demise of refinement, quality and variety in music and beyond. I will demonstrate this through a consideration of newspaper advertisements later. Crucially, in their view, this was an issue of public concern and not merely an internal labour dispute to the arts.

Despite numerous and sustained articles, editorials and public appearances putting forward the AFM argument, by the time *Sound Waves* entered its second year of publication in 1929, the situation had clearly moved on in favour of recorded sound. Multiple speaking parts had begun appearing in Hollywood movies, thus removing one of the strongest objections actors had to recorded sound, namely that it greatly reduced the number of speaking parts[12]; theatre architecture was beginning to adapt to the new sound requirements, studios were investing heavily in producing talkies and, crucially, box office was unequivocal in rewarding talkies and even until the then stubbornly silent MGM lion roared proudly on screens for the first time. This is the stage upon which the MDL emerged, a point in time when the battle for the hearts and minds of the general public, let alone those of studios heads, looked certain to slip away from the AFM. Setting aside a considerable budget of $500,000, in 1930, the AFM began paying publishers across the country to print one-page spreads in the press. At first, though aggressive in tone, the rhetoric employed and the language used to convey it remained relatively conciliatory. One of the earliest of these one-page spreads, published in June 1930, is at pains to avoid extreme language.[13] Although it is unequivocally titled 'Trampling Art for Profits', the spread suggests that: 'If you agree that theatre patrons are entitled to real music—in addition to talking and sound motion pictures, for the price they pay–HELP SAVE THE ART FROM RUIN. Enroll with millions of others in the Music Defense League. *When the public's voice is raised its will must be served!*' (italics and capital emphasis are from the original advert). Although sanguine in its defence of live music, also suggesting that '300 musicians in Hollywood supply all the "music" offered in thousands of theatres. Can such a tiny reservoir of talent nurture artistic progress?', the advert avoids the use of overtly inflammatory language.

However, it is the imagery used in such adverts that would rightly make the MDL's spread infamously known: even in this early, 'mild' version of the MDL's argument, the advert is headlined by a disturbing image. A large, grotesque figure of a man, symbolizing profit, appears to incite a mechanical, robotic figure playing canned music towards movie theatre patrons. The latter appears to be fleeing in fear, dwarfed by the gigantic figures of both the profit maker and the robotic figure. The use of the robot as a proxy is central to understanding the reigning feelings towards recorded sound. The robot quickly became identified not merely as a mechanical performer but as the originator of music itself, thus raising the spectre of soulless automation replacing human imagination. The introduction of recorded, synchronized sound to the movies represented, in the view of the MDL/AFM, a direct threat to human creativity and inventiveness. In a further attempt at appealing to the public, the robotic humanoid was also given a 'black face' in a non-too-subtle attempt at adopting popular racial discrimination tropes. The fear of mechanization as a threat to jobs and industry was certainly not new but the figure of the humanoid robotic automaton had only recently gained public appeal following the success of the Czech play *RUR*, the first of such works to use the word robot and present automatons that had human feature. The AFM mobilized the spectre of mechanization in ways that they hoped would help rally the support of both core union membership and, more crucially, the general public.

However, the campaign had little or no impact on either the studios or the public: the success of *All Quiet on the Western Front* (Lewis Milestone, 1930) (still regarded as one of the first 'great' sound movies) was a stark reminder of this. The film represented Universal's greatest investment to date (costing over $1 million) and was a great success both at the box office, where it became the 1930s greatest hit (grossing over $3 million) and with critics, with the film winning four Oscars, including a best picture and best director Oscar for Lewis Milestone.

Most alarmingly for the AFM and the MDL campaign, Milestone had clearly thought carefully about sound in the movie and overcame some of the camera limitations of the time (often encased to avoid the noise of the camera motor to be picked up by the microphone on stage recording the action) by shooting some of crane sequences as silent, only to add and synch sound to those sequences in post-production. Most damagingly for the AFM's efforts to defend live music in the cinema and a clear signal of the changing times, Milestone filmed two versions: in the silent version, music accompanies the pictures as per expectation and tradition (though with some sound effects and even snippets of dialogue synched in); however, in the vastly more successful sound print, the director chose to use no music reportedly to avoid detracting from the tension he had created through dialogue and sound effects.

In view of the popular and critical success of movies like *All Quiet on the Western Front* and the successful drive to resolve all technical issues that had characterized the early days of recorded movie sound, the MDL escalated the tone and viciousness of its campaign accordingly. Following a steady flow of one-page spreads in 1930, all increasingly aggressive in message and tone, 1931 saw the MDL take on more than just canned music and expand their target to sound overall. In a March 1931 spread, titled 'The Robot at the Helm', the text reads: 'Are you content to face a limitless expanse of "sound" without a sign of music?'[14] The (unequivocally black) robot also takes a much more aggressive stance by literally wrestling away from the rudder the (unmistakably white) musical muse of old, thus introducing a theme of violence and threat that the MDL would pursue in other spreads.

Indeed, by this time the robot is portrayed as posing a physical, even sexual threat. In August 1931 when a new spread title appeared, 'When is that young man going home?', the transformation had reached its peak. Less of the spread is dedicated to language than in previous adverts with images doing the talking: the father of the same musical muse portrayed in earlier spreads, stands on top of the family home's stairs aghast at what he sees, namely the black robot with his arm around the muse pulling her towards him in a clearly sexualized move, as the text reinforces by suggesting that 'this unwelcome suitor has been wooing the music for many dreary months without winning her favour'.[15]

Moreover, far from being confined to Hollywood alone, the campaign against recorded sound and canned music waged across the USA, in some cases becoming the excuse for organized crime to intimidate theatre owners. San Francisco was the stage of some of the most infamous of these instances:

> As the talkies started to move into theatres, a group of unnamed 'racketeers' began making threats and bombing movie theatres. In June 1930, a bomb tore a four-foot hole in the metal roof of the Royal Theatre (...) four months later, a janitor found a bomb at the Alhambra Theatre, planted behind the ticket kiosk, with enough dynamite to blow up the entire theatre and damage buildings within a block. (Poletti, 2008, p. 138)

Just as the MDL had suddenly appeared in 1930, so it vanished in late 1931, no more spreads were published and the AFM ceased its campaign. There is no record of discussion or decisions to this effect available from the AFM archives or other sources, indicating that the most probable cause of this was simply that the money expired and no more funds were made available.

By this time, the issue of who would represent sound technicians had become a central union concern as the numbers of filmmakers, technicians and musicians in this field and related 'mechanical trades' grew exponentially:

> An organizing campaign in 1928 and 1929 resulted in almost complete unionization of the different mechanical trades as well as of several additional groups such as wardrobe workers, costumers, engineers, and cameramen. The introduction of sound aided Musician Local No. 47, as many instrumentalists migrated to the West. By 1930 this union was the third largest in the United States. (Perry & Perry, 1963, p. 326)

## A Long Hurricane Tail-End

The 2011 *Priscilla, Queen of the Desert* dispute becomes easier to understand when placed against the backdrop of the early developmental stages of the relationships between the music industry and the film industry. In this important sense, *Priscilla* works as but the latest reminder that the MDL was only the starting point of a long history of contention between music and (recorded) sound. It showed the strength of feelings that were emerging and it would come to represent a hindrance to the development of full cooperation between musicians and sound artists as they drove a wedge between the emerging sound department and the established practices of live music and performers.

What is perhaps most striking, in this short but tempestuous period, was quite how long lasting its effects would be. The answer lies partly with the AFM itself: as the fight against recorded sound was evidently lost, and sound people were beginning to develop a whole new film department, it could be argued that the AFM could have secured its future role in shaping the development of sound by bringing sound men and women under their wing and asking them to join the AFM to work together with musicians. The considerable sum of money the AFM invested in the MDL campaign could have been directed towards lobbying both the other key unions and the studios: in the absence of a paternal figure, the emerging sound department eventually joined the 'electricians department' in the IA. Much as sound personnel were influential within the IA (it represented a considerable number of film professionals), it never had the muscle to influence the kind of action around the negotiating table that would have signalled sound's intention to become established as a leading force in the industry.

Whether this missed opportunity was due to a lack of foresight on the part of the AFM's leadership or simply a historical accident is difficult to assess and would certainly warrant further research, particularly around the dynamics of unionization that characterized the 1930s in the wake of the Great Depression and the National Labour relation Act of 1935, when virtually all of the guilds as we have them today were formed.[16]

What is indisputable is that the AFM did have the perfect opportunity to suggest closer collaborations between musicians and sound artists but instead chose to reiterate their position against recorded sound. Nowhere did this became clearer than on Monday, 29 September 1930, when a special meeting of sound technicians and union representatives was held to approve a new charter document that would create Local 695 in Hollywood to represent sound workers in Hollywood. Several invited guests from related locals and organizations spoke in support of the new charter: amongst them was J.W. Gillette the film representative for the AFM. His remarks were recorded as follows:

> After congratulating the members on their new Charter, he went on to state that 'conditions generally were bad and that there were 9 million men out of work in the United States, regardless of all the propaganda by the Los Angeles

Times-Chamber of Commerce and others'. He said that 'the situation is critical and breadlines are being filled to greater length every day.' (...) Spoke on 'the control of machines which are so rapidly replacing man power' and 'believed organized labor must overcome the situation.' Said that 'if a question is not answered within the next two years, one-half of the men sitting in this room will be replaced by machines.' Said that 'out of a membership of 4000 Musicians, 2000 were out of work and he had personally aided men financially whose feet were actually on the ground, that they might take bread home to a hungry family.' Spoke of 'the close affiliation of organized labor through the American Federation of Labor and the American Legion, the greatest political power in the country today and one that can bring about the results for economic betterment of the country.' In closing, asked that 'the Brothers seriously consider the machine problem' and wished them the greatest success in the world. (Smith, 2010, p. 21)

Arguably, the AFM's campaign waged through the MDL defined the relationship between musicians and those working in recorded sound in ways that were difficult to reconcile; while this is perfectly understandable in the climate of fear about the future of musicians at the time, this kind of 'all-or nothing' strategy in effect slammed the door on closer integration of music and sound in the cinema right at the very moment when sound departments were being established. When sound finally became fully represented, under the newly formed Motion Picture Editors Guild in 1937, it had become self-evident that the future of film sound (and thus film music) lay firmly within cinema and increasingly away from the AFM, thus sealing a division that, in many respects, continues to this day. This move away from the music industry and into the film industry was not just the domain of sound artists. Film music composers also chose a similar route a few years later when they formed the Screen Composers Association (1945), later to achieve guild status in 1953 as the Composers Guild of America. The move was a direct challenge to ASCAP to recognize the value and rights of film music composer, particularly with regard to film music royalties, and acted as a powerful reminder of the division that characterized the relations between the film industry and the music industry.

## Notes

1. The outcome of the arbitration is not yet known at time of writing, but a 2013 Tour Agreement contract from the AFM shows *Priscilla* as touring in the USA with a nine-live-performer crew. Contract agreement available at: http://www.afm.org/uploads/file/Priscilla.pdf
2. The website for the 'Save Live Music Campaign' is available at http://savelivemusiconbroadway.com and their survey can be access ad http://savelivemusiconbroadway.com/wp-content/media/Broadway-Poll-Data-4-20-11.pdf
3. It is of course not accidental that debates around the nature and end objectives of mechanical reproduction of sound and images should emerge at a time when music and cinema in particular were maturing into fully formed and extremely popular forms of entertainment. Although a fully articulated position, most famously in the postulations of Adorno and Horkheimer, was not developed until the 1940s and 1950s, it ultimately originated at roughly the same time as the

emergence of cinema as an industry in the work started in 1920s at the Frankfurt School in Germany and in the 1930s at the Chicago School in the USA.
4. Randy Thom and Gary Rydstrom are two of the most successful sound men in Hollywood over the past 30 years.
5. For an excellent account of that period see Eyman, S. (1999).
6. The fight for jurisdictional supremacy between the International Brotherhood of Electrical Workers (IBEW) and the IATSE in 1921 is one of the most well-known of these early West Coast disputes. Studios fuelled these divisions in a sort of 'divide and conquer' approach that proved very successful thanks to the combined efforts of individual studios and their official representative, the Motion Picture Producers and Distributors of America (MPPDA).
7. For an excellent account of early representation of filmmakers, see Laurie Pintar (2011).
8. This was a time of considerable boundary transparency between production departments where writers got training in sound, costume, cameras and direction, no doubt assisted by having all relevant department and artists under one roof.
9. For a succinct and effective account of this period, see Wierzbicki (2008).
10. For an excellent account of early sound effects troupes and techniques see Altman, R. (2004, pp. 145–155). For a similarly compelling account of the arrival of synchronized sound to the cinema see Crafton, D. (1999) and Gomery D. (2005).
11. *Sound Waves* was published by the Sound Waves Publishing Co., Cedric E. Hart. There is extremely little information on Hart and his motivations but he worked as a representative to opera stars and was close to both performers and theatre owners, something that is apparent in the publication's drive to represent both camps in the debate over sound.
12. For an account of the divisions between actors with speaking parts and those with nonspeaking roles following the introduction of sound, see Chapter 6 in Slide, A. (2012).
13. Image available at http://public.media.smithsonianmag.com/legacy_blog/1930-June-5-Bradford-Era-Bradford-PA-sm.jpg, last accessed 1 July 2014.
14. Image available at http://2.bp.blogspot.com/_sGYULzoQCgA/RyVjxyZT_iI/AAAAAAAABJA/7twI9CSPeOs/s1600-h/1931-March-9---paleofuture.jpg, last accessed 1 July 2014.
15. Image available at http://public.media.smithsonianmag.com/legacy_blog/1931-Aug-24-Centralia-Daily-Chronicle-Centralia-WA-sm.jpg, last accessed 1 July 2014.
16. To name but a notable few, the Writers Guild of America and the Screen Actors Guild formed in 1933, the Directors Guild of America in 1936 and the Society of Motion Picture Editors, now the Motion Picture Editors Guild, representing both editors and sound men and women, in 1937.

## References

Altman, R. (2004) Silent Film Sound (New York: Columbia University Press).
Crafton, D. (1999) *The Talkies—American Cinema's Transition to Sound, 1926–1931* (Berkeley and Los Angeles: University of California Press).
Eyman, S. (1999) The Speed of Sound: Hollywood and the Talkie Revolution, 1926–1930 (Baltimore: Johns Hopkins University Press).

Fones-Wolf, E. (1994) 'Sound Comes to the Movies: The Philadelphia Musicians' Struggle Against Recorded Music', *Pennsylvania Magazine of History and Biography*, 118 (1/2, January/April), 3–32.

Gomery, D. (2005) The Coming of Sound (London and New York: Routledge).

Healey, P. (2011) 'Broadway Union Takes On 'Priscilla' Over Music', *New York Times* [Online] 15 May, http://www.nytimes.com/2011/05/16/theater/broadway-union-takes-on-priscilla-over-recorded-music.html?_r=1&pagewanted=1, date accessed 1 July 2014.

Hershon, R. (1997) 'Film Composers in the Sonic Wars', *Cineaste*. Vol. 22, No. 4 (March), 10–13.

Laslett, J. H. M. (2012) Sunshine Was Never Enough: Los Angeles Workers, 1880–2010 (Berkeley: University of California Press).

Moore, H. P. (1928) Letter to the Publisher, *Sound Waves*, Vol. 1 (1 August).

Oderman, S. (2000) Lillian Gish: A Life on Stage and Screen (London: McFarland & Company Inc).

Perry, L. B. and E. S. Perry (1963) Early Labour Struggles in A History of the Los Angeles Labor Movement, 1911–1941 (Los Angeles: University of California Press).

Pintar, L. (2011) 'Bronco Billy and Open Shop Hollywood' in T. Sitton and W. F. Deverell (eds) Metropolis in the Making: Los Angeles in the 1920s (Berkeley: University of California Press).

Poletti, T. (2008) Art Deco San Francisco: The Architecture of Timothy Pflueger (New York: Princeton Architectural Press).

Scott, A. J. (2005) On Hollywood: The Place, the Industry (Princeton: Princeton University Press).

Slide, A. (2012) Hollywood Unknowns: A History of Extras, Bit Players, and Stand-Ins (Jackson: University Press of Mississippi).

Smith, S. D. (2010) 'Beginnings of Local 695' in *695 Quarterly*, Vol. 2, No. 4 (Fall), 16–26.

Thom, R. (n.d.) A Few Notes on Music in the Final Mix, http://www.filmsound.org/randythom/finalmix.htm, date accessed 1 July 2014.

Valentine, M. (1996) The Show Starts on the Sidewalk: An Architectural History of the Movie (New Haven and London: Yale University Press).

Wierzbicki, J. (2008) Film Music: A History (New York and London: Routledge).

Xanthia (1928) 'Mlle. Ana Xanthia answers Union statement', *Sound Waves*, Vol. 1 (1 August).

CHAPTER 5

# Mixing as a Hyperorchestration Tool

*Sergi Casanelles*

The music for the opening credits of *The Social Network* (David Fincher, 2010) begins with the intriguing combination of an unsettling drone, generated by processing diverse electric guitar samples, and a solo piano line. According to the director David Fincher, 'It was kind of astounding, because it seemed to talk about this loneliness, the piano was this lonely and also so childlike ... and yet it had this seething anger, vitriol that was sort of bubbling under it' (Fincher, 2011). Fincher also explains that he chose the opening music from a set of musical ideas the composer team, Trent Reznor and Atticus Ross, sent him as the starting material. In addition to choosing the track, Fincher envisioned a triptych of scenes that would include the same track. The music begins the first time just at the moment when Zuckerberg's (Jesse Eisenberg) girlfriend, Erica (Rooney Mara), leaves after breaking up with him for being arrogant (0:05:19).[1] The second time we hear it is during a deposition scene when Zuckerberg is telling a lawyer that he cannot have his full attention because he doesn't deserve it (0:49:00). Finally, the third and last time that the theme appears (1:43:00), it accompanies Zuckerberg's betrayal of his only friend Eduardo Saverin (Andrew Garfield). The piano theme evolves during these scenes: the first time the sound is recorded by placing a microphone close to the instrument, the second time the microphone is placed further away and the third time even further than in the second scene (Fincher, 2011). These three scenes are examples of a mode of scoring that generates meaning just by applying aural modifications to the musical content of a piece. The music serves to symbolize the increasing detachment that the main character experiences during the process of abandoning his initial ethical principles. Although the harmonic content and the melody remain much the same in all three versions, the changing sound of the piano signifies the process of detachment.

Music for contemporary film and television has drastically changed with the incorporation of computer-aided technology, which has greatly expanded the

S. Casanelles
NYU Steinhardt, USA

© The Editor(s) (if applicable) and The Author(s) 2016
L. Greene, D. Kulezic-Wilson (eds.), *The Palgrave Handbook of Sound Design and Music in Screen Media*, DOI 10.1057/978-1-137-51680-0_5

possibilities afforded to composers. As the example from *The Social Network* illustrates, by utilizing a variety of microphone positions of the piano recording, the music is able to imply a meaning that would have otherwise required harmonic or instrumental variation. In this chapter, I aim to show how procedures derived from the practice of music mixing have become part of the creative process of scoring. I call these methods *hyperorchestration tools* because they involve the utilization of a *hyperorchestra*, a virtual music ensemble that inhabits hyperreality, a product of the combination of virtual instruments (sampled and synthetic), real live recording sessions and sound processing. My use of the term hyperorchestra encapsulates the processes of music creation that transcend the limitations of the physical world. Jean Baudrillard defined hyperreality as 'the generation by models of a real without origin or reality' (1994, p. 1). By extension, the hyperorchestra is a musical ensemble able to produce music that might sound realistic even though it could not have been generated by physical means alone. Sound recording is, by nature, a process of virtualization that allows the recorded sound to be transformed beyond what would be possible in the physical world with acoustic instruments alone. Therefore, any process of sound recording involves a certain degree of bringing sound into hyperreality.

The hyperorchestra expands the possibilities of the traditional Western orchestra, which has been the dominant mode of musical expression for film and television music. The orchestration practices for the Western orchestra, or the strategies of instrumental combinations, have always been linked to Western music practices based on notation and utilization of the musical score. Writing for the hyperorchestra allows the composer to surpass the limitations imposed by the score. In order to provide some theoretical context for my discussion, I will describe the properties of traditional orchestration. This will serve as a means to better explain how the hyperorchestra is able to produce music that transcends this limited framework typical not only of Western traditions of classical music but of screen music practice as well.

## Music and the Western Score

In *Understanding Media*, Marshall McLuhan argues that Western society was given 'an eye for an ear' (1994, p. 91). Although McLuhan's thesis focuses on the phonetic language, his thoughts are directly applicable to the Western score, as I will describe below. For McLuhan, the phonetic language is key to understanding the development of human intelligence because 'language does for intelligence what the wheel does for the feet and the body. It enables them to move from thing to thing with greater ease and speed and ever less involvement' (p. 89). Western society evolved with the utilization of the phonetic language, a form of communication that separates the visual and the auditory experience. A phonetic language is a symbolic system that represents language where its written symbols directly correspond to its spoken sounds. To put it in McLuhan's words, 'semantically meaningless letters are used to correspond to semantically meaningless sounds' (p. 83).

In McLuhan's vision, the phonetic language became key to the development of civilization since it allowed the creation of rational thinking that could be easily transmitted and reproduced. In order to explain the consequences of the implantation of this communication system, he utilized the graphical representation of the American flag as an eloquent example:

> Suppose that, instead of displaying the Stars and Stripes, we were to write the words 'American flag' across a piece of cloth and to display that. While the symbols would convey the same meaning, the effect would be quite different. To translate the rich visual mosaic of the Stars and Stripes into written form would be to deprive it of most of its qualities of corporate image and of experience, yet the abstract literal bond would remain much the same. (p. 82)

This example highlights two main consequences of the introduction of the phonetic language. First, by separating 'both signs and sound from their semantic and dramatic meanings' (p. 91), there is a detachment 'from the feelings or emotional involvement that a non-literate man or society would experience' (p. 89). Second, it is precisely by separating the emotional part from the content of the phonetic language that it becomes a tool for rational thinking. Moreover, the rationalization of the language allows it to be easily reproducible and to be systematically taught and learnt.

The Western musical score shares a considerable amount of features with the phonetic language, as described by McLuhan. Unquestionably, employing a musical score facilitates the distribution of and permits a systematic approach to learning music. In addition, the musical score creates the concept of discrete pitch, associating each of the 12 possible tones to a sound frequency. At the same time, it discretizes the dynamics to just a few levels (derived from just two dynamic levels: *piano* and *forte*) and restricts the notation of dynamic transitions to a vague idea of *crescendo* and *decrescendo* (progressive increase or decrease of the dynamic). In the case of dynamic variation, the Western score becomes an especially weak notation device.[2] Let's examine a common *crescendo* from a *piano* (soft) dynamic to a *forte* (loud). The common notation that represents a *crescendo* is unable to specify the evolution over time of the dynamic increasing process. In Fig. 5.1, there are three different possible interpretations of the same *crescendo* represented utilizing the Piano Roll notation system from the program Apple's Logic X, a widely used software program that falls under the umbrella term of Digital Audio Workstations (DAWs) which include the potential to write, record, edit and mix music and sound in the one work station. In Fig. 5.1, the vertical axis shows the musical instrument digital interface (MIDI) values of a continuous controller that modifies the dynamics of the sounds, whereas the horizontal axis corresponds to time. The first example shows a linear increase of the dynamics. The second graphic shows an uneven dynamic increase. The last graphic represents a *crescendo* that mainly increases the dynamic at the end of the process. These three images illustrate the range of graphical shapes that can represent a *crescendo*. The same ambiguity applies to creating variations in the metre and in the tempo.

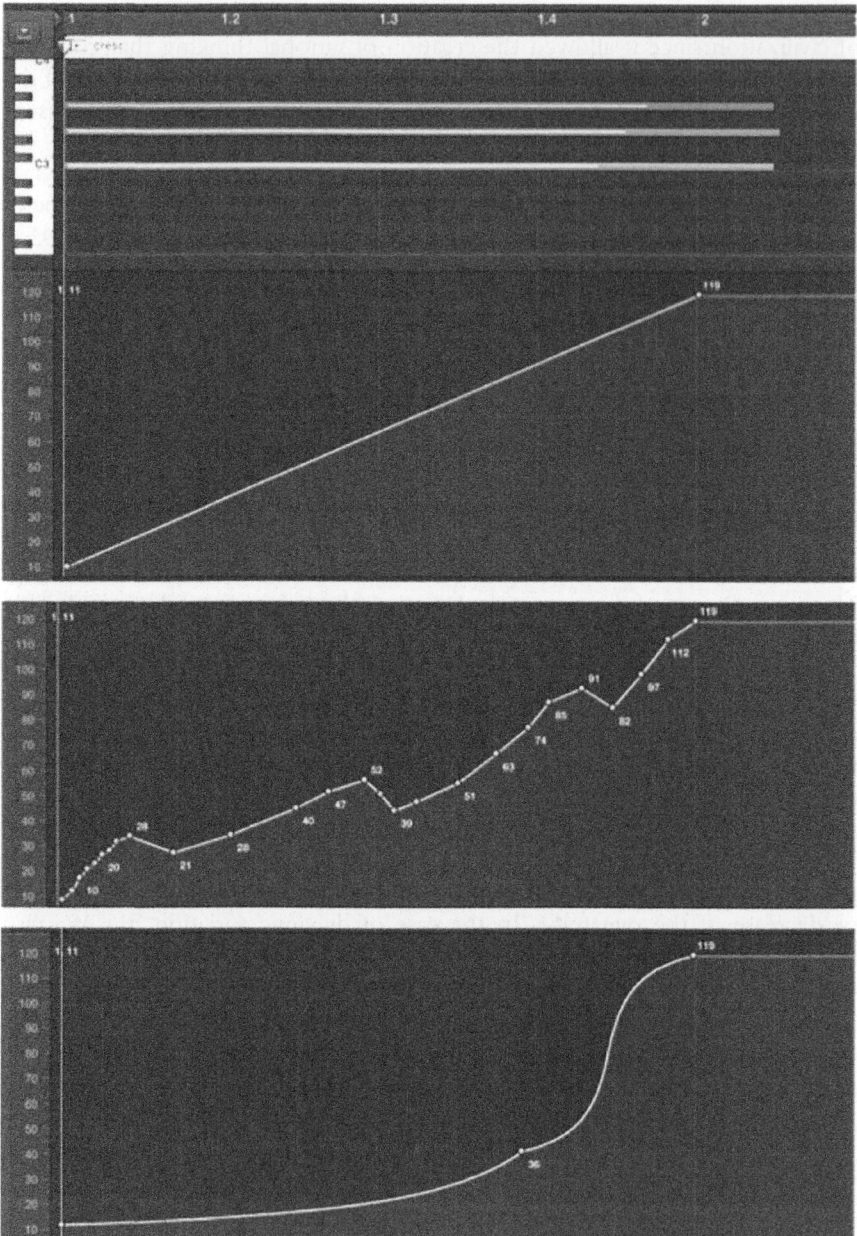

**Fig. 5.1** Different interpretations of a crescendo using the Piano Roll notation system from Apple Logic Pro X (Digital Audio Workstation)

The impossibility of precisely shaping a *crescendo* might not be extremely relevant in concert musical scores, but it is highly relevant in music for the screen, which relies on precise synchronization in order to accurately generate meaning.

Although the score is just a blueprint for performance, a set of instructions designed to guide the performer in how to produce a series of sounds over time, traditional musicology and music analysis assume that the score has a certain representational capability. Musicologist Nicholas Cook, who advocates an approach to musical analysis that encompasses all the audiovisual aspects involved in a musical performance, states:

> Traditional musicological approaches, following the nineteenth-century aesthetics of absolute instrumental music, force a distinction between the 'musical' and the 'extra-musical', where the 'musical' is essentially defined in terms of notation: everything that Michelangeli does before he plays the first note, then, falls into the category of the 'extra-musical'. (2013, pp. 72–3)

Traditional music analysis has utilized the score as the primary source to describe a musical experience. A traditional harmonic (chord) analysis or a Shenkerian reduction are performed by just looking at the score alone. However, the score cannot represent the overtones that would emanate from a note, nor can it graphically distinguish between different timbres.[3]

In lieu of this situation, it is important to comprehend how the score has become a useful tool for music creation and performance in Western society. The score extends the standardization process of music into performance and music creation. In other words, composers create music for predefined ensembles (especially the orchestra) that is performed in relatively similar concert halls. Therefore, the concert hall has become the accepted medium in which to perceive music. For orchestral music, the placement of the instruments onstage was also standardized, which generated a template for orchestral writing. The process of music creation also adapted to the restrictions of the score. For instance, pitches were mostly written using the tempered scale, which divided the octave into 12 tones, whereas the rhythm followed a temporal grid. Moreover, traditional Western harmonic principles, which started to develop during the eighteenth century and got established during the nineteenth century, incorporate chord distribution practices that are designed to overcome the hidden presence of overtones. From this viewpoint, the score represents an acceptable notational system to generate orchestral music created and performed in an extremely controlled environment. Therefore, instead of a representation of the sound, the score is really a blueprint for the instrumental performers to produce sound. However, modelling Western music as a controlled environment comes at a price: it neglects an extensive array of musical features that do not fit within the restrictions imposed.

The definition of music as a subset of sound has been culturally established. In other words, the distinction between what is sound and what is music is a product of pure cultural convention. As the notion of what constitutes music changed significantly during the second half of the twentieth century, so the limitations of the traditional score expanded to include graphic notation, aleatoric notation and the utilization of the studio as a means to produce a recording based on improvised material. Moreover, spectral composers created pieces for orchestra and traditional ensembles based on the analysis of sound spectra.[4] The concept of hyperorchestra is another way of broadening the boundaries of what is considered music. With the hyperorchestra, it is possible to surpass the limitations of the score, as its modes of expression, centred on computer programs such as Apple's Logic X, do not require traditional score notation in order to produce music. Thus, the domain of the hyperorchestra is the full sound spectrum. From this perspective, as I will argue later, the process of music composition is just a subset of sound design. Moreover, the subset is defined symbolically by the aesthetics of a given culture. Therefore, a sound might be considered music when it obeys the parameters that a culture defines as acceptable for music.

## Extending the Orchestra with Sample Libraries

One of the most relevant additions that the hyperorchestra offers is the possibility of utilizing sample libraries as a source of sound creation. A sample library is a sophisticated collection of recordings from a musical instrument, an instrumental section (e.g. violin section) or even a group of instruments (e.g. low brass or even the whole orchestra) that is able to virtually reproduce the sound of that instrument (or group) by performing it on an electronic keyboard, or any virtual device. This is possible because sample libraries utilize MIDI for input communications. In order to construct the sample library, each note might be recorded multiple times, in multiple dynamics, with multiple levels of vibrato, articulations and techniques. In addition, recordings might include transitions between two notes, the beginning and the ending of a note, the sound of a bow change and so on. With this aggregate of information, a piece of software called a sampler is built and scripted in order to generate the sounding result. Dynamics, vibrato and other similar musical features are crossfaded or layered in order to achieve smooth transitions, and scripting tools are used to successfully connect the different pieces of information. There are multiple companies that produce sample library products, which are sold as software packages. The immense range available includes virtual and extremely realistic versions of all the orchestral instruments. The advantage of scripting is that a composer interacts with the sampler, which automatically takes care of a significant amount of operations (triggering the correct sample, looping, crossfading, implementing a round robin algorithm for repeated notes, etc.). This means that the sampler generates virtual versions of instruments that can be controlled using diverse MIDI messages which react in a similar manner to how a physical instrument would. Virtual instruments might model individual orchestral instruments, full sections or orchestral gestures among many other possibilities. In addition, it is possible and fairly easy for the composer to create custom-made sample libraries by using a sampler such as Native Instruments' *Kontakt* or Apple's *EXS24*. Considering the purpose of this discussion I would argue that there are no significant ontological differences between using and manipulating virtual instruments from an existing sample library or doing the same with a custom-created one. In other words, once the virtual instruments are created, both types of libraries become similar compositional tools for music creation, open to further processing or sound modification. However, there are some practical differences between a commercial product and a custom-made one, especially when the composers have limited resources.

Sample libraries generate virtual musical instruments that might be modelled on existing physical instruments. From a certain perspective, they invert the process of composition and recording, allowing the creation of music with already recorded sounds. This increases the amount of sound processing that can be utilized as an intrinsic part of the compositional process. In addition, most of the sample libraries produced right now offer a high degree of flexibility in terms of shaping the final sound of the virtual instrument. A remarkable example of this is *HZ01: Hans Zimmer Percussion London Ensembles* released at the end of 2013 by the British sample library production company Spitfire Audio. It is a sample library that mainly contains epic drums and percussion which replicate the aesthetic approach to drum writing that Hans Zimmer developed for the scores he composed in the first decade of this century, such as *Gladiator* (Ridley Scott, 2000) or *Pirates of the Caribbean: Dead Man's Chest* (Gore Verbinski, 2006). The promotional material specifies how each sound in the library was recorded:

> Recorded at Air Studios via an unsurpassable signal chain. 96 rarefied microphones, into Neve Montserrat pre-amps, the world's biggest Neve 88R desk (which was exhaustively re-gained at every dynamic layer for optimum signal quality), via a dual chain to HDX and Prism converters running at 192k. Well over 30 TB of raw material from these sessions alone. (Spitfire Audio, 2013)

The microphones were placed in diverse locations to capture the sound of each drum from multiple positions. Commonly, the sound engineers responsible for the creation of one of these libraries would mix some of these microphones to produce different sound perspectives (they will generally create a close, a mid-range and a distant perspective).[5] This particular library offers a set of different perspectives produced by different engineers and Hans Zimmer himself. For example, each engineer produced their own version of what a close perspective recording should sound like, thus generating multiple possibilities for those working with these samples. This is the reason why this library is exemplary in showing how the same recording and the same aesthetic intention (creating a close perspective) may generate completely different sounds. This is the result of different approaches to mixing different microphones in order to create the perspective in addition to utilizing a different set of sound processors. For instance, Zimmer's own close perspective mix tends to sound thick and dense, whereas the mixes of score recordist and engineer Geoff Foster, who worked on all the Christopher Nolan films scored by Zimmer, tend to be as naturalistic as possible. Therefore, selecting an instrument is not just a generic decision anymore, as is specifying the name of the instrument on the score. Instead of asking for just a Taiko Drum hit, the contemporary composer utilizing sample libraries needs to be more specific. First, the composer needs to select a specific taiko drum virtual instrument from a variety of offerings. For instance, EastWest's *StormDrum 3* (2013), 8dio's *Epic Taiko Ensemble* (2013) or Spitfire's *Hans Zimmer percussion* (2013) offer diverse taiko virtual instruments recorded with multiple microphones. Once the instrument is selected, the composer will customize the resulting sound by creating a mix of the different microphone positions available, which can be further modified by the utilization of different sound processors inside of the DAW they are working with. Finally, each of these virtual instruments has been recorded at different dynamic levels several times, which will allow to produce a varied performance that will not sound repetitive.

Sample libraries are broadly used in soundtracks composed nowadays for cinema, television and videogames. Sample library companies, such as the ones mentioned above (EastWest, 8dio or Spitfire Audio), boast some of today's top composers as their users. For instance, 8dio claimed on their Facebook page that four of the five nominated original scores for 2015 Academy Awards utilized their libraries: 'Congratulations to all the Oscar scores tonight. They are all winners in our ears—and luckily 8Dio is featured in both [sic] Zimmers, Desplats and Johannssons magical works. Love you all!' (8dio, 2015).

Although composers tend to be secretive about which libraries are utilized in their film and television programmes, their interviews commissioned by the sample library companies provide some clues about their compositional processes, as exemplified in this interview with composer Blake Neely (*Everwood, Arrow, The Mentalist*)[6]:

> Specifically, in my orchestral template, I use the beautiful woodwinds you've created [8dio]. The Adagio Violins, specifically, are often featured on 'Arrow', as are all of the Epic drums, of course. Some real favorites I use a lot in 'The Mentalist' are the Propanium, Cylindrum and Hangdrum libraries. And I'm about to start working on a big new show for the Fall, which I think will heavily feature the new 8W Black library. It's such a huge and unique sound. (Folmann & Neely, 2014)

## Hyperinstruments

Analogous to the hyperorchestra, a *hyperinstrument* is the result of bringing a musical instrument to the hyperreal. The piano from *The Social Network*, an instrument whose sound perspective changes depending on the intentions of the narrative, is a good example of this. Figure 5.2 presents a conceptual diagram for the generation of a hyperinstrument. Once the sound source is chosen (a virtual instrument from a sample library, a synthesized sound or a

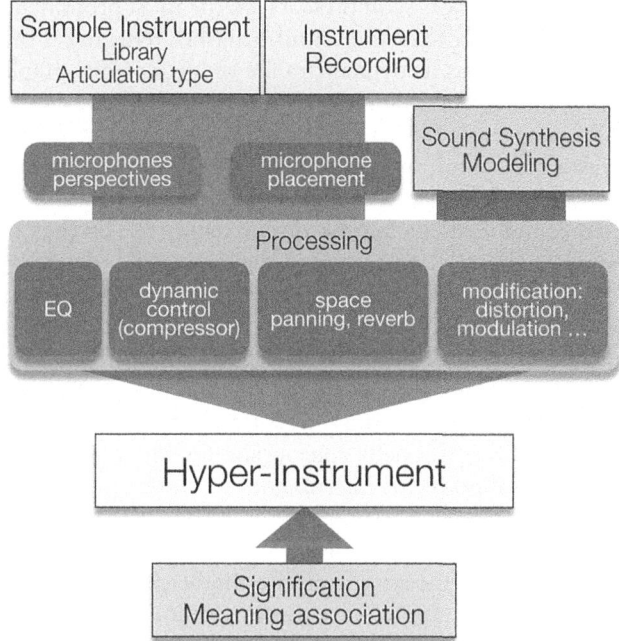

**Fig. 5.2** Conceptual diagram for the hyperinstrument

traditional recording), there are two main processes involved in its definition: generation of a sound perspective and creative processing. Hyperinstruments utilized in film and television become virtually tailored instruments that fulfil a precise purpose in terms of giving meaning to an audiovisual work.

In terms of the first process, sound recordings are necessarily mediated through the microphones used to record them, which generate a set of different possible perspectives. Using different sound processing techniques may further modify the instruments. Sound processors can be grouped in four main areas: equalization, dynamic control, spatial placement and sound alteration.[7]

The term equalization (EQ) describes the original purpose of these processors, which is to restore the *original* sound of the instrument altered due to the recording process. In contemporary usage, EQ does not necessarily serve as a tool to restore or balance a sound. Instead, it can be used to significantly alter it by boosting, reducing or even filtering specific frequency areas. For instance, cutting the high frequencies of a hyperinstrument (low-pass filtering) will make the recording sound muted, as if the instrument was played either very far away from the microphone or inside a closed room. This is the result of the physical nature of high-frequency waves which are greatly attenuated by distance or when attempting to cross walls. By employing EQ, it is possible to fine-tune the instrument in order to generate a particular sound that could better be associated with the intended meaning of the music. Dynamic control includes a group of processors (compressors are the most prominent ones) that modify the dynamic response of the sound by either reducing it or expanding it. A compressed sound has its dynamic range reduced, which implies that the difference between the quietest and the loudest sounds diminishes.[8] Percussion sounds that are compressed have a longer presence, which results in them having a longer sustained sound, making them more noticeable. Spatial placement involves the process of placing the sound in a particular position in either the stereo or the surround field, at a precise distance from the listener and in a specific hall. The microphone placements and their mix will influence this area, as they naturally provide spatialization. Finally, processes that are grouped under the umbrella term of 'sound alteration' relate to all the processors designed to alter a sound by distorting or modulating it. Sound distortion is probably the most common effect in this group. Similarly, the tremolo effect, which modifies the amplitude (volume) of a sound over time by using a very slow sinusoidal wave (LFO) becomes especially appropriate for music for the screen, as it attaches a constant motion to the instrument.

For instance, in *Interstellar* (Christopher Nolan, 2014) the church organ (recorded) is merged with a synthesized sound that expands when Cooper (Matthew McConaughey) is located—inside the black hole—in a neo-Gothic three-dimensional representation of a five-dimensional space. When analysing the soundtrack, one realizes how the organ sound blends with undulating synthesizers (which have a tremolo-like sound processor added to them) that sustain some of the organ's notes, interacting with the frequencies that emanate from the recording of the organ, creating the impression that the physical organ is fluctuating in a much larger space. The merging between the organ and the synthesizers becomes a single hyperinstrument that helps to signify the location of the character, which is meant to transcend human perception.

When necessary and when there is a big enough budget, recording new samples offers the additional possibility of creating new sound combinations onstage, which will result in a particular sound recording. For example, in *The Man of Steel* (Zack Snyder, 2013), the composer Hans Zimmer recorded a drum track by bringing together 12 of the top drummers in LA and requesting that they play together. The drummers were asked to start each take by playing a given rhythm together, which they later personalized by incorporating elements of their own drumming style (Water Tower Music, 2013). The result of the recording session became a mix of different elements: first, a rhythmic pattern that evolves into a varied but cohesive mix of cultural traditions; second, an overall drum sound; and third, the concept of a sectional sound (mimicking a string section) applied to drums. The recording of these hyper-drums highlights a process of music creation that has abandoned the sense of performative linearity. The recording did not involve screening scenes from the film. Instead, it served to create a custom-tailored sample library that generated a unique sound for the movie. Obviously, most projects can't afford such time-consuming recording sessions in order to produce their own sample libraries, which is the reason why a significant amount of the percussion used in music for media is created by using pre-existing sample libraries.

In order to demonstrate how hyperinstruments operate, I will briefly return to my example from *The Social Network*. This example showed how the main piano melody was recorded from three different microphone positions. These different versions of the melody were employed as a means to portray the evolution of Zuckerberg's character during the film. In contemporary composition practices that involve the utilization of sample libraries similar to what I described earlier, sound perspectives (or microphone positions) are regularly employed as compositional and orchestrational strategies. The effect of microphone placement significantly alters the recorded sound to such a degree that it may even seem that different instruments were used in each perspective. Composers that utilize these libraries will typically mix these perspectives in order to achieve the sound that is appropriate for the music they are working on.

The use of hyper-drums in *The Man of Steel* is another good example of the utilization of highly complex sound perspectives. The sound of the hyperinstrument retains part of the clarity and the intensity of a drum recorded employing microphones located close to the instrument, yet is much more powerful. This was achieved by placing microphones close to all the drums in addition to general microphones. All these recordings were then mixed in order to create a perspective that generated 'one giant machine of energy' (Water Tower Music, 2013). The resulting sound of the hyperinstrument does not represent a physically possible perspective, but rather a blend of sound sources with the objective of creating a unique sound for the movie.

## Hyperorchestration Principles

The above description of hyperinstruments serves to provide a ground for the generation of the virtual instruments that constitute the hyperorchestra, and the possibilities of producing them by employing mixing procedures. In this environment, the options in terms of sound choices for the hyperorchestra expand exponentially. Composers can be specific in defining exactly the instrument, type of performance, articulation, microphone perspective and sound processing that will be required for a given situation, thus generating a tailored hyperinstrument that exactly fits the needs of the screen work. In other words, orchestration becomes a process of deciding how to sculpt an instrument and how the instrument will contribute to the final sound in terms of how it adds to the different regions of the sound spectrum.

Traditional Western music orchestration could be defined as a set of techniques related to writing for orchestra utilizing an orchestral score. These techniques explore the different possibilities, in terms of sound combinations, available when using orchestral instruments. Hence, orchestration is inseparable from instrumentation, which studies the techniques required to effectively write for orchestral instruments. Instrumentation is also tied to the score, as it explores the different notation conventions that express, to some extent, the diverse array of performing techniques available to each instrument. Hyperorchestration principles, however, expand the traditional orchestration approaches, by considering concepts which are especially relevant to the process of screen scoring.

I'll first address the concept of aural fidelity or 'the extent to which the sound is faithful to the source as we conceive it' (Bordwell & Thompson, 2012, p. 283). Aural fidelity does only imply that the sound is perceived as verisimilar: 'we do not know what a laser gun "really" sounds like, but we accept the whang they make in *Return of the Jedi* as plausible' (p. 283). Hence, the fidelity of a sound does come from it being perceived as realistic. I argued earlier that a particular sound perspective would tend to sound realistic even though it might not be reproducible in the physical world. Thus, this sound would be considered as truly faithful. Conversely, filtering a frequency range, distorting or compressing an instrument will generally affect its aural fidelity. In the context of screen work, a low degree of aural fidelity might be desirable. Therefore, from a hyperorchestration point of view, aural fidelity becomes a tool for producing meaning and emotions instead of simply being an objective that needs to be achieved.

Secondly, focusing on the sound spectrum allows music and its instruments to interact more easily with the rest of the soundtrack (dialogue, voiceover and sound effects). Contemporary film music has been recently expanding its boundaries, embracing a wider range of possibilities that were not considered 'music' before. As a consequence of this process, music and sound design are not considered separate entities anymore in some practices. Moreover, the capacity to actively modify the sound properties of the music and to adjust the frequency spectrum of the sound facilitates the interaction with the rest of the soundtrack. A hyperinstrument might have a frequency range filtered in order to better integrate with a sound effect in that frequency range. The result will blend the boundaries between the sound produced by the hyperinstrument and the sound effect, generating a much more integrated and interconnected soundtrack.

Thirdly, music becomes a process of sound sculpting, where the sound details are relevant. This propels the search for and creation of precise and particular sounds (the drummers from *The Man of Steel*, the piano from *The Social Network*) by employing diverse recording and sound manipulation processes. Therefore, the music for the movie or television programme will be custom-made, in part because some of the sounds that will constitute the soundtrack will be sculpted specifically for it. This is true regardless of the sound source utilized in the generation of the hyperinstrument, as there are diverse methods, which I described before, used for fine-tuning the sound of an instrument. In addition, hyperorchestration also encourages a multicultural approach to instrumentation, which increases its timbral possibilities and expands its network of signification.

Fourthly, in modern discussions on film music and film diegesis (Cecchi, 2010; Winters, 2010, 2012; Yacavone, 2012), it is commonly accepted that music which would traditionally be qualified as nondiegetic is able to shape the diegesis as if it were a diegetic element. For instance, Ben Winters (2010) correctly states that the main theme for *Indiana Jones* franchise is as essential for the creation of the diegesis of the character as any of his iconic attire.

By expanding the sound world of the music and by sculpting the sounds to custom-fit the necessities of the narrative, the capacity of the music to shape the diegesis increases. Moreover, an approach to music making, where melody, pitch and harmony are not dominant, facilitates the generation of a musical soundscape that stays in the background, helping to shape the overall diegetic space, which is equivalent to what Winters describes as 'musical wallpaper' (2012).

Lastly, hyperorchestration facilitates the conception of the music creation process as non-linear. Different hyperinstruments and instrumental sections are generally recorded at different times—some of the recorded material may be used as samples and part of the music will originate in the computer. Everything is then mixed and processed together.

Hyperorchestration not only expands the number of techniques available to composers but also redefines the foundations from where these techniques come from. Since the hyperorchestra transcends the limitations of the score, the compositional palette becomes the sound spectrum. Hyperorchestration adds, at the very least, a new dimension to music: it unlocks the dimension of space. The process of hyperorchestration allows the generation of a multidimensional performing area that not only goes beyond the concert stage but also goes beyond what is possible to achieve with acoustic instruments in reality. The virtual performing stage becomes, thus, hyperreal. It is important to emphasize that, by becoming hyperreal, the virtual stage transcends the laws of the physical world. Using a specific mix of perspectives that would not be achievable in reality can create a hyperinstrument if the virtual stage is flexible enough to allow the sound of an instrument to partially emanate from different virtual areas at the same time.

Hyperorchestration implies above all an attitude towards sound that focuses on the spectrum and its different features. Hyperorchestration means thinking about music in terms of sound, becoming a sculptor of the soundscape. Further, in sculpting sound, it is possible to create form in a manner similar to what one would do when using harmony or melody. Thus, to hyperorchestrate is to think musically beyond the Western concepts of harmony, melody, rhythm or pitch. For instance, a simple D minor chord may signify completely different meanings depending on how it has been hyperorchestrated. Therefore, to hyperorchestrate does also imply that producing music is a way to transmit meaning that is significant and understandable for a given culture at a given time.

## Conclusion: Composition as Sound Design

In this chapter, I have described how mixing techniques become a means to hyperorchestrate in a musical framework that transcends the foundations of Western classical music based on the musical score. If music is a subset of sound and sound designers utilize the full sound spectrum without any specific limitations, then music becomes a subset of sound design. Being a composer implies the design of a series of sound combinations over time that we call music. Therefore, the process of creating music has always been a form of sound design in a culturally defined and controlled environment. The Western score, the predesigned orchestral ensemble and the principles of Western musical theory acted as isolation booths that created an overly controlled sound space inside the whole sound spectrum. The nature of the association between music and sound design is ontological: there are no essential differences that justify, from the point of view of a philosophical distinction, the separation of the process of sound design and the process of composition that are not culturally grounded. However, this ontological equivalence does not imply that screen composers and sound designers have not been two distinct and separate professions that produced separate results in the post-production process of filmmaking. Nevertheless, the absence of an ontological distinction between music and sound design allows nowadays the conception of a soundtrack that is much more integrated, in part thanks to how screen composers interact with and treat sound. Composers are aware of their role as sound sculptors and they have an array of tools focused on the transformation of music as sound. In utilizing a model based on a hyperorchestra and a set of hyperinstruments, the aesthetics of the music for audiovisual media has expanded to incorporate a vast new array of different sounds. This process has narrowed the distance between what we call music and what we call sound design in film, elucidating even more that, as I stated before, composition has always been sound design. In other words, if music is a subset of sound, then creating music has always been a process of designing sound in time. Acknowledging that has implications that go beyond issues of semantics, as it opens the door to a process of music making for audiovisual media that is highly and naturally integrated with the rest of the sounds present in the soundtrack.

## Notes

1. This is the timing of the scene as played on a digital video file of the movie from iTunes.
2. The relatively limited amount of musical symbols is one of the factors that explain the high efficiency of the recording session for film music, which is normally never rehearsed. Thus, this limited framework for music writing served as a useful tool for recording efficiency to the first generations of film composers.
3. The timbral distinction is interpreted by reading the names of the instruments and deducting their timbral properties.
4. Spectral composers employed technical knowledge and, ultimately, the aid of technology in order to unveil the physical properties of sounds. In *Did You Say Spectral?* Gérard Grisey, who is considered one of the founders of the movement, reviewed the emergence of the Spectral movement, which 'offered a formal organization and sonic material that came directly from the physics of sound, as discovered through science and microphonic access' (Grisey, 2000, p. 1). The spectral movement is a good example of the change in how composers negotiated the sound, from being the result of a rational process of notation to being the main focus of music creation. In addition, the dependence of spectral composers

upon technology is relevant. The hyperorchestra utilizes a musical model that is closely related to what spectral composers designed a few decades before.
5. A close perspective aims to reproduce the sound of an instrument which was recorded from close proximity. The mid-position is a recording that assumes a position similar to that of a conductor. Finally, the distant position records the instrument from far away in the hall. In addition, there is a whole set of unusual microphone positions.
6. It is important to mention that the production time for music from a TV show is significantly shorter than the time allowed for completing the music for a movie. Therefore, composers for television have traditionally relied on computer-generated sounds to produce music as fast as possible. This means that they are more open to rely mainly on sample libraries for creating music compared to big budget movie composers, who still extensively use recording sessions in the creation of their scores.
7. For more details about the particularities of the processes of mixing see, for example, David Gibson's *The Art of Mixing* (2005).
8. The effects on the sound of an instrument might be significant. For example, a percussive sound usually has a sharp attack and a fast decay. By using a compressor, the attack will become less sharp and the decay will be significantly more present.

## References

8dio (2013) *Epic Taiko Ensemble*, http://8dio.com/instrument-category/percussion/#instrument/epic-taiko-ensemble-vst/, date accessed 20 April 2015.

8dio (2015) Facebook Post, 22 February, https://www.facebook.com/8dio.productions/posts/791857724183411, date accessed 20 April 2015.

Baudrillard, J. (1994) *Simulacra and simulation*, trans. S. Glaser (Ann Arbor: University of Michigan Press).

Bordwell, D. and K. Thompson (2012) *Film Art: An Introduction*, 10th ed. (New York: McGraw-Hill).

Cecchi, A. (2010) 'Diegetic Versus Nondiegetic: A Reconsideration of the Conceptual Opposition as a Contribution to the Theory of Audiovision', *Worlds of Audiovision*, http://www-5.unipv.it/wav/pdf/WAV_Cecchi_2010_eng.pdf, date aaccessed 20 January 2015.

Cook, N. (2013) 'Bridging the Unbridgeable? Empirical Musicology and Interdisciplinary Performance Studies' in N. Cook and R. Pettengill (eds) *Taking It to the Bridge: Music as Performance*, (Ann Arbour: University of Michigan Press), 70–85.

EastWest Sounds (2013) *StormDrum 3*, http://www.soundsonline.com/SD3, date accessed 20 April 2015.

Fincher, D. (2011) 'DVD Extras, Trent Reznor, Atticus Ross, David Fincher: On the Score', *The Social Network*, Sony Pictures.

Folmann, T. and B. Neely (2014) 'Interview with Blake Neely', *8dio Artist Spotlight*, http://8dio.com/blog/blakeneely/, date accessed 20 April 2015.

Gibson, D. (2005) *The Art of Mixing: A Visual Guide to Recording, Engineering, and Production*, 2nd ed. (Boston: Artistpro Publishing).

Grisey, G. (2000) 'Did You Say Spectral?', *Contemporary Music Review*, Vol. 19, No. 3, 1–3.

McLuhan, M. (1994) *Understanding Media: The Extensions of Man* (Cambridge, Mass.: MIT Press).

Spitfire (2013) *HZ01: Hans Zimmer Percussion London Ensembles*, http://www.spitfireaudio.com/hz-percussion-london-ensembles, date accessed 20 January 2015.

Water Tower Music (2013) 'Man of Steel Soundtrack—Percussion—Hans Zimmer' [Online Video], https://www.youtube.com/watch?v=QTOMIyynBPE, date accessed: 20 January 2015.

Winters, B. (2010) 'The Non-diegetic Fallacy: Film, Music, and Narrative Space', *Music and Letters*, Vol. 91, No. 2, 224–244.

Winters, B. (2012) 'Musical Wallpaper?', *Music, Sound, and the Moving Image*, Vol. 6 No. 1, 39–54.

Yacavone, D. (2012) 'Spaces, Gaps, and Levels', *Music, Sound, and the Moving Image*, Vol. 6, No. 1, 21–37.

CHAPTER 6

# Emotional Sound Effects and Metal Machine Music: Soundworlds in *Silent Hill* Games and Films

*K.J. Donnelly*

While film and video games are not the same thing, there is a common core of audiovisual perception, technology and aesthetic techniques, and essence at the 'join' of moving image and sound. The *Silent Hill* franchise relatively effortlessly moved from video game to film and illustrates this explicitly. The adaptation to film brings something of video game audio to film, yet the games themselves already evinced a significant influence from horror films. In audiovisual culture, sound can often adopt a more 'musical' character. Indeed, sound tends to take on an aesthetic character, in other words acquiring a distinctly musical aspect. This is beyond evident in the *Silent Hill* games and films, where not only can sounds take on an emotional character but music can also adopt a cold, mechanical character more akin to the traditional character of sound effects.

## SILENT HILL ADAPTATION

*Silent Hill* is a successful and remarkably singular series of video games produced by Japanese company Konami. On the face of it, it concerns a third-person character's navigation through the misty ghost town of Silent Hill, under threat from various grotesque creatures while attempting to solve a central mystery. It is a 'third person survival horror game', where the player's avatar explores a three-dimensional (3D) navigable environment, solves puzzles, collects items, stays alive and strives to solve a central mystery. The game has a persistent subtext of psychological disturbance, suggesting that it may all be a fantasy of the protagonist. The game world oscillates without warning between a seeming normality and the terrifying 'Otherworld' of fire and imminent

---

K. Donnelly
University of Southampton, UK

threat by large enemies ('pyramidheads'). The music *and* the entire sound design for each of the early games was written and produced by composer Akira Yamaoka, a specialist in video game music. The game has appeared for a number of different gaming platforms:

*Silent Hill* (protagonist Harry) (1999) [for Playstation, later versions ported for PC]
*Silent Hill 2* (James) (2001) [Play Station 2, PC, Xbox]
*Silent Hill 3* (Heather) (2003) [PS2, PC]
*Silent Hill 4: The Room* (Henry) (2004) [PS2, PC, Xbox]
*Silent Hill Origins* (Travis) (2007) [PSP handheld]
*Silent Hill: Homecoming* (2008) (Alex) [PS3, XboX, PC]
*Silent Hill: The Escape* (2008) [iOS]
*Silent Hill: Shattered Memories* (2009) (Harry, again) [Wii, PS2, PSP]
*Silent Hill: Downpour* (2012) (Murphy) [PS3, XboX]
*Silent Hill: Book of Memories* (2012) (choosable character) [PSVita]
*Silent Hills* (announced 2014 for PS4)

An 11th game in the series has been mooted, a collaboration between *Metal Gear Solid* creator Hideo Kojima and film director Guillermo del Toro. The films are based on the earliest most iconic games. The first *Silent Hill* film, directed by Christophe Gans, was released in April 2006, while the second film followed in 2012. *Silent Hill: Revelation* was made in 3D and directed by Michael J. Bassett. The first concerns Rose, who follows her adopted daughter back to Silent Hill and finds out about her past. The second is about teenager Heather, who discovers she is not who she thinks she is and visits Silent Hill to find the truth.

*Silent Hill* (2006) is a direct attempt to translate the video games to film, but significantly, this transposition takes place around the original music which is retained from the Konami game as a skeleton upon which to rebuild the character of the game into film form. The game music thus embodies an 'essence' of the *Silent Hill* character. Indeed, the film's director Christophe Gans initiated the film project by creating a 'demo' which he sent to Konami. Its visuals were cut to the game's music, so the music was a given for the project: it was there from the very start.[1] Game players will have heard this music constantly; indeed the repetitive nature of video game playing means that pieces of game music can be heard more repeatedly than any other music. Thus, the music needs certain qualities to allow for repeated listenings. Equally, though, the situation of game playing—and its aim at psychological immersion—allows music to insinuate itself significantly into the game player's mind, a situation which seems particularly apt in that *Silent Hill*'s world appears to emanate from the neurotic mind of the game's central character. Indeed, the constant dislocation of sound and image establishes the sense of aberrant psychology at the heart of the game.

When it came to the film adaptations, the film makers were faced with a familiar problem: how to translate the game's elements into a film format, enhancing and adding 'cinematic' elements while retaining an essence of the game's character. A crucial decision was that the music and soundscape from the games would be adopted as the foundation upon which to build the films. The experience of the *Silent Hill* films, and notably their sounds and music, will clearly be different for an experienced game player from the manner in which it will be apprehended by someone coming to the film 'cold'. The films of *Silent Hill* work differently for aficionados of the game: most notably, the music triggers a memory (and a feeling) of the world of the game.[2]

## *Silent Hill* Game Sound and Music

The music *and* the sound design for each of the games was written and produced by Akira Yamaoka, a specialist in video/computer game music.[3] He was trained at art college rather than music college (so he was not 'classically trained'). He joined Konami as a roster composer and musician at the age of 25 in 1993. The video game industry tends to have music by 'workers' who are contracted (either short term or long term) to the game developing company. This is similar to the heyday of the Hollywood Studio system, where music was produced industrially rather than the more recent system of freelancing composers like in contemporary film production. It very much retains the character and rhetoric of an industry rather than seeing itself as 'art'.

Yamaoka produced not only the music but also the sound effects for the *Silent Hill* games, credited with being not only composer but also sound designer and sound producer and director. By the time of *Silent Hill 3* in 2003, Yamaoka had become the game producer for the PC version of the whole game.[4] The game's music includes 'indie rock'-type songs, atmospheric ambient music and noisy music that sounds much like an amalgam of machine-like and natural sounds. Although there are some female vocals and electric guitars, the vast majority of the music clearly was produced on computer software. This is evident not only in the clear and simple textures but also in the principle of the loop as the musical structural basis of most pieces. Apart from the indie-type songs, some of the music is reminiscent of the subgenre of dark ambient or darkwave (particularly groups such as Bocksholm), while some of his other music is vaguely reminiscent of Japanese artist D. J. Krush. Also influential was Brian Eno's vaguely programmatic *Ambient 4: On Land* (1982), which evinced a lack of purposeful progression or development, alongside an evacuation of melody/harmonic movement. This form of stasis foregrounds texture and sonority, and inspired later so-called 'Dark Ambient' music (such as Cold Meat Industry artists Raison D'Etre, Desiderii Marginis and Deutsch Nepal). It also takes something from 'industrial' rock music such as Nine Inch Nails, who used loops and mechanical sounds on the mini album *Broken* (1992).[5]

Yamaoka's incidental music for *Silent Hill 2* and *Silent Hill 3* has a notable 'trip hop' flavour particularly in the first game,[6] as well as including a darker and more noise-based score. This latter music is not 'score' in the traditional sense for games or for films. Indeed, it includes austere 'noise', often mixed with echoed notes, deep chords, metallic sounds, although these also often appear in isolation and in succession. This is at least partly due to the structure of the score, as tracks are overlayed and not so obviously comprising relatively short loops of music. One of the sonic characteristics is the use of disjointed rhythms, which sound like the functioning of broken machines.[7] Indeed, the video games intermittently use music of an 'avant-garde' character, which at times sounds closer to what we would expect of sound effects. Indeed, the 'musical sound design' of the games and films is remarkable in that supernatural events involve sounds that are neither clearly sound effects nor music.

The *Silent Hill* game soundtracks evince an overlap between incidental music and sound effects, delivering a soundscape of ambiguous ambience. David Bessell noted that in video games '... the boundaries between music and sound effects start to become more blurred' (2002, p. 139). This was far from uncommon, indeed something of a video game tradition, perhaps partly due to sounds and music being produced by the same chip and using similar sonic component parts. *Silent Hill*, as a matter of strategy, aims to put the player in a state of some confusion and the soundtrack ontology is one of a number of representational points of ambiguity. In *The Terror Engine*, his book about the *Silent Hill* game, Bernard Perron notes: '... the games of *Silent Hill* are really "audio-video" games, and it is important to note, the audio precedes the video in the expression. [It was] ... designed with sound in mind (which is not always the case in video games)' (2012, pp. 87–8). The games exploit the phenomenon of 'acousmatic' sound, which Michel Chion discusses in *Audio-Vision*, using Pierre Schaeffer's definition, as sound with an unapparent source or origin (1994, p. 71). There is an essential ambiguity to such sounds. Their origins are immediately obscure, although their source may be understood later. In psychological terms, such sounds are perceived as a potential threat in that they hang in uncertainty for the perceiver. The use of these makes for disturbing gameplay as the player is uncertain of what these sounds indicate and where they are located. However, the protagonist/avatar has a radio which indicates imminent attack through crackling with static, while the appearance of the diegetic siren announces the onset of the transformation from normality to the nightmarish 'Otherworld' and sets the player in anticipation of being attacked. These are occasional but there is a more regular wash of sonic atmosphere, mixing music and what appear to be sound effects. Zach Whalen discusses the crucial acousmatic effect of the radio in the game, where an imminent threat is signalled by a burst of static from the radio:

> Below the static sound, the dominant base sound in *Silent Hill* is a chilling ambient wash which throbs with the sound of machinery and sirens. The volume level of this ambient sound is low, but its ubiquitous presence keeps the player on edge and sets an ominous tone for the visual environments of both worlds of *Silent Hill*. Its mechanical tone also blends smoothly with the machine-produced static of the radio such that the sonic texture of the atmosphere remains consistent. (2007, p. 76)

In *Silent Hill*, evil is associated sonically with the appearance of white noise. In terms of sound, white noise represents a primordial soup out of which other sounds can emerge. Significantly, it also suggests a mental state of being overwhelmed by 'noise', and marks a homology of the 'immersion' at the heart of the game. In the game, the appearance of static on the radio carried by the protagonist warns that monsters are approaching. Similarly, in the first film, there is sonic distortion on Chris's (Sean Bean) telephone message from Rose (Radha Mitchell). The sound mixes static and breakup. Also in this film, there is a sound reminiscent of that generically used to represent radiation, which appears first when Rose begins to look for Sharon (Jodelle Ferland) in the main street. This latter sound is ambiguous about its status. There is nothing indicating that it is diegetic in origin, or indeed non-diegetic. This sound appears to come from an 'elsewhere', manifesting an irruption from the unconscious, or at least a sonic concretization of a fundamental psychology of fear. The sounds and music emanate from the white noise like life from a 'primordial soup' of basic elements, and the monsters from traces of earlier culture or repressed memories. This sonic continuum provides something of a general 'sonorous envelope' that cocoons the game player.[8] While the whole of the *Silent Hill* universe might be construed as an interior fantasy, inside the disturbed mind of the protagonist, sound plays an essential role in the game's aim to homologize interior states.

Music is usually conceived as having conventional melodic, harmonic and rhythmic structures. Here, much of the 'music' lacks these and comes across as ambience or sound effects, in a continuum of sounds that are sustained and loop based, making a bed of continuous sound alongside occasional periodic interjections.[9] Zach Whalen notes a lack of dynamics and lack of melody, which suggests something like the 'filler material' in classical film scores (2007, p. 77). Incidental music in video games often avoids distinct dynamics or gradual and logical development, as this might not match the game event which it accompanies but *Silent Hill* is in some ways exceptional. Rob Bridgett suggests that this use of visual uncertainty allows the soundtrack to pervade forward and indicate the 'unseen world of danger that may be lurking within the darkness' (2008, p. 130). The intermittent movement between 'normality' and the 'Otherworld' allows for a movement between standard aesthetics and the transmission of an idea of the 'abnormal' through non-standard approaches to aesthetics. The sound world is the counterpart and equivalent of the visual dreamscape in the games, consisting of empty buildings, fog-wreathed streets. The soundtrack is landscape-like, enveloping and unsettling, mixing both beauty and ugliness. The outside is dominated by distant acousmatic bubbling sounds and other indistinct sounds. However, the insides of buildings tend to be very quiet, indeed sometimes completely silent.

## SILENT HILL FILM SOUND AND MUSIC

The *Silent Hill* films owe much sonically to their video game counterparts: they 'port' a number of game music aspects into the film situation. The first film's music consists of a pre-existing repertoire of music, from which effective pieces could be drawn. That repertoire is, of course, the music written for each of the four games by Akira Yamaoka, cementing the film and game soundtracks (Mundhenke, 2013, p. 117). Pieces were chosen from this reservoir of Silent Hill sound and then they were fitted to new contexts in the film. However, it is worth noting that they were used for different situations.[10] For example, the piece called 'Magdalene' is used for repose at the resolution of the film's concluding massacre, yet in *Silent Hill 2* game, the piece plays after the death of James's female companion. In the film *Silent Hill*, it offers a moment of reflection after the demise of the evil cult, while in the game it overlays the continuation of the game with a sense of sadness for her seeming death. Both situations certainly call for some 'repose', and similarly the music for the so-called 'boss battle' at the conclusion was also used for the climactic final fight in the film. The film was not 'scored', however, and therefore music to a lesser or greater degree articulates the image. Pre-existing music inspires images to be cut to 'fit' its dynamics, and one might even argue that the pieces of music, arranged in succession, provide the temporal and motoric direction of the film as much as any narrative impetus. However, the film's music makes the film a fragmentary experience. It contains little in the way of clear and memorable repetition, and little sense of a sonic continuity. In other words, the score is not orchestral, does not consist of songs and does not follow a particular musical style or genre. Yet, for someone who has played these games and interiorized the game music, the experience is a constant evocation of memories of the game and feelings associated with the game. The music becomes like a long finger probing the memory and gaining direct access to feelings stemming from the game experience.

Strangely, on the film's credits, the incidental music was credited solely to Canadian composer Jeff Danna. Akira Yamaoka, the actual composer of almost all the incidental music that appeared in the film, instead was credited as 'executive producer' of the film itself. Although initially seeming like some sort of bizarre contractual anomaly, this suggests that music's role in the transition from small to large screen was more important than its merely incidental status. Much of the film appears simply to 'port' Yamaoka's game soundtrack into the film, to simply compile and cut it into the film like a 'temp track'.[11] As Yamaoka's pieces tend to be atmospheric loops devoid of sudden changes in dynamics,[12] there is a temptation to think of the film's incidental music as being a divide between distinct 'pieces' (that were written by Yamaoka) and stingers or rare points where music matches action (by Danna).

The soundtrack is unlike traditional film scores and separate sound effects. In terms of music, there is no action matching and the recordings appear much more like 'pieces' with their own integrity (including songs) rather than as film 'cues' which are crafted to fit action. *Silent Hill* mixes up noisy austere pieces from *Silent Hill 1* noise, using mechanical loops and scraping sounds, and more conventional musical pieces derived directly from the first four games.

In the first film, there is sonic distortion on Chris's telephone message from Rose. The sound mixes static and breakup. Similarly, the 'radiation' sound appears first when Rose enters Silent Hill's main street in search of her daughter Sharon. The status of the sound is ambiguous. There is nothing indicating that it is diegetic in origin, or indeed non-diegetic. This sound appears to come from an 'elsewhere', manifesting an irruption from the unconscious, or at least a sonic concretization of a fundamental psychology of fear.

The second film, *Silent Hill: Revelation*, moves away from building its sonic world around sound and music taken directly from the game. However, it uses a recognizable sound world and short excerpts from music in the games, usually developed into something closer to film music cues. Indeed, the film's music is much more like a series of 'variations' on and developments of Yamaoka's original music from the game. While it remains sound based and often appears to lack traditionally 'musical' aspects, it most clearly was written as a score for the film. Like the first film, *Silent Hill: Revelation*'s many visions and dream sequences allow for unconventional sonic as well as visual aesthetics. For instance, the opening dream sequence set at a fairground incorporates prominent slashing noises on edits, a mickeymoused 'stinger' noise matching the large toy rabbit moving its head. Indeed, many movements are accompanied by sounds that follow the logic of sound effects but break the convention of sound effects. For example, the armless monster that is the first to threaten Heather at the school is accompanied by an electrostatic sound. This appears to be diegetic sound as it matches the monster's bodily movement; however, there is a question mark over its status. It may simply be a musical emphasis, akin to a stinger. Similarly, in the manikin store room before the attack of the manikin creature, Heather's tense wanderings are accompanied by atmospheric sounds, which are not clearly either score or diegetic ambience. There are intermittent echoed sounds, scraping sounds and sustained single notes, which appear to be part of the disturbing environment although they could equally be construed as music. Early in the film a day-dream sequence near street stalls with a clown evinces isolated and exaggerated single sounds with the film focusing in detail on a succession of individual aspects of what appears to be a straightforward but strange day. Although this is not uncommon in certain films, here it might be an aspect of the film's 3D production, where exaggerated, foregrounded images are matched by a similar process in the soundtrack. Each sound is given a strong sense of detail with space around it supplied by electronic reverb effects.

As the second film is based on the game, three themes from *Silent Hill 3* are used in *Silent Hill: Revelation*. The film opens with 'Never Forgive Me Never Forget Me', which appears a few times later in different arrangements. 'Innocent Moon', a repetitive piano theme appears regularly in the first film including when Chris is looking on the Internet for information about Silent Hill, when Rose first enters Silent Hill and when he senses but cannot see Rose passing him. It appears in *Silent Hill: Revelation* when Chris sees Rose in the mirror, when Heather (Adelaide Clemens) has visions in Midwich High School and at the end of the film. 'Clockwork Little Happiness' is based on a mechanical rhythm and keyboard chords. In addition to these, 'Promise (Reprise)' from

*Silent Hill 2* is also used. In the first film, it appears as a theme for Sharon and Alessa (both played by Jodelle Ferland). In *Silent Hill: Revelation*, it appears when Rose looks at the drawing by her younger self (Sharon), when Alessa appears at Midwich Elementary School, in the empty Sacrificial Chamber and as Rose sees Alessa in Brookhaven Hospital. The transposition of the video game sound world to two films illustrates differences between the two media but perhaps more clearly illustrates the correspondences between film and video game. Films have certainly influenced video games and video games now are asserting themselves on film. The *Silent Hill* films are a rarity in so directly using music that derives from different gaming functions (the interactive character of games means that music often loops and overlays and is not fixed) in a film context. They certainly 'work' as film music but excelling in the 'scene setting' atmospherics that are central to both the films and the games.

The sounds are similar to the game, making for a distant ambience of acousmatic noises, against which there are isolated, foregrounded sounds. There are sounds for actions (loud, featured sounds analogue to the film's 3D effects) and sounds that are 'just there' (as its ambient soundscape). The soundtrack is derived directly from the game, but it also evinces some distinct film conventions. There is less in the way of unexplained ambient sound and more in the way of direct synchronized sound effects that are louder than the background continuum of sound/music. The sequence at Brookhaven Asylum includes distant acousmatic shouts and groans, presumably from the inmates but this is never made specific. The soundtrack is ambiguous about whether it is music or sound effects. It consists of rumblings and resonances, echoed sounds and what could be diegetic sounds of electricity. However, these sounds have more of the character of music in that they appear used as much if not more for their physical texture as signifying ability. Some of the sustained tones clearly are more like music, yet these are indifferent to the events on screen and merely provide a disturbing ambience.

## The Unified Soundtrack: Game–Film Continuum

Video game sound and music, while having some similarities with film sound and music is not the same.[13] Some game music draws very directly upon the orchestral film scoring tradition, in terms of both sounds and functions, but other game music emanates decidedly from its own traditions, particularly where concerns are with general atmosphere and interaction rather than music fitting the precise temporal requirements of on-screen developments.[14]

In terms of game music's relationship to film music, there tend to be assumption of some key similarities (and inspirations) that have entered game music from film music (and also its close relation television music). However, the interactive nature of video games means that they cannot be 'scored' in the manner of fixed-time, linear films or plays. In other words, the game player controls how long a certain 'scene' might take. Should they so wish, they can take their time and loiter at a certain point in the game. Thus, the nature of games disallows the use of significant 'cues' in the filmic sense. Apart from the occasional 'cut scene', the game's temporal dimension is controlled by the player and thus cannot easily be matched or underscored by the music.[15] Instead, the music logic of the game is that of looping, where a piece will repeat during an extended playing time, until the triggering of the next piece of music or silence by the character's progress in the game world. While such gameplay cannot be scored in the traditional sense, 'cut scenes' owe a great deal to film. These are pre-constructed sequences triggered by the player arriving at a certain point in the game, and which are not controlled by the player in any way. In the vast majority of cases, these look very similar to films and in effect are the same as animated film. Consequently, they are scored precisely and provide sometimes a rare opportunity for game music composers to write music to match action and dynamics on screen. Most of the time, they have to provide music in the form of loops, which can be repeated endlessly to accompany certain sections of the game. Thus, the music needs to be sensitive to certain aspects that have not been important in other forms of music.

In recent times, there has crept into film-making a certain ambiguity about what is 'music' and what is 'sound effects', breaking the strict demarcation between the two that characterized dominant forms of film-making post-production.[16] We should not forget, however, that there was always a strong convention that film scores would bolster diegetic sounds, which is embodied in its most crass form by 'mickeymousing' imitation of screen activity. In a seeming reverse of this, it might be noted that in some films sound effects now are becoming 'film music', losing their tethering to on-screen causality in favour of an 'emotional' function and 'musical' organization within films as an aesthetic rather than representational object. According to James Lastra when discussing film, '... the founding gesture of sound design ... [is] the complete severing of sensory experience from representation ...' (2008, p. 135). Losing simple representational values sound effects become 'texture'. Indeed, one might argue that horror film music and sound design has influenced the sound of video games and that in turn has fed back into horror films.

While the *Silent Hill* films are a well-developed example of how non-diegetic music and diegetic sound effects can be merged, in a way, it has always been impossible to fully separate musical score from sound effects in audiovisual culture. Music has always mimicked, emphasized or suggested certain sounds in the diegesis. Similarly, sound effects in films are regularly of more importance than simply fostering the illusion of the diegetic world on screen constructed by the film or video game. Sound effects regularly have symbolic or emotional values that outweigh any simple representational status. To compound this further, music has a tradition of taking inspiration from the natural world and mimicking natural sounds, and in more recent years, mimicking mechanical sounds such as trains and gunfire, for example.

Technological developments have enabled and encouraged the mixing of sounds and music. Video game sound and music has greatly been enabled by the use of musical software, such as sampling software and digital sound equipment developed originally for use in music. It often has been produced quickly and easily.[17] Digital audio workstations (DAWs), also known as sequencers or 'softstudios', allow the easy integration of music and sound effects. Indeed, many of the composers for computer games are also the game's sound designers. These 'softstudios' have everything run through them (recording, sequencing, temporal editing and precise adjustment, even synchronization to image). Logic, Cubase, Reason, Ableton Live, FL Studio, Orion and ProTools, to name probably the most prominent, can all be used as the hub of a home computing set up, with some being more sophisticated than others (Cubase 4, for example, allows musical scoring directly to images). The vast majority of the music and diegetic sound in the *Silent Hill* games clearly was produced on a DAW. This is evident not only in the clear and simple textures but also in the principle of the loop as the musical structural basis of most pieces.[18]

Digital technology (and the process of 'digital signal processing') has enabled a concerted focus on the qualities of sound itself. Such developments in musical sequencing software (often the centre of 'Music Technology') have inculcated composers with an awareness of sound and an ability to manipulate it electronically: sound for sound's sake—for example, adding reverb, habitually using filters and placing sounds in a stereo mix. These musical skills are not directly related to the traditional virtues of conventional training of composers for producing traditional music for traditional ensembles (what is often called 'classical training'). As an essential part of these digital developments, the use and manipulation of sound samples has become central. This means that raw sound recordings are wielded as starting material, which allows the integration of recorded 'sound effects' with music.[19] Contemporary sound designers by and large are using the same (or very similar) software as musicians, and often have some musical knowledge, or at the very least approach sound in a manner tuned-in to music.

Inspired at least partially by the game's sound design, the film *Silent Hill* tends to concentrate on ambient sound which emphasizes the uncertainty of traditional status between diegetic sound effects and non-diegetic music. This not only provides a highly distinctive sound world but also furnishes a level of sonic ambiguity and uncertainty to the *Silent Hill* landscape and soundscape. Considering that most of the music in the first *Silent Hill* film consists of pre-existing pieces, we might expect a certain 'disconnection' between image track and sound track, yet the asynchrony evident in the first film far exceeds expectation. Indeed, the dominance of musical asynchrony invokes a feeling of unease, a feeling of disconnection and uncertainty. In addition to this, the lack of repeated 'themes' of many traditional scores encourages a feeling of schizophrenia (where each successive second is made anew) rather than intermittent return and the repose offered by the use of repeated themes or related musical material.

The music embraces a wealth of disturbing and disconcerting sounds. The ambient sounds include deep drones, sub-bass-like rumbles, distant clunked metal, sounds like bowed metal/microphone feedback, and a plenitude of electronic echo and reverb. The regular dissolution of the traditional distinction between non-diegetic incidental music and diegetic sound effects often leads to a seemingly unified sonic field. While this is not unique, it has a history of isolated instances, such as the Barron's 'electronic tonalities' for *Forbidden Planet* (Fred. M. Wilcox, 1956), where sounds are strictly not sound effects or incidental music, but both simultaneously, or perhaps more pertinently in David Lynch's *Eraserhead* (1977), where Alan Splet's disturbing background ambiences appear to be a diegetic sound effect although have more of an effect akin to that of unsettling incidental music.[20] *Silent Hill*'s locations inspire almost constant music and ambient sound, the presence of which serves to demonstrate the sonic importance of Silent Hill's 'otherness', and the imminent presence of threats and uncertainty. This last point is crucial. We hear a metallic sound and think it probably non-diegetic, until the metallic 'pyramidhead' monster appears. This questions the status of the diegesis and, significantly, adds to a sense of ambiguity of environment through confusion of sound and image. Similarly, there are regular bass rumbles (almost sub-bass rumbles) on the film's soundtrack. Are these diegetic? That information is never furnished by the film. The disturbing effect of such ambiguous sound is discussed in *Audio-Vision* by Chion when discussing 'acousmatic' sound. Their origins are immediately obscure, although they may become apparent later. In psychological terms, such sounds are perceived as a potential threat in that they remain an uncertainty for the perceiver.

Now, on one level, this discussion might seem naïve. Austere music might well sound like 'sound effects' but there is art music that sounds like this as well. I am aware of this—but there is a tradition of sound effects in film (and video/computer games), and these scores engage those traditions more than they come from outside (from art music). A number of recent films offer very rich sonic landscapes that work on their own independently of their film. This might be related to the tradition of programmatic music, illustrating vistas and places through sound, a tradition reinvigorated by certain ambient music and new age music. However, there might also be an input from sound art, which has been a burgeoning area of the art world over the past couple of decades. In terms of film, Sergei Eisenstein discussed the notion of 'non-indifferent nature', where the setting is more than simply a realistic backdrop but becomes an emotionally charged landscape.[21] Indeed, the most complex of audiovisual art includes elements with more than simple relevances and valences.

The *Silent Hill* games are premised less upon action and excitement than atmosphere, with extended sections of potentially aimless wandering about through a deserted town shrouded in mist. According to the film's screenwriter Roger Avery, the first film focused on atmosphere to the point where the initial script looked thin and lacking to potential backers.[22] Like the games, the film concentrates on attempting to build an intensely immersive atmosphere—potentially at the cost of narrative and characterization. There is less in the way of functional (signifying) music, while focusing on atmosphere rather than action, movement and direction, is further enabled by a sense of stasis in music. Therefore, like sound effects, the music tends to be tied to place rather than mobile like a traditional score. *Silent Hill*'s focus on atmosphere aims at a high degree of emotional involvement in the game through a strong sense of immersion, with often limited vision but enveloping sound. Akira Yamaoka (2005) notes that one of game's central aims was to '… to get more in-depth into the subconscious of the characters …'. Indeed, the games appear to delineate an interior (mental) landscape, and the mixture of music and sound veers away from conventional representational duties in order to constitute a sense of interiority.[23]

In the games and films, there is a high degree of sound that is not directly representational. This is not to suggest it is without function. It is crucial in the provision of space as well as having a 'geographical function', that of delineating the particularities of a place. Silent Hill as a location has a bizarre sense of space. Music works as a spatial aid to sound design that does not match the visual illusion of 3D space—sounds can often lack reverb, echo or presence. Thus, a progression through the game is a progression not only through a series of distinct spaces (hotel, hospital, park, amusement park), but also through a series of distinct musical pieces. Hence, the difficulty of building a thematic and coherent experience from the music alone.

Often now bracketed under the term 'delay', echo is a more extreme version of reverberation. Reverberant spaces have reflective surfaces which bounce sounds off them. This means that a small reverberant space will give a certain amount of isolation to a sound, with a slightly harsh edge of reverb that makes it stand out slightly. The larger and more reverberant the space, the more a sound will echo, to the point where there are distinct repeats of sound (sometimes called 'slapback' in the recording industry). However, the use of electronic echo and reverb is often more of an emotional effect than one of communicating the 'reality' of a screen space. It can often indicate more of a state of mind rather than representing diegetic 'reality. According to Peter Doyle, '… echo as encountered by the human listener is an uncanny phenomenon, as if the sound has been emitted by the mass that reflects it' (2005, p. 108). He goes on to suggest that there is something of the transcendent and divine, particularly in echo as used in film. Indeed, one could argue that electronic reverb and echo embody technology as a psychological state in audiovisual culture.

Video games largely have inherited their use of echo and reverb from film and radio, where it often indicated memory or dream. Since the 1930s, processing of sound effects such as reverberation (colloquially known as 'reverb') have been used to figure interior states, either for memories of spoken words, as voices in the mind or as indication of supernatural activity. The sound effect of echo, which normally involves some sort of repeated sound reflection, tends to have a more 'realistic' usage, although its extreme use indicates either massive space or a situation of abnormality.

A constant ambience is evident in the films more than in the games, although arguably it is derived from the logic of the games. It is not continuous, and changes constantly, but almost always there is a continuum of vague sound-music-noise present. In most cases it illustrates a sense of deep space through echo and reverb, more often than not at a similar distance rather than rendering a succession of sounds at different distances. In the *Silent Hill* games and films there is an almost constant use of subtle reverb and echo effects whether in Silent Hill or in the Otherworld. This indicates the abnormality of these spaces, but suggests that they take place in the mind of the protagonist. However, electronic reverb and echo is less of an indicator of diegetic space than it is a musical aspect of the soundtracks. The sense of events taking place at distance is disturbing but constructed as something of a continuum in many sequences and manifests a form of aural accompaniment rather than delineators of the game world and film space. This can lead to something of a mismatch between the expansive, reverb-drenched music and sounds and misty (what should be sound-muffled) images.

## Conclusion

The two *Silent Hill* films (2006, 2012) were constructed around the existing soundtracks of the source video games, particularly the early ones. As a consequence, they have highly singular soundtracks, on the one hand cementing the films' relationship to the games while on the other sometimes appearing bizarre in relation to mainstream film soundtrack norms. In the games, *Silent Hill*'s world appears to emanate from the neurotic mind of the game's central character. This translates to the films. Indeed, the constant dislocation of sound and image establishes the sense of aberrant psychology at the heart of the game. The *Silent Hill* films follow the games in having a soundtrack that, although it adopts some film aspects, reverses some of the film conventions, most notably in having sound effects that have an emotional cast and music that is unemotional and mechanical, like an inanimate object.

There is a degree of equivalence between sonic ambience and images/ideas. The deserted town of impossible geographies and mysterious apparitions involves electronic delay on sounds and music, while the relentless mist and falling ash inspire continuous sounds that simply remain rather than developing. Echo and reverb here are less components of representation than very direct emotion and psychology, in other words not communication so much as pure aesthetics. These are characteristics not only of the unified soundtrack but also of all sounds being organized in a musical manner and having essentially emotional valence.

## Notes

1. As stated by Gans in the DVD commentary. *Silent Hill*. Fox Home Entertainment, 2006. B000GHRCEE.
2. Furthermore, the importance and status of the game's music is evident in CD releases of selections from each game, and also on a DVD called 'Lost Memories—The Art and Music of *Silent Hill*', which includes music from the first three games, as well as trailers, artwork and production material.

3. 'Every sound and every line of sound that is in the game is done by me. And, I make all my own sound effects ...' Akira Yamaoka (2005).
4. Earlier, he had worked on *Castlevania: Symphony of the Night* (1997), where he programmed drums, and supplied songs for a number of games including *Dance Dance Revolution* (1999) and *Beatmania IIDX* (2002). For those games, Yamaoka predominantly composed songs, although he has composed all the music for *Road Rage* (aka *Speed King*) (1998).
5. Nine Inch nails leader Trent Reznor went on to produce the soundtrack for the video game *Quake* (1996), while member Chris Vrenna, supplied the music for the game *American McGee's Alice* (2000).
6. Yamaoka (2005) refers to a 'Bristol-influence' (trip hop) in *Silent Hill 2*, moving to 'more American' pop songs in *Silent Hill 3* and then back to a 'more British sound' in *Silent Hill 4: The Room*.
7. The ambient sounds and mechanical loops suggest a musical notion of the 'post-industrial', figuring the ghost of the industrial past, with Silent Hill as ghost town, possibly an old mining town, and thus, this 'industrial music' embodies nostalgia for blue collar work.
8. Cf. Gorbman's (1987, p. 63) use of the term 'sonorous envelope' (taken from Didier Anzieu) to describe one of the central functions of film underscore.
9. In a recent dedicated article about sound in *Silent Hill 2* Andy Kelly notes, 'The audio design is rarely talked about with the same adoration as the wonderfully dark story and surreal, twisted art style, but it's just as important. ... Can you imagine a major publisher taking a risk on such a bizarre, slow-paced game today? ... Whenever I listen to [Yamaoka's score] I'm instantly transported to those misty streets' (2014, pp. 126–7).
10. Of course, this is nothing particularly new to film. Famously, Ridley Scott took sections of Jerry Goldsmith's score for *Alien* (1979) and shifted them to sections for which they had not been written.
11. Temp tracks might be approached as a musical foundation plan for films, setting out a structure of action and emotion before the film is constructed. Good examples would include Stanley Kubrick's *2001: A Space Odyssey* (1968) and Quentin Tarantino's *Reservoir Dogs* (1991).
12. Some of the music has been remixed and some re-recorded. As the film's credits inform us, this took place at Metalworks Studio, Toronto, although Kevin Banks's credit as 'music editor' suggests that there nevertheless was a need to cut pieces together.
13. 'Games are not film! But ...' section. (Collins, 2008, p. 5).
14. The notion of 'gameworld' denotes the distinct character of the illusory world and space on screen. It is similar to film's illusory diegesis, although it also includes the limitations upon and 'feel' of playing the game.
15. It can match the action through certain activities triggering the appearance of certain music or signalling developments in the ongoing music.
16. See, for example, Kulezic-Wilson (2008, pp. 127–131).
17. While mainstream films tend to use orchestral scores, DAWs are often used to sketch what the score will sound like when played by an orchestra. For video/computer games, DAWs tend to produce the final product.
18. Yamaoka's Equipment on the early games was Emagic Logic, Emagic EXS24, Emagic amt8, Phrazer Infinity, Roland JD-800, Roland JP-8080, Roland TB-303, Roland MKS-80, Roland DJ-70, Roland VP-9000, Sequential Circuits

Prophet 5, Oberheim OB-MX, Ensoniq VFX, Akai VX-600, Korg Prophecy. There were no acoustic drums and guitars except on one or two tracks. These sounds have a strong 'retro' sense to more recent listeners.
19. Indeed, one might argue that in aesthetic terms this has been ongoing for some decades, particularly if one thinks of the rock tradition which includes records like the Shangri Las's *Leader of the Pack* (1965) with its motorcycle sounds or the recordings of animals at the conclusion of The Beatles's *Good Morning* (from *Sgt.Pepper's Lonely Hearts Club Band* [1967]), or the extensive use of field recordings on Pink Floyd's *Dark Side of the Moon* (1973). These amongst others helped establish a solid tradition that denies any significant divide between 'music' and 'sound effects'.
20. In fact, in its lack of regular synchronization and background continuity, Splet's ambience resembles many 'horror' game soundtracks. Interestingly, Lynch's regular production designer Carol Spier worked on *Silent Hill*.
21. Evident in his discussions of 'nonindifferent nature', the 'musicality of landscape' and the 'musicality of color and tone' (Eisenstein, 1987, p. 389).
22. According to screenwriter Roger Avery, like Gans he is a video game player and was impressed by Gans's knowledge of *Silent Hill*. He notes that it was '… a very difficult script for the studio to accept. … we had long moments where seemingly nothing happens. It's all atmosphere …' (Davidson, 2005). [http://uk.movies.ign.com/articles/658/658291p1.html accessed 03/0407].
23. This is a process that is evident perhaps in some 'space rock', such as Klaus Schulze's *Mirage* (1977) or Brian Eno's foundational ambient album *Ambient 4: On Land* (1982).

## References

Bessell, D. (2002) 'What's That Funny Noise?: An Examination of the Role of Music in Cool Boarders 2, Alien Trilogy and Medievil 2' in G. King and T. Krzywinska (eds) *ScreenPlay: Cinema/Videogames/Interfaces* (London: Wallflower), 136–144.
Bridgett, R. (2008) 'Dynamic Range: Subtlety and Silence in Video Game Sound' in K. Collins (ed.) *From Pac-Man to Pop Music: Interactive Audio in Games and New Media* (Aldershot: Ashgate), 127–134.
Chion, M. (1994) *Audio-Vision: Sound on Screen* (New York: Columbia University Press).
Collins, K. (2008) *Game Sound* (Cambridge, Mass.: MIT Press).
Davidson, P. (2005) '*Silent Hill*: A Movie Made by Gamers' [interview with screenwriter Roger 'Pulp Fiction' Avery] in *IGN*, 13 October, http://uk.movies.ign.com/articles/658/658291p1.html, date accessed 3 April 2007.
Doyle, P. (2005) *Echo and Reverb: Fabricating Space in Popular Music Recording, 1900-1960* (Middletown, Conn.: Wesleyan University Press).
Eisenstein, S. M. (1987) *Nonindifferent Nature: Film and the Structure of Things*, trans. H. Marshall (Cambridge: Cambridge University Press).
Gans, C. (2006) DVD commentary. *Silent Hill*. Fox Home Entertainment, B000GHRCEE.
Gorbman, C. (1987) *Unheard Melodies: Narrative Film Music* (London: BFI).
Kelly, A. (2014) 'How Sound Makes *Silent Hill 2* a Horror Masterpiece', *PC Gamer* 262, February.

Kulezic Wilson, D. (2008) 'Sound Design is the New Score', *Music, Sound and the Moving Image*, Vol. 2, No. 2, 127–131.

Lastra, J. (2008) 'Film and the Wagnerian Aspiration: Thoughts on Sound Design and History of the Senses' in J. Beck and T. Grajeda (eds) *Lowering the Boom: Critical Studies in Film Sound* (Chicago: University of Illinois Press), 123–138.

Mundhenke, F. (2013) 'Resourceful Frames and Sensory Functions—Musical Transformations from Game to Film in *Silent Hill*' in P. Moormann (ed.) *Music and Game: Perspectives on a Popular Alliance* (Wiesbaden: Springer VS), 107–124.

Perron, B. (2012) *Silent Hill: The Terror Engine* (Ann Arbor: University of Michigan Press).

Whalen, Z. (2007) 'Film Music vs. Game Music: The Case of Silent Hill' in J. Sexton (ed.) *Music, Sound and Multimedia: From the Live to the Virtual* (Edinburgh: Edinburgh University Press), 68–82.

Yamaoka, A. 'GDC 2005: Akira Yamaoka Interview' *Game Informer magazine*, www.gameinformer.com/News/Story/200503/N05.0310.1619.39457.htm, date accessed 7 March 2007.

PART II

# Presence, Immersion, Space

CHAPTER 7

# Towards 3-D Sound: Spatial Presence and the Space Vacuum

*Miguel Mera*

An enduring auditory trope in science fiction cinema is the concept of 'silence' within a vacuum. Mechanical sound waves can travel only through matter. Since there is almost no matter in interstellar space, sound cannot travel through it. Yet, that reality presents particular challenges to filmmakers. It may be true that 'in space no-one can hear you scream', as the tagline to the film *Alien* (Ridley Scott, 1979) proudly declared, but literal representations of the silence of space rarely make for an engaging cinematic experience. Indeed, filmmakers have grappled with environmental verisimilitude in different ways, frequently ignoring physical laws or creating their own. This chapter considers some cinematic responses to the concept of the vacuum in space. I hope to advance the idea that the physical reality of the vacuum presents a particularly fascinating and challenging site for audience 'immersion'. Even though, to date, very few people have had any actual experience of space travel, filmmakers' desire to convince the audience that they are physically located within a mediated environment governs cinematic representations of outer space. The vacuum, therefore, presents a fruitful example of the conflict between scientific rationality and immersive impact, a scale that slides between knowing and feeling.

Immersion is a term that has gathered purchase in recent audiovisual scholarship, particularly in relation to videogames (Grimshaw, 2007; Lipscomb and Zehnder, 2004; McMahan, 2003), yet it remains insufficiently explored and under-theorized. The more technically accurate psychological term is *presence*, the experiential counterpart of immersion. In this chapter, I will adopt Wirth et al.'s (2007) theory of *spatial presence*, which provides a framework for understanding how immersive media can inspire users to believe they are personally and physically present in the represented environment. This desire to 'be there' is clearly a central concern for many movies set in space. As Cara Deleon

M. Mera
City, University of London, UK

observes: 'The medium's goal is to create an environment in which the audience is fully immersed, no longer aware of the two-dimensionality on the screen' (2009, p. 10). By tracing some of the ways in which this two-dimensionality has been extended by sound design and music, and their absence, it is possible to examine evolving strategies for spatial presence, which are married to shifts in technology and cinematic aesthetics.

We begin with Stanley Kubrick's *2001: A Space Odyssey* (1968), which established the idea that music can replace the vacuum of space. Growing from this fundamental concept, we can trace an historical evolution in representations of outer space. Michel Chion's concept of the superfield described the sensation of complete space produced by multichannel ambience outside of the visual frame. Mark Kerins' subsequent development and revision of this term for the digital age, the ultrafield, sought not to 'provide a *continuous* aural environment, but rather to *continuously* provide an *accurate* spatial environment where aural and visual space match'. The ultrafield is, therefore, explained as the 'three-dimensional sonic environment of the diegetic world, continuously re-oriented to match the camera's visual perspective' (2011, p. 92). I argue that we are moving beyond these conceptualizations from the superfield, via the ultrafield, to something that I will call *three-dimensional (3-D) sound*. This is an expansion and development of the characteristics of the ultrafield, partly afforded by the increased visual and spatial depth of 3-D cinema, requiring a more dynamic use of both music and sound. In particular, the emancipation of music from its traditionally fixed sound stage spatialization offers the most striking indication of an aesthetic and technological turn. The result is that divisions between music and sound design collapse when the spatial domain is enacted as the dominant feature in the construction of a soundtrack. This is best illustrated by the film *Gravity* (Alfonso Cuarón, 2013), which redefined many of the unwritten rules of aural spatialization and motion. A film governed by the scientific principles of the vacuum offers an interesting glimpse into the future of the integrated soundtrack. This chapter examines the relationship between two types of spatial presence: the spatial presence that articulates the audience's suspension of disbelief and their subsequent location within a film's narrative world, and the spatial presence of sound and music within a multichannel cinema environment.

## Spatial Presence

The term *immersion* has become a catch-all phrase to describe user experience, particularly in the Humanities. Conversely, *presence* has been studied primarily by computer scientists and psychologists evaluating the effectiveness of virtual reality systems. Both terms have often been used somewhat interchangeably and it is worth clarifying an important difference and the implications of this for the study of the integrated multichannel soundtrack.

Immersion is achieved by replacing as many real-world sensations as possible with the sensations of a virtual environment. It is an objective description of what can be delivered by particular technologies (Slater and Wilbur, 1997). The aim of immersive technologies is to generate a sense that one has left the real world and is 'present' in the virtual environment. If immersion is the technologically driven, objective aspect, presence is the perceptual outcome of that immersion. It is the psychological perception of 'being in' the virtual environment in which one is immersed; the impression that a mediated experience is 'real'. As Lombard and Ditton explain in their frequently cited essay, presence is 'the artificial sense that a user has in a virtual environment that the environment is unmediated' (1997).[1]

The distinction is not just semantically expedient, because the perceptual/technological split reveals value judgements that frequently disconnect technical and aesthetic innovation, particularly in relation to movies. New film technologies have frequently been considered tawdry or gimmicky, restricting rather than enlivening, and somehow damaging to the purity of the cinema. Tim Recuber, for example, identifies a range of high-fidelity audiovisual technologies designed to enhance the kinaesthetic experience of the audio-viewer, which he calls 'immersion cinema'. He argues that these emphasize 'technical achievement to the detriment of social or artistic relevance' while simultaneously embedding a 'passive, consumerist ideology within the spaces of contemporary movie going' (2007, p. 316). Critical responses consistently state that artistic integrity is drowned by the immersive technologies of spectacle. The recurrent historic discussions around stereoscopic cinema are a case in point (Holmberg, 2003; Kermode, 2009).

It is telling that Neuendorf and Lieberman, on the other hand, seek to identify and celebrate the correspondences between technology and aesthetics in their adoption of the term presence. They suggest that cinema was 'the original medium of presence' and that the history of film is one of 'striving for an ever-greater level of presence through technological innovation, changes in aesthetic form, and developments in narrative structures and performance styles' (2010, p. 9). The significant difference in their stance is that presence is understood as a cognitive process, it is the result of perception rather than just a series of physical sensations, and it is recognized as multimodal and experiential. Presence can happen in different kinds of films, not just those that avail themselves of the most advanced immersive technologies, because mental constructions are more important than the mechanics of the stimuli.

By aligning ourselves with this position we are able to identify and dismantle some common fallacies. The first is that the more pervasive the technology—further surround sound channels, a larger screen—the more complete the mediated world will seem and the more immersive the experience will be. I am sure that I am not alone in experiencing deep engagement and effective suspension of disbelief while watching small screens and listening to a limited stereo field. In line with Bracken and Skalski (2010), therefore, I am inclined to identify presence in a range of conventional and everyday media. This will be significant when it comes to our discussion of *Gravity*, because it is not automatically the technical innovation of Dolby Atmos[2] or the increased number of surround sound channels that make spatial presence more probable, but rather the bold aesthetic decisions that derive from the way that this technology has been applied.

Furthermore, because the mediated environment is a precondition for presence, we can identify ways in which the experience is different from the real world. Some scholarly definitions of immersive experiences are close, if not identical, to descriptions of nonmediated reality (Mantovani and Riva, 1999). But *spatial presence*, as defined by Wirth et al., requires an appreciation and acceptance of the 'rules' of a media environment, a process of self-orientation in relation to it, and entry to and exit from the mediated world. It is an experience that can be enriched but does not entirely depend on external mediatized information. It is the term *spatial presence*, then, that comes closest to what I suspect film audiences think of as immersion. For spatial presence to occur, the technology disappears, at least to some degree. Consequently, spatial presence must be understood as a cognitive and experiential process, rather than defining the technologies of immersion as automatically engrossing or engaging. There is, indeed, sophisticated interplay between the mental and the experiential where technology and aesthetics are unified.

Wirth et al.'s 'Process Model of the Formation of Spatial Experiences' (2007) is useful, therefore, because it integrates a range of existing theories from psychology, communication and virtual reality into a clear and unified procedural structure. It identifies how audio-viewers can be made to feel like they are leaving the real world behind. Importantly, the authors argue that 'spatial presence is not bound to virtual reality, but can also occur in users of conventional media, such as books or television' (2007, p. 495). Wirth et al. argue that spatial presence requires a journey across two levels. At the first level, a Spatial Situation Model (SSM) is created. High levels of involvement and suspension of disbelief result in spatial presence at the second level. At the risk of oversimplification, the two stages of the model could be summarized as follows:

1. Audio-viewers develop a *mental representation* of the space or world that the media presents to them and form an SSM.
2. Audio-viewers begin to *favour* the media-based space as the point of reference for where they are 'located'. The mediated space then becomes the Primary Egocentric Reference Frame (PERF).

These stages can be explored in a little more detail. Interrelated audiovisual objects and assumptions about the represented world based on real or mediated 'personal spatial memories' (2007, p. 501) help audio viewers form a mental model of the film's mediated space. There is a continual process of interpretation and mental construction that evaluates the congruence of the perceived spatial environment with the SSM. This process, therefore, highlights 'how many aspects/details are salient that fill the imagination as well as how plausible and coherent the imagined space is' (2007, p. 502). The various spatial and sensory elements must be appropriately rich and, since film is multimodal, the 'information provided must be consonant across the modalities in order to increase consistency' (2007, p. 502). Richness in this context means rich *enough*, but not necessarily a direct replication of actual reality. Richness could be achieved, for example, by strong narrative structure as much as by the completeness of sensory information. Wirth et al. sum this up as follows: 'A variety of concise spatial cues (preferably within different perceptual channels), which are linked in a consistent and plausible manner, should evoke both richer and more internal consistent SSM's than those presenting only a few, diffuse or inconsistent cues' (2007, p. 504).

Once the mental model has been created, the audio-viewer must subconsciously decide whether they feel like they are in the imagined world or in the real one. This is conceptually different from stage one because SSMs are 'mental representations, whereas Spatial Presence is regarded as an experiential state' (2007, p. 504). Wirth et al. consider the state of spatial presence as binary (on/off) and, at its emergence, the audio-viewer aligns their spatial perceptions within the mediated environment rather than any other possible frame. This is what has been labelled the PERF. An audio-viewer accepts the mediated environment as the PERF, because 'perceived self-location, perceived possible actions and mental capacities are all bound to the mediated space' (2007, p. 506). Various media factors and user characteristics can enhance or hinder both stages of the processes that lead towards the state of spatial presence, but it is important to note that this is a fluid state that can be entered and exited repeatedly.

This process model presents one way to understand what is necessary for spatial presence to take place, but it also presents a particular challenge when we consider the filmic representation of interstellar space, especially in relation to the concept of the vacuum. In cinematic representations of, for example, spaceships travelling through space, knowledge of reality suggests that these shots should be presented in silence, but this is rarely the case. The lack would immediately pull the audio-viewer out of any mediated spatial presence, or in Wirth et al.'s formulation, the audio-viewer's PERF would return to the auditorium or other environmental frame. The lack of sensory completeness, the loss of an important channel of information, the inconsistent behaviour from the represented world (unless the film is completely silent throughout), and the creation of a cognitively less demanding environment would point towards incompleteness, a loss of richness and a break in the illusion of the mediated reality. The cinematic space vacuum frequently presents a clash between what audiences know *about* reality and what they must feel in order to believe the representation *as* reality. Mediated sensory completeness is in direct conflict with nonmediated reality, plausibility is in conflict with imagination and credibility of one kind is challenged by credibility of another. Wirth et al. hint at this when they suggest that 'spatial knowledge and spatial imagination become more relevant if the mediated representation of the space is less intuitive and more fragmented' (2007, p. 502). It is unsurprising, therefore, that filmmakers have consistently found interesting ways to fill the gap.

## Ye Cannae Change the Laws of Physics[3]

In a striking scene in *2001: A Space Odyssey* (1968), 'suspicious' supercomputer HAL cuts Dr Frank Poole's (Gary Lockwood) oxygen hose while the astronaut attempts to reinstall a component of a faulty antenna and he is sent spinning into the void to his death. We see the tiny figure of the rotating astronaut, but we hear nothing. For a very brief moment, the soundtrack is completely and eerily silent. Stanley Kubrick's determination to ensure that the film was scientifically accurate is well documented (Kolker, 2006; Kirby, 2013). Several technical advisors were hired, including experts in aerospace engineering and artificial intelligence. This realistic depiction of outer space resulted in the very carefully controlled representation of the propagation of sound. Chion describes the strategy as follows:

> For the sequences of space travel, when the camera is filming from without like an eye floating in the void, Kubrick appears to apply a simple principle faithful to physical reality: since there is no sound in a vacuum, there will not be the slightest sound linked to operations or movements of machines. (Chion, 2001, p. 98)

Despite this governing principle, the use of absolute silence is confined to Frank Poole's death scene. Elsewhere the film employs music to replace the silence of the vacuum or, alternatively, as the Jupiter Mission progresses, there is an increasing use of 'objective-internal sound', which Chion describes, in this context, as the sound of breathing inside an astronaut's helmet (2001, p. 99), but this term could also be applied to heartbeats or other sounds that correspond to the physical and mental interior of a character. It seems to me unlikely that the audience would experience spatial presence for much of this film, because Kubrick constantly places the audio-viewer 'outside' the action, and the film requires continuous contemplation and questioning. But we do move further towards spatial presence, I suggest, in the stargate sequence where Dave Bowman's (Keir Dullea) psychedelic sound and light journey allows him to travel to another dimension. The rather literal representation of the silence of the vacuum at Frank Poole's death, therefore, marks the point at which the film shifts from the realistic to the experiential, where the limits of our knowledge of space travel define the perceptual framework.

Let us explore that trajectory. Roger Ebert argues that in the famous 'Blue Danube' docking sequence 'even the restless in the audience are silenced, I imagine, by the sheer wonder of the visuals' (1997). Silenced perhaps, but not spatially present. Even though the Strauss waltz replaces the sound of the vacuum and, therefore, partially supports the sensory completeness that Wirth et al. argue is required for spatial presence to take place, the music and image are not consonant. Royal S. Brown has described the music in *2001* as a 'parallel emotional/aesthetic universe' (1994, p. 239) and other writers have also noted the deliberate sense of dislocation between music and visuals (Gorbman, 2006, pp. 4–5). For Chion, despite the breathtaking brilliance of the sequence, 'something is missing in all this dancing plenitude' (2001, p. 94). It is music that creates an expressive contrast by its very indifference to the situation on the screen; it is *anempathetic* (Chion, 2001, p. 94). The combination of music and image, then, in this and other scenes in *2001*, demands a cognitive process that distances the audio-viewer from the representation of mediated reality. In terms of the SSM, the audio-viewer cannot progress to stage two because even though a mental representation of the presented world is encouraged, it cannot become the point of reference while the PERF is held in suspended animation by the discordant audiovisual choreography.

The sequences of Frank Poole's space walk and manoeuvring using the extravehicular activity (EVA) pod move somewhat closer towards spatial presence, it seems to me, because of a closer internal association with the character. It is aural design that might imply greater subjectivity, but Chion is right to call this 'objective-internal sound', because even though we hear Poole's breath—accompanied by the continuous hiss from the air supply—it is always presented from the same aural perspective. The visual construction of shots, on the other hand, radically alters the spatial perspective. The sound remains fixed regardless of whether we are inside or outside of Poole's spacesuit, inside or outside of the EVA pod, or whether we see wide shots of spacecraft or close-ups. Therefore, breath sounds function like ambiance, generating an objective rather than subjective aural perspective.

When Bowman attempts to rescue his colleague, we see external shots of the EVA pod and Poole's body floating in complete silence. These are some of the most ghostly scenes in all cinema. There is an accurate representation of movement through the silence in the vacuum, but this does not encourage spatial presence. The lack of sound, though scientifically accurate, stands in opposition both to the multimodal nature of human existence and the multimodal nature of the cinema as we know them. The presentation of isolated moments of emptiness is in stark contrast to the 'complete' spatial environments elsewhere in the film. We are so attuned to the synchrony of sound and image in our world that in this filmic context a lack can only be read as a lack.

The contrast between this painful, beautiful and eerie silence and the plenitude of the stargate sequence is marked. When Bowman enters the stargate, a psychedelic audiovisual journey begins. The visceral and sensory experience encourages spatial presence. The audio-viewer is persuaded to enter the infinite corridor of light and sound rather than to act as objective observer of that space. Chion suggests that at this point in the film, 'all notions of realism or unrealism become irrelevant' (2001, p. 100). He is right, up to a point, but realism in this context relates to what the audience is prepared to accept. It is a credible representation of a fantastical environment, allowing a mental representation to be formed. It could be argued that the use of manipulated versions of Ligeti's *Atmospheres* and *Adventures* in this sequence act as the 'voice' of the monolith. Yet, Ligeti's music functions in a different way in the stargate sequence. In two previous mysterious presentations, the monolith is enacted by the music, which gives it weight, depth and scale, but in the stargate sequence, the music and image are enacted by their interaction with each other. The music is given greater energy by the light fields rushing towards the audience and the corridor of light is given depth and perspective by the music. It is a rich, multimodal spectacle that places the audio-viewer directly at the centre of the experience and aligns spatial perceptions within the mediated environment.

To be sure, Kubrick did not seek to create a film that encouraged spatial presence throughout, although it certainly aimed for the spectacular. *2001: A Space Odyssey* preserved and prioritized environmental verisimilitude while also moving towards spatial presence, yet for much of the film's duration, the audience is kept at a deliberate intellectual distance.

It is very rarely noted that *2001*'s première and Roadshow Theatrical Release featured a six-track stereo magnetic soundtrack.[4] HAL's voice issued from the surrounds and generated an effective acousmatic all-seeing and all-knowing authority.[5] In its 35-mm anamorphic general release format, however, the film included either a four-track magnetic stereo soundtrack or an optical monaural soundtrack.[6] Audiences in the late 1960s, therefore, experienced very different spatial manifestations of the sound of the film, defined by both the nascent technology and exhibition limitations of the time.

Only a few years later, the refined surround capabilities offered by the Dolby Stereo format presented a new challenge to director George Lucas and the sound team for *Star Wars* (1977) (see Sergi, 2004).[7] How could immersive surround technologies be effectively deployed if sound could not travel in space? Thus, fidelity to the laws of physics was abandoned, the vacuum was filled with air and sound could once again propagate. This 're-inflation' partly reflects the hybrid science fiction/fantasy genre of the film, but I also suggest that the abandonment of scientific rationality was primarily at the service of spatial presence. In the first few minutes of the film, following the opening titles, the concept of the silent vacuum is, quite literally, blown apart by a series of explosions as a rebel ship flees from an Imperial Star Destroyer. Travelling overhead we hear the mechanical whirr of the rebel ship and a series of directional laser bolts. These sounds are engulfed by the low rumble and roar of the Star Destroyer, which travels from the back to the front of the auditorium. The audio-viewer is encouraged to feel the spatial location, size, scale and weight of these vessels. There is an immediate sense of being at the heart of the skirmish.

Later, in the battle that eventually destroys the Death Star, ships zip from left to right, a torrent of lasers and blasts are heard around the auditorium. Enemy craft chase Luke Skywalker's (Mark Hamill) X-wing starfighter through a narrow trench. He must fire proton torpedoes into a thermal exhaust port at exactly the right moment in order to destroy the Death Star. The design of this sequence seems to be a precursor of the racing videogames that would become prevalent in the 1980s. William Whittington acknowledges this perspectival approach suggesting that 'sound design allows the filmgoer to ride the film rather than simply view it' (2007, p. 108). The audio-viewer frequently experiences a first-person perspective with the gaze drawn towards the centre back of the screen, while credible environmental directionality is provided by the sound. At key moments in this film where, rationally speaking, silence in the space vacuum should prevail, we find the exact opposite. In terms of the potential for spatial presence, the construction of the SSM is carefully controlled to direct the audio-viewer's attention. But it is not simply the plenitude of the local multimodal experience that encourages this. At this point in the film the audio-viewer is narratively empathetic, having followed Luke's development from cocky teenager to rebel hero. Obi-Wan's (Alec Guinness) sacrifice has set Luke free to understand how to use the 'Force'. Therefore, the climax of the film, the peg on which the narrative resolution hangs, is also the point of greatest potential spatial presence. We might also observe, retrospectively, that a similar narrative principle is in action in the stargate sequence in *2001*.

Gianluca Sergi notes that the key innovation of *Star Wars* was the conviction that it provided a 'unique opportunity to change radically sound exhibition' (2010, p. 15). It was released in the Dolby Stereo format in over 50 per cent of its first release theatres and it had a profound impact on both aesthetic practices and exhibition technologies in the years immediately following (Kerins, 2011, p. 32). Sergi also notes that in *Star Wars*, the surround channel was 'less a means to provide music and some rare ambiance effects, than a source of primary sound information' (2010, p. 17). This description seems to straddle and problematize the borderline between Chion's notion of the superfield and Kerins' concept of the ultrafield.

## Pseudo-Silence: Houston We Have a Problem

Chion describes the superfield as the 'space created, in multitrack films, by ambient sounds, city noises, music, and all sorts of rustlings that surround the visual space and that can issue from loudspeakers outside the physical boundaries of the screen'. He argues that the ensemble of sounds have a 'quasi autonomous existence with relation to the visual field' (1994, p. 150) because it does not depend moment by moment on what we see onscreen. If Chion's concept can be applied to the use of analogue surround technologies and the aesthetic approaches that relate to them, Kerins extends this concept in light of developments in Digital Surround Sound. It does not render the superfield extinct; rather, it is an evolution beyond the limits of Dolby Stereo. Sound now leaps even further off the screen and extends to the whole of the cinema auditorium:

> I dub this updated superfield the *ultrafield*. It differs from the Dolby Stereo-based superfield in two key conceptual ways. First it sacrifices the 'invisibility' of sound editing and mixing to embrace digital surround's aforementioned capabilities to exploit active and changing sounds. Where the superfield maintains a sonic continuity, the ultrafield constantly shifts sounds around the multi-channel environment. Second it encompasses a much broader array of sonic elements than its predecessor. Where Chion limited the superfield to ambient sounds and noises, the ultrafield encompasses not just these background sounds but the entire aural world of the film including sound effects, dialogue and diegetic music. (2011, p. 92)

Why only diegetic music? In Kerins' definition sound moves but non-diegetic music does not. The ultrafield, then, defines its boundaries in the 3-D sonic environment of the diegetic world, but does not resolve the use of non-diegetic music in spatial terms. For this innovation, we must wait until the aesthetic and technical developments of 3-D sound. What we have witnessed thus far in the challenge of depicting the space vacuum is an historical trajectory where pure objective internal sound or music replaces the void of space, next the principles of the vacuum are simply ignored and sound design rejects environmental accuracy in the service of spatial presence. As we shift from the superfield to the ultrafield era, we find increased efforts to reconcile scientific fact with dramatic fantasy. I call this hybrid attempt to find a representational middle-ground *pseudo-silence* (which could also be understood as pseudo-science). It is, of course, always designed to enhance spatial presence.

A film such as *Apollo 13* (Ron Howard, 1995), which won an Academy Award for sound, makes effective use of exhibition technologies and flexible digital tools for sound manipulation early in the ultrafield era. Sound and music primarily remain spatially fixed and maintain sonic continuity. Yet, there is also some exploitation of active and changing sounds within digital surround systems. This partly reflects the fact that *Apollo 13* is a docudrama, which implies a greater emphasis on realism. In comparison to *Armageddon* (Michael Bay, 1998), David Sonnenschein argues that '*Apollo 13* is more reality-based and takes this interpretation of space literally by having the ship move silently' (Sonnenschein, 2001, p. 127). The Apollo 13 is certainly quieter than spacecraft in *Armageddon*, yet it is not accurate to state that the ship moves silently. External shots of the spaceship are, in fact, always accompanied by 'whooshes' from gas thrusters, or other rumbles. Any static external shots of space are always filled with front-focused quiet music and/or radio chatter. Flying debris is always accompanied by sound. Even a shot showing an overboard dump is accompanied by its own 'spray' sound effect, astronaut Fred Haise (Bill Paxton) calls this 'constellation urine'. It is interesting to note, therefore, that Sonnenschein perceives silence in this film's representations of outer space. I suggest that this is, in fact, carefully crafted *pseudo-silence*. It is an attempt to imply absence through a marked reduction in ambient sonic material but not through its entire omission. Furthermore, individual spot sound effects remain, but these are not particularly dynamic in terms of their movement in the surrounds. Conversely, on Earth we find a greater use of the surrounds and considerable digital manipulation of 'sound materials' that is typical of the ultrafield era. For example, after Jim Lovell (Tom Hanks) reveals that the Apollo 13 is venting oxygen into space, we witness mission control's shocked reaction followed by a flurry of nervous activity. There is an eruption of sound that envelops the audience: radio chatter, panicky conversations, a polyphonic mass of dialogue in all auditorium speakers that reflects the chaos of the situation. The earthbound directional use of sound is, therefore, often more adventurous than the sound in space because of the challenge of representation in the space vacuum.

One scene in *Apollo 13*, however, radically challenges the notion of pseudo-silence in the space vacuum and points some of the way towards 3-D sound. This is a nightmare sequence representing Marilyn Lovell's (Kathleen Quinlan) fears for her husband's safety. Following an unspecified problem aboard the ship, numerous alarms are heard (in the full spatial speaker array), glass smashes, a pod bay door is sucked out into the void and the cabin is depressured. Jim Lovell is dragged out of the spaceship. The amplitude and complexity of the soundscape increases and there is a powerful spectral fusion of sound design and music. The increased use of the surround speakers and, especially, increased use of sound in the low-frequency effects (LFE) channel (sometimes also called the subwoofer) helps generate a kind of distorted wind effect. There is extensive use of reverb in all channels, a rhetorical device that signals that the scene does not represent 'reality'. This bold aural representation suggests the potential for integration of music and sound in cinematic representations of the space vacuum.

Moving ahead some 15 years, towards what I suggest is the beginning of the end of the ultrafield era, we see the continuation and development of the principle of pseudo-silence in J.J. Abrams' reinvention of *Star Trek* (2009). Early in the film a Klingon vessel blows a hole in the hull of the U.S.S. Kelvin and a woman is sucked out into space. When the unnamed crewmember is outside of the ship, a state of pseudo-silence is heard. Furthermore, the sound and music are directionally sucked out with her as an aural representation of the vacuum. Whistling wind is heard, yet the screams of the doomed crewmember stop. The full visual perspective of the battle is displayed, yet explosions and phaser fire are absent. Later and throughout the film, however, the audience does hear explosions, weapons fire, crashes and engine rumbles in outer space. These sounds are directional and take full advantage of the surround speakers.

A further hybrid approach to pseudo-silence is heard when Kirk (Chris Pine) and two other crewmembers 'space jump' from a shuttle in outer space into the Romulan atmosphere, falling at considerable speed towards the alien planet. The sequence begins in pseudo-silence featuring quiet 'wispy', 'wailing' sounds that develop inharmonic ambiguity with shifts between intervallic pitch and noise. Then breath is introduced to the sound mix, and finally wind, gestures of bodily movement and vocalizations are included. The sound design becomes fuller as the characters fall further into the atmosphere and more air is available to conduct the sound. Nowhere in the sequence is there absolute silence.

Attempts to encourage spatial presence in the ultrafield era frequently employ an aural middle ground that carefully manages the amount, frequency and spatialization of audio material. Whittington suggests that every film since *Star Wars* has ignored the vacuum. The decision to render space with sound has coloured 'the sound tracks of every subsequent science fiction film' (2007, p. 108). In fact, illusions both of silence and of the physical reality of the vacuum are created, but audio material is never reduced to the extent that spatial presence may be compromised. I argue that this represents an aesthetic desire and drift towards 3-D sound, which is finally afforded by developments in digital sound and visual technologies in the late 2000s. Neuendorf and Liebermann suggest that creating a convincing 3-D soundscape is one of the most valuable aspects of the role of sound design in the creation of spatial presence, but if the soundscape does not match the two-dimensional (2-D) image it might 'be a deterrent to a sensation of full immersion' (2010, p. 23). This is, indeed, the defining boundary characteristic of Kerins' notion of the ultrafield where the 3-D sonic environment of the diegetic world is 're-oriented to match the camera's visual perspective' (2011, p. 92). Yet, in 3-D Sound, just as the visual perspective is dimensionally extended, so is the soundscape.

## 3-D Sound or the Gravitational Pull of *Gravity*

*Gravity* is a film governed by the space vacuum. It is also deeply concerned with the spatial organization of its audiovisual materials. Director Alfonso Cuarón's solution to the challenge of presenting a narrative within the vacuum was to acknowledge the fact that sound cannot travel through the atmosphere but can be transmitted through the 'interaction of elements, meaning that if our characters grab, or touch stuff, the vibration of that will travel into their ear, and so they will get a muffled representation of that sound' (Coleman, 2013). The sound design team recorded many of the sounds using contact (transducer) microphones, which are attached to the surface of objects and record their vibrations rather than the vibration of air. Stuart Bender describes the impact of this approach in terms of its defamiliarization (2014). Furthermore, Cuarón explains that, '*Gravity* is a film that has designed itself for a surround system. The sound is constantly traveling, it is very dynamic' (Coleman, 2013). The film was released in the majority of cinemas in 7.1 surround (7.1 splits the existing Left Surround and Right Surround channels of 5.1 into four 'zones'), but also in Dolby Atmos in theatres that were equipped with the new technology.[8] Atmos is the first commercial audio format based on audio objects rather than channels. This means that any sound can exist as a discrete audio object, free of channel restrictions, and can be precisely spatially located anywhere in the auditorium, including overhead, and can be fluidly and seamlessly moved through space (Dolby 2014).

This technical development runs parallel to the mainstream resurgence of stereoscopic 3-D visuals from 2009 onwards. However, it is not the innovation in audiovisual technology, on its own, that encourages spatial presence in *Gravity* but rather the connection between technical advance and aesthetic lucidity deriving from the way that technology has been deployed. Sound design's place in the aural environment of the movie is justified through haptic perception; in order to be heard, sound must be quite literally touched. This immediately ties the sound design to the embodied experience of the characters. In the physical and conceptual gap vacated by this approach, music is suddenly free to move spatially in a way never before achieved in commercial cinema. Furthermore, the clear criteria given to sound design and music result in their detailed integration within a symbiotic soundscape. Metaphorically, we could refer to the 'gravitational pull' of the film, which attracts physical bodies of sound and music to each other with the result that they are able to interact in radically new ways. The movie's composer, Steven Price, identifies how this hybrid conception affected his scoring parameters: 'Alfonso wanted me to try to express things that ordinarily would be sound in a musical way. So the composition serves a dual purpose' (Schweiger, 2013). *Gravity*'s soundtrack generates exceptional integration between sound design and music precisely because the aesthetics of spatialization have been foregrounded in the space vacuum.

One of the defining characteristics of what I call 3-D sound, then, is that music is emancipated from a fixed sound stage representation. Indeed, music begins to function with a similar kind of directional freedom that has been typical of sound design in the ultrafield era. At the same time, music is not tied to environmental 'reality' in quite the same way as sound design, so music is, in some ways, able to move *more* freely. All in all, this means that the borders between what have traditionally been considered sound design and music are collapsing which, I argue, is also primarily at the service of spatial presence. This conceptualization aligns with and extends recent discussions suggesting that the boundaries between diegetic and non-diegetic music are also disintegrating, in theoretical terms, if they were ever valid to begin with (Kassabian, 2013; Winters, 2010). So, it is interesting that a film defined by the scientific principles of the vacuum in space, perhaps the most challenging aural environment for encouraging spatial presence, points the way forward to the fusion of sound and music.

Of course, there are consequences associated with this kind of approach. In order for music to move, it must remove some of its spatially fixed characteristics. These are typically associated with the perception of real musicians playing real instruments. Audiences find it unnerving, for example, to hear a flute melody moving around an auditorium, because the sound of the instrument automatically conjures mental perceptions of human performers in traditional static performance spaces. *Gravity*'s music editor, Chris Benstead, confirms that one of the stipulations Cuarón gave the music team was that he did not ever 'want to feel like there was an orchestra behind the screen' (Mera, 2014). The result is that there is a great deal of digital manipulation of live recorded orchestral material and the music approaches sound design in its spectromorphological capacity, particularly in the use of what Denis Smalley would have described as graduated continuant textures (Smalley, 1986, 1997). Orchestral recordings are no longer aurally sacrosanct; they become source materials ready to be transformed. Benstead notes that the composer 'did a lot of editing and reversing of little bits within phrases, in order to delineate it from that more traditional sound' (Mera, 2014). Indeed, one of the central and recurrent aural motifs in the film was created by digitally manipulating and cutting off double bass passages that were recorded separately. Benstead reports: 'We had seven or eight bass players in Abbey Road just doing those little figures' (Mera, 2014). The passages were conceived and recorded specifically so they could then be manipulated in the digital audio workstation.

In terms of process, sound designers typically record a range of source sounds in order to combine and manipulate them in the creation of the soundscape. Composers (when working with orchestras) tend to treat the recording session as the final realization of the ideas that have been painstakingly mocked-up during the compositional process. In *Gravity*, the compositional approach to recording approximates the working practices of sound design by modularizing orchestral recordings and using them as source materials for digital manipulation. It is significant that Price's experience as a music editor seems to have encouraged some of this aesthetic working method.

The film also encourages spatial presence throughout. In fact, the very first sounds of the film are designed to 'suck' the audience into the vacuum of space. As we see a series of titles describing the harsh environmental realism—'There is nothing to carry sound. No air pressure. No Oxygen' and 'Life in space is impossible'—the amplitude of the music and sound gradually increases in all speaker channels, including the LFE, creating an enormous enveloping soundscape that suddenly falls to absolute silence when we see the first shot of Earth. This powerful aural gesture, which the sound design team called 'the hoover' (Mera, 2014), overwhelms the audience. Benstead reports that the film was especially bold in its use of dynamic range: 'We start out literally at silence with that initial 30–40 second piece, and by the end, in 7.1, I think all the channels hit 0dbfs, and it is really quite a harsh sound as well' (Mera, 2014). The audio-viewer is literally pulled into the film's environment, but unlike similar 'hoover' depressurization-type gestures in *Star Trek* or *Apollo 13*, the audio-viewer experiences the movement themselves rather than through the distance of observing another character. The SSM here bypasses rational process and forces the PERF into the mediated environment. Benstead also highlights the fusion of sound and music in this gestural passage: 'Steve came up with that idea, but there is a sound effect element to it and without that it is not what it is. There is a brilliant low end thing in the sound effects and Steve's stuff is in the top of the frequency range, so the marriage in instances like that is absolutely crucial' (Mera, 2014). Figure 7.1 shows the increasing amplitude in the opening sequence and the sudden drop to silence at 37 seconds using materials derived from the commercially available DVD, which features a 5.1 reduction of the cinema soundtrack.[9]

Figure 7.2 shows a surround vectorscope representation of the loudest moment at 37 seconds just before the cut to silence. The ascending concentric rings relate to amplitude bands (−30db rms, −20db rms, −10db rms and 0db rms).[10] This diagram provides a stylized visualization of how the surround's audio channels may be perceived by the audience, particularly demonstrating each individual surround channel's presence relative to others. The location of the dot represents the summed surround location of all the surround channel's signals. The significant point is that amplitude is, more or less, equally spread across the auditorium space, generating a complete enveloping sound, represented by the shaded area.

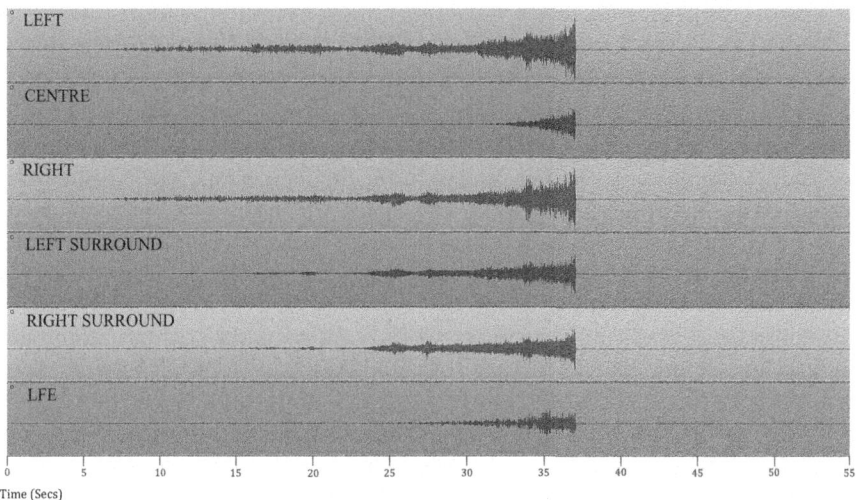

**Fig. 7.1** *Gravity* (Alfonso Cuarón, 2013) opening sequence, 'The Hoover' (Logic Pro)

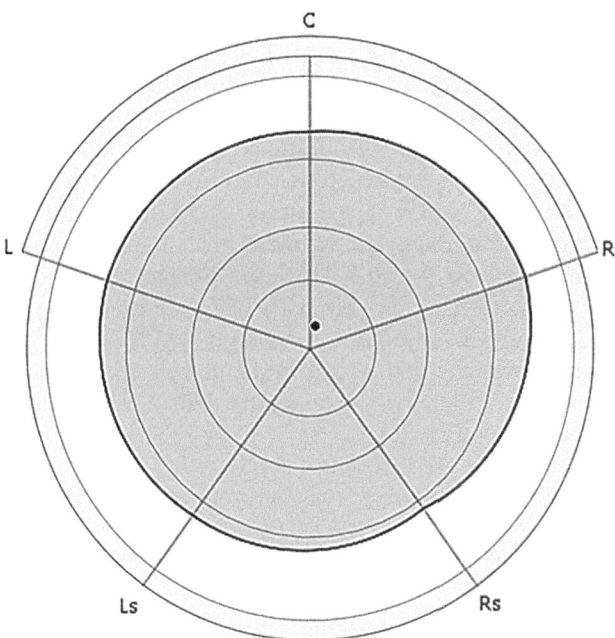

**Fig. 7.2** *Gravity* (Alfonso Cuarón, 2013) opening c. 37 seconds, surround vectorscope representation (5.1) (Izotope Insight Vectorscope)

The sound in *Gravity* is not only enveloping, however, it is also dynamic and, as I have already suggested, the music is unusually dynamic. The film's events result from a missile strike on a satellite, which inadvertently causes a chain reaction sending a speeding cloud of debris towards the astronauts who are performing repairs on the Hubble Space Telescope. When we first see the fragments of wreckage approaching the astronauts, we do not hear sound effects associated with their movement through space, or of impacts as the debris collides with the Telescope and The Explorer. However, music does enact movement of the debris. We first hear a rising glissando tone, which matches Kowalski's (George Clooney) eyeline as he sees the approaching debris, and gradually transforms from E flat to A flat with an attendant increase in volume. This is further animated by a pan from left to right that matches the directional movement of the debris. In fact, the music moves not only from left to right but also around and across the auditorium, in essence a circular shift in energy from the front left to the right surround speaker array. Furthermore, as the glissando tone reaches the high A flat the music also shifts from F minor to A flat minor, further marking the dramatic significance of the moment. Dynamic music has replaced some of the functions undertaken by sound design.

Later, as Ryan Stone (Sandra Bullock) attempts to disentangle a parachute that prevents the Soyuz from separating from the International Space Station, the debris field completes its orbit and, once again, crashes into the ships. Again no sounds of explosions are heard. The camera reflects the increasingly chaotic movement and, extraordinarily, the 'distorted' orchestral music spins a complete circular 360°. It provides a powerful sensation of disorientation and terror. In this moment, notions of traditional musical sound stage spatialization are completely destroyed. Much as sound design moved to match the visual orientation of the camera in the ultrafield era, here the music moves to represent visual disorientation of the central character and becomes as dynamic as sound design at its most extreme. However, Benstead also notes an important difference and qualifying characteristic of music in motion compared to sound design. Though the music is not as closely tied to 'reality' as traditional sound design, its movement still cannot be random, it must function within a musical framework and, therefore, the panning demands musicality:

> I did it in tempo, almost like balancing a pop record, if something was pinging from left to right surround, I'd have something opposing the other way to fill it in, so it is immersive but it never feels too narrow. There was always a temporal period to those pans. I always felt that it had to obey the rhythm of the sound, it was the rhythm more than anything. (Mera, 2014)

The focus in this section on musical movement could lead us to forget, momentarily, the importance of its function in *Gravity*. Spatial presence is the ability to make audio-viewers believe that they are physically present in the mediated environment. Above all else, *Gravity*'s integration of music and sound in fictional interstellar space and auditorium space attempts to make the audience feel what the central character, Ryan Stone, feels. Whereas earlier films frequently employed Chion's notion of objective-internal sound in the vacuum, *Gravity* radically plays with point of view and point of audition so that the soundscape moves beyond a purely objective internal perspective and encourages the audience to *become* Ryan Stone. Music in rotation, for example, clearly embodies Stone's disorientation. Through these devices, the audio-viewer's perceived self-location, perceived possible actions and mental capacities are firmly bound to the character within the mediated space. The soundscape enacts the PERF within the mediated environment. Indeed, dexterous and subtle shifts in aural perspective invite us to become Stone as she observes the terrifying emptiness of space from inside her helmet, and also to experience her reaction externally so that we may perceive the environment and empathetically engage with her situation. This is only possible because of the thoughtful and detailed spatial alliance between sound and music.

There are many moments of integration from the film that could be highlighted, but a useful example is when Stone drifts away from The Explorer following the first debris strike. We see her spinning and hear her increasingly panicky breathing, which approaches hyperventilation. Kowalski's voice shifts its location. For example, the successive phrases 'Give me your position' and 'Report your position' are heard primarily in the right front and right surround speakers, respectively. We become increasingly aware of the sounds of a heartbeat in the soundscape, much of its energy contained within the LFE. The musical gestures begin to spin in circular waves around the auditorium. Mid-frequency musical delay lines turn into muffled lower frequency textures as the camera travels inside Stone's helmet, her breathing and dialogue becomes more intimate, we experience her desperation. As we travel out of the helmet and eventually see her drift away into the distance, the music again employs a rising glissando tone and higher-frequency range textures. The heartbeat sounds become more prominent and a sung female voice emerges. Stone says: 'I am off structure and I am drifting, do you copy, anyone …'. At this point, the soundscape, which has employed dynamic use of the entire speaker array, folds itself into the mono centre speaker channel as Stone's spinning body drifts into the distance. We experience the fear and chaos of the situation as Stone and the soundscape recede into the screen. Benstead notes that mixing was developed initially against 2-D images but then checked in the latter stages of post-production against the 3-D visuals where adjustments needed to be made, because 'pans needed to be a bit deeper, some things needed to be louder or quieter' (Mera, 2014). This sequence demonstrates the harmonious unity between music and sound, using the full range of surround tools available, in order to locate the audio-viewer within the terrifying environment.

It is not uncommon for films set in space to create claustrophobic, lonely or isolated atmospheres. The emptiness of the void frequently signals emptiness within the characters themselves, something with which they must struggle in a journey of self-awareness. In *Gravity*, the audio-viewer is taken with Stone on that journey. It generates moments of genuine silence and exceptionally intimate pseudo-silence that draws the audio-viewer into the narrative world, and it employs radical, dynamic 3-D sound and music that are carefully designed to encourage spatial presence.

## Conclusions

Despite my claims for *Gravity*'s groundbreaking status, I am cautious about ascribing it more importance than is appropriate. In many ways, it remains an exceptional example, with a very particular set of circumstances that permitted its bold approach. Nonetheless, the cat is out of the bag, so to speak, and ever-increasing sophistication in directionality and movement in both music and sound seems like the inevitable next step in the historical evolution of both sound technologies and film aesthetics. Of course, some movies will not require or provide the framework for such audacious treatment. Yet, each era develops films that undertake the boldest experimental approaches and, nonetheless, trickle down to influence general practice. Overall, I suggest that *Gravity* marks a turning point where we begin to see a drift towards 3-D sound. The gravitational pull of *Gravity* is strong and, I suspect, inexorable. The most significant shift is that music is freed from its traditional sound stage spatialization and, as a result, we move towards more dynamic uses of music in auditorium space. Furthermore, the historic divides between music and sound begin to dissolve when the spatial domain articulates the primary relationships between soundscape elements, resulting in a multifaceted, multivalent and integrated soundtrack.

This chapter has examined several kinds of spatial presence. I have argued that the term *immersion* does not accurately account for what takes place when an audio-viewer feels as if they have entered the mediated environment. I have also attempted to demonstrate how cinematic spatial presence works by applying Wirth et al.'s model to various challenging examples. It is not simply the nature or scale of the technology that is key but rather the way it has been developed within a clear aesthetic framework that results in more effective spatial presence experiences. At the very least, I hope to have demonstrated that spatial presence is more significant than film sound scholars have acknowledged thus far. By showing the continuous evolution and negotiation between sound and music within the cinematic space vacuum, I have also attempted to demonstrate how representations of the interstellar space have been at the centre of aesthetic challenges relating to notions of spatial presence in cinema. We have witnessed silence, pseudo-silence and dynamic sound in various developing forms. The scientific reality of silence within the space vacuum has resulted in representational experiments that have constantly sought to help us leave our own world behind.

## Notes

1. It is also worth noting that within virtual reality studies there has been detailed discussion about the appropriateness of the use of the terms *presence* and *telepresence*. See Bracken and Skalski (2010) for an overview of these debates.
2. Dolby Atmos is the name of a surround sound technology announced by Dolby Laboratories in April 2012. It delivers a supported soundtrack to conventional speakers in the cinema and also to speakers in the ceiling to give extra height to the soundscape.

3. Montgomery Scott, or 'Scotty', never actually said: 'You cannae change the laws of physics' in the *Star Trek* television series. In episode 1, season 1 'The Naked Time' (1966) Scotty clearly states: 'I can't change the laws of physics! I've got to have thirty minutes!' The preference for the Scottish vernacular has become a recurrent meme/cliché, which was at least partially reinforced by The Firm's parody song 'Star Trekking' (1987).
4. A Roadshow Theatrical Release, sometimes also known also as a Reserved Seat Engagement, describes the Hollywood studio practice of pre-release in state-of-the-art cinemas in large cities for a specific period of time before nationwide general release. The practice had largely ended by the early 1970s. See Holston, K. R. (2013).
5. This spatialization was not so heightened in the Subsequent 5.1 mix, in the 1990s.
6. The original 70-mm release, like many Super Panavision 70 films of the era, was advertised as being in 'Cinerama' in theatres equipped with special projection optics and a curved screen. In standard cinemas, the film was identified as a 70-mm production. The original release of *2001: A Space Odyssey* in 70-mm Cinerama with six-track sound played continually for more than a year in a handful of venues, and for 103 weeks in Los Angeles.
7. This was subsequently renamed *Star Wars Episode IV: A New Hope*.
8. The technology was first used in Disney Pixar's *Brave* (2012). At the time of writing, there are currently 300–600 Atmos-enabled theatres. At the end of 2014, Dolby announced that Atmos would be available for home theatres.
9. It is worth noting that it was not possible to access the 7.1 or the Atmos mix materials, partly because of commercial sensitivity. It remains an obstacle to detailed sound analysis, particularly film surround sound, that such materials are not archived or easily available for scholarly analysis.
10. Db (FS) is decibel full scale, which refers to digital full scale readings. Zero is the top of the scale and cannot be exceeded. Db (RMS) is root mean squared and refers to the average level, not the peaks which can be much higher than the average level.

## References

Bender, S. (2014) 'There is Nothing to Carry Sound: Defamiliarisation and Reported Realism in *Gravity*', *Senses of Cinema*, 71 (July), http://sensesofcinema.com/2014/feature-articles/there-is-nothing-to-carry-sound-defamiliarization-and-reported-realism-in-gravity/, date accessed 12th December 2014.

Bracken, C. C. and P. D. Skalski (eds) (2010) *Immersed in Media: Telepresence in Everyday Life* (London and New York: Routledge).

Brown, R. S. (1994) *Overtones and Undertones: Reading Film Music* (Berkeley: University of California Press).

Chion, M. (1994) *Audio-Vision: Sound on Screen* (New York: Columbia University Press).

Chion, M. (2001) *Kubrick's Cinema Odyssey* (London: Palgrave Macmillan).

Coleman, M. (2013) 'SoundWorks Collection: The Sound of *Gravity*', http://vimeo.com/76123849, date accessed November 24th 2014.

Deleon, C. M. (2009) 'A Familiar Sound in a New Place: The Use of the Musical Score Within the Science Fiction Film' in M.J. Bartkowiak (ed) *Sounds of the Future: Essays* on *Music in Science Fiction Film* (Jefferson, North Carolina: McFarland and Company).

Dolby (2014) *Dolby Atmos: Next-Generation Audio for Cinema*, White Paper, Dolby Laboratories.

Ebert, R. (1997) '2001: A Space Odyssey', http://www.rogerebert.com/reviews/great-movie-2001-a-space-odyssey-1968, date accessed 12th December 2014.

Gorbman, C. (2006) 'Ears Wide Open: Kubrick's Music' in P. Powrie and R. Stilwell (eds) *Changing Tunes: The Use of Pre-Existing Music in Film* (Aldershot: Ashgate).

Grimshaw, M. (2007) 'Sound and Immersion in the First-Person Shooter' in Q. Mehdi, P. Estraillier and M. Eboueya (eds) *Proceedings of CGAMES'2007*. 11th International Conference on Computer Games: AI, Animation, Mobile, Educational and Serious Games, Université de La Rochelle, France, 21–3 November.

Holmberg, J. (2003) 'Ideals of Immersion in Early Cinema', *Cinémas: revue d'études cinématographiques/Cinemas: Journal of Film Studies*, Vol. 14, No. 1, 129–147.

Holston, K. R. (2013) *Movie Roadshows: A History and Filmography of Reserved Seat Limited Showings 1911–1973* (Jefferson, North Carolina: McFarland & Company).

Kassabian, A. (2013) 'The End of Diegesis as We Know It?' in J. Richardson, C. Gorbman, and C. Vernallis (eds) *Oxford Handbook of New Audiovisual Aesthetics* (New York: Oxford University Press).

Kerins, M. (2011) *Beyond Dolby (Stereo): Cinema in the Digital Sound Age* (Bloomington and Indianapolis: Indiana University Press).

Kermode, M. (2009) 'Come in Number 3D, your time is up', http://www.bbc.co.uk/blogs/legacy/markkermode/2009/12/come_in_number_3d_your_time_is.html, date accessed 12th December 2014.

Kirby, D. A. (2013) *Lab Coats in Hollywood: Science, Scientists, and Cinema* (Cambridge, MA: MIT Press).

Kolker, R. (ed.) (2006) *Stanley Kubrick's 2001: A Space Odyssey New Essays* (Oxford: Oxford University Press).

Lipscomb, S. D. and S. M. Zehnder (2004) 'Immersion in the Virtual Environment: The Effect of a Musical Score on the Video Gaming Experience', *Journal of Physiological Anthropology and Applied Human Science*, 23, 337–343.

Lombard, M. and T. Ditton (1997) 'At the Heart of it All: The Concept of Presence', *Journal of Computer-Mediated Communication*, Vol. 3, No. 2, http://onlinelibrary.wiley.com/doi/10.1111/j.1083-6101.1997.tb00072.x/full, date accessed 12th December 2014.

Mantovani, G. and G. Riva (1999) 'Real presence: How different ontologies generate different criteria for presence, telepresence and virtual presence', *Presence: Teleoperators and Virtual Environments*, Vol. 8, No. 5, 538–548.

McMahan, A. (2003) 'Immersion, Engagement, and Presence: A Method for Analyzing 3-D Video Games' in M. Wolf and B. Perron (eds) *The Video Game, Theory Reader* (New York: Routledge).

Mera, M. (2014) 'Interview with Christopher Benstead', Unpublished. Pinewood Studios. 29th August.

Neuendorf, K. A. and E. A. Lieberman (2010) 'Film: The Original Immersive Medium' in C.C. Bracken and P.D. Skalski (eds) *Immersed in Media: Telepresence in Everyday Life* (New York: Routledge).

Recuber, T. (2007) 'Immersion Cinema: The Rationalization and Reenchantment of Cinematic Space', *Space and Culture*, Vol. 10, No. 3, 315–330.

Schweiger, D. (2013) 'Interview with Steven Price', http://www.filmmusicmag.com/?p=11881, date accessed 12th December 2014.

Sergi, G. (2004) *The Dolby Era: Film Sound in Contemporary Hollywood* (Manchester: University of Manchester Press).

Sergi, G. (2010) 'Tales of the Silent Blast: *Star Wars* and Sound', *Journal of Popular Film*, Vol. 26, No. 1, 12–22.

Slater, M. and S. Wilbur (1997) 'A Framework for Immersive Virtual Environments (FIVE): Speculations on the Role of Presence in Virtual Environments', *Presence—Teleoperators and Virtual Environments* Vol. 6, No. 6, 603–616.

Smalley, D. (1986) 'Spectro-morphology and Structuring Processes' in S. Emmerson (ed.) *The Language of Electroacoustic Music* (London: Macmillan).

Smalley, D. (1997) 'Spectromorphology: Explaining sound-shapes', *Organised Sound* Vol. 2, No. 2, 107–126.

Sonnenschein, D. (2001) *Sound Design: The Expressive Power of Music, Voice and Sound Effects in Cinema* (New York: Michael Wiese Productions).

Wirth, W., T. Hartmann, S. Böcking, P. Vorderer, C. Klimmt, H. Schramm, T. Saari, J. Laarni, N. Ravaja, F. Ribeiro Gouveia, F. Biocca, A. Sacau, L. Jäncke, T. Baumgartner and P. Jancke (2007) 'A Process Model of the Formation of Spatial Presence Experiences', *Media Psychology*, Vol. 9, No. 3, 493–525.

Whittington, W. (2007) *Sound Design and Science Fiction* (Austin: University of Texas Press).

Winters, B. (2010) 'The Non-diegetic Fallacy: Film, Music, and Narrative Space', *Music and Letters*, Vol. 91, No. 2, 224–244.

CHAPTER 8

# Inner and Outer Worlds in the Film *Gravity*: A Multidisciplinary Approach

*Gilbert Gabriel and David Sonnenschein*

In his interview with Michael Ondaatje, Walter Murch describes our attempts at cinematic transcription as 'stumbling around in the "pre-notation" phase of its history' (Ondaatje, 2002, p. 51). He speculates on whether there will be the cinematic equivalent of music notation. This might be one where it becomes a means to embrace its multimodal semiotic apparatus (in the way that music notation enables contemporary musicians to understand the different 'technical and emotional aspects' of twelfth-century and eighteenth-century music). As cinema is a multimodal medium, it requires more than just a textual reading to decode its composite nature. In order to engage in the description, analysis or transcription of film soundtracks, it is necessary to integrate an amalgam of several elements that include a film's visuals, speech, music, sound and cultural influences. These elements signify meaning both independently and conjointly as part of the whole multimodal process.

For the purpose of studying the soundtrack of *Gravity* (Alfonso Cuarón, 2013), this study coalesces four different approaches that are drawn from film sound theory and film practice in order to investigate how the soundtrack is used to signify Ryan's (Sandra Bullock) subjective experiences. Following the concepts of social semiotics (the study of signs in culture) and sound semiotics, it collects data and coalesces information from several different sources in order to yield meaning/s. It thus becomes what Theo van Leeuwen (1999, p. 194) describes as an 'inter-subjective' activity where a variety of sources are used to stimulate ideas to help to shed light on a topic or 'text' without necessarily arriving at an absolute or 'right answer'.

---

G. Gabriel
Composer, Sound Semiotician and Lecturer, UK

D. Sonnenschein
Sound Designer at iQsonics LLC, USA

The focus of this essay is on how speech, sound and music are used to signify physical and psychological aspects of Ryan's attempts to survive in space and her eventual return to Earth. It uses four different approaches to unpick the multilayered soundscape used to signify Ryan's different subjective experiences: 'terror', 'dream states' and 'joy'.

Firstly, this chapter uses Chion's concepts of 'vococentrism' and 'on-the-air' sounds as a means of explaining the use of the voice as a semiotic resource for verbal and non-verbal communication. Secondly, it deploys van Leeuwen's sound semiotic techniques as a means of exploring how the soundtrack of *Gravity* is used to signify the character's subjective experiences and investigate what makes the uses of sound in the film apt signifiers for Ryan's different states of mind. Van Leeuwen's approach is used to investigate how the reduction, increase or neutrality of aural parameters such as pitch, dynamics, volume and reverberation are configured to suggest dramatic tension or the reverse of that. How many times has a film audience recoiled from a sudden high-pitched and dissonant blast of sound and then been calmed by the introduction of consonant sounds when they are out of harm's way? In *Gravity*, these kinds of sonic gestures permeate its soundtrack as the deployment of speech, music and sound are used to dramatize Ryan's adventure in space. Thirdly, it uses Sonnenschein's (2011) concept of *Sound Spheres*. This is an audio-visual model that contextualizes how the psychology and geography of sounds are perceived by both audience and characters within the film's story world. *Sound Spheres* consists of six levels of sonic experience that begin with the 'inner personal sphere' and expand towards the most 'outer' and 'unfamiliar'. Lastly, this study of *Gravity's* soundtrack utilizes Gabriel's *Dream States* model to illustrate how dream states soundtracks are configured. By using these different approaches to interpret the narrative and dramatic arc of *Gravity's* soundtrack, this chapter sets out to illuminate how speech, music and sound are employed to signify meaning as well as examine the process of soundtrack analysis itself.

## The Sound of Terror

The following section investigates how Ryan's voice is used to signify her terror after her communication is lost with Earth after a space accident. According to Chion's concept of vococentrism, the voice in narrative cinema is foregrounded and dialogue prioritized over music and other sounds in order to assist in creating meaning. *Gravity* conforms to Chion's notion of the voice's central role in cinema 'where it is not only a carrier of textual information' but is also a means of the conveyance of psychological and emotional information that is expressed through its spatial, material and sensory aspects as vococentricism (1999, p. 6). Chion points out that 'During filming it is the voice that is isolated in the sound mix like a solo instrument ... we are not talking about voice of shouts and moans, but the voice as medium of verbal expression' (p. 6). Ryan is the main protagonist and harbinger of information, her voice functioning as the main signifier and fulcrum of the film's narrative. As the story unfolds, the audience becomes finely attuned to her subjective experiences via subtle modulations of her vocal tones, non-verbal utterances and breathing. The combination of Ryan's speech and non-verbal utterances encourage the audience to empathize with her different emotional states as she moves from feeling isolated to experiencing pure terror when she is left to fend for herself in space. The breakdown in communication between the crew and NASA becomes apparent with its digital distortion and intermittent dropouts.

In the opening scene (00:07:30), Ryan, her fellow astronauts and NASA ground control have their voices treated with low-cut filters that reduce the bass frequencies to a telephone-like quality, termed as 'on-the-air' voices that are 'transmitted electronically by air, radio, telephone and so on' (Chion, 1994, p. 76). This technique is used to signify their respective social distances from one another. The same equalization (EQ) technique is used later in the film to signify the distance between Ryan and her communication with NASA as well as in her attempt to talk to an Inuit fisherman back on Earth. The use of 'futzing' (the application of digital distortion and a low filter EQ to simulate radio and telephone voices) makes these long-distance voices seem almost unintelligible at times. From the time the space station has been hit by space debris, Ryan's world has been thrown into turmoil. Her precarious situation is further heightened by the sounds of laboured breathing, gasps of panic and an automated voice counting down her oxygen supply level as she is catapulted around in space.

From the beginning of the film, the audience is encouraged to marvel at the wonders of man-made technology that seems to defy the hostile environment of space. However, when the technology fails, Ryan and Matt (George Clooney) experience extreme disorientation and a sense of terror as they fight for their lives. Ryan's narrative and vocal utterances as well as music and sound design are used to heighten the drama not only of her inner world but the outer turmoil of the space station being torn apart. In contrast to the hyperbolic use of sound effects and orchestral crescendos found in space action films such as *Star Wars* (George Lucas, 1977), this study of *Gravity*'s soundtrack reveals that the use of music and sound design is instead more focused on creating a realistic depiction of Ryan's subjective experiences. The combination of her gasps, heartbeats and electronic alert sounds that are both actual and also metaphorical all combine to signify her psychological and physical discomfort as she attempts to conquer her fears and return to Earth.

When Matt and Ryan are informed by NASA that they must abandon their work because of a space collision, the urgency of the situation is heightened by the sound of a low rumble and then later with higher electronic sounds that function as 'activation sounds' (increased effort of a character or object). An ominous rumble (00:09:49) signals to the audience that there is a potentially dangerous incident about to occur. The combination of a low disturbing electronic drone and a wavering synthesizer sound in the mid-range heightens the frantic exchange between Matt and ground control as radio interference obstructs the clarity of their conversation.

Van Leeuwen introduces the concept of 'fluctuation range' that highlights the 'close association of vibrato and emotionality' (1999, p. 175). At 00:10:16, 'fluctuation' is observed as an oscillating sound helping to signify the crew's heightened sense of fear and uncertainty as space debris flies towards them. As this scene develops (00:10:24), the combination of fluctuating sounds, white noise and reverberation adds a sense of increased drama and tension. Ryan's terror is signified through her close-miked gasps and breathlessness as she is flung around in space. Whereas Matt's voice appears controlled and rational (i.e. gender stereotype of a strong male character), Ryan's voice is initially presented as being more vulnerable and feminine with her less controlled non-verbal utterances that signify her sense of fear and terror, as she gasps 'I can't breathe'. The music score (00:12:32) also heightens both her physical and psychological sense of falling and loss of control with its 'descending' sounds. The score then builds dynamically to signify her danger and ultimate release from her belt with the climax of a synchronized loud thumping sound as she becomes free. At 00:14:24, the use of extreme compression and EQ signal her sense of claustrophobia. The combination of an alarm sound, a pulsing electronic heartbeat and a strong rhythmic string motif with stabbing brass, all combine to heighten the drama of the scene and her experience of terror.

The drama of Matt and Ryan's precarious situation becomes increasingly heightened as more space debris flies towards them. This is achieved through the additional sounds of radio interference and the ominous electronic soundscape that accompanies the chaos that ensues. The sound of Ryan's closed-miked verbal and non-verbal utterances illustrate how the audience is drawn into Ryan's subjective world. The rise and fall of the underscore's dynamics combines both electronic sounds and choral voices to echo her vulnerable state as a lone female who is flung helplessly around in space. As Ryan reacts to the horror of seeing a dead astronaut with his face blown-off, the scene is intensified by a dramatic 'stinger' that heightens this moment and then shifts to feature more ethereal tones that signify her sense of shock, loss and vulnerability. At the end of this scene, a further 'stinger' acts as a 'hit-point' that marks out the intense trauma that Ryan experiences when she witnesses the astronaut's dead body floating in front of her face. Matt tries to distract her from this horrific experience by engaging her with memories from her own life on Earth.

## THE SOUND OF DREAM STATES

The following section investigates *Gravity's* soundtrack through Sonnenschein's *Sound Spheres* model (2011) demonstrating how the sound of dream sequences is organized to signify the progression from reality to dreams. The six layers of sound represented in the Sound Spheres model are as follows:

*I Think*—Subjective and internal (thoughts, mental rehearsal, memories, dreams, auditory hallucinations).

*I Am*—Produced by the self or protagonist (speaking, breathing, chewing, coughing, snoring, sneezing).
*I Touch*—Contact made with the external world (physical vibrations like hammering, walking, vocal transmission to deaf people through touch).
*I See*—Synchronization of image and sound (mouths moving with speech, identification of the speaker or sound producing object/event).
*I Know*—Identification of source, information, and/or emotional impact without image (speech outside our vision, familiar audio-only electronic transmission, alert signals).
*I Don't Know*—Unidentifiable sounds, generating potential surprise or fear (unknown human or non-human origin, ambiguous information or emotion, foreign language) (Fig. 8.1).

The entrance into the *I Know* sphere occurs at the beginning of the dream sequence (1:02:06) when Ryan turns off her oxygen supply with its hissing sound that slowly fades away and is visually supported by Ryan's actions as she turns a dial on the control panel. However, when Matt carries out the same procedure within the dream sequence (1:03:38), the oxygen hiss is buried under the alarm and therefore plays a subordinate dramatic role.

The whole sequence could be considered within the *I Think* sphere because of its imaginary subjective dream nature. This is only revealed at the end of this sequence when Ryan turns her head to see that Matt is not there. The movement from the *I Think* to the *I Am* sphere includes dialogue, non-verbal

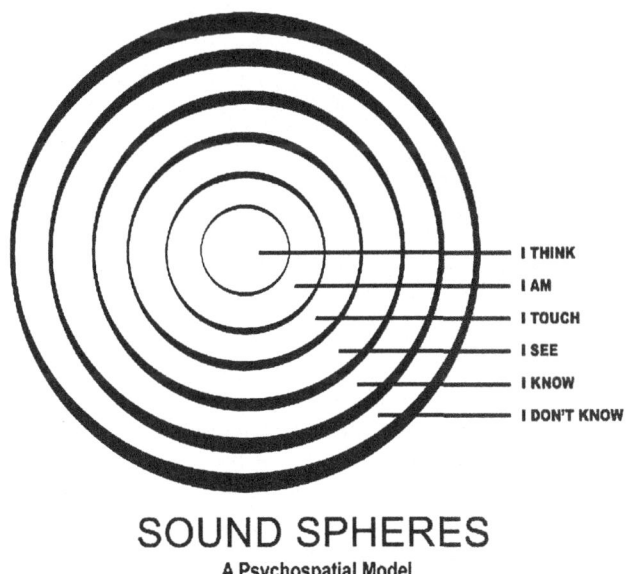

**Fig. 8.1** Sound Spheres—David Sonnenschein (2011)

vocalizations and Ryan's heavy breathing which are visually expressed by the vapour exuding from her mouth. In the *I Touch* sphere, the characters' actions create sound with their operations of the control panel as well as when Matt unclips his helmet (1:03:40). These sounds draw a focus to the shifting technological drama of this scene and the characters' attempts to survive.

The visceral sounds of Matt opening the vodka bottle (1:04:21) in the *I Touch* sphere encourages the audience to believe that this is reality and not a dream. From the beginning of this scene (1:02:39), Ryan hears a knocking sound in the *I Don't Know* sphere and she turns her head to see Matt appear outside the capsule window in the *I See* sphere (1:02:46). Once inside the capsule, Ryan is surprised by Matt's return as he matter-of-factly operates the controls and speaks to her in the *I See* sphere (1:03:40). Towards the end of the scene Ryan closes her eyes and Matt drifts off-screen with his voice panning towards the right as he enters the *I Know* sphere (1:06:03).

The *Sound Spheres* model provides a useful means of showing how sound and image are configured in this scene to reveal the link between technology and survival, the emotional connection between Ryan and Matt, as well as the difference between dreams and reality.

In *Altered States Altered Sounds*, Gabriel (2013) reveals a common pattern that is used to denote how transitions from 'reality' to dream states and back again are configured. Using Mladen Milicevic's definition of the terms 'hypnagogic' (representing the state of falling asleep or drifting away from the reality world) and 'hypnopompic' (representing the state of waking up or coming back to the reality world) (n.d., pp. 2–3), Gabriel shows how the soundtracks of dream sequences often follow a familiar trajectory. Frequently normative sounds from the diegesis (the storyworld) are replaced by music or sensory sounds that represent the meta-diegetic (character's mind). These may be sounds that are heightened, a change of music or even complete silence.

1. *Hypnagogic state* (falling asleep). Audio-visual resources that signify a character falling asleep.
2. *The Dream*. Audio-visual resources that signify a character is dreaming.
3. *Hypnopompic state* (waking up). Audio-visual resources that signify a character is returning to 'reality' (Fig. 8.2).

In the hypnagogic stage of the dream sequence, normative sounds of the spacecraft's functions (oxygen supply, computer hums, etc.) are removed and signal the onset of Ryan's dream sequence. Ryan (01:02:06) is seen preparing for sleep with the sound of an Inuit fisherman's lullaby coming from her radio. The beginning of this dream sequence is signalled at 01:02:46 by a complete removal of normative sounds as a window of the spacecraft is blown in. Absolute silence at 01:03:00 heightens the impact of Matt's return after the audience imagined that he had already died. The scene appears then to return to reality as 'normative' sounds are heard (i.e. country music in the

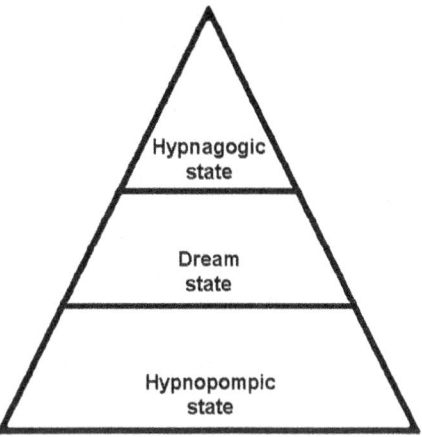

**Fig. 8.2** Dream States—Gilbert Gabriel (2013)

form of 'Angels Are Hard to Find' by Hank Williams Jr. and Foley sounds). These sounds correspond with Matt's return. The audience (01:06:23) then realizes that Ryan was dreaming as she is seen operating a computer and the hissing sound of her oxygen supply is heard once again. The soundtrack now signifies a return to reality as the 'hypnopompic state'.

Gabriel's model adapts Milicevic's (n.d.) conception of sound in cinema in order to structure dream sequences into a tripartite form of the entrance to dream states where normative sounds of 'everyday reality' are removed (the 'hypnagogic' state), the dream itself (often sensory or featuring a complete removal of sound) and, lastly, the exit from a dreamstate as normative sounds return ('hypnopompic' state). Similarly, the *Sound Spheres* (2011) interpretation of the soundtrack in Ryan's dream sequence follows six stages that range from her own 'internal' sounds to those that lay beyond her range of direct identification as 'outer sounds'.

## The Sound of Joy

It is interesting to note that Alfonso Cuarón (the film's director) reveals how Robert Bresson's classic *A Man Escaped* (1956) influenced the ending of *Gravity*. Following *A Man Escaped* narrative format, the main protagonist escapes from seemingly insurmountable physical and mental shackles. Cuarón describes *Gravity* as a 'metaphor of rebirth; literally, at the end as "she goes from a foetal position as she floats after undressing in the space station" and eventually stands on her own two feet and "walks again"' (Lee, 2013). As well as sharing the existentialist concerns of 'metaphysical walls' with Bresson's film, *Gravity* is highly reliant upon the soundtrack to signify its main protagonist's subjective experiences which transport her from the depths of terror and hopelessness to ultimate joy as she survives and experiences rebirth on terra firma.

Although the film's director sets out to avoid the usual Hollywood clichés, as far as the soundtrack is concerned, there is evidence in the 're-entry' scene that this notion is somewhat abandoned. In keeping with more traditional Hollywood scores, it marks out the epic return of its heroine to Earth with grandiose gestures that conjoins with sensory sound design as her space vehicle is battered by the atmosphere on re-entry. The audience experiences the soaring and surging sounds of the orchestral soundtrack that features a wordless soprano that is reminiscent of Morricone's music for Sergio Leone's Spaghetti Westerns. The use of sensory sounds ('heightened sound') has become an established practice amongst many filmmakers that wish to portray characters' subjective experiences in a range of genres such as thrillers and horror films. This can be observed in *Gravity* as musical hyperbole and a sensory 'heightening' of events. The final scene begins with a more naturalistic approach with Ryan's aural underwater perspective. This character-orientated listening position (01:20:11) is signified by higher frequencies being reduced from the sound mix. The sound mix (01:21:05) then becomes a high-fidelity range of naturalistic sounds that includes birdsong and insects that are reminiscent of Tarkovsky's film *Solaris* where *musique concrète* is used to signify an astronaut's aural perception of Earth when he returns from a space mission. The soundtrack foregrounds Ryan's visceral experience of natural sounds as she swims to the surface and begins to walk again having been weakened by being in zero gravity. The detailed portrayal of all the natural sounds around her includes the sounds of water-lapping, birds and insects. A final Hollywood orchestral gesture signifies her achievement of surviving her ordeal in space and being able to stand once more upon Earth's soil.

## Conclusion

This research reflects upon the complexity of decoding the soundtrack of *Gravity* that is inextricably part of a multimodal process where visuals, speech, music and sound are used to signify Ryan's psychological and physical experiences. Although this chapter employs four different approaches to unpicking the semiotic content of the film's soundtrack, it readily acknowledges that this is by no means the only interpretation. Film practitioners also make unconscious or intuitive choices on their route to creating a final product that matches a soundtrack with visuals.

Firstly, Chion's conception of vococentricism is observed with Ryan's verbal and non-verbal utterances being a central part of the film's enunciation. As Ryan is the only surviving member of the space mission, her words, heavy breathing and gasps become a central form of enunciation alongside the film's sound design and music. Chion's notion of on-the-air sounds also features as an integral tool that helps to signify the vast geographical distances between the astronauts and NASA on Earth. Secondly, the use of van Leeuwen's sound semiotic resources provides a useful means of investigating how increases or decreases of aural parameters of pitch, volume and so on help to signify Ryan's subjective experiences. For example, when she becomes anxious, her voice becomes louder and terse and she breathes much faster, whereas when she decides to give up on life and go to sleep her voice becomes slower and more regulated and the tone of her voice becomes softer. Thirdly, Sonnenschein's *Sound Spheres* model decodes the characters' psychospatial experiences and thus demonstrates how the audience can be immersed into the subjective realities of this story world. Finally, Gabriel's (2013) description of dream phases explores how music and sounds are placed both metaphorically and literally to 'make meaning' and also help immerse the audience into the film's narrative through its music and sound design. In conclusion, this research has pointed to the value of using a multifaceted approach to investigate how soundtracks may help to imbue film with meaning through various different semiotic resources. It also urges future researchers to find ways of interpreting cinema's sound codes as a part of a multimodal medium where visual information and sound and music do not only produce meaning in isolation but also simultaneously.

### References

Chion, M. (1994) *Audio-Vision: Sound on Screen*, ed. and trans. by C. Gorbman (New York: Columbia University Press).

———. (1999) *The Voice in Cinema*, trans. by C. Gorbman (New York: Columbia University Press).

Lee, D. (2013) 'Alfonso Cuarón Answers All Your Questions About *Gravity*', *Vulture*, http://www.vulture.com/2013/10/alfonso-cuaron-answers-your-gravity-questions.html, date accessed 12 May 2015.

Gabriel, G. (2013) *Altered States, Altered Sounds* (Saarbrücken, Germany: LAP Lambert Academic Publishing).

Milicevic, M. (n.d.) *Film Sound Beyond Reality: Subjective Sound in Narrative Cinema*, http://filmsound.org/articles/beyond.htm, date accessed 3 February 2007.

Ondaatje, M. (2002), *The Conversation: Walter Murch and the Art of Editing Film* (London: Bloomsbury).

———. (2011) 'Sound Spheres—A psychoacoustic model', *The New Soundtrack*, Vol. 1. No. 1, 13–27.

Van Leeuwen, T. (1999) *Speech, Music, Sound* (London: Macmillan).

CHAPTER 9

# Intertwining Music and Sound in Film

*Martine Huvenne*

Walter Murch argues that sound has the potential to become pure music: 'Sometimes a sound effect can be almost pure music. It doesn't declare itself openly as music because it is not melodic, but it can have a musical effect on you anyway' (2005, p. 10). By way of contrast, the soundscape composer Hildegarde Westerkamp emphasizes that even if a recorded sound is integrated into a (musical) soundscape composition, it always refers to the sound environment and thus never can become totally 'abstract': 'The essence of soundscape composition is the artistic, sonic transmission of meanings about place, time, environment and listening perception [...] soundscape composition is always rooted in themes of the sound environment. It is never abstract' (1999). On first reading, Murch and Westerkamp seem to contradict each other, but using the experience of listening to recorded sounds in an audiovisual context, we can put the two quotations together and question if the same recorded sound can be heard as a musical element or/and as a sound effect. In this chapter, I will argue that the recorded sound does not exist in its own right, but that it is in the listening that the perception of sound can either become 'pure music' or can still refer to the sound environment. Using *Atonement* (Joe Wright, 2007) and *Last Days* (Gus Van Sant, 2005) as case studies I will discuss this question from a phenomenological perspective of perception.

In phenomenology, perception is not a simple reception of information, but it involves an interpretation which frequently changes according to the context. Phenomenology starts with experience rather than by what we expect to find, given our theoretical commitments. It asks us not to let preconceived theories form our experience, but to let our experience inform and guide our theories. In phenomenology, we are interested in how the things appear as correlates of our experience (Gallagher and Zahavi, 2008).

M. Huvenne
KASK & Conservatory, School of Arts, Gent, Belgium

Applying this idea to the experience of listening to a sound, I put the question about the intertwining of sound and music as follows: is it possible to experience and to listen to the same recorded sound differently in such a way that the same recorded sound can be both a musical element, and with a different experience of listening, a sound rooted in a sound environment? When sound and music are considered in relation to the image in film, the situation can become even more complex. In the act of perception, it is possible to relate the sound to a situation, the visual space on screen (diegetic sound) or to integrate the sound in the soundtrack.

For example, let us take the opening scene of *Atonement*. In this scene, the sound of the typewriter is introduced off-screen. We can hear the sound before we see the 13-year-old Briony Tallis (Saoirse Ronan), an aspiring writer, finishing her play. At first the sound of the typewriting fills the children's room. A camera movement takes us towards the source of the sound. Till now the sound is related to what happens within the diegesis. But in a subsequent scene, Briony runs through the house to show her mother her finished play. In this scene, the sound of the typewriter has become a percussive sound that is fully integrated into the music composed by Dario Marianelli. How can we describe the difference between the sound experienced as a sound effect integrated in the audiovisual context and the sound (related to the same source, the typewriter) experienced as a musical element? Integrated in the musical composition, the sound of the typewriting conforms to the pace and metrical rhythm of the music. The source of the sound is still the same, but the rhythm and the dynamics of Briony's gestures of typewriting are not audible any more in a new musical context.

Even more intriguing example can be found in *Last Days* in which Van Sant uses Westerkamp's soundscape composition *Doors of Perception* (1989), created for Ars Acustica[1] in Linz. In this composition, Westerkamp used field recordings and other recorded sounds. In *Last Days*, this composition is integrated into an audiovisual context, which makes it hard to distinguish between sounds originating in the diegetic space and sounds from Westerkamp's original composition. Without knowledge of Westerkamp's original, the audience tries to find the sources of the sounds within or in relation to the visual images. For example, at a certain moment, we hear a motorbike passing by when the main character Blake (Michael Pitt) is walking on a road. In combination with the image, our listening strategy changes: rather than listening to the motorbike as an auditory event, as is the case in Westerkamp's soundscape composition *Doors of Perception*, we take it as an off-screen event, not paying the same attention to the musical features of this sonorous event as we may have done while listening to Westerkamp's soundscape composition.

Some questions arise from this: how can we interpret the intertwining of the sound of the motorbike as a musical element in Westerkamp's soundscape composition and as a sound effect in *Last Days*? How can we distinguish between sound as a sound (effect) within an audiovisual context and sound as a musical element within a soundscape composition? Do we have to start from the experience of sound itself, or rather from the compositional context of the sound? Or do we focus instead on the act of listening rather than on the characteristics of the sound itself? Bearing in mind the example of the motorbike in *Last Days*, and the typewriter in *Atonement*, do we treat the perception of the same sound in a sonorous and an audiovisual context differently?

To find answers to these questions, I propose to focus on listening in three stages. The first stage concerns the act of 'listening'. As opposed to starting from the image or the narrative, I propose to start from listening and sound in order to understand how sound can be perceived or experienced in film. Second, I propose to delve into the music history and more precisely into the *musique concrète* of the French composer and musicologist Pierre Schaeffer to understand better the integration of recorded sound in a musical composition. Inspired by Edmund Husserl's phenomenology, Schaeffer developed a music theory with a focus on the correlation between sound and listening, more precisely the correlation between the *sound object* and *reduced listening* and between *musical object* and *'musicianly' listening* (*écoute musicienne*). Schaeffer makes a distinction between *musicianly listening* as a form of listening with the refined ears of a musician and a *traditional musical listening* (*écoute musical traditionelle*) supposing musical structures of reference.[2] But Schaeffer does not take the phenomenological first-person perspective into account. This leads us to the third stage, in which I explore *embodied resonating* listening (a listening that takes the resonating body of the listener into account and considers it as the centre of reference) in correlation with *felt sound* (a bodily experienced sound that does not refer to any source or meaning).

## A Focus on the Act of Listening

The fact that sound has always been discussed in relation to image is being more and more criticized. Don Ihde (2007 [1976]) and Casey O'Callaghan (2007) are very clear in their criticism. O'Callaghan suggests we abandon visuocentrism. He argues that sounds are entities in their own right, revealing different aspects of the world other than visual elements: 'Freedom from focus on the visual encourages us to eliminate confusion about the place of sound and to capture the character and usefulness of auditory awareness' (p. 9). Ihde outlines a 'history of philosophical visuocentrism' in the West and concludes that listening can deal with the invisible. He proposes a phenomenological approach to sound and listening:

> The rationality of the West owes much to the clarity of its vision. But the simple preference of sight may also become, in its very richness, a source of the relative inattentiveness to the global fullness of experience and in this case, to the equal richness of listening. (p. 8)

However, both authors agree that sound and listening are crossmodal and connected to visual perception, as does Michel Chion when he argues that

'Cinema is not solely a show of sounds and images; it also generates rhythmic, dynamic, temporal, tactile, and kinetic sensations that make use of both the auditory and visual channels' (1994, p. 152). Chion proposes to start a film analysis with a 'masking method' of observation to distinguish the different audio elements of speech, music and noise (p. 187). He presents a descriptive analysis that avoids any symbolizing interpretation of a psychoanalytic, psychological, social or political nature. He states that the (referential) interpretation of a sound may follow as a second step, based on the findings of the analysis. His main interest lies in the relationship between sound and image. In order to focus more on sound, I propose to go deeper into different modes of listening.

In a short article, Roland Barthes distinguishes three modes of listening (1976). Each listening mode establishes a new connection with the world; in each listening mode, our attention is directed in a different way. First, Barthes defines alert listening as related to survival and how attention can be paid to the source of the sound in a situation. Next, there is a mode of listening that seeks to understand the world and discover the meaning of sound. The third mode of listening Barthes calls 'panic listening', referring to the Greek god Pan; it is a non-intentional listening mode, different from listening to indices or signs (p. 228). With this listening mode, Barthes refers to the field of art and more specifically to the listening required by the composer John Cage: a listening to 'each sound one after the next' rather than 'its syntagmatic extension'. Barthes suggests that in 'panic listening' the individual textures and notes are more important to consider than understanding the work as a whole because the work does not necessarily possess meaning. (Behr, 2014, p. 115) I would like to comment further on this term relying on phenomenological concepts.

In phenomenology, the intentional object is constituted in the intentional act. This means, for instance, that when we listen with the intention to discover the source of the sound, our intentional act is directed towards the discovery of the source of the sound. Hence, we are listening in a different way (with a different strategy) than when we do in order to understand the meaning of the sound. I would like to return to the typewriting in *Atonement*. While listening to someone writing on a typewriter, I direct my attention to the different aspects of this act of typing. Where is the sound coming from? What kind of typewriter is used? What is expressed by the gesture of pressing the keys? By directing my attention when listening to the same sound, I discover different features of this typing. In an audiovisual context, the sound of the typewriter is introduced off-screen in *Atonement*. We are wondering where the sound is coming from (the position of this sound in the diegetic space). Following the sound and the camera movement, we reach the source of the sound: we see Briony pressing the keys. Along with the visual gestures, we follow the pace and the phrasing of her writing. However, the perception of this sound changes radically in the following scene when the sound of the typewriting is integrated into the music. In this scene, the sound and the rhythm of the sound are disconnected from the act of writing, which is replaced by the act of rhythmically percussive typing in a regular measure of 4/4. Even though the pace of the music is still referring to the character of Briony, her real act of writing is no longer expressed. Even if the typing still refers to the previous scene, the act of typing becomes an act of a musician rather than from a character in a film writing a play. Therefore, I would like to argue that listening to the sound of the typewriter in Marianelli's music can be compared to 'panic listening'.

To understand better what 'panic listening' means, I propose to make a clear distinction between the music without a filmic context and the music integrated in the film. Marianelli composed the opening theme for *Atonement* by using the sound of the typewriting as a starting point, integrating its musical features into his piece (Huvenne, 2013b).

Without the filmic context, the sound of the typewriting becomes an energetic sounding movement on its own, not revealing a specific action of a character positioned in space. Here, even if we can hear that the source of the sound is a typewriter, we can listen to it in its 'abstraction'. The typewriting is sounding as a percussive element in a broader musical context, absorbed by the regular and metrical rhythm of the musical composition. The rhythm and the pace of the music within the film can be considered expressions of the decisive energy of the main character Briony who is finishing her play. Integrated into the music, the space in between the sound of typing and the listener is not defined anymore through distance. Our attention is now visually directed, following the movements of Briony through the house. The audience is immersed in the music and no longer spatially positioned in relation to the typewriting sound.

The listening to the sound of the typewriting within a musical context can be indicated as an instance of Barthes' panic listening, as a non-referential listening (not referring to the source or the meaning of the sound). But then another question arises: how can we define the listening to the sound of the typewriter as a musical gesture? How is it possible that the sound of the typewriter becomes a percussive sound within the musical context? Some answers can be found in the western music history of the twentieth century.

## 'OPEN LISTENING' IN THE CONTEXT OF MUSICAL HISTORY

The distinction of Barthes' panic listening from a listening to indices or signs brings us to the 'reduced listening' introduced by composer Pierre Schaeffer. In his 1966 collection of essays *Treatise on Musical Objects*, Schaeffer proposed a new music theory starting from a new listening strategy. Inspired by the (static) phenomenology of Husserl,[3] he proposed to concentrate on a de-contextualized way of listening to create an openness to new contexts. He introduced the concept of sound object (*objet sonore*) as the basis of his compositions. This sound object is a gesture, an audible movement rather than a note, correlated with 'reduced listening',[4] referring to Husserl's phenomenological reduction as a method. In Schaeffer's interpretation, reduced listening is a mode of listening to sound for sound's sake, by removing its real or supposed source and the meaning it may convey.

Schaeffer's theory can be situated in the historical movement of the twentieth century, which broke down the fundamentals of the tonal musical composition. This movement was accompanied by the questioning of 'listening to music', a listening free from expectations of what 'music' should be. *Prélude à l'après-midi d'un faune* (1894) by Claude Debussy is considered to be at the beginning of this musical movement, slightly predating the twentieth century. Inspired by Indonesian gamelan music, Debussy puts the compositional focus in this work on timbre, rather than on pitch and a metric rhythm, playing with the notion of tonality. In *Trois nocturnes: Nuages* (1899), he requires an 'open listening', sensuously affected and solicited by the sounding music (Lockspeiser and Halbreich, 1989, p. 670).

It is clear that Debussy goes in the direction of Barthes' 'panic listening': the listener is sensuously affected by the sounding music rather than searching for musical references in the listening to this music. After Debussy, the composers Luigi Russolo, Erik Satie, Arnold Schoenberg, Edgard Varèse, Schaeffer, Cage, Mauricio Kagel and György Ligeti all contributed to the expansion of music to cover the entire field of sound.

In a letter to Richard Strauss, who conducted his piece *Farben* (five pieces for orchestra op. 16, 1909), Schoenberg explains that the score has to be performed through blind faith, without analysis or understanding of the compositional space. He promises something colossal, especially in sound and mood (Slonimsky, 1971, p. 207). In fact Schoenberg asks for a 'passive' and 'open' listening attitude, avoiding analysis from the perspective of classical compositional rules or an 'understanding' of the musical composition. Here the liberation of musical parameters from the classical hierarchy (with pitch as the dominant musical feature) can be understood as listening to the sound as an energetic movement rather than de-contextualized listening to musical sounds.

In 1913, the Italian futurist Luigi Russolo published his manifesto *The Art of Noises*. For Russolo, musical sound was too limited in its timbre. He propagated an infinite variety of noise-sounds, designed the new musical instruments as *intonarumori* and classified noise-sound into six families: the family of rumbles, roars, explosions, crashes, splashes and booms; the family of whistles, hisses and snorts; the family of whispers, murmurs, mumbles, grumbles and gurgles; the family of screeches, creaks, rustles, buzzes, cracks and scrapes; the noises obtained by percussion on metal, wood, skin, stone, terracotta, etcetera and the voices of animals and men (Russolo, 2013). The focus of Russolo was to integrate daily sounds into music. By proposing the pitch, rhythm and energy of a daily sound as the basis of a musical composition, he opened a way to de-contextualize the daily sounds and re-contextualize them in a musical context.

In the same period, Erik Satie integrated the sounds of a typewriter, a pistol shot, steam whistles and sirens into *Parade* (1917), a ballet based on a scenario by Jean Cocteau. Satie uses sounds with a reference to their sources, which is different from Futurism. We recognize and define the sounds in the composition. They are used as *objets trouvés* and are integrated into the music through rhythmical characteristics. *Parade* is still a musical composition, based on the musical parameters of pitch, rhythm, dynamics and timbre. The sounds from non-musical sources in it are rather an abnormity.

The intention to pay attention to daily sounds as musical elements and to redefine 'listening to music' became even more extreme in the work of Edgar Varèse and John Cage who argued for an extension of 'timbres' and an integration of noise into music. Inspired by the treatise by Ferrucio Busoni, *The Sketch of a New Aesthetic of Music* (1907), Varèse expresses the need for a collaboration between an electrician and a composer to invent new instruments with new timbres (1983). He composed *Poème electronique* for the Philips pavilion at the 1958 World Fair. That very year Cage stated in an article on experimental music: 'New music: new listening. Not an attempt to understand something that is being said, for, if something were being said, the sounds would be given the shapes of words. Just an attention to the activity of sounds' (1971, p. 10). It is to this 'new listening' that Barthes refers to in his article on listening.

In 1948, Schaeffer began to compose his *musique concrète* with a sound recorder. Schaeffer's *musique concrète* starts off from the same fundamental idea as image editing: a recorded moving object. The technique and mechanical manipulation of recorded visual or auditory material includes possible modifications of the material: cutting, sticking together, reversing, accelerating, decelerating, and so on, instead of starting from the classical musical parameters such as pitch, rhythm (tone duration), timbre (tone colour) and intensity (loudness).

In one of his first *musique concrète* compositions, *Etude aux chemin de fer* (1948), Schaeffer uses railway sounds to compose (edit) them in an unusual musical way. Schaeffer takes the recorded sounds as the basis of his musical composition, takes them away from their 'context', and thus preventing the source or meaning of the sound from being heard.

Considering the music history of the twentieth century, the 'emancipation of listening' can be interpreted twofold. On one hand, Debussy and Schönberg require an open (embodied) listening by which the listener is sensuously affected (Debussy) away from the 'understanding' of the musical composition (Schönberg). This means that listening to music is not defined anymore by the listening to the musical form. On the other hand, the emancipation of listening concerns also the de-contextualization and integration of the daily sound in a musical context (Russolo, Satie, Varèse, Schaeffer) with an attention to the qualities of the sound itself (Cage). With recorded sounds being the basis of *musique concrète*, the question arises how can a recorded sound, which is part of a musical composition, be perceived as a 'musical object' in an audiovisual context?

## *Musique Concrète* as the Basis of the Intertwining of Music and Sound in Film

To what degree are Schaeffer's concepts of *sound object* and *reduced listening* the basis of both musical composition and sound design? To answer this, I would like to go back to the sound of the motorbike in Westerkamp's composition *Doors of Perception*. In her soundscape composition, Westerkamp disconnects the sound from its original environment. She uses the sound of the motorbike as a *sound object*. Listening to the piece, this sound is perceived as a clear energetic sonorous event, rather than as an evocation of the image of a motorbike passing by. The church bells and the prayers are associated with 'church sounds', stemming from the same environment. We do not try to position them in a concrete referential visual space.

This changes profoundly in the audiovisual context of the film: within this context, we try to 'understand' or interpret each sound: we make an effort to link the sound of the motorbike to an imaginable object that is positioned off-screen, as we do with the church bells. The source and the positioning of the sound source are somewhere present in our audiovisual perception. The bells are considered an off-screen sound, related to the visible environment. The sound of praying is less easily understood in relation to what we are looking at. Unable to give them a place in relation to the images on screen, the audience interprets them as happening in the mind of Blake. Compared to our listening of Westerkamp's composition outside of the film context, we discern different 'groups of sounds'.

In his article 'Clear Density-Dense Clarity', sound designer Walter Murch makes a distinction between 'encoded' and 'embodied sound'. He indicates speech as the clearest example of encoded sound and music as the clearest example of embodied sound. In speech, sound is the vehicle for codes—one has to know the code of the language to extract meaning. Murch's encoded sound implies a semantic listening mode. With an embodied sound, the sound is experienced directly 'without code intervening between you and it. Whatever meaning there is in a piece of music is "embodied" in the sound itself' (2005, p. 8). I suggest that in the audiovisual context of *Last Days* the sounds of the bells and the motorbike are more 'encoded sounds' while in the soundscape composition of *Doors of Perception* they are more 'embodied sounds'. This brings us back to Barthes's 'panic listening' and its relation to *embodied listening*.

## Embodied Resonating Listening and the First-Person Perspective in Film

In her remarkable essay on listening to film, 'L'écoute filmique' (1999), the French philosopher Véronique Campan starts from Barthes's 'panic listening' to develop her theory on filmic listening. In her approach, the embodied perception of the sound as an energetic movement takes a central position.[5] Campan interprets Barthes's panic listening as a listening mode in which the listener is moved. The meaning is not given, but emerges from the experience of being moved by the sound. With Campan's interpretation of Barthes's panic listening an enactive approach[6] to filmic listening is introduced. Her description of listening to sound in film ties in with Maxine Sheets-Johnstone's 'thinking in movement' as our primary way of making sense of the world:

> To think in movement is to think in terms of dynamics, to be witness to the qualitative nature of the form one is creating, its waxing and waning, its now vibrant, now hushed character, the way in which it flows, the way in which it builds, the way in which its parts interconnect—in short, its overall spatio-temporal-energic character. Whatever the art, its creator thinks in dynamic terms, which is to say in movement. (2013, p. 22)

Sheets-Johnstone also argues that there is no mind-doing and body-doing: perception and movement are seamlessly interwoven (2009, p. 32). Applied to sound it means that listening to a sound does not necessarily imply a reflective way of listening. The sound can also be felt. A pre-reflective way of listening exists. But what does that actually mean? In a phenomenological approach to sound and listening, the first-person perspective is dominant.[7] This perspective has to do with the 'position of the listener in space', and is also related to the fact that each person listens with his own experiences, knowledge, sensibilities, and so on.

Although embodied perception and the perspective of the first person are developed in the phenomenology of Maurice Merleau-Ponty, I propose to go back to Husserl's phenomenology using an interpretation by Dan Zahavi (2003). Husserl argues that the intentional act is triggered by the kinaesthetic experience and motivated by the fact that we are affected by things. Being affected or moved, the listener is thus always at the centre of his listening. Consequently, the description of listening should be from a first-person perspective. For instance, when I have the impression that I am just moved by a sound in a passive way, there is also an active component to the act of listening. I am not confused by different vibrations—instead, I actively distinguish noise from voices or music. Listening from a first-person perspective, I make these choices in the act of listening itself, without reflecting on the listening or on the sound. According to Husserl, experience (a non-thematic kind of self-awareness) precedes reflection. This implies that reflection is characterized by disclosing, not by producing its theme (Zahavi, 2010, pp. 325–7). According to Zahavi's interpretation of Husserl's later writings, it can be said that I am listening on a pre-reflective conscious level to distinguish sounds through 'feeling' them. In other words, I can be aware of different types of sounds without the sounds being intentional objects. An embodied resonating listening is listening to a sound without attending to the meaning or the source of the sound.

But how can we describe this 'embodied resonating listening' and the 'felt sound' in an audiovisual context? Although the 'first-person' is a given for the perceiver (the fact that the listener is always at the centre of his listening) and is implied in several scholarly works concerning sound and music in film, it is rare that the situatedness of the listener is included in the analysis of film sound. Again Murch points to an interesting pathway: 'I like to think that I not only record a sound but the space between me and the sound' (2011). Implicitly he poses the question of where we are when we listen to a sound in film. In a recording not only the sound but also the position of the listener can be transmitted. The audience takes the position of the recorded listening, which means that any change of distance can play an important role which is rarely the case in the recording of music.[8] Is the position of the listener in relation to the sound then a key concept in distinguishing between a sound composition (effect) and a musical composition?

In her soundscape composition *Doors of Perception*, Westerkamp combines different auditory spaces, using the sounds of opening and closing doors to link recorded spaces. Interior and exterior spaces are combined in a poetic way, rather than merely evoking a reality. The listener follows a virtual (unrealistic) path that runs through different spaces. The listener is at the centre of the action itself through his first-person perspective of listening and enactive perception. Westerkamp invites us to situate ourselves in the middle of the dynamic world created through her compositions, by listening to them and by experiencing the sound. Inner and outer worlds are interlaced, and by extension, listening to the (outer) environment is also interlaced with *listening from within* (Petitmengin et al., 2009).

## Listening from Within as an Embodied Listening

The expression 'listening from within' refers to an article edited by Claire Petitmengin, devoted to the experience of listening. In this article, a threefold generic structure of auditory experience is examined: the attention of the subject directed towards the event which is at the source of the sound, the experience of listening independent from listening to the source, and, the felt sound.

In 'listening from within', two interpretations of an 'open listening' are presented: a way of listening which Schaeffer defined as a *musicianly listening* and an *embodied resonating listening* correlated to the felt sound. The process of becoming aware of the pre-reflective dimensions of auditory experience seems to be associated with a gradual loss of intentionality. This loss of intentionality is in turn accompanied by a gradual synchronization between the space perceived as 'inner' and the space perceived as 'outer', a synchronization that makes the distinction between the two spaces permeable. This is mostly the case when listening to music. In other words, the more our attention is detached from its absorption in outward objects to enter into contact with the inner experience, the more the distinction is reduced between 'inner' and 'outer'.

In listening to Westerkamp's *Doors of Perception*, we do not need images of doors opening or closing. They are evoked in our mind's ear by listening to the acoustics of different spaces. Nor do we need images to create a path in a virtual space. This composition is not the representation of a space, but invites us to create imaginary spaces. Being at the centre of our listening, we are travelling through these evoked spaces. For the spectator/listener, the sounds in the composition are combined in a different way in Van Sant's *Last Days* than in Westerkamp's composition: some of them relate to the diegetic visible world on the screen, others evoke Blake's 'the mental space'. Not integrated into a musical composition, as is the case of *Atonement*, Westerkamp's composition *Doors of Perception* is entangled with the images and the other sounds from the film.

Randolph Jordan remarks that even when you know the work of Westerkamp quite well it remains difficult to distinguish the sounds coming from the sound design and the sounds coming from Westerkamp's composition (2007, p. 255). Jordan relates Westerkamp's music to Blake's mental space. He argues that the scene using Westerkamp's piece illustrates how Blake is no longer connected with his direct environment:

> Westerkamp's work is directly engaged with issues in the relationship between internal experience and external environments, [...]. As such her compositions are ideally suited for helping to flesh out Van Sant's portraits of young people adrift in worlds from which they are seemingly detached. (2010, p. 234)

Here I would like to pose some complementary questions. What happens with the felt sound and our embodied listening in Westerkamp's soundscape composition in the audiovisual context of the film? What happens with the space in-between the listener and the sound evoking virtual images in an audiovisual context? What happens with the 'thinking in movement', our virtual travelling through Westerkamp's composition? Is it possible that while looking at images, we employ different listening modes simultaneously, while having the impression that we are only looking at the images? Differently put, what happens with Westerkamp's composition in *Last Days*? Within audiovisual perception, the audience experiences the sounds from Westerkamp's composition as if they were created based on the image. Even if there are not any synchronized sounds, the audience tries to find their source. The church bells and motorcycle are imagined off-screen. Sounds we cannot place in relation to the visual (screen) space, for instance the voices of praying churchgoers, we situate indeed in Blake's mind (the mental space). But in our perception, we connect not only with the experience of an inner space in Blake's mind but also with his alienation from the 'outer' space.

To enable this, Van Sant has invited us from the start to move with Blake. We see him from a distance on a nature walk. Yet, acoustically we are in a very intimate relation to Blake, by hearing his murmuring. In this way, we are already 'with' him. Unable to hear his footsteps, we integrate Westerkamp's music into this situatedness. *Doors of Perception* is introduced at the same time (0:07:00) as Blake's murmurings. We hear a door opening and some musical notes. When Blake walks through a gateway, we see a car and hear a motorcycle. The association works. Not reflecting on the 'truth of this referential sound', we continue to move with Blake and accept Westerkamp's composition as part of his experience. In fact we accept the coexistence of two different experiences: our situatedness in Westerkamp's music (which is not interrupted in the audiovisual perception) and our moving with the character. When we hear a door squeak (0:08:30) as a sound effect, this sound is integrated as a *felt sound*. Our attention is visually directed towards Blake. But acoustically Blake's (non) being-in-the-world experience is transmitted through our situatedness in Westerkamp's composition. We are not switching from listening to sound design to a more musical listening. Focussing on the experience of sound, the combination of *musicianly listening* and *embodied resonating listening* enables the connection of the sound as an energetic movement with both sound design and music. Beneath our audiovisual perception, an embodied listening is always present.

Starting from listening strategies, it is possible to combine directional listening and embodied listening. It is our experience of listening and sound that can change and reveal different intentional objects, or can be embodied without revealing an intentional object. In changing and combining listening modes, sound design and music can be intertwined within the same material.

## Conclusion

Looking for a better understanding of the intertwining of sound design and music in film, I proposed to develop a more precise understanding of listening modes in relation to audiovisual perception. I explored the meaning of Barthes's 'panic listening' and explored two different approaches to the concept of listening, which both play a role in the intertwining of sound and music in film. The first approach relies on the *musique concrète* and music theory of composer Schaeffer. Inspired by Husserl, Schaeffer put the correlation between *reduced listening* and the *sound object* and between the *musicianly listening* and the *musical object* at the basis of his music theory. The second approach considers phenomenology and listening inspired by Husserl's insights in the motivation of an intentional act. I proposed to add the notion of correlation between the embodied resonating listening with the felt sound to the other listening strategies in film perception. This is rarely mentioned in film theory, but plays a crucial role in any embodied perception of film.

Discussing Murch's ideas on the recorded space between the listener and the sounding object, I introduced the importance of the situatedness of the listener in his listening. This aspect of listening to recorded sound was mentioned in Schaeffer's music theory, but was not applied in his *musique concrète*. In *Atonement*, the sound of the typewriter is integrated in a musical context and invites us to a *musicianly listening* to the sound of the typewriter as a percussive musical element. But in Westerkamp's compositions, the transmission of a listening experience and the listener's first-person perspective in listening comes into account. With the listening, the situatedness of the listening in the auditory space and an embodied listening are transmitted. This enables an exceptional intertwining of music and sound in film: the situatedness of the listener in Westerkamp's music is sustained in the experience of the felt sound, even when some sounds find their place in relation to the visual image and can be interpreted as off-screen sound, revealing a source and meaning.

## Notes

1. Ars Acustica is a group of producers and editors of radio art programmes in national-public broadcasting corporations in Europe. Founded in 1989 within the European Broadcasting Union EBU, the Ars Acustica group aims at initiating and realizing projects, promoting radio art, exchanging productions between European radios, and eventually open up a space for debate on the future of radio, of art and of radio art as such. (http://radioartnet.net/11/2011/11/08/20-years-ebu-ars-acustica-cd).

2. 'On pourrait dire, et ce serait mieux qu'un jeu de mots, que l'écoute musicale traditionnelle est l'écoute du sonore des objets musicaux stéréotypés, tandis que l'écoute musicienne serait l'écoute musicale de nouveaux objets sonores proposés à l'emploi musical'. [We could say—and this is no word play—that traditional musical listening (*l'écoute musicale*) is a listening to the sonorous aspects of the stereotyped musical object, while listening like a musician (*l'écoute musicienne*) would be a musical listening to the proposed sonorous objects in function of a musical use of them.] (Schaeffer, 1966, p. 353) Translation M.H.
3. In the early 1920s, Husserl places static phenomenology in contrast with genetic phenomenology. According to Mary Jeanne Larrabee, static analysis is that which 'analyzes a constituted object without dealing with the flowing temporal process in which the object is constituted' (1976, p. 164).
4. Michel Chion describes 'reduced listening' as follows: "According to the author of the *Traité des objects musicaux* [Schaeffer 1966], this is listening in a mode that intentionally and artificially ignores causes and meaning (and, I would add, effects) in order to concentrate on the sound itself, in terms of its sensory properties including pitch, rhythm, texture, form, mass, and volume (2009, p 487).
5. Chion refers to the French composer François Bayle's idea of sound as an energy in movement (2010, pp. 198–9) and the fact that our body 'co-vibrates' in listening (p. 217), but he does not accept Campan's proposition to start with sound and listening in the analysis of film (2003, pp. 203, 208, 211, 234, 439). His critique of Campan is not included in the English version of the book.
6. In an enactive approach of perception emotions and motor actions in the world are considered (Thompson, 2007). In this embodied approach, the Husserlian idea of passive genesis, underlying active synthesis, becomes crucial in an account of experience and perception. Central in this approach are movement and the embodied sense of movement. Husserl argues that the intentional act is motivated by kinaesthetic experience, preceding a thematic experience. The active genesis of the intentional object presupposes, in other words, always a degree of passivity, meaning that the subject does not decide that he or she is affected by something.

    The thought behind active/passive distinction is that our active orientation toward things in practical and theoretical reason, or artistic creation, presupposes a deeper and more fundamental openness to the world. It is an openness to being sensuously affected and solicited by the world through the medium of our living body, and responding by the attraction and repulsion. Investigating these sensorimotor and affective depths of experience leads phenomenology to the notion of passive genesis. (pp. 29–30)
    For an enactive approach of film perception, see also Pia Tikka (2008).
7. For further reading on 'first-person perspective' see Gallagher and Zahavi (2008).
8. For further reading on the importance of the listening aspect in sound recording, see Deshays (2010).

## References

Barthes, R. (1976) 'L'écoute' in R. Barthes, *L'obvie et L'obtus* (Paris: Les éditions Seuil), 217–230.

Behr, E. (2014) 'Something inaudible: Antony Burgess's Mozart and the Wolf Gang and Kirsty Gunn's the Big Music as Literary Music through Roland Barthes's Concept of Listening', *MUSe*, Vol. 1, No. 1, 114–124.

Cage, J. (1971) *Silence: lectures and writings* (London: Calder and Boyar).
Campan, V. (1999) *L'écoute filmique: l'écho du son en image* (Saint-Denis: Presses universitaires de Vincennes).
Chion, M. (1994) *Audio-vision: Sound on Screen*, trans. C. Gorbman (New York: Columbia University Press).
Chion, M. (2009) *Film, a Sound Art*, trans. C. Gorbman (New York: Columbia University Press).
Chion, M. (2010) *Le son: traité d'acoulogie*, (Paris: Armand Colin).
Chion, M. (2003) *Un art sonore, le cinéma* (Paris: Cahiers du cinema).
Deshays, D. (2010) *Entendre le cinéma* (Paris: Klincksieck).
Gallagher, S. and D. Zahavi (2008) *The Phenomenological Mind: An Introduction to Philosophy of Mind and Cognitive Science* (London and New York: Routledge).
Huvenne, M. (2013a) 'Sound in Film as an Inner Movement: Towards Embodied Listening Strategies' in H. De Preester (ed.) *Moving Imagination* (Amsterdam: John Benjamins Publishing Company), 133–48.
Huvenne, M. (2013b) 'Interview with Dario Marianelli', *Film Fest Gent*, 18 October.
Ihde, D. (2007) *Listening and Voice: Phenomenologies of Sound* (New York: State University of New York Press).
Jordan, R. (2007) 'The Work of Hildegarde Westerkamp in the Films of Gus van Sant: An Interview with the Soundscape Composer (and some added thoughts of my own)' *Offscreen*, 11, Nos. 8–9 (August/September), http://offscreen.com/view/jordan_westerkamp, date accessed 16 February 2015.
Jordan, R. (2010) *The Schizophonic Imagination: Audiovisual Ecology in the Cinema*, PhD Thesis (Montreal: Concordia University), http://spectrum.library.concordia.ca/7060/1/Jordan_PhD_F2010.pdf, date accessed 16 February 2015.
Larrabee, M. J. (1976). 'Husserl's static and genetic phenomenology', *Man and World*, Vol. 9 No. 2, 163–174.
Lockspeiser, E. and H. Halbreich (1989) *Claude Debussy* (Paris: Fayard).
Murch, W. (2005) 'Dense clarity—clear density', *The Transom Review*, Vol. 5, No. 1, 7–23.
Murch, W. (2011) Workshop 'Sound in Film', School of Arts, Gent, 17th-19th October.
O'Callaghan, C. (2007) *Sounds: A Philosophical Theory* (Oxford: Oxford University Press).
Petitmengin, C., M. Bitbol, J.M. Nissou, B. Pachoud, H. Curalucci, M. Cermolacce, J. Vion-Dury (2009) 'Listening from within', in C. Petitmengin (ed.), *Ten Years of Viewing from Within: The legacy of Francisco Varela* (Exeter: Imprint Academic), 252–84.
Russolo, L. (1913) *The Art of Noises*, http://www.unknown.nu/futurism/noises.html, date accessed 23 August 2014.
Schaeffer, P. (1966) *Traité des objets musicaux: essai interdisciplinaire* (Paris: Seuil).
Sheets-Johnstone, M. (2013) 'Bodily resonance' in H. De Preester (ed.) *Moving Imagination* (Amsterdam: John Benjamins Publishing Company) 19–36.
Sheets-Johnstone, M. (2009) *The Corporeal Turn: an Interdisciplinary Reader* (Exeter: Imprint Academic).
Slonimsky, N. (1971) *Music since 1900* (London: Cassell).
Thompson, E. (2007) *Mind in life: biology, phenomenology and the sciences of mind* (Cambridge and London: The Belknap Press of Harvard University Press).
Tikka, P. (2008) *Enactive Cinema: Simulatorium Eisensteinense* (Helsinki: University of Arts and Design Helsinki).

Varèse, E. (1983) *Ecrits* (Paris: Christian Bourgois).
Westerkamp, H. (1999) 'Soundscape Composition: Linking Inner and Outer Worlds', Talk for *Soundscape before 2000*, 19–26 November, Amsterdam, http://www.sfu.ca/~westerka/writings%20page/articles%20pages/soundscapecomp.html, date accessed 14 February 2014.
Zahavi, D. (2003) *Husserl's Phenomenology* (Stanford: Stanford University Press).
Zahavi, D. (2010) 'Inner (Time-) Consciousness' in D. Lohmar and I. Yamaguchi (eds) *On Time—New Contributions to the Husserlian Phenomenology of Time, Phaenomenologica 197* (Dordrecht: Springer), 319–39.

CHAPTER 10

# Interview 2: Reality and Representation—An Interview with Dario Marianelli

*Miguel Mera*

Born in Pisa but now living in London, Dario Marianelli is an Academy Award-, Golden Globe- and Ivor Novello-winning film composer. His film scores include *The Boxtrolls* (2013), *Anna Karenina* (2012), *Atonement* (2007), *V for Vendetta* (2006), *Salmon Fishing in the Yemen* (2011), and *Pride and Prejudice* (2005). Marianelli has worked with numerous prominent filmmakers, but has developed a particularly close collaborative relationship with British director Joe Wright.

MM: One of your longest and most productive collaborative relationships has been with Joe Wright. In your work together you constantly seem to question the fictionality of film. Why is that a concern for you? Can you trace the development of those ideas?

DM: The first film I did with Joe was *Pride and Prejudice* and this subject of truth and fiction came up in our very first conversation. Especially because, as a period drama, you would see people playing an instrument in the world of the film. There was a very obvious question to answer: What would they be playing when you see them? Would they play authentic music from the period? Would you use music from the period when *Pride and Prejudice* was first drafted or, perhaps, when it was first published, which was fifteen years later? Whichever way, you would have to do some research and find music that was possible at the time, so perhaps early Beethoven sonatas, or late Mozart sonatas, or Clementi, or something like that, possibly played on a fortepiano rather than a modern piano. Or the other way to go about it would be to write something original, while still having to answer the question about period or modern instruments. This is a very pragmatic instance of making decisions

M. Mera
City, University of London, UK

MM: about truth and authenticity, but I think the conversation was, and has been over the years, of a philosophical nature.

MM: Philosophical? In what way?

DM: It is an interesting conversation that comes up, for example, very strongly when I write something for a true story. I'm working on something now for a film about the 1996 tragedy on Mount Everest where a lot of people died. You recreate a world that did exist, but you do that with CGI, with special effects, with green screen, and then with actors pretending to be somebody else, and then you put music on it, which even further fictionalises the truth. So when you read 'based on a true story', by the time filmmaking has finished, is it still true or has it somehow been transported to another level of reality? The level of that reality is very interesting for me, because it has to do with a certain philosophical take on the world. What is the reality of abstraction or of 'universals'? When you try to touch a universal with art, are you touching something real? It is the old Aristotelian/Platonic dichotomy: Are ideas something that really exist somewhere, and are they as real as physical things, or are they completely human constructs that have no tangible being. They don't live somewhere, they live in our minds. Even if that was the case and they were completely manufactured man-made objects, they are still objects, whether you can touch them or not. You can say that of anything you cannot touch, friendship for example. You cannot put it under the microscope, but it would be silly to think that it does not exist, it is able to have an effect on the world, on real things, on the way people make decisions and live their lives. So there is still a very concrete level of reality in these intangible, untouchable things. And I think music is very interesting because it lives half way through those worlds. You cannot touch it but it is tangible, it is audible, it is part of the real world and also part of the abstract world. A lot of what music does, at its best, is to give a sound or a body to some abstract feeling or idea. You know, you probably can't see friendship or freedom on the screen, but maybe you can try to give it a sound, and then it becomes something that can travel through the movie with the ability to change, to have experiences, to interact with characters, and maybe throw light on something that the characters do, or even make them do something in a very weird way. Music is a very strange thing that lives right in-between worlds of fiction, reality, abstraction, ideas, and concrete effects upon people's lives.

MM: You said that you can't touch music, but I'm very struck by the fact that in many of your scores there are very clear tactile elements, I'm thinking of the typewriter in *Atonement*, for example, but there are many other examples of sounds that are in some way embodied. Can we talk a bit about that typewriter, because *Atonement* is also about blurring reality and fiction. Can you tell me how you approached that film sonically?

DM: What I remember was that it was a bit of a journey of discovery for me and for Joe. Part of it was expanding on some experiments we had done in *Pride and Prejudice*, where something in the frame would be absorbed in the score. There was one particular dance, for example, with a solo violin that was in the room and then the orchestra comes in and it becomes the accompaniment to the violin, but it goes at a different speed. So it is obviously separate. It created a little bit of tension and a split between the room and a more interior, introspective sound.

MM: This is the second ball at Netherfield house?

DM: Yes, that's the one. But then if you take the direct amplification of that experiment it would be the beach walk in *Atonement*, where there is a choir of soldiers singing on the beach. This would be the equivalent of the solo violin in the dance, and then the music somehow comes in. Actually the score starts first, but the principle is the same. For me, it was important that the speed of the two musics was different. That was my first port of call. You know, create some kind of split, musically, between what you see and hear and what you hear but don't see. It is magical when it works. They work together but they also work separately, and they stay separate. That is a musical equivalent of those moments; maybe we've all felt from time to time, where your mind is a bit split. You're there but you're also watching yourself being there. There's a kind of estrangement, an out-of-body experience. The two types of music are really doing that, one is really there, the other is observing and they are not going at the same speed.

MM: Could we just dwell on that sequence for a moment, because the soldiers are singing 'Dear Lord and Father of Mankind'?

DM: Yes, it's Hubert Parry.

MM: It is also an extended scene comprising just one shot. How did this audiovisual interaction come about practically through your discussions with Joe? How do conceive of something that works on this kind of scale?

DM: Joe had this idea for the very long shot from the beginning and he knew there would be a group of soldiers singing the hymn. That was in the script.

MM: But were you involved in that?

DM: I wasn't involved in the choice of the hymn. I've been involved in other movies with Joe in the choice of the kinds of materials we see on screen. On *The Soloist* I chose all the music that was played and I was involved at the script level. But on *Atonement* I wasn't. So I found it there. Joe was quite convinced that the hymn would be the music of that scene. There wasn't going to be the need for anything else, in the same way that he was convinced that the solo violin would be enough for the dance in *Pride and Prejudice*. I suggested that we could bring in some score that would interact in an interesting way with the music that was already there. I remember very well that experiment in *Pride and Prejudice* because it was a very successful experiment for me, so I wanted to try something similar. I remember my first attempt was not so successful because you could see the idea but you could not really see how it could work. Joe was very shrewd in knowing how far he could push me, so we threw away that idea and I went at it again and we ended up with what is there now, which I was very pleased with.

**MM:** Why didn't that first attempt work?

**DM:** I think the reason why the first attempt didn't work so well was that the music I created was too dependent on the music that was already there. It wasn't disassociated enough. The trick, really, was to come in with music that was very different from the hymn, then the two merge and fall apart, and that was the way to create that interior sense of disassociation. We were very conscious that there is a breaking point, you know, you push things too far and then they become gimmicks, they become clever for the sake of cleverness. They lose their emotional relevance and their storytelling relevance. We had to keep checking with each other whether we thought we were doing something gimmicky or relevant. After you've done it and everyone agrees that it is not a gimmick it seems easy, but when you are there in the middle of it you feel like you are shooting in the dark, you don't how people are going to register it.

**MM:** You've built that relationship over time with Joe and you have developed a language that you both understand. So, are you worried about the fact that other directors might see that kind of approach and come to you to try these ideas because they are part of the 'Marianelli sound', but perhaps without the depth?

**DM:** Yes, but, I think … we don't have a copyright on those kind of ideas. From my side, if I do something like that I would always be conscious of the risks and I wouldn't want to be pushed away from being comfortable about being honest. There has to be some kind of rationale. It can't be gratuitous, you know, bring in the typewriter because it is cool. It has to do with storytelling and if it doesn't help I would be resistant.

**MM:** You also said that Joe was pushing you. How does he push you? How do you push each other?

**DM:** On that particular occasion he said: 'I like it but I think you can do something better.'

**MM:** But was he not more specific? 'You could do it better this way, or did you think about trying this?'

**DM:** Actually, he almost doesn't need to say anything. I can see when I have missed the mark a little bit, but I still feel that I have to send music to him because he's waiting to hear something. So I'll send it, but in the back of my mind I'll be thinking: 'I can do better than this and if there is time I will go back and improve it.' Even if he hadn't said anything I would have gone over it again, because I knew that there was some headroom there.

**MM:** How do you push him then?

**DM:** On *Atonement* there was a brilliant push-me-pull-you where he was very convinced that the main love theme, or romantic theme, should have been a tune from the 1940s, a Flanagan and Allen song that he wanted me to adapt to become the main tune of the score. I thought, 'that is great, but what space does that leave me to do something original.' So I kind of resisted it, but my way of resisting was that every time there was a cue in that vein I would present two versions, one with the Flanagan and Allen tune and one with my own tune. And I kept telling him: 'Joe, I know a good tune when I hear one, I think my tune is better than Flanagan and Allen.' Finally he gave in. I don't know if it was out of tiredness, or he couldn't bear carrying on with the charade, or that he really came round to think that my tune was better, but I think he was happy to have it in the end.

MM: That's interesting, because I'm thinking of my own experience as a film composer. I think I might have given up more quickly than you in that case. What gives you the resilience to go for three or four months holding on to this idea and fighting for it?

DM: I have found myself, on occasion, working on movies where I don't believe in them as much, in those situations I probably would give up earlier. But in something that I really think is so good, that has great potential, I would never give up, I would fight, and I think you would too.

MM: You were talking about originality and how you would not want to be involved in a score where your 'voice' is not present and yet, in *The Soloist*, Beethoven looms large for the whole of that film. So why is that different?

DM: Because it would have been a hybrid otherwise, and I don't like hybrids. I like clean things. The book from which the film was taken is called *Imagining Beethoven* and the main character of the story, which is based on a true story is a homeless, black schizophrenic musician whose obsession in life is Beethoven. Now, Dario Marianelli needs to get in there and write some music, but what is he doing there? What has Marianelli got to do with somebody who is obsessed with Beethoven, probably even more than I am?

MM: Yes, you're a Beethoven fan aren't you?

DM: Yes, I'm a huge fan. I think most composers are fans. It's the struggle.

MM: The constant reminder of your inadequacy in comparison.

DM: Yes, and the desperate hope that you can overcome it at some point. But I just thought, if there is Beethoven's music in the film but I also have to write music cues that are mine, it is going to be a mish-mash of things. Anyway, one way or another, I convinced everyone that my job as a composer on that project was not to write a single note of original music, but to adapt Beethoven's music for the film. It wasn't easy actually. It has been one of the least rewarding projects from a public exposure point of view, because I've made myself totally invisible, and I've tried to turn Beethoven into a film composer, which is quite a task because Beethoven's narrative is so stringent. You can't bend it very easily to the narrative of the movie, which needs to happen if you want to use it as film music. It was hard work. I remember agonising, trying to turn a seventeen-minute movement of a quartet into a two-and-a-half minute piece. You know, what do you cut out and how do you shape it?

**MM:** So, is there anything you can say about that process? What do you distil from Beethoven?

**DM:** For weeks I listened to a lot of music by Beethoven, but mostly string quartets and the third symphony because I was hoping I could derive the whole score from just one piece and I thought the third symphony was a good candidate. What I was looking for was the 'shiver' moment. Moments that take you by surprise and I tried to zoom in on those moments and make something out of them. There are a couple of bars in one movement of a string quartet that no matter when I hear them or where I am they always have the same effect on me. So, I expanded those bars to a three-minute piece. Essentially it is two bars that are inflated into a film cue.

**MM:** In that example there are those two bars that give you 'shivers', but they surely do that in the context of the whole piece? And when you are thinking of those two bars you are thinking of them in the context of the whole narrative? So, is it a process of deconstruction?

**DM:** I guess it is. I have met people who have told me that I had found a moment that had given them shivers too and they were still getting the shivers from the expanded or the shrunk version. Somehow there is something in those two bars, even out of context...

**MM:** There is an essence to it...

**DM:** There is something that is able to stand away from the piece. I don't know, maybe it does that to people who know Beethoven and have their memory of the original piece. It's a really good point. I don't know the answer to that. If you had never heard the whole piece or had never heard Beethoven would it still register in the same way? Maybe not.

**MM:** In *The Soloist* the actors have to play instruments, were you involved in that process? Presumably there are things that have to be composed or arranged in time for shooting and they have to be credible?

**DM:** For example, there is one scene where the main character, Nathaniel, is given a cello for the first time in many years and he takes it out of the case and he tries it.

**MM:** This is the scene in the underpass?

**DM:** Yes, it's a tunnel, an underpass, a very busy road junction. So you hear a lot of traffic noise and he takes the cello out of the case and he starts playing a few notes, and tentatively starts playing the tune. But the tune, which he plays from memory, is not actually a cello tune at all, because the piece we had chosen for that scene was one of the late string quartets. I couldn't just let him play the cello part of the string quartet, because we would not recognise the tune. So, I transcribed the main tune for cello and when the rest of the music started drifting in, it is actually played by the L.A. Phil, it is not played by a string quartet. There is an expansion of the music. But even then, he still doesn't play the cello part that was written by Beethoven; he plays the main theme of the string quartet, which is a very odd and fake thing to do, but it was the only way really to focus on him playing, because the cello part of the string quartet would have been less focusing.

**MM:** But that's a development, surely, in your working relationship with Joe, because presumably in the early days you did not have that level of detail for these kinds of interactions?

**DM:** It was much more detailed. While Joe was in pre-production in LA, because the film was entirely shot in LA, and the LA Phil was in fact one of the characters in the movie, I went over for weeks at a time and I worked with Joe, playing him mock ups of Beethoven arrangements. And he was trying to work out timings and trying to visualise what the camera would do, until we got to the point with the music where we could record it with a real cello. We decided to do it that way rather than recording the music after.

**MM:** So, in a way, the film was editing around the music.

**DM:** Yes. It's more like a musical, you do the music first and then you shoot the images to music, so everybody can hear it while they are acting. It was the only way to get Jamie Foxx to move his hands in a plausible way.

**MM:** You were talking about the very noisy underpass, and it made me wonder about your relationship to the interaction between music and sound design. How do you deal with that?

**DM:** Mostly I don't have to manage that. Mostly it is in the hands of the dubbing mixer and the sound designers. The interaction doesn't happen nearly as much as I would like it to happen. Very often I am involved before the sound people start their real work. I would very rarely be at the dubbing stage to interact with the dubbing mixer, because I don't believe the composer is very useful on those occasions, and should really take a step back.

**MM:** Why?

**DM:** Because the composer has a very skewed ear, not a very objective ear at that point. In a sense the dubbing mixer who has come in fresh onto the project is the best person. He doesn't know anything about what the sound designers have done, he doesn't know anything about what the musicians have done, he doesn't know anything about what the director wants. He just comes in and he has got all these elements to balance with a fresh ear, and it is not biased in a particular way.

**MM:** So you never attend the dub?

**DM:** I had one experience with Terry Gilliam when I was invited to a dub and he let me make suggestions to the dubbing mixer for the whole day about what I thought the level of the music should be. So, cue by cue I did that and I was very smugly pleased with myself, and then we watched the whole thing from beginning to end and it was awful. It was like a musical. The music was so overbearing. I discovered that it was very hard to maintain perspective over the course of the whole movie.

It's a very hard job. You might be able to do a good job on one cue or another, but to keep things from escalating into hysterical loudness is very hard and that's what dubbing mixers are good at, and that's what they do all the time. The other way to do it, which sometimes works, is to let them do it, come in and listen to what they've done from beginning to end and maybe give some notes. Mostly I feel that the music is too loud and ask them if they could take it back a little bit. There are some pieces I write that are intended to be very subliminal and dream-like, but the dubbing mixer doesn't know and the director has maybe forgotten that this was the idea and has not noticed that, for example, you've got a solo clarinet line that sounds as loud as the orchestra that is coming up in the next scene. Otherwise, I stay out of the way.

MM: But what about interaction with the sound-designers? Is there an interaction as you are working on something?

DM: Mainly I have found that the interaction, for me, is when they do something that is a bit musical and it fights the key of my music. I might have to say: 'Can you re-tune that church bell, it really is jarring in a bad way.' I mean I don't mind jarring if it's expressive, but if the harmony is on a drone or a pedal note and you add another drone that completely contradicts what I am trying to do musically, I have to say something. So that's the kind of interaction.

MM: You were talking before about a kind of estrangement as a device and that is certainly something that strikes me about *Anna Karenina*. The whole way that film is constructed seems to be approaching a kind of Brechtian distanciation. Can you tell me a bit about how the music works in that film?

DM: What happened was that we had the script, which didn't really say anything about Joe's visual idea for the film. Joe's conceit eventually was to place the whole story in an abandoned theatre and treat it like a play. So my initial reaction to the script was more traditional. All it took, really, was to go and see Joe in his studio and he took me through the film, and there were bits of paper stuck on the wall as a kind of rough storyboard, and by the end I was in tears. Just seeing how he had conceived it and how he had turned reality on its head, transforming it into something that was completely non-literal. I don't know why it moved me so much, especially the ending. It had grass and flowers sprouting from the floorboards of the theatre. It was a totally topsy-turvy approach. It was yet another blurring of the boundary between what is real and fictional, but done with elegant poetry. It was just a really powerful image and it gave me the parameters for the film. We could do absolutely what we wanted with this movie. It was a totally open space for the music to come in and be poetic and non-literal, to be over the top if it needed to be, to be completely abstract. If I wanted the music not to comment on what you could see but on something completely different and lateral, I could do that. I had worries about *Anna Karenina* as a pillar of literature with all the weight that comes from that and all the different versions that have been attempted. Suddenly there was a space there to fill with the music that was completely free. It was brilliant sleight of hand on Joe's part, to free everybody, which you never expect on a story like that. You feel completely constrained by period, costume and everything. He just wiped that out, which is the reason that I love him so much.

**MM:** How did you get started?

**DM:** I started from the pieces that were needed for the dances because there was a choreographer, Sidi Larbi [Cherkaoui], who had been asked to choreograph some waltzes in a contemporary way, not just people moving their legs. They moved their arms and everything is just so unrealistic. So I wrote a couple of waltzes and a mazurka, trying to find a way to bring something ... I listened to a lot of those waltzes, and I felt that they were very shallow. You know, young Strauss waltzes, I love them as fluff and light-hearted things, but I find them very shallow, they don't have a lot of soul for me. So I wanted to write something that had potential, the seed of a soul, that could then expand into something that could also work later as the more soulful part of the score, and the more dramatic, traumatic part of the score. So, I guess my waltzes are a little more melancholic. For example they do not tend to have the tune on the top and the 'oom pah pah' on the bottom, they have a counter theme....

**MM:** And layers fighting with each other?

**DM:** Yes, there are layers fighting, exactly. There is some conflict already in there.

**MM:** And also they never quite resolve...

**DM:** I'm very bad at resolving. I just can't write endings.

**MM:** But it's not just a weakness, there's a dramatic purpose to it, right?

**DM:** That's my excuse then. But that's why I think it is Schumann and not Beethoven who would have made a great film composer, it is the lack of resolution. You start things as if you are in the middle of a sentence and you end them without ending. That's life isn't it? There's no beginning or end, well there is, but still...

**MM:** So, you obviously had to work closely with the choreographer on this project.

**DM:** Closely enough. We had a first meeting together, but meetings with composers are kind of pointless. Composers need to write the music and then let you hear what they've done. There's no point describing the music you are going to write, you have to write it.

**MM:** But at least on the level of synchronisation of that extraordinary waltz scene there must have been some detailed discussion?

**DM:** The main thing was for me to have a rough idea of the length of the scenes. So there were two waltzes and a mazurka. What I really needed to know was how long they were. Within that, at least for one of the waltzes, Joe had the idea that something would happen half way through. So I knew I had to mark it in some way. I had done a mock up which was just for piano at that point but it was good enough, you could hear what the waltz was doing. Joe tried to imagine how he would film it and said: 'Can we have an extra eight bars here? Can you delay this moment?' or 'Can you expand this moment so it has a longer build up?' So, I made those changes and then I went to Antwerp to meet with the choreographer, who is based there, and he tried the new versions of the waltzes. Then eventually things settled and the shoot arrived. It was shot over three days, they shot the two waltzes and the mazurka. Then, of course, the editor is set loose on them and starts chopping things and when I got them back it was a bit of a headache, partially of my own making, because I didn't want to keep the pulse steady. Things invariably had gone off what we had agreed, the climax came in a different place, and moments that had to be marked were in different places. The second waltz and mazurka were separate pieces, but at some point during the edit the ballroom scene was too long and it was decided that the two pieces would merge. So, I had to find a way to combine them and go smoothly from one to the other. Then Joe had this idea, that he had already tried in *Pride and Prejudice*, where all the lights and all the people disappear and there is a moment just with the two main characters locked into each other, forgetting whatever else is going on, and that had to be treated musically in some special way. There were a number of exercises that were quite interesting for me. And then there was how to derail, to derange a waltz into something distorted and increasingly anxious. So you start with the 'oom pah pah' and end with this massive schizophrenic thing with the train smashing through the ballroom. I was trying to find a way to do that as a smooth progression, so you don't quite know when it started to happen.

MM: That thematic material becomes the basis for a lot of the rest of the score of the film. So it all starts from the waltz?

DM: That is the thing I have tried on every film with Joe. It has become a concern for me over the years, to have material within a film that is interrelated. Both waltzes, in fact, contain either as the main theme or counter theme, virtually all the themes that you are going to hear in the rest of the score, except for one theme that is completely separate. But most of the music in *Anna Karenina* comes out of those two waltzes. And again, it was a way to build a self-consistent world. I think it had its own rationale. It was justified because every time the tune from the waltz comes in you know that everything that happens to Anna is going back to that moment. It all connects to that waltz.

MM: I'm just thinking about some of the other scenes where you had to work with the choreographer, like the bureaucrats stamping, or the transition scene through the theatre where you see musicians playing in the frame. What is the purpose of bringing that into the world of the film?

DM: I think the rational explanation would be that Joe was trying to give some kind of visual and musical counterpart to the idea that the aristocracy in the years before the revolution were living a totally fake life, as if they were in fact actors on a stage, or characters in a musical. There was nothing genuine and honest about their lives. For one thing they wanted to be French, they didn't want to be Russian. The contrast between their life immersed in bureaucracy, you know that scene you mentioned with the stamping, is a reflection of the true soul of the Russian Aristocracy. There is the character of Levin, who is maybe an echo of Tolstoy's own feeling about being an aristocrat who was uncomfortable about the bureaucracy. Levin is the enlightened farmer who questions why the land doesn't belong to the peasants, and why peasants are treated as cattle, owned by their masters, and he goes to visit Anna's brother, who is in fact completely immersed in the bureaucratic emptiness of Russian life, the pretend life. The desire to show the split between what I would call the true life, or at least the aspiration towards a true life, is what prompted Joe to put that on the stage and for the music to be stage music. It's a total fake.

**MM**: So, you have 'fakeness' that can be represented by those devices, making us aware of their own construction. But how is the truth reflected in the score?

**DM**: It was complicated and it turned out to be layered, but my first impulse was to do exactly what Russian musicians in the late nineteenth century had done when they found themselves with the desire to develop a national school, and stop writing French-imitation music, or German-imitation music. What they did was to look at folk music. You know Balakirev went off in the 1840s or 1850s and on several trips he transcribed as many folk tunes as he could find and then he started publishing them. So, I also tried to research what they had researched. I tried to get close to the real thing. We found a Russian singer who knew a lot of these songs, and she came and sang for us and we picked a couple. Unconsciously I picked one that Tchaikovsky had used in his fourth symphony. It was probably in the back of my mind because of that. It has something familiar about it. When I realised that Tchaikovsky had already used it, it didn't put me off, it felt like a good omen. I felt like a slightly too late composer of The Five, the group of people who were trying to create the national school.

**MM**: The five-and-a-half?

**DM**: The fifth-and-a-half Italian that no-one knew about! That was quite interesting for me. First to try and distil in my own mind what makes Russian tunes different from Armenian tunes or from Middle Eastern tunes. You can't quite put your finger on it, but there is something in the way they use certain intervals and rhythms and it immediately sounds Russian. I hoped that by doing that it would be reflected in some way in the rest of the music that I would write. Keeping that at the back of my mind, using fourths and fifths in a certain way. I ended up using this tune and bending it, actually I did some violence to it to make it do what I wanted. That was one of my bridges connecting to the late nineteenth century Russian school.

**MM**: The thing that strikes me most about the film is that it has a musicality to it. That's partly because of your evolving relationship with Joe, and the various other things we've been talking about. I see it as very musical and balletic rather than cinematic, if I can put it that way.

DM: Well I take that as a great compliment. For me if I can write music that doesn't refer directly to other film music, I am very happy. I don't particularly want to write 'film music', in the same way that when I think of a Stravinsky's ballet I don't think he was trying to consciously obey the parameters that are inherent to ballet music, or Bach ... These are unholy comparisons, by the way, but I'll make them anyway, you don't write church music trying to make it sound 'churchy' you write music that amplifies a certain type of experience or connects to a certain type of idea. I don't think Bach wrote church music with the idea of connecting to what, in his mind, was church music. He was trying to connect to the idea he had of God. It's a different thing. And for me there is a certain idea that I have of music that I try to connect with, it is not an idea that I have of film music, or of film even. In *Anna Karenina*, I was trying to connect to ideas that have to do with more underground themes. What does it feel like to live a fake life?

MM: But you said you didn't want to do 'film music' and by implication that means that there is an understanding of what film music is, and what you're trying to do is consciously to go against that.

DM: I can see I am digging myself a very deep grave here potentially.

MM: Well, no, I think it is an interesting point that you see a distinction there. So what is it that 'film music' does that you are trying not to do?

DM: I don't think there is such a thing as film music really. There are certain films where I can feel that the music is very functional in a slavish way. So, I guess for me the difference is whether I am able to get the music to relate to the same underlying themes to which everybody else in the film is relating. So when an actor has to inform their performance they have to dig deeper. It cannot be done by numbers, by pulling muscles in the face, you have to connect to something deeper. It is that conversation you and I have had a few times in the past about what style is. How do you write a piece of music that is not pastiche and is not just empty style, that has some kind of heart or depth, and that can connect you as a human being to some kind of human experience that is independent of music? There are certain universals and so we go back to the idea of truth, with a capital T. There are some universals that we connect to and they might be abstract and intangible, but nevertheless they are there. For me, if my music can connect to and comment on those then it might have an integrity and honesty that I recognise. I suppose what I am trying to say is that I do not always recognise music in films in that way. Sometimes I do not hear that desire to connect to something deeper and it remains superficial for me. It sounds great, it is beautifully recorded, well-orchestrated, it provides tension or atmosphere or colour, whatever you want, but doesn't quite do what I aspire to do in my own music which is to try and go deeper.

PART III

# Listening: Affect and Body

CHAPTER 11

# Sound Effects/Sound Affects: 'Meaningful' Noise in the Cinema

*James Wierzbicki*

Every sound has meaning.

When the hammer on a wind-up alarm clock begins its clangorous beating against metal chimes, the sound means that the clock's hour hand and minute hand have together reached the precise configuration that represents the time for which the alarm had been set. When a dog barks, the sound means that a canine creature has simultaneously expelled air from its lungs and constricted certain muscles in its throat in such a way that its vocal cords vibrate. When wine goblets clink in the dining area of a café, the sound means that two glass objects have been brought together forcefully enough to trigger bell-like resonances but not so forcefully as to cause the objects to shatter.

But these same sounds can have meaning of a different sort. The ringing of the alarm clock can be a signal, most likely one that reminds its owner that it is time to wake up. The dog's bark can be a sign, a gesture whose communicated content might range from a warm greeting to a fierce threat. The clink of wine glasses can be a symbol, perhaps one that represents nothing more than routine cordiality amongst people who work together day after day, perhaps one that represents—after long months of tentative flirtation—the establishment of a potential couple's first bit of common ground.

The real world teems with sounds that have meaning in and of themselves and at the same time potentially have meaning as elements in a shared or private semiotic system. During our waking moments, those of us equipped with normal hearing absorb such multivalent sounds constantly. Our physical survival demands that we be aware of *all* these sounds; our psychic survival demands that we attend, lest we be overwhelmed, only to those sounds that for one reason or another seem to matter. Like all animals, we are equipped

---

J. Wierzbicki
University of Sydney, Australia

with a 'filter' that allows us to sift through everything that our ears *receive* and identify those isolated bits of sonic information that our brains in fact *perceive*, to shuffle quickly through the myriad sounds whose meanings have to do only with the facts of their existence and pick out those relatively few sounds whose meanings, for their individual hearers, hold significance.

The mechanism of this 'filter' is for the most part subconscious, but it nonetheless involves a thought process. In the real world, the separation of sound that is somehow significant from inconsequential background noise is always done—consciously or not—by us. In the fictional world of narrative cinema, the separation is typically done *for* us, by the filmmakers.

\*\*\*\*

Cinematic sound is constructed, but this is not to say that the sound one encounters in films it is entirely artificial. To be sure, many cinematic sound 'effects' bear little resemblance to the real-life sonic events they purport to represent. In the first half of the 1930s, when the industry was still exploring the potential of the new sound-on-film medium, filmmakers learned quickly that the dull thud of hooves on the ground did not communicate the sense of urgency that they wanted in their 'horse chase' scenes. Likewise for the sounds of pistol shots, and the sounds of brawlers' fists smashing into one another's jaws, and the sounds of knives plunged into the chests of murder victims. Even if they could have been properly recorded, the actual sounds of galloping, shooting, punching, stabbing, and so on were simply not theatrical enough for the filmmakers' needs, and so they were replaced by sonic simulations of the sort that earlier had been used in radio dramas and the accompaniments to 'silent' films[1] but whose roots date back, at least, to the days of Elizabethan theatre.

'We have had spoken dialogue and sound effects on stage for longer than we have had novels', notes the literary historian Raymond Tallis (1985, p. 60). To the persnickety critic of Shakespeare's time, both the tone of language at the Globe Theatre and the acoustic details of the back-stage sound effects surely would have been perceived as false; to most members of the ticket-buying public, the language and the sound effects—like the costumes and the sets and the fight choreography—likely would have been accepted not as really 'real' but as 'real enough' to give the customers their money's worth. The contract by which suspension of disbelief is exchanged for a few hours of engaging entertainment has been entered into by audiences for centuries, in venues ranging from Paris's Théâtre du Palais-Royal to Tokyo's *kabuki-za*, from the Covent Garden stalls that hosted the first Punch-and-Judy shows to the Jakarta storefronts that still host performances of *wayang* puppet drama.

Audiences of the sound film—today as much as in the 1930s—have followed in this tradition of responding to patently fake sound effects as though the sounds were genuine. And it is not always a case of the audiences merely *deigning* to treat sonic fiction as though it were sonic fact; empirical research has shown that persons exposed to non-cinematic film clips sometimes take studio-produced sound effects to be more 'real'—more convincingly communicative of whatever objects or actions appear in the clips' visual imagery—than the real thing (Heller and Wolf, 2002). As the French sound theorist Michel Chion reminds us: 'Sound that rings true for the spectator and sound that *is* true are two very different things. In order to assess the truth of a sound, we refer much more to codes established by cinema itself, by television, and narrative-representational arts in general, than to our hypothetical lived experience' (Chion, 1994, p. 107; emphasis original).

The cinema is thus rich with manufactured sounds that by theatrical convention 'ring true' but which, upon scrutiny, are not true at all. At the same time, the modern cinema is fairly loaded with sounds that *are* true, but only to an extent.

In a scene involving an automobile, for example, the sounds of the front door slamming shut, of the engine firing to ignition, and of the tyres screeching as the vehicle leaps into action are probably sounds not created by a 'Foley artist'[2] but generated by an actual door, engine, and set of tyres. It might well be, however, that these sounds were not generated by the car that the film's audience sees. Indeed, the filmmakers might well have experimented with dozens of recordings—collected by themselves or borrowed from commercial sound-effects libraries—before deciding that for their purposes the fictional scene featuring a teenager's hot rod would be most effectively accompanied by a combination of noises emanating from, say, a family sedan, a Rolls Royce, and a Ferrari.

The idea that filmic sounds are 'true', but only to an extent, applies even to the voice of the character who, just before entering the hot rod, says something along the lines of 'Well, I guess I'd better go'. Audiences will not doubt for a moment that the voice belongs to the famous young actor who plays the part, for they will have heard this recognizable voice in the actor's earlier films and during his various television interviews; they will see the actor's lips move precisely as his character utters the words, and if the cinematic illusion is successful they will think not so much that the combination of image and sound is a documentation of an enacted performance but, rather, that it is reality transpiring right before their eyes and ears. Only the actor and others involved in the making of the film will know that the phrase heard by the audience is just one of numerous versions of the same phrase spoken in the controlled environs of a recording studio, with the actor mimicking again and again what he actually said in front of the camera and its companion microphone. By the time the film reaches its audience, the actual on-set sound recording of the actor's voice, low in fidelity and likely cluttered with accidental noise, will long have been discarded; in its place will be a constructed bit of soundtrack, featuring in its foreground a filtered and equalized treatment of one particular take from the 'dubbing' sessions and in its background a collage of pre-recorded or invented sounds—representing the whoosh of wind, perhaps, or the chirping of birds, or the distant whine of an emergency vehicle—likely chosen by technicians but ultimately approved by the director.

All of this artifice—the replacement of a spontaneously spoken phrase with a well-rehearsed version of the same, the substitution of store-bought or custom-made recordings for genuine background noise, the use of tradition-sanctioned and theatrically potent 'fake' sound in lieu of mundane natural sound—is brought into play for the sole purpose of infusing a scene with credibility. Along with the camera's filters and the make-up department's wigs and the actors' acting, the soundtrack contributes significantly to narrative cinema's grand illusion. Regardless of its actual source or substance, most sound in the so-called classical-style film is supposed—by its hearers—to be real.[3]

But what of film sound that, in the hearing, is somehow *more* than real?

\*\*\*\*

This chapter explores affective filmic sound, that is, sound that has the potential to trigger in its listeners emotional responses, or affects, at least as deep as those stirred by a film's extra-diegetic music. Affective sound of the sort discussed here almost never occurs whilst underscore is in progress, for the impact of the one would cancel out the impact of the other. Almost always, affective sound is isolated from everything else that makes up a film's soundtrack; affective sound works best, filmmakers have learned, when it is somehow 'framed'.

In his 1975 article 'The Unattainable Text', Raymond Bellour distinguishes between what he calls 'motivated noise' and 'arbitrary noise'. The former is motivated, even necessitated, by the circumstances of the filmic scene; its purpose is to flavour the scene with a sense of realism, to convince the audience that the sound indeed results from whatever actions figure into the scene's on- or off-screen content. In contrast, 'arbitrary noise' is noise/sound whose presence is similarly warranted by a scene's circumstances but whose treatment is somehow exaggerated or highlighted, for the explicit purpose of furthering the film's narrative (Bellour, 1975, pp. 23–4).

Bellour's terminology is perhaps unfortunate, for there is nothing whimsical or happenstance about the existence in a film of sound of the sort that he labels 'arbitrary'. Such sound is invariably the result of conscious decisions on the part of the filmmaker, and invariably it is sound that resonates far beyond the limits of a simple semiotic index. Like lines of dialogue that mark turning points in a plot, and even more like those visual images whose slow or sudden revelations in effect 'speak volumes', incidents of what Bellour terms 'arbitrary' noise—what I prefer to call affective sound—stand very much apart from the norm of any film's audio content. Relative to the entirety of information that a film offers its audience, affective sound/noise—the sound effect that results in sound affect—is often deeply meaningful.

\*\*\*\*

Consider the cliché-ridden horror film. Such a film bristles with quasi-realistic sounds that indeed contribute much to the film's overall 'feel'; although perhaps more because of the genre than because of the specific needs of the plot, the soundtrack fairly teems with the noise of squeaking doors and whistling winds, of sobs and shouts and moans and groans. Most of these noises relate directly to on-screen images, yet few of them demand attention; most often they blend, along with the extra-diegetic music that likely accompanies their articulations, into the fairly dense blanket of predictably 'edgy' sound in which fans of such films take comfort. Here and there, to be sure, something will emerge from the stereotypical sonic mix for the sake of giving audience members an exaggerated frisson. For the experienced consumer of horror films, however, even the most spine-tingling of these sound effects are really not all that special.

Sound affect, on the other hand, *is* special. Sound affect of the sort that prompts this chapter—as opposed to the cumulative affect roused by all the many sound effects appropriate to a horror movie—is within the course of its film a phenomenon that is singular, or very nearly so. But it is more than its relative scarcity that makes sound affect so powerful. In contrast to the expected emotion-provoking results of a genre film's quotidian sound effects, sound affect as defined here typically strikes filmgoers not just as a sound-related surprise but as a surprise that in some way alters the filmgoers' relationship towards the unfolding on-screen drama. Whereas well-executed sound effects help make a story seem credible, sound affect helps tell the story.

Like most cinematic sound effects, the triggers of narrative-propelling sound affect typically 'ring true'. Two early examples of realistic sounds that contribute much to the flow of their films' narratives can be found in the pre-Hollywood works of Alfred Hitchcock, a director who throughout his long career paid keen attention to the potential of the carefully timed realistic sound effect not just to grab hold of the audience's attention but also to change the audience's perspective vis-à-vis a film's plot.[4]

In Hitchcock's 1935 *The 39 Steps*, the cleaning lady for a London rooming house discovers a dead body in the parlour of one of the tenants; the camera focuses on her shocked face, and as she opens her mouth the audience hears not the expected scream but, instead, the shrill blast of a steam whistle. In the second scene of Hitchcock's 1937 *Young and Innocent*, the collective shriek of seagulls similarly replaces the joint scream of a pair of young women who stumble across the victim of what at first seems to be drowning. The whistle and gull noises are introduced precisely at moments when audience members expect to hear screams, and because human beings in real life have a strong tendency to identify sounds with the presumed sources of those sounds, human beings in the cinema very likely think that they are indeed hearing whistle-like or gull-like screams.[5] Misidentification of the sources of the sounds lasts only for the briefest of moments, of course. A mere split-second or two after the simultaneous close-up showings of open-mouthed women and the loud sounding of whistle/gull noise, just at the point when the observant listener might conclude that the noise in fact results not from female vocal cords but from something else, quick cuts in the imagery reveal the actual sources of the strident noises: in *The 39 Steps*, the source is the locomotive that pulls the train on which the rooming house's tenant, innocent yet fearful of accusation and arrest, is escaping London, and in *Young and Innocent* the source is the flock of seabirds that regularly populate the beach on which the corpse has washed up.

One of the most famous affective sound effects—so famous that its essential on-screen component has become a jargon term for filmmakers keen on injecting tension into their works—is heard slightly more than halfway through

Jacques Tourneur's 1942 *Cat People*. By this time, one of the film's female characters wonders if the peculiar woman who recently married her colleague might be telling the truth; she wonders, seriously, if this young Serbian woman might indeed be the victim of an ancient curse that causes her, when moved by anger or jealousy, to morph into a vicious panther. As she walks home late at night after a perfectly innocent meeting with the Serbian woman's husband, this wary character becomes increasingly anxious about the footsteps of someone who is following her; the footsteps, which the audience knows belong to the Serbian woman, accelerate and then stop; as the female character runs to escape what she fears will be a life-threatening attack, the erratic clicking of her own heels on the pavement is overwhelmed by a growl whose rapid crescendo climaxes in a savage hiss; a heart-stopping moment later, the character (along with the film's audience) *sees* that the growl-hiss emanates not from a panther but from an approaching, and suddenly braking, bus.

For persons new to *Cat People*, *The 39 Steps*, and *Young and Innocent*, the noises described above are quite literally *double entendres*, that is, single 'sound objects' that not just *can* be but in fact *are* heard—and thus understood—in two very different ways. But even persons long familiar with these films will find the noises to be at the very least bracing. And even if the bracing noises were not offered as *double entendres* but simply as unambiguous aural concomitants of a bus and a locomotive and a flock of birds, they would still be both special and meaningful.

The noises would be special because neither their sonic content nor their high volume level exists anywhere else in their films' soundtracks. Val Lewton, the producer of *Cat People* and other low-budget but expertly crafted 'thrillers' that the RKO studio released during the World War II years, told an interviewer that a single film should never have more than just a handful of 'busses', or 'horror spots' (Siegel, 1972, p. 32; Hanson, 2007, p. 44). That astute advice—although not often enough heeded—applies as well to films whose genres have nothing at all to do with horror. As suggested above, the potency of affective cinematic sound seems to be inversely proportional to the frequency with which similar sound, or similar use of sound, occurs in the context of a particular film. The 'bus' in *Cat People* works as well as it does in large part because of the scene's deft editing, but it also works because, in the entirety of the film, there are simply no other sounds that even remotely resemble those of a bus's growling tyres and hissing airbrakes.[6] Likewise for the train whistle and gull cries in Hitchcock's *The 39 Steps* and *Young and Innocent*, and likewise for almost every bit of filmic noise that transcends the category of mere sound effect and serves as a trigger of sound affect.

The noises would be meaningful both because in and of themselves they jolt audience members to attention and, more important, because they signal to audiences that the films' narratives have been ratcheted up to new levels of intensity. In *Cat People*, the bus noise that audiences likely mistake for cat noise is heard well into the story, and it marks the turning point at which the hitherto discounted legend of 'cat people' is first given credibility; in *Young and*

*Innocent*, the gull cries that masquerade as human screams imply that the body stumbled upon by beachcombers is the victim not of an accidental drowning but of murder. The train whistle that in *The 39 Steps* covers the scream of the charwoman goes even further, for the revelation of its actual source illustrates not only that the film's dramatic pitch has been raised but also that the film's theatre of action—and perhaps the pace of action as well—is now much different to the one in which the noise was first articulated.

A paradigmatic example of pace-changing sound affect happens early in Terrence Malick's 1978 *Days of Heaven*. There is no *double entendre* here, just a fierce burst of realistic noise that communicates—as clearly as did any fanfare in an Elizabethan play—that the prelude has ended and the drama has begun. In this case, the film's gentle prelude consists of a two-minute title/credit sequence accompanied by a lush orchestral version of the 'Aquarium' segment of Camille Saint-Saëns's *Carnival of the Animals* and then a nine-second scene, accompanied by tinkly diegetic sounds, that depicts female workers collecting pieces of scrap metal from a stream that flows alongside a World War I-era Chicago steel mill. The mill's hellish interior is where the drama starts, for it is here that the film's hot-headed male protagonist, with fiery furnaces as his backdrop, commits an accidental murder that prompts him, along with his girlfriend and younger sister, to abscond to a farm deep in the American heartland. It is surely remarkable that the mill scene's industrial noise sustains for almost a minute and a half. Had this unrelenting din been sustained for just a fraction of that length, however, the affect likely would have been the same: together with the quick cut from a medium-long shot of the almost pastoral streamside activity to close-ups of sweaty men shovelling coal into furnaces, the sudden onset of oppressively loud noise is quite enough not just to catch the audience's attention but also to announce, boldly and inarguably, that what had come before was just a set-up.[7]

\*\*\*\*

Bold 'announcements' of this sort are not often to be found in the classical-style films that dominated Hollywood and European film production in the 1930s, 1940s, and 1950s. Even in the 1960s, when studio executives pushed hard for 'hip' scores that supposedly reflected the musical tastes of their hoped-for younger audiences, screenplays tended to ease their way into whatever stories they had to tell. Title sequences in films from the 1930s, 1940s, and 1950s typically featured an orchestral score that with an array of stereotyped musical symbols not only straightaway informed audiences as to the plots' geographical and chronological settings but also, with a neat combination of contrasting themes, in effect presented synopses of those plots; title sequences of pop-flavoured films from the 1960s by and large did away with the overture-like title sequence and opted instead for generically upbeat mood music. Regardless of the genre, title sequences throughout this long period of film history most often faded smoothly into the film's action, and thereafter for the film's entire length the action was typically fitted only with sound effects whose sole purpose was to grace the on-screen action with credibility.

That situation started to change in the late 1970s with the introduction into cinemas of the so-called Dolby system of high-fidelity multi-channel sound. In a 1978 article aptly titled 'The Second Coming of Sound', Triumph Films president Charles Schreger offered 'a short list of sound-conscious directors' who were using the new technology to their advantage. His list of course included Malick, and it included as well Robert Altman, Michael Cimino, Francis Ford Coppola, Miloš Forman, Philip Kaufman, Stanley Kubrick, George Lucas, Alan J. Pakula, Ken Russell, Martin Scorsese, Jerzy Skolimowski, and Stephen Spielberg (Schreger, 1978, p. 34). These filmmakers were drawn to Dolby in part because it could add impressive 'realism' to sound effects that audiences for decades had accepted as realistic enough. They were also drawn to Dolby because, significantly, it encouraged them to use realistic sound effects for the purpose of stirring in audiences a wide variety of sound affects.

Sound recorded on magnetic tape by means of Dolby's patented 'noise-reduction' technology was of course cleaner than what had previously been available; the more impressive novelty, however, had to do with the fact that such sound, once transferred to a film's optical soundtrack, could be played to an audience via an array of loudspeakers located both behind the screen and along the theatre's walls. Stereophonic sound had been introduced to American cinema as early as the 1950s, a decade during which Hollywood struggled desperately to win audiences away from the free entertainment available on their new television sets, but the studios' efforts—supported by budgets both high and low—amounted to so many gimmicks whose realization for most theatre owners in the long run proved to be prohibitively expensive, and by the 1960s filmgoers were, once again, content with monophonic sound. With a limited frequency range and a tendency to distort loud or complex noises, the monophonic installations that had been the norm since the introduction of sound to cinema led filmmakers to 'give aural priority to music and the human voice' (Sergi, 2002, p. 108). Films with stereophonic soundtracks were indeed made throughout the 1960s, but most often they were exhibited in theatres equipped only with monophonic sound systems.

Indications that audiences wanted something more were evident early in the 1970s, when market-spurred architectural innovations that led to the establishment of multiple theatres under a single roof led as well to the setting up, in the more prestigious of any cineplex's relatively small auditoriums, of high-quality stereo sound systems. By the middle of the decade—after initial experiments with Dolby in Altman's *Nashville* (1975), Russell's 1975 *Tommy* and *Lisztomania* (both 1975), Michael Anderson's *Logan's Run* (1976), and Frank Pierson's *A Star Is Born* (1976)—it was clear that at least some filmgoers were willing to pay premium prices for movies that supposedly sounded as good as they looked. By the end of the decade, audiences in general had cultivated an appetite for high-quality cinematic sound.

The change in audience demand, and with it the change in filmmakers' attempts to meet that demand, came in 1977, with George Lucas's *Star Wars*. Over initial objections voiced by Twentieth Century-Fox, which had agreed to distribute the independently produced film, writer/director Lucas insisted that *Star Wars* feature four-channel Dolby sound, and theatre managers who wished to exhibit this much-publicized and thus potentially lucrative film had no choice but to spend the $5000 or so that it took to fit their venues with the necessary equipment. The managers were not disappointed. As the legendary sound editor Walter Murch told an interviewer: '*Star Wars* was the can opener that made people realize not only the effect of sound, but the effect that good sound had at the box office' (Murch, in Biskind, 1998, p. 335).

It is possible that some of the filmgoers who flocked to *Star Wars* received three-dimensional and sometimes bone-jarring sound effects, along with a superbly recorded orchestral score by John Williams, simply as an auditory bonus attached to what they expected to be a more or less 'normal' science-fiction/ adventure film. It is likely that for many audience members at the time, however, the situation was the other way round. Notwithstanding whatever entertainment value they might have gleaned from the plot of *Star Wars*, many filmgoers bought tickets—again and again, it seems—primarily because of the opportunity that *Star Wars* gave them to experience technology-enhanced sound effects not just with their ears but with their guts, at visceral levels much deeper than could be plumbed by television or earlier films, or even by real life. Aware that audiences would be willing to pay for physically sensational cinematic sound effects for the same reasons they had long paid for scary rides at amusement parks, studios encouraged both the development of ever-more sophisticated 'surround sound' installations and the production of films that exploited those installations to the fullest.[8]

This profit-driven trend has continued through the present day, and one of its results has been a surfeit of would-be 'blockbuster' films whose sonic content, although certainly sensational, is by and large unremarkable. Like the cliché-ridden horror film of the 1950s and 1960s, the cliché-ridden action film of the Dolby era fairly teems with sound effects of a sort that help define its genre. Instead of monophonic moans and screams, patrons of the modern action film expect (and usually get) a subwoofer-powered stereophonic earful of blazing gunfire and soaring or crashing vehicles. All of this high-decibel sonic stimuli of course contributes to the package of thrills and chills for which the patron, when he or she paid for admission, had bargained. As with the noises in most horror films, however, there is nothing really 'special' about the noises in most action films. Spectacular sound effects in the run-of-the-mill 'blockbuster' are indeed many and varied, but their range of affect—by and large a cumulative affect, and usually from film to film the *same* cumulative affect—tends to be quite limited.

*****

The mill scene that announces the start of the drama in Terrence Malick's *Days of Heaven* would have been impossible without Dolby sound. A monophonic soundtrack might well have contained the very same industrial noises, but in the pre-Dolby days the mix of these noises could not have been played at the same intensely high volume level, and it could not have been presented with the clarity that results from recorded sounds emanating from five discrete sources within the auditorium. More significant, without Dolby the film would not have been able to deliver its powerfully affective *quiet* noises.

Hardly a commercial success—indeed, a box-office flop that many critics berated as an over-produced exercise in directorial self-indulgence—Malick's debut Dolby effort features moments when the audience simply has no choice but to focus not just on the sight but also on the sound of such natural phenomena as wind, insects, and water. The film is certainly not filled with such moments; whether or not he was aware of producer Val Lewton's admonition that a good horror film should never have more than just a handful of 'busses', Malick certainly knew, because he was gifted with common sense, that to saturate a film with detailed attention to sonic minutiae would be to overtax the audience's ears and thus to lessen the audience's ability to attend to whatever story a film might be trying to tell.

Since the story of *Days of Heaven* takes place mostly in America's rural Midwest, objects moved by wind, naturally, figure into many of the scenes. Only in one scene, however, when the three protagonists first arrive at the farm and try to adjust to a world vastly different to the squalid city from which they have escaped, is emphasis placed on visual and sonic wind imagery. Insects and water are also natural components of the film's setting. But only in the introduction to the climactic scene, which involves the farm's crop being destroyed by a swarm of locusts, do the sight and the sound of insects dominate. And only at the start of the conclusive scene—when the male protagonist, after having committed a second murder, is hunted down and killed near his riverside campground—does the film concentrate on the visual and the aural properties of flowing water.

At the beginning of these three scenes, the characteristic noises are presented in such a way as to make them *seem* very, very quiet. But it is only because of an illusion that one hears as quiet the wind's 'gentle' gusts and whooshes, the insects' 'minuscule' chirps and buzzes, and the water's 'delicate' splashes and trickles. The illusion of *pianissimo* is conjured in part by eliminating from these segments all hints of noises that audience members might assume, based on their experience with the real world, to be considerably louder than the sounds of wind, insects, and water that at least for the moment are the focus of the film's attention. In larger part, the illusion of *pianissimo* is conjured by means of clever audio engineering.

Dolby's 'noise-reduction' method allows for the supposedly distortion-free recording of sounds that hitherto had been regarded, perhaps not by scientists but certainly by persons in the sound departments of Hollywood film studios, as impossibly 'tiny'. Typically with left, right, and centre channels at the front of the theatre, with 'surround' channels both at the rear of the theatre and along the side walls, with the low frequencies of everything bolstered by non-directional subwoofers, Dolby's stereophonic playback system allows for the spreading of such closely recorded 'tiny' sounds throughout the auditorium. There is plenty of decibel strength behind each and every one of those sonic phenomena, which of course are not really the sounds of wind or insects or water but, rather, vibrations in the air triggered by the movement of various loudspeaker diaphragms. In the cinema's public physical space, the sounds in fact are quite loud; in the audience members' private psychological spaces—because of their three-dimensional distribution, because of the individual sounds' framing by silence—these very same sounds are likely perceived as the very opposite of loud.

Along with the just-mentioned scenes involving microscopic sonic images of water, insects, and wind, the small handful of truly affective moments in *Days of Heaven* of course includes the mill scene described earlier. It is surely not by mere coincidence that these four instances of potent sound affect occupy the very beginnings of scenes that for the film's central characters represent new environments and which for the film's audience hint at soon-to-be-revealed new dramatic situations. Always combined with quick cuts in the visual imagery, these sudden deliveries of wide-spread arrays of sharp-focused sound announce—not just loudly but clearly—that something important is about to happen.

Comparable ear-catching 'announcements' occur in many films from the early Dolby years. Although the successful blockbusters—*Star Wars*, for example, or Richard Donner's 1978 *Superman*, or Stephen Spielberg's 1981 *Raiders of the Lost Ark*—tend to privilege music-supported 'surround sound' action sequences over everything else, even these films at least occasionally follow their sonically spectacular moments with scene changes that begin with sonic intimacy. More striking is the use of ear-catching sound affect in the period's war movies. Michael Cimino's 1978 *The Deer Hunter* and Francis Ford Coppola's 1979 *Apocalypse Now*, and later Oliver Stone's 1986 *Platoon* and Stanley Kubrick's 1987 *Full Metal Jacket*, remain justifiably famous for their frighteningly loud depictions of combat in Southeast Asia, but they also feature scenes whose intense dramatic content is prefaced by environmental sounds that seem frighteningly 'quiet'.

In all these films, and in Dolby-rich films right up to the present day, the standard trope of affective sound that coincides with changes of scene involves three components. First, in the segment that immediately precedes the sound affect, there is the establishment of a situation whose aural content emanates primarily, as would be the case with a non-Dolby film, from behind the screen and which audience members accept as 'normal'. Then there is the affect-producing shift, realized by the sudden introduction of highlighted three-dimensional sounds and a single quick cut in the visual imagery, into a situation that audiences likely do not immediately recognize and thus have reason to suspect is in some way *not* normal. Finally, as the novelty wears off and as the highlighted sounds both decrease in volume level and gravitate towards the speakers at the front of the cinema, there is a relaxation into this new situation whose relevance to the drama is after a while revealed, primarily by character-based action in combination with screen-centred dialogue and sound effects, and perhaps also by extra-diegetic music.

Just as the trope itself has three components, the trope's central component—the one that so crucially depends on sound—has three requirements. In the first place, the sounds featured at the very moment of transition must be, within the context of the film's narrative, extraordinary (that is to say, they need to be—like the pre-Dolby noises of the bus in *Cat People* and the train whistle in *The 39 Steps*—elements that are not at all common to the film's soundtrack). Secondly, the aural focus on these 'special' sounds must be extreme (in other words, the sounds need to be treated in such a way that, for as long as they last, they fairly dominate the audience's attention). Thirdly, the amount of time allotted to the highlighted sounds must be, relative to the film's overall pace of editing, extended (the 'special' sounds that are abruptly thrust into the foreground need to be kept in that foreground for longer than would be necessary if the filmmakers had sought to create a scene that was not affective but merely credible).

A condensed version of the Dolby era's standard affect-provoking trope is sometimes found in films, most of them quite recent, whose narratives are for the most part straightforwardly linear but which nevertheless feature moments during which audience members are left confused. Usually placed at the film's start or just before a post-climactic dénouement, this alternate trope involves a quick succession of very brief scenes that contain seemingly unrelated audio-video content. Götz Spielmann's 2008 *Revanche*, for example, opens cryptically with a sustained audio-visual focus on a rural pond, its stillness violated first by the loud splash of something thrown into the water and then, after a jump cut reveals both the interior and the exterior of a house, by the even louder noise of a lawnmower. Before its first words of dialogue are softly spoken, Guillermo Arriaga's 2008 *The Burning Plain* opens with a set of three eight-second scenes: a long and quiet view across a Mexican plain of something on fire, a close-up of a burning mobile home introduced with both a jump cut and a blast of flaming roars, a medium view of the dark interior of a motel room introduced by a jump cut and a plunge into near-silence. Just as Nicolas Roeg's pre-Dolby 1973 *Don't Look Now* early in its story depicts the edginess of its grief-wracked central male character by means of the sudden noises of shattering glass, an electric drill, and spilling water, with similarly disorienting affect Agnieszka Holland's 2002 *The Healer* features, as the story moves into its final act and focuses on the love-related distress of the central female character, a series of shots that without transitions and with exaggerated focus on sound show the character sitting alone in her living room, taking a shower, vacuuming, and tentatively typing a letter.

Instead of seizing the audience's attention for the purpose of signalling that the course of the drama is about to undergo an important change, the sharply contrasting affective noises in these sequences of 'short cuts' seem only to alert audiences that what follows—usually filmic drama whose sound effects and editing are in most ways fairly conventional—is worthy of sustained, but not necessarily heightened attention. As with the 'announcement' trope, however, relative to the film's treatment of sound in general, the noises in the 'alert' trope are typically extraordinary, extreme, and extended.

****

All of the meaningfully affective noises described above—no matter how extraordinary they might be in content, no matter how extreme and extended they might be in treatment—are in essence 'realistic'. For that matter, almost all filmic sound effects are 'realistic', for they are intended by their overseeing filmmakers first and foremost to 'ring true' and thus to lend credence to story-telling. Even the most far-fetched of filmic sounds—associated with light sabres, alien spacecraft, genetically engineered dinosaurs, worm-eating troglodytes, and so on—give the impression that they indeed emanate from their on-screen sources. Regardless of the technology that has made them possible, sound effects in the Dolby era as much as in the sound film's formative years typically contribute to, not detract from, their films' believability.

But some filmic sounds are *not* believable, at least not at first listen. To be sure, they are based on sounds from the real world, and necessarily so, for it is their resemblance to mundane sounds that allows them to function as signs, symbols, or signals within the context of a narrative. For dramatic reasons, however, these sounds are in some way enhanced or distorted to the extent that they seem not at all 'real' but, rather, hyper-real or even surreal.

Most filmic sound, and most filmic visual imagery, invites the audience member only to 'observe'—from one detached perspective or another—whatever transpires in a constructed on-screen situation. In marked contrast, the hyper-real or surreal sound fairly demands that the audience member 'hear' a certain sound from a perspective that is not at all detached. Just as the camera technique long known in film-studies parlance as 'POV' forces the film's spectator to momentarily adopt the 'point of view' of one of the film's characters, so the hyper-real or surreal sound forces the film's listener to adopt, for so long as the exaggerated sound occupies the soundtrack, a particular character's 'point of audition'.

Like the 'bus' that figures so powerfully in the films produced by Val Lewton, the POV shot is a gimmick that works best when it is used sparingly. The same applies for the POA sound effect, but in this case the admonition should be stronger. Whereas the POV camera shot requires only that for a moment or two audience members receive (via their eyes) whatever visual information is supposedly being taken in by a particular fictional character, the POA sound effect asks audience members not just to *receive* sonic information (via their ears) but also to *perceive* that information (via their brains) in the same way that it is perceived by the character who at the moment stands in the narrative's foreground.

Because they invite the audience to briefly 'get inside the head' of one of the film's characters, hyper-real and surreal filmic sounds almost by definition are much more 'meaningful' than the quotidian noises that constitute the bulk of any film's soundtrack. Such sounds are usually semiotic indicators of something or other, and what they tend to indicate, because they stand so far apart from their film's sonic norm, is an abnormality on the part of the character with which they are linked. Sometimes the abnormality represented by the enhanced or distorted sound is neurological, like the various forms of deafness that afflict the protagonists in Anand Tucker's 1998 *Hilary and Jackie*, Miloš Forman's 2006 *Goya's Ghosts*, and Alfonso Cuarón's 2006 *Children of Men*. More often, perhaps because its owners are more easily limned, the abnormality is not neurological but psychological.

Sonically illustrated examples of psychological abnormality range from simple anxiety (the exaggerated thump of a suitcase landing on a hotel bed and the squeak of the hotel room's window in the Coen brothers' 1991 *Barton Fink*, the equally exaggerated ticking of a clock as the title character in Baz Luhrmann's 2013 *The Great Gatsby* awaits the arrival of his long-lost love) to heightened sensitivity (the intense sounds of a buzzing insect, of the cracking of the shell of a hard-boiled egg, and of wine being swallowed that represent the POA of a girl who 'hears things that others miss' in Park Chan-Wook's 2013 *Stoker*) to drug-induced delirium (a great many larger-than-life sounds—perhaps too many—that in Danny Boyle's 1996 *Trainspotting* have a darkly comic effect and which work towards quite the opposite goal in Darren Aronofsky's 2000 *Requiem for a Dream*) to genuine mental illness (severe manic-depression in the case of Mike Figgis's 1993 *Mr. Jones*, schizophrenia in the cases of Ron Howard's 2001 *A Beautiful Mind* and Joe Wright's 2009 *The Soloist*, psychosis in the cases of David Fincher's 1999 *Fight Club* and Richard Kelly's 2001 *Donnie Darko*).

In these films and many more, hyper-real or surreal sound effects invite the audience member to experience not what a film's central character 'actually' hears but, rather, what the character 'thinks' he or she hears.[9] Sound-related revelations about the inner workings of a character's mind can be powerfully affective, but they are theatrically effective only when used sparingly.

\*\*\*\*

The real-life jangling of my wind-up alarm clock 'means' that the clock is functioning properly, but it also 'means' that it is time for me to get out of bed. In a filmic context, this noise could easily have nothing more than those two very basic meanings. Treated as just another 'realistic' sound in a constructed soundtrack that contains many such sounds, the ringing could 'mean' simply that a fictitious alarm has been triggered and has served as wake-up call for the fictitious character in whose room the fictitious clock resides.

If the ringing of the fictional alarm were unusually loud, however, and if it started immediately after a jump cut from a shot showing a person smashing the window of a parked automobile, the sound could be a momentarily puzzling *double entendre*, a noise that members of the film audience might 'hear' as coming from the car's security device in the split-second before they realized that in 'fact' the noise was coming just from a bedroom clock. If the clock's very loud ringing interrupted a lengthy filmic scene whose sonic components up to this point consisted only of the quietest imaginable nocturnal noises, it could well be an 'announcement' of an imminent and significant change, not of the film's scenery but of the course of its dramatic flow. If the alarm sounded loudly but briefly as part of a sequence of jump-cut shots accompanied by noises of starkly contrasting volume levels, the sequence in itself could be a discomforting 'alert' that the narrative was about to take a turn for the serious. If the sound of the ringing were wrapped in reverberation, or somehow muffled or muted, or drastically slowed down, it could be a symbol for the clock owner's somehow disturbed state of mind.

In most films, the ring of a fictitious alarm clock—or the bark of a dog, or the clink of wine glasses—would likely be an unremarkable noise, one familiar element amongst many that together constitute a sonic *mise en scène* designed primarily to make its action and dialogue seem credible. But treated in a way that makes it somehow stand apart from the film's norm, the ring or the bark or the clink can be something quite remarkable.

Thrust even for a moment into the equivalent of the sonic spotlight, what might have been just a sound effect can trigger a sound affect; instead of simply blending into the background and therefore having little meaning beyond the mere fact of its existence, the affect-producing sound effect—the filmic noise—can be, indeed, quite meaningful.

## Notes

1. For details on sound effects in 'silent' films, see, for example, Bottomore (1999).
2. A 'Foley artist' is a person who by various (usually low-budget) means generates sounds that, when heard on a film soundtrack, are likely to taken by the audience for the 'real thing'. The term is named after Jack Foley, a 'sound man' first for radio and then for the Hollywood studios. For details on Foley's career and contributions, see the first several chapters of Ament (2009).
3. Cultivated since the late 1930s in Hollywood and elsewhere, the classical-style film is one in which virtually everything that is presented to the member of the audience—acting, dialogue, sets and costumes, accompanying music, and—importantly—sound effects—is designed to make clear, and not obscure, the film's narrative. For a thorough definition, see the entry on 'classic Hollywood cinema/classic narrative cinema/classical narrative cinema' in Hayward (2000, pp. 64–8).
4. For extensive commentary on Hitchcock and his attitudes on sound effects, see, for example, Weis (1982); Truffaut (1984); Sullivan (2006); Schroeder (2012).
5. Pierre Schaeffer, the French composer/theorist who in the years following World War II explored the idea of *musique concrète*, used the term 'causal listening' to describe the mode of listening in which human beings, by instinct, connect sounds with their likely causes. See Chion (1994, pp. 25–8, 32–3).
6. After the 'bus' that features the eponymous vehicle, *Cat People* features only three more 'horror spots'. These occur when the nervous female character fears that she might be set upon whilst relaxing in her apartment building's swimming pool, when she and her married colleague worry that the kitten that inhabits their office might actually be a vicious beast, and when, near the film's end, a panther that may (or may not) be the transformed Serbian woman attacks and kills a ne'er-do-well psychiatrist. These 'horror spots' utilize powerfully affective sound effects, but in all cases the sounds are unique to relevant scenes.
7. For more on the 'affective' qualities of this scene and others in *Days of Heaven*, see Wierzbicki (2003).
8. For more on the intimate relationship between Dolby sound and the box office, see Sergi (2004) and Kerins (2011).
9. Hyper-real or surreal sound effects, perhaps not surprisingly, occur most often not just in films whose central characters experience emotional/psychological distress but also in films that in some way violate the traditional norms of linear narrative. For more on such films, see Booker (2007) and Buckland (2009).

# REFERENCES

Ament, V.T. (2009) *The Foley Grail: The Arts of Performing Sound for Film, Games, and Animation* (Abingdon: Focal Press, 2009).

Bellour, R. (1975) 'The Unattainable Text', *Screen*, Vol. 16, No. 3, 19–27.

Biskind, P. (1998) *Easy Riders, Raging Bulls: How the Sex-Drugs-and-Rock 'n' Roll Generation Saved Hollywood* (New York: Simon & Schuster).

Booker, K. (2007) *Postmodern Hollywood: What's New in Film and Why It Makes Us Feel So Strange* (Westport, Ct.: Praeger).

Bottomore, S. (1999) 'An International Survey of Sound Effects in Early Cinema', *Film History* Vol. 11, No. 4, 485–98.

Buckland, W. (ed.) (2009) *Puzzle Films: Complex Storytelling in Contemporary Cinema* (Oxford: Blackwell).

Chion, M. (1994) *Audio-Vision: Sound on Screen*, trans. Claudia Gorbman (New York: Columbia University Press).

Hanson H. (2007) 'Sound Affects: Post-production Sound, Soundscapes and Sound Design in Hollywood's Studio Era', *Music, Sound, and the Moving Image*, Vol. 1, No. 1, 27–49.

Hayward, S. (2000) *Cinema Studies: The Key Concepts* (New York and London: Routledge).

Heller, L.M. and L. Wolf (2002) 'When Sound Effects Are Better than the Real Thing', *Journal of the Acoustical Society of America*, Vol. 111. No. 5, 23–39.

Kerins, M. (2011) *Beyond Dolby (Stereo): Cinema in the Digital Sound Age* (Bloomington: Indiana University Press).

Schreger, C. (1978) 'The Second Coming of Sound', *Film Comment*, Vol. 14, No. 5, 34–37.

Schroeder, D. (2012) *Hitchcock's Ear: Music and the Director's Art* (New York and London: Continuum).

G. Sergi (2002) 'A Cry in the Dark: The Role of Post-Classical Film Sound' in G. Turner (ed.) *The Film Cultures Reader* (New York and London: Routledge), 107–14.

Sergi, G. (2004) *The Dolby Era: Film Sound in Contemporary Hollywood* (Manchester: Manchester University Press).

Siegel, J. (1972) *Val Lewton: The Reality of Terror* (London: British Film Institute).

Sullivan, J. (2006) *Hitchcock's Music* (New Haven: Yale University Press).

Tallis R. (1985) 'The Realistic Novel versus the Cinema', *Critical Quarterly*, Vol. 27, No. 2, 57–65.

Truffaut, F. (1984) *Hitchcock* (New York: Simon & Schuster).

Weis, E. (1982) *The Silent Scream: Alfred Hitchcock's Sound Track* (Rutherford, NJ: Farleigh Dickinson University Press).

Wierzbicki, J. (2003) 'Sound as Music in the Films of Terrence Malick' in H. Patterson (ed.) *The Cinema of Terrence Malick: Poetic Visions of America* (London: Wallflower Press), 111–22.

CHAPTER 12

# Listening to Violence: Point-of-Audition Sound, Aural Interpellation, and the Rupture of Hearing

*Tony Grajeda*

In the far-flung global landscape of *Babel* (Alejandro González Iñárritu, 2006), with its multiple narrative threads entwined and traversing some three continents, the segments in Japan are distinguished in particular by the film's use of sound in staging its narrative concerns. Within the noisy, shimmering environment of Tokyo, a teenage girl named Chieko (Rinko Kikuchi) makes her way through city life seemingly by sight alone, since she and her friends attend a school, as we learn from the subtitles, for deaf students. For this multilingual film, as the title itself implies, sign language is yet one more form of communication that as often as not inhibits interaction and understanding. In a sequence that finds Chieko and her friends partying with some boys, boys who belong to the wider society of verbal speech and hearing, a nightclub scene serves to exacerbate the breach already separating these communities. A series of medium close-up shots contribute to an initial sense of togetherness as the group of teenagers join the crush of bodies on the dance floor, swathed in a maelstrom of sight and sound: shards of light reflected off a rotating disco ball, impossibly rapid strobe lights, pulsing, deafening music. To this point, the film's diegetic sound has remained more or less objective rather than subjective, offering a generalized aural perspective over favouring that of any particular character. Without warning, however, the dance music pounding away with a shot of Chieko in the frame is abruptly severed by dead silence, cut with a simultaneous matching shot from Chieko's point-of-view, a view captivated by swirling overhead lights, club land smoke, and the exuberant faces of friends and strangers crowded on the dance floor. The unexpected shock of silence, the film's startling attention to sound and its absence, is repeated a few

T. Grajeda
University of Central Florida, USA

© The Editor(s) (if applicable) and The Author(s) 2016
L. Greene, D. Kulezic-Wilson (eds.), *The Palgrave Handbook of Sound Design and Music in Screen Media*, DOI 10.1057/978-1-137-51680-0_12

more times, allowing the spectator to make the connection: a basically neutral shot accompanied by loud music cuts to Chieko's perspective and near silence, and then back again. These altogether jarring alternations between sound and silence—a kind of whiplash effect in which each sonic event attaches to an aural perspective—are mostly in sync with visual perspective, forcing the audience to careen between what Chieko hears and what she can't hear. And what she does presumably hear, the absence of sound, effectively fuels her growing sense of separation and alienation.

Although *Babel*'s thematics of global interconnectedness and local disconnection of emotional attachment and detachment, of communication and miscommunication, have been well established by this juncture in its narrative, the Tokyo 'story' is perhaps the most striking realization of *hearing* that struggle, where the desire for communication and the inability to achieve it has been made audible.

The rendering of sound here in *Babel* instantiates one of the key concepts in film sound theory—that of 'point-of-audition sound'. This particular sound design practice has been taken up by a handful of scholars since at least the early 1990s and formulated as one of the primary but overlooked ways in which film generates spectatorial identification, a strategy reached by aligning the audience with a particular auditor in the filmic text. As film scholar Rick Altman explains, 'point-of-audition sound always has the effect of luring the listener into the diegesis not at the point of enunciation of the sound, but at the point of its audition', adding, 'We are asked not to hear, but to identify with someone who will hear for us' (1992, p. 60). Along the same lines, filmmaker and sound theorist Michel Chion, in the first of his books to be translated into English, *Audio-Vision: Sound on Screen*, also emphasizes the subjective aspect of such sound practices, asking, 'which character, at a given moment of the story, is (apparently) hearing what I hear?' (1994, p. 90). But despite the widespread convention of using point-of-view shots to forge subjectivity visually, what, we might ask, happens in films that confuse the 'all-hearing ear' of the microphone and more subjective point-of-audition events? Against the common but largely unexamined impression that point-of-view always aligns with point-of-audition, how do we read those instances when a break between seeing and hearing has taken place? Is it always clear from whose perspective we are being asked to identify with as a listener? Who, indeed, is supposed to be hearing?

This chapter takes up the relation between sound design and subject positioning by exploring cinematic moments that dramatically stage point-of-audition sound, focusing in particular on a range of films that ask us to listen to the sound of violence. These occasions when sound draws attention to itself—bursting forth in such volume as to jolt us, or submerging us in near silence, or subjecting us to the kind of noise said to simulate damaged hearing—provide an opportunity to listen closely to film sound as it invites us, as Altman suggests, 'to identify with someone who will hear for us' (1992, p. 60), even if such a hearing itself tests the limits of aural interpellation. In such films as *Saving Private Ryan* (Steven Spielberg, 1998), *Three Kings* (David O. Russell, 1999), *The Pianist*

(Roman Polanski, 2002), *There Will Be Blood* (Paul Thomas Anderson, 2008), *Children of Men* (Alfonso Cuarón, 2006), and *Cop Land* (James Mangold, 1997), point-of-audition sound is foregrounded through moments of trauma, when the sound of violence poses a physical threat to a body, and where hearing faces its own annihilation. By considering those moments when subjectivity through sound is experienced as a privileged position, one geared not towards clarity and intelligibility but rather confusion and pain—in short, as a form of rupture—I want to argue that listening to violence on screen may be heard most clearly, ironically enough, precisely at the moment when hearing itself is endangered—both within the frame for characters suffering from their loss of hearing and beyond to an audience asked to experience that very same (temporary) loss.

In considering point-of-audition sound in relation to the art and science of sound design, it should be stated from the outset that the discussion to follow is less concerned with the production process in creating a film's sound design and more concerned with the reception of sound. My interest here in listening to cinema is oriented by sound theory attentive to the ways in which sonic effects shape affective relations, identification mechanisms, and mediated subjectivity.[1] As such, I will engage with the relevant scholarship as it informs my analysis. One such scholar, as already noted, is Rick Altman, who provides a non-specialist's definition of our topic at hand: 'point of audition sound is identified by its volume, reverb level, and other characteristics as representing sound as it would be heard from a point within the diegesis, normally by a specific character or characters'. This 'impression of auditory perspective' effectively 'locates us', he writes, 'in a very specific place—the body of the character who hears for us' (1992, p. 60). In this way the spectator is interpellated as an 'internal auditor', what James Lastra calls an 'embodied perceiver' within the filmic text (2000, p. 141).

One of the more high profile examples of point-of-audition sound can be found in the opening D-Day sequence in *Saving Private Ryan*. Following the framing prologue of an elderly James Ryan (Harrison Young) in the present visiting the Normandy American cemetery, at the end of which an extreme close-up on his eyes lingers long enough to insinuate that his recollection will take us back to June 1944, the film begins in earnest. Accordingly, one of the very first shots, a close-up on a pair of hands shaking uncontrollably, hands as the camera reveals that belong to Captain Miller (Tom Hanks), initiates a process of identification, which will soon enough meet its acoustic equivalent. The ensuing chaos of the storming at Omaha Beach is rendered through a series of quick shots, often taken from an angle at ground level along the beachhead or bobbing on the surface of the water, as a number of amphibious military vehicles transporting US forces attempt to withstand the incessant bombardment and make it to shore. The lack of any significant establishing shots magnifies the pandemonium of the landing, as does the overwhelming noise of warfare, with the sound of bombs that seem to drop from out of nowhere producing a sense of fear rooted more in what could be heard than could be seen.[2] The hand-held, nearly cinema verité-like camerawork during this sequence places the audience in the midst of the battle, with the composition staged from among the troops dominated by medium close-up shots and, as Shaun Farley notes, a 'constricted field of vision'.[3] This disorienting visual landscape is further compounded by a cacophony of sounds—bombs exploding, relentless gunfire (especially machine gun noise), bullets ricocheting off metal or rifling past the frame (indicated by a rapid Doppler effect that is also frightfully close), and, of course, the yelling and screaming of troops. Both sight and sound, then, immerse us in the action, which is nothing if not an unbearable stream of gruesome images and sonic terror—a harrowing confrontation with what happens to bodies in warfare, the deliberate intent of which is, in Elaine Scarry's words, 'to alter (to burn, to blast, to shell, to cut) human tissue' (1985, p. 64). As Miller's unit attempts to disembark, the first few rows of troops in the landing craft are mercilessly cut down by machine gunfire. Miller is shown shouting to whoever is left to jump overboard. The cut to the next shot is also a cut to a drastically different sound design, shifting from mostly diegetic sound to more specific point-of-audition, and henceforth becoming roughly associated with Miller's perspective.

As he struggles underwater while helplessly watching a number of his comrades get shot in the water, the sea turning a sickly red, Miller's view is matched by what can only be termed underwater sound, where the sounds of warfare from above the water are suddenly smothered by the sea, nearly but not quite dampered by the ambient sound of what it's like to hear under water. Echoing the oscillation of hearing in *Babel*, the effect here is heightened by Miller bobbing up to the surface, with the sound returning to full force and volume, and then back underwater, with the sound submerged once more, reduced to a low hum that mimics water pressure on the eardrums.

As Miller staggers to shore, bearing witness to still further carnage, a bomb lands within such proximity that the deafening sound immediately drops out, suddenly signalling that Miller's hearing has been damaged, which also means that we are now hearing (or not hearing) what the character ostensibly is experiencing. Although the underwater shots provided a spatial sense of point-of-audition, the auditory perspective now becomes unmistakably tied to the stunned and wounded Miller (indicated by the sight of bleeding from his ears). This moment of subjective point-of-audition, unlike what occurred in *Babel*, could be said to approximate what happens to hearing when it has been subjected to the extreme violence of ear-splitting sound; the impact not only sutures the spectator-auditor to a specific figure on screen but also imposes on us the sonic effect of dreadfully losing one's own hearing. The camerawork here cements the process of identification, with several hand-held shots from Miller's point-of-view further positioning us *as* Miller, even if the film resorts to slow-motion footage that heightens as it mitigates the realist imperative.

This arresting inscription of subjective point-of-audition sound lasts for less than a minute, but it's long enough to secure an affective and sensorial connection between audience and character through sound, a connection seized by a traumatic experience—one shattering the so-called fourth wall—binded by a phenomenologically shared sense of damaged hearing. The moment passes with a close-up shot of a fellow soldier screaming at Miller (still in slow motion), who seems to just as suddenly snap out of his near-catatonic state, with the auditory field quickly returning to full volume and the film itself resuming the speed of real time. The battle thus continues, with Miller at the centre of the storm, so to speak, entirely immersed in the violence and, in keeping with the notion of the sonorous envelop, insolubly a part of it. And having locked identification through an economy of affect and sensory assault, the film's palette of sound returns to mostly diegetic sound.

What is curious, finally, about this portion of *Saving Private Ryan*'s sound design is the degree to which it cuts against the grain of the film's putative message. Relying on a time-worn convention of classical narrative cinema, which in its standardized form requires a 'protagonist' with whom an audience is beckoned to take the unfolding journey, *Saving Private Ryan* offers a paradoxical if not contradictory experience. The text's ideal of self-sacrifice to which the narrative leads is realized at the film's end by the ego-centred drive of its narrative structure. That is to say, the lesson of selflessness is delivered by the formal mechanism of individuality, as identification is engendered through the construction of cinematic building blocks of both a point-of-view field of vision and an auditory field of point-of-audition sound.

A less familiar but no less intriguing example of point-of-audition sound occurs near the end of the Persian Gulf War film *Three Kings*, when sniper fire suddenly hits US soldier Troy Barlow (Mark Wahlberg), dropping him to the ground; just as suddenly the sound drops out. The camera then assumes his perspective, now looking up at Chief Elgin (Ice Cube), who can faintly be heard saying, 'Can you breath?'. With the sound distinctly muffled, what can be heard is Barlow struggling for breath, accompanied only by the 'internal' sound of his heartbeat and the muted voices of his comrades. Until his hearing returns, the film's audience is momentarily placed in the position of this particular character through sound, presumably hearing as he does. Yet we are sutured not merely as an 'internal auditor' in the text but moreover as an 'interiorized' one—listening from within a damaged body that sounds as if it's taking its last breath.

What is also compelling about this scene is the confusion or elision of two forms of point-of-audition sound that Chion outlines in *Audio-Vision* and elsewhere, when he draws a distinction between a spatial designation and a subjective one. For Chion, a spatial sense of point-of-audition sound arises from a rather specific 'point in the space represented on the screen or on the soundtrack', very often a 'camera's position rather than a character's' (1994, p. 90). A subjective sense of such sound-work on the other hand, as Chion describes it in his *Film, A Sound Art*, presents 'a character through whose ears it is suggested that we are hearing a sound' (2009, p. 485).

The slippage between the spatial and the subjective point-of-audition perspectives enacted in *Three Kings* intimates a somewhat more complicated relationship with regard to subject positioning, for as spectator-auditors we are asked to simultaneously identify as and with a character (which also happened more briefly in the second point-of-audition event in *Saving Private Ryan*, as my reading conveyed). This dual movement of hearing both from within a body and outside its somatic limits, across the space it inhabits, is further overdetermined by a third point-of-view: an internal graphic shot of the character's chest cavity as his lungs fill with fluid from the bullet wound. The camerawork here offers then three perspectives: Barlow's point-of-view, those surrounding him as they attend to his wound, and the internal view of his bodily organs. Even as the image-track jumps across all three perspectives, the point-of-audition remains linked to Barlow's perspective, a rather impossible auditory experience taking in both spatial and subjective modes of listening, one that in effect sunders the aural equivalent of the point-of-view shot.[4]

While war movies elicit a certain kind of hearing, where audiences expect to brace themselves for the sound of violence, other genres and cinematic experiences provide a somewhat less predictable form of listening. In both *Saving Private Ryan* and *Three Kings*, point-of-audition events are mobilized for affective relations between audiences and figures within the film's narrative space. Other films, such as *The Pianist*, *There Will Be Blood*, and *Children of Men*, have incorporated point-of-audition sound to function *within* the narrative itself, with the more extreme aural moments where the sense of hearing is ruptured, as we will find, contributing to character development or advancing the plot, even as such ruptures also work to interpellate us as auditor-spectators.

Less a war movie than a historical drama set during war time, *The Pianist* is based on the true-life story of famed Polish-Jewish pianist and composer Wladyslaw Szpilman (Adrien Brody), who against all odds survived the Nazi occupation of Poland in World War II. Given its bio-pic bearings, both diegetic and non-diegetic music are featured prominently, yet its non-musical elements merit attention as well.

About mid-way through the film, during the Warsaw ghetto uprising sequence, Szpilman is depicted as more a witness to than a participant of the armed resistance by Polish partisans, often framed as watching events unfold on the street below from an upstairs apartment window. When Nazi soldiers surround the building where he has been hiding, threatening to blow it up, Szpilman discovers he is trapped in the apartment, becoming visibly agitated with nowhere to run. Frantically trying to open the door, he pauses upon hearing the sound of a tank's motor rumbling and, more ominously, the hydraulic whirring sound of its gun turret. Moving back to the window overlooking the street, a close-up on Szpilman's face captures the look of fear, as the tank fires its artillery hitting the apartment building not far from Szpilman's window. He scrambles back to the door in a futile attempt to escape, just as a second explosion blows out most of a wall in the apartment. The ear-shattering sound of the explosion does just that: the diegetic sound immediately disappears, replaced by the distinct sound of high-frequency ringing, as the audience is thrust into Szpilman's 'head-space'. The auditory sensation at this moment feels as if all the sound has been sucked out of the narrative (and theatrical) space, with the distinct sound of tinnitus rushing in to fill the void. A shot of the smoke-choked room cuts to Szpilman, hand held to his right ear, stumbling away from the door and towards the massive hole in the wall. With the high-pitched squeal piercing the air, we also hear more explosions, now muffled and thus sounding deceptively distant, along with the faint sound of feet stumbling over rubble, as Szpilman makes his way through the hole and into the adjoining room. More disturbing still is the sound of coughing, which is muffled like the other diegetic, *external* sounds (artillery fire, gun turret, falling debris), in contradistinction to the sound of tinnitus which seems *internal*, dominating the sound design here in both volume and the spatial characteristics of 'close-up sound'. Another explosion furnishes the opportunity to accentuate (rather unrealistically) the quick recovery in Szpilman's hearing, as the muffled sound is swiftly lifted, returning to full frequency and volume. The subtle inclusion of Szpilman coughing, sounding external to him and at some distance, has the alarming effect of being physiologically separated from his own body, to which the audience had just been attached aurally. Not unlike what happens in *Three Kings*, we share Szpilman's audible experience in our conjoined rupture of hearing, even if we seem located both inside his body and outside it at once.

Since the audience had been positioned all along to identify with the pianist, the focal point from the beginning, the subjective point-of-audition patch of Szpilman's loss of hearing (which lasts for about a half a minute) only enhances what had already been secured by narrative structure. But the sound of damaged hearing has thematic resonance, given that the pianist needs his faculty of hearing not only to play, of course, but also to survive, to listen for danger. In other words, the rupture in hearing suffered by the character and shared by the spectator-auditor contributes to the affective work of the film, amplifying the pathos of the pianist dependent on the ability to hear for both his livelihood and his very survival.

Unlike the use of point-of-audition sound in *The Pianist*, which services the narrative development of the title character, the narrative deployment of point-of-audition in *There Will Be Blood*, at least in its most extreme moments, fastens instead to a secondary character as a way to shed light, so to speak, on one of the film's two principal leads. For my purposes here, the relationship between Daniel Plainview (Daniel Day-Lewis) and his adopted son H.W. (Dillon Freasier) is of primary interest, since it is the son who, in suffering from noise-induced hearing loss, will demand audible focus and not the father, who otherwise commands narrative centrality along with his antagonist and dialectical other, the preacher Eli Sunday (Paul Dano).

In order to recognize how point-of-audition sound works to complicate that filial relationship, though, it bears emphasizing that from the very beginning of the story of Plainview, the self-described 'oil man', he has been irredeemably marked by greed, deceit, and single-minded self-interest. Indeed, Plainview is even given to instrumentalizing his relationship to H.W., who essentially functions as yet one more means to an end. Although Plainview appears to adopt H.W. out of a passing sense of guilt, following the industrial accident of the boy's father (who was part of Plainview's work crew), the narrative barely hesitates in depicting how the surrogate father uses the boy. In his pitches to potential investors or in his dealings with landowners whose property he wishes to lease for drilling, Plainview is prone to speak of himself as one of the people—'I'm a family man, I run a family business'—and that he works alongside H.W.—'my son and my partner'—who is supplied with an origin story founded upon Plainview's lie that the boy's mother died in childbirth. 'It's just me and my son now', he says to those who inquire. Therefore, when another industrial accident occurs, this time wounding the adopted son, a begrudging sense of sympathy slides to Plainview, whose contemptible disposition had by then built up instead a desire for cosmic justice.

The sequence in question begins when an oil well blows up, hurling young H.W., who had been nearby watching the work, off a wooden structure bracing the oil derrick. His body violently landing with a thud is concurrent with the diegetic sound suddenly stifled, as the image-track cuts to a medium close-up of H.W. curled up with hands over his ears. The shot quickly cuts to Daniel rushing to his fallen son, with the roar of the gushing oil well just as suddenly overwhelming the momentary silence. As one of the workers reaches H.W., the diegetic sound is once again stifled, although the accompanying shot frames the boy's wounded body—a clear case of mis-aligning point-of-view and point-of-audition, exemplifying a disjuncture between seeing and hearing. With the sound quickly resuming, now dominated by a menacing, percussive score (the film's music is composed by Radiohead's Jonny Greenwood), Daniel is shown tending to his son, who lies on a floor in what looks like a state of shock. A close-up on his oil-smeared face, with his father kneeling over him, is once more cut to relative silence. The camera then briefly switches to H.W.'s point-of-view, now staring at a close-up on Daniel's face, framed as shouting but without any sound, his voice altogether muted as the point-of-audition here aligns with H.W.'s perspective.

In a subsequent scene, which began with a physician checking the boy's ears and confirming the damage, we find Daniel and his son alone together in a barren room. A shot of H.W. lying on a bed, with Daniel sitting next to him, is accompanied by the same scored music that had propelled the scenes of the accident. Daniel is shown speaking to his son but again the voice issues only silence. We are here placed once more in H.W.'s partial point-of-audition, subjected to the condition of deafness, which means the spectator-auditor is now inhabiting both the narrative space of the film and that which lurks outside it, since the non-diegetic music, in a classic illustration of continuity editing, has been flowing throughout this scene. But then the music abruptly ends, leaving the scene in what feels like total silence. A shot of Daniel still moving his lips—as if he could be heard but blithely unaware of being denied a listener, for neither the son nor the audience can hear a word—only heightens the effect that we are for the moment sharing H.W.'s deafness.

While the rest of the film offers few more such subjective point-of-audition events from the son's aural perspective, his deafness still figures in the narrative entanglements, for H.W.'s tragic disability, the consequence in no small measure of Plainview's insatiable greed, nonetheless garners a sense of pity as it cloaks him in the kind of victimization too often associated with the deaf community. Meanwhile, the sympathy that at least temporarily had accrued to the father, shown at one point cradling his wounded son and humming (perhaps futilely) a song to comfort him, soon enough evaporates. In the war waged between Plainview and Eli Sunday, the unrepentant capitalist and the religious charlatan, H.W. is instrumentalized all over again, this time as Plainview's proof that the evangelical preacher is a hoax, much as the audience is made to wish for at least one undeserving miracle.

Although rather fleeting and perhaps even forgotten eventually by the film's audience, the choice use of subjective point-of-audition in *There Will Be Blood* worked to distance us from Daniel Plainview and his megalomaniacal trajectory. Moving in the opposite direction, the narrative emplotment of point-of-audition sound in *Children of Men*, however, works to not only stitch the spectator-auditor into the text, attaching us to the lead figure aurally; it also transforms that figure, nudging him from a character holding events at a distance to one utterly moved to action.

The dramatic use of sound in *Children of Men* sets its narrative in motion, which takes place in a dystopian future when the blight on humanity is infertility. The opening scene frames a crowd of people in a London coffee shop, faces glued to the televised report of the death of Baby Diego who, at the age of 18, is reported to have been 'the youngest person on the planet'. The only patron to appear indifferent to the news, Theo (Clive Owen), grabs his coffee and leaves the shop. The next shot frames Theo walking down a busy city street, the din of traffic crowding the soundtrack. Out of nowhere a massive explosion tears out a side of a building, barely missing Theo who is within reach of flying debris. The boom of the blast and its nearly instantaneous aural aftermath—rubble crashing, glass breaking, people screaming—is just as quickly overtaken by an unanticipated form of stillness, a backdrop of quiet against which can be heard the piercing sound of high-pitched ringing—a shattering of both eardrum and audible stillness. No sooner do we recognize the sound of damaged hearing than the image-track fades to black, with the title of the film filling the screen as the ringing continues, acting as a sound bridge to the next scene, Theo entering his place of work at the Ministry of Energy. Although the tone of tinnitus soon dissipates, retreating into a mix of diegetic sound and non-diegetic scoring, Theo's ruptured hearing comes up a few more times in dialogue, including as a joke with an old friend. Yet in a key sequence that initiates Theo's reluctant involvement in the plot, escorting the world's only known pregnant woman to safety, sound once again plays more than a bit part.

The turn of events begins when Theo is kidnapped by a rebel group fighting the government. He is brought to a large, cavernous space (which looks like an abandoned train station) and is confronted by Julian (Julianne Moore), his estranged wife and now a leader of the rebels. After Theo refuses to help their cause, he is dragged back to a waiting vehicle. This physical separation between

Theo and Julian is dramatized by the sound design. As Theo is dragged away, Julian's voice, which had dominated the auditory mise-en-scene in volume and reverberating throughout the empty building, begins to diminish in proportion to her relation to the frame; she remains stationary within the shot, as the camera tracks back and away from her. The audience is placed visually and aurally into Theo's position, as we hear Julian's voice recede while gaining more echo, in keeping with the growing separation in audio-visual space. As her final words trail off, followed by the return of the high-pitched tone of tinnitus, we hear her say: 'You know that ringing in your ears? That "eeeeeee…"? That's the sound of the ear cells dying, like their swan song. Once it's gone you'll never hear that frequency again. Enjoy it while it lasts'.

Theo soon enough agrees to help the rebels, but for a price, still too cynical to care about much of anything. But a transformation finally takes place when the car that carries Theo, Julian, the pregnant refugee girl Kee, and two other rebels is attacked by a marauding gang. In the chaos of trying to escape the mob, Julian is fatally shot through the windshield. And what had been an unyielding blare of sounds—mob yelling, car engine racing, gun shots, shattering glass, screaming—is quickly quelled, dimly heard in the background as the by-now familiar sound of tinnitus returns once more. The horrendous violence here—Julian shot through the throat and Theo desperately trying to stop the bleeding—seems to shake him into finally being moved by more than selfish reasons, thereafter committed to the cause. Thus, the narrative development of the character essentially can be heard as much as seen, shared by an audience asked to inhabit the auditory space of Theo's ruptured hearing.

Where subjective point-of-audition sound in *Saving Private Ryan* and *Three Kings* primarily worked in terms of aural interpellation, suturing character and spectator-auditor through a coextensive experience of violence against our faculty of hearing, and where point-of-audition sound functioned within the narratives of *The Pianist, There Will Be Blood,* and *Children of Men,* acting as a crucial element in motivating character development, the final film under consideration here offers a mix of both strategies in sound design. Out of all these films, perhaps the most elaborate treatment of film sound and subject positioning takes place in *Cop Land*, an otherwise fairly standard genre film about corrupt police in New York City and their small town refuge across the river in New Jersey.

Sylvester Stallone plays Sheriff Freddy Heflin who, according to an opening voice-over, is a 'wanna-be who couldn't get on the force on account of his bad ear', having suffered partial loss of his hearing as a result of an incident, we learn later in the narrative, when a teenaged Freddy rescues a girl whose car had veered off a bridge and into the river below. This hearing impairment is treated as a disability in the story—what separates him from the 'real' cops—and is continuously referenced throughout. One scene even opens with a close-up shot of a record player and turntable, as a Bruce Springsteen song plays diegetically. The woman Freddy saved years earlier, and for whom he still pines, says, 'You know, you can get this on CD, in stereo'. To which he responds, 'It wouldn't matter to me'. Her reply: 'Oh yeah, right'. Since the soundtrack here maintains its uniform acoustic dimensions in volume, scale, frequency, and fidelity (i.e., it *doesn't* simulate monophonic sound), the point-of-audition ostensibly remains spatial rather than subjective.

But in a key sequence near the end of the film when Freddy is about to uncover the network of corruption running his town, the already hearing-impaired sheriff suffers considerable loss of the rest of his hearing when the eardrum of his 'good' ear gets damaged by a close-range gunshot. With some members of the police force who are on the take, as they say, assaulting Freddy, one of the cops places his revolver against Freddy's head and says, 'This is the good ear, right?' before firing a round. The crack of the gun shot and the scene of brutal violence triggers a shift in the film's sound design, where diegetic audible elements—car doors slamming, tyres squealing, Freddy writhing in agony on the ground—slowly but assuredly fade to quiet, a sparse musical score filling in the 'blank space' left by the world of the film going mute. The incident also precipitates the film shifting to slow motion, with a shot of Freddy clutching his bloodied ear, staggering down the street, and giving chase on foot after his assailants. A close-up on Freddy, his face contorted in pain, is set at first to relative silence, with the score diminishing in volume, but the audible space becomes noticeably shot through with high-frequency ringing. We have now assumed Freddy's point-of-audition, enveloped in all but the inescapable range of a damaged eardrum. As Freddy rambles towards the home of one of the corrupt cops, the piercing tone slowly ebbs, giving way to the film's score, which plays low in the background. At one point the music, itself laden with the sound of regal, muted trumpets, has the faint ringing of tinnitus mixed in, a merging of interiorized sound and non-diegetic sound (to which we will return).

As the sequence continues, which is still shot in slow motion, Freddy arrives at the house where the cops are holed up, one of whom appears, wielding a gun and yelling at Freddy. Since the film is now almost entirely staged from his auditory space, the voice cannot be heard, functionally muted to inaudibility. An exchange of gunfire ensues, with the sounds distinct but muffled as well. The scene of violence, blood spurting from bodies, faces silently expressing pain beyond measure, moves inside the house. The shoot-out continues, until the last bad cop is felled, fatally shot and futilely yelling at Freddy, who can be heard in close-up sound, 'I can't hear you, Ray'. The soundscape heard here—dampened musical score, ambient noise, muffled voices, somewhat muted gunfire, the noticeable ringing of a shattered eardrum—is of course entirely tied to the bodily perspective of Freddy. Yet while the point-of-view veers among and between several characters, the point-of-audition remains that of Freddy's, once again mixing spatial and subjective perspectives. Moreover, the trauma of damaged hearing is also shared by the spectator-auditor, who is subjected to dampened sound pierced only by a high-frequency tone signalling a severe rupture to one's hearing, essentially simulating the sound of tinnitus.

What qualifies the auditory connection established between figure and audience, as it has in the other films discussed here, is a series of point-of-view shots from different perspectives, with Freddy in the frame and thus severing point-of-view from point-of-audition. What is compelling, nonetheless, is *Cop Land*'s soundscape comprised mostly from the internal dimensions of what's left of Freddy's hearing, the audible space shared with the audience but not with the rest of the characters in the film. For a nearly five-minute-long sequence, the film has created a kind of auditory canal in which hearing takes place, directly cathecting a character and the spectator-auditor. This moment of subjective point-of-audition sound also tenders a challenge to the conventional dichotomy between diegetic and non-diegetic sound, a neither/nor moment of sound both inside and outside the audio-visual space of the film, one that reverberates with our cinematic experience, attaching us as it repels us through sound.

The work of sound in such scenes recalls what Theodor Adorno termed 'the nonobjectiveness of the sense of hearing' (1976, p. 51), whereby aural phenomena becomes suffused and dispersed, blurring the distinction between screen and reception, between inside and outside, and, in the more radical examples here, between interiority and exteriority. As listeners, we ineluctably become immersed in sound; it permeates our bodies, suggesting the possibilities for a relational and intersubjective experience with an other. As philosopher Don Ihde poses it, we are never really very far from a state of listening within an auditory field, what he calls a bounded, 'situated context', which acts as 'an "opening" to the World' (1976, pp. 72–3). Which is to say, we may indeed be within proximity of an empathic experience through sound.

Such conditions take on additional resonance with regard to the figure of the body in contemporary culture. As Vivian Sobchack contends in the afterword to her 1974 article on the representation of violence in the movies, a period she calls 'The Postmorbid Condition', we find ourselves subjected to, if not immersed in, increasingly pointless displays of violence in contemporary cinema (with particular reference to Quentin Tarantino's films). Sobchack asks, what remains of the significance of the human body in an era of violent cinema, one shot through with savage bodily destruction, devaluation of human flesh, the cruelty of torture as a form of entertainment, the extinguishing of even a fictionalized life—all of it drenched in irony (Sobchack, 2000, pp. 120–1). Moreover, such observations take on a certain urgency in time of war, when real bodies are mutilated, scorched beyond recognition, shredded but concealed, while others are detained, deported, disappeared.

But not all screen violence is absurd or funny or 'senseless'—impervious to meaning. Occasionally we are summoned to perceive violence as a way of engendering meaning, even to share it, as it so happens, through sound and the faculty of hearing. And in such cinematic moments of extreme point-of-audition sound, I've tried to suggest here, subjectivity through sound is amplified through its near absence, when we are asked to experience a privileged perspective aurally as paradoxically a form of rupture. For, listening to violence on screen in a current cinema may be heard most clearly precisely at the moment when hearing itself is imperilled, at the very moment when we all experience a loss of hearing.

## Notes

1. For my purposes here I am relying on Edward Branigan's work on subjectivity which, as he puts it, 'may be conceived as a specific instance or level of narration where the telling is *attributed* to a character in the narrative and received by us *as if* we were in the situation of a character' (1984, p. 73; emphasis in original).
2. On the emotional trauma induced by the sound of warfare, it is worth noting the historical record, such as the highly-acclaimed memoir by E.B. Sledge, *With the Old Breed*, upon which the HBO miniseries *The Pacific* was partly based. In his reflections on his first major combat experience on the island of Peleliu, Sledge writes: 'To be under a barrage of prolonged shelling simply magnified all the terrible physical and emotional effects of one shell. To me, artillery was an invention of hell. The onrushing whistle and scream of the big steel package of destruction was the pinnacle of violent fury and the embodiment of pent-up evil. It was the essence of violence and of man's inhumanity to man. I developed a passionate hatred for shells. To be killed by a bullet seemed so clean and surgical. But shells would not only tear and rip the body, they tortured one's mind almost beyond the brink of sanity. After each shell I was wrung out, limp and exhausted' (2007, p. 79).
3. Farley's (2012) insightful reading of *Saving Private Ryan*'s sound design for the D-Day sequence is based on Walter Murch's notion of deprivation, which differs somewhat from my emphasis on point-of-audition sound as a kind of binding agent between characters within the film and the spectator-auditor.
4. The disruption of point-of-audition sound in *Three Kings*, which is also its insistence on being heard, resonates with Anahid Kassabian's analysis of point-of-audition in *The Cell*, which, according to her reading, 'insists on being heard as not only subjective but also troubled, unreliable, and incoherent' (2008, p. 304).

## References

Adorno, T. W. (1976) *Introduction to the Sociology of Music*, trans. E.B. Ashton (New York: Continuum).

Altman, R. (1992) 'Sound Space' in R. Altman (ed.) *Sound Theory/Sound Practice* (New York: Routledge), 46–64.

Branigan, E. (1984) *Point of View in the Cinema: A Theory of Narration and Subjectivity in Classical Film* (Berlin: Mouton Publishers).

Chion, M. (1994) *Audio-Vision: Sound on Screen*, ed. and trans. by C. Gorbman (New York: Columbia University Press).

———. (2009) *Film, A Sound Art*, trans. by C. Gorbman (New York: Columbia University Press).

Farley, S. (2012) 'Ideas in Sound Design: Deprivation and Barriers—Part 2', *Designing Sound: Art and Technique of Sound Design*, March 9, http://designingsound.org/2012/03/ideas-in-sound-design-deprivation-and-barriers-part-2/, date accessed 28 November 2014.

Ihde, D. (1976) *Listening and Voice: A Phenomenology of Sound* (Athens, Ohio: Ohio University Press).

Lastra, J. (2000) *Sound Technology and the American Cinema: Perception, Representation, Modernity* (New York: Columbia University Press).

Kassabian, A. (2008) 'Rethinking Point of Audition in *The Cell*' in J. Beck and T. Grajeda (eds) *Lowering the Boom: Critical Studies in Film Sound* (Urbana and Chicago: University of Illinois Press), 299–305.

Scarry, E. (1985) *The Body in Pain: The Making and Unmaking of the World* (New York: Oxford University Press).

Sledge, E.B. (2007) *With the Old Breed: At Peleliu and Okinawa* (New York: Ballantine Books).

Sobchack, V. (2000) 'The Violent Dance: A Personal Memoir of Death in the Movies' in S. Prince (ed.) *Screening Violence* (New Brunswick: Rutgers University Press), 110–124.

CHAPTER 13

# Acoustic Disgust: Sound, Affect, and Cinematic Violence

*Lisa Coulthard*

As J. David Slocum has noted, screen violence is a 'lazy signifier', a 'notoriously expansive notion' that refers broadly to coercive acts, threats, physical, and psychological violence (2001, p. 2). While it is true that what we mean when we talk of screen violence is widely varied and frequently contested, there is nonetheless a sense of when boundaries are violated, when cinematic violence is seen to go too far, when it verges on excess, extremism, or perverse brutality—in short, on the 'unwatchable', as a new book by Asbjørn Grønstad (2011) designates a recent extremist trend in contemporary European cinema. This 'going too far' is frequently ethically defined, as it is in Grønstad's book, as a kind of spectatorial confrontation or assault—the *'razorblade gestures* ... slicing open the gaze of the spectator' (2011, p. 6). As this description suggests, the terms used and analysis offered are ocularcentric—the confrontation is one aimed at the spectator's vision, interrogating the limits and impact of what he or she is viewing and questioning what is ultimately 'unwatchable'.

Against this ocularcentrism, this chapter considers the imperative role of sonic techniques in cinematic violence, particularly in violence that is deemed excessive or unwatchable. In the same way that there is an 'unwatchableness' tied to films that go beyond the boundaries of taste to interrogate ethical and formal issues of violence, the sounds of film violence can be extreme, unbearable, or unlistenable. More precisely, in what follows, I investigate what I contend is a key aspect of the sonically unbearable: acoustic disgust. Not only is acoustic disgust as important as visual revulsion in film violence but arguably

---

I would like to thank SSHRC's Insight Grant program for their generous funding of this research.

L. Coulthard
University of British Columbia, Canada

the envelopment and intimacy associated with hearing create a particularly fecund environment for this affective impact, one perhaps even more powerful than sight. Sonic disgust not only represents violence but also has the potential to create a kind of violent revulsion in the viewer, attaining an affective and sensation-based impact beyond that of the violence depicted.

And yet, the idea of acoustic disgust is almost never mentioned in theories and accounts of the affect. In his seminal work on disgust, Aurel Kolnai contends that sonic disgust simply does not exist, because sound has a remoteness, an 'analytical' character that always ties the sound heard with an object being sounded (2004, p. 49). For Kolnai, aural disgust is always moral disgust, because, for instance, the sound of a boozy voice carries with it associations of lifestyle and visual images of the person behind the voice. He asserts quite definitively that sound lacks the proximity and intimacy of smell, taste, touch, or even vision: 'One would search in vain for any even approximately equivalent parallel in the aural sphere to something like a putrid smell, the feel of a flabby body, or of a belly ripped open' (2004, p. 49). Signalling rather than exhibiting the 'ontological object' (2004, p. 102), sound lacks the invasive over-proximity necessary to have the direct affective impact associated with the immediacy of disgust.

Ignoring the direct and corporeal physiology of hearing, Kolnai's understanding of sound too easily discounts it as a distant affect. Anything but remote, sound directly impacts the body of the listener and its potentialities for crowd dispersal, weaponry, and torture suggest the extent of its ability to act as a very direct and powerful affect. Moreover, it is important to note that Kolnai is addressing sound in the world, not cinematic sound, which are two very different things. Sound scholars, critics, and everyday listeners have commented on the eerie intimacy of post-Dolby cinema sound where voices, breath, or small inconsequential sounds have a volume, presence, and impact far beyond what would exist in everyday life. For us to hear quiet breath or a whisper loudly and clearly—amplified and resounding in a theatre auditorium—is an impossible sonic presence in everyday life. Theorists and scholars alike note the almost unbearably intimate sounds of the cinema, where voices 'too large for any body' (Dyson, 2009, p. 136) resound, whispers and breath are impossibly loud, and actions that are virtually soundless resonate with sonic presence.

In surveying approximately 100 violent scenes in contemporary film and television, I found that although sound played a key role in the effects and impact of violence, the acoustic dominants focused on music or noise, rather than on the act of bodily wounding itself. By far, the most popular current trope is for overwhelming music cues, with some scenes of violence so heavily scored that diegetic sound is eradicated entirely. Frequently paired with slow motion visuals, this musical dominant creates uncanny effects by dislodging the violence from realism and placing it in a musical realm that highlights its stylization and artifice. This uncanniness is occasionally intensified by the use of upbeat, incongruous music at odds with the action depicted, which creates anempathetic effects that can render impact more intense through incongruous juxtaposition or, contrarily, contain it by directing audience enjoyment in a manner akin to a laugh track. In addition to these musical conventions for scenes of brutality, many scholars including myself have written on the use of silence and low frequency noise as sonic elements capable of intensifying cinema violence: silence can make us aware of complicity, our presence as listening subjects, and low frequency hums and drones create a feeling of nausea in the viewer, impacting his or her body in a direct and often unconscious way through infrasound.

In addition to these sonic intensities are sounds of the body wounded by violence, sounds that can be over-amplified or incongruous, turning the human form into object, thing, or mass by an act of violence. It is these sounds that I contend are most closely aligned with acoustic disgust: silence, noise, and music all have significant impact on the effects of scenes of sonic violence, but the sound of the body itself, its materiality and moisture is where sonic disgust thrives. For a *Slate* magazine article on 'The Sounds of Violence' (2012), Daniel Engber contacted me to discuss what he saw as the auditory excess of the violent elevator scene in Nicolas Winding Refn's *Drive* (2011). In this scene, the main character (Driver played by Ryan Gosling) brutally stomps on a potential attacker's head. Following a slow motion kiss with accompanying romantic music, the scene is one of abrasive and extended violence, with an astounding head blow count of 17. But what drove Engber's inquiry was the squish itself: he wanted to know if this was an innovation in sound, an unusual appearance of wetter, grosser horror sounds in a mainstream film, or merely the result of the combination of sound and visual elements in the film that worked to foreground disgust in listening to a '*thud* turn into a *crunch* on its way to a *squish*'.[1]

While there may be something to the idea that violent sound has become increasingly moist in recent years, which perhaps relates to both shifts in genre and technological sophistication, it is also evident that the squish itself is not entirely new. In discussing a scene in Liliana Cavani's *The Skin* (1981), Michel Chion notes the traumatic sound of a tank running over an Italian boy, producing 'a ghastly noise that sounds like a watermelon being crushed' (1994, p. 22). This traumatic squish renders the body an inert mass through a 'humid, viscous' sound that fits with the audience's imagination of what this might sound like, even if it does not adhere to sonic realism (1994, p. 22). Even more traumatic is the idea that the sound may have been produced 'precisely by crushing a melon' (1994, p. 22), an inert, unfeeling watermelon battered in a Foley studio to substitute for a human head. The crushing of a human head may not in fact sound like a melon, but the affective impact of the sound emphasizes the softness, vulnerability, and fragility of that element of the human body most associated with subjectivity and being—the head. Like the punch, that synchretic *point de capiton* (1994, p. 6) that stands in for what is not there and that has no relation to realism or reality (a punch is virtually noiseless, not the loud sonic event we hear in film), the crushed head is about the effect of the noise and not about its realism.

When discussing this Foleyed crushed melon, Chion goes on to suggest that it is not the sound that is disturbing, but the context. The sonic crushed head could as easily be a crushed melon in a film comedy that no listener would find the least bit disturbing let alone violently disgusting, traumatic, or nauseating. Rather than seeing this sonic neutrality as an argument for context in scenes of violence, I suggest that we take this duality seriously to consider the uncanniness of sonic violence itself, and to consider it within the frame of over-proximity in the auditory close-up. That is to say, perhaps a part of the disgust in this sonic crushed head is precisely because it is also on some level heard as a melon, or at least some other squishy object, but heard at such a close range and with such amplification that it becomes defamiliarized. Fortunately, most of us have never heard a human head being crushed. And yet there is a strange, unfamiliar familiarity when we hear the sound—a certainty that yes, this is what a crushed head might sound like, but also an awareness that this sounds like something we have heard before (crushed fruit) and a recognition that what we are listening to is a rendered, constructed, artificial, and even metaphorical sound ('his head was crushed as if it were a melon'). As any Foley artist will tell you, the object used in the image is not necessarily representative of what will sound most effective or even convincing: the squish of a melon has the correct emotional, tonal, and affective impact and that is the most significant thing. This disjuncture between sound and vision is precisely the point. As a sound that we know is not real but feel on some level as too real, as recognizable as an everyday object, the crush of a head in Chion's example has a disorienting familiarity. Because the sound is that of a thing and not living human matter, there is a disjunction between what is heard and what is felt: the sound is not realistic, but its affective impact may be all the more extreme precisely because of this artifice.

But if we return to the *Drive* example, we notice that it is not merely the squish and its overly amplified presence that invites disgust—the 'humid, viscous' quality, combined with thuds and elevator rattles from the brutality of the stomping, certainly contribute to the level of violent revulsion in the scene. However, even more disturbing than the squish is the visual/auditory close-up on Driver's face as he is perpetrating the violence. Sound editor Lon Bender comments that it is not merely the sounds of the impacts that construct this scene's violent effect but the overlaid and amplified sound of Driver's breathing and spittle that comes to foreground of the scene: 'Rather than play the scene for more and more gore, we brought it back inside his head. We hear the sounds of his breathing. We hear his body react' (Business Wire, 2011). Arguably it is this intensified breathing, the wet, moist sounds of Driver's breath and spittle that push the scene's violent acoustics over the edge into disgust. It is significant that the intimacy of Driver's breath, snorting, and spittle heard over the thuds and squishes of violence refers back to the previous moment of pre-violence romance. Featuring romantic music, subdued lighting, and leisurely slow motion cinematography, the elevator kiss between Driver and Irene (Carey Mulligan) sets up an intimacy that carries over into the violence that follows. What we did not hear in the romantic kiss (mouth sounds, lips, moistness, breath), we now hear in the scene of violence, pushing the two actions together and intensifying an uncomfortable intimacy that veers into disgust.

This intimacy of cinema sound is missing in Kolnai's account and it is what prevents him from recognizing the considerable role of sound in disgust, particularly in its relation to violence. As Eugenie Brinkema notes, disgust 'is a spatial operator, delimiting zones of proximity that are discomforting versus acceptable': it is a 'threatening proximity from which one recoils … an exteriority without distance' (2014, p. 131). This 'coming-too-close' is inseparable from a sense of 'going-too-far' (p. 131) and both are yoked to the close-up, a formal device of disturbing over-proximity and 'unwelcome nearness' (p. 139). Brinkema's project seeks to place form at the forefront of affect; in attempting to 'dethrone the subject and the spectator', she treats 'affects as having and inhering in form' (p. 36). For Brinkema, affect is in form, to be read and analysed as much as experienced. The privileged form of disgust is the close-up, the viscerally powerful impact of which can magnify the negative and is tied to the 'worse than the worst' -ness of disgust (p. 141)—what is worse than a cinematic image of vomit? a close-up of vomit![2] Citing Sergei Eisenstein's assertion that a cockroach in close-up creates more terror than a long shot of 100 elephants, Brinkema uses as examples 'the claustrophobic proximity to the bisected eyeball in *Un chien andalou* [Luis Buñuel, 1929] or the affective intensity of the maggots on the meat in Eisenstein's *Potemkin* [1925]' (2014, p. 140) to support the links between disgust and the close-up. Julian Hanich neatly sums up the relation between the close-up and disgust when he comments that 'filmmakers simply have to choose a disgusting object, put it in front of a camera and film it in close-up; the result will most likely elicit some degree of disgust' (2011, p. 12).[3]

Curiously, the audio close-up is left out of discussions of disgust, even though sound theorists and scholars repeatedly stress the link between sound and affect as substantiated by the physiology of hearing, psychoacoustics, and perception studies. In recent years, sound scholars and technicians have discussed the envelopment of post-Dolby sound, its ability to surround and embrace the listener and to create an immersive proximity with both positive and negative effects. Many have commented on the immediate, physiological phenomena of hearing, where air acts directly on the ear and creates resonances and vibrations that are felt throughout the body.[4] As theorist Jean-Luc Nancy notes, 'the sonorous is omnipresent, and its presence is never a simple being-there or how things stand, but is always at once an advance, penetration, insistence, obsession, or possession' (2007, p. 15). Sound 'that penetrates through the ear propagates throughout the entire body something of its effects', which, as Nancy notes, 'could not be said to occur in the same way with the visual signal' (p. 14). This language of penetration is further developed by Nancy when he contends the sonorous is 'methexic', involved with 'participation, sharing, or contagion' (p. 10), the latter term taking on special significance when we consider the obtrusive nearness and immediacy of acoustic disgust.

Many have noted this corporeality of sound and several have commented on the potential for sonic hapticity, but the sensory-based relation between the aural close-up and cinematic violence, particularly as it is conveyed through disgust, demands consideration. In her analysis of sensation in new extremist cinema, Martine Beugnet recognizes the 'uncanny intimacies' of the auditory close-up as well as its wavering between sensuality and violence: an 'audio close-up pulls the viewer in and envelops him or her with a sensuous or uncanny sense of intimacy or gives full power to the feelings of repulsion brought forth by excessively close contact with the object' (2007, 91). Stressing the repulsion of audiovisual over-proximity, Beugnet correctly points to the way in which sound opens onto the over-proximity of the corporeal close-up. While Beugnet is discussing only a specific moment in a single film, we can extend this observation further to consider the question of how the auditory close-up and the sonorous resonance of the body work together to create this sense of sonic over-proximity. It is equally important not to generalize; although one can discuss feelings of repulsion with the audiovisual close-up, we must also recognize the particularity of sounds and their affective impacts—even within the frame of the films of new extremism, not every audiovisual close-up is read as 'too close', overly intimate, or repulsive.

However, Chion's and Engber's comments suggest moistness appears to be one sound that holds a particular place in acoustic disgust. Even more specifically, I contend that the *Drive* example is indicative of a wider revulsion associated with auditory close-ups involving mouth sounds (breath, spittle, slobber, moisture). The over-intimacy of moisture-based mouth sounds in a cinematic context appears to be a key precipitator to the unwanted intimacy of disgust.[5] In Hanich's (2011) article on filmic disgust, he notes the appearance of the first close-up shot of the alien in *Alien* (Ridley Scott, 1979), but if we recall that scene, the cue to revulsion is the moisture, slime, and wetness of the alien's movements, especially as they are focused on its sizable mouth. Suggestive of intimacy, immersion, and contagion, mouth sounds are associated with both sex and horror and carry with them a particularly evocative 'too close' -ness that seems crucial to conceiving sonic disgust. In the same section where he discusses the watermelon, Chion comments on an 'atrocious sound of gargling, which makes the skin crawl' (1994, p. 23) in the torture scene from Andrei Tarkovsky's *Andrei Rublev* (1966): it is as if this combination of moistness and squishiness associated with the human head and mouth offers particular access to the uncanny sonic disgust of the body in pain and distress.[6] It is no surprise that sufferers of misophonia tend to suffer most from mouth sounds: chewing, slurping, sipping, smacking, drinking, breathing, and chewing gum. Those who have this condition describe extreme agony at these (and other) sounds and react with fight or flight aggression, panic, and rage.

For the average non-misophonic listener, these sounds are not disturbing; however, their cinematic rendering—played loud over auditorium speakers or in headphones, amplified beyond realism—may make them so by creating overwhelming and dislocating loudness, unwanted intimacy, and over-proximity.

When I worked in a Foley studio years ago, there was only one sound that without fail required me to remove my headphones—the Foleyed kiss. The stir of nausea this sound created had nothing to do with a kind of misophonic revulsion for everyday kisses: it had everything to do with the amplification, over-proximity, uncomfortable intimacy, and artificiality of the sound itself— its loudness, wetness, and overly emphatic sonic presence (real kisses, like real punches, are not very loud) were the disturbing elements. The intensity of the playback headphones only increased this disgust. Over the years, we worked on countless scenes of physical violence and graphic sex, but it was the Foleyed kiss that produced revulsion every time. Bringing together the sounds of breath, moisture and squishiness, kissing sounds carry an alluring repulsion that combines with a kind of auditory discomfort with the mouth itself. Taste, eating, swallowing, but also vomiting, are tied to these mouth sounds, and redoubling these positive or negative connotations, there is the intimacy of the sounds themselves—these sounds are quite simply too close and too loud in a post-Dolby cinematic context.

The link between sex and violence created by overly amplified mouth sounds is crucial to conceiving acoustic disgust. In a scene from Claire Denis's *Trouble Every Day* (2001), Coré (Béatrice Dalle), who is suffering from a disease that turns her sexual urges into cannibalistic ones, strokes, kisses, then murders a young man who has broken into her home. The scene begins with an intense close-up on his skin as we hear the breath of both lovers and the sounds of her hands moving over his skin. As the music (a recurring melancholic melody by Tindersticks) comes up in the mix, we hear the breaths and gasps of pleasure turn into garbled moist screams, painful gasps, and a kind of strangled yell. After a cutaway, the music has ceased and we are left with the victim's extremely loud and disturbingly laboured breathing and moisture sounds of blood and skin as Coré plays with his bloodied wounds with her fingers and mouth. The audio and visual close-ups work in concert and both invite revulsion as a scene of desire veers into violence and disgust.

Like the elevator scene from *Drive*, much of the disgust in this *Trouble Every Day* scene arises because of the slippage from the erotic into the brutally violent, and the uncanny similarity of the sounds of both. Both preface violence with music that could be read as romantic, or at the very least pleasing and melodic. In both scenes, music fades away as the sounds of violence take over, but the effects of the music linger to create an added dimension of intimacy. In neither instance is music eradicated and replaced abruptly by sounds of violence; rather, the music fades out slowly so that its tonality stays with the listener and carries over to intensify the discomfort of the sounds of violence that follow—the veil of romance lingers over the mouth sounds, breathing and moistness, in a way that reminds us on some level of the intimacy of the sounds themselves.

In Jean-Luc Nancy's 'Icon of Fury', an essay on *Trouble Every Day*, he contends that the film interrogates the kiss and its associations with devouring, biting, and consuming: 'it is not a question of any particular kiss, but rather that the kiss, in itself, opens on to the bite, and the taste of blood' (2008, p. 1).

Nancy asserts that *Trouble Every Day* asks 'what is a kiss?' (2008, p. 1). The film begins with an anonymous couple kissing in the dark in a romantic location (a car near the banks of the Seine), sonically paired with the mournful and repetitive title song featuring Stuart Staple's crooning baritone serenading the couple, before quickly turning to a narrative of vampirism and cannibalism. The kiss as bite reveals the truth of the body, its existence as matter filled with fluid, its lack of secrets and inner truths, and its inexorable move towards death and decay. Blood and breath within the body become mere objects once outside: 'Once the skin has been bitten to draw blood (to the depth of the blood and at the level of the blood), the blood becomes cruor, spilled blood, a jet which no longer irrigates but which spurts out like one or other of the sexual liquids' (Nancy, 2008, p. 6). As Chelsea Birks summarizes the scene, Coré's 'desire to expose the lifeblood coursing through the body of her victim is automatically self-refuting in that once she bites through his skin, his lifeblood becomes *spilled* blood', the nothingness of pure liquid and matter (2013, p. 54).

Acoustically this kiss that devours, that turns the body inside out and exposes its interiority as 'a little puddle of matter' (Nancy, 2005, p. 25), is inseparable from overly proximate and overwhelmingly tactile mouth sounds (breath, screams, licks, kissing noises) and sonic wetness associated with the moist and viscous liquid of his spilled blood. Crucial to this impact is the slippage from desire to disgust, where sounds that could fit a sexual, erotic, romantic register go 'too far', and come 'too close'. We hear similarly breathy and moist mouth sounds in other scenes of violence associated with excess and extremism: the elevator scene from *Drive* already mentioned (which recently made an online 50 most disgusting movie scenes list); the sex/brutality scene in *Antichrist* (Lars von Trier, 2009) where She (Charlotte Gainsbourg) batters He's (Willem Dafoe) penis then masturbates him until He ejaculates blood; the penultimate scene of *Dans ma peau* (Marina de Van, 2002) where Esther (Marina de Van) shuts herself in a hotel room to explore (and cannibalize) her own bodily boundaries and transgress the thinness of skin as a boundary of inside and outside, life and death. These films are not unique in eliciting affective disgust through auditory close-ups of sounds redolent with desire, but they are illustrative examples. This slippage between desire and disgust is crucial to affective impact: disgust, as Brinkema reminds us, is both 'revolting and alluring' (2014, p. 131); Kolnai references its 'macabre allure' (2004, p. 42); and William Miller posits that 'the disgusting itself has the power to allure' (1997, p. 111).[7] But this alluring nature of disgust is one dependent on spatial proxemics, which, as I have discussed, tread a fine line of cozy intimacy and atmospheric immersion on the one hand, and unwelcome penetration and claustrophobic envelopment on the other.

To return once again to Chion's melon example, the disturbance of these moist sounds is found in their defamiliarization in terms of loudness, amplification, and proximity as well as in their sonic qualities that are at least in some way unpleasant if not outright disgusting. Whether in comic or tragic circumstances, the squished melon sound carries with it a fragility, moistness, and viscous sonic quality that in everyday perspective and acoustics is not disturbing or disgusting; however, miked close and played loud in an auditory close-up, the sound invades and contaminates all the senses. Mouth sounds, breathiness, and squishiness discussed within the frame of an auditory disgust are not merely results of spatial proxemics, but are also uncanny sound objects, both familiar and unfamiliar. The audio close-up proves cinematic sound's potential for intimacy, invasive envelopment, and sonorous penetration and resonance. But even more than this, the already disturbing intimacy of the mouth in addition to the discomfiting defamiliarization of the ordinary (breath, mouth sounds, food sounds) combines with the audio close-up to create the 'too close' and 'too far' of violent disgust and excessive violence. There is something to these sounds that pushes them over the edge to extremism and excess: voice and not voice, breath is life, but inarticulate life tied to desire and effort; the squished melon sound is one of taste and food, but resonant of an over-ripeness and, when associated with a head, terrifyingly fragile and fluid; mouth sounds of eating, licking, and tasting suggest an openness that, as Jean-Luc Nancy reminds us apropos of the kiss as bite, suggest the limits of the human itself. Significantly, they are also sounds that recall that sense most associated with disgust—taste. Mouth, saliva, and fruit: the moist sounds associated with these objects work transsensorially to call to mind taste, tactility, and smell. It is no accident that the most disgusting sounds of violence are resonant of and frequently created by food; from the punching of meat to the squishing of melons, the Foley studio is rife with the acoustics of food and these sounds dominate in scenes of physical brutality, quite literally turning the human form into meat and matter.

Contrary to Kolnai's assertion that sound is too distant for disgust, these intimacies of cinematic violence suggest an intensified relation between sonority and revulsion. Sound is closer to smell, touch, and taste than vision: when considering cinematic violence, it is imperative to not only consider the sonic aspects of violent affects but also privilege them because of the potential for disturbance, disgust, and intimacy—affects crucial to the impact of film violence. All theories of disgust foreground taste and smell, with touch and vision as secondary and with hearing rarely mentioned at all. And yet, like smell and taste, sound permeates, penetrates, and invades the human body. Bringing together the tactile, the gustatory, and the olfactory, the mouth is central to any theory of disgust. This is its unlistenableness: the over-amplification and unwanted intimacy of something so tied to life (breathing, eating, sex) rendered emphatic and disgusting in scenes of brutal violence and destruction.

## Notes

1. The perception that sounds of violence have become more moist, squishy, viscous and fluid, and hence more disgusting, in recent years is one repeated frequently online in posts, blogs, discussions and articles on videogames, film and television. See, for instance, Lejacq (2012), Vancouver Film School [Blog] (2011).

2. Brinkema is here drawing on Jacques Derrida's 'Economimesis' ('the disgusting can only be vomited' [Derrida, 1981, p. 23]), which she then applies to Laura Dern's vomit in David Lynch's *Wild at Heart* (1990).
3. However, he also notes that disgust is not always quite so simple.
4. Comments on the intimacy of film sound are found throughout scholarship: Mark Kerins notes 'sound's inherently intimate nature' (2011, p. 131); Kevin J. Donnelly comments that because it lacks 'the physical distance between the viewer and film on screen', 'hearing is more immediate than vision' and 'seems to take place "inside" our heads' (2005, p. 94); and Frances Dyson comments on 'the impossibly intimate sounds of the big screen' (2009, p. 136).
5. The sound of vomiting has recently been declared the 'most horrible sound in the world' by *The New York Times* news blog, *The Lede* (Zeller, 2007).
6. The scene is one in which boiling oil is poured down the victim's throat.
7. With this slipperiness of desire and disgust in mind, one might not be surprised to find online various audiovisual clips featuring mouth sounds, whispering, breathing, and eating as a source of acoustic pleasure. Viewers (over nine million of them on YouTube for a clip from user 'GentleWhispering') report that ASMR (Autonomous Sensory Median Response) videos give them feelings of well-being, pleasure, and relaxation. For the most part, these clips feature dry sounds, with viewers even commenting negatively about the sounds of saliva interfering with their pleasure. https://www.youtube.com/watch?v=RVpfHgC3ye0

## References

Beugnet, M. (2007) *Cinema and Sensation: French Film and the Art of Transgression* (Edinburgh: Edinburgh University Press).

Birks, C. (2013) *Violent Subjectivity: New Extremist Cinema and the Philosophy of Jean Luc Nancy*, unpublished MA dissertation, University of British Columbia.

Brinkema, E. (2014) *The forms of the affects* (Durham: Duke University Press).

Business Wire (2011) 'The Sound of "Drive": Soundelux Creates "Emotional Truth" for Nicolas Winding Refn's Cerebral Action Film' [Press Release], http://www.businesswire.com/news/home/20110928006344/en/Sound-Drive-Soundelux-Creates-Emotional-Truth-Nicolas, date accessed 10 February 2015.

Chion, M. (1994) *Audio-Vision: Sound on Screen* (New York: Columbia University Press).

Derrida, J. (1981) 'Economimesis', trans. R. Klein, *Diacritics* Vol. 11, No. 2, 2–25.

Donnelly, K.J. (2005) *The Spectre of Sound: Music in Film and Television* (London: BFI).

Dyson, F. (2009) *Sounding New Media: Immersion and Embodiment in the Arts and Culture* (Berkeley: University of California Press).

Engber, D. (2012) 'The Sounds of Violence', *Slate Magazine*, http://www.slate.com/articles/arts/culturebox/2012/02/drive_the_sound_editing_in_the_elevator_stomping_scene_.html, date accessed 10 February 2015.

Grønstad, A. (2011) *Screening the Unwatchable: Spaces of Negation in Post-Millennial Art Cinema* (Basingstoke and New York: Palgrave Macmillan).

Hanich, J. (2011) 'Toward a Poetics of Cinematic Disgust', *Film-Philosophy* Vol. 15, No. 2, 11–35.

Kerins, M. (2011) *Beyond Dolby (Stereo): Cinema in the Digital Sound Age* (Bloomington: Indiana University Press).

Kolnai, A. (2004) *On Disgust* (Chicago: Open Court).
Lejacq, Y. (2012) 'The Sounds of Violence', *Kill Screen Daily*, http://killscreendaily.com/articles/sounds-violence/, date accessed 10 February 2015.
Miller, W.I. (1997) *The Anatomy of Disgust* (Cambridge: Harvard University Press).
Nancy, J. (2005) *The Ground of the Image*, trans. J. Fort (New York: Fordham University Press).
——. (2007) *Listening*, trans. C. Mandell (New York: Fordham University Press).
——. (2008) 'Icon of Fury: Claire Denis's *Trouble Every Day*', *Film-Philosophy* Vol. 12, No. 1, 1–9.
Slocum, J.D. (ed) (2001) *Violence and American Cinema* (New York: Routledge).
Vancouver Film School [blog] (2011) 'The Man Behind Super Meat Boy's Squishy Sound', http://blog.vfs.com/2011/01/14/the-man-behind-super-meat-boys-squishy-sound/, date accessed 10 February 2015.
Zeller Jr., T. (2007) 'Most Horrible Sound in the World', *The Lede* [blog], http://thelede.blogs.nytimes.com/2007/01/24/most-disgusting-sound-in-the-world/, date accessed 10 February 2015.

PART IV

# Time and Memory

CHAPTER 14

# Mad Sound and the Crystal-Image: The Soundtrack of Rivette's *L'Amour fou*

## Byron Almén and James Buhler

New Wave director Jacques Rivette's third feature-length film *L'Amour fou* (1969) represented an aesthetic turning point both for Rivette and for the New Wave directors in general. Rivette is perhaps the least well known of the five 'canonical' *nouvelle vague* directors, in part because his most celebrated filmic experiments occurred after the movement's heyday in the late 1950s and early 1960s and after each of his four *Cahiers* colleagues had secured themselves a breakout film—Claude Chabrol's *Le beau Serge* (1958), François Truffaut's *Les quatre cents coups* (*The 400 Blows*, 1959), Jean-Luc Godard's *À bout de souffle* (*Breathless*, 1960), and Éric Rohmer's *La collectionneuse* (*The Collector*, 1967). Not that Rivette was completely unknown; his first film, *Paris nous appartient* (*Paris Belongs to Us*), in production as early as 1957, was actually released four years later (due to financial delays in filming) and received some critical attention, if not popular success. His follow-up, *Suzanne Simonin, la Religieuse de Denis Diderot* (1966), often called *The Nun* in English language distribution, was the center of a cultural scandal when it was banned by the French minister of information, Yvon Bourges, after complaints that it was anti-Catholic. (For a review of the dispute, see Jackson, 2002.) And of course, Rivette had a solid reputation as a critic (culminating in his editorship of *Cahiers* starting in 1963), with an encyclopedic knowledge of both film and current avant-garde trends in other arts, including music (Morrey and Smith, 2009; Wiles, 2012; and, on music, McMahon, 2014).

But Rivette's characteristic directorial approach really emerged at the end of the 1960s with the release of *L'Amour fou* (Lloyd, 1971). In part, this film was a natural outgrowth of stylistic and formal concerns dating back to *Paris nous appartient*. The tension between freedom and control, for example, makes its first appearance in that earlier film, most characteristically in the character of

B. Almén • J. Buhler
University of Texas at Austin, USA

Gérard (Giani Esposito), a theater director who not only struggles to bring his production out of the rehearsal process, but who also seems ambivalent about establishing a definitive shape to the work. The same tension appears in other, more subtle ways: the vague conspiracy plot that both organizes and fails to motivate the film's temporality, and the disjunction between the atonal musical score and the visual elements.

One can think of Rivette in the 1960s in part as searching for an appropriate vehicle to express this tension. In that light, Rivette attempted various metaphorical solutions inspired by then more or less current developments in modernist music (Bartok, Stravinsky, Boulez, Stockhausen). For example, in *Paris nous appartient*, composer Philippe Arthuys supplied a Bartok-like score with a 'slightly decadent romanticism … which was meant to be grating' (Aumont et al., 1977). It appears that Rivette intended this music to rub uneasily against the visuals and narrative situation, giving rise to subliminal implications that would echo the film's thematics of a vast but unfocused conspiracy that extended well beyond what was given in the immediate narrative representation. The non-coincidence of visuals, plot development, and music—the refusal of underscoring to clarify or even to align with narrative or visual elements—pairs with the music's dysphoric topical associations to create a sense that what we are watching has been undermined by some immense force that exceeds the representation, that in fact even the director's (whether Rivette's or Gérard's) control is only partial. In this film, then, what is borrowed from music, what emerges as its contribution is just that dysphoric topical representation—a usage, however, that remains firmly within the tradition of scoring contrapuntally against the picture. Its function in the finished film is equally traditional: to generate a mismatch between soundtrack and visual elements in order to suggest an additional layer, a narrative motivation or action that goes beyond what is shown.

In *La Religieuse*, Rivette attempted a different kind of metaphorical transfer on the soundtrack. Here the point of departure was Boulez's notion of cellular construction that discrete musical passages should contain discrete parametric elements: 'The idea was that each shot had its own duration, its tempo, its "colour" (that is, its tone), its intensity and its level of play' (Aumont et al., 1977). Rather than evoking topical associations, this *metacompositional principle* of parametric seriality was appropriated from musical aesthetics to become the guiding constructive principle of the film[1]: 'The original idea of *La Religieuse* was a play on words: making a "cellular" film, because it was about cells full of nuns' (Aumont et al., 1977). The atonal score of Jean-Claude Eloy, a student of Boulez, does supply musical topical elements of unease, but it is only one component of a rich palette of sounds comprising 'varying degrees from pure direct sound to pure music, with all the other variations in between, such as real sounds mixed together, slowed down, [played] backwards, with percussion instruments, more or less clear, loops of music at various speeds' (Aumont et al., 1977) and nature sounds (running water, wind, birds) introduced at intense levels to dramatize the contrast with the heroine's imprisoned status. What results is both a reinforcement of Rivette's cellular conceit and an expansive mapping out of possible sound design strategies along multiple axes. Thus, pure music stands at one pole of a representational structure that stretches across a number of axes: 1) from the maximally concrete to the maximally abstract; 2) from onscreen placement of synchronized 'realistic' sound to the absolutely offscreen (i.e., non-diegetic) placement of pure music; and 3) from the radical interiority of purely subjective fantasy to the radical exteriority of purely spiritual transcendence—with the difference between this radical interiority and radical exteriority becoming ultimately indiscernible.

With *L'amour fou*, Rivette feints at another kind of metaphoric transfer, again to exploit the tension between freedom and control. The film's opening credits feature a sequence of unconnected sound elements (trains, folk music, Zen chanting, water drops) that he claimed was intended as 'an equivalent in the cinema for Stockhausen's recent research: this mixture of what is constructed and what is by chance' (Aumont et al., 1977), referring in particular to that composer's work *Telemusik*. Chance is also a procedure for uncovering new linkages, discovering those unexpected threads that connect even the most disconnected points, and testing to find expressive potential in novel configurations. But it also anticipates the theme of the contingency of relationships, the way two bodies that come into proximity display bonds that can attract or repel. Most importantly, however, this mixture of chance sound elements is realized in the film in its own terms—except for the initial hint, the idea is carried over from music without the necessity of realizing it through music. Given that the specifically musical elements in the opening credits are only lightly developed by anything else in the film (see below), Rivette and Eloy pull away from the thread of music–topical associations to something far more subtle, non-traditional, and inherently filmic; something that seems in fact to follow a line that organizes these sounds along a parametric series that condenses into a hard, crystalline face that initially appears only opaque. These opening sounds and music are constructed perhaps by chance; but they also form a series that will stretch the thinnest of lines across the length of the film. The soundtrack may still refer topically, but those topics dissociate, seeming to run on another plane from the film itself.

Where *La Religieuse* uses the cell of the cloister as an architectural metaphor that determines both the structure of the film and the music on several levels, *L'amour fou* does something similar with respect to the idea of a couple. The relationship between soundtrack and image has long been conceptualized by both practitioners and theorists as a 'marriage', a problematic metaphor whose gendered implications have been frequently examined and criticized in the scholarly literature. Mary Ann Doane, for instance, documents how sound technicians use the metaphor of marriage and mating to insist on the sound's subordination to the image (Doane, 1980). The uncritical application of the marriage metaphor has the effect of naturalizing the relation of subordination contained within it. (For a summary, see Buhler, 2014.) If the idea that precedes the metaphor is one of two equals coming together to produce a new unity, that unity in fact emerges only by allowing one to dominate, with the other becoming subordinate. In this way, the structure of filmmaking comes to reproduce naively at a filmic level the accepted sexual politics of society at large. This is the situation that *L'amour fou* confronts and uses its narrative of marriage to critically examine, displace, and perhaps subvert. Indeed, by insisting at the outset that sounds and music can take flight—not just from the image but from each other—and concatenate in strange and provocative ways, the film calls into question the utility of the sound–image 'marriage', which seems to lock everything into conventional, predetermined roles.

*L'Amour fou*, in the process of narrating the unraveling of a marriage between a stage director (Sébastien) and an actress (Claire), therefore makes provocative thematic use of this venerable metaphor in a way that obliquely anticipates the feminist scholarly critique of the image–sound relationship. Across the four hours of the film, this relationship is marked as fraught if also structurally obscure. Robin Wood astutely notes that 'each stage in [Sébastien's] progressive abdication as controller of the performance is counterpointed with the deterioration of their relationship and Claire's withdrawal into insanity' (1981, p. 5). And something similar happens on the soundtrack: the dissolution of the relationship between the couple is reflected in an increasingly disjointed treatment of sound, which develops toward exactly that disconnected use of music and sound anticipated in the opening credits. The film also uses sound among other things to distinguish three types of settings: 1) the space of the theater, primarily associated with Sébastien (Jean-Pierre Kalfon); 2) the space of the apartment, primarily associated with Claire (Bulle Ogier); and 3) other public spaces, generally coded as neutral with respect to the couple. The conflicted sound designs of the apartment and the theater especially serve to reflect the troubled psychological interiors and antagonisms of the couple.

The theater stands as Sébastien's space and its sounds are dominated by dialogue; an important subsidiary sound is the accompaniment of percussion used to punctuate the delivery of lines during the rehearsals. (And, as described below, the symbolic pairing of protagonist and percussion is dramatically emphasized in the diegesis by Sébastien's hobby of drumming.) The theater itself has two distinct settings: 1) the stage, characterized by rehearsal and the reading of lines from Racine's *Andromaque* (which Kalfon was actually directing) and 2) offstage and backstage, characterized by informal dialogue and documentary interviews. In addition, the representation is split between the 35 mm procedures belonging to the general film and 16 mm footage from a purported diegetic documentary (directed by the actual producer-director André S. Labarthe) being shot on the stage production. As Wood recognizes, this situation produces a dazzlingly complex series of representational reflections: 'We have, then, Rivette making a film of Labarthe shooting a documentary of Kalfon producing a play by Racine reinterpreting a Greek myth' (1981, p. 5). Importantly, and running counter to those crystalline reflections,[2] the theater is also the space where fractures in the relationship between Sébastien and Claire first appear. Claire, while rehearsing the lead role in the play, grows tired of Sébastien's constant dissatisfaction with her performative decisions and quits the production. Although seeming to initiate the film's dramatic trajectory, her action here also foretells its end, as she will also make the decision to end their marriage. In any event, Sébastien quickly and insensitively hires an old girlfriend to replace Claire. Sébastien's behavior both before and after this incident also suggests that he lacks self-understanding to adequately perform his role as director. After Claire leaves the troupe, she appears in the space of the theater only once.

The other major location is the apartment, which becomes increasingly defined as Claire's space after she leaves the production. Claire spends the vast majority of her time in isolation here, leaving to visit the theater once, going on a quest to find a dog, and occasionally joining Sébastien and others at restaurants. Early in the film, the apartment is characterized by silence and ambient sound, marks of Claire's separateness and Sébastien's absence. Later, Claire begins to experiment with filling the aural space, first by playing with a tape recorder, then adding radio broadcasts. After Claire quits the production, Sébastien returns to the apartment regularly, but each successive return feels increasingly like an intrusion. Indeed, on several occasions, Sébastien rudely invites members of the cast and crew to the apartment to rehearse and unwind. As Rivette notes, 'I think these are rather important scenes, because it is the intrusion of the theatre upon Claire, while excluding her even more than the fact that she isn't participating in the play. Not only is she pushed out of the theatre, but the theatre comes and chases her right into her refuge' (Aumont et al., 1977). Indeed, these intrusions seem almost to incorporate the apartment into the reflections of the theater, as though it too is being enfolded into the crystalline structure, leaving no space between theater and life.

Although the film opens on Claire, and Claire and Sébastien have roughly equal screen time (Wood, 1981, p. 6), it is ultimately Sébastien's film; Claire's motivations remain relatively opaque throughout. As Rivette notes,

> It's true, [Sébastien] is the central character. But in the same way that there is a balance for him between the theatre and the flat, I wanted there to be a balance between the two of them. But the point of departure was that we were only to see [Claire] in relation to him. What we see of Claire is perhaps only Sébastien's own idea of her: there are passages about her, especially towards the end, where one may think that he is imagining it all. In any case, it is necessarily a man's idea of a woman (Aumont et al., 1977).

Insofar as the film tells the story of the dissolution of a marriage, the images of that relationship are all retrospective reconstructions of Sébastien, or at least they can easily be read that way. This is not to say that there are no scenes of Claire alone, for there are. But the scenes we see all relate back in some fashion to Sébastien and to their marriage in a way that Sébastien's scenes *sans* Claire do not. Moreover, Claire's scenes, when read this way—as retrospective reconstructions—suggest an interesting compartmentalization of Sébastien's interior psychological life, a self-fracturing of awareness: he is at all moments both aware and unaware and in moving through filmic space both his awareness and lack of awareness shift.

The result is a kind of structure of cells, but the structure is not a formal architecture like the cloister of *La Religieuse*, which has similar thematics in this respect. Sébastien's relation to this cellular structure is also the inverse of *La Religieuse*. If interiority and exteriority remain indiscernible in *L'amour fou*, this is because Sébastien hardly registers a distinction between inner and outer life—or even between theater and apartment—until after Claire leaves. This is related to his fundamental passivity. Although Claire's isolation would seem to draw her as a fairly passive agent in the film, it is Sébastien who in fact proves the passive one. Or rather, he plays an active public role but is in reality extraordinarily passive, the primary cause of the difficulties not only in his marriage but also in his ambition to be a director. Claire appears to play a rather passive public role, but she is also a keen observer and indeed comes to serve as the active and creative spirit in the film. In a film about the creation of an artistic work, it is also worth noting that only Claire, not Sébastien, manages to create and complete a work.

Ultimately, Claire makes the decision to leave, and Sébastien is left in a dissociated state wandering down the street to the one long non-diegetic music cue in the film. Of this moment, Rivette writes:

> Just because there wasn't any music at all, I thought there had to be some important music at some point, because all rules should be broken once, and also, for it to take off, for the passage really to soar, to go beyond the rest, to the other side.... I wanted this passage not only to have music, but, to borrow a term from Boulez, for the music to be the carrying wave, with the image being a simple accompaniment, almost accidental, with no importance (Aumont et al., 1977).

Wood, for his part, finds this moment unconvincing. This scene, 'marked by subjective shots and overwrought music, culminating in his self-confrontation in a mirror-window, has always troubled me, its rupturing of the film's overall tone and method seeming arbitrary and unproductive' (1981, p. 6). However overwrought its music, this moment is not, as Wood seems to imply, one of psychological underscore and the laying bare of subjective interiority but rather of disjunction and dislocation in the sound/image relationship. It is also paradoxically a quintessential theatrical moment, a moment of reversal and revelation when the self-contained crystalline structure of the theatrical situation shatters, and Sébastien is left to wander aimlessly, the music offering no guidance except the promise of an exterior to the self-enclosed world of the theater. In narrative terms, Sébastien at this moment finally comes to recognize that the rupture in his relationship with Claire is irreparable and perhaps that even his revised conception of his play will yield only the closed world of madness so long as he remains, indispensable, at its center.

*****

With the important role that music plays in this climactic scene of wandering, it is instructive to consider the variety of ways that Rivette employs sound (or even simply the concept of sound) in relation to other elements of the film, to plot, form, structure, or the development of character. What is striking is just how often these relationships turn out to play a pivotal interpretive or evocative role.

Indeed, by unpacking the film's sound design in relation to its chronological unfolding in the film, Rivette's editing aesthetic and strategies become clear in a manner that reinforces Rivette's own penchant for combining freedom, flexibility, improvisation, and cast input during filming with considerable care during editing to create a subliminal, enabling structure. If Sébastien's theatrical performance fails, Claire's tape piece, created like film through recording and editing, succeeds, and so, too, does Rivette's film, which takes its form as Sébastien's recollection provoked by the latter's encounter with Claire's tape. In addition to the sonic contrasts engendered by the film's diegetic spaces (theater, apartment, exteriors), several important threads emerge as narrative foci. Most important is a kind of parallelism between the two characters' contrasting experiments with sound: Sébastien's aestheticized, even passive–aggressive, use of percussion to direct his actors' text declamations is shown to be impoverished in relation to Claire's construction of a new persona through acute observation, which she is able to cast in material form through the reel-to-reel sound recording. Reinforcing this contrast is Sébastien's irritating hobby of drumming, which intrudes into the apartment scenes and stands for his immaturity and insufficiency as a marital and creative partner.

The opening scene—actually one of the latest in the film's chronological time—shows an empty stage and a sparsely populated audience space, against which is heard the sound of a baby crying. Given that much of the film was recorded using direct sound, this aural element was seemingly a fortuitous accident that Rivette seized upon in his edit, resulting in an initial impression of primitive wounding and loss that foreshadows both Sébastien's primitive self-awareness and the charged and combative space created by the dissolution of his relationship with Claire.

The film then passes to Sébastien in his now-deserted apartment—also the last scene before the film-spanning flashback—and this establishes the primacy of sound in *L'amour fou*. Here we learn about the reel-to-reel tape recording that Claire labors over throughout much of the last half of the film. Although we do not yet understand its significance, we hear Claire's voice speak the phrases 'This desire to find still water again; the courage to separate; in the morning we'll awaken…'. Sébastien then rewinds the tape, which emits the rapid chirping of the recording at high speed. At this point, the film jumps back 19 days from the 2nd of a nameless month to the 14th of a previous (31-day) month. In a sense, then, the rewinding of the tape enacts the rewinding of the film itself and of Sébastien's memory—which calls into question the balance of subjectivity and objectivity in what follows.

Sound plays an important role in marking off and inflecting the physical spaces and psychological 'beats' from Day 1 (the 14th), when Claire leaves the production and the couples' estrangement begins, to Day 20 (the 2nd), when Claire leaves Sébastien and Paris by train. Days 1–3 acquaint us with the film's 'direct sound' aesthetic and its primary spaces: the subtle alternations of background 'tone' between the 16 mm and 35 mm footage and the ubiquitous creaking of floor boards during rehearsal scenes (occupying parts of 16 or 17 days over the narrative's three-week span), the intense presence of street noise in outdoor scenes (as when Claire returns to the apartment after quitting) or the clattering of dishes and background chatter in café, restaurant, and bar scenes, and the claustrophobic ambience of the apartment scenes (occasionally enlivened by the sounds of traffic or church chimes wafting in from the balcony door). In all these examples the noise of the exterior is insistent and intrusive, and ultimately it seems to beckon, to call her to break one set of links (with Sébastien) in order to forge new ones—a procedure that she will use the tape recorder to experiment with.

Beginning on Day 3 (the 16th), more explicitly symbolic, characterological, and narrative elements begin to appear in the sound design. During the first of several impromptu 'rehearsals' of some of the play's cast members—described by Rivette as causing Sébastien's problematized theater space to 'chase' Claire into her own home—Sébastien is shown and heard playing drums while others listen or study their lines. This is a most peculiar scene, in that it positions Sébastien as a troubled mixture of indifference and disconnectedness (he is providing very little direction to his cast), narcissism (his drumming forces the others to attend to his needs in a somewhat passive–aggressive manner), dilettantism/indecisiveness (he has considered giving up his theater work for a career in drumming), self-delusion (he does not have an accurate sense of his own abilities), and heedlessness/selfishness (he either does not notice or does not care that Claire in particular is bored by his behavior)—traits that will reveal him as the more problematic member of the couple. The drums become both an index of Sébastien's mood and a marker of his need to control his environment without having to look too overtly directive (the latter behavior of which would violate his—and Rivette's—stated aesthetic values).

Beginning on Day 4 (the 17th), Claire begins to express her displeasure with Sébastien by accusing him, not incorrectly, of being attracted to virtually every female member of his cast and crew—Madly (Maddly Bamy), Michel (Michel Delahaye), and Marta (Josée Destoop) (the latter is Claire's replacement in the play and Sébastien's ex-lover). At their dinner party with the cast that night, Sébastien again plays the drums. This time, however, he uses them to silence Claire, who has continued her insinuations in the group setting. She asks him sarcastically whether he is 'giving us a concert', to which he acerbically replies that he is denying them one—that is to say, keeping her from her own 'performance'. Both members of the couple admittedly behave badly here. Claire, hurt by the ease with which Sébastien has moved on without her in the play and feeling isolated, conspiratorially announces to the guests that he is hiding something and cheating on her, to which he responds with annoyance and discomfort. Sébastien, for his part, drums more and more loudly, making his playing into a provocation that drives first Claire and then Marta from the room.

That night, as Sébastien sleeps (or actually, appears to sleep), we hear the faint sounds of the Zen chanting from the opening credits. Rivette had initially intended this sound as a kind of *leitmotiv* but had abandoned the idea. In its sole appearance within the body of the film, then, the chanting (apparently accompanied by the ticking of a clock or some other regular noise) presages psychological distress, as Claire hovers a needle over one of Sébastien's closed eyes until Sébastien opens them and moves the needle aside, compelling her to embrace him somewhat reluctantly. As it turns out, this will be the last appearance of Claire for some time—a deliberate editorial decision to make us forget about her for a time before bringing her back in a more disturbed state.

Over the course of Days 5 and 6, Sébastien actively retreats from his home environment, seemingly disaffected by his wife's behavior, and throws himself into his work and into more or less overt episodes of flirtation with the female cast members. The sound design is full of contrast and frenetic activity—the competing cameras in the rehearsal space, café, and street scenes, interviews by the documentary director Labarthe with Sébastien (where the latter reveals his ambivalence about directing—he wants to be kindly and collaborative, leaving his actors free to make their own choices, but is frustrated by the lack of progress; this statement reflects his domestic ambivalence as well), and the awkward small talk accompanying a seemingly unsuccessful tryst with Marta in her apartment.

It is during this period (Day 6) that Sébastien hits upon an aural solution to his problem of providing an effective nuance to the delivery of lines in the play. It begins when one actor is shown clapping at certain points along with his lines to emphasize a certain declamatory flow. This is soon replaced by a cracking noise as Sébastien takes up the practice more generally. By the time of the play's (abortive) performance, this technique will have morphed into a full array of exotic percussion to accompany the actors. Sébastien tells Labarthe that he is trying to 'efface the actor's ego' to find the 'unity' and 'rhythm' of the author's thoughts and words. Although he appears to feel that this tactic allows his directing to be less manipulative, it actually shifts the manipulation into another register, an approach that is emblematic of Sébastien as a character.

Finally, a phone call late at night in the dressing room where Sébastien is sleeping brings him news of Claire's suicide attempt. The ringing phone is a sonic motif in this film, first appearing near the opening of the film during Day 20 when Sébastien, alone in the apartment and realizing that Claire has abandoned him, ignores the frantic calls of the cast awaiting his appearance for opening night. The phone is also a vehicle by which Sébastien's separate worlds are brought into connection or conflict. For example, he calls home on Day 5 to tell Claire that he will be sleeping at the theater.

Claire's suicide attempt and its aftermath are strangely elided. Not a single scene from Day 7 is shown; instead, Sébastien from Day 20 is shown listening to Claire's taped, mantric reverie. This is the first return of Claire's stream-of-consciousness speech, hinting at the suicide attempt as a breach in the wall separating interiority and exteriority, in which the two become indiscernible as she begins to process her observations, her growing estrangement from Sébastien, and to give voice to a new self that is independent of him.

The film sets this development to one side for a time, however, as the next scene (Day 8) shows the couple as seemingly happy and untroubled. Rivette's editing strategy of showing very little of the suicide attempt and recovery appears to position it as less important—at any rate evidently unimportant to Sébastien— as part of Claire's strategy to reclaim Sébastien's attention, a strategy that momentarily seems to have paid off. Nevertheless, the cracks in the couple's relationship soon appear once more, and again it is sound (or potential sound) that marks, and in some respects, creates the cracks. Claire and Sébastien, looking for some way to spend the day, decide to put on a 'love record', but can't agree on what to play. It transpires that Sébastien has purchased a 45 single because he liked the picture of the dog on the jacket, but the song turned out to be no good. The dog's face had—rather unflatteringly—reminded him of Claire (the nose, eyes, and ears), and he expresses a desire to own a dog like that. Despite its somewhat infantilizing subtext, this appears to please Claire at first, because it shows Sébastien's continued interest in her. As they elaborate on the fate of the imaginary dog, however, Sébastien cruelly backpedals, joking that it would put on weight and would be 'out the door' or that they could 'eat him' after fattening him up. This darkens Claire's mood considerably, although it subsequently leads her into an extended search for a dog resembling the one in the photo—apparently an attempt to re-establish connection. The search for a suitable dog continues into Days 9 and 10: at one point, Claire even attempts to steal another man's dog. When instead of a dog Sébastien returns home with a kitten that he thinks will please her, she becomes very angry. She sees Sébastien's failure to notice her interest in a specific *species and breed* of dog as evidence that any woman will do for him, and she henceforth ignores the kitten.

During this same period in the film, Claire embarks in earnest on extended experiments with sound and dialogue. On Day 9, while cleaning the house, she discovers their reel-to-reel tape recorder, which apparently contains recordings of Claire reciting lines from the play. As if to erase and repudiate this identity, she begins to rewind and record over these lines. At first, she replaces them with other lines of dialogue more reflective of her current situation ('What pain devours me? Can I not know whether I love or hate?'), and Rivette cuts away frequently to ironic scenes of Marta reciting the same lines in rehearsal.

As the days progress, however, she diverges from the script and uses the recorder to become both more observing and more creative. She gives up on reciting lines from the play when she notices sounds beckoning from the open balcony doors. As though hearing afresh the larger world outside her cloistered space, she at first closes off the ambient sounds and begins to repeat, then to fragment the lines, and finally to add her own: 'Ridiculous, rotten, shitty Don Juan … I hate him! I hope he rots! I hope he dies! Excuse me. It's not you. It's my fault. It's funny … I'm the guilty one…'.

At this point, Rivette makes explicit the parallel between Claire's recordings and Sébastien's punctuated accompaniment of the play's dialogue. In the rehearsals, the clapping or cracking has given way to the sound of blowing into a Coke bottle. Rivette's parallel editing at one point carries the Coke-bottle sound over into the next scene in Claire's apartment. The point of comparison is that both Sébastien and Claire are experimenting with sound. But while Sébastien's efforts are becoming more aestheticized and abstract and have the effect of manipulating others (the effect of which he is strangely ignorant), Claire's are more constructive and directed toward self-examination and redefinition. By Day 10, Claire makes her first attempt to break with Sébastien by asking for a divorce. As if to reflect this wider outlook, Claire's recordings in Day 11 involve narrating her observations, what she sees and hears out the window of the apartment. She adds description of passersby, gives the scene she sees direction and significance, and seems to be gaining confidence. Meanwhile, Sébastien's rehearsals are characterized by an ever more frenetic sense of amorphous directedness.

Later, after the film's 'Intermission', Claire's experiments are extended to recordings of static and fragments of music from a radio that she numbers like exhibits in an art show ('New series no. 1' over an orchestral work, 'Number 2' over plainchant, 'Number 3' over ambient sounds like a plane flying overhead, 'Number 4' over a flute-like instrument playing some exotic folk music, and 'Number 5' over the same music with Claire blowing into the microphone; the Parisian music scene is obviously quite eclectic!).

The couple's two sonic threads represent important constitutive elements in subsequent days, continuing the trends described above. Claire enters a new phase by Day 12, an inner confidence seemingly generated by certainty that Sébastien has been unfaithful. Her recordings are filled with 'new evidence against S', and she begins calling her old boyfriends, looking for opportunities to even the score (although it brings her little pleasure when she eventually succeeds). Meanwhile, the cast and crew of the theatrical production are becoming increasingly bored and unproductive, as Sébastien withdraws completely from giving any feedback during rehearsals.

Now it is Sébastien's turn to break down. After an argument with Claire where she again announces her intention to leave, he begins cutting his clothes off his body with a razor, mimicking Claire's suicide attempt; horrified, Claire comforts him. On the night of Day 13, Sébastien appears to force himself sexually on Claire. The next morning, we hear Claire's cryptic sentences on tape playing in the background as Sébastien holds Claire in their bed. She retreats almost catatonically to the bathtub for the day as Sébastien once more invites the cast to the apartment for an ill-situated rehearsal. Sébastien recalls his physical violation of Claire with an aural violation when he shuts the window in the bathroom and turns off the radio that she had been listening to while in the bath. By the morning of Day 15, Claire is huddled in the corner of her bedroom, accompanied by sounds of water dripping. This is the last sonic element from the opening credits to have made an appearance, subtly revealing the extent to which the latter's abstract collage of sound elements was in fact foreshadowing, presenting almost a condensed version of the film's narrative through abstract sonic motifs that accrue a particular signification for Sébastien and Claire's crumbling relationship. She begins to scrape and pound on the walls as she becomes more frantic, bringing Sébastien to her aid once more.

The film's climax occurs on Days 16 and 17. Here, Sébastien and Claire isolate themselves in their apartment in an apparently shared manic state of overexuberance. They repeatedly engage in lovemaking and then systematically destroy virtually everything in their apartment, writing on and knocking down walls, moving and breaking furniture, and engaging in role play. Some of the most jarring elements in this sequence involve the sound design. For example, as they rock back and forth in bed at one point, reciting lines and talking about Racine and (the biblical) Noah, we hear—as if from nowhere—the sound of loud, crashing waves. Rivette seems to be breaking the conventions of direct sound here, creating a kind of (shared?) subjective space that emerges out of their creative merging. We cannot be certain of the 'author' of this space, and Rivette allows the ambiguity to open a corresponding interpretive space. (Rivette will increasingly turn to this effect later in his career; in fact, a similar use of rushing waves and seabirds in his early 1980s film *Love on the Ground* has by this time become a way to represent the uncanny spatial permeability of the film's central mansion location.)

A further example of destabilizing the source of the sound in the image is the use of Claire's recorded voice on the tape speaking her mantric lines as the couple lies in bed together: 'Sébastien wants me back. He wants to kill me. It's easy to kill someone. You are my childhood, my love, cradle me. I'm happy in my water … Come, come closer to me. I'm cold to you'. Though these words seem to emanate from the diegetic world, they do not appear to belong to the moment of the visuals but seem instead to come from an earlier or later time that is impossible to specify. This is part of a process of decoupling the recorded sounds from sources in the diegesis, and it becomes increasingly difficult to discern their temporal origin, that is, whether a sound is a flashback, a recording played in the present, a flashforward, a mental image, or even absolutely removed from the diegesis.

For much of this climactic, destructive sequence, the couple seems at last of a single purpose, in sync. Both appear manically happy. But while Sébastien, comparatively unaware, seems to feel re-engaged and enchanted by this new dynamic, as though he had come to life, Claire seems to be using it to cathartically expel her last feelings of connection and desire. Yet a tiredness has defined their relationship almost since the beginning of the film. Claire recognizes the tiredness, and so seeks to purge the relationship. Oblivious as usual, Sébastien simply does not recognize it. In essence, Claire exhausts the madness, in order to diminish its power over her. Throughout the scene Claire directs the couple in a regression to childhood. Sébastien, missing the art, takes the act as real; Claire, embracing the art, understands it as artifice. Sébastien is attracted by Claire's art, then, because he senses in it at some level what he wants but can't accomplish himself. Claire contains, channels, and releases chaos in a productive way. When, by Day 17, Sébastien is contentedly drumming again, Claire recognizes Sébastien's mistake and gains insight into their incompatibility, his basic indifference and lack of artistic feeling, and perhaps thereby knows that she must move on, must make other linkages with other people in other places if she is to continue her art or even if she is just to find life. In any event, Claire responds to their extended siege of the apartment by declaring herself 'done' and asking him to leave. Sébastien returns to work, rehearsing all night, the clapping now replaced by wood blocks, gongs, bells, and the like.

By the end of the film, Rivette has increasingly decoupled Claire's taped dialogue from its diegetic visual counterparts. The couple's last joint appearance (Day 18) features Claire on the floor with a razor cut on her face and a further stream of dialogue on the tape: 'I'll breathe with your mouth, breathe through your skin. Stay with me, don't look anywhere else. Don't go back for ... Why do you turn your back? You're not here—you're far away. No one sees you as I do. I don't care ... that you won't find anyone else. You'll always search for me. Stay with me! ... We're alone. Don't be afraid. I've been so far away, alone. Don't worry, I'll protect you'.

When Sébastien returns from the dress rehearsal on the morning of Day 20, Claire is gone, having taken the train that we see her in at the beginning of the film. As noted, Rivette here breaks his rule of avoiding non-diegetic music. An atonal, fragmentary, and dysphoric orchestral track accompanies Sébastien as he wanders the streets of Paris. The music grows more intense, sometimes effacing the street noises, as he finally stares intently at himself in the window of a building. Sébastien's comparative self-ignorance has apparently been breached, allowing him to see at last that the crystalline structure of his theatrical production has trapped him in its endless reflections. Claire's journey of self-repair, though seemingly requiring her to traverse a dark face of the crystal, has allowed her art to follow a crack in the crystalline structure and escape with renewed health, whereas Sébastien remains locked in a series of reflections that dazzle but continue to isolate him tragically in his own lack of awareness. His sudden coming to awareness of the dark reality of the reflection—accompanied by music from the absolute 'outside'—is thus the tragic counterpart to Claire's laborious recording process. When Sébastien sits alone in the wrecked apartment listening to Claire's recording (a replay of the opening scene)—we are able to feel the full force of what the film's opening only hinted at. The excessive length of *L'amour fou* renders this revelation all the more forcefully for having been so painstakingly developed and chronicled.

*****

Through most of the film Sébastien is deluded; and he seemingly thrives on this delusion. His life is compartmentalized but he believes he's creating a singular self. Rivette notes:

> The story is about someone who is torn between two places, two separate enclosures, one where he rehearses and the other where he is trying to save—so to speak—the couple which he forms with his wife, without anyone being able to tell whether it is because the couple is not working out, that the play is not working out or vice versa. In fact, for him, it's all connected; he is caught in a muddle, being pushed into a corner from both sides (Aumont et al., 1977).

From Sébastien's perspective, the problems in his marriage become indiscernible from the problems in his play. But in proposing that particular doubling, Rivette here is perhaps too kind to Sébastien. His work at saving the couple is in fact minimal, and he fails as a director for the same reasons he fails in his marriage. In fact, Sébastien seems primarily concerned with avoiding recognition of problems either in theater or at home, and he is continually cycling from one place to the other, fleeing, whenever the pressures of the one grow too strong. His flight moreover is into the familiar patterns, into clichés.

The structure of the film both reproduces and critiques Sébastien's constructions. This is particularly the case with the music and sound and its relation to image and narrative. The sound overall is sparse, the music even more so. This sparseness seems to subordinate sound to visuals and narrative, and in this respect it demonstrates how easily direct sound simply falls into the customary pattern of marrying sound to image in order to domesticate and subordinate the former. Yet, throughout *L'amour fou*, the soundtrack reveals things that happen nowhere else. The dictatorial intention of Sébastien's drums are one instance; the artistic freedom of Claire's tape recorder is another. Sound in this sense is subversive, analogous to the figure of Claire. Sébastien believes that he is egalitarian but the way he uses his drums indicates he is in fact a tyrant, or if not a tyrant at least a control freak. Claire, by contrast, observes, allows the world to unfold, and then finds novel ways to recombine its disparate matter, to locate those fine threads that bind the most distant parts of the great open whole together. If that seems too metaphysical, we can point to the way that sound that strays from a 'proper' relation to the image forces attention: an inner voice that needs to be attended to but is not. Here, then, the exterior sound comes to represent and call forth the interior in a way that the two become indiscernible.

Sébastien's theater is a space of endless and dazzling reflection, a crystal-image in Gilles Deleuze's typology and the reflections here capture a tragic mood, a mad world without apparent escape (1989, pp. 68–97). Sébastien's profound lack of self-reflection and self-understanding of the way he compartmentalizes his life means that he is both unaware of the boundaries he has erected and the way that those boundaries themselves create reflections that make the spaces permeable. The life he has constructed requires boundaries that are secure, yet the reflections between theater and the apartment continually cross in ways that sabotage both work and home. The play of reflections therefore mostly incapacitates Sébastien, who is particularly unaware of how all of this is structured, of how he has structured his life to dazzle himself.

Claire, who begins in the theater, withdraws, but does not initially escape its reflective geometry, which drives her into the madness of the darkest face of this crystal. After some setbacks, Claire eventually discovers how to observe this dark face, to make it first artistically productive, and then ultimately to use it to escape. The instrument that allows Claire to explore this dark face is the tape recorder. Wood interprets her tape, negatively, understanding it only as a 'record of disintegration' (1981, p. 5), as a report of her fall into madness. Her engagement with the tape recorder perhaps begins that way as it leads her to confront and observe the dark face, but she soon turns the recorder into a productive tool of self-creation, as she learns to detach sounds from their origin and rework them to discover novel combinations. (Wood also does not recognize the strong parallel the film draws between Sébastien's stage and Claire's tape recorder, as though Wood cannot hear the artistic possibilities in it. Here, Sébastien proves ultimately a better listener than does Wood.) Claire uses the tape recording to locate a 'crack' along this dark face of the crystal, one that allows her to escape and perhaps makes the crack audible for Sébastien as well. In his most productive move as a director, Sébastien, Wood notes, had intuited the need for actors to 'speak as themselves', and to make a performance that satisfied them rather than being calculated to please an audience. But so long as the performance remained trapped in the crystalline play of limpid reflection, this shift of directorial emphasis merely assured that the difference between theater and life was ever more indiscernible. The crazy, absurd paradox is that Claire creates an art out of mechanical reproduction as the key to escape the reflective art of the live theater.

It is in this sense that Claire's departure is in fact a final gift to Sébastien, as through it he at last experiences the world taking flight. He wanders down the street, his failed production abandoned, and he lets go; music unmoored from his world sounds, beckoning him (or is it us?) to make other connections to the open whole that is revealed. That thought reverberates all the way back through the film to the opening scene, which folds back, as Sébastien discovers Claire's tape, recollects, and begins to see the dark face of madness amidst the reflections. 'Rivette needs theater for cinema to exist', Deleuze writes (2007, p. 261). Like Jean Renoir, who also needed theater and for similar reasons, Rivette produces a crystal that is cracked and so leaves open the possibility of escape. Sébastien, staring at his own reflection after his aimless stroll, perhaps sees the film *L'amour fou* flowing out of his recollection and through the crack of his theatrical crystal. 'I've been so far away, alone. Don't worry, I'll protect you'.

## Notes

1. Noël Burch explores at length the analogy between the parametrical serial design of music and film (1981, esp. Part II, pp. 51–101). He also explores the relationship of film to chance composition (pp. 105–21).
2. The reference here is to the crystal-image as elaborated by Gilles Deleuze (1989). The crystal-image appears when reflections produce an image where the difference

between virtual and actual becomes indiscernible. This indiscernibility, Deleuze writes, 'constitutes an objective illusion; it does not suppress the distinction between the two sides, but makes it unattributable, each side taking the other's role in a relation which we must describe as reciprocal presupposition, or reversibility' (p. 69).

## REFERENCES

Aumont, J., J. Comolli, J. Narboni and S. Pierre (1977) 'Time Overflowing: Interview with Jacques Rivette', trans. Amy Gateff, in J. Rosenbaum (ed.) *Jacques Rivette: Texts and Interviews* (London: British Film Institute), 9–38. Originally appeared in *Cahiers du Cinema* 204, 1968.

Buhler, J. (2014) 'Gender, Sexuality, and the Soundtrack' in D. Neumeyer (ed.) *Oxford Handbook of Film Music Studies* (New York: Oxford University Press), pp. 366–82.

Burch, N. (1981) *Theory of Film Practice*, trans. H. R. Lane (Princeton: Princeton University Pres).

Deleuze, G. (1989) *Cinema 2: The Time-Image*, trans. H. Tomlinson and R. Galeta (Minneapolis: University of Minnesota Press).

Deleuze, G. (2007) *Two Regimes of Madness* (Los Angeles: Semiotext(e)).

Doane, M. A. (1980) 'Ideology and the Practice of Sound Editing and Mixing' in T. de Lauretis and S. Heath (eds) *The Cinematic Apparatus* (Milwaukee: MacMillan), 47–56.

Jackson, K. (2002) '"Carnal to the point of scandal": On the Affair of *La Religieuse*' in R. Mayor (ed.) *Eighteenth-Century Fiction on Screen* (New York: Cambridge University Press), 139–56.

Lloyd, P. (1971) 'Jacques Rivette and *L'amour fou*', *Monogram* 2, 10–15.

McMahon, O. D. (2014) *Listening to the French New Wave: The Film Music and Composers of Postwar French Art Cinema* (Oxford: Peter Lang AG, Internationaler Verlag der Wissenschaften).

Morrey, D. and A. Smith (2009) *Jacques Rivette* (Manchester: Manchester University Press).

Wiles, M. M. (2012) *Jacques Rivette* (Urbana: University of Illinois Press).

Wood, R. (1981) 'Narrative Pleasure: Two Films of Jacques Rivette', *Film Quarterly* Vol. 35, No. 1, 2–12.

CHAPTER 15

# The Sonic Realm in *The Quatermass Experiment*: Medium and Genre and Sound

## Robynn J. Stilwell

Only the first two of the six episodes of *The Quatermass Experiment* (BBC, 1953) still survive. The results of the experimental kinescope recording process were considered so unsatisfactory and prohibitively expensive that it was discontinued for the last four episodes (Pixley, 2005, p. 12). This ephemerality of early television is one of the challenges to understanding the history of the medium. Another is that television is a space of crossing, merging, and blending of institutional practice, technological structures, aesthetic fields, personnel, and genre across media.

Television is a broadcast medium like radio, largely built on the infrastructure of radio networks already in place, whether the BBC in the UK or the array of commercial networks in the USA. Like radio, television is composed of a heterogeneous flow of shows and advertisements; the musical sutures and announcing voices both provide 'continuity' (their nominal function) and disruption. Individual programmes exhibit aesthetic parameters (mise-en-scène, soundscapes, narrative tropes) that have been inherited from many sources. Radio created the game show (arguably, a descendant of parlour games), soap opera (a dramatization of the human desire for gossip), the procedural (a writerly form blending reportage and the mystery novel), and the situation comedy (a generic mash-up of vaudevillian sketches and classical comedy). The concert hall or theatre shapes live performance in a variety of ways across genres. Drama bears the marks of both theatrical and cinematic influence, although with the passing of the live broadcast era, the latter became more predominant.

As the above précis suggests, television exhibits a strong correlation between genre and medium. Science fiction, however, is a genre that spreads widely across media, and shows an unusual dynamic of interchange between

---

R.J. Stilwell
Georgetown University, USA

them. Like television, science fiction had existed before World War II, but became a mainstream force in the post-war years. Pulp magazines generated a community of authors, fostering the short story and novella alongside the novel. Cinematic science fiction in the 1930s and 1940s had largely been bifurcated into monster/horror films and the Saturday morning serials like *Buck Rogers* and *Flash Gordon* (both by Universal) that were a clear precedent for the early, action/adventure-based shows geared towards children: *Captain Video and His Space Rangers* (Dumont, 1949–55); *Tom Corbett, Space Cadet (*appeared on ABC, CBS, NBC, and Dumont at various times during its 1950–55 run); and *Stranger from Space* (BBC, 1951–52).[1] An exception was the 1936 British production of H.G. Wells's prescient *Things to Come*. In the USA, 1950 is the year when horror and sheer adventure started to shade into genuine speculative fiction with films like *Destination Moon* (Irving Pichel, 1950), *Rocketship X-M* (Kurt Neumann, 1950), and *The Day the Earth Stood Still* (Robert Wise, 1951).[2] On radio, *2000 Plus* (Mutual, 1950) and *Dimension X* (NBC, 1950–51; later *X-Minus One* 1955–58) both debuted in 1950, with the former presenting original stories and the latter presenting adaptations of stories by such writers as Isaac Asimov, Ray Bradbury, Robert A. Heinlein, and Kurt Vonnegut.

Although the BBC had produced some literary adaptations, like *The Time Machine* (1949), *Quatermass* was an original science fiction television production aimed primarily at adults, built around the character of rocket scientist Professor Bernard Quatermass. Three stories of six 30-minute episodes each were produced by the BBC: *The Quatermass Experiment* (1953); *Quatermass II* (1955); and *Quatermass and the Pit* (1958–59). Each story was then adapted by Hammer Films, into *The Quatermass Xperiment* (US title: *The Creeping Unknown*, Val Guest, 1955), *Quatermass 2* (*Enemy from Space*, Val Guest, 1957), and *Quatermass and the Pit* (*Five Million Years to Earth*, Roy Ward Baker, 1967). A fourth miniseries, simply titled *Quatermass* (four one-hour episodes), was produced by Thames Television (1979). Finally, *The Quatermass Experiment* (Sam Miller) was adapted into a two-hour telefilm, broadcast live for Channel 4 in 2005.

*Quatermass* as a whole then offers fertile ground for exploring the generic tropes and aesthetic parameters of science fiction in television and film at mid-twentieth century. Radio provides a robust model for the operation of music, sound, and mise-en-scène in television, while in cinema, the generic pull towards horror would influence not just the Quatermass films but also the direction of Hammer Films as a studio (Hutchings, 1993, p. 25). And in the 2005 version, live television itself is 'remade'—that which was a given in 1953 becomes the special attraction in 2005, and a half-century of science fiction television stands between. Thus, the original television series *The Quatermass Experiment* (1953), the first Hammer film *The Quatermass Xperiment* (1955), and the 2005 live version of *Quatermass* form a useful baseline for exploring the interactions and intersections of genre, medium, and soundscape.

## But First...

Orson Welles's infamous 1938 radio adaptation of *War of the Worlds* (Koch) may or may not have been an influence on *Quatermass*, but it was certainly a precedent. The use of music and the frames in which the speaking voice is deployed would find many echoes in science fiction radio and television in the post-war era.

At the top of the hour, a Columbia Broadcasting System (CBS) announcer identifies the network and announces the *Mercury Theatre on the Air*'s presentation of Orson Welles's adaptation of *War of the Worlds*. These kinds of announcements are both logo (a discrete sonic identification badge for the network) and continuity, claiming that which comes before and after. The strains of Tchaikovsky's First Piano Concerto form another sound-logo, marking the identity of the specific show.

The announcer introduces the director of Mercury Theatre, who then begins his opening monologue, based closely on the opening paragraphs of H.G. Wells's novel. The novel's voice is that of the unnamed protagonist—a writer—setting the stage for the invasion:

> No one would have believe in the last years of the nineteenth century that this world was being watched keenly and closely by intelligences greater than man's and yet as mortal as his own; that as men busied themselves about their various concerns they were scrutinised and studied, perhaps almost as narrowly as a man with a microscope might scrutinise the transient creatures that swam and multiply in a drop of water. (Wells, 1898)

The powerful imagery of this opening destabilizes the world of the reader, as the human race's frame of reference is suddenly expanded to encompass other worlds, and by simile, humanity is reduced to microscopic size. Every fictional world must be constructed, but with science fiction, the stakes are much higher: for something as brief as an hour or half-hour program, there is little time to ease the audience into the world. Until at least the 1990s (the early seasons of *Quantum Leap*, NBC, 1989-93), almost every radio or television science fiction show would begin with such a monologue: those from *The Twilight Zone* (CBS, 1959–1964), *The Outer Limits* (ABC, 1963–1965), *Battlestar Galactica* (ABC, 1978), and *Star Trek* (NBC, 1966–1969) are part of pop culture's canon.

Welles's monologue extends an authorial ambiguity present in many of these prologues: director of the theatre company and director of the radio play, Welles will also portray Prof. Pierson, eventually merging with the novel's anonymous author in the final act. Similarly, the monologue itself straddles the external continuity of the broadcast flow and the internal coherence of the story, carrying listeners from the everyday into the world it is tasked with building.

*War of the Worlds* is unusual in that the hour-long play is in three distinct sections, each demonstrating a different 'texture' determined by information distribution, constellation of characters, and relationship to time. The first mimics the flow of a network radio broadcast during breaking news; the second, military communication during battle; and the third, the internal monologue of a survivor.

The most significant change in the opening monologue is in the very first phrase: from H.G. Wells's 'No one would have believed', which is past perfect and conditional, to Orson Welles's 'We know now' the assertive *present*, which leads us into the experiential 'now-ness' of the first, and arguably most famous, section of the play. The alternation of musical performance, recordings, news bulletins, field reports, and on-the-scene interviews is mediated by a continuity announcer, giving a sense of immediacy—although even moderate attention would betray the temporal impression of real time, as breakaways for music last only about 20 seconds a time, and reporter Carl Phillips manages to get around to several locations in New Jersey before he is killed by a heat ray, and identified at a Trenton morgue mere minutes later.

The second act is implicitly 'overheard', as the radio facilities are handed over to the state militia. An officer gives orders, a gunner ranges his sights, and an observer reports damage, against distant sounds of battle, foreshadowing both wartime military coverage and science-fiction 'technobabble' to come. Like the first act, the timeline is compressed, but the less fragmentary texture fosters an even greater sense of real time.

A dirge-like musical cue introduces the third, most reflective and literary act, Pierson's journal of events. Story time is indeterminate, extending over months until the aliens have been wiped out by the 'transient creatures that swarm and multiply' beneath a microscope.

Welles, as Welles, takes us back out of the show in the reverse order that we came in. His epilogue is followed by the Tchaikovsky logo theme for the series and a continuity announcer offers network identification. The broadcasting stream has 'flow', but it also has structure, a syntax that both organizes information and guides the audience.

## Opening Sequences

The opening sequence of *The Quatermass Experiment* series is very like the opening of *War of the Worlds*, and for that matter, the opening of the American kids' program *Captain Video*, with a classical music 'logo' and a scene-setting monologue. Both television shows have simple title cards, essentially static images that cede motion and activity to the music, a clear example of 'radio with pictures'.

The screen is black for the first, pounding iteration of the 5/4 bolero rhythm of Gustav Holst's 'Mars, Bringer of War' from *The Planets*, then fades up on a black title card emblazoned with the words 'The Quatermass Experiment'. The militaristic but asymmetrical rhythm and the low, ominously surging brass are a striking combination, a motto that is instantly recognizable as a musical object (a closed unit), as well as a forward-driving musical trajectory that builds through upward melodic sequencing and increasing orchestration. A cross-fade to the second title card, 'A Thriller for Television in Six parts by Nigel Kneale', is followed by a blackout as the pyramidal sequencing and orchestration builds. 'Episode One Contact has been Established' appears as the trumpets repeat the

'Mars' rhythm on the same pitch. The low brass drops out, only to restart the building as the image cross-fades to a rocket launch. The sound of the rocket blurs over the abrupt ending of the musical cue, and the image cuts to a shot of the earth from above, as if from a window of the rocket. First, we rise above a scrubby desert, and another cut takes us to an elevation where the curvature of the earth is visible against the blackness of space.[3]

A male voice starts speaking, calmly but with a faint lilt that connotes 'storytelling' as opposed to a more detached 'reportage', aided by the vague temporal indication of the two opening clauses.

> One morning, two hours after dawn, the first manned rocket in the history of the world takes off from the Tarooma Range, Australia. The three observers see on their scanning screens a quickly receding Earth. The rocket is guided from the ground by remote control as they rise through the ozone layer, the stratosphere, the ionosphere, beyond the air. They are to reach a height of 1500 miles above the earth, and there learn [pause] what is to be learned.
> [A haze of lens flare leads to a fade to black]
> For an experiment is an operation designed to discover some unknown truth. It is also a risk.
> [Fade up to British Experimental Rocket Group signage, pan down to chart of curving flight paths]
> When it is 1400 miles up, all contact with the rocket is suddenly lost.

In the 1955 Hammer film, the narration-free title sequence consists of an original cue by composer James Bernard and credits superimposed on an image of clouds, thicker than summer fluff but not yet storm clouds. A low rustle of strings forms an amorphous bed of sound, suggesting the wind that sets the clouds drifting from right to left across the screen. A gradual crescendo crests with the title and the entry of low monophonic brass. Midrange strings take up a rocking conjunct motion with an erratic circling that, through its lack of predictability, creates a sense of uneasy anticipation.

The difference in the music encapsulates the versions' tonal difference almost immediately. Holst's 'Mars' creates a powerful, rising, even aspirational tone, even with its edge of menace, whereas Bernard's wavering score emphasizes suspense.

The 2005 live *Quatermass* is a relatively faithful adaptation of Kneale's original script, with an initial nod to the original. The broadcast begins with the BBC kinescope, but as the low brass of 'Mars' starts to rise, the black-and-white shot of the Earth's curved horizon is replaced by a modern, colour image and the music fades almost seamlessly to a higher-quality version, in which the snare drum beats out the asymmetrical bolero, increasing intensity as the images of earth whirl faster. During the narration, we pan across a star field through a few wisps of atmosphere, putting the POV above Earth looking out through the upper reaches of the atmosphere, something of a negotiation between the two earlier versions—a pattern we shall note again.

## Initiation of the Action

While the momentum of the television version and film version already differ significantly because of the opening narration (or lack thereof) and the musical profile, the initiating onscreen action creates a further divergence of tone. In the television versions, we essentially enter the story from above. In the Hammer film, we enter the story from below, the alien threat literally dropping down on us, a directional nuance that highlights the difference between suspense and horror.

In the 1953 version, transition between the opening narration and the action is dovetailed, both narratively and audiovisually. After the blackout, the image fades up to a wall sign declaring British Experimental Rocket Group, and tracks down to a chart of curving flight paths; especially since we had been travelling through space 'with' the rocket in the credit sequence, this creates contrary motion and competing lines of inertia, thus a subtle sense of suspension as the narrator reports, 'All contact with the rocket is suddenly lost.' The music settles into a drone in the lower strings and brass with a descent of a step on the fourth beat of every four-beat bar; this regulates the rhythm of 'Mars', with the lower note acting as a steady flat-seventh flex, or breath. The tension is sustained but with less forward drive than the asymmetrical rhythm with the rising brass.[4]

The first person we see is a woman in a lab coat. Before her is a lighted globe wrapped with delicate arcs of glowing tubing, a device that appears both technological and artistic. Cued by the wall chart and the way she moves her fingertips along the tubes with concern, we may infer that these fiberoptic tubes mark the rocket's orbits. She is Judith Carroon (Isabel Dean), a flight engineer married to one of the astronauts, Victor Carroon (Duncan Lamont), who will be at the centre of the story's crisis.

The camera continues to pull out, revealing two banks of desks of the type we would now immediately recognize as mission control, arranged as if they might be facing a large monitor offscreen right. Judith is at the far end of the front desk, and beside her is a distinguished-looking gentleman. The music fades down as he looks back at rear bank. The music gives way to his action, underlining his significance: this is Professor Bernard Quatermass (Reginald Tate), the man behind the rocket's design.[5]

Following a concerned exchange between Quatermass and Judith about the rocket's loss, Quatermass fields a phone call from 'The Ministry', a character named Blaker (W. Thorp Devereux) for whom Quatermass demonstrates little patience. Quatermass argues for full disclosure to the public, while Blaker is worried about public support. Both characters are shot in medium close-up, vaguely angled towards one another as the image cuts from one speaker to the other. Neither a cinematic split screen nor theatrical blocking, where two conversants face each other but cheat their bodies towards the audience, this sequence has elements of both.

The reliance on the mediation of technology—radio communication, telephone—is a common trait of radio drama, as it provides a rationale for detailed verbal communication, including descriptions of objects and actions for the audience in the guise of being for the person on the other end of the line. Early television adopts it as well—whole segments of *Captain Video* are spent on a variety of communications devices, with the only visual action in Captain Video's movement from one part of his simple headquarters set to another.

The conversation is interrupted by a high-pitched whine that alerts them to new communication, and Quatermass and the two men at the upper bank gather around the microphone mounted there, even though the sound seems to emanate from a speaker behind their heads as Tarooma reports the re-entry of the rocket, after having travelled 380,000 miles. 'That's more than we ever planned for', exclaims Judith; 'Half as far again as the moon', muses Quatermass before a fade to black (Fig. 15.1).

The only moment in this scene that transmits information visually is when Blaker asks, 'Frankly, is there any chance of their survival?' and we see a mid-close-up of Judith, looking anguished. When Quatermass responds angrily, 'Equally frankly, I don't…' Judith's head turns slightly towards Quatermass, but she does not look at him. He drops his voice and asks softly into the telephone receiver, 'How can anybody answer a question like that?'.

This sequence plays transparently, but the exchange is a moment of slippage: nothing indicates that anyone but Quatermass can hear Blaker; Judith is possibly attuned to the situation enough so that Quatermass's agitation piques her attention, but the timing of her reactions suggests that she hears both sides of the telephone conversation, as the audience does. The diegesis is variable and permeable.

Images start to participate more frequently in the next scene. Against visual darkness, mid-range strings and flutes rock back and forth on a major second and string harmonics slide downward in modernist dissonance as the 'lights come back up' on Judith and Quatermass still at their posts. Quatermass

**Fig. 15.1** Futuristic and retrograde technology (*The Quatermass Experiment*, BBC, 1953). Left (**a**), Judith Carroon follows the rocket's orbits on a futuristic fiberoptic device; right (**b**), Quatermass and the technicians in mission control gather around a bulky stand microphone to follow the report from Tarooma Range, even though the sound appears to be coming from the small round speaker behind their heads

uses a model rocket and a chart on the wall to give the now-present Blaker (and the audience) an update on the mission in theatrical imitation of a classroom lecture or academic paper.

A low electronic hum indicates contact with the rocket, and a slight pulsing creates tension as Quatermass turns to the controls—for the first time, oscilloscopes and aviation dials provide the visible semblance of telemetry. The uneasy seconds and sliding harmonics return for another blackout. These time elisions and the uneasy music build tension as they track the rocket. As an urgent Quatermass requests emergency services, a dissonant electronic hum with audible frequency-difference beats heralds the nearing of the rocket to earth, and its sudden cessation marks the rocket's crash in Wimbledon. A silent blackout closes the first act/half of the episode.

The television version thus builds suspense through verbal information and the aural signature of the lost craft, punctuated by transitional music that relies on familiar tropes of uneasiness and concern. These, however, are moderate, restrained affects; horror is not.

The television show's trajectory from 'Mars' to unease is almost flipped by Bernard's ominous, monophonic credit music for the film, which rocks on a monophonic low tonic/supertonic with an occasional minor third, echoed by the higher strings. As the credits end, we descend (via blackout and the momentary cessation of sound) to an idyllic country road at twilight. A young couple is walking along it towards the camera to the lilting, compound-metre strains of violins in thirds, a folkish dance gesture that fades quickly under their laughter. Their literal tumble in the hay is interrupted by a whooshing sound that catches his attention; she thinks it's a jet, while he is certain that it is not—thus the first words are about the sound and its mysterious provenance. He points to the sky and demands, 'Look!'. He tries to shelter her in the haystack, but she takes off towards the apparent safety of a farmhouse where her father urges them inside. From within, we see lights flashing through the windows before the roof falls in. A horse whinnies[6] and a dog barks as we follow the father, now armed with a shotgun, outside. Only then do we see an explanation of the noisy destruction—a rocket is buried tip-first into the ground, three minutes into the film; we first see the rocket in the television version at over 14 minutes, at the beginning of the second act, buried fins-first in the rubble of a row house in suburban London. The direction of the crash underlines the difference in the threat, not just the direction of its entry; the image of the half-buried rocket has particular resonance for a British audience only a decade removed from World War II as the loaded threat of an unexploded bomb.[7]

A quick cut takes us to sometime later, with crowds gathering, a fire brigade hurtling through a village street, and a calm voice on a loud hailer requesting that people return to their homes for safety. This quick succession of images, along with the collapse of the farmhouse, has a strong resonance with the *War of the Worlds* novel as well, evoking the scene described around the crash of one of the Martian cylinders on Horsell Common.

Exposition is given to a newsreader in an austere radio studio, emphasizing his words (but, true to cinematic fashion, welded to his image) as he reads a bulletin about the event, while a Volkswagen bus hurtles towards the scene, bearing government officials and a gruff American Quatermass (Brian Donlevy). A man in the back seat frets about the Home Office's concerns (Fig. 15.2). Their exchange, in the same space even if not exactly face-to-face, is the equivalent of the phone call with Blaker, and is more immediately about the threat to public safety than about the public reaction to the failure of a government-funded project. In the film, Judith Carroon (Margia Dean) is reduced primarily to her role as Victor's wife and is a much more stereotypical concerned, and at times terrified, woman. In the television versions, Judith Carroon is married; in the film, she is a wife—it is not an insignificant difference.

Although Quatermass knows some of what has occurred, the audience does not. Whereas the emphasis in the television version is 'What will happen?' that

**Fig. 15.2** Quatermass and the Man from the Ministry (*The Quatermass Experiment*, BBC, 1953; *The Quatermass Xperiment*, Val Guest, 1955). In the television production (top left and right), the intercutting and body orientation suggests a semblance of face-to-face dialogue mediated by the telephone; the film (bottom) takes a more cinematic (and hostile) approach, with Quatermass and the man from the Ministry in the foreground, in the front and back seats, respectively, and other characters in the vehicle beside them

in the film is 'What just happened?'. The latter is more disconcerting and concerning because of lack of knowledge.

## Tell Me What Happened Here?

In *War of the Worlds,* Wells dispenses information about the invasion with a combination of show (first-hand description of events witnessed by the unnamed narrator) and tell (second-hand narration by characters like his brother and the Artilleryman) who have seen things the narrator cannot. This difference is somewhat flattened in the novel because it is all related in words, but if we as readers stand in the place of the narrator (the equivalent of a camera, recording events), there is a difference in immediacy between the first-hand and second-hand exposition. When Orson Welles adapted the novel for radio, he used on-site reportage, military radio communication, and finally a reflective personal testimony, increasing in first immediacy and then intimacy in relating events.

Show versus tell is an obvious difference between cinema and radio. Television can logically fall between the two, but, especially in its early stages, is 'mostly tell, show a little'. While technology has improved to a point commensurate with cinema, the generally smaller budgets and shorter production periods still constrain what is representable in television.

The manner in which the crash is reported in the various versions highlights this difference. While we never see the crash, in the film we do see the lights, hear the crash, see the destruction of the farmhouse before emerging with the characters to gawp at the rocket in the field, then the bustle of humanity coming to watch or help. The crash essentially initiates the action. By contrast, the second act of the 1953 television version begins sonically—the barking of a dog is joined by the crying of a baby as the image fades up on a flat theatrical set. A wooden fence along the front of the set suggests a gardening allotment in the space between the fence and a row of houses, the façades of which have been stripped off, exposing the interiors like dollhouses. A segment of the rocket cylinder tilts into the left-hand corner, explaining the destruction. This set will serve the second half of the episode, with characters from the neighbourhood moving mostly behind the fence and the scientists, police, reporters, and gawkers moving in front of it.

With the exception of short interstitial scenes vectored to intersect with the scene of the crash—Judith and Quatermass coated up to leave mission control, an editor dispatching a reporter at a newspaper office, and a newsreader in a studio—the second act is largely the story of the crash related in highly theatrical fashion. First, the audience experiences it through a local couple's immediate reaction to danger, then an old woman relating the crash to a policeman, and then these witnesses giving their stories to reporters. The primacy of radio is signalled by the short inset of the newsreader: despite the frontal blocking and the careful arrangement of microphone to his side and clock over his head, his head-down reading signals 'radio' rather than television. As a reporter conducts on-site interviews, the characters cluster theatrically around the microphone. It would have been easy to elide the broadcast camera for a news camera, but representing *radio* as the means of transmission of information fits into the larger pattern of recalling the Blitz as a reference for the crash.

The 2005 version has an amusing synthesis of the two versions of this sequence, with the original witness couple and the young rural lovers melded into a middle-aged married couple canoodling in a car when the crash occurs—even the rocket lands on its side, which almost seems like a cheeky compromise between fins and nose, though it may have just been a practicality for constructing an outside set piece. In this version, characters are interviewed by a *television* reporter in a hyperaware media deployment: the live broadcast camera takes in the entire set-up, with the lighting, cameraman, security tape, and portable monitor for the in-story report creating a stage and television screen within the larger image.

## Sonic Space

In each iteration of *Quatermass*, certain spaces are invested with sonic profiles that have significant narrative and affective impact, mingling sound effect, voice, and music. These places are those most implicated in the mysterious circumstances of apparent sole-survivor Victor Carroon's transformation into an amalgamation of all the living material on the ship (the astronauts and even some plant samples). Carroon begins to take on more plant-like characteristics while suffering disorientation and shock from the melded psyches, and the transmogrified 'monster' is eventually killed by the rebellion of the absorbed humans called out by Quatermass. These significant spaces are the ship, the medical area in which he is tended, and Westminster Abbey/The Tate Modern Museum, 'sanctified' public spaces for the sacrifice.

## The Ship

In the 1953 series, our first entry into the spaceship is musically silent. The moment that Quatermass and his assistant Marsh (Moray Watson) start to look around the quarters (their eyelines followed by the camera), soft tremolo strings (midrange with harmonic overlays) begin, moving in slow, stepwise fashion up two steps and then down; a soft celesta (or vibraphone) arpeggio chimes as focus falls on an empty spacesuit, an important clue—the spacesuit is made such that it has to be taken off in layers, and so the intact but empty spacesuit means that it wasn't taken off, but that the astronaut disappeared from inside it. The simple, rocking phrase is repeated, and this time on the chiming arpeggio, Marsh exclaims, 'Mr. Greene! Doctor Reichenheim! I don't understand! How could they ?' The chime thus links the clue (the spacesuit) with the symptom (the disappeared men).[8]

Later, as the scientists explore an organic colloid found in the rocket's cockpit, the suspenseful cue thickens, with slowly rising bass notes added to the tremolos and almost waltz-like chimes, the arpeggio now in rippling chord structures. Pianissimo flute flourishes tumble down in anticipation of the invocation of 'centrifugal force' forcing the colloid into the grillwork of the rocket-ship. The clues become more overt, and the music evoking the incident that merged the organic material in the ship less tenuous. The parallel scene takes place in the medlab in both the Hammer film and 2005 live broadcast.

In sharp contrast to the television versions, no music at all is used in the ship sequence in the film. The hollow clanks and clangs of a submarine-like metallic structure are the only non-dialogue sounds, emphasizing the emptiness of the vessel. The 2005 version relies even more than the first on the old radio suspense (and early horror film) concept that what you *don't* see is most powerful. We never see inside the cockpit; however, we hear it. The black-box recording is electronically salvaged in a scene that echoes the colloidal investigation. Flashback close-ups of the space-helmeted crew depict them speaking, but their voices are obscured by a white-noise hiss and a sucking, garbling distortion.

At the crash site itself, a low synthesized string drone lies underneath the cordoned-off scene of the crash; joined by a higher drone, Quatermass (Jason Flemyng) asks 'Are they alive?' and his colleague Paterson (Mark Gatiss) replies, 'I don't know.' An erratic metallic banging almost sounds like a percussive element of the score until Judith (Indira Varma) calls for everyone to stop and listen, and the music stops too, exposing the banging's diegetic source. Victor Carroon (Andrew Tiernan) climbs out of the opened hatch to a low drone, walks towards them, and falls to the ground. A disjunct but long-lined cello lament descends, repeats, then rises in its consequent phrase to an unstable cadence and starts to shift tonality. As Quatermass, Judith, and Lomax (Adrian Dunbar) of the MOD gather around Carroon in the foreground, Paterson peers inside the hatch, later to declare it empty. The low drone continues throughout, then moves up a perfect fourth (interpretable as a perfect cadence) as they call for medical care. The low string line becomes more melodic before we then cut to the interview of crash witnesses, when the music drops out entirely for the imbedded televisual segment.

## Medlab

The most distinctive element of the 2005 version is the ambient soundscape of the medlab; the blindingly white, sterile space pulses with quasi-musical life. Every moment of every scene in the medlab features a low, steady pulsating beat like a heartbeat, usually mixed with soft, higher, faster bleeping synthesized sounds. These sounds could conceivably be coming from instruments within the lab, but they are never cued to a visual source, and at times work against that assumption. Intensity is added through the layering of low synthesized drones, or volume, as when Judith admits that she and Victor weren't happy in their marriage; by contrast, in a moment of tenuous contact between Judith and Victor, the sound reduces just to that inexorable beat. Yet the pulsing 'heart rate' never rises in tempo, even when Victor reacts aggressively.

Repeatedly, the medlab scene cuts to a television screen and a shot of a newsreader summarizing events, and the music smooths into a chord, the pulse drops out, and then will cease entirely in the next scene. The newsreader scenes are transitions, an efficient adaptation for switching sets/locations in a live broadcast.

The extraordinary sonic nature of the medlab sequences in this version highlights subtler but significant treatments in earlier versions. Because only the first two episodes of the original television series exist, time in the medical lab is limited, but telling. Music underlines those moments that reveal Victor's absorption of the other crewmembers. As Judith and Quatermass ask about the fate of the other astronauts, the glassy harmonics and bell-like arpeggio of the 'ship' soundscape return, growing more dissonant as Quatermass urges an increasingly upset Victor to elucidate. A rich, emotive cello line underlines Victor calling Louisa Greene (Tracy O'Flaherty) 'Lou', a nickname only her husband used, and his sudden ability to speak German. The music dies out in a silent accentuation when Carroon is asked his name and replies weakly with the name of fellow astronaut Ludwig Reichenheim. Even in the sequence when Judith confesses that she had intended to leave Victor upon his return, there is no music, leaving its function purely to evoke what happened to the men in the spaceship.

In the Hammer film, the room in which Victor is tended is associated with a wavering whole step in high strings and winds surrounded by a slight haze of dissonance. The music crescendoes and becomes deeper and more ominous as Victor displays distress, but fades immediately as we return to the outer office and Quatermass enters to converse with the doctor, Gordon Briscoe (David King-Wood). Through the glass partition, we see Victor struggle from the bed and (dimly) hear the crash of a vase of flowers; a napping Judith awakens and rushes to the French doors, and as she opens the doors, the music crescendoes quickly to a trill, as if the sound has been suppressed behind the glass. Soft trills mickey-mouse Victor's twitching fingers and a low-level, suspenseful *agitato* persists as Judith confronts Quatermass over Victor's condition. The cue peaks slightly when Briscoe declares that he is sending Victor to a hospital. A slight, bittersweet mordent accentuates Briscoe's departure from the room, and with a high flutter, the music evaporates with the visual cross-fade to the next scene.

## Sanctified Space

Only the teleplays remain to hint at the finale of the original version, in which the compound 'Thing' is killed in Westminster Abbey. Notable sonic elements in the scripts include the agitated rustling of the tentacled moss/fern creature, Quatermass's hypnotic calling out of the three individual astronauts in turn, and the increasing electronic sound that rises as Quatermass has the television van (there to broadcast a live architecture documentary on the Abbey) play back the recording of what happened in the rocketship. Quatermass urges the three men to 'dissever' themselves from the evil that will destroy their world, and Judith recognizes ' That noise! It's the thing itself!' (Kneale, 2005, Ep. 6, p. 43). The electronic sound rises in volume and pitch as the Thing gathers itself as if to leap; then 'The sustained shrill note suddenly sweeps down the scale—not electronic sound now but into a mighty rushing wind!' (p. 44). The sound continues to decrease in pitch while at full volume, and the Thing stills. Quatermass breaks off a tendril that falls with the sound of a dry leaf. Exhausted, Quatermass declares, 'They won', and the end credit music fades back up. In this finale, the polyphony and interplay of Quatermass's voice and the playback sound of their own voices recall the three men to vanquish the composite Thing, whose simple electronic hum can only rise and fall in resistance and death.

This version builds suspense across the gap between the fifth and sixth episodes by having the Thing creeping into view of the documentary television cameras within the television show, doubling the 'liveness'. Sound is the Thing's 'voice'. In the Hammer version, music creates a visceral tension in the audience, typical of horror, and represents the means of defeating the monster.

A workman falls from the scaffolding, dead; a shot from outside shows a slimy trail across the cobblestones and brickwork of the exterior; a small raft of busy, wavering, stuttering strings rises over Westminster Abbey as we first see the monster in the scaffolding, and then descends into low, rhythmic pulsations in strings and percussion that increase in intensity until a volume fade when power is cut all over London. A timpani softly beats and rolls in 3/4 alternation as Big Ben chimes and we hear the creaking of the scaffolding as it is wired up to the electrical grid. String tremolos layer octaves over the timpani as the last workman runs outside to contact Battersea Power Station. Sudden musical silence clears the aural palate before the electricity is turned on, and shrieks come up from the violins, the electricity in the wires, and the monster, fading to a soft electronic hum and silence as the Thing falls dead. In contrast to sound as a manifestation of the life force of the creature in the television show, the sound is (primarily) the force that kills it and chronicles its death in the film. And at the end, the main title cue is reprised as Marsh asks Quatermass what he is going to do; Quatermass replies he is going to start again, and we get a shot of a rocket lifting off into space—the first time we see the rocket in flight. If the music were different, we could project a more successful subsequent flight, but the musical rounding of the reprise suggests something far more ominous, a common trope of horror fantasy: the possibility of it all happening over again.

At the climax of the 2005 version, Paterson enters the Turbine Hall of the Tate Modern Museum (standing in for Poet's Corner) and is overwhelmed by an electronic musicalized scream reminiscent of that of the Martians described in *War of the Worlds*, although somewhat more sonically complex, and certainly more complex than the electronic sound suggested by the Kneale's original script. A hollow rumbling suggests breathing in the enormous space even when the screaming stops. But it is Paterson's shrieks we hear from outside the building, along with Quatermass and the others.

Quatermass then decides to enter, as Briscoe (David Tennant) plays the cleaned-up black-box recording. Some distortions remain, consisting of quasi-musical effects like enveloping tones and burbling. Percussive rumblings at first seem to be part of the recording (they seem to be the sounds that the voices on the tape are reacting to), but the amount of reverb suggests that they are in the cavernous hall. A low drone begins as a spotlighted Quatermass addresses the three men, and he physically reacts to an invisible force. Howling sounds increasingly take up the sonic space; they are heard by those outside, but inside, there is only a drone as Quatermass says, 'It can only exist through your submission', and he turns to see Carroon in his space suit, lit from underneath in another spotlight. As the other two astronauts step up from the darkness, Quatermass urges, 'You must dissever from it. Send it out of this earthly existence!'. A low pulse sounds softly under high, gently dissonant vocal timbres as Quatermass falls to the floor in slow motion. In this version, the monster is thus entirely invoked by sound, and defeated by sound, with a choir of alien angels cushioning Quatermass's fall.

Synth string music picks up as we see a twitching Quatermass lying alone on the floor, then a cut takes us outside where Briscoe surmises, excitedly, that the Thing must be dead, and Quatermass walks unsteadily out of the building. The score is overtaken by 'Mars' as the credits roll and we see folks milling about in a manner that could be either relief from the 'real' dramatized events or the actors breaking character in a post-performance round of hugs and smiles.

## Genre, Medium, and Sonic Space

Science fiction is a genre that stretches across modern media from the short story to the video game; it is also a genre that requires the kind of leaps of imagination that sound is particularly adept at suggesting and shaping, not just creatures, objects, and ideas, but space and time. Radio and television are media that rely heavily on sound to transmit information, and while cinema is widely conceived and construed as a visual medium, it is nonetheless susceptible to sound's manipulation. The horror genre relies especially on sound to condition the audience response, and as the genre overlaps with science fiction, it isn't difficult for the same story to slip through that permeable boundary when crossing media.

The near-contemporaneous re-versioning of *Quatermass* from television to film in the 1950s demonstrates how the same story emerged quite differently in the two media, each version illustrating a representative configuration of sound. In the television version, sound effect, music, and speech interact dynamically, transmitting information at the same time as they build suspense; the traces of radio are still strongly visible (yes, visible, in the staging of characters around a microphone, or the blocking and editing of a telephone conversation); in the film version, a science-fiction tale slips easily into the grooves of the horror genre, letting sound effect and music shape our response while the image teases with withheld information. Half a century later, it is the modern medium of television itself that serves a structuring function in a live broadcast, a throwback to earlier times.

In all three versions of *Quatermass*, sound defines key spaces; it gives information about the mystery and agency to the characters merged into the 'monster'. And in the end, it is the combination of electronic sound and the human voice that delivers the finale in a grand space in part defined by its vaulted acoustic aliveness. In the original television version, electronic sound represents the life-power of the monster; in the Hammer version, it represents the power that kills the monster. In the more complex soundworld of the 2005 version, electronic sound represents the alien force in the great hall, enveloping the voices of the astronauts in the corporate creature; but in the end, it is the human voice—that of Quatermass and their own cockpit recording—that recalls the astronauts to life.

## Notes

1. A 1954 West German–French–American co-produced *Flash Gordon* [syndicated in the USA] has unusually high production values and storylines that offer some more thoughtful nuances than the usual kids' fare.
2. The 1950s cycles of flying saucer and monster-mutation movies arguably straddle and/or blend the horror and speculative fiction divide.
3. The slightly glassy curvature of the image is an artifact of the primitive cameras, but suggests looking out through the window of the rocket. (Pixley, 2005, p. 10).
4. *Quatermass* was largely scored with library music, but the concern here is with affect rather than authorship. Pixley lists the provenance of many of the cues (2005, p. 12).
5. The 2005 television version makes the transition from above earth to control room through a transparent heads-up display in front of the mission control banks. The characters, introduced as a group rather than a succession, face the camera, creating a closer intimacy through the near-direct address through the glass.
6. This sound's association with horror is underlined by the running joke in *Young Frankenstein* (Mel Brooks, 1974)—whenever Frau Blucher's name is mentioned, it is accompanied by the terrified whinny of a horse.
7. This similarity is a major plot point in the third *Quatermass* miniseries *Quatermass and the Pit*.
8. A shortened version of the scene is repeated at the beginning of the second episode, coming out of the short narrator recap; it is cut after the shot of the spacesuit and the chiming arpeggio, thus getting the clue in and preserving musical coherence.

## References

Hutchings, P. (1993) *Hammer and Beyond: The British Horror Film* (Manchester: Manchester University Press).

Kneale, N. (2005) 'DVD Extra: The Quatermass Experiment, Teleplays for Episodes 4–6', *The Quatermass Collection*, British Broacdasting Corporation, DVD1478.

Koch, H. E. (adaptation) 'The War of the Worlds Radio Script', http://www.sacred-texts.com/ufo/mars/wow.htm, date accessed 29 March 2015.

Pixley, A. (2005) 'Viewing Notes', *The Quatermass Collection,* DVD, British Broadcasting Corporation, DVD1478.

Wells, H.G. (1898) *The War of the Worlds*. Atria Unbound e-books, date accessed 24 March 2015.

CHAPTER 16

# Sound, Music and Memory in Jia Zhangke's 'Hometown Trilogy'

*Philippa Lovatt*

> Music cannot exist in isolation from a broader geography of sound and the very idea of music as a separate category of sonic experience depends on this cultural politics. The struggle between authorised and unauthorised sound constantly raises these issues as spatial questions. Such issues include the subversive role of sound to create alternative and semiautonomous spaces, as well as the sociopolitical mechanisms for enforcing silence. (George Revill, 2000, p. 602)

A shrill, sustained note pierces the darkness of the black screen of the opening credits of Jia Zhangke's *Platform* (*Zhantai*, 2000). A moment later, the melodious sounds of traditional Chinese instruments can be heard as the musicians in the performance troupe about to play begin to tune up: first, the lute-like strings of the sanxian, joined then by the fiddle sound of the erhu and then a bamboo flute—the lilting, bird-like dizi. These sounds interweave with the ambient expectant hum of the auditorium and the voices of a group of peasants talking and laughing nearby, waiting to take their seats. As the musicians warm up their instruments, playing different variations of arpeggios and glissandi, the formal properties of the exercises, which are by their nature repetitive, convey stilted movement. The ascending notes seem to embody a sense of forward projection that is drawn back as the notes descend, encapsulating sonically a feeling of temporal suspension. These first three minutes of screen time capture the mood of expectation that pervades the entire film, and Jia Zhangke's 'Hometown Trilogy', through sound.

The 'Hometown Trilogy': *Xiao Wu* (1997), *Platform* (2000) and *Unknown Pleasures* (*Ren xiaoyao,* 2002) is set in the Shanxi Province of rural northern China where Jia was born and grew up in the 1970s and 1980s. The three films chart that period from the end of the Cultural Revolution to the early days of

---

P. Lovatt
University of Stirling, UK

© The Editor(s) (if applicable) and The Author(s) 2016
L. Greene, D. Kulezic-Wilson (eds.), *The Palgrave Handbook of Sound Design and Music in Screen Media*, DOI 10.1057/978-1-137-51680-0_16

the reform era, focussing as Michael Berry notes, on 'the plight of marginalised individuals—singers, dancers, pickpockets, prostitutes and drifters—as they struggle to navigate through the radically transforming terrain of contemporary China' (2009, p. 20). Although fictional, as Jin Liu has observed, the films offer a '"supplementary history", a documentary-based representation of a contemporary Chinese underclass' (2006, p. 164).

Ching Kwan Lee and Guobin Yang have argued that since the reform era, popular memories have gained particular currency and momentum in the People's Republic of China (PRC) as people have tried to find 'moral and cognitive frameworks to understand, assess, and sometimes resist [the] momentous changes in their lives' (2007, p. 1). In this context, they assert, through 'television series, documentaries, novels, songs, theatre, music, and memorabilia in street markets, the purveyors of public and commercial nostalgia for China's revolutionary past have produced a "memory industry"' (2007, p. 1). The films of the Fifth Generation produced a very particular 'version' of the past through their use of epic narratives, often demonstrating a similarly nostalgic attitude towards the Cultural Revolution. By contrast, leading Sixth Generation director, Jia Zhangke, is concerned with making films that reflect the 'ordinariness' and heterogeneity of 'unofficial' memories (*minjian de jiyi*) (Jia Zhangke, 1999).

In an interview in 2007, Jia discusses the significance of music and sound for his films and for the memories he has of that time growing up. As he explains:

> One overwhelming memory I have of Fenyang ... is the vast numbers of loudspeakers that filled the air with a rich soundscape of political propaganda and music. Most factories had a tannoy system that would broadcast revolutionary songs or announce which new official had come to work there, or which party member had recently been pardoned or sanctioned. In the mornings, the workers who slept in dormitories at the back of the factory would file out to its bugle call. Such sounds transport me instantly back to that era, and my childhood reality is reflected in the multiple layers of sound that I use in my own films. (Jia Zhangke, 2007)

Jin Liu argues that in Jia's films the acoustic realm helps to establish both the period and the region in which they are set: popular music is like 'cheap wallpaper' of the time, he argues, while the sounds of local Jin opera (*Jin ju*) denote the specific geographical location (2006, p. 175). As I have discussed elsewhere, it is through this layering of acoustic space that the films communicate the ways in which social and personal memories are connected; their rich sonic texture expresses the dialectic between the public and the private, by establishing both the atmosphere of an era within the diegetic space of the film through music, radio or television broadcasts, for example, and by setting the (sometimes conflicting) emotional tone for each scene (Philippa Lovatt, 2012, p. 420). In the 'Hometown Trilogy' the complex diegetic soundscapes, which are often recorded using the documentary method of 'direct sound', are represented as 'occupied' spaces: acoustic realms that are densely layered with the competing discourses of reform era China. This chapter explores how this experience of lived space during the period of China's rapid transformation in the years following the end of the Cultural Revolution is articulated through sound and music.

## REVOLUTIONARY SOUNDS

*Platform*, the second film in the trilogy (although the earliest in terms of its period setting), follows the lives of the members of the Fenyang Cultural Group: a state-run Maoist propaganda troupe that perform plays and music around remote areas of Northern China. The film chronicles their journey from the early days of the reform era in 1979 to the end of the 1980s, when the group have been transformed through privatization into the All Star Rock n' Breakdance Electronic Band. Documenting this period of rapid societal change (chronologically, the period leading up to the first film of the trilogy, *Xiao Wu*), the film expresses the relationship between memory and history through the transforming soundscape of the era: from revolutionary songs of the early post-Mao period, to illegal Taiwanese gangtai, to the sounds of Bollywood emanating from the local cinema, to the nihilistic electronic rock music of the reform era, and finally to the 'easy listening' sounds of 'Travelling in Suzhou' (*Gusu xing*) that sonically encode the domesticity of the film's closing scene.

The sense of expectation established on the soundtrack in the first few moments of *Platform* is violently ruptured as the house bell rings out over the acoustic space of the auditorium, calling to attention the start of the performance. One of the members of the performance troupe, Yin Ruijuan (Zhao Tao), walks onto the stage (dressed in a traditional Maoist jacket and cap) and introduces the play: 'Train to Shaoshan' (*Huoche xiangzhe Shaoshan pao*). The audience applauds enthusiastically in recognition of Shaoshan's significance as the hometown of Mao Zedong. Ruijuan continues: 'A southbound train races across the sunny land; it is heading for Shaoshan, Chairman Mao's hometown. Look, here they come!' According to Elizabeth J. Perry, during the revolutionary period theatre played a crucial role in 'eliciting an emotional reaction that was used intentionally to solidify popular commitment' (2002, p. 112). While discussions of the Cultural Revolution have tended to focus on the role of ideology, organization and social structure, the mass mobilization of emotions through staged theatrical performances, as well as performative 'struggle sessions', was critical to the campaign's initial success, and to its sustained level of support. Perry writes that 'such techniques drew creatively upon dominant themes in Chinese political discourse that emphasize group—more than individual—bases of morality' and that building 'a sense of collective solidarity … was a fundamental element of revolutionary mobilization' (2002, p. 112).

Significantly then, in this scene in *Platform*, the point of audition during the mise-en-abyme is from within the space of the diegetic audience itself, as the camera films the performance in extreme long shot from the back of the auditorium. The slight reverb of the speaker's amplified voice resonates around the space and seems to merge with the subdued ambient sounds coming from the stalls: the coughs, chatter and laughter of the audience. This effect is further underscored as the mellifluous rhythm of Ruijuan's words and warm tonal quality of her voice seem to be *absorbed* into the ambience of the general room tone. This aural confluence creates an impression of wholeness—an emotional quality that captures the ideal essence of collectivism. Along with the mobilizing lyrics of the song, which project a sense of dynamism through the evocation of travel, this scene demonstrates the extent to which Maoism continued to be a cultural force, particularly in rural areas, even after the death of Mao Zedong, while highlighting the importance of the role played by emotion in mobilizing the masses during the revolutionary period.

As the play begins, the troupe's flautist plays a soaring, joyful melody while a group of actors (bent down over wooden chairs pretending to be the wheels of the train) enter from stage right singing in harmony with the flute: *Wheels flying, whistles blowing, train heading for Shaoshan, over mountains across rivers toward the radiant sun.* A ripple of laughter flows across the audience in response to this comical sight. Then one of the characters on stage asks how much longer the journey will take, as he says that one of the older passengers is finding it too slow. Somewhat affronted by this, the old man in question steps up and says in response, 'Young folk, don't you know?' before bursting into song: '*Learn from Dazhai Commune, where poor farmers raised the red flag. They united in action—fearless and practical they acted as one*'. The last line of the song is emphasized as the group repeats it, raising their arms in unison. The dynamism evoked by the lyrics and performance style is also made concrete through the motif of the train which, first introduced here, becomes a pivotal, structuring motif in the film. The verbal exchange described above betrays an anxiety over the tantalizingly slow pace of change as experienced by young people in peripheral communities during this period. However, the theme of train travel also resonates more broadly within the film as a powerful indicator of the changing perceptions of space and time during this decade of rapid industrialization, as well as the changing horizons of personal expectation that followed.

According to Arnold Trachtenberg, during the process of industrialization in the West the railway introduced 'a new system of behaviour: not only of travel and communication but of thought, of feeling, of expectation … the Utopian promise implicit in the establishment of speed as a new principle of public life' (Trachtenberg cited in Schivelbusch, 1986, p. xiii). While in China at the end of the 1970s, this utopian promise was almost tangible in the country's economic centres, in places like Fenyang, being as it was on the cusp of such great change (but always just out of reach), it manifested itself in a feeling of suspension. This is articulated in the scene that takes place shortly after the performance where the troupe's leader, Lao Xu (Liu Juan), berates Cui Mingliang (the film's central character played by Wang Hongwei) for keeping them waiting, saying that he lacks 'discipline' and does not understand the principles of collectivism. Interestingly, he focuses his annoyance on Mingliang's impression of the train during the performance:

| | |
|---|---|
| *Mingliang*: | Give me a break I'm not that late. I didn't spoil the show. |
| *Lao Xu*: | Didn't you? What the hell were those train sounds? |
| *Mingliang*: | I don't know how a train sounds! |
| *Lao Xu*: | Never taken a train? Even if you've never tasted pork you must have seen a pig! |
| *Mingliang*: | I've only heard one! |

[Everyone laughs].

As their hometown Fenyang is not on a railway line, it is likely that none of these characters would have ever heard a train and so their only reference points against which to measure their performance are fictional. Driving into the darkness, the group playfully mimic the toot of a train's whistle, producing an antiphonal response to the sustained note heard at the very beginning of the film. We then hear the group vocalize the chugging noises of the train's engine and the steady rhythm of the wheels on the tracks, which bring a close to the film's prologue.

The title of the film refers to the platform of a train station (an image that connotes both movement and stillness), but also comes from a pop song of the late 1980s by Liu Hong. This song appears later in the film in a scene in which the performance troupe's truck gets stuck in wet sands in a remote area of northern China while they are on tour. Realizing that they may be there for some time, Mingliang puts a tape of the song on the truck's cassette player. As the other members of the troupe gather round to listen, the absence of dialogue focuses our attention on the song's lyrics, which seem to speak of the characters' own subjective experience of suspended time. In the song, a character waits for a train that seems like it will never arrive: '*The long and empty platform/Lonely, we can only wait/All my love is out-bound/Nothing on the in-bound train*'. As well as signalling a particular time period, the wistful lyrics and melancholy music (a guitar-based soft rock sound) convey the frustration of unfulfilled expectation that characterized the experience of modernity in those communities peripheral to the dynamic centres of change in this period in China's recent past, as information about the radical social and economic developments being experienced in China's coastal cities (such as Shanghai, Guangzhou and Wenzhou) gradually filtered through.

One of the group catches the sound of a distant freight train making its way closer towards them. Whooping and screaming, they run to get close to it before it passes by. On the soundtrack, the volume of the diegetic pop song is heightened as it continues over the noise of the train blowing its whistle and rumbling loudly over the tracks before coming into view. This aural juxtaposition emphasizes both the symbolic weight of the motif in the film and in the characters' lives at this pivotal moment. As Jason McGrath observes, as well as being 'a literal industrial emblem of modernisation' the train is also an 'abstract symbol of modernity actually experienced largely as an absence and a longing' (2007, p. 98). The characters' longing is tangible as we see them filmed in extreme long shot climb the hillside and run up onto the railway bridge, calling out the train sounds they had performed earlier in the opening scene as the train itself speeds out of view.

During the course of the film, the wonder demonstrated in the scene on the bridge turns into one of silent resignation as the 'utopian' promise of the earlier moment never materializes. While in the scene described above, the train's whistle symbolizes new (albeit unattainable) opportunities for travel and experience, by the film's final scene it has become an emblem of thwarted ambition. Framed within a small interior domestic space, Mingliang dozes on the sofa while Ruijuan, now his wife, entertains their young child as a kettle boils on the hob. The soporific atmosphere created by Mingliang's faint snore and the traditional sounds of 'Travelling in Suzhou' (*Gusu xing*) playing in the background is shattered by the kettle's whistle blasting into the acoustic space. This sound, a homophone of the piercing note that began the film, now brings it to a close. The symbolic use of antiphony here suggests that in the space of the ten years, despite the official rhetoric of progress and transformation, for them, nothing has really changed (see Ying Bao, 2013, p. 214).

The rhetoric of synchronicity encapsulated in the train motif in *Platform* forms a dialectic in the film with the discourse of productivity and industry associated with revolutionary mobilization. Both discursive frameworks privilege the regulation and productive use of time and the notion of a forward trajectory (literally and ideologically). As the improvised sound of the train (by the performance troupe) cuts abruptly to the fast, regimented rhythm of a sewing machine, we see a woman dressed in Maoist clothing, bent over the machine steadily operating its foot pedal, moving her body slightly in synchrony with its beat as she listens to revolutionary music on the radio: the 1948 propaganda song 'We Workers Have Power' (*Za men gong ren you li liang*). The music has a similarly upbeat rhythm and a 'rallying' energy (resulting from the different voices singing together in harmony) that interweaves with the rhythm of the machine, thereby also forming a connection with the movement of the woman's body.

George Revill contends that the 'physical properties of sound, pitch, rhythm, timbre seem to act on and through the body in ways which require neither explanation nor reflection' (2000, p. 602). For him this means that music has a particular ability to 'play on the emotions' in order to 'arouse and subdue, animate and pacify'—an ability exploited by nationalist music, he suggests, as it 'draws cultural authority from the apparently shared intersubjective qualities of sound' (p. 602). Nationalist music, he argues, draws together social and political messages and incorporates them into 'an aesthetic of bodily involvement' encouraging participation through 'its rhythmic and melodic qualities' (p. 602). The mention made here of bodily movement has a particular significance in relation to this scene in *Platform* while also resonating with Perry's discussion of the role of 'emotion work' in 'mobilizing the masses'. Both of these arguments are at work in this scene in *Platform* as the 'intersubjective qualities' of 'We Workers Have Power' (its timbre and harmony) demonstrate this ability of music to 'harness' the emotions and produce 'participatory' subjects. Moreover, the synergic relationship between the mobilizing force of this music and the repetitive rhythm of machine noise in this scene suggests that the body's rhythms can similarly be 'harnessed' by those of industry, thereby creating a regulated 'productive body' for the 'participatory subject' characteristic of the socialist era. Yet, it soon becomes clear that times are changing in Fenyang, as Mingliang, who is the woman's son, pesters her to finish the bell-bottom trousers that she has been sewing for him. When Mingliang jokes that he is an 'art worker' who uses his brain, she answers incredulously: 'Really? Here you follow orders'. Later when the father criticizes his 'bourgeois' trousers and accuses Mingliang of sounding like a 'capitalist roader', their dialogue highlights the tensions between the competing ideologies of communism and individualism that began to circulate in the early days of the reform era: a pivotal socio-cultural shift that Jia's film here articulates through the layering of sound.

## 'A New Mode of Listening'

Describing the soundscape of the PRC between 1949 and 1979, Nimrod Baranovitch argues that the state's monolithic structure, which 'imposed unity in almost every domain', resulted in there being only one audible voice within the public sphere, that of the Communist Party (2003, p. 1). Reaching a crescendo in the decade of the Cultural Revolution, the party's message, he writes, 'was disseminated, through every possible medium—film, radio, recordings, television, live performances, and public address systems—and [was] heard and seen "everywhere" and "at all times"' (p. 1). During the reform era, however, the soundscape of the PRC also began to change. As he explains:

> One of the immediate consequences of the ... 'open door policy' was the flooding into the country of foreign cultural products, among which was popular music. As foreigners could move into and out of China more freely, cassettes and records of contemporary pop started to be smuggled in and soon swept the entire mainland. (p. 1)

The introduction of new (comparatively) inexpensive tape recorders and cassettes, particularly 'gangtai' music from Hong Kong and Taiwan, Baranovitch argues, had a 'decentralizing and democratizing effect' as for the first time since the establishment of the People's Republic, people could choose what they wanted to listen to (pp. 12–13). As more people started to own tape recorders, he explains, a 'new mode of listening' began to be experienced as the reception of music no longer needed to be restricted to public spaces where the sounds heard were dependent on the choices made by the state, but now 'individuals could create [their own] intimate sonic space' (p. 13).

In an interview with Michael Berry, Jia describes the impact that popular music had on his generation as he recalls the first time he heard illegal gangtai music from Taiwan by the pop phenomenon Teresa Teng:

At the time, I was quite young and couldn't really say what it was about her voice, but it was so moving ... Later when I went to college and reflected back on this time, I realised that her music represented a massive change in our cultural landscape. When I was a child we used to ... sing 'We Are to Carry on Communism' (*Women shi gongchanzhuyi de jiebanren*) or in the eighties ... 'We are the New Generation of the Eighties' (*Women shi bashi niandai de xin yidai*), both of which highlighted the 'we'—the collective. But Teresa Teng's songs were always about 'me'—the individual. Songs like 'I Love You' (*Wo ai ni*) and 'The Moon Represents My Heart' (*Yueliang daibiao wo de xin*) were something completely new. So people of my generation were suddenly infected with this very personal individual world. Before that, everything was collective: we lived in a collective dormitory, our parents worked as part of a collective, and our schools were structured in the same manner. In our educational system the individual belonged to the nation and was part of the collective. But in the eighties everything changed, and it all started with popular music. (Jia Zhangke in Michael Berry, 2005, pp. 189–90)

Geremie R. Barmé writes that: 'The threat of popular music from Hong Kong and Taiwan had been recognised for nearly a decade, and in the early 1980s, Teresa Teng (Deng Lijun) cassettes were confiscated and burned in an attempt to deter people from nonmainland music' (1999, p. 117). Just as rail travel evokes the changing conceptualizations of time and space in Jia's films, the presence of diegetic pop music therefore also signifies fundamental shifts that occurred at this time in the perception of space-time and the limits of experience, particularly across the three films of the Hometown Trilogy which recurrently turn to pop music to convey the changing mood of the era.

Later in *Platform*, when Mingliang's friend Jun (Liang Jingdong) returns from a visit to Guangzhou (an economic centre in the south) he brings with him the 'new sounds' of the city: pop music from Taiwan and Hong Kong. Carrying a ghetto blaster, he walks along the path towards the troupe's rehearsal space: the centre of the sound *moving with him* as opposed to *surrounding him*. The music he is listening to is 'Genghis Khan' (*Cheng ji si han*)—a poppy rock 'n' roll number by Zhang Di with twangy guitars and a stomping bass line (the lyrics tell us Zhang Di is '*always asked if Taiwan girls are better than Singapore girls*'). Highlighting a connection made between sound and travel in an earlier scene in Jun's bedroom, Mingliang walks towards him pointing a gun and joking: 'Stop! Foreign Devil!' When the rest of the troupe rushes out to see him, they are all excited to hear about life in the south and listen to the new sounds he has brought back with him. A cut to an interior 'disco' scene shows the group dancing energetically and expressively, foregrounding a sense of autonomy that vividly contrasts with the regimented 'machine-like' movement of Mingliang's mother at the sewing machine earlier. This diegetic sound then bleeds into the next scene, which takes place the following day as Zhang Di is still being played on Jun's ghetto blaster as he and his friends do their chores; importantly, bringing the sound with them, they are able to create their own autonomous acoustic world. This 'new world' also reaches out into the wider world with the promise of travel and adventure, as indicated on the diegetic soundtrack by the overlaying of this song with a 'Teach-Yourself-English' tape playing loudly in the aural mix, seeming to bring this 'other world' closer to home.

From 1978 onwards, with the impact of Deng Xiaoping's economic reforms, China experienced 'a radical break' with its revolutionary past, which led to a questioning of the framework of experiences, values and ideologies associated with that past (Dirlik and Zhang, 2000, p. 8). This sense of flux is expressed at several points in Jia's earlier film, *Xiao Wu*, through its use of sound and music. The film begins with an audio recording of a kind of comic skit (*xiangsheng*) set against the black screen of the opening credits (Berry, 2008, p. 250). A clipped, fast-paced, staccato exchange between a man and a woman speaking in northern Chinese dialect is intercut with the disembodied sound of an audience's laughter and applause which ripples warmly across the non-diegetic soundtrack. This then merges with the diegetic sound of the distant rumble of a truck coming closer as it makes its way along the dusty country road towards a family who are waiting by the roadside. In the distant background behind them, stark, branchless trees visually echo the tall industrial chimneys also in the frame, of a factory formerly run by the people's commune, a grim image, argues Xiaoping Lin, that recalls Mao's disastrous Great Leap Forward launched three decades previously (Xiaoping Lin, 2005, p. 191). *Xiangsheng* became very popular during the reform era in response to the rapid changes being experienced. While many Chinese lost patience with the slow-paced didacticism of traditional Maoist drama, the quick-paced, lively entertainment offered by these sketches reflected more closely their own lives and concerns, deploying parody or satire to critique state corruption as well as contemporary social phenomena (Mackerras, 1981, p. 103). In this opening scene, the quick-fire pace of the satirical soundtrack conflicts with the slow (even static) pace of life shown on screen where we see characters standing, watching, waiting while 'China's post-socialist project ... passes them by' (Berry, 2008, p. 251).

Like *Platform*, *Xiao Wu* documents a period of turbulent transition in China's recent history. Set towards the end of the 1990s, the film focuses on Xiao Wu (Wang Hongwei), a pickpocket from Fenyang, who has lost touch with his former best friend Xiaoyong (Hao Hongjian) now a successful business man, a 'model entrepreneur' (and local gangster), who no longer wants to know him, and his values seem to have no place in the fast changing world of the 'new China'. In *Screening the Past: Memory and Nostalgia in Cinema*, Pam Cook defines nostalgia as 'a state of longing for something that is known to be irretrievable, but is sought anyway' (2005, p. 2). As Cook suggests, there is something intrinsically melancholic about nostalgia and this is a mood that pervades *Xiao Wu* enhanced by the use of diegetic pop music in the film. In particular, Xiao Wu's ideological dislocation is evoked at several points in the film by diegetic music that becomes slowed or distorted. The first instance of this occurs outside Xiaoyong's home when we hear the pop song 'Farewell My Concubine' (*Bawang bieji*) by Tu Honggang, which at first seems to be non-diegetic. The soft-rock ballad has a soaring melody, and questioning existential lyrics 'Who is the hero now?' that perform an important narrative role in that they convey Xiao Wu's emotional state, and more specifically, his profound sense of loss and alienation as he tries to function in a world he no longer recognizes (Jin Liu, 2013, p. 195). The scene, which takes place just before Xiaoyong's wedding, begins with the piercing sound of his mobile phone ringtone as a mutual friend calls to try and persuade him to reconsider inviting Xiao Wu. Unsettled by this reminder of his old life, Xiaoyong paces backwards and forwards in front of a wall outside his house that has been scored with height lines and inscribed with the date '1982'. As he hangs up, he reaches up to touch the lines on the wall. We later see Xiao Wu mirror this gesture as he drunkenly walks past while we hear 'Farewell My Concubine' again on the soundtrack (see Lovatt, 2015, p. 192). The mood created by the stretched out, distorted sound of the music (suggestive of a kind of sonic resistance to the passage of time) heightens our sense of Xiao Wu's 'obsessive desire to recapture the past', which we know is doomed to fail (Cook, 2005, p. 8).

As the film cuts to a shot of Xiao Wu standing in a busy street opposite a stall selling ghetto blasters (bearers of the reform era's burgeoning potential for a more heterogeneous soundscape), the music's source is located and the song ends abruptly when the stop button is pressed on one of the machines. After pick-pocketing one of the stall's customers, Xiao Wu walks home whistling the song to himself and on the way passes a group of children who are singing a skipping rhyme. This layering of sounds, against the memory of the song's questioning lyrics, suggests that like the demolition of Fenyang's old town centre where nothing is built in its place, Xiao Wu's inability to position himself within the discourse of the new China makes him a spectral presence—a residual figure from the past who continues to 'haunt' the present. The song is heard again at the very end of the film after he is caught red-handed and arrested.

Another song that communicates the characters' emotional state is 'Heart Rain' (*Xin yu*), which is heard several times in the film. The song's mournful lyrics (about a lover who will '*become someone else's bride tomorrow*') foreshadow the failure of Xiao Wu's relationship with Meimei (the karaoke singer and prostitute with whom he falls in love, played by Zuo Baitao) who eventually leaves town with some wealthy businessmen. The melancholic tone however also relates to the breakdown of the bond between Xiao Wu and his former friend; tellingly, it is first heard as a background to some celebratory messages to Xiaoyong on his wedding being broadcast on local state television, and then later when a young couple sing it in front of a funeral parlour to a small gathered crowd.

In *The Space of a Song*, Richard Dyer argues that: 'Song ... is at the intersection between individual feeling and the socially and historically specific shared forms available to express that feeling, forms that shape and limit and make indirect what can be expressed and even with any degree of consciousness felt' (2011, p. 2). In this way, songs can not only communicate feeling but can also provide a way of giving form (or 'voice') to emotions that could not otherwise be expressed. For example, when Xiao Wu goes to visit Meimei at home when she is ill, she tells him how she loves to sing, and had dreams of becoming a star, but knows that she won't succeed. He asks her to sing for him and she sings a Faye Wang song, 'The Sky' (*Tian kong*), making him promise not to laugh: '*Why is my sky always weeping, why does my sky always look so sad?*'. For Meimei, singing her idol's song has an aspirational quality that elevates her above the drab reality of her everyday life. The act of singing itself opens up an imaginative, even utopian, space in which she can envisage a very different reality (a desire made evident at another point in the film when she telephones her mother and pretends that she is studying to be an actress in Beijing). Describing the scene, Jason McGrath writes: 'As the ambient exterior noises of traffic fill the silences in their conversation, Xiao Wu and Meimei struggle to penetrate each other's loneliness. When Xiao Wu asks Meimei to sing for him, her choice of song ... vocalizes the feelings of solitude and desire they cannot otherwise express' (2007, pp. 92–3). It is worth noting that Xiao Wu only finds the courage to sing the song later when he's alone and naked at a public bathhouse. But, while still in her room, when she asks him to sing, he refuses, and instead asks her to close her eyes before playing her the weary electronic version of 'Fur Elise' on his cigarette lighter, which similarly acts as a surrogate for his voice in moments of deeply felt emotion. First heard as he waits to give Xiaoyong a wedding gift (that is rejected), it plays again while Xiao Wu drunkenly watches Xiaoyong being interviewed on television. The scene ends with the lighter running out of battery and the tune whirring down to a halt while the image fades to black. Like the worn cassette tape playing 'Farewell my Concubine', 'Fur Elise' becomes therefore another aural evocation of the death of the friendship and the socialist values that it represented (to Xiao Wu at least).

## Acoustic Space and Power

Deploying the documentary method of recording 'direct sound', *Xiao Wu*'s sound designer Zhang Yang produces a disorientating acoustic space that emphasizes texture over clarity. Elena Pollacchi has argued that the use of on-location sound recording in 1990s Chinese cinema is also indicative of a wider historical and industrial shift in the use of sound more generally in Chinese film. She describes how the old system of state studio production (1950s onwards) deliberately expelled natural sound 'in order to emphasise, through dialogue and music, the ideological message' whereas since the mid-1990s the increasing use of natural sound (as opposed to dubbing) points to changing production structures which have recently started to allow on-location filming (2008, p. 193). Adopting the *xianxhang* (shooting live) aesthetic first used by the New Documentary Film Movement, these films place far greater importance on the pro-filmic and the contingent. This filming practice and its aesthetic have significant political implications in relation to the representation of the power dynamics of lived space in China's recent past.

Jacques Attali argues that 'the monopolization of the broadcast of messages, the control of noise, and the industrialization of the silence of others assure the durability of power' (1985, p. 6). Control over acoustic space is illustrated at several points in *Xiao Wu*, firstly when Xiao Wu arrives in Fenyang near the beginning of the film. In this scene, the first sounds we hear are of an authoritative male voice interrupting the sound of a pop song being broadcast over public loudspeakers in the street. While Xiao Wu stands with a crowd of people reading from a notice board about the 'crackdown' on criminal behaviour in the town, an acousmatic voice begins: 'This announcement is presented by Public Security and the Justice Department concerning the self-denunciation of criminals'. As the voice reverberates around this space, other street sounds such as the rumble of car and motorbike engines combine with it to produce a cacophonous acoustic environment that sets the tone for the entire film.

The ability of sound to make material the abstract notion of power, and to both map out and 'occupy' territory, asserting control over its 'subjects', is demonstrated in the latter part of this scene when Xiao Wu hitches a lift on the back of a friend's bicycle. As the camera films them in a tracking shot as they cycle along, they are shown to be physically moving further away from the source of the voice (projected from the overhead speaker), and yet, the sound of the broadcast does not quieten as we would expect, but remains at a constant volume. This effect suggests that the town's inhabitants cannot escape the auditory regime of the Party and alludes to the omnipresence of its voice, which although produced from a centre of power that is *elsewhere* is at the same time perceived by the subject *everywhere*. Although we do see the speaker from which the voice is being projected, the effect is similar to Michel Chion's description of the acousmatic voice in cinema. Occupying an ambiguous place, 'being in the screen and not ... the acousmêtre brings disequilibrium and tension' (1999, pp. 23–4).

The pervasive atmosphere of control in *Xiao Wu* continues into the third film in the trilogy, *Unknown Pleasures* (*Ren Xiao Yao* ironically translates as 'Free of All Constraints'—a poem by Taoist philosopher Zhuangzi that was also a pop hit by Taiwanese singer Richie Jen in 2001, the year in which it is set). The film takes place around the post-industrial mining town of Datong in northern Shanxi in the northeast of China. Xiaoping Lin notes that at this time, while China's economic boom had brought prosperity to some, 'it polarize[d] a society shaped for decades by Mao's egalitarian socialism'. While foreign trade, the domestic market and living standards, he explains, had been 'boosted' by China 'embrac[ing] capitalist globalization ... China's efforts to build a free market economy forced countless state-owned enterprises into bankruptcy, resulting in mass unemployment and grave social problems unprecedented in the nation's socialist history' (2010, p. 1). Datong's lack of infrastructure reflects this particular historical moment: it is a living graveyard of decaying buildings, semi-completed construction work and unfinished roads-to-nowhere. On the edge of town, tomblike industrial chimneys litter the barren post-socialist landscape, while electricity pylons stand nearby like scarecrows. This location is experienced by the two central protagonists, teenagers Bin Bin (Zhao Weiwei) and Xiao Ji (Wu Qiong), as a space of dislocation and inertia. As Michael Berry notes: 'the physical landscape of destruction … works as a powerful metaphor for the emotional, cultural and moral desolation of the characters as they blindly drift through towards an unknown destination' (2009, p. 94). Lacking the enthusiasm and hopefulness of the young people in *Platform*, in *Unknown Pleasures* the characters seem lost and aimless. Born in the 1980s during the Open Door era (and a result of the state's single child policy) they are the first generation to have no direct memory of Maoism, and look instead to global pop culture as a way out: the gangsters in Quentin Tarantino's *Pulp Fiction* (1994) and Hong Kong action movies, for example, provide key role models for the two boys.

In contrast to *Xiao Wu* and *Platform*, figures of authority have only a peripheral presence in *Unknown Pleasures*, appearing just once near the beginning when petty crook Xiao Wu (also played by Wang Hongwei who appeared in the earlier film) is arrested by plain-clothes police, and again later at the very end of the film when one of the central characters, Bin Bin is arrested. And yet, the acoustic space of Datong appears similarly 'occupied' but here less by official sounds of authoritarianism than by the Siren-like calls of consumerism, reflecting the changing mood of the time. Maurice Meisner has described how, in response to the ideological and political void that followed the collapse of the Cultural Revolution, Deng Xiaoping's government 'offered no great social and political ideals but rather promises of a better material life, encouraging the purchase of the new consumer goods rapidly appearing on department store shelves and on billboards that formerly displayed revolutionary slogans' (1986, p. 457). This ideological shift is treated ironically in the film as at the time of Xiao Wu's arrest, a promotion for the Datong Lottery is broadcast over a nearby loudspeaker outside the bus terminal building, while the protagonists are shown in long shot standing idly in front of the building's entrance. Firstly, a male voice announces: 'Try the lottery and make your leisure time pay'. With obvious irony, just at the moment when two policemen run up to Xiao Wu to handcuff him, a woman's voice joins in and in a spoken harmony they proclaim: 'The Shanxi Charity Lottery wishes you the best of luck!'.

The film focuses on the experiences of Bin Bin and Xiao Ji, two unemployed teenagers who live with their parents. While Bin Bin has a girlfriend (at least at the start of the film), Xiao Ji ill-fatedly falls in love with Qiao Qiao (Zhao Tao), a singer and prostitute who works for her boyfriend and pimp promoting Mongolian King liquor. The town is not completely without hope—at one point we see a group of textile workers celebrating the news of Beijing's successful 2008 Olympic bid—but overall, the atmosphere is bleak. As with the earlier films in the trilogy, in *Unknown Pleasures* pop songs perform an important role in expressing the emotional state of the characters. Richie Jen's *Ren Xiao Yao* is heard at several key points in the film, but each time conveys a slightly different mood. It is first heard booming out from the speakers next to the stage where the Mongolian King Liquor Troupe are performing, and again later when Bin Bin and his girlfriend Yuanyuan (Zhou Qingfeng) meet at a karaoke hotel, where they hold hands and softly sing along to the lyrics: '*Whatever sorrows come ... I follow the wind, I roam happy and free*'. Yet, the sorrows come more quickly than expected for Bin Bin: while Yuanyuan gains a place at the University of Beijing to study international trade, Bin Bin himself misses a chance to also make a new life in the city as a 'Beijing soldier' when a blood test indicates that he has hepatitis. After a failed (and pitifully executed) bank heist towards the end of the film, Bin Bin is caught and arrested while his best friend Xiao Ji makes an escape on his motorbike and heads for the new Datong-Beijing expressway, only to break down on the outskirts of town.

At the police station, Bin Bin reveals his naïvity about the legal system and is shocked to learn that the punishment for bank robbery is execution. Irritated by Bin Bin's insolence when he disputes the likelihood of this sentence (because it was 'only *attempted* robbery'), the police sergeant attempts to reassert his authority by ordering Bin Bin to sing: 'Stand up and sing a song', he commands him. After a short silence, he orders him again. Drawing a blank, Bin Bin asks, 'Sing what?' to which the sergeant answers simply, 'Something you know well'. With painful awkwardness he delivers a fragile, a cappella version of 'Ren xiao yao'. Rather than implying some kind of 'inner' freedom, the absurdity of hearing the song's lyrics within this hostile environment only serves to heighten our awareness of his vulnerability within the system. Martin Cloonan and Bruce Johnson have argued that the tendency of early popular music studies to 'celebrate the power of music to empower the construction of individual and social identities' belies music's equal capacity, as part of a general campaign of sonic oppression, to displace or destruct identities (2002, p. 27). Citing historical cases where music has been used as a means of torture, they write: 'Disempowerment and oppression can be brutally imposed through state terror, but they are quietly naturalised through the channels of everyday life and through means barely registered at the moment of their implementation' (p. 37). This scene, which takes place at the very end of the film, and therefore marks the conclusion of the trilogy, clearly illustrates how state control over modes of expression continued during the post-Mao period.

Unlike the earlier films, in which the dissemination of official discourse comes mostly from audio sources, most of the official voices in *Unknown Pleasures* are heard via news broadcasts shown on television sets in a range of different environments: in the home, the workplace and in public outdoor spaces. Beijing's reaction to the discovery of an American surveillance plane in sovereign air-space, for example, is shown in Bin Bin's mother's apartment; in Xiao Ji's father's workshop (which is also their home), we hear of the arrests of Falun Gong protestors after setting themselves on fire in Tiananmen Square on 23 January 2000; we hear of the planned Beijing-Datong highway in a hairdresser's salon and its successful completion later in the local police station; and, as mentioned above, on the street outside an open air pool hall, we witness the announcement of Beijing's successful Olympic bid. Nonetheless it is through the evolving soundscapes of the era, whether broadcasts or pop songs, that the Hometown Trilogy conveys the mood of the period in which the films are set: post-revolutionary China. I have argued that by alerting us to the cultural politics embedded in the auditory realm, these films articulate the 'struggle between authorised and unauthorised sound' within social space, and at the same time, express the subversive potential of sound and music in creating 'alternative and semiautonomous spaces' (Revill, 2000, p. 602). Through my discussion of the films' use of sound and music therefore, I hope to have demonstrated how these elements work together to articulate what Revill calls the 'broader geography of sound' by communicating the sonic experience of lived space during this turbulent period of China's recent history.

## References

Attali, J. (1985) [1977] *Noise: The Political Economy of Music*, trans. by Brian Massumi (Manchester: University of Minnesota).

Bao, Y. (2013) 'Remembering the Invisible: Soundscape and memory of 1989', *Journal of Chinese Cinemas*, Vol. 7, No. 3, 207–222.

Barmé, G. R. (1999) *Into the Red: On Contemporary Chinese Culture* (New York: Columbia University Press).

Baranovitch, N. (2003) *China's New Voices: Popular Music, Ethnicity, Gender and Politics, 1978–1997* (Berkeley and Los Angeles: University of California Press).

Berry, C. (2008) '*Xiao Wu*: Watching Time Go By' in C. Berry (ed.) *Chinese Films in Focus II* (Basingstoke, Hampshire and New York: Palgrave Macmillan), 250–257.

Berry, M. (2005) *Speaking in Images: Interviews with Contemporary Chinese Filmmakers* (New York: Columbia University Press).

———. (2009) *Jia Zhangke's 'Hometown Trilogy'* (London: BFI).

Chion, M. (1999) *The Voice in Cinema*, trans. by C. Gorbman (New York: Columbia University Press).

Cook, P. (2005) *Screening the Past: Memory and Nostalgia in Cinema* (Abingdon, Oxon and New York: Routledge).

Dirlik, A. and X. Zhang (2000) *Postmodernism and China* (Durham: Duke University Press).

Dyer, R. (2011) *In the Space of a Song: the Uses of Song in Film* (Abingdon, Oxon and New York: Routledge).

Cloonan, M. and B. Johnson (2002) 'Killing me softly with his song: an initial investigation into the use of popular music as a tool of oppression', *Popular Music*, Vol. 21, No. 1, 27–39.

Lee, C. K. and G. Yang (eds) (2007) *Re-visioning the Chinese Revolution: The Politics and Poetics of Collective Memories in Reform China* (Washington, D.C.: Woodrow Wilson Center Press).

Lin, X. (2005) 'Jia Zhangke's Cinematic Trilogy: A Journey across the Ruins of Post-Mao China' in S. H. Lu and E. Yueh-yu Yeh (eds) *Chinese-Language Film: Historiography, Poetics, Politics* (Honolulu: University of Hawai'i Press), 186–209.

———. (2010) *Children of Marx and Coca-Cola: Chinese Avant-garde Art and Independent Cinema* (Honolulu: University of Hawai'i Press).

Liu, J. (2006) 'The Rhetoric of Local Languages as the Marginal: Chinese Underground Films by Jia Zhangke and Others', *Modern Chinese Literature and Culture*, Vol. 18, No. 2, 163–205.

———. (2013) *Signifying the Local: Media Productions rendered in local languages Mainland China in the new millennium* (Leiden: Brill).

Lovatt, P. (2012) 'The Spectral Soundscapes of Postsocialist China in the films of Jia Zhangke', *Screen*, Vol. 53, No. 4, 434–5.

———. (2015) 'Life is Cheap: Chinese Neo-Noir and the Aesthetics of Disenchantment' in Chi-Yun Shin and M. Gallagher (eds) *East Asian Film Noir: Transnational Encounters and Intercultural Dialogue* (London and New York: I.B. Tauris), 179–196.

Mackerras, C. (1981) *The Performing Arts in Contemporary China* (Abingdon, Oxfordshire: Routledge).

McGrath, J. (2007) 'The Independent Cinema of Jia Zhangke: from Postsocialism to a Transnational Aesthetic' in Z. Zhen (ed.) *The Urban Generation: Chinese Cinema and Society at the Turn of the Twenty-first Century* (Durham and London: Duke University Press), 81–114.

Meisner, M. (1986) *Mao's China and After: A History of the People's Republic* (London: Collier Macmillan Publishers)

Perry, E. J. (2002) 'Moving the Masses: Emotion Work in the Chinese Revolution', *Mobilization: An International Journal*, Vol. 7, No. 2, 111–128.

Pollacchi, E. (2008) 'The Sound of the City: Chinese Films of the 1990s and Urban Noise' in A. Webber and E. Wilson (eds) *Cities in Transition and the Modern Metropolis* (London and New York: Wallflower Press), 193–204.

Revill, G. (2000) 'Music and the Politics of Sound: Nationalism, Citizenship, and Auditory Space', *Environment and Planning D: Society and Space*, 18, 597–614.

Schivelbusch, W. (1986) *The Railway Journey: The Industrialization of Time and Space in the 19th Century* (Leamington Spa, Hamburg and New York: Berg).

Zhangke, J. (2007) in 'Life in Film: Jia Zhangke', *Frieze Magazine*, Issue 106 (April) http://www.frieze.com/issue/article/life_in_film_jia_zhangke/, date accessed 15 December 2014.

Zhangke, J. (1999) 'The Age of Amateur Cinema Will Return' first published in *Southern Weekend* (*Nanfang Zhoumo*). [See full translation by Yuqian Yan at http://dgeneratefilms.com/critical-essays/jia-zhangke-the-age-of-amateur-cinema-will-return], date accessed 18 December 2015.

CHAPTER 17

# Vinyl Noise and Narrative in CD-Era Indiewood

*Ian Garwood*

Mason (Ellar Coltrane), the protagonist of Richard Linklater's *Boyhood* (2014), is, like his sister Samantha (Lorelei Linklater), a digital native. The film begins in 2002, with Mason aged six, following his development over 12 years. Stage by stage, Mason and Samantha are shown interacting with the digital technologies of the time: in terms of music, they are seen listening to an iPod via headphones, docked on a portable speaker, and listening through a mobile phone. Even their father (Ethan Hawke), a lover of the 'analogue' genres of blues and country rock, becomes a digital convert, selling his vintage car, the in-built cassette player of which is highlighted as a key feature, and presenting Mason with a homemade CD, authored from a computer.

The film is focalized predominantly through Mason, favouring everyday detail over major dramatic contrivance. As such, it is appropriate that he and his family are associated with music-playing technologies that a child of his age would use and encounter, at the particular time and place (Texas) within which the narrative is set. In this context, it is unsurprising that the dominant music format of the twentieth century, the record, is treated as obsolete media. A record player *is* seen in the background when Mason's father takes his kids back to the apartment he shares with his guitarist flatmate, Jimmy (Charlie Sexton). This amounts to no more than a glimpse: the player is not heard and, given that it is only brought into view by the father's solitary movement into a backroom, there is no indication that it is registered by Mason.

In the era immediately preceding the film's starting point, however, record playing was a significant trope of films produced in the same Indiewood context as *Boyhood*, that is, to say an 'independent' arena dominated, from the early to mid-1990s, by the specialty divisions of major studios (King, 2009,

I. Garwood
University of Glasgow, UK

p. 4). In the 1990s and at the very turn of the millennium, vinyl listening was becoming an ever more specialist activity, but at a point that was still pre- iTunes and the iPod. The dominant format making vinyl obsolete in this period was the CD rather than digital downloads and, in this chapter, I argue this is an influential context for the representation of vinyl listening in some of the movies of the time. To recognize particular tendencies in the films' depiction of record playing, I focus on three high-profile Indiewood films: *The Royal Tenenbaums* (Wes Anderson, 2001); *Pulp Fiction* (Quentin Tarantino, 1994); and *Ghost World* (Terry Zwigoff, 2000).

The recurrence of vinyl in films of this era has not gone unnoticed.[1] Robynn Stilwell (2006) and Tim J Anderson (2008) have both focused on record playing in (predominantly) American films of the period, with a particular crossover in their analysis of *Ghost World*. Reflection on their commentary on this film is helpful in defining the contribution my chapter makes. Stilwell studies girls' rites-of-passage films that feature record playing as an aspect of identity building for the female protagonists, within a cultural context that characterizes record collecting predominantly as male. Her commentary on *Ghost World* focuses on teenage protagonist Enid's (Thora Birch) playing of Skip James' 1931 recording 'Devil Got My Woman', passed on to her by obsessive record collector Seymour (Steve Buscemi). Stilwell concentrates on the way Enid uses the song to realize her identity through deflection, via 'a voice that comes from someplace entirely *other*' (2006, p. 159). Anderson's interest is similarly in identity building, this time in relation to an argument about the debilitating effects of nostalgia. He suggests that Enid's and Seymour's different relationships to vinyl recordings demonstrate the distinction between them as characters, Enid representing a figure who 'is able to move forward through the use of these records in a manner that Seymour never does' (2008, p. 69).

In both cases, the critical attention is on the characters' *act of* playing the records (and, in Seymour's case, his collection of them). There is very little focus on the quality of sound used to represent the records when they are played. Stilwell does claim that the 'materiality of the record matters' (Stilwell, 2006, p. 158), but the aspects she emphasizes, in terms of the argument being made about characterization, are visual ones. The privileging of the visual is also a feature of McNelis' and Boschi's study of visible playback technology in film, which analyses characters' uses of on-screen record players, amongst other types of music media (2013).

An original feature of this chapter is its attention to the sound of vinyl in the films under review. This does not entail a retreat from the narrative and character analysis employed by Stilwell, Anderson, McNelis, and Boschi. Rather it involves a consideration of the contribution of noise to such matters, a critical approach that is distinctive within the wider study of pop music in film. Indeed, this constitutes a new avenue in my own investigations of the pop soundtrack, which have tended to prioritize attention to the choices made in the selection of specific songs to soundtrack particular film moments (e.g. Garwood, 2000, 2006, 2009). By contrast, this chapter foregrounds choices in sound design that are format- rather than song-specific, whilst still relating these to individual narrative scenarios.

What are the sounds of vinyl? Each film defines them in their own way, but each is also drawing on then-contemporary cultural assumptions about the sounds that sought to distinguish records from other music formats. Discussing vinylphiles' valorization of the record over the CD specifically, John D. Davis highlights the following aural qualities:

> For vinylphiles, the sacred element surrounding vinyl is connected to the format's *authenticity* ... the vinyl record is the quintessential recorded-music format, providing a more authentic listening experience than the CD. The listening experience includes ... the sound of the vinyl record, from its scratches and pops to the perception of its more-extensive bass range. (2007, p. 404)

Emily Yochim and Megan Biddinger, again analysing vinylphilic statements, suggest that signs of fallibility, such as scratches and pops, are prized because they bestow upon the format a 'mortality' that connotes the sound's possession of human qualities such as 'warmth' and being 'alive' (2008, pp. 183, 188). They note that vinyl imperfections only become valued in the context of other music media and, in particular, in relation to the CD, a format that, upon its introduction in the 1980s, was marketed aggressively in terms of its 'perfect fidelity and infinite durability' (p. 184), that is to say, its infallibility and immortality.

The films under review appear at a point when these qualities of vinyl sound had become increasingly fetishized, in the face of the overwhelming dominance of the CD within the commercial market. Davis identifies 1989 as a key turning point for the vinyl format, with the seven major US labels significantly downscaling their support of new vinyl releases and unloading their back catalogue at reduced prices (p. 399). This consolidated the CD as the mainstream music industry's format of choice. In this context, as Davis also notes, adherence to the vinyl format became a matter of subcultural affiliation (p. 399).

The vinyl aficionado becomes, therefore, a more keenly defined cultural figure in the 1990s, and, as such, more readily available for reference as a 'type' within films of the period, particularly those with an indie sensibility. As Michael Z. Newman argues, the term 'indie' identifies a taste culture, in which affiliation to certain types of cultural objects and practices mutually reinforce one another (2009). As adherence to vinyl became a niche option, defined against the mainstream movement to CDs, it followed that this would become available as the sign of an indie sensibility that differentiated itself from mainstream values. In their work in the 1990s and early 2000s, the following key names on the American independent scene all made at least one reference to vinyl in their films: Quentin Tarantino, Hal Hartley, Jim Jarmusch, Richard Linklater, Wes Anderson, Whit Stillman, Allison Anders, Spike Lee, Sofia Coppola, David Lynch, Todd Haynes, the Coen brothers.

Amidst a myriad of choices, *The Royal Tenenbaums*, *Pulp Fiction* and *Ghost World* have been selected for closer study because they all pay particular attention to vinyl's distinctive aural signature, as it became understood in the CD era. Each film audibly references the signs of vinyl's fallibility—its surface noise, scratches, crackles, and pop—to establish its status within the film's fictional world. CD sound's positioning as vinyl's 'other' is relevant, in more or less explicit ways, to all of these examples and the case studies are sequenced according to the extent to which vinyl is allowed an expressive weight, in terms of narrative commentary and characterization, against this backdrop.

## Squeezing Out the Vinyl: *The Royal Tenenbaums*

Wes Anderson's *The Royal Tenenbaums* focuses on the lives of the titular family, which includes troubled tennis pro Richie (Luke Wilson) and his adoptive sister Margot (Gwyneth Paltrow). The film spans a number of years, revealing early on that Richie and Margot share an unrequited love. In the present-day narrative, Margot is married to a neurologist (Bill Murray), whose suspicions lead to him teaming up with Richie to hire a private detective to investigate her. After Richie hears the detective's report, detailing Margot's involvement in a string of affairs, he attempts suicide. Checking himself out of hospital, he returns to the family house, where Margot is hiding out in his childhood tent, listening to records on *her* childhood record player. The sequence covering Richie's journey and his subsequent encounter with Margot includes three songs, each connected somehow with the record player. However, the sound of the music is only intermittently attributed to the sound of vinyl. This leads to a squeezed quality in the representation of vinyl and its sounds, which is in keeping with the inhibited view of Margot offered overall.

After Richie discharges himself from hospital, he catches a bus, whereupon Nick Drake's 1970 song 'Fly' begins, mixing with engine noise. His estranged father, Royal (Gene Hackman), witnesses this and he is then seen commenting on Richie's condition, his dialogue overlaying the introductory passage of the song. Drake starts singing and there follows a minute-long passage, covering the first verse, in which other sounds are subdued and the film cuts between Richie on the bus, Royal in a taxi, and Richie disembarking and climbing into the family home via a window. In a surprising twist, the quality of musical sound then changes, as 'Fly' becomes characterized as a song Margot is playing on her record player from within the tent.

Despite not being introduced as a vinyl recording, the aural movement at the beginning of the song from 'music plus competing sound' to 'music dominance' aligns with a common practice in films' handling of record-playing moments. Tim J Anderson notes:

> records are often loaded with large reserves of social memory, able to spark affections and release intense mnemonic charges. In many cases this aspect is intentionally amplified through supra-diegetic mixing techniques that quickly

dispose of any strict concerns of 'cinematic realism'. In the quest to sensually reveal the emotional importance we deposit on these objects, the result is a privileged point of audition wherein the 'clarity' of the record's details are often much clearer for the auditor than the discernible perspective offered to the on-screen listener. (2008, p. 60)

Retrospectively, it becomes clear that the record playing of 'Fly' by Margot has been subject to this kind of supra-diegetic mixing, attributing it a privileged point of audition. On first listen, however, the assumption is that the song is playing out non-diegetically to lend emotional resonance to Richie's situation. The normal formula of moving 'quickly' from realist diegetic vinyl sound to privileged audio clarity has been reversed.

If, as Anderson argues, this rapid movement to audio clarity works sensuously to enhance the recording's affective charge, how is the reversal of the effect experienced? Firstly, the twist is teased out, the film revealing the diegetic status of the song through a change in sound quality, without moving into the tent to show its exact source. Instead, the camera follows Richie's exploration of the room, with the music eventually being stopped with an off-screen click.

It is only after hearing this sound that the viewer is allowed to see inside the tent, where Margot sits, record cover on her lap and record player behind her. To reinforce that we have been listening to vinyl, Richie asks 'what are you doing in my tent?', to which Margot replies, 'just listening to some records'.

Shortly afterwards, Margot lifts the record sleeve and turns towards the player. As it proceeds, however, this movement is blocked from view by Richie who has entered the tent. At the very end of this shot, a click is heard, followed by an overhead view of the record player, with a disc spinning and Margot's hand lifting the needle onto a groove towards the middle of the record. Crackle is heard before being drowned out by the organ intro of the song, The Rolling Stones' 'She Smiled Sweetly'. An intimate conversation follows, in which Richie confronts Margot about what he has learned of her past, they confess their love for each other, kiss and then reflect on Richie's suicide attempt, which he admits was triggered by his feelings for Margot, to her evident distress.

The overhead shot of the record player and its accompanying sounds attribute a special status to vinyl that has been suppressed by the previous cues offered in the sequence. The square shape of the record player is precisely centred within the frame. This contrasts with the preceding visualization of Richie's and Margot's interactions, in which the camerawork prioritizes Richie's movements. The sound of the moment is fetishistic, featuring aural cues associated with record playing.

The attribution of the music to Margot may suggest it speaks for her in some way, fulfilling the 'identity-building' function explored by Anderson and Stilwell. However, any sense of agency in Margot's playing of 'She Smiled Sweetly' is compromised. The 'needle-drop' moment is isolated from its surroundings, partly due to the disparity between the moment's concentrated vinyl-centricity and the quite lengthy obfuscation of the music's vinyl origins that precedes it. The continuity of the overhead view of the record player with Margot's actions towards it is also disrupted. This is partly because her movement to the record player becomes blocked by Richie's body entering the tent, so that the film performs a conventional 'cut-on-action' (Margot lifting her hand towards the player) without the viewer gaining full view of the action to which the editing is choreographed.

The sense of dislocation is reinforced by the implausibility of this record now being on the turntable. Once on-screen, Margot is not shown taking the Nick Drake record off the player and she would not have been able to do so in the time that elapses between her stopping it off-screen and Richie's entrance. These continuity issues may seem trivial, but attention is drawn towards them due to the initial decision to hide, for almost two minutes, any visual and aural markers of vinyl, only then to suggest that this is how 'Fly' is actually being heard.

This contributes to a feeling that Margot is not truly attached to the music with which she is diegetically associated. The details of the needle-drop moment are, on the one hand, scrupulously authentic. Conversely, Margot's physical interaction with the record and player is effaced. The moment follows a whole passage which attaches 'Fly' to Margot's diegetic listening as an afterthought, following a substantial sequence in which it has leant an emotional charge to Richie's actions.

The compromising of the needle-drop moment as a way of characterizing Margot is cemented by the manner in which the scene ends. After Richie confesses his suicide attempt was linked to his feelings for Margot, the song comes to a 'natural' stop. At this point, Margot asks, 'you're not going to do it again are you?', to which Richie says, 'I doubt it'. This equivocal response is very distressing to Margot who starts crying. The Rolling Stones' 'Goodbye Ruby Tuesday' then begins.

Without knowledge of the running order of 'Between the Buttons', the album playing on the record player, the viewer could assume that this is simply the next song on the album, as the pause between tracks mimics what would be expected from an LP. However, the sonic profiling of 'Goodbye Ruby Tuesday' disabuses this notion immediately and further isolates the needle-drop moment from the musical representation that surrounds it. The song is heard with the same clarity associated with the initial non-diegetic airing of 'Fly'. This reinforces the diegetic playing of 'She Smiled Sweetly' as an isolated moment of vinyl signification, with all the visual and aural signifiers of its vinyl status crammed into the overtly stylized overhead shot of the record player. This is sandwiched between two instances of songs being emphasized in the sound mix without any diegetic or vinyl markings.

'Goodbye Ruby Tuesday' *does* begin by soundtracking Margot's crying, her decision to walk out of the tent and her declaration to Richie that they can only remain secretly in love. In this sense, it appears to be attached to the agency of Margot, lending emotional resonance to her actions. However, this, too, is momentary. The song reaches full affective power with the raising of volume (just after Margot's words) exactly as it reaches its famous chorus. This accompanies the insertion of one of the film's title cards, featuring a hand-drawn picture of Richie and a few lines of prose that describe what Richie did the next morning (which we then see, with the music continuing powerfully).

At its most sonically emphatic, 'Goodbye Ruby Tuesday' becomes attached to Richie's response to Margot's actions, just as 'Fly' is initially presented as a song connected to Richie, even though it is 'really' Margot's music. This corresponds to a theme in the film whereby the association of Margot with vinyl recordings is consistently 'squeezed'. For example, when the private detective reveals his findings about Margot to her husband and Richie, these are visualized in a montage accompanied by the Ramones' 'Judy is a Punk'. The recording bursts in after a low-key affirmation from Margot's scholarly husband that he would like to see the contents of the file. The song possesses the vitality associated with the 1970s punk single, a quintessentially vinyl format. It is allowed to play for almost a minute, with no competing sound, but is then cut off mid-line as the film returns to Margot's husband, who has evidently read enough. The abrupt introduction and sudden silencing of the vinyl is of a piece with the 'sandwiching' effect described in relation to the needle-drop moment in the tent, whereby Margot's association with vinyl is squeezed between longer and more sonically emphatic musical moments attached to Richie. Here the 'awkward fit' is between the bursting-at-the-seams vitality of the song and the languid aura of near silence that surrounds it.

Arved Ashby argues that the 'Judy is a Punk' scene 'fills out a depressive and hitherto one-sided character, and our seeing it proves salutary' (2013, p. 196). This becomes harder to accept if it is understood as part of a general tendency to bestow upon Margot a special connection with vinyl sound, only for that to be treated as something that has to fit within another character's script. This is, after all, a sequence visualizing a report on Margot that has been made without her consent, and the song is switched on and off at her husband's behest. Instead, the scene chimes with the co-opting of Margot's record playing in the tent for the purposes of characterizing Richie, a process in which choices in sound design play a major part.

## Vinyl and the CD: Fantasies of Co-Existence in *Pulp Fiction*

The record player is the only music playing technology diegetically present in *The Royal Tenenbaums*. It is brought to attention only to highlight vinyl's marginal position, the difficulty it has 'fitting in' with the dominant emphatically heard non-diegetic musical soundtrack. As such, the cultural obsolescence of vinyl is alluded to in a deflected manner, the pristine audio values of more contemporary musical media suggested by the clarity of the non-diegetic soundtrack, rather than represented directly. The two remaining examples discussed in this chapter tackle the relationship between vinyl and other musical formats head-on, referencing other musical media, including the CD, alongside the record player, within their diegetic worlds.

Ken Garner discusses the 'vinyl-centricity' of Quentin Tarantino's films from *Kill Bill: Volume 1* (2003) as a unique turn in his soundtrack style (Garner, 2013). I will return to his observations on these later films, but, for now, I want to suggest that there is more to say about the representation of vinyl, aurally and visually, in his 1990s films, as exemplified by *Pulp Fiction*.

The record-playing moment in the film occurs when the mob contract killer Vincent (John Travolta) arrives to collect his boss' wife Mia (Uma Thurman), a scene accompanied by Dusty Springfield's 'Son of a Preacher Man'. Garner analyses this moment in an earlier piece of writing on Tarantino's musical choices. Consistent with the argument he develops later, Garner focuses on the situational aspects of the moment. For example, Garner notes that the scene:

> foreground[s] the central female character's music selection and control of the aural environment, by featuring extreme close-ups on her music technology; the needle lifting from the groove of Mia's copy of the *Dusty in Memphis* LP ... Tarantino's original script had the Dusty album more plausibly being played from a CD (Tarantino, 1994a: 45), but the stopping-and-starting of a CD's internal laser cannot be shown as a physical, fetishized act. (Garner, 2001, p. 200)

Garner suggests that the switch from CD in the script to a vinyl recording in the film is motivated by the desire to show Mia exercising agency in the scene, through her control of the record player's tone arm. Garner does not consider the aural qualities of this scene. In addressing this element, I want to suggest that the CD player imagined in the script is still a presence on the soundtrack, and is also insinuated visually.

The scene occurs half an hour in, at the beginning of a music-laden passage featuring Vincent and Mia, culminating in Mia's overdose from cocaine use. Garner recognizes this as a turning point in the film's scoring practices, a sequence that marks the high-point of the film's overloaded musical sensibilities, from which it then steps back: '[j]ust as Mia is snapped out of drug-induced coma, so is the audience rudely awaken from its musical haze' (2001, p. 201). This is an astute observation, but, in relation to the 'Son of the Preacher Man' scene, his attention to the specific connotations of the song mean that other elements that contribute to this 'overdosing' quality are overlooked, in particular around sound design.

The sequence establishes a principle of aural eclecticism on its non-musical soundtrack. Vincent approaches Mia's house and finds a note written on white paper stuck to the door, which is displayed in close-up as Vincent holds it: 'Hi Vincent, I'm getting dressed. The doors open. Come inside and make yourself a drink. Mia'. The viewer requires no more information to understand what is being asked of Vincent, and, yet, the film still elects to supply a voiceover from Mia (the first time we have heard her), reiterating the writing in a clear, conversational tone. This is heard centrally in the stereo mix, cushioned between insect sounds in the left and right channels that indicate the heady climate of the setting.

The voiceover is narratively redundant, existing solely to introduce Mia's voice in a lustrous setting. The sensation of being bathed in sound is also represented visually as a burst of white light covers the cut to Vincent walking into the open-plan building. It is in this moment of pure light that the musical intro of 'Son of a Preacher Man' emerges emphatically, dominating the soundtrack and acting as a continuation of the lustrous aural qualities just established, as well as a complement to the visual ones.

Springfield's opening singing is heard without competing sound, meaning that her celebrated soulful voice is allowed maximum exposure. By the second line, the film has cut to Mia in the control room, from which she is watching Vincent's movements through a range of monitors. There is an intercom microphone in front of her which she speaks through in an extreme close-up that features the head of the chrome mic, light bouncing off its top-side, and Mia's painted red lips as close as they can be without touching it. As a piece of technology specifically associated with the vocal and as the body part that projects the voice, the two elements continue to connote a lustrous representation of sound, reinforced by the continuation of the song.

Mia says 'Vincent' into the mic and the sound design of its rendition is significant. It is mostly heard clearly to give the viewer the ideal audition of the word that issues from Mia's lips. However, there is a cut, at the very end of the word, that takes the viewer back to Vincent and that represents Mia's voice as it is heard through the downstairs intercom. This results in a phased effect on the closing 't'. She repeats his name, in a more drawn-out fashion this time, and this allows the full word to be heard projected into the large open-plan space via the small speaker of the intercom, with a reduction in clarity faithfully reproduced.

Although we have only seen glimpses of Mia, by this point we have heard her voice technologically mediated in three different ways: as closely miked non-diegetic voiceover, as clearly relayed diegetic sound, and as sound subjected to diegetic technological interference. In this context, the unrelentingly pristine quality of the song becomes an example of one option, amongst many, of how sound can be conveyed in films.

The cut to Vincent downstairs does not just reveal a new dimension to the sound quality associated with Mia's voice. It also exhibits a new part of the diegetic space, which houses different types of music technology. Specifically, we now see that the apartment holds a reel-to-reel tape recorder, which sits upon a hi-fi unit housing, presumably, other types of music playing systems: it is clear that there are other slots on the machine and it is also apparent that a record player is not present. The implication that the system also includes a CD player is reinforced by the stack of CDs that are positioned on the shelf below.

Up until this moment, there has been no indication that the song is being played diegetically. The revelation of the music equipment gives the song a possible diegetic source, the most plausible being that we are hearing a CD (as the reel-to-reel is not turning, there is no record player in view and there is a stack of CDs on the shelf).

After a relatively lengthy segment in which the song is allowed to be heard without competing aural elements, the music, and the sequence, is brought to an end in a surprising way. A close up of Mia's bare feet walking across the ground floor space indicates that she has moved out of the control room. The next shot is a close-up of the tone arm being lifted from a record, framed so tightly that no hand is visible operating the mechanism. The music stops, there is a cut to Mia's bare feet and we hear her voice saying 'let's go'. The scene ends.

It is impossible to place the tone arm, and the record player it represents, within the geography of the space. This is surprising, given how much of the open-plan ground floor we have seen, due to Vincent's exploration of it. The withholding of a full view of Mia's body and the exclusion of a hand in the shot of the tone arm lifting also makes it impossible to say for sure that Mia is responsible for stopping the record. This ambiguity is exacerbated by the surprise that 'Son of a Preacher Man' was playing diegetically on a record player at all.

To counter-balance the ambiguity, there is a simultaneous overload of inferential cues to persuade the viewer that Mia's actions and the performance of the song are all centred around a diegetically located record player at this point: we see Mia walking towards something, we hear music stopping as the tone arm is lifted (presumably what Mia was walking to) and we then hear Mia saying it is time to go, as if she has put a stop to the music in order to facilitate this. At this point, we even see Mia lifting one foot and then setting it down, as if to mimic the action of lifting and setting down the tone arm she has just performed.

However, a detail in sound design works to unsettle the viewer's acceptance of these highly concentrated inferences. The lifting of the tone arm is accompanied by a concise 'thwipp', so concise, in fact, that it hits the ear as a library effect rather than a naturalistically rendered sound. The sense of contrivance around the moment is exacerbated by the fact that the song has already halted before the needle is raised. Springfield is singing a declamatory 'oh yes she was' in a call-and-response section of the song. The music is halted on 'was' just before the needle is lifted, but still makes its presence felt over this action due to the use of reverb to 'round out' the moment of its cessation.

A needle-lifting, rather than more conventional needle-drop moment, the uncanny appearance of vinyl into this scene suggests the sequence as aural fantasy, controlled equally by a diegetic figure (Mia) and an authorial one (Tarantino and his sound crew), who stages a scene that showcases the diverse qualities of sound that can be achieved in film. Like Margot in *The Royal Tenenbaums*, Mia's relationship with record playing technology is made strange through the construction of discontinuities in performance and the deliberate exclusion from sight of certain physical actions relating to the characters' handling of the technology. However, the consequences this has for the viewers' understanding of the characters is quite distinct. In her opening scene, Mia acts as a magical presence, orchestrating different types of sound from within the diegesis, as a complement to the authorial manipulation of sound that is also being foregrounded. The result is a scene of aural decadence, in which all shades of sound are allowed to mingle, including CD clarity with vinyl aura. The overdosing of sensory stimulus this involves cannot be sustained, as Garner suggests, but the attribution of consequences is a matter for a later scene.

## Surface Noise and Deep Characterization in *Ghost World*

A more conventional needle-drop moment occurs in Tarantino's *Jackie Brown* (1998), when the titular protagonist (Pam Grier) invites her bail bondman (Robert Forster) into her home. She plays the Delfonics' 'Didn't I Blow Your Mind' on her turntable, as the couple have an exchange about the fate (and value) of vinyl in the face of the 'CD revolution'.

This is an example of the CD versus vinyl debate coming to the narrative surface of an Indiewood film of the era, rather than being alluded to through different forms of deflection, as occurs in *The Royal Tenenbaums* and *Pulp Fiction*. A version of this discussion also occurs in *Ghost World*. Enid has persuaded her friend Rebecca (Scarlett Johansson) to attend a 78s collectors' party, involving her new record-collecting acquaintance, Seymour. The scene is introduced by the following exchange, between two subsidiary characters:

> JEROME: There are some records I will pay serious money for, provided they're a sincere V plus. Other than that I'd prefer to just have them on CD.
> STEVEN: CDs will never have the presence of an original 78.
> JEROME: WRR-ONG! A digital transfer adequately mastered will sound identical to the original. Do you have a decent equalizer?
> STEVEN: I have a Klipsch 2B3.
> JEROME: Obviously the problem! You expect a ten-band equalizer to impart state of-the-art sound? Dream a little dream, it's never going to happen. (LAUGHS)

For a 78s collector, Jerome is surprisingly liberal-minded about the virtues of the CD, but the comedy stems from his ability to still articulate a technological condescension, through his comments about equalization. Despite the comic tone, this passage, played out by two characters who are not otherwise featured, acts as a keynote for understanding the manner in which the sound of records are represented in the film. The 78s are not, as might be expected, attributed aural qualities in opposition to the perceived cleanness of the CD: they are actually the cleanest sounding records played in the film. The 'presence' to which Steven refers, that is to say the supposedly 'human' qualities of vinyl sound (rather than the technical definition Jerome imposes on the term 'presence'), are much more apparent in the 33 1/3s and 45s played in the film. Whereas the playing of records in the previous case studies is marked by either restriction (*The Royal Tenenbaums*) or unsustainable intensity (*Pulp Fiction*), the representation of records in *Ghost World* is much more sustained, allowing for the construction of a micro-system of vinyl and, in the case of the 78s, shellac sounds.

Seymour is the only protagonist with a record player that can play 78s, so all of these scenes take place in his house. The 78s are played during the party scene, on a later occasion when Enid and Seymour talk in his record room, and during the scene in which Enid and Seymour kiss.

Considering that Seymour is identified so strongly as a collector of old records, very little attention is given to the way they are played. There are no needle-drop moments in these scenes: in all three, we join the action *in (music) media res*, each time with a shot of a record already spinning on a turntable. Even though each scene features a change of record, the viewer never sees this process being enacted.

With no special attention given to the act of playing the records, the 78s generally function as conventional underscoring, providing an appropriate yet unobtrusive musical backdrop. The tracks are purely instrumental and this adds to the sense they are functioning like a composed score. The usual aural signifiers of old records are generally notable by their absence. There is some surface noise audible in the opening shots of the first two record-playing scenes, but, in both cases, this is not generally a feature of their aural presentation as they settle into the background.

There is one point during these scenes that surface noise is made more apparent. As Lionel Belasco's 'Venezuela' plays in the background, Enid discovers that Seymour owns an old poster advertising the chicken franchise for which he works. The poster is clearly racist, featuring a cartoon caricaturing the features of a smiling African-American man. Seymour explains that he has collected it as a historical curiosity and he shows Enid a folder that documents the history of the fast food chain. On the cut to a close-up of the folder, whose pages are being turned by Enid, the volume of 'Venezuela' becomes louder and the surface noise much more present. A pause in dialogue allows the now markedly 'old' music to be heard in tandem with a view of racist memorabilia. As Enid reaches a page that documents the franchise's more modern, less obviously racist, era, the conversation picks up again, with the music receding to its earlier background position.

Enid asks to borrow the poster from Seymour and, in the next scene, we see that she has co-opted it as a piece of 'found art' to present to her summer school art class. The increased 'presence' of the music as she looks through the folder is significant as it attaches this quality of the music to Enid rather than its ostensible owner, Seymour: this is a moment where Enid sees a way of making use of Seymour's collection for her own purposes and it is to this realization that the momentary heightening of the music's auratic qualities refers.

Surface noise is, therefore, connected to Enid's subjectivity, rather than presented as an intrinsic property of an old record or as a quality that illuminates the character of Seymour. This idea is pursued consistently across the film, with Enid's own playing of records registering as a notably more 'noisy' affair than Seymour's.

In the key moment Stilwell analyses, Enid has an evidently revelatory experience listening to Skip James' 'Devil Got My Woman', which is featured on a compilation album she has bought in a boot sale from Seymour, in their first face-to-face encounter. The album is a standard 33 1/3. Playing the album for the first time on her record player in her bedroom, we initially hear the opening seconds of the first track, 'Let's Go Riding' by Mr Freddie. The viewer sees Enid putting the disc onto the turntable and lifting the tone arm onto it, but this is represented in long shot, rather than fetishistically. Enid walks away from the record player to get on with colouring her hair. The song is heard quite emphatically (there is little competing sound) with some audible crackle, but fades out quickly as Enid closes her bathroom cabinet door onto the camera, creating a 'natural' fade to black.

To put on the record, Enid has made a choice to turn off a cassette recording of the more contemporary (but still retro) Buzzcocks' track, 'What Do I Get?'. The crackle on 'Let's Go Riding' does mark out the song as belonging to a different age and format to the Buzzcocks' cassette, but the difference is not registered emphatically. However, when the image returns after the fade to black, it reveals a different depiction of the record. The album has now arrived at the narratively key track, 'Devil Got My Woman', the sound rolling in towards the end of the musical intro, accompanied by a close-up at turntable level of the needle on the spinning disc, which is quite badly warped. The surface noise for this track is much more pronounced than was the case for 'Let's Go Riding'. A cut to Enid at her sink, now with black hair, shows her turning, intrigued, towards the source of the sound. The scene then plays out visually in the way Stilwell describes it, with the camera gesturing towards a circular movement around Enid, who is standing transfixed, that complements the close-ups of the warped disc spinning on the turntable (2006, pp. 158–9).

There is a dissolve from a close-up of the needle to a later point in the evening, with Enid lying on a beanbag, still captivated by the song, which, magically, continues undisturbed by the passage of time that has elapsed. This dissolve is covered aurally by a phase where there is no singing and a relative lull in the attack of the music. This means that surface noise is the main aural element covering the dissolve, a visual/narrative cue that is important in conveying the extent of Enid's immersion in the song. Surface noise becomes, therefore, a key aural indicator of the song's hypnotic effect on Enid. When it comes to an end, all the viewer can hear is the crackle of the needle playing out in the groove between songs. Enid immediately lifts the needle and places it back on the groove at the start of the song, producing a click. At the end of this pivotal record-playing scene, the viewer is made to hear as much pure surface noise as they are music.

Enid's response to the song leads her into a relationship with Seymour that eventually ends in a misguided sexual encounter. At the same time, Enid has grown distanced from her friend Rebecca, although she holds onto their plan to move in together. In the course of packing her belongings to take over to the new apartment, Enid comes across an old record of her own—this time a 45. She puts it on her record player but drops the needle on the turntable, rather than disc, resulting in a scraping noise. When she does place the needle correctly, 'A Smile and a Ribbon', a tinkly children's tune from the 1950s, sounds out in a fashion both tinny and crackly. During the song, Enid's body language indicates that hearing it, in the process of going through her old things, has made her introspective. As the song comes to an end, she stops what she is doing, stands for a moment and then slumps onto her bed. This is accompanied by ten seconds of pure surface noise as the run-out groove of the disc continues to spin under the needle.

It is unclear what Enid is thinking at this moment or what the song means to her. It is apparent, however, that record surface noise is connected with key moments of insight for her character: the broadening of her horizons represented by her first encounter with 'Devil Got My Woman'; the realization that she can make use of Seymour's collecting obsessions for her own ends; and the revelation that the way forward may lie in reflecting on her own cultural memories (the childhood record found in a box) rather than relying on someone else's (Seymour's collection). Soon after listening to 'A Smile and a Ribbon', Enid makes her peace with Seymour and then takes the bus out of town.

As such, the surface noise of the records Enid listens to gets noisier the more her character develops a sense of the path that lies ahead. This plays on the term 'presence' used by Steven in the opening exchange of the party scene. Through the course of the film, 'presence' comes to mean not only the particularly fallible and mortal sound made by the records associated with Enid, but also takes on a more literal sense. Surface noise becomes attached to the concept of 'being present', a sonic signifier of the ability to use music to move forward that Tim J Anderson identifies as the defining difference between Enid and Seymour (2008, p. 69).

## Conclusion: Vinyl Representation in Film in the Age of the Digital Download

Characters are still playing records in films. The movies of the 1990s and early 2000s do not have the monopoly on such representations, although I have suggested that the films under review were drawing on an understanding of vinyl sound that was developed quite particularly during the era of CD dominance. Nevertheless, the contrasts in meanings attributed to vinyl in the three films I have discussed should caution against regarding movies as direct conveyors of a musical zeitgeist. Just as there is always the potential for specific pop songs to act as a type of dramatic film music when they are applied to fictional film scenarios, it is also true that less particular music format noises, like vinyl crackle and pop, can take on a narrational role. This means that the significance of such noises in films can only be fully assessed on a case-by-case basis, an attempt I have made in this chapter.

That said, there may be a general point of distinction to be made between the vinyl-related films of the 1990s and millennial turn and those 'born digital' in the music download and streaming era that has followed. As Davis notes:

In this age of digital media, the vinyl record format *is* obsolete, in the technological sense. *Obsolescence*, as used here, reflects both a formal status of technical incompatibility with popular and widely used digital media such as CDs, iPods, and various PC-based media systems, but also a symbolic status. (2007, p. 400)

Davis' italicization of 'is' is significant. It represents a definitive distinction between the overwhelmingly digital musical environment of the twenty-first century and the obsolete analogue format of vinyl; by contrast, in the 1990s, vinyl was not at this radical stage of obsolescence. It was also competing with formats that were material in their own right, in contrast to the immateriality that is often attributed to the digital music file (e.g. cassettes are attributed material sonic imperfections like hiss, akin to the crackle of vinyl, and CDs are still objects to be handled, like records).

In the contemporary context, featuring record playing scenes in films becomes an even more anachronistic or niche choice than it was in the 1990s. On the other hand, the ability of the digital domain to act as a repository for all previous music formats offers new possibilities in representation. Digital technology can store, or create from scratch, the imperfect sounds that were previously only possible through the tactile operation of vinyl on a record player. The possibility of listening to vinyl sound without the presence of records or the need to lift a tone arm provides a new context with which filmmakers can choose to engage.

It is the 'disembodied' representation of vinyl sound that Ken Garner laments in his appraisal of Quentin Tarantino's move away from 'character-based selection of music within the diegesis' to a more diffuse use of 'vinyl surface noise, scratches, and soundtrack wear and tear' (2013, p. 175). Garner attributes a nostalgic impulse to this development in Tarantino's sound aesthetic, the director deploying such sounds to ensure 'that we are conscious of the authentic physicality of the sound' and to underline 'the historical audio experience that we are going to get' (p. 175). However, my analysis of *Ghost World* demonstrated that, even in a film that does depict characters using old-fashioned record playing technology, there is not an intrinsic link between a particular device and a specific sound: the intensity of surface noise at different points in the film is an externalization of Enid's consciousness, rather than the result of distinctions between the playback qualities of different types of records. It could be that Tarantino's less situational use of vinyl noise in his more recent films is not purely backward-looking. Rather it may be responding to a new situation, in which digital technology has liberated the requirement that vinyl sound must be seen to issue from a particular material source.

## Note

1. For a whistle-stop tour of many examples of record-playing moments in American Independent Cinema, see my audiovisual essay 'Indy Vinyl: Close Ups, Needle Drops, Aerial Shots—Records in US Independent Cinema 1987–2015': https://vimeo.com/162847038

# REFERENCES

Anderson, T.J. (2008) 'As if History was Merely a Record: The pathology of nostalgia and the figure of the recording in contemporary popular cinema', *Music, Sound and the Moving Image*, Vol. 2, No. 1, p. 51–76.

Ashby, A. (2013) 'Wes Anderson, Ironist and Auteur' in A. Ashby (ed.) *Popular Music and the New Auteur: Visionary Filmmakers after MTV* (New York: Oxford University Press), 180–202.

Davis, J.D. (2007) 'Going Analog: Vinylphiles and the consumption of the "obsolete" vinyl record' in C. R. Acland (ed.) *Residual Media: Residual Technologies and Cultures* (Minneapolis: University of Minnesota Press), 398–427.

Garner, K. (2001) '"Would You Like to Hear Some Music?" Music in-and-out-of-control in the Films of Quentin Tarantino' in K.J. Donnelly (ed.) *Film Music: Critical Approaches* (Edinburgh: Edinburgh University Press), 188–205.

Garner, K. (2013) 'You've Heard This One Before: Quentin Tarantino's Scoring Practices from *Kill Bill* to *Inglorious Basterds*' in A. Ashby (ed.) *Popular Music and the New Auteur: Visionary Filmmakers after MTV* (New York: Oxford University Press), 157–179.

Garwood, I. (2000) 'Must you remember this?: Orchestrating the "standard" pop song in *Sleepless in Seattle*', *Screen*, Vol. 41, No. 3, 282–298.

———. (2006) 'The Pop Song in Film' in J. Gibbs and D. Pye (eds) *Close Up: Volume 1* (London: Wallflower Press), 89–166.

———. (2009) 'Great art on a jukebox: the romantic(ized) voice of Bob Dylan in *I'm Not There*', *Film International* Vol. 7, No. 6, 6–22.

King, G. (2009) *Indiewood, USA* (London: I.B.Tauris).

McNelis, T. and E. Boschi (2013) 'Seen and Heard: Visible Playback Technology in Film' in M. Quinones, A. Kassabian and E. Boschi (eds) *Ubiquitous Musics: The Everyday Sounds That We Don't Always Notice* (Aldershot: Ashgate), 89–106.

Newman, M. (2009) 'Indie Culture: In Pursuit of the Authentic Autonomous Alternative', *Cinema Journal*, Vol. 48, No. 3, 16–34.

Stilwell, R. (2006) 'Vinyl Communion: The Record as Ritual Object in Girls' Rites-of Passage Films' in P. Powrie and R. Stilwell (eds) *Changing Tunes: The Use of Pre-existing Music in Film* (Aldershot: Ashgate), 152–166.

Yochim, E. and M. Biddinger (2008) '"It kind of gives you that vintage feel": vinyl records and the trope of death', *Media, Culture and Society*, Vol. 30, No. 2, 183–195.

CHAPTER 18

# Interview 3: Mixing Punk Rock, Classical, and New Sounds in Film Music—An Interview with Brian Reitzell

*Meghan Joyce Tozer*

Brian Reitzell is a composer, producer, and music supervisor best known for his collaborations with filmmaker Sofia Coppola including *The Virgin Suicides* (1999), *Lost in Translation* (2003), *Marie Antoinette* (2006), and *The Bling Ring* (2013) and for the NBC series *Hannibal*. He has toured as a drummer with Redd Kross and Air, among other bands, and released his first solo album in 2014 entitled *Auto Music*.

MJT: My first question is in reference to your descriptions of your approach to writing film music as a 'collage', using synthesizers and orchestra and also pre-existing music in different styles. I'm wondering if you could just expand on what you mean by that.

BR: What I do depends on the project, which sometimes just depends on the money. Sometimes I'm scoring completely and not using any existing music. Other times, I'm mostly using existing music. And that would be the case with one of Sofia's movies. With her, the music is coming along with the script oftentimes. So I would make her a mix, based either on a story idea that she had or from a script that was in varying stages of completion. So a movie like *Marie Antoinette*, I started way before there was a script because it was being based on that historical character and I had read the Antonia Frasier book, so I knew the history. But they're all different. With *Lost in Translation*, it was mostly me using my record collection and making a mix CD for Sofia for her to listen to and get an idea of what I thought the reality of the film should be, and it just sort of riffed from there.

M.J. Tozer
The Ronin Institute, USA

And the first movie was the one where we just kind of learned how to work together. In *Virgin Suicides,* some of the songs were in the book, and I think only two of them maybe were in the book, during that phone conversations when the sisters call the boys and they play records. So I licensed two that were from the book and then two I filled in. We got every song we wanted for that movie, and it was her first film, but we had to do some very creative things. You know, I had to have her write letters sometimes to the artists. Getting Jeff Lynne to agree for us to license an ELO song was really tricky, because he had just licensed a song to *Boogie Nights* and he got a lot of money for it and we didn't have that kind of money, so I had to show the movie to him. And we showed the movie to most people—a lot of the artists were there or their managers or lawyers or record companies or whatever—and after the screening, Jeff Lynne walked up to Sofia and said that we could have the song for fifty cents.

MJT: Oh, wow!

BR: Yeah, he loved the movie so much! The way the music is used in that movie is different, in a way, than the other ones. But that's because it was scored—and I was also part of the scoring process, working with Air in France—and we weren't really working to picture, the way I normally do. If you listen to the record and then you watch the movie, you'll notice the music is completely different in the movie than it is on the record, and that's because those tracks, they weren't really made for the movie so much as they were made as pieces of music that fit the tone and the overall concept and story of the movie, but they were a way too built up. So the stems of the music were sent to the mix stage in San Francisco where Sofia (worked with) Richard Beggs, our sound mixer and sound design guy, who's done all of Sofia's movies with me. So we all went to the Cannes Film Festival, and we went to the screening and that was the first time we'd heard the music that had been completely edited and changed and my heart just sank. I was shocked. But then, you know, after watching it again and sort of resigning myself to the fact that this was part of the process, I realized, I learned so much. Even though I deliver stems, I've never had them taken apart and moved around like that. I'm really proud of what Richard and Sofia did to the music 'cause they fixed it and they made it all work. They just pulled everything out, they just left one sort of mellotron voice pad and the bass. And I had played drums on it and there's like, no drums for the most part, so maybe I was the most shocked.

MJT: In one interview you mentioned that you were influenced by Cage and Morton Feldman. Could you talk a little bit about your history there? And how you came upon these composers who are now becoming part of the classical music canon?

BR: I'm a huge [Toru] Takemitsu fan, and I think that's because I love a lot of those Eastern textures, and really it's all about timbre for me. Ravel, I think, was such a master of timbre. I think he was obsessed with it. And people like (Krzysztof) Penderecki. I love those orchestrations!

I've been working on films now since '99 I guess. So when you're doing films, you certainly learn about classical music, because I wasn't a classical music guy. I was a drummer in a punk rock band for a while! I've been studying music for as long as I can remember, reading books and making chords and learning rhythms and things like that. But I'm every day trying to create something that sounds new, and I think a lot of those guys were doing that too, but in a more 'composed' way. Penderecki would never use a synthesizer. I'm not a purist by any means—I don't care how I get a sound, I'm just looking for that sound. So we do use lots of sounds that wouldn't be considered, you know, made by an instrument. Using water, and having things made that aren't necessarily tonally precise. And I think growing up as a drummer, even as a little kid, I had like saw blades and Freon tanks as part of my drum kit because I wanted more sound colors. And I think a lot of that happened in the '80s, which is when I was a teenager, with very adventurous, new wave music.

MJT: You mentioned briefly your history as a punk rock drummer. Would you think of yourself as a punk composer now?

BR: I think what I'm doing now is probably the most punk of any musical thing that I've done, aside from just playing very loud, fast music that was sloppy. But what's happening now is super punk. When we did *Lost in Translation* and when we did *Virgin Suicides* early on, music in movies was not really … it wasn't what it became with the use of say, bands, and integrating musicians who grew up listening to the Beastie Boys, [who] became these artists that are scoring these Hollywood movies. It's very common now, but when we started it, when we jumped into that stream there were only a few other people swimming in it, if you know what I mean.

MJT: Could you go into a little more detail about your composition process when you were writing music and compiling music for *Virgin Suicides* and *Lost in Translation*?

BR: When (Sofia) is writing, I make her a mix, a playlist on a CD, of what I think the movie could sound like. And she often will have a couple of places for me to start from. So with *Virgin Suicides*, she knew she wanted to hire Air to score the movie. I didn't know the Air guys. I knew the EP. *Moon Safari* wasn't even out yet. It was just the EP *Premiers Symptômes*, so it was pretty underground at the time. That was really cool of her, because here it was, her first movie. She didn't want a film composer, but remember, film music was not really at a very good place, I think. And the music in that movie, the '70s music, only plays when one of our characters could be listening to it on the stereo. There are a couple of places where we cheat that, with two Heart songs—with 'Magic Man' and 'Crazy on You'—both of those really scored Josh Hartnett's character. And Richard put vinyl scratches on it, so it sounds like, you know, the record's playing, even if it's in the car. There are vinyl scratches when Josh Hartnett is listening to Heart on the radio, and it really gives the overall texture of that movie a super cool '70s vibe.

The thing that we did with that movie, that I mentioned to Sofia, is that I didn't want to use the stoner stuff. I didn't want to use the '70s stuff that everybody else used. Like *Boogie Nights*—as much as I love Paul Thomas Anderson, the music in that movie just kills me because it beats you over the head so hard, it's like song after song after song, it's just every trick in the book, and he kind of dirtied the water for everybody else to use those songs, because once somebody uses something in their movie, you want to find your own stuff, and do your own thing, at least I do. So every piece of music that he put in that movie, I wasn't going to be able to touch. And then around the same time, or just after we did *Virgin Suicides*, the movie *Almost Famous* came out. The only song I wasn't able to get for *Virgin Suicides* was the Elton John song, 'Tiny Dancer', which Kirsten Dunst was going to be singing off-camera.

MJT: Yeah, that's in the screenplay.

BR: Yeah. I got permission from Elton John and I got permission from Bernie Taupin. I even talked to Bernie on the telephone and they gave me their blessing for me to use it, but the woman at the publishing company, who it just so happened, was also the publishing company that I was signed to as an artist, which was Paula Graham, she refused it. I didn't have a computer at the time I made *Virgin Suicides*, I only had a turn table, an eight-track hard-disk recorder that I think I borrowed from Sofia's brother Roman, I had a four-track reel-to-reel tape machine that I used, and a CD player and lots of CDs and records. There was a record store down the street from my house called Rockaway. And I would spend the entire day sitting on the floor just looking at records and making notes. And I didn't have a lot of money, so I had to be smart about what I chose. And I did that for probably four or five months. And then in that process, about halfway through I guess, I met the two Air guys 'cause they came out here to LA to do a music video with a guy named Mike Mills. I literally knocked on the door when they were trying to figure out who was going to play drums, and I think Mike answered the door and said 'Oh, Brian would be perfect!' So then I ended up doing their Moon Safari tour. And then *immediately* after the tour, we went into the studio in Versailles and recorded the score (for *The Virgin Suicides*). They had already started on it, so they had some sketches, some things they just wanted me to play on top of, but really I think everything on the record that has drums on it was something that we did while I was there. But again, we weren't like, scoring the picture. We had a little, teeny, like, maybe 12-inch video monitor that had a built-in VHS tape. And it sat down next to my left foot, and the drums were completely surrounded by blankets, to get that super dead sound, and the only way I could see those guys was through a crack directly in front of where the blankets met, these big packing blankets. And I could cue them—one of them was in front of my line of sight playing bass, and the other one was just behind him playing piano. And I would give them head movements to sort of cue them in, while I was looking at the picture down by my hi-hat foot. And that's how we scored that movie.

With *Lost in Translation*, I made Sofia two mix CDs. I never give her a lot of stuff, and that's one of the reasons our relationship works. I think most music supervisors, at least from what I hear from other directors, they give the director just entire CDs by bands. And it will be 50, 100, basically they turn over their mail and they give it to a director. Because we, all us music supervisors, get sent tons and tons—every record you can think of that's released. So with that movie, there were two mix CDs. And 80 %, really, of the source music of that movie came from those two CDs. And then I wanted to build it around the nucleus, sort of, sound. 'Cause for me, every movie that I've done with Sofia is based around the sound of one song, really, and then everything connects to that song. And as long as it connects to it, then they all flow together in a way that I think works. It's kind of like, you know, the way you would modulate if you were going to switch keys if you were playing chords, there's gotta be a connection to it, you know, you always gotta have one piece holding over into it, to make it work.

Some of the karaoke songs that we picked—that was tricky. That was tricky because I had to pick the song, get Sofia to approve it, and then record it, and then get on a plane and go to Japan. I sat with the actors and I kind of coached them on the song they were going to sing, so they knew it, because if you're going to karaoke something, chances are it was something that you knew, so we prerecorded those pieces and I studied karaoke music so I had to be sure they sounded just cheesy enough, you know. The song 'More Than This', that was something that Sofia and Bill did on the fly there. That was not in the script. All the other ones were. Not in the script, but I mean, we knew what we were going to shoot. But Sofia, loving Roxy music, and then Bill, after we had done everything else, and I think he was probably pretty drunk, 'cause he was drinking the sake—he was in character! I mean, imagine going to a 12-hour karaoke party—once he sang that, it sounded like Joy Division, I mean it was incredible. Again, he was able to take this super cheesy recording of a wonderful Roxy music song, but his voice is what actually connected it with, say, The Jesus and Mary Chain, and for me, that was just magic and I give Sofia and Bill full credit for that one.

**MJT:** So for *Lost in Translation* then, what was the 'nucleus'?

**BR:** That was really Kevin Shields. I was touring with Air on, I think, the second tour. I did a lot of *Lost in Translation* from the back of a tour bus, literally. The problem with that is, you know, Sofia said that she wanted me to just score the whole movie with records. There wasn't going to be a composer. But I convinced her that I'd bring Kevin in and like, do something. You know, really we didn't need Kevin, but it would be cool if he would contribute to it and be part of it and kind of further weave together the fabric of the music.

You know, the way that I work with Sofia, too, a lot of credit has to go to Sarah Flack, who edits Sofia's movies. She didn't do *Virgin Suicides*, but she did *Lost in Translation, Bling Ring, Marie Antoinette*, etc. So I'll send my mix to Sofia and to Sarah, and they'll both be quite familiar with that. We gave the DP, the cinematographer, Lance Acord, he had a mix. The actors had a mix. So everybody sort of knew what that movie was gonna sound like while they were shooting it. Which is really cool, to do that, and I love being able to do that with Sofia. I love Sarah's editing. She's a musical sort of editor.

With Kevin, I sat there and tried to coach this guy, who had never scored a movie by the way, and it was only really *my* third movie and I hadn't really *scored* those other movies—I had been involved in the scoring of them, but, you know. So we just approached it the way you would make a record. We were in a recording studio. We had stuff that Sofia was shooting, like dailies. They would FedEx it to us while she was still in Japan. It took a lot to get just the five pieces that are in the movie, 'cause everything that we did is in the movie. There's no excess.

**MJT:** So you've been talking a lot about how integrated the process is, working with Sofia and Sarah and Richard. In your interactions with Sofia, and in the way you guys have presented your process publicly, do you think it's important for Sofia to come across as having the cultural currency of the connection with you, and being a 'musical' director? Or do you think that's coincidental?

**BR:** It's no coincidence. I think Sofia learned from her father some really great lessons. You hire the people that you trust to make you look good in every way. And Sofia gets the credit for having this musical style with her films that she deserves full credit for that—and that's because she hired me! I may be the one who's out there sort of picking the vegetables, chopping them up, and prepping them, but at the end of the day, she's the head chef.

She did a movie without me, *Somewhere* (2010). Originally I was going to work on that movie. But I think she was kind of fed up with people having this idea that her movie was going to be another sonically rich mix-tape—which *Lost in Translation* is, and *Marie Antoinette* is, but that's her style! That's how she uses music—and she, I think, wanted to try to *not* do that. So with *Somewhere*, the idea was there wouldn't be any music in the whole movie, other than when it's playing. But of course, she had to have a moment or two. And then that track, I remember hearing that Phoenix song ['Love Like a Sunset'] for the first time at Roman's house at a little party just for all us friends. And that song was just so great, I loved it so much, and it's so cinematic. And starting the movie with it and ending with it, I thought was just so great. And again, that's Richard Beggs.

I don't always represent Sofia when it comes to music. I think back then, you know, some magazine had asked her to pick her ten favorite records, and I think she asked me to do that for her. But you know, that doesn't happen anymore. She's got her own records. I still make her mixes. I just made her a mix because when I listen to music I sometimes think, you know, Sofia would like this, because I think I really know what she likes.

MJT: When you're creating music, have you already read drafts of the screenplay?

BR: With Sofia, I've gotten scripts in varying stages. It's more like an outline. With *Virgin Suicides*, she had worked on that script for a while because she was adapting the book. And I don't mean a long time, because Sofia's actually very fast. And one of the things I love about her so much is, she's very good about trusting herself, and listening to that voice inside and trusting her gut. So she doesn't go back and forth. Once she says she loves something it's done, and I try to be the same way with my work.

What I always do when I read a script is, I read it in one go. I don't ever read a script where I'm gonna be interrupted and I have to stop and start again. So I always try to do it at night, and I make notes the entire time about music stuff. If there's anything in the script, I'll mark it yellow. And for everything else, I'll put little green or orange marks and those are areas where I want to put something. And I have all those scripts, just full of all these Post-It Notes! But it's great how so much stuff is that very first idea, where it sparks for you. There's always a couple of cues that are the hardest ones to get.

I'll tell you, the 'Just Like Honey' (The Jesus and Mary Chain) scene (in *Lost in Translation*), that track, I wanted to use in a different place. Where the My Bloody Valentine song 'Sometimes' is. That scene was a little bit different in the script. And I thought The Jesus and Mary Chain song would be great there. And then I remember trying it at the end, with Sofia at my house, I only had it as a record, so I'm just dropping the needle while we're watching a little VHS tape. But when that thing hit, it was just perfect, it just worked so well. So that was instant, and I wasn't even looking for that at the time. It's kinda like if you ask different songwriters about writing a song and they tell you that it just, you just gotta be listening for it. But if you sit and try to make it happen, it often doesn't work. It has to come to you.

What Sofia likes to do is, when she goes location scouting, she likes to listen to the music. And I think that's really smart. So with *Marie Antoinette*, she'd sometimes have to drive an hour outside Paris to location scout, and she'd listen to some of that Aphex Twin, and Windsor for the Derby and Radio Department and all those bands that were new to her, and I think if you have that thing in your head when you're in that place, you can get a really solid feel for it. And then it's just done, you know what I mean? It just works.

And with *Bling Ring*, we played those songs live in the room while those kids would dance to them. So I was on set, and I don't think there were songs in the script for that specific scene, so those were things that I had to do and figure out. And they weren't figured out at that time. I loved the song 'Two-One-Two' by Azaela Banks and I really liked how that worked. The Avicii song that's in there starts this big montage, and I don't like that track. There's been a couple of instances where Sofia and I actually disagreed, and a compromise was reached. And I took that Avicii song and then right on the downbeat where that hook comes in, you know it sounds like *The Hills* or it sounds like *Jersey Shore*—it's just so, it's bad is what it is. And I don't like to use bad music in a movie ever! Even if the scene requires something bad, let's say, it needs to be *good*. So I time-stretched the piece. So I'm still using the Avicii track, but instead of it playing in real time, I've time-stretched it over like, seven hours. So by doing that, it just creates ambience, air, atmosphere, a giant synth pad. And then I'd record a bass on top of it and a few other instruments and then Richard Beggs would put wind chimes on it. But you know, that was not in the script, but she knew that she wanted like, this one-minute, atmospheric, slow-motion dance. You know, she had that scene in her head. But that was one of those moments where we had to do it afterwards.

It's a really tricky job. The *Bling Ring* was a good example because it was the hip-hop world, and I don't ever want to deal with hip-hop again. It's so difficult and it's a completely different playing field. And everything worked, I got everything that I needed, but I was dealing with people like Kanye West. And dealing with someone like Kanye is very different than when you're dealing with someone like Kevin Shields.

It's pretty scary to take on a movie. For *Marie Antoinette* I did several months of research. I lived in Paris and I would go to the libraries and go to museums and go to performances, you know, I was studying music of the late 1700s from there! So, those things are really interesting. That was the first time I got to work with a musicologist. I worked with a woman who's on the east coast, I can't remember her name. I never met her, I only talked with her on the phone and did emails. But we were trying to figure out, there's a song that I was having Marie Antoinette sing in the movie. And she was the one helping me figure out if she had indeed written the song, and a few other things.

It was really important to me that I was spot-on with that music. And all the opera cues in the movie, all the music that's playing when they're eating dinner, that is all music that could have been played at that time in Marie Antoinette's life. The harpsichord piece is by Scarlatti, and the Boccherini pieces, you know, so for about three months I got to study all that stuff in France. And I also, of course, studied a bunch of it here. By the end of it, I think I spent close to three years working on *Marie Antoinette*.

You know, sometimes finding the perfect song is the hardest thing there is. It's like needle in a haystack—you just never know which one's going to be the easy one and which one's going to be the hard one. But I have really labored over finding the right song, and it's much easier just to create it. I think scoring is easier than supervising. But I also think music supervising is done really poorly. I don't think there are many people that do it very well. 'Cause part of that job—it's the weirdest job—what a music supervisor is supposed to do is to clear songs, so you do paperwork. It's like being a lawyer. And I did it on *Virgin Suicides*, I did some of it so I could learn how to do it. And I've not done it since. I hire someone to do all of the paperwork. And that way, I can just deal with the creative. And that's fantastic. But really, for most music supervisors, their biggest job is just doing the paperwork. You know, when you've got somebody like Wes Anderson or whoever it is, somebody that has got their opinions, and is able to—or Scorsese, or whatever—they don't really *need* somebody picking things for them, they just need someone clearing them.

MJT: I've read that you prefer to be listed as 'music producer', rather than 'supervisor', because you feel it's more appropriate.

BR: Well, that was Sofia's idea. When we did *Lost in Translation*, she wanted to credit me with that. And, I tell you, that was very kind of her, because I think she felt like the music really played a strong role in that movie. Plus, I produced Kevin Shields! So Sofia felt like she wanted to credit me as music producer, and she had to write a letter to the DGA (Directors Guild of America) to get approval for it. And the fact that Kevin and I were nominated for a BAFTA for music, that couldn't happen now. If 50 % or more of a film comes from existing music, it doesn't qualify for Oscars or for BAFTAs or things like that. It did *then*—we didn't have enough music to qualify for the Oscar, but the BAFTA didn't have the same restrictions. So if someone did a movie like that, which I think you and I both agree is an interesting way to score a movie or to just add to the layer of the movie, those organizations don't consider it legitimate, which is silly, but maybe it will change. And I do a lot of different things—so whether it's a video game, whether it's a TV show, whether it's a movie, or a song, or whatever it is, you should be able to try to do it *any* possible way to get what you want from it. And you know it's interesting, Sofia's dad,

Francis—if you take a look at what he did with *American Graffiti*, I think a lot of the things Francis was doing were so new. Even with *Apocalypse Now*, I mean there was no credit for sound design until that movie! Because Francis wanted to give them some sort of proper credit but that job didn't exist. And they did the same thing with *American Graffiti*, it's a radio station that's constantly playing. And I just think that being creative about making music and film work together and what the feeling is gonna be, can be anything, really.

MJT: It seems like a lot of the pre-existing music you use, especially in *Lost in Translation*, is alternative music that a mainstream viewer might have heard of, but won't necessarily have associations already embedded. What's the difference in your approach between coming in with the assumption that the audience is going to recognize a piece, and building on their assumptions, or using something that's brand new, which is what you've been talking about so far?

BR: Well, that is my tool, right there. Which is, what do I want the song to do? Do I want the audience to have a connection with it? Do I want them to have any sort of baggage from it? 'Cause that's really dangerous. So I try to find stuff that's special in that way. Sometimes you *want* them to know that it's a Cure song. You know, sometimes you *want* them to know that it's, you know, The Rolling Stones! And again, it's connections with things that can be dangerous. When I put in 'Just Like Honey', nobody knew who Sébastien Tellier was in this country when his song ('Fantino') is in *Lost in Translation*, or the Squarepusher track ('Tommib'), for example. And I think most people wouldn't even think that was a licensed song. But again, 80 % of the music in that movie is licensed.

In *Lost in Translation*, there's a cue called 'On the Subway', I think it's called. And there was a track that we couldn't get, so I did something that was similar to it. And it was a Cure song. It was 'All Cats Are Grey', which is the only Cure song that Robert Smith does not play guitar in. It's just a synthesizer, bass, drums. So when I did *Marie Antoinette*, I put that song in it. It played in the main credits. And I told Robert Smith, 'cause I got to give him a tour of Versailles, which was one of the most surreal things that's ever happened to me, I told him that I knocked his song off for *Lost In Translation*, but yet now, lo and behold, I'm going to license it from him. Those things are fun.

Also, with *Marie Antoinette*, I met with every single artist that I licensed a song from. With the exception of Adam Ant, because Adam Ant had already just agreed to it. But I feel like when I'm gonna put someone's song in a movie, it's kind of like I'm going to babysit their kid, or I'm going to alter their legacy in some way. I am very respectful and careful about that process. So I always try to show it to the artist and say, 'This is what I'm doing. Do you approve?'

PART V

# Breaking Conventions

CHAPTER 19

# From Analogue to Digital: Synthesizers and Discourses of Film Sound in the 1980s

## Katherine Spring

> We're a new breed of artist; we combine music and effects. And someday, I don't think you'll be able to tell the difference between the two. It'll be such an abstract kind of art form that you'll wonder whether it's music or sound.
> Frank Serafine (Armbruster, 1984, p. 16)[1]

Although Frank Serafine's prophecy, published in a profile on the film sound designer in *Keyboard* magazine, may seem overstated to readers today, the notion of an integrated approach to the production of film sound and music was shared by many of Serafine's contemporaries. One reason for this was that recent experiments in the application of the techniques of *musique concrète* to film sound, such as those used by Walter Murch for the soundtrack of *Apocalypse Now* (Francis Ford Coppola, 1979), had demonstrated the creative possibilities in the musical treatment and organization of recorded sound effects.[2] These experiments were bolstered in the 1980s by a second and ultimately permanent factor: the diffusion of digital instruments for sound recording and editing. The widespread embrace of digital audio devices in the early 1980s not only galvanized the production of synthesizer scores in Hollywood films but also ushered in a period during which the potential for eroding the boundaries between non-diegetic film music and diegetic sound effects seems to have been especially pronounced.[3]

This chapter considers how the transition from analogue to digital technologies influenced the ways in which two distinct groups of Hollywood film sound

---

Part of the research undertaken for this study was funded by the Social Sciences and Humanities Research Council of Canada's Insight Development Grant program. The author thanks Margaret Clark and Katherine Quanz for their assistance.

K. Spring
Wilfrid Laurier University, Canada

professionals, composers and sound editors/designers, approached their craft.[4] Scholarship on digital post-production sound is heavily skewed towards the period of the 1990s and early 2000s, when digital audio workstations (DAWs), such as Pro Tools, became commercially widespread (Sadoff, 2013; Wright, 2011), and digital formats replaced magnetic tape as the primary media for editing film sound. Yet, as this chapter seeks to show, the seeds of the now ubiquitous DAWs were planted in the 1980s, when the digital instruments that replaced analogue devices functioned as integrated platforms for real-time sound synthesis, sampling, recording, storage, and playback. Although these nascent digital synthesizers retained the physical hardware controllers of their analogue predecessors (the buttons, joysticks, sliders, and faders that gave the user a physical connection to the machine and that subsequent DAWs would replace by way of onscreen images of controllers), they also were used to create two discrete elements of the film soundtrack: diegetic sound effects and non-diegetic music. The early 1980s thus represents a period of film history in which technological resources facilitated the conflation of labour in post-production sound, even if it did so on a small scale.[5]

In order to shed light on this formative period, I will consider first how the nuts-and-bolts design of the earliest digital synthesizers appealed to composers and sound editors alike. Then, I look at how discourse in contemporaneous trade magazines shaped reader expectations of the relationship between the new technologies and traditional practices of post-production film sound. The second part of the study is based largely on a survey of reports and interviews published in trade papers of the entertainment industry (*Variety* and *Billboard*) and audio production and engineering (*Mix*, *Keyboard*, *dB*, and *Recording Engineer/Producer*).[6] Although historical information supplied in the interviews runs the risk of distortion on account of the subjects' potential biases and inaccurate memories, and although product reviews may well favour the companies who supplied the papers' advertising revenue, the trade papers nonetheless offer a valuable means by which to gauge industry discourse of the 1980s. Such discourse centred on a number of debates, including the authenticity of synthesized sound, the new agents of film sound (humans or machines), and the disintegration of the distinct labour practices of sound editors/designers and film composers. At a time when 'all the world became a musical instrument' (Tully, 1987, p. 51), we may ask, to what extent did the interfaces of the nascent digital synthesizers influence film sound professionals' perception of their creative roles?[7]

Because digital synthesizers were designed not for film sound professionals but rather for musicians and audio recording engineers, a useful concept for approaching this research is 'transectorial innovation', described by Paul Thèberge as a phenomenon in which 'innovations developed to meet the needs of a specific industrial sector come to play an important role in the creation of new innovations and commodities in formerly unrelated industries' (Thèberge, 1997, p. 58). In his book *Any Sound You Can Imagine: Making Music/Consuming Technology*—a masterful study to which this chapter is indebted—Thèberge evokes the concept of transectorial innovation in order to explain how the musical instrument industry of the 1980s adopted innovations in digital technology stemming from the computer industry. Thèberge also introduces the concept of 'transectorial migration', which he defines as 'the movement, from one industry sector to another, of individuals with particular forms of technical knowledge and expertise' (p. 59). I contend that these lines of transectorial innovation and migration extended to the motion picture industry, because the same digital instruments used by recording artists and engineers in the early 1980s transferred, along with their standards and protocols, to the work environment of film sound professionals. While this line of development, from audio recording to sound editing, may be unsurprising given the American film industry's established history of using technologies invented and innovated in other industrial contexts,[8] the profound and lasting impact of the 'digital revolution' on post-production film sound merits our attention.

## 'THE GREATEST THING SINCE SLICED VOLTAGE CONTROL': MICROPROCESSORS, MIDI, AND SMPTE SYNCHRONIZATION

Two essential properties distinguished analogue synthesizers from the digital synthesizers that would follow.[9] First, most analogue synthesizers were modular, meaning that they consisted of separate hardware units, each of which was responsible for a distinct task of sound production: oscillators generated a basic sound signal (e.g. a sine wave or a sawtooth wave); filters modified the harmonic content of the signal; amplifiers controlled the volume of the signal; and envelope generators shaped the signal's properties of attack, decay, sustain, and release. Second, analogue synthesizers were voltage-controlled, which meant that a user-operated device such as a keyboard, joystick, or button sent a metered amount of current to a module in order to change its settings. One other important controller, a sequencer, could record and playback a programmed series of notes at a rate sent by an internal clock.

Although modules and voltage controllers dominated the synthesizer's design through the 1970s, they suffered from three limitations. First, the task of connecting modules to one another, or 'patching', was cumbersome, for it typically entailed multiple and elaborate networks of cables. Second, analogue synthesizers were not programmable, meaning that they could not store module settings in an efficient way. Third, they were largely monophonic, or able to produce only one note at a time. Some early polyphonic synthesizers, such as Moog Music's Polymoog and Korg's PS-3000 series, proved to be overly expensive and unreliable, primarily because in order to achieve polyphony, every component of the synthesizer's controller—for instance, every key of the keyboard—required a dedicated 'articulator' consisting of at least one filter, amplifier, and envelope generator. The sheer number of articulators increased the likelihood of technical failure (Reid, 2000). A noteworthy alternative was the polyphonic and programmable Prophet 5, released by the California-based company Sequential Circuits in 1977 and used in the production of both sound effects for *Star Trek: The Motion Picture* (Robert Wise, 1979) (described in Serafine, 1980a) and musical scores for *Escape from New York* (John Carpenter, 1981) and *Scanners* (David Cronenberg, 1981). However, despite its impressive capacity to digitally store up to 40 sounds, the Prophet 5's polyphonic range was limited to five voices and, more fatefully, it lacked the Musical Instrument Digital Interface (MIDI) protocol that I discuss below.

The analogue synthesizer's limitations of monophony and non-programmability were overcome with the advent of the microprocessor, a programmable circuit that integrates electronic components onto a single chip, or microchip as it is more widely known. As synthesizer components, microprocessors translated analogue sound into binary data that represented the frequency, amplitude, timbre, duration, and envelope of a sound, and transmitted this data as a digital file that could be stored, accessed, and manipulated at any time, hence instantaneously changing the rendered sound. The microchip's high speed, small size, relative affordability, and capacity to render complex sound sequences with efficiency propelled their rapid integration into synthesizers, and by the early 1980s, portable synthesizers that could both generate and control sounds through digital means became commercially available.

In order to stave off consumer fear of both product obsolescence and technical incompatibility among different synthesizers, manufacturers were compelled to develop a universal protocol that would enable their products to communicate with one another and with computers via the transmission of digital data. The MIDI protocol was introduced in January 1983 (and remains the standard today for communication between digital instrument networks). MIDI, which Larry Oppenheimer would later call 'the greatest thing since sliced voltage control' (1987, p. 32), permitted the use of a computer to control other synthesizers in the studio, such that music written on a master synthesizer could be reproduced on other instruments. The binary data that was transmitted from one instrument to another represented not the sound waves themselves but rather instructions for rendering sound, such as a note's pitch and duration. That MIDI was designated a non-proprietary technology afforded a degree of stability to the synthesizer market and further incentivized manufacturers to incorporate microprocessors into synthesizer design (Thèberge, 1997, pp. 84–6).

The portability, affordability, and efficiency of fully digital synthesizers stimulated their almost immediate uptake by musicians and sound professionals. Yamaha's DX-7, a synthesizer whose ubiquity in recording studios led a *Mix* reporter to dub the device the 'Rhodes of the '80s' (Jacobson, 1987, p. 168), weighed just over 14 kilograms, boasted a slim profile of four inches, and cost $1995 when it was released in 1983. Endowed with a five-octave keyboard, circuitry for FM (frequency-modulated) synthesis, and an unprecedented capability to replicate the sounds of acoustic instruments, the DX-7 was a worldwide commercial success, selling 200,000 units in three years. By the mid-1980s, the majority of popular synthesizers produced by leading manufacturers in North

America (ARP, E-mu, Moog, Rhodes, Sequential Circuits), Western Europe (Crumar, RSF, PPG), and Japan (Roland, Yamaha) were priced well below $2000 ('Buyer's Guide', 1986, pp. 49–53), helping to drive synthesizers from studios into homes and in turn stimulating the 'electronic cottage' industry that thrives to this day.

While the relatively low price point was an important factor in the early commercial success of digital synthesizers, the two devices that pioneered post-production film sound were also the most expensive, pitched as they were to the high end of the audio consumer market. These were the Synclavier, designed by New England Digital Corporation and released in 1977, and the Fairlight CMI (Computer Music Instrument), designed by the Fairlight Corp. of Australia and first demonstrated in 1979. With a base price of approximately $25,000, and add-ons driving costs up to $200,000, these machines were prohibitively expensive for the amateur sound engineer or composer.[10] Yet their features were impressive and by 1983, updated versions of each device included polyphonic voicing (of up to 128 distinct voices in the Synclavier); samplers that enabled the real-time manipulation of recorded or preset sounds, the latter of which numbered 400 on the Fairlight; circuitry that could effect various forms of sound synthesis, such as additive, granular, and FM; a memory device for storing digitized audio so that users could have random access to sampled or synthesized sounds; a velocity-sensitive keyboard controller that could be programmed such that each key played a different sound and was responsive to the speed at which the player struck the keys; a printer; MIDI compatibility; and computer terminals that offered graphic representations of sound. The Fairlight even came equipped with a light pen that allowed users to control the parameters of a sound wave by drawing on the screen of the machine's computer terminal. Within roughly a decade, the predominance of less expensive and sophisticated digital instruments forced Fairlight and New England Digital (NED) out of business, but in the interim, these all-digital sound recording and editing machines—NED even trademarked the name 'Tapeless Studio' for the Synclavier—constituted the first DAWs that permitted the recording, manipulation, and playback of sampled or synthesized sounds.[11]

Although they were purposed for professionals in the audio recording industry, the Fairlight CMI's and Synclavier's expansive range of functions, in particular the feature of non-linear access to digitized sounds, made them popular tools with film sound editors. Renowned sound designer Ben Burtt (*Star Wars*, *WALL-E*) recalls of the Synclavier:

> Here was an interface with keys like a piano but I could put sounds on, like glass crashing or a pick-up truck exploding ... Then I could play them at different pitches. I could improvise by playing the keyboard ... I've always been an improviser. With the Synclavier, and the ability to perform and improvise, I could try things very quickly. I could put different animal recordings on keys and start playing around with them. [The Synclavier] opened up a line of creativity that I still use to this day'. (Spring, 2015)

While the creative efficiencies of the Synclavier (and Fairlight) should not be overlooked, Burtt's allusion to improvising on the keyboard is worth considering for its suggestion of the music-oriented aspects of the machine. Indeed, the popularity of digital synthesizers among sound editors must have owed at least in part to the 'transectorial migration' of practitioners who traversed the domains of music composition and film sound. For instance, NED sought out a classically trained keyboardist to serve as a product specialist at the company's outpost in Los Angeles, so that consumers of the costly synthesizer, be they musicians or sound effects editors, could be trained 'on the very same box' (Callery, qtd. in Karlin, 2013, p. xxiv). A glance at industry magazines reveal numerous profiles of composers who imported their knowledge of electronic music and synthesizers to the tasks of sound editing—a phenomenon to which I return in the next section.

Yet another reason why digital synthesizers appealed to motion picture professionals was their incorporation, after 1983, of a circuit card that could read and generate the time-code standard of the Society for Motion Picture Technicians and Engineers (SMPTE). The card allowed synthesizers to be programmed to play sequences of music or sound effects triggered by SMPTE time-code, and also, crucially for the purpose of motion picture sound editing, to synchronize audio tracks with one another and with video, with frame-by-frame accuracy. By placing the SMPTE time-code signal both on the audio track of a video recorder and on one track of a multi-track audio recorder, the audio and video recorders could play in synchronization with one another. The capacity for SMPTE synchronization was trumpeted as yet another feature in the integrated, all-in-one digital synthesizers. By 1987, an 11-page advertising insert in *Mix* touted the Synclavier's 'total computerized recording environment that is flexible enough to meet the needs of a diverse range of production and post-production applications: music scoring, recording, video sweetening, sound design, effects edit-to-picture, Foley, ADR and film-style mixing' (Synclavier advertisement, 1987, p. 15).[12]

In the context of integrated devices in the digital revolution in film sound, it's worth mentioning the SoundDroid or Lucasfilm Audio Signal Processor, the result of the first concerted investment by a film industry stakeholder in the development of a DAW. Conceived by a team of computer scientists who were commissioned by George Lucas' production company Lucasfilm, SoundDroid was intended not only to make unprecedented quantities of audio available for instantaneous random access but also to integrate into a single, programmable station the five usually disparate tasks of music composing, music recording, film editing, sound effect production, and film sound mixing (Moorer, 1982; Moorer, Abbott, et al., 1986). The prototype was powered by a Motorola 68,000 computer and equipped with a high-resolution graphic display, a Winchester disk drive with one megabyte storage capacity (capable of storing up to 15 minutes of eight-track audio), and eight digital signal processors, each of which could handle up to eight channels of audio at a sampling rate of 48 kHz. The SoundDroid's software foreshadowed DAWs of the subsequent decade in that it could shift the function of each hardware component (for instance, buttons and knobs) and thereby obviate the need for literally hundreds of components that otherwise would have been required to effect the number of sounds afforded by the digital signal processors. Although the SoundDroid was never commercialized, and in 1993 its proprietary technology was acquired by pioneering editing technology company AVID in a six-year partnership with Lucasfilm (Rothman, 1993), the 'All-Digital Sound Studio in a Box' (The Droidworks, 1985, p. 1) was an important harbinger of later DAWs used by sound practitioners.

## 'THE LINE IS NOW A BLUR': THE SOUND EDITOR AS COMPOSER

One of the most celebrated features of the new digital synthesizers was their expansive sonic palettes, which consisted of recognizable sounds, unrecognizable sounds, and uncanny hybrids of the two (Shatz, qtd. in Pasquariello, 1986, p. 60). Such an unprecedentedly broad range of sounds contributed to the perception that the synthesizers could conflate sound effects and music. For example, composer Jeff Rona described his recording of sounds of billiard balls, brake drums, and garden weasels, and his subsequent manipulation of them with an Akai S-900 digital sampler 'until they become as musically useful as possible ... This gives you a new sonic palette that didn't exist before and extends the definition of what a musical instrument is' (Tully, 1987, p. 51). Freelance composer and sound editor Rich Macar likewise attributed the blurring of the boundaries between effects and music to digital sound design software, which allowed users to 'explore the most intricate details of the sounds we take for granted every day. We can further extract elements or sections of these sounds to create musical sound effects as well. These boundaries can expand as far as you desire' (Macar, 1987, p. 112).

The synthesizer's capabilities for disintegrating the ontological distinction between music and sound was reflected by the 'transectorial migration' of professionals from audio and music production into film and video production, a process that in turn inspired some sound editors to adopt a new understanding of his or her job in musical terms—specifically as 'sound composers'. As Macar reported in 1987, 'Over the last five years the bridge between sound and music [has] become shorter and shorter to the point where the line is now a blur. As a result, I have to accept the label of sound composer as well as music composer' (1987, p. 112).

The early career of Frank Serafine, who described himself as having 'had one foot in the record industry and one foot in the film industry' when he began working on *Tron* (Steven Lisberger, 1982), qualifies as an example of the process of 'transectorial migration' (LoBrutto, 1994, p. 221). Trained in North Indian classical music at the Ali Akbar College of Music in San Rafael and in jazz at Denver University, Serafine acquired a handful of Moog synthesizers before being hired by the Walt Disney Company in 1977 to compose and perform music for the grand opening of the Space Mountain Pavilion at Disneyland in Anaheim, California. Two years later, in 1979, Paramount Pictures hired him to create sound effects for *Star Trek: The Motion Picture*, a task that, according to Serafine, was aided by his musical training in the ways in which tone clusters (or chords) can be shaped in order to cue an audience's psychological and physiological responses (Serafine, 1980b, p. 796). Serafine was again employed by Disney in 1981, this time to work with supervising sound editor Michael Fremer on the production of the sound effects for *Tron*. After forming Serafine FX, Inc., a company specializing in post-production sound for motion pictures, Serafine was credited variously in the early 1980s as a sound effects editor, sound effects synthesist, and sound designer.

Particularly when discussing the sound effects for *Tron*, Serafine distinguished his work from conventional practice by explaining how new technologies could enable the sound editor to work like a musical composer or performer. At the time, post-production sound editing typically required the physical splicing of sound effects into 35 mm magnetic tape, a task that was usually performed on a Moviola or flatbed editing machine that synchronized the tape to a work print or videotape of the picture's edit (details in Barnett, 1982 and Mosely, 1981).[13] By contrast, for *Tron*, Serafine used synthesizers and computers not only to create the film's sound effects but also, in the process of recording, to *perform* the effects to picture in 'real time', in much the same way that a studio orchestra or Foley artist performs while simultaneously watching a video monitor during a recording session. As Serafine told an interviewer shortly after *Tron*'s release, 'Real time sound effects means mainly to compose the sound directly to the picture, laying it down with the video and multi-track recorder in sync together' (Larson, 1983, republished online; see also Oppenheimer, 1986, p. 43). Serafine attributed his 'playing to picture' ability to the superior equipment available at Lion's Gate Sound, a recently opened facility owned by Robert Altman's production company and where most of the post-production sound editing for *Tron* took place. The studio was not only staffed by personnel from the audio recording industry but also integrated devices from both the video and recording industries; the system that Serafine used (and dubbed the Electronic Sound Assembly) consisted of a Sony U-Matic videotape editing machine (for ¾" videotape, which was of higher quality than the ½" tape of VHS), two 16-track recorders, an Atari 800 computer, an Apple II computer, and a handful of synthesizers, including the Fairlight CMI, Prophet 5, and Minimoog (Serafine, 1982, pp. 830–2; Halfhill, 1982, p. 18). The sound effects, which comprised recorded acoustic sounds, existing videogame sounds, and synthesizer creations, were digitized and sampled into the Fairlight, where, using the synthesizer's light pen and other feature, Serafine could tweak the sounds before transferring them as digital files to the FileManager 800, a database software program on the Atari computer. The files were then catalogued according to title, number, category, reel number (corresponding with the film's picture reels), track number, description, and what the sound relates to visually. By depressing a key on the Fairlight or Atari, any stored effect could be retrieved almost instantly and, because a track on one of the multi-track recorders had been encoded with SMPTE time-code, inserted and synchronized to the video picture with frame accuracy. Serafine praised the time-saving quality of the system, writing in a feature article published in *American Cinematographer*: 'We can invent on the spot and get to the material within seconds [...] There is no wading through ¼ inch tapes looking for the proper effect, no waiting until the next day to get it transferred on to 35 mag' (Serafine, 1982, pp. 833–4).

Serafine's enthusiasm for integrating technologies from audio recording and film industries may have resulted in his overstating of the extent to which *Tron*'s sound effects were performed in real time and reliant on SMPTE-driven synchronization of computers, synthesizers, and editing suites. Another account, based on interviews with Fremer and the film's composer, Wendy Carlos, suggests that roughly two-thirds of the sound editing process depended upon the more conventional method of cutting and splicing, and that the synchronizers used to control the videotape playback unit and 16-track recorders were cumbersome and fraught with technical problems (Moog, 1982, pp. 54, 57). Nevertheless, Serafine persisted in not only touting the integration of technological devices from various media industries (Serafine, 1982, p. 830) but also comparing the role of the sound designer to that of the film composer, referring in various sources to the processes of 'orchestrating the (film) sound' (Larson, republished online) and performing sound effects to the picture 'like a musician would be playing music' (Petrosky, 2009, online; see also LoBrutto, 1994, p. 224).

Another sound professional whose 'transectorial migration' seems to have inspired a self-described musical approach to sound design is Alan Howarth, one of Serafine's collaborators on *Star Trek: The Motion Picture*. A versatile musician who played in rock bands during his adolescence and most of his 20s; Howarth was hired in 1976 as a synthesizer technician for the Los Angeles-based jazz fusion ensemble Weather Report. Following one of the band's tours, Howarth settled in Los Angeles, where his experience with synthesizers landed him a job on the sound effects team for *Star Trek*. In 1981, Howarth became one of John Carpenter's regular collaborators when he both wrote the score and created special synthesized sound effects for *Escape from New York*. In an interview conducted at the end of the decade, Howarth effaced the distinction between composition and sound design, claiming:

> I'm a composer/sound designer, meaning that I compose with sound [...] In a lot of ways it's all the same to me. It comes out of the same machine. You're using musical instruments in a different way to create these sonic textures, and actually in some ways there's an argument for the fact that these sound effects are really music (Larson, n.d., online).

Both Serfaine's and Howarth's accounts betray a discourse that implicates the synthesizer in the potential disruption of the hierarchy of sound professionals, one that subsumes the status of the effects editor to that of the composer. By likening themselves to music composers who were using identical digital instruments, sound effects practitioners accorded their work a degree of artistry traditionally reserved for composers. As Serafine has stated elsewhere, 'Most sound designers don't know music—they know how to make a door slam, but they're not musicians, so composers don't work with them. The sound guy is the low man on the totem pole, while politically, the composer always has the upper hand' (Armbruster, 1984, p. 20).[14] Indeed, unlike film scoring, sound effects editing was categorized by the Director's Guild of America and the Academy of Motion Picture Arts and Sciences as a technical craft, and not an artistic activity[15]; moreover, sound effects were denied copyright protection despite, as Horwath argued, the practitioner's expenditure of similar amounts of effort on the same digital machines (Larson, n.d., online). The multifunctional digital synthesizer, used by musicians and editors alike, was a crux in the case for legitimizing the creative work of sound editors.

## The Human Element: Luthier or Computer Programmer?

As noted above, many film sound practitioners held that the musical treatment of sound effects, and, conversely, the incorporation of unfamiliar sounds into musical scores, owed to the digital synthesizer's extensive range of sounds. However, this same feature was considered by some to be a threat to creativity and to employment. In 1983, the American Federation of Musicians (AFM) launched a campaign to curtail the displacement of traditional musical instruments with electronic ones (Kirk, 1984, p. 1).[16] In so doing, the AFM took a position that at least one composer seems to have espoused: 'My goal is not to replace traditional music and traditional musicians with electronic sound, but to use it on its own musical terms for its own musical qualities', David Kurtz told an interviewer. He continued, 'If you want the sounds of trombones, you'll be far ahead of the game by hiring trombone players' (King, 1986, pp. 54, 57; see also Soifer, 1986, p. 181).

While Kurtz's stance does not seem to have been a ubiquitous one, film composers and sound editors nonetheless unified their rhetoric concerning the 'human element' around a traditional, romantic distinction between science/technology and art/creativity. On the one hand, at least one dissenter complained that digital instruments threatened to 'erode the human element in music', making music 'less an art ... and more a science' (Prager, 1986, p. 10; see also Parker Jr. qtd. in Gibbs, 1984, p. BM16). On the other hand, the vast majority of sound professionals praised the instruments, not least for their facility in empowering users with the means to achieve creative results with great efficiency. Thus Larry Oppenheimer, in his article 'Visions of the Digital Beyond', asked and answered, 'Have the machines then taken over the music? Of course not!', while John Appleton, professor in Dartmouth's music program (progenitor of the Synclavier), observed, 'People are afraid that in the future only machines will make music and that's wrong ... The designer of digital instruments is the luthier of our time. And these instruments are making music more accessible' (Daley, 1987, p. 69).

As is to be expected, product advertisements emphasized the role of human creativity in the new digital context, although they did so in ways that underlined not the division between individual creativity and mechanistic technology but rather the potential unification of the two categories, positioning the synthesizer as an unparalleled site of convergence of art and science. A survey of advertisements in *Mix* and *Keyboard* magazines clearly show how the Synclavier, Fairlight, and other digital instruments of the early 1980s were to be understood as devices for the cost-conscious professional who wanted to reduce routine tasks and focus on the creative side of her business. A promotional piece placed by NED in *Billboard* offers this assertion by Brad Naples, the company's director of marketing and sales: 'You can't stop technology and you can't stop the arts from borrowing from it … People are doing more combining of music and computers, and it's very important to see the human element involved' ('Synclavier Marries', 1982, p. 31).

These advertisements and endorsements betray what Thèberge, citing piano historian Craig H. Roell, has been identified as a 'contradictory ideology' in the promotion of new musical instruments, wherein 'the personal sense of individual achievement and creativity' is countered by modern modes of consumption that emphasize the 'easy to play', allegedly democratic aspects of the instruments (Thèberge, 1997, p. 29). Similar to the pianola (or piano player) described by Thèberge in the early twentieth century, digital synthesizers of the 1980s found immediate success in part because they 'required no particular skill on the part of the operator' (p. 29). Synthesizer interfaces were designed to maximize user accessibility, a quality highlighted by many advertisements and also mentioned by some practitioners (such as David Kurtz's comments about the Fairlight in King, 1986, p. 57). But the promise of universal accessibility was consistently counterbalanced by the prevailing rhetoric of sound professionals, which claimed that mastery of the instruments would require a new set of skills, namely those of a computer programmer or operator. In 1984, composer and audio producer Shelton Leigh Palmer observed that 'the smart synthesist/composer added engineering programming and producing to his list of required crafts' (1984, p. 30). A few years later, Serafine advised that 'engineers are going to have to get hip to MIDI' and that his own audio engineer would no longer be a tape operator but rather a 'computer operator' (Davidson, 1988, p. 18; see also DiMauro, 1987). In a two-part interview published in *Mix*, sound designer Leslie Shatz commented on the impact of the transition from magnetic tape to hard disks and other storage devices for digital media. Alluding to the enduring nature of analogue post-production within the new digital environment, he stated:

> The people who [are responsible for producing film sound] will have more of a multi-purpose background. They won't just be the dialog editor or the assistant editor or the Foley editor. There will be more people who can create a little bit of sound, mix a little bit of sound, work on dialog a little bit, thread up tape machines and generally work their way around this equipment … There isn't a lot of room for compartmentalization. The people who work in this process have

to know how to mix, how to clean the tape machine, how to select the sound and how it should sync up with the picture. The division of labor is diminishing and gradually disappearing because of the hardware (Pasquariello, 1987, p. 143).

The same 'easy to play' technical features that eased digital synthesizers from the audio industry into the motion picture industry portended changes to the labour of film sound professionals.

## Conclusion

At the outset of a January 1987 *Mix* article titled 'A Sampling of Sampling', author Tim Tully summarized the controversy surrounding the 'lightning-fast development' of electronic music machines with a theatric flair nonetheless conveying more than a kernel of truth:

Depending upon who's got the floor, the sampler can be the demon that will de-humanize music; the most exciting and flexible instrument since Cro-Magnon plucked his bowstring for fun instead of food; [or] an immoral, unethical and soon-to-be illegal ripoff of *real* musicians' performances on *real* instruments or the wave of (what else) the future (p. 49).

As I hope to have shown, the critical tensions described in this passage emerge throughout trade industry magazines in relation to both digital technologies and the creative status of those who recorded, assembled, programmed, and edited film sound content. Whereas the influx of digital synthesizers in the early 1980s gave rise to predictable anxieties over the displacement of musicians by electronic instruments, the majority of trade paper content pertaining to the role of digital instruments in film sound focused on the likening of sound editors to composers (a comparison that was predicated on the disintegration of the ontological distinction between sound effects and music) and the role of individual creativity in the context of technological innovation.

As Benjamin A. Wright has noted, the adoption of digital instruments and workstations by film sound professionals was by no means linear, and the early 1990s marked a period of technological instability owing to the array of competing analogue, digital, and analogue–digital workstations that would not be supplanted by fully digital, non-linear workstations, featuring integrated third-party programs (or plug-ins), until the early 2000s (2011, pp. 135–6). And yet the restoration of industry stability may have occurred at a cost, to the extent that present-day DAWs are seen by some to eradicate the physical connection between artist and machine. Serafine, for instance, laments the loss of the hardware that he once used in order to 'perform to picture'; DAWs such as Pro Tools encourage the simple insertion of library sound effects rather than the manipulation of sampled sounds with hardware controllers and 'all the fun stuff that we [Serafine and his peers] had back then: turning the sound backwards, affecting the pitch, manipulating all the elements' with a keyboard (Petrosky, 2009, online). In addition, despite the promise of digital technology to usher in a more integrated workflow across the tasks of sound editing and music composition, contemporary practices still tend to treat the two as discrete processes. Considered from this perspective, the post-production sound industry's transition from analogue to digital instruments, and ultimately the effect of that transition on the blending of music and sound effects in Hollywood cinema of the period, remains ripe for future study.

## Notes

1. This quote is included with the permission of *Keyboard Magazine* published by NewBay Media.
2. *Musique concrète* is a technique of musical composition that consists of the selection and editing of sounds recorded to magnetic tape, which may then be manipulated in a variety of ways, including tape reversal, speed variation, and the application of filters. Popularized after World War II, when the works of pioneering practitioners Pierre Schaeffer and Pierre Henry were broadcast on Paris' Radiodiffusion-Télévision Français, *musique concrète* is generally credited as a precursor to electronic and computer music and is frequently cited by Murch as a chief influence on his 'sound montages' in *THX 1138* (George Lucas, 1971), *American Graffiti* (George Lucas, 1973), *The Conversation* (Francis Ford Coppola, 1974), and *Apocalypse Now* (Francis Ford Coppola, 1974). See LoBrutto, 1994, pp. 83–100.
3. Although discussion of synthesizer scores in Hollywood cinema is inevitably addressed in historical overviews of film music (e.g. in Brown, 1994, pp. 65–6; Burt, 1994, pp. 241–4), a thorough analysis of their formal and stylistic functions has yet to be written.
4. Some readers may object to my use of the phrase 'sound editor' to encompass a wide range of tasks associated with post-production film sound, including not just the creation and recording of sound effects but also Foley work, sound mixing, and, at times, conceptual sound design. Yet the primary sources that I consulted often did not discern among these labels, lending credence to Benjamin A. Wright's argument that a quality of pluralism has characterized the role of the Hollywood sound designer (2013). It is further telling that the Academy of Motion Picture Arts and Science's award for Best Sound Editing, which is given to a production's Supervising Sound Editor who sometimes is accompanied by the Sound Designer, has undergone different names: Best Sound Effects (1963–1967, 1975), Best Sound Effects Editing (1977, 1981–1999), and Best Sound Editing (1979, 2000–present). The award for Best Sound Mixing is usually given to sound mixers and rerecording mixers even though sometimes a production's sound designer oversees the final mix.
5. As Benjamin A. Wright points out, most Hollywood sound and picture editors used analogue systems well into the 1990s (2011, p. 135).
6. On the role of music periodicals in the marketing of digital instruments, see Thèberge, 1997, pp. 106–130. Many issues of *dB* and *Recording Engineer/Producer*, as well as scores of magazines from the broadcasting and engineering industries, are available at the American History Radio website (http://www.americanradiohistory.com) and the Internet Archive (http://www.archive.org).
7. The question is inspired in part by K.J. Donnelly's observation that 'technological determinism is hardly the critical flavor of the month, but we have to accept

that technological capabilities set the horizons of aesthetic capabilities, and in the vast majority of cases, users adopt the technology's path of least resistance' (2013, p. 358).
8. For instance, Hollywood studios converting from silent to synchronized sound production benefited from contemporaneous innovations in the field of thermionics or vacuum tube technology (Crafton, 1997, pp. 27–34).
9. For comprehensive histories see Appleton (1989), Holmes (2012) and Vail (2014).
10. Among the earliest consumers of the Synclavier were established musicians Frank Zappa and the band Genesis. Early adopters of the Fairlight included Kate Bush, Peter Gabriel, and Stevie Wonder.
11. Peter Manning notes that the Fairlight and Synclavier also 'established some very important operational criteria that have influenced the development of commercial computer music systems to the present day', such as the use of proprietary software that cannot be accessed and modified (2013, p. 227).
12. The glossary of *Sound-on-Film: Interviews with Creators of Film Sound* defines the Synclavier not as a digital music synthesizer but, perhaps more aptly, as 'a digital, multichannel editing system' (LoBrutto, 1994, p. 286).
13. When Serafine created sound effects for *Star Trek: The Motion Picture*, a working picture edit was not available. Serafine later recalled, 'I never had a video … I'd sit at the Moviola in the editing room at Paramount with (supervising sound editor) Richard Anderson, go home at night with timings, create the sounds, come back the next day, give it to (the editors), transfer it, they'd cut it in, they'd adjust it and cut it if it was a few frames off here and there' (LoBrutto, 1994, p. 223).
14. Composer James Di Pasquale echoed Serafine's sentiment when, in a feature article penned for *Variety*, he commented that the practitioners who called themselves sound designers were 'technically-oriented people who were proficient computer programmers and mediocre musicians' (1985, p. 248).
15. Arguably, sound practitioners who espoused the label 'sound designer' aimed to imbue their reputedly technical craft of sound editing with a connotation of artistry (Beck, 2008, p. 73; Wright, 2013, p. 140).
16. Notably, the AFM did not object to the use of electronic instruments as a means of creating ethereal, 'unusual' sounds. Its proposed provision in 1984 permitted the use of electronic instruments 'for the unusual sound these instruments are capable of producing' (Kirk, 1984, p. 1). See also Terry, 1983, pp. 1, 67; Daniels, 1984, pp. 13, 15. George Burt claims that synthesizers led to significant job losses among musicians (1994, p. 241).

## References

Appleton, J. H. (1989) *21st Century Musical Instruments: Hardware and Software* (New York: Institute for Studies in American Music, Conservatory of Music, Brooklyn College of the City University of New York).

Armbruster, G. (1984) 'Frank Serafine: Designing Harmonious, Hallucinatory, & Horrifying Sounds for Hollywood Hits', *Keyboard*, Vol. 10, No. 9, 16– 17, 19–21.

Barnett, S. (1982) 'Film Sound Editing Techniques, Part 2', *Recording Engineer/Producer*, Vol. 13, No. 1, 56, 58, 60, 62, 64–7.

Beck, J. (2008) 'The Sounds of "Silence": Dolby Stereo, Sound Design, and *The Silence of the Lambs*' in J. Beck & T. Grajeda (eds) *Lowering the Boom: Critical Studies in Film Sound* (Urbana: University of Illinois Press), 68–83.

Brown, R.S. (1994) *Overtones and Undertones: Reading Film Music* (Berkeley and Los Angeles: University of California Press).
Burt, G. (1994) *The Art of Film Music* (Boston: Northeastern University Press).
'Buyer's Guide: Synthesizers and Computer Software,' (1986) *dB*, Vol. 20, No. 3, 49–56, 59.
Crafton, D. (1997) *The Talkies: American Cinema's Transition to Sound, 1926–1931* (New York: Charles Scribner's Sons).
Daley, D. (1987) 'Ivy League Goes Digital', *Mix*, Vol. 11, No. 7, 64, 69–70.
Daniels, B.D. (1984) 'Synthesizers Fan Controversy in Music Field', *Variety*, 14 November, 13, 15.
Davidson, C. (1988) 'Paramount's Electronic Cottage', *dB*, Vol. 22, No. 3, 13, 16–19.
Di Pasquale, J. (1985) 'Synthesizers, Composers Almost Inseparable', *Variety*, 29 October, 245, 248–9.
DiMauro, P. (1987) 'Digital Synth Consultants Help Artists In Studio Expertise', *Variety*, 14 October, 219.
Donnelly, K.J. (2013) 'Extending Film Aesthetics: Audio Beyond Visuals' in J. Richardson, C. Gorbman and C. Vernallis (eds) *The Oxford Handbook of New Audiovisual Aesthetics* (New York: Oxford University Press), 357–371.
Gibbs, V. (1984) 'The Synthesizer: Instrument, Not The Player, Changes Music', *Billboard*, 16 June, BM6, BM16.
Halfhill, T.R. (1982) 'The Sounds of TRON', *Compute!*, Vol. 4, No. 9, 18, 20, 22.
Holmes, T. (2012), *Electronic and Experimental Music: Technology, Music, and Culture*, 4th ed. (New York: Routledge).
Jacobson, L. (1987) 'Synths in the Studio', *Mix*, Vol. 11, No. 7, 168–174.
Karlin, F. and R. Wright (2013) *On the Track: A Guide to Contemporary Film Scoring*, 2nd ed. (New York: Routledge).
King, M. (1986) 'The Modus Operandus of David Kurtz—Part II', *dB*, Vol. 20, No. 2, 54–7.
Kirk, C. (1984) 'Proposed AFM-Producers Pact Would Limit Tuner Work Loss to Technology', *Variety*, 1 March, 1, 22.
Larson, R.D. (1983) 'An Interview with Frank Serafine', *Soundtrack: The CinemaScore & Soundtrack Archives*, http://www.runmovies.eu/?p=9186, date accessed 15 March 2014.
Larson, R.D. (n.d.) 'HYPER-REALITY: ALAN HOWARTH's Synthesized Scores and Specialized Sound Effects', *Alan Horwath*, http://alanhowarth.com/press-articles.html, date accessed 1 September 2014.
LoBrutto, V. (1994) *Sound-on-Film: Interviews with Creators of Film Sound* (Westport: Praeger).
Macar, R. (1987) 'Post-Script: Putting the Synclavier into "Overdrive"', *Mix*, Vol. 11, No. 1, 112, 115.
Manning, P. (2013) *Electronic and Computer Music* (New York: Oxford University Press).
Moog, R. (1982) 'Wendy Carlos & Michael Fremer Reveal the Secrets Behind the Soundtrack of *Tron*', *Keyboard*, Vol. 8, No. 11, 53–7.
Moorer, J.A. (1982) 'The Lucasfilm Audio Signal Processor', *Computer Music Journal*, Vol. 6, No. 3, 22–32.
Moorer, J.A., C. Abbott, P. Nye, J. Borish and J. Snell (1986) 'The Digital Audio Processing Station: A New Concept in Audio Postproduction', *Journal of the Audio Engineering Society*, Vol. 34, No. 6, 454–463.
Mosely, J. (1981) 'Motion Picture Sound in Record-Industry Perspective', *Journal of the Audio Engineering Society*, Vol. 29, No. 3, 114–125.

Oppenheimer, L. (1986) 'Serafine FX: Midi in the Movies?', *dB*, Vol. 20, No. 2, 43–4, 46.
Oppenheimer, L. (1987) 'Speculation on the future of Musical Instruments: Visions of the Digital Beyond', *Mix*, Vol. 11, No. 1, 29–32.
Palmer, S.L. (1984) 'The Creative Interface: Computers and Music Production', *Recording Engineer/Producer*, Vol. 15, No. 1, 30, 32, 152.
Pasquariello, N. (1986) 'Leslie Shatz: Sound Design for the Japanese', *dB*, Vol. 20, No. 2, 60, 63–4.
Pasquariello, N. (1987) 'Trends in Film Sound (Part Two)', *Mix*, vVl. 11, No. 12, 90–4, 96–8, 143.
Petrosky, M. (2009) 'Interview with Frank Serafine', *Tron Wiki*. http://tron.wikia.com/wiki/Tron_Wiki:Frank_Serafine_Interview, date accessed 15 June 2014.
Prager, B. (1986) 'Music by the Numbers: Surrendering Creative Control', *Billboard*, 15 February, 10.
Reid, G. (2000) *Synth Secrets, Part 20: Introducing Polyphony*. http://www.soundonsound.com/sos/dec00/articles/synthsec.asp, date accessed 6 June 2014.
Rothman, M. (1993) 'Lucas takes an Avid interest in digital firm', *Daily Variety*, 21 April. https://variety.com/1993/film/news/lucas-takes-an-avid-interest-in-digital-firm-106109, date accessed 15 June 2014.
Sadoff, R.H. (2013) 'Scoring for Film and Video Games: Collaborative Practices and Digital Post-Production' in C. Vernallis, A. Herzog and J. Richardson (eds) *The Oxford Handbook of Sound and Image in Digital Media* (New York: Oxford University Press), 663–681.
Serafine, F. (1980a) 'Probing the Sounds of *Star Trek*', *Studio Sound*, Vol. 22, No. 8, 30–2.
Serafine, F. (1980b) 'The New Motion Picture Sound', *American Cinematographer*, Vol. 61, No. 8, 796–799, 846.
Serafine, F. (1982) 'Sound Effects Design and Synthesis for *Tron*', *American Cinematographer*, Vol. 63, No. 8, 807, 830–4.
Soifer, R. (1987) 'The American Federation of Musicians: A Study in Contrasts', *Mix*, Vol. 11, No. 8, 175–7, 179, 181–2.
Spring, K. (2015) 'Telephone Interview with Ben Burtt', 30 January.
Synclavier advertising insert (1987) *Mix*, Vol. 11, No. 1, 14–24.
'Synclavier Marries Art and Technology' (1982) *Billboard*, 20 March, 31.
Terry, K. (1983) 'Synthesizers Change Music Biz: Musicians See a New Era Dawning', *Variety*, 6 July, 1, 67.
The DroidWorks (1985) *SoundDroid: The All-Digital Sound Studio in a Box*, The DroidWorks, North Hollywood.
Thèberge, P. (1997) *Any Sound You Can Imagine: Making Music/Consuming Technology* (Hanover and London: Wesleyan University Press).
Tully, T. (1987) 'A Sampling of Sampling', *Mix*, Vol. 11, No. 1, 49, 51–2, 181.
Vail, M. (2014) *The Synthesizer: A Comprehensive Guide to Understanding, Programming, Playing, and Recording the Ultimate Electronic Music Instrument* (New York: Oxford University Press).
Wright, B.A. (2011) 'Sound from Start to Finish: Professional Style and Practice in Modern Hollywood Sound Production', Ph.D. thesis, Carleton University.
Wright, B. (2013) 'What Do We Hear: The Pluralism of Sound Design in Hollywood Sound Production', *The New Soundtrack*, Vol. 3, No. 2, 137–157.

CHAPTER 20

# Unlearning Film School: The 'lo-fi' Soundtracks of Joe Swanberg

*Nessa Johnston*

## INTRODUCTION

One of the salient features of post-2000 cinema is the sheer increase of very low-budget feature-length film production, widely heralded as a 'digital revolution' in filmmaking (Tryon, 2009; Jenkins, 2010; Munt, 2008). The use of cheaper digital technologies instead of expensive film stock has lowered the budgetary threshold for shooting. The landscape of film production has changed considerably, and the means by which film school graduates make inroads into production has changed to reflect this landscape. Micro-budgeted digitally shot feature productions, often produced entirely at home or self-financed, are getting completed at an advancing rate but are jostling for exhibition at film festivals and beyond. But what are the ramifications of this technological shift for the soundtrack? This chapter presents a case study from the US independent filmmaking sector, that of writer-director Joe Swanberg. What is interesting, and possibly ironic in the context of a book such as this, is that Swanberg has risen to prominence via his association with the press-hyped 'mumblecore' label—a filmmaking movement renowned for (and named with reference to) its 'bad' sound.

Elsewhere, I have explored and interrogated the critical status of sound in mumblecore films, not only in the films of Swanberg but also in those of other US directors associated with mumblecore, including Aaron Katz and Andrew Bujalski (Johnston, 2014a). Arguably, their work has entered a 'post-mumblecore' phase, in which a number of the directors initially associated with the movement are asserting more distinct individual identities. Swanberg's work stands out as an exemplar of a particular set of possibilities presented

N. Johnston
Edge Hill University, UK

© The Editor(s) (if applicable) and The Author(s) 2016
L. Greene, D. Kulezic-Wilson (eds.), *The Palgrave Handbook of Sound Design and Music in Screen Media*, DOI 10.1057/978-1-137-51680-0_20

by post-millennial filmmaking. As Brigitta Wagner notes, Swanberg has a particularly visible critical status within mumblecore, often cited as exemplifying its worst or particularly emblematic tendencies: 'As anonymous contributors wrangle over [...] Mumblecore, Swanberg emerges as the undisputed bullseye of a more general critique that this cinema is un-cinematic or cinematically uninteresting' (2011). His prolific rate of output, filmed on cheap digital video, along with its lackadaisical improvisational style, and sometimes gratuitous nudity, have contributed to a degree of critical scepticism. For example, the critic Amy Taubin has dismissed Swanberg's films as 'smug' and 'lazy', and accused the director of 'clueless narcissism' (Taubin, 2007). Nevertheless, he has earned a cult following and his films are seen by indie distributers and festivals as increasingly bankable (Robinson, 2014). Carrying out a more academic assessment of Swanberg's work, James Lyons views mumblecore screen performances more positively, arguing that they 'deploy playful personification, suitably dual coded to allow for a cult-like appreciation of the controlling presence of a director/actor' (Lyons, 2012, p. 174). Hence, Lyons suggests that Swanberg's 'smug' and 'lazy' frequent appearances in his own films contribute to his films' increasing cult following. Meanwhile, Swanberg's career is achieving a more financially sustainable level of success (Robinson, 2014), and he has found a few notable champions amongst critics—including the relatively highbrow critic Richard Brody of *The New Yorker*—earning him a greater degree of artistic and commercial legitimacy.

From a more production-oriented standpoint, Swanberg's work is noteworthy given that he has fully embraced digital video as a medium that affords the ability to shoot with very minimal crew, potentially allowing actors greater freedom to improvise. In addition, he has taken full advantage of the low cost and shortened, simplified workflow of digital shooting and editing to produce a considerable quantity of work. He is remarkably prolific—since 2005, he has made sixteen feature-length films, plus short films, feature film segments, TV episodes, vodcasts and web series. In 2010 alone, he shot *six* feature-length films (all released in 2011). All can be described as naturalistic comedy-dramas, heavily improvised, and often sexually explicit. A few flirt with the horror genre, such as *Silver Bullets* (2011) and *24 Exposures* (2013), with which Swanberg is further associated via his parallel acting career in the films of Ti West (*The House of the Devil*, 2009; *The Sacrament*, 2014) and Adam Wingard (*You're Next*, 2011). Chuck Tryon (in interview with Henry Jenkins) cites mumblecore as an example of the importance of collaboration 'in an era of democratized media production' (Jenkins, 2010). The work (whether mumblecore, post-mumblecore or horror) of Swanberg and his collaborators substantiates Tryon's assertion: *Silver Bullets* sound designer Graham Reznick also writes and directs, and Ti West and Joe Swanberg act in each other's films. Swanberg is conscious of this collaborative shift too, and says of Ti West and others:

> We're not specialists in a sense that like one person's the director, there's one person who's just the cinematographer, somebody's just a writer. I think our

generation really approaches it from the point of everybody knowing how to do every different job and kind of be willing to help sort of work with their friends in different capacities. (*Coming Soon*, 2013)

Similarly, despite having worked as a sound designer on over thirty ultra-low-budget films, Reznick describes himself as a filmmaker and writer, and does not identify with the professionalized sound personnel sector, referring to the world he occupies as a 'film scene' rather than a 'film industry' (Johnston, 2014b). The idea of a film 'scene' might be a useful way to reconceptualize the workings of ultra-low-budget filmmaking. We already speak of 'music scenes' as distinct from 'music industries'; thus a 'film scene' is a potentially meaningful way to describe some filmmaking cultures. While distribution and exhibition channels for Swanberg's earlier films were initially limited to self-distribution via DVD, as well as screenings at small festivals (most notably South by Southwest in Austin, Texas), via these festival connections, Swanberg has more recently secured a video on demand (VOD) distribution deal with IFC (Independent Film Channel) in the USA (Tzioumakis, 2012; Robinson, 2014). Additionally, for the duration of his career to date, he has been based in Chicago rather than either of the US film industry centres of Los Angeles and New York, therefore providing an interesting case study of production contexts beyond these more mainstream locations.

In this chapter, I want to focus on Joe Swanberg's films as a distinct body of work and further explore his working methods, focusing on sound. Three of his 2011 films (*Art History, Silver Bullets* and *The Zone*) form the self-reflexive *Full Moon* trilogy, in which Swanberg plays a parodic version of himself, making films within these films. This trilogy is of particular interest because, to some extent, it acts as a documentary representation of Swanberg's shooting methods, albeit as overseen by the character of Swanberg as Swanberg. Furthermore, a more recent film *Drinking Buddies* (2013) represents a shift from these stripped-down production methods to working with a full crew, allowing this chapter to consider to what extent Swanberg's approach to sound has changed as he has moved into a 'post-mumblecore' phase with his more recent work. Nevertheless, what is striking and informative about Swanberg and his work (in general) is a lack of interest in the possibilities of sound design. Therefore, it is my contention that this lack of interest can offer an insight into the process of creating the soundtrack in his ultra-low-budget production methods, as well as allowing the opportunity for renewed consideration of production methods that do not entirely fit within a narrowly defined model of industrial norms.

## The Noise and Labour of 'lo-fi'

A particularly striking feature of Swanberg's work is the fact that the bulk of his films, up to *Drinking Buddies*, have minimal sound credits, and sometimes none. Swanberg has spoken in previous interviews about his working methods

(Wagner, 2011) but only mentioned his approach to sound in passing. To clarify his approach, I carried out an interview with him in August 2014 in which he expanded on his pre-*Drinking Buddies* sound production methods, as follows:

> I didn't have sound people on set. I was using microphone stands and hiding mics in certain places—just a lot of low budget tricks for getting really good sound on set without a dedicated sound person or a boom operator or anything like that. [...] So over the years there have been different techniques—there's been using lavelier microphones on the actors, there's been combined techniques of using a boom mic that's either held by somebody or held on a stand, and then using wireless H2 Zoom recorders, and placing one or two or three of them around the room in different locations, so that as the characters move around, there's always a microphone somewhere near picking up something, and occasionally on some of the small movies I have had sound people, or at least a boom operator, a dedicated sound person. But in all of those different scenarios I'm just looking for clarity of voice. The soundtracks aren't very deep; the movies are very dialogue driven, so just the voices have been the primary concern. (Johnston, 2014c)

As he explained in another interview, 'for the most part I've let the camera follow the actors and not the other way around. [I've] wanted the actors to be free to just inhabit a space and let the camera move around them' (Bibbiani, 2014). The emphasis on Swanberg's production methods seems to give actors complete freedom to improvise, with camera and microphone capturing spontaneous action as it unfolds.

Swanberg's model of capturing sound on set may appear to follow a paradigm as old as sound recording, which James Lastra identifies as the 'fidelity' paradigm, as opposed to the 'intelligibility' paradigm:

> the former sets as its goal the perfectly faithful reproduction of a spatiotemporally specific musical performance (as if heard from the best seat in the house); the latter, like writing, intelligibility or legibility at the expense of material specificity, if necessary. (2000, p. 139)

Despite Swanberg's assertion that his primary concern is 'clarity of voice', which would imply that he is following the intelligibility paradigm, that is not entirely the case; in fact, the two paradigms are not mutually exclusive. Rather, Swanberg's emphasis on 'picking up' sound on set suggests a preference for the spatio-temporal specificity of the fidelity paradigm; and overall, his is an approach that is not regarded as industry standard. As Sandra Pauletto asserts in her article 'The Sound Design of Cinematic Voices', speech is rarely an object of discussion in consideration of sound design, even though it is typically very heavily designed. In production, a skilled team of boom operator and sound recordist will attend carefully to microphone placement and mixer levels in order to capture as intelligible a recording as possible; and in post-production, the dialogue editor will assemble the dialogue track from a composite of sources including multiple takes and Automated Dialogue Replacement (ADR) (Pauletto, 2012). In contrast, Swanberg expressed that he did not feel the need to provide a clean dialogue track separate from other tracks:

> It was understood that because of the way that I work, most of the audio was on the dialogue track, and it was unrealistic to expect a Foley-filled M&E track, so those movies just went out—those ones that went out into the foreign marketplace—they went out with that caveat that—almost like a documentary or something like that—you just weren't gonna be able to dub the movie. It was gonna have to be subtitled. (Johnston, 2014c)

In other words, the sounds heard in Swanberg's earlier films are based on the kind of relatively 'raw' sound associated with documentary, rather than the carefully edited, mixed, reconstructed and designed soundtracks associated with fiction films' intelligibility paradigm.

A notable feature of the Swanberg films that do not credit sound crew, such as *Art History, The Zone* and *Uncle Kent* (2011), is that the background noise level is unstable, with the quieter, more intimate scenes having louder background noise, arising perhaps from crude normalization of sound levels in a desktop editing program. However, as I have argued in relation to mumblecore generally, background noise carries connotations beyond mere technical sloppiness (Johnston, 2014a, p. 75). Jeffrey K. Ruoff has described the intrusion of noise as a characteristic of documentary sound (1992); thus noise lends fiction films an authenticating aura of documentary. Indeed, Michel Chion has observed a tendency for some filmmakers to regard direct sound as a 'moral choice'; ergo, noise can connote 'truthfulness' in realist filmmaking (Chion, 1994, p. 108). Similarly, the manifesto of the Dogma 95 movement contains a rule outlawing post-production sound editing and mixing, including clean-up of raw, location-recorded sound. It states: 'The sound must never be produced apart from the images or vice versa. (Music must not be used unless it occurs where the scene is being shot)' (Hjort and MacKenzie, 2003, pp. 199–200); and the manifesto as a whole declares that these technical restrictions will help 'force the truth out of my [the filmmaker's] characters and settings'. Overall then, we can understand the audible noise in these films as having a heritage of cultural connotations relating to a vague yet persistently rearticulated notion of sonic 'truth'.

The dim sludge of background noise that characterizes Swanberg's ultra-low-budget soundtracks is particularly interesting when considered within broader contemporary trends of soundtrack editing and mixing. Even thirty years ago, it was observed that soundtracks were using less musical scoring, instead putting more creative work into designing backgrounds. As Stephen Handzo argues in the foundational edited collection *Film Sound: Theory and Practice*: 'If there is any single trend that can be observed in sound effects practice, it is toward a much more detailed background sound ambience [...] On the whole, sound effects have gained at the expense of underscoring' (1985,

p. 408). More recently, Robert Walker has written extensively on the design of background ambiences in the 'gritty' HBO TV drama *The Wire* (2002–8), underlining its strategy of aiming to keep the medium transparent, in the service of sonic verisimilitude. Walker places this aesthetic approach in contrast with more opaque uses of direct sound:

> Jean-Luc Godard's *Vivre sa vie* (1962) is often cited as a key work in the progression towards the use of a more detailed, direct soundtrack, though in direct opposition to classical Hollywood there is a deliberate foregrounding of the apparatus and medium of filmmaking. This is evident in audible changes in the directionality of the microphone during shots and sound cuts that have not been smoothed. (Walker, 2013, p. 49)

Here, Walker articulates two ever-present 'fidelity versus intelligibility' approaches to the realist soundtrack, and aligns the 'intelligibility' approach with Hollywood practice, and the 'fidelity' model with Godard's use of sound in *Vivre sa vie*. Similarly, Swanberg can be regarded as opting for this widely problematized fidelity model, though without the avant-garde, oppositional stance of Godard. Rather, his view confirms that he regards the 'fidelity' model as somehow an 'obvious' choice, with his reluctance to take a reconstructive approach to the soundtrack along the lines of the 'intelligibility' model arising from a lack of interest in sound design (or indeed sound design as he conceives it):

> It's not artistically exciting for me to create a bed of soundscape and play with drones and all that stuff. I would just rather hear the sounds of a kitchen and a car driving by and birds chirping, and if we can get that on set along with the dialogue then it seems to me why would we go out of our way to recreate something to try and sound natural when it's already there? (Johnston, 2014c)

Hence, Swanberg articulates a clear preference for the 'fidelity' model, and disdain for an 'intelligibility' model that he postulates in the above statement as redundant.

That noise is ever present in Swanberg's films, given his approach, is perhaps unsurprising, but also leads to interesting conceptual slippages. Noise can be a by-product of adhering to Lastra's fidelity model of sound recording, yet noise is also associated with 'lo-fi' sound, as articulated in indie music discourse. Noise reduction is also a constant pursuit in sound production and post-production. Walker's article extensively discusses editing and mixing processes designed to minimize noise, rendering it unnoticeable and keeping the medium transparent. Indeed, Andy Birtwistle goes so far as positing noise reduction as the key driver behind technological development in sound mediation: 'the promise of noiseless recording … has been with us since the very beginnings of commercial film sound technology' (2010, p. 87).

The term 'lo-fi' requires further explanation. In sound studies, R. Murray Schafer's influential work has discussed 'lo-fi' sound in terms of increasing levels of industrial noise pollution (1993); however, in indie music cultures 'lo-fi' signifies a particular type of minimally mediated, opaque production values, with connotations of authenticity and sincerity (Grajeda, 2002). These issues are not unrelated—drawing upon David Hesmondhalgh on music (1999) and Michael Z. Newman on film (2011), Jessica Lynn Trimble has posited independent music and independent film as 'cultural cousins', given the popular and industrial understanding of the term 'indie' and the shared trajectories of the term in both contexts (2013, pp. 44–9). With respect to film sound, it is therefore helpful to consider work in popular music studies to clarify what 'lo-fi' might mean in the similarly 'indie' working context of Swanberg's work. In this respect, Emily Dolan argues the appeal of the lo-fi sound aesthetic as a marker of authenticity in indie pop, differentiating it from the higher production values of mainstream pop:

> The lo-fi sound world […] draws attention to the mediating technologies at work. Just as scratches on an old record or the hiss of cassette tape break the illusion of an unmediated experience with the music, so too the outdated instruments and amateur playing draw attention to the technologies behind the production. Here the 'honesty' of this music does not arise from the illusion of unmediated communication […] but rather from openly emphasizing the process of mediation. (2010, p. 464)

Dolan compares two versions of 'I Don't Believe You' by The Magnetic Fields (a.k.a. Stephin Merritt), one an obscure early 7" release with messy production and occasionally unintelligible (yet witty) lyrics, the other a more recent, more professionally produced, and more easily available version, concluding:

> the higher production values attempt to cast the song as something lofty, but the very act of polishing it transforms the flaws which, in the original version, had charm into something negative. (2010, p. 467)

Low production values have 'charm'; hence the occasional unintelligibility of dialogue, the rising and falling noise levels, and general lack of 'polish' in the sound of Swanberg's films have an authenticating function, signifying 'indieness', which would be negated were the soundtracks more detailed, less noisy and more 'professional' sounding. According to Swanberg, this fits with the overall audio–visual aesthetics of his films: 'The idea has been to arrive in a place where the sound is serviceable to the movie and seems to fit also with the visual aesthetic which is just low budget, the realities of low budget filmmaking' (Johnston, 2014c).

Swanberg's preference for aesthetically 'serviceable', raw, location-recorded sound posits itself, in a relational fashion, as opposed to the more polished, more fully realized (more than merely 'serviceable') Hollywood sound:

> It's always been important for me to capture natural sound on set and stick with that sound in the editing process […] it wouldn't feel right to then go back through and then add a bunch of Foley and ADR and things like that. (Johnston, 2014c)

However, this aesthetic preference has budgetary and labour implications. Benjamin Wright emphasizes how the work of Foley artists is crucial within Hollywood sound aesthetics' emphasis upon detail, clarity and intelligibility:

> as if sound practitioners intend audiences to hear the unhearable. These aural closeups are not so much exaggerated from their real-world context as audibly distinguished to convey narrative details that otherwise would be lost in the din of a film's busy soundscape [...] the level of detail and definition present [...] is symptomatic of the complexity and ambition of modern sound style and practice. (Wright, 2013, p. 204)

Wright adds, though, that: 'The attention to such textural detail and the degree of intentionality behind the rendering of sound suggests that Foley represents a kind of "heightened reality". There is nothing inherently natural about Foley (or cinema sound in general) and its function on the soundtrack' (p. 217). In other words, the differences in production methods result in two contrasting benchmarks of sonic 'reality'—one 'lo-fi', with an unfinished yet 'serviceable' quality and minimal labour input, and one 'heightened', more crafted, professionalized, skilled and labour intensive (not to mention more expensive).

### 'THE POINT' OR MERELY 'WHAT HAPPENED': IMPROVISED PERFORMANCE AND SONIC CONTINGENCY

*Art History* is a film about the making of a bad mumblecore film (sexually explicit, with lengthy improvisational scenes) in which Swanberg plays 'a spoof of [him]self' (Wagner, 2011) and demonstrates a spoof of his filmmaking process ('Joe Swanberg Interview', 2012). He has elaborated on the shooting methods used in both *Art History* and *Silver Bullets* in interview: 'There's no sound person, just me and the actor. Or, in scenes I'm not in, I do the shooting. The mics are hidden in the room. In that sense, these films are completely accurate representations of our productions' (Wagner, 2011). In a later interview with me, he further confirmed that he did not use any dedicated sound crew (Johnston, 2014c). So although the film is a spoof of Swanberg's filmmaking, the technical process we see portrayed is not (according to Swanberg). There is no sound credit in the credits of *Art History*, in line with Swanberg's description of his working methods.

*Art History* opens provocatively with a sexually explicit scene between the two lead characters, Eric (Swanberg regular Kent Osbourne) and Juliette (Josephine Decker). The picture is flatly lit and shot somewhere between close-up and medium close-up; the soundtrack has an unprocessed, unsweetened, 'raw' quality, made up of dull and incoherent noises of breathing, jewellery jangling, bodies shifting on sheets. After a minute or two, the soundtrack betrays the film-within-a-film nature of the scene, as we hear the director Sam's voice (Swanberg) directing the couple's physical actions. The film then cuts to a static, low-angled camera perspective just outside the room, revealing in full the apparatus of filmmaking and Sam/Swanberg's figure. The sound is expressive of the contingencies of the shooting process—quiet, yet messy. In interview with me, Swanberg stressed the importance of capturing such sonic contingency and equates it with a performative register of 'reality', emphasizing a goal of capturing sound as it happens on set and an aversion to post-production fixes:

> It's the performances that I'm focused on and the movies are built entirely around those performances—that's the thing that we can't get later. It needs to all work. Because I'm my own editor I tend to know which bits of takes I'm going to use, and if a car drives by over the top of a line in the middle of a take that's not a big deal to me because it's contextualized. I'm happy to let the reality of the world into the movie. (Johnston, 2014c)

For Swanberg then, unexpected noises that might interfere with the sonic intelligibility of a scene are equated with reality or rather 'the reality of the world', which he further considers to be contextualized by his emphasis upon capturing spontaneous performances that he can't 'get later'.

*Art History*'s narrative revolves around Sam shooting a film about a relationship between characters played by Eric and Juliette. As Eric develops an attraction to Juliette, it becomes apparent that Sam desires her too. While as a director, Sam initially welcomes this strengthening of the actors' on-screen chemistry, he gradually becomes jealous. A later scene shows Eric and Juliette lying in bed in the dark, embracing and (suitably) mumbling to one another, cross-cutting to similarly darkened shots of Sam at his laptop. The perspective and quality of the sound of the couple's mumbles shifts to sound like it could be emanating from Sam's laptop's speakers. However, the temporal and diegetic status of this asynchronous sound is unclear, as is the status of the visuals of the couple in bed. Whether Sam is editing an earlier scene while the actors recover from the earlier shoot, or whether the shots and sounds of the actors are temporally displaced and reference the footage Sam is editing, is unclear. This is only clarified when Sam and his friend (a nameless character played by horror director Adam Wingard) chuckle and raise the volume on Sam's laptop, seemingly in an effort to drown out the sounds of the couple in the next room.

Although *Art History* overall appears to champion minimal mediation of the soundtrack and the contingencies of crudely recorded location sound, the use of asynchronous sound in the scene just discussed, and the spatio-temporal ambiguity of the diegesis or order of scenes, actually highlights the mediated quality of allegedly minimal mediation. Furthermore, a moment in the final twenty minutes of this film not only shows the working microphone set-up but also depicts Sam/Swanberg filming a love scene between the two main actors, one of whom is his on-screen girlfriend. In the scene, Sam gets aggravated because he thinks he hears Eric say 'I love you'. But no such line is audible, which underlines distinctions between the subjective experience of listening, the mediated film within a film we are viewing, and the contingent character of the profilmic event. Overall then, *Art History* oscillates between embracing a 'lo-fi' minimally mediated sonic aesthetic and foregrounding uncertainties around the 'lo-fi' apparatus of sound production. Furthermore, this tension is paralleled within the film's narrative, in which Sam/Swanberg at first welcomes the building chemistry between the two actors as an opportunity to capture authentic emotional 'chemistry', then becomes jealous and aggravated by the very 'chemistry' he seeks to capture.

Questions of realism and mediation recur throughout Swanberg's ultra-low-budget oeuvre. With *The Zone* (also a film about making a mumblecore-esque film) and *Uncle Kent* (which incorporates iPhone footage alongside HD), Swanberg situates his films within wider contexts of audio–visual communication such as the aesthetics of web video and increasingly widespread media literacy, in concurrence with his credo to make movies that 'look like whatever right now looks like' ('Joe Swanberg interview', 2012). Although Swanberg's remark is not referring specifically to sound, if we consider everyday mediation of experiences via web video, iPhone cameras and their ilk, this includes sound that is 'lo-fi', noisy and imprecise. While the 'lo-fi' noisy sound in Swanberg's films stresses the contingent character of the loosely planned, improvised film shoot, this is not simply deterministic. Noisiness and 'lo-fi-ness' can be performed as a stylized contingent, which is posited throughout the *Full Moon* trilogy by virtue of its self-reflexive structure. Indeed, the final scene of *The Zone* opens up the film's reality like a Russian doll, showing Swanberg and his wife Kris, playing themselves, negatively critiquing the film that has just happened:

KS: …your past few movies have been about you complaining about making movies, it's sort of like another one that's just you complaining about making movies about complaining about making movies […]

JS: … I definitely feel like it runs out of steam, but I almost sort of felt like that became the point … it's like I just didn't have the energy or enthusiasm to finish the movie so it just sort of doesn't get finished…

KS: Is that *the point*, or is that *just what happened*?

It is my contention that this self-reflexive critique crystalizes issues surrounding the status of performance in these works, their 'lo-fi' sound, and Swanberg's authorship and critical status. The contingency emphasized by the soundtrack's aesthetics is further highlighted by Swanberg and his wife's exchange. It articulates a confusion regarding a balancing act of capturing actions as they unfold, as having some sort of 'point' versus the perceived effort of 'making' a film. Indeed, we can see this balancing act played out in *The Zone*'s critical reception. In some quarters, it is panned for its 'rudimentary lighting, uninspired camerawork and rote editing' (Lowe, 2011); in stark contrast, Richard Brody (2012) praises it as a work of 'terrible elegiac power' and draws comparisons with the work of Pier Paolo Pasolini.

## Post-production Sound Design: Genre and Sonic Authorship

Arguably, Joe Swanberg does not 'author' his soundtracks, and neither does a sound designer—instead, he creates an environment in which his actors improvise freely and thus 'author' a soundtrack passively captured on set without the aid of any credited sound personnel, let alone a sound designer. The lack of post-production sound work, including Foley, speaks also to a conceptualization of the authenticity of screen performance in his films and the contingency of the 'raw' location sound captured during shooting.

Although *Art History* has no sound person credited, the second film of the *Full Moon* trilogy, *Silver Bullets*, does. I mentioned earlier that this film flirts with the horror genre, which it does in quite a metatextual way—the horror director Ti West plays a version of himself named Ben, directing a werewolf film that stars Swanberg's parody character's girlfriend Claire (Kate Lyn Sheil). Tension and jealousy build between Ethan (Swanberg as 'Swanberg') and Claire, exacerbated by his professional jealousy of Ben, and by Ethan's decision to cast Claire's friend in one of his own films. The sound credit goes to Graham Reznick for 'special sound design', which refers to a heavily stylized, dream sequence-like horror scene, dominated by electronic music and a few background drones. Another characteristic feature of the sound in *Silver Bullets* is a heavily used string-driven score by Orange Mighty Trio. Compared with *Art History* and *The Zone* then, *Silver Bullets* has manifestly more non-diegetic post-production-added sound and music.

Alongside *Silver Bullets*, Swanberg's more recent horror film *24 Exposures* (starring Adam Wingard) and his contribution to the anthology film *V/H/S* (2012) are slightly more heavily financed, have larger casts and crews, and are more explicitly positioned within the horror genre, distributed by IFC's genre subdivision, IFC Midnight. As Swanberg clarified in interview with me, in his opinion, the larger budget and genre positioning go hand in hand with a contrasting sound aesthetic and a greater amount of post-production sound work:

> With *24 Exposures* and *V/H/S* those definitely went through full creative mixes and there was a lot of additional sound brought in. Those are the demands of the genre and there is an expectation from the audience of a score and a certain level of sound design, and also creatively it's important—you can really play with people's emotions and heighten things very effectively and cheaply using sound, and so that's been a really fun part of doing that genre work. In a way I consider it something very different from something like *Art History*, which was conceived of as something very sparse and never having music. [...] Those genre films I made like *Silver Bullets* and *24 Exposures* and *V/H/S* were really not realistic at all [...] and they got more experimental with the sound but for the most part

> I just want the sound to not draw attention to itself, to not be an interesting, complicated sound mix. (Johnston, 2014c)

It is interesting to note that Swanberg emphasizes sound design as part of the demands of genre, rather than either a key part of film storytelling technique, or as an area in which he can exert creative control or impose his signature style or auteurist stamp. Furthermore, rather than describing a directorial 'vision' of the soundtrack, Swanberg stressed the collaborative nature of his working methods, including collaboration with composers and sound designers: 'I work with composers the same way I work with my actors. I really like to give them a lot of freedom and trust their instincts, and my feeling is—hire the right person and they'll do the right work for it' (Johnston, 2014c). This is a potentially contradictory stance considering that Swanberg de-emphasizes the creative autonomy of the sound production and post-production process in the films discussed earlier in this chapter yet also likes to give creative 'freedom' to collaborators in other instances. Essentially, this contradictory stance reinforces the notion of sound 'design' as manifested through noticeable creative effort, and what is easily recognizable as stylized designed sound is generally associated with genres such as horror, not with the 'un-cinematic or cinematically uninteresting' (Wagner, 2011) realm of Swanberg's relationship-focused mumblecore comedy-dramas. It is similarly recognizable in the more professionally produced, intelligible soundtracks beyond the ultra-low-budget sector. In contrast, the 'raw' lo-fi sound described earlier in *Art History* and *The Zone* is automatically posited as a manifestation of a lack of obvious creative or professional effort, the term 'raw' inviting the assumption of work remaining to be done to 'cook' ('cut', 'mix', 'process', 'sweeten') the sound. In 'The Poetics of Signal Processing', Jonathan Sterne and Tara Rodgers examine this metaphorical usage of 'raw', arguing that in fact the act of recording sound is what makes it raw—sounds themselves are never 'raw'—'sounds are thus rendered raw through human action—and do not simply exist in a raw state out in the world' (2011, p. 41). Yet '"cooking" with sound can be figured as a creative, expressive act or as a labor or service' (p. 48). The 'raw' aesthetic is a key component of the 'lo-fi' indie aesthetic; whereas 'cooking' with sound can connote either the stylization associated with particular genres such as horror or Hollywood-style sonic verisimilitude (Lastra's 'intelligibility' model).

In contrast to the *Full Moon* trilogy, Swanberg's *Drinking Buddies* made use of a full crew and an industry standard post-production sound mix. It was Swanberg's first opportunity to work in this manner, and he has posited his previous work as a learning process building up to a point in which he could enter a fully professionalized working environment for the first time:

> The way I felt about it while I was doing it was that I was finally making my first feature. My films from *Kissing on the Mouth* to *All the Lights in the Sky* were [...] like a workshop/laboratory environment, and I was totally freely playing with the medium, and unlearning things I was taught in film school at Southern Illinois

University. Coming out of film school, I rejected having a crew and big productions. [...] With *Drinking Buddies* I was ready to re-embrace the 115-year history of cinema, and this system that Hollywood invented and that people have been trying to perfect since then. (Kramer, 2013)

However, as clarified in interview with me which focused on this shift to working with a full crew from a sound perspective, Swanberg did not see the process of constructing the soundtrack of *Drinking Buddies* particularly as an artistic opportunity and conceived of it primarily as 'a deliverables concern, rather than an artistic concern':

> as my career has gone along and the expectations of the movies have changed, like on *Drinking Buddies* and *Happy Christmas* [2014], the two most recent ones, we've just had to do some ADR and we've had to do various things just because those movies are going to play in a foreign market and a lot of countries still want to dub. So separate from the movie itself, we've had to hire sound places to create Foley and create an entire M&E track. I never had to do that with the earlier movies. [...] And so, nowadays that stuff happens. But it happens separate from me. I'm supervising the final mix, but I'm not supervising the M&E mix that's gonna be used for dubbing, because I don't care. Y'know, it's gonna sound terrible anyway, so I don't feel like I need to, like, run a fine-toothed comb through the footstep Foleys for some Italian version of *Drinking Buddies* that I'm never gonna watch. (Johnston, 2014c)

Swanberg implies that the earlier, ultra-low-budget films are subject to a greater level of personal control in all aspects of their production, including sound—whereas in the case of *Drinking Buddies*, he grants autonomy to collaborators in the sound department. However, Swanberg's stance on the role of post-production sound in this context downgrades it to that of a technical process, as opposed to a creative process—hence, he grants the autonomy largely due to an expressed lack of interest.

In addition to considering sound production and post-production, I wish to briefly reflect on sound and exhibition contexts at this point. Swanberg has stated that although he believes in watching films theatrically (because he enjoys hearing the audience's response), he is not convinced that his own films are necessarily best experienced that way: 'I don't know if I'm making those kinds of movies; I actually think that the kind of intimate character films that I'm making can be really great experiences on a laptop with your headphones on [...] I'm kind of open to people seeing them in any way that they want' ('10 Questions for Joe Swanberg', 2012). As Yannis Tzioumakis has recently emphasized, 'alternative' channels of digital delivery and exhibition are an increasingly important part of the market and 'in recent years some of them have started generating more revenue for films than the theatrical exhibition market' (Tzioumakis, 2012). Swanberg's reliance on VOD deals and DVD subscription packages, and only very recent and minimal use of cinema exhibition, attests to a shift in cinema consumption along the lines he describes. There are therefore potential ramifications for film sound studies and further analysis of soundtracks. For example, Walker describes the television program *The Wire* as having a 'cinematic aesthetic' because it's mixed to 5.1 surround—but what happens with sound's 'cinematic aesthetic' when we take the various different channels of delivery and modes of reception of the digital era into account? In the case of Swanberg's pre-*Drinking Buddies* films, his production methods and lack of concern with taking a meticulous approach to the soundtrack can be linked to how he interacts and conceives of his audience, presumed to be audio-viewing his films 'on a laptop with your headphones' rather than in a cinema.

## Conclusion

This chapter offers one filmmaker's perspective on the soundtrack but opens up a range of questions regarding the status of sound in low-budget cinema. I have demonstrated how Swanberg's work and its 'lo-fi' sound functions within a tradition that holds unpolished, noisy location-recorded sound as somehow more 'truth'-ful within the context of his ultra-low-budget relationship-focused comedy-dramas such as *Art History* and *The Zone*. The 'lo-fi' quality of these soundtracks authenticates Swanberg's status as 'indie' practitioner, yet has the potential to deprioritize and efface sound specialist labour. His description of his chosen approach demonstrates a preference for a 'fidelity' paradigm of sound recording (fidelity to a contingent sound event), which is paralleled by a preference for capturing the contingent qualities of semi-improvised actors' performances as they unfold spontaneously. The reflexive qualities of the *Full Moon* trilogy, with its films within films, highlight many of the tensions inherent in these preferences. However, as Swanberg scales up his productions and works within different genres, he emphasizes the importance of the labour of sound personnel and the aesthetic, narrative and technical potential of 'good' sound design, while simultaneously lacking much interest in its potential as a mechanism for his own creative control or directorial 'vision'.

Swanberg's lack of overt creative interest in the possibilities of sound design and his opinions regarding sound production illuminate issues around the critical and cultural status of sound, as well as broaden the scope of film sound studies research beyond the institutionally recognized film industry and into the semi-professionalized, post-film school indie 'film scene'. Typically, scholarly research in film studies has distinguished between amateur and professional production. Much ultra-low-budget work occupies a grey area, but one that is increasingly visible to audiences. In exploring filmmaking practice beyond the conventionally recognized 'film industry', that is, the industrially and institutionally organized sphere, I am aware of the danger of effacing the real labour of film sound production, yet this is certainly not my objective. Instead, I have documented these examples to enable a more nuanced understanding of film sound practices that occur not quite inside the industry or at its fringes, but between the two. As the landscape of production, post-production and exhibition continues to shift, it is important for film sound studies to develop a more nuanced understanding of how these blurred boundaries impact upon the creative and industrial practices of sound personnel.

## References

'10 Questions for Joe Swanberg' (2012) *IUCinema*, vodcast (Indiana University Cinema YouTube Channel), 19 September, date accessed 10 January 2014.

Bibbiani, W. (2014) 'The Sacrament: Joe Swanberg on Ti West's Directing Style' *CraveOnline*, 06 June, http://www.craveonline.co.uk/entertainment/film/interviews/701279-the-sacrament-joe-swanberg-on-ti-wests-directing-style, date accessed 7 July 2014.

Birtwistle, A. (2010) *Cinesonica: sounding film and video* (Manchester: Manchester University Press).

Brody, R. (2012) 'Go See Tonight: Joe Swanberg's *The Zone*', *The New Yorker*, 18 June, http://www.newyorker.com/culture/richard-brody/go-see-tonight-joe-swanbergs-the-zone, date accessed 1 August 2014.

Chion, M. (1994) *Audio-Vision: Sound on Screen* (New York: Columbia University Press).

*Coming Soon* (2013) 'Interview: DIY Filmmaker Joe Swanberg on Working with Others' *Coming Soon*, 27 November, http://www.comingsoon.net/movies/features/107924-interview-diy-filmmaker-joe-swanberg-on-working-with-others, date accessed 15 January 2014.

Dolan, E. I. (2010) '"... This little ukulele tells the truth": indie pop and kitsch authenticity', *Popular Music*, 29, 457–469.

Grajeda, T. (2002) 'The Feminization of Rock' in R. Beebe, D. Fulbrook, and B. Saunders (eds) *Rock Over the Edge: Transformations in Popular Music Culture* (Durham, NC: Duke University Press), 233–254.

Handzo, S. (1985) 'A Narrative Glossary of Film Sound Technology' in E. Weis and J. Belton (eds) *Film Sound: Theory and Practice* (New York: Columbia University Press), 383–426.

Hesmondalgh, D. (1999) 'Indie: The Institutional Politics and Aesthetics of a Popular Music Genre', *Cultural Studies*, Vol. 13, No. 1, 34–61.

Hjort, M. and S. MacKenzie (2003) *Purity and Provocation: Dogma 95* (London: BFI Publishing).

Jenkins, H. (2010) 'Reinventing Cinema: An Interview with Chuck Tryon (Part Two)' *Confessions of an Aca/Fan: the Official Weblog of Henry Jenkins*, 19 July, http://henryjenkins.org/2010/07/reinventing_cinema_an_intervie.html, date accessed 5 January 2014.

'Joe Swanberg Interview' (2012) *The Seventh Art* Issue 5, vodcast, http://www.theseventhart.org/main/videos/issue-5-joe-swanberg/, date accessed 23 July 2014.

Johnston, N. (2014a) 'Theorizing "Bad" Sound: What Puts the Mumble into Mumblecore?', *The Velvet Light Trap* 74, 67–79.

Johnston, N. (2014b) 'Graham Reznick: Skype interview with author', 10 June.

Johnston, N. (2014c) 'Joe Swanberg: Skype interview with author', 24 July.

Kramer, G. (2013) 'Interview: Joe Swanberg', *Slant Magazine*, 2 August, http://www.slantmagazine.com/features/article/interview-joe-swanberg-2013, date accessed 28 December 2013.

Lastra, J. (2000) *Sound Technology and the American Cinema: Perception, Representation, Modernity* (New York: Columbia University Press).

Lowe, J. (2011) '*The Zone*: Film Review', *The Hollywood Reporter*, 14 November, http://www.hollywoodreporter.com/review/zone-film-review-261252, date accessed 1 August 2014.

Lyons, J. (2012) 'Low-Flying Stars: Cult Stardom in Mumblecore' in K. Egan and Sa. Thomas (eds) *Cult Film Stardom: Offbeat Attractions and Processes of Cultification* (Basingstoke: Palgrave Macmillan), 163–178.

Munt, A. (2008) '"Am I crazy to make a film for only $100,000 or am I crazy not to?" Kriv Stenders goes Micro-budget Digital for Boxing Day', *Senses of Cinema*, Issue 46, http://sensesofcinema.com/2008/australian-cinema-46/kriv-stenders-boxing-day/, date accessed 05 April 2015.

Newman, M. Z. (2011) *Indie: An American Film Culture*, (New York/Chichester: Columbia University Press).

Pauletto, S. (2012) 'The sound design of cinematic voices', *The New Soundtrack*, Vol. 2, No. 2, 127–142.

Robinson, E. B. (2014) '*Happy Christmas*: Director Joe Swanberg on the Financial Life of the Independent Filmmaker', *Filmmaker Magazine*, 25 July, http://filmmaker-magazine.com/86888-happy-christmas-director-joe-swanberg-on-the-financial-life-of-the-independent-filmmaker/, date accessed 28 July 2014.

Ruoff, J. K. (1992) 'Conventions of Sound in Documentary' in R. Altman (ed.) *Sound Theory, Sound Practice* (New York: Routledge), 217–34.

Schafer, R. M. (1993) *The Soundscape: Our Sonic Environment and the Tuning of the World* (Rochester, VT: Destiny Books).

Sterne, J. and T. Rodgers (2011) 'The Poetics of Signal Processing', *differences: A Journal of Feminist Cultural Studies*, Vol. 22, No. 2–3, 31–53.

Taubin, A. (2007) 'Mumblecore: All Talk?', *Film Comment*, November/December 2007, http://www.filmcomment.com/article/all-talk-mumblecore, date accessed 5 February 2015.

Trimble, J. L. (2013) '"More Than Just Film": Rebranding Independence on IFC', MA thesis, University of Texas at Austin.

Tryon, C. (2009) *Reinventing Cinema: Movies in the Age of Media Convergence* (New Brunswick, NJ/London: Rutgers University Press).

Tzioumakis, Y. (2012) 'Reclaiming Independence: American Independent Cinema Distribution and Exhibition Practices beyond Indiewood', *Mise au point* 4, https://map.revues.org/585, date accessed 3 August 2014.

Wagner, B. (2011) 'Accidental Cinema and the YouTube Sublime: An Interview with Joe Swanberg', *Senses of Cinema* 59, http://sensesofcinema.com/2011/feature-articles/accidental-cinema-and-the-youtube-sublime-an-interview-with-joe-swanberg/, date accessed 3 August 2014.

Walker, R. (2013) '"Don't pump up the emotion": The creation and authorship of a sound world in *The Wire*', *The New Soundtrack*, Vol. 3, No. 1, 45–59.

Wright, B. (2013) 'What do we hear? The pluralism of sound design in Hollywood sound production', *The New Soundtrack*, Vol. 3. No. 2, 137–157.

CHAPTER 21

# The Janus Project: Cristobal Tapia de Veer's *Utopia*, Anempathetic Empathy and the Radicalization of Convention

*Annette Davison and Nicholas Reyland*

Giving a recent keynote lecture on moments in film scoring where music is undeniably 'heard', Claudia Gorbman[1] identified a recurring strategy in the films of Paul Thomas Anderson: music so wrong it is right (2014). To be specific, there are passages in *There Will Be Blood* (2007) and *Punch-Drunk Love* (2002) where music's sensuous and symbolic cues feel so misplaced that, paradoxically, they incur a stronger, more appropriate emotional response from the audio-viewer than a more conventional scoring strategy could induce. Such responses are not merely more active forms of critical engagement cued by the audio-viewer's experience of anempathetic, ironic or otherwise symbolic distance between music and action; nor are they an active disengagement with the narrative discourse, triggered by an unconventional gesture's puncturing of the storytelling apparatus's putative realism—although both of these effects can be mobilized, amongst others, by such gestures. Rather, a primary function of these moments is to revivify screen scoring's conventions for the arousal of emotion, retooling one of Gorbman's famous fundamentals of screen scoring—'[s]oundtrack music may set specific moods and emphasize particular emotions suggested in the narrative, but first and foremost it is a signifier of emotion in itself'—for savvier postmodern ears. Convention can thus be achieved unconventionally, albeit often—as in these films—in narratives that are far from conservative.

---

A. Davison
University of Edinburgh, UK

N. Reyland
Keele University, UK

Cristobal Tapia de Veer's score to seasons one and two of *Utopia* (Channel 4, 2013–2014) is one of the more significant recent achievements in television scoring because, in part, of its unconventional conventionality. The serial's music energizes a continuum of possibilities between heard and unheard, the expected and the surprising, cueing responses that range between straightforward empathy and the induction of what, developing Gorbman's line of thinking, we might term anempathetic empathy for characters and situations in the show. This strategy, as the analysis below will argue, parallels storylines and character arcs in the serial, many aspects of which relate, thematically, to the name and purpose of the sterilization serum, Janus, central to the plans of the show's meta-governmental conspirators The Network. (Taking its title from the Greek god with two faces, Janus's components are designed to sterilize most of humanity in order to combat overpopulation, reset the Earth's ecosystem, and save the species.) *Utopia* thereby represents a shocking fictional solution to a terribly real problem: our planet's population will reach an unsustainable 10 billion by the end of the present century (Emmott, 2013). Tapia de Veer's strategies encourage the audio-viewer to experience the Janus-like discomfort of crisscrossing empathy and anempathy. Conventional subject positions are destabilized as one's fictional loyalties and personal views are called into question by the show. The journeys into and out of the darkness of The Network's envisaged solution (or *is* it darkness?) for characters, including Wilson Wilson/Mr Rabbit No. 2 (Adeel Akhtar) and RB/Pietre (Neil Maskell),[2] create concomitant experiences of sympathy/disavowal, the audio-viewer's allegiances changing suit like the characters' names and allegiance to The Network/humanity. This, then, is one source of the show's political heft: its dramatization of questions about overpopulation and humanity's fate, and the manner in which, amplified through the show's developments of televisual style, it induces the audio-viewer to join in the questioning. Tapia de Veer's scoring, allied with other televisual innovations in *Utopia*—such as its extravagant art design (all those eye-popping chromatic polarizations of yellow and blue) and landscape cinematography (long shots isolating lonely figures in the countryside open many episodes)—energizes this polemical process.

The significance of Tapia de Veer's *Utopia* score, therefore, is not merely its bringing of art film strategies into recent network television (albeit relatively avant-garde cult television on the publicly owned, commercially funded public service broadcaster, Channel 4). It is significant because, unlike the vast bulk of original music in productions from the new 'golden age' of serial television drama, it actually does something interesting with the musical conventions of the medium. A peculiar facet of the prestige tradition emanating, above all, from HBO's influential *The Sopranos* (1999–2007) and *The Wire* (2002–2008), is that original non-diegetic music is often absent from 'TV3' drama. Indeed, its absence is a hallmark of these flagship HBO productions, in much the same way that using no non-diegetic music, or using it sparingly but unconventionally, is a hallmark of pockets of art cinema including films directed by Mike Leigh, Krzysztof Kieślowski and the Dardenne Brothers.

This may be, in part, an attempt to signify difference (from more mainstream texts), and thus quality, by demonstrating a commitment to avoiding obvious strategies of audience manipulation.[3] There are, of course, exceptions in recent long-form TV drama—for example, W.G. Snuffy Walden's *Friday Night Lights* (NBC, 2006–2011), Bear McCreary's *Battlestar Galactica* (Sci-Fi, 2004–2009) and Sean Callery's *24* (Fox, 2001–2010)—where one can argue that a show's development of the medium included significant innovations in scoring style. The utilization of pre-existing popular music (not least in main title and end credit sequences) has also created new forms of musico-narrative sophistication in these shows. Nonetheless, it is rare to hear original non-diegetic scoring that troubles televisual conventions to the extent of, say, *The Wire*'s politically motivated manipulations of televisual grammar and audio-viewer empathy/anempathy. Indeed, many critically lauded shows contain poor musical moments (e.g., *Boardwalk Empire*'s attention to historical detail in all, it seems, but the disruptively implausible miming of its 'diegetic' musicians /HBO, 2010–2014/, or *Forbrydelsen*'s over-use of key cues to the extent that they begin to tip spoilers, for example, the 'Sarah Lund is about to make a breakthrough' high piano ostinato /DR1, 2007–2012/). As such, it is important to study fusions of drama and purpose as radical as *Utopia*, in which musical aspects of the televisual discourse are as innovative as the plot and other elements of the storytelling, in order to theorize the foundations of their radicalism and more fully critique the serial.

In the present chapter, we frame and situate this investigation as follows. First, Tapia de Veer's musical background, career before *Utopia* and first major TV soundtrack for director Marc Munden (*The Crimson Petal and the White*, BBC, 2011) are examined, the latter introducing a number of stylistic and aesthetic traits that develop in *Utopia*. The show's plotlines are then more fully detailed, in the context of a survey of *Utopia*'s critical reception. As with his previous work on *The Crimson Petal and The White*, reviewers often highlighted his music's contribution without, notably, being able to define exactly what the nature of that contribution had been or, indeed, to find words adequate to the task of describing its sound world. Cues from the earlier score are discussed briefly, before a more detailed analysis of *Utopia*'s music commences, moving between close analysis of individual scenes and broader trajectories in the scoring across both seasons, and between observations about audio-visual style and interpretation of the music's contribution to the serial's storytelling and subtexts.

## Before *Utopia*: Scoring *The Crimson Petal and the White*

Cristobal Tapia de Veer is a Chilean-born Canadian film and television composer, arranger, producer and multi-instrumentalist based in Montréal. As a child, he built himself a drum kit and invented percussion instruments (Anon., 2015). He graduated from the Conservatoire de musique de Québec with a master's degree in music, and was awarded a prize for percussion performance. He began to experiment with a 4-track recorder, producing avant-garde soundscapes, formed a band (The Blokes) and built a career as a music producer. He co-founded the eclectic pop trio One Ton, which had a number one hit in Canada with 'Supersex World', and produced an album, *Abnormal Pleasures*, that straddled 'dance-pop, reggae, funk, cabaret, and hip-hop' (LeBlanc, 2002). At this point Tapia de Veer began working with the French-Canadian singer Jorane, co-composing music and arranging songs for several films. His first feature-length solo score was for Martin Frigon's documentary *Mirages d'un Eldorado* (2008), an exposé of the damaging practices of Canadian mining companies in Chile.

Tapia de Veer's debut television score was for an adaptation of Michael Faber's 2002 neo-Victorian novel *The Crimson Petal and the White* (2011), directed by Marc Munden, and co-produced by the BBC and the Montréal-based Canadian production company, Cité-Amérique. Here the composer established a soundscape for the audio-visual representation of literary neo-Victorianism, a fiction genre '*about* the Victorian age, rather than *of* the Victorian age', as Iris Kleinecke-Bates highlights (2014, p. 1). The neo-Victorian text 'plays with and explores its own distance to its object of scrutiny' and thus 'asks questions concerning the fictionalization of the past and its situatedness vis-à-vis the present' (Kleinecke-Bates, 2014, p. 1). Thus, Faber's novel opens with a meta-fictional warning from its omniscient narrator to the reader. Screenwriter Lucinda Coxon provides a similar warning to the audio-viewer in the first of the adaptation's four episodes, via an embodied voice-over by the 19-year-old prostitute, Sugar (Romola Garai), whose rise the novel charts:

> London, 1874. Keep your wits about you. This city is vast and intricate and you do not know your way around. You imagine from other stories you've read that you know it well, but those stories flattered you. You are an alien from another time and place altogether. You don't even know what hour it is, do you? Nor do most where you're going. Here people go to sleep as soon as the gin takes effect. You've allowed yourself to be led astray and there's no hope of finding your way back.

There is no main title sequence to orient audio-viewers, though an 'overture' of sorts accompanies Sugar's warning and the show's opening.[4]

The overture begins with a howling wind and the determined scratching of Sugar's ink pen. The sustained ringing of a pitched metallic sound emerges, but is interrupted suddenly by a loud synthetic cello figure in a minor key, which produces an insistent ostinato. A three-note theme is heard on electric bass, then a sustained solo wordless voice enters, menacingly shape shifting, its timbre manipulated by the changing envelope of the mouth that produces it. Intimate close-ups of parts of Sugar's body appear in sharp focus, while extreme blurring obscures parts of the image. As Sugar departs her attic room, the camera follows via a series of jump cuts. We glimpse a cello as we hear the instrument, but its sound is quickly submerged beneath guttural screams and the squelching of mud as Sugar emerges from the house into the squalor of St Giles. The sounds of scissors and a doorbell form part of the texture.

The move from interior to exterior is signalled via a momentary harmonic lightening to the major, but this is soon trodden back down. Dizzying (then slower, dazed) handheld camera work focuses on those who live and work in the slums of St Giles, alternating with slow-motion shots of Sugar's silky shawl flowing behind her—a punctuation of vivid colour amidst the darkness. The camera is distracted by the unfolding spectacle of a traffic accident involving a horse and cart, but finally catches up to Sugar. The soundscape is now more rhythmically layered with electroacoustic sounds (including 'unheard' vocal samples of open vowel sounds and sibilance), which drive the tempo forward. The music gradually dissipates as Sugar enters another house, the transition bridged by cries, murmurs and sound effects visibly sourced from the new location.

The sound world of this overture is harmonically static, fixed around the tonic minor, yet perpetually in motion. The dizzying cacophony of the image sequence is balanced by the persistent rhythm of the ostinato, but also matched by the layering of sound effects, and a variety of musical sources and textures: acoustic, synthesized and electric instruments are juxtaposed alongside non-linguistic vocals and vocal samples. The orientation provided by the musical soundscape is that of disorientation. It sets in motion a jarring juxtaposition of twenty-first-century sensibilities and the Victorian novel to create an audio-visual identity for this neo-Victorian text, and for the characters and issues it moves from the margins of the Victorian novel to the show's centre. In retrospect, *The Crimson Petal and the White*'s audio-visual destabilizations of theme, style and audio-viewer response anticipate strategies developed in *Utopia*.

## *Utopia*: Story, Production, Reception and Its Sound

The production company, Kudos, approached screenwriter Dennis Kelly to explore an idea for a conspiracy series based around a graphic novel. From this *Utopia* emerged. In the series, a graphic novel by Mark Deyn (later revealed to be Philip Carvel) depicts 'The Utopia Experiments', which in turn mobilize a number of conspiracy theories. A small group of Utopia fanatics discuss *Utopia* in an online forum, and arrange to meet in person. One of the group members obtains a copy of the novel's manuscript, and tells another about his find: Grant, an 11-year-old boy with a fictional internet identity. Grant locates the manuscript holder and arrives at his apartment, only to witness his murder. The boy steals the manuscript and runs. Pursuit begins. The cards are not stacked in the favour of the shambolic group of conspiracy theorists, however, as each one in turn is either brutally tortured or framed by The Network for shocking and violent crimes. It becomes clear that The Network's henchmen, who carry a squeaky yellow holdall, will stop at nothing to locate the manuscript and someone called Jessica Hyde. The first episode closes as Jessica (Fiona O'Shaughnessy) presents herself to the fugitives. Meanwhile, a deadly strain of Russian flu hits the Shetland Islands.

Over the course of the serial, the conspiracy is revealed as fact: The Network have a plan to solve the population crisis by releasing a drug, Janus, to sterilize 90–95 % of the world's population. The company Corvadt (makers of a Russian flu vaccine) have been working on an approximation of Janus, but it is missing crucial final adjustments made by Carvel; to make those, they need Carvel's manuscript. But Milner (whose allegiance has been questionable from the start) knows that the secret is not in the manuscript: it is in the blood of Jessica Hyde, Carvel's daughter.

Season 2 takes us back to the beginning, to the moment when a young Milner met a young Philip Carvel and together they formed a brave plan to save the human race. But whereas Milner believes it is not for them to decide who Janus's victims will be, Carvel asks, 'why not?' Hence, the adjustment Carvel made to the protein in Jessica's blood. The Network's new plan is to unleash a potentially fatal strain of flu to ensure everyone takes the vaccine (to which Janus has been added). Elsewhere in the world, Janus will be released via crop-duster planes. But does it even work as a vaccine? And does this matter? We discover that Carvel is alive: he's speaking Romany and has a concentration camp tattoo on his arm. He decided that his own race, and especially his daughter Jessica, should survive.

Channel 4 commissioned digital agency TH_NK to create a 'multiplatform content experience' for *Utopia*—The Utopia Inquiry—with a stated aim of blurring the boundaries between fact and fiction, but also to personalize the consumer's experience.[5] After handing over some basic personal information, the Inquiry revealed to participants how long it would take *them* to find you, provided information about new developments in technology and invited participants to decide how overpopulation might be managed, before examining the possible repercussions of each decision. The factual basis of some of the show's conspiracies was also revealed. Fans were e-stalked (with their permission), and invited to telephone the Grant Letham is Missing telephone line for 'Easter Eggs'.[6] Tapia de Veer created an 8-bit version of the Utopia theme to accompany 'The Lost Game' that formed part of this paratextual realm.[7] A soundtrack album was released on CD and on vinyl for each season (500 copies on yellow vinyl for the Season 1 release).

*The Guardian* placed *Utopia* third in its 'best TV of 2013' review, describing it as 'Bold, theatrical and unlike anything else on the box at the moment', drawing attention to Munden's 'incredible visual tone [...] his use of acid colours and startling symmetry' and to Tapia de Veer's 'queasy wub-wub soundtrack' (Raeside, 2013). The critic also highlighted the shifting ground on which the show places its audio-viewers:

> It's a drama cleverly peopled with truly likable yet totally unknowable characters. You invest in them, then they do something unspeakable. You're constantly

asked to adjust your moral take on what you're seeing. Each one of them reaches a moral impasse, as in *Breaking Bad*, and they have to make difficult decisions without completely losing the audience's sympathy. In a world where it's never clear who is bad and who is good—we're constantly shifting allegiance. It's the opposite of a passive viewing experience and almost a physical workout at times.

Several broadsheet critics worried about *Utopia*'s extreme violence, notably the eye-gouging torture scene and the school massacre, but balanced their anxieties with praise for the show's 'great visual style' or its 'original, weird and exciting' drama (Sutcliffe, 2013; Smith, 2013). Mark Monahan of *The Telegraph* commended the 'slick score and sleek widescreen camerawork', describing the first episode as 'a dark, tantalisingly mysterious overture, with serious-minded and at times even tender-hearted observations on our age lurking beneath the lurid surface' (2013). The second season of *Utopia* courted further controversy over the decision to interweave fact with fiction by incorporating the real life murder of the MP Airey Neave into the show's conspiracy plot; a decision condemned by Neave's family and some members of the press. Despite garnering high praise alongside some notoriety from critics, *Utopia* gained only a rather ordinary proportion of audience share.[8] Nonetheless, the show won an International Emmy Award in 2014 for 'best drama series'.

As with *The Crimson Petal and the White*, Munden created a highly stylized approach to filming the real world: 'a bit like being on the North London line and seeing the houses from the back, things that you've never seen before. It was an attempt to see that real world in a very different way' (Munden in Anon., 2014). Foregrounded sound effects also play a role in this, notably the impossibly creaky leather jacket worn by RB, his asthmatic wheeze, and the rattle of the raisins in the boxes he carries with him. Our relationship with RB is first and foremost mediated by the sound effects associated with him, which also serve to humanize him somewhat. He doesn't speak much (in the first episodes), and when he does, it is slow and deliberate: the show's most conspicuous audio leitmotif is his persistent enquiry 'Where is Jessica Hyde?'[9]

For *Utopia*, Munden knew he 'wanted the music to be quite uplifting in some sort of way' and notes that Tapia de Veer provided him with 'a whole album of stuff, samples and things' before the editing began. Drones featured heavily, and 'we took elements of those from this thirty minute album of pop songs he's made'. There were 'lots of samples and we took the quirkiest bits of that for the first series' (Munden in Anon., 2014). Tapia de Veer has described his approach to the first season as 'like a birth, very minimalistic and crude, the characters were naive, childish, like kids in a videogame', whereas Season 2 had 'more established mayhem, more "knowledgeable" characters, in your face political conspiracy, a much heavier, darker and complex sound' (in Murphy, 2014).[10] The composer came to the UK for six months to produce the music for Season 2, bringing with him a number of analogue synths to accommodate the 1970s setting of the opening (Anon., 2014). He apparently also brought some dried out rhino dung and a bone, playing the first *Utopia* tune to Munden 'with chopsticks on the rhino dung' (Anon., 2014)[11]; the score also features a Chilean trutruka, recorded in Borough tube station (Anon., 2014b). Despite developing a darker palette in the music for the second season, Tapia de Veer re-used some of the samples from the first, creating a sense of sonic coherence across the show's run.

The score for *Utopia* won a Royal Television Society Craft and Design Award for 'best original music' in 2013: it was judged to be a 'startlingly original scoring of hyper-reality, and unlike anything we've heard before. The winner's work blurred the lines between sound design and score, creating a soundtrack that the jury said felt like it was being played inside your head' (RTS, 2013). *Mojo* placed the album fourth in its Best Soundtracks of 2013 (*Mojo*, 2013).

## 'Janus Is Inside Me'

*Utopia* leaves many moments of dramatic and emotional significance unscored or, at least, musically underplayed. For instance, the suggestion at the end of S1E2 that one of the protagonists, Becky, might be working for The Network is emphasized by the gradual *removal* of music (0:45:44–0:47:05).[12] Beforehand, a richly textured and delicate waltz—its layers including flutey Mellotron, gently performed non-western percussion, musical box loops and, eventually, soft female vocal samples—plays on the semiotic conventions of screen scoring to create a maternal haze around Becky as she meets and hugs one of her online collaborators, Grant (having just discovered that he is not, in Wilson's terms, a city trader and thus 'bound to be a cock', but instead a frightened boy). The cue's layers are then stripped away, forming a subtle diminuendo and connotative vacuum around the telephone call Becky makes, in which she tells someone (unknown) that 'the manuscript exists… the boy knows where it is'.

This cue, however, also plays a role in establishing the musical thread that emphasizes S1's symbolically charged subplot about murdered, damaged, or otherwise imperilled children. Furthermore, it is an example of some of the ways in which Tapia de Veer's scoring explores the continua and tipping points between 'unheard' audio-viewer manipulations and 'heard' (or at least more pronounced) provocations to active interpretation. His trademark vocal samples, for example, are not ostentatious here. Yet by nature of being a distorted, denaturized human sonority, their peculiarity is simultaneously difficult to miss. The many hooks within Tapia de Veer's meticulously rendered textures, in turn, may also make such cues more noticeable—in part, because they are such a pleasure to perceive as music. Other facets of the cue, however, create embodied responses in the audio-viewer that do not approach the threshold of conscious recognition—such as the way in which one might sway with its waltz rhythms (either literally or in terms of one's automatically firing mirror neurons mimetically replicating its gestures), and thus, in a sense, be embraced by music extending the 'family' in this sequence to include the audio-viewer. This 'unheard' (but felt) manipulation is achieved with appropriate subtlety (the fairly quick waltz rhythm subdivides the cue's previous 4/4 beat pattern).

This section will explore the continuum of positions between unheard and heard, conventional and unconventional, introduced by *Utopia*'s cues.

Given the noticeability and catchiness of much of Tapia de Veer's music, it is important to observe that he produced an extensive body of cues in *Utopia* that achieve the stealthily manipulative 'unheard' effects necessary, in particular, to support the show's more chilling scenes. Such cues often sound like electroacoustic textures; they lack well-defined hooks or melodies and evince a marked absence of beats. The textures creep in and out, not unlike a classical Hollywood score, but the materials are self-effacing. Indeed, while an increasing emphasis on 'secondary' compositional parameters (e.g., timbre, texture, dynamics, spatiality) is a broader trend in recent mainstream screen scoring, Tapia de Veer's cues sound more indebted to avant-garde electronica from Karlheinz Stockhausen and Trevor Wishart to Tangerine Dream and Boards of Canada. Some of these 'unheard' cues are short, adding a throb of momentum or intensity to a sequence. When Jessica stops Milner from killing Dugdale in S2E4 (0:42:09–0:42:39) and then prepares to shoot her, a pulsing, metallic synth pad quickly builds up. A foreground of antiphonal, detuning, reverb-saturated motifs gives way to a thickening of the background sonority. At the peak of tension, the entire texture then begins to slide microtonally upwards with an increasing dynamic level, before cutting to silence abruptly at Milner's last-ditch reveal to Jessica: 'Your father is still alive'. If the basic function here is conventional, its musical realization is not.

The closing moments of the same episode are sculpted in a similar yet even subtler manner, fusing aspects of composition and sound design into sinisterly unified purpose. In this pivotal scene, Wilson finally embraces The Network's agenda and executes Ian's brother's guards and then Ian's brother (0:47:17–0:48:30). As the camera approaches a seated Wilson along a grimy industrial corridor, and then jump cuts to Wilson upright and retching, the disgust mechanism cued by the sonic foreground (i.e., his retching and subsequent spitting) intensifies the already unnerving quality of the audio: the cue begins with bassy fibrillation that sounds like an impossibly accelerated heartbeat. Again, conventionally one could argue that the soundtrack creates continuity across the cuts in the anything but conventional action (the next two cuts occur as Wilson checks his gun and then heads towards his victims). If the visual cuts hint at his fracturing subjectivity, however, the music suggests the inexorability of his new persona's rise. A mid-range cloud of higher timbres subtly accentuates the tension just before Wilson shoots the two guards, at which point the pulsing stratum stops. Then, as the gunshots' reverberation fades, a higher stratum of sonority, somewhere between whining train brakes and sonoristic strings, enters above the nebula, and the whole texture increases in volume as the camera swings from Ian's pleading and terrified brother to frame Wilson preparing to deliver the next musical punctuation mark: a final gunshot. When he fires, both strata stop, and the massively reverberant gunshot echo gradually makes way for a sickening Foley effect: blood dripping out of the man's head and splattering onto the floor. Perhaps the most astonishing thing about this sequence, however, is the range of emotions it might provoke (or fail to provoke) in the audio-viewer. On the surface, the music helps one to feel the pain of Wilson's decision to join The Network and his immediate struggle in this sequence. On the other, despite the lurid violence and disgust the story and discourse generate, one might feel oddly unmoved or even unsympathetic. This is not merely because *Utopia*'s violence, from its very first pre-credit sequence, has gradually prepared one for the likelihood of such acts: the serial's storytelling has begun to convince one of their necessity.

Aside from the narratively motivated diversion into Krautrock created by the start of Season 2 (the flashback episode tracing the origins of The Janus Project), there is a broad trajectory to the scoring across the two seasons of *Utopia*. This moves towards the dramatic necessity of 'unheard' scoring as discussed above and away from the type of material that dominates Season 1 and much of Season 2: ultra-quirky and upbeat, or bizarre yet emotive, music demanding our attention. Sometimes, as with the electroacoustic cues, these tracks perform conventional roles unconventionally; sometimes, the most outwardly conventional music in the show performs truly peculiar functions. And therein lies a key to the serial's overarching manipulation of subject position.

In S1E3, Jessica says, 'Some of us don't get to have childhoods'; in S2E4, her brother RB/Pietre states, 'It's all about family'. Initially, *Utopia* positions the audio-viewer's sympathy firmly on the side of its (broken) angels. Jessica and Pietre are the children of Philip Carvel, the genius who, aided and abetted by Milner, conceives and creates Janus. Their father damaged both of them. Pietre's lack of empathy in S1, which makes him such an effective and apparently sociopathic killer on behalf of The Network, is revealed to have been in part the result of a drug trial gone wrong at the hands of his father. Jessica's damage is primarily psychological, but a crushing blow arrives in the discovery that her father hid the code for Janus's all-important trigger molecule not in The Utopia Manuscripts—the graphic novel created by Carvel after he has been driven insane, and which initially drew the story's protagonists together—but inside Jessica. He injected her with Janus, rendering her infertile, but also saving her from the carnage to be wreaked when Janus is launched on the world. Grant and the show's other child, Alice, and in their own ways Becky, Ian and Wilson, are also literally children or childlike. In S1 Tapia de Veer's cues for this group, as noted above, often articulate style topics with connotations of the feminine, tenderness, maternity and childhood.

Aside from the delicate waltz, a series of vocal cues confirm this association and, in turn, its tragic nature. Those tragic connotations accrue over the course of S1 and help reveal what seems, initially, to be the show's relatively conventional subtext: the archetypal plot of damaged children looking for a father figure and/or redemption. When Jessica reveals the truth (as she knows it up until this point) about The Network and the graphic novel's origins to Becky and Ian in S1E2 (0:14:40), an electroacoustic texture builds out of a ticking clock sound and a bed of quiet wind swirls beneath Jessica's dialogue. There are two musical anchors: a moderate heartbeat bass pulse, and the soft timbre of a repeating minor mode riff on a relatively clean synth, which sounds like a Fender Rhodes electric piano. The riff stops, however, and the hitherto tonally centred harmonic layers warp, as Jessica makes the show's first big reveal: that she is Carvel's daughter and has been on the run since she was four years old. (Lonely cries seep into this musicscape here and, while not exactly elided, the vocal source of these interjections is not foregrounded—that happens with the shift to vocal harmony.) As she says this, Jessica is framed to the right of the widescreen medium shot in a domestic set lit with warm yellows; the next shot is of Grant, who has yet to meet up with his friends. He is hiding alone in an industrial unit lit with (admittedly wan and more sickly) yellow-green tones and framed in exactly the same position in the shot as Jessica. As if this did not make its point clearly enough (i.e., that more than one broken child is at the heart of this story), a powerful new musical idea drops into the vacuum created by the vanishing stability of the previous musical texture. Just before the cut to Grant, a choral melody begins, forward in the mix and closely harmonized with sampled and treated voices that are either children's voices or voices manipulated to sound like children. The soundtrack having given voice to its damaged infants, the riff returns, echoing back and forth across the mix on a delayed and reverberant, cleaner electric guitar. This riff's delicacy is somewhere between an angel's lyre and the plucked accompaniment to a lullaby.

While scored in a minor key, this vocal cue is not entirely saturated with topics of lament. That function is left to the cue's developmental cousin in Season 1: a recurring melody of lament, usually beginning with a single female voice. Both are part of a developmental trajectory of the vocal, requiem-like music first audible, in an ironically soft and understated form, when Wilson is tortured and his eye is gouged out in S1E1. (The contrast between the empathy thus generated and the complexities of the cue when Wilson executes Ian's brother is starkly indicative of his character arc.) The requiem thread then develops under the bizarre suicide at the start of S1E2 and Jessica's big reveal in the same episode; it moves to the organ to set up the shocking school shooting at the start of S1E3; it then begins to fray sonically, the looping pitches of sustained vocal samples receiving glitches and other electroacoustic degradations, as we see RB exhibiting remorse for killing and framing Grant, and thus his first Pietre-like (i.e., humanistic) behaviour. These manipulations of the 'natural' voice, as stated above, call attention to themselves through their acts of alienation. The show's gradual repositioning of audio-viewer sympathy, shifting us from empathy for the main characters towards a tenser view of the necessity of loss, is reflected, microcosmically, in such timbres.

At 0:11:11 of S1E3, *Utopia*'s fraying requiem coalesces into its archetypal form. Jessica is framed against a window in an otherwise darkened room, dust particles dancing around her like an angel's halo, replete with twinkling chimes. She begins to tell Grant some home truths ('People always let you down'), while nonetheless offering to protect him; the cue begins, initially for a solo alto voice. The unbroken vocal lines (the first is soon joined by a high tenor counterpoint) appear to have been constructed from a sampled female singer (most likely Tapia de Veer's wife),[13] looped and then bent with a pitch shifter to achieve the melodic movement. A higher soprano voice, clearly feminine, leads the affective ascent as Jessica promises to protect Grant. Already, the combination of dialogue (people let you down/I'll protect you) and music (pushing towards melodrama) feels purposefully wrong. This sense of wrongness develops later in the episode, when Jessica and RB meet for the first time, and RB cannot compute that he has finally found his big sister: 'Where is Jessica Hyde?' he asks her, surreally but poignantly, his vocal leitmotif returning to underscore the past traumas that stop him from recognizing that his sister is standing right in front of him. All these broken children: *Utopia* works hard to make one care for them during its first season, and music, both up to and beyond this moment, is central to that manipulative errand. The requiem cues fray and warp further as the season and its sequel unfold. Yet simultaneously, it already insinuates a need to disavow such sympathies—local-level sympathy, as it were, for individuals and small familial groups—if one is to be led towards sympathizing with The Network's solution to the large-level problem of impending population and climate catastrophe, and thus with the plight of the entire human family.

*Utopia*, then, is setting its audio-viewers up for an audacious reversal. Having started on the side of its angels, its sympathies begin to shift, and our allegiances are pulled along with them—towards its devils. For this is a show, one begins to realize, not about families but the biggest family of all: humanity. And that family's survival, in the face of the historically unparalleled threat of overpopulation, requires sacrifice beyond compare. Extraordinarily, therefore, having sucked its audio-viewers into unquestioning loyalty to its broken children, *Utopia* will now persuade one of the necessity of such breakages in order to achieve the greater good. Tapia de Veer's scoring is central to enabling one to entertain that kind of doublethink. Indeed, it has been laying the groundwork since the very first cue of the serial.

*Utopia* effects its radical repositioning of audio-viewer empathy through music so wrong it is right. The opening scene of the serial occurs in a comic book shop. The initial shots of the show depict swaying fields of wheat overlaid with a radio news item about the spiralling cost of food and related unrest (inevitable outcomes of overpopulation we may see within our lifetimes). The radio broadcast forms a bridge between the shots of the countryside and the interior of the shop. Once the action is inside the shop, it becomes clear that the broadcast audio has been treated to sound like a transistor radio located in the store. RB and Lee enter by crawling beneath the shutters of the apparently closed emporium. They are looking for *The Utopia Manuscript* (The Network believes it contains the secret to completing Janus) and, through it, Jessica. Shockingly, because it comes out of the blue, Lee kills one customer with a lead pipe, then another customer and the owner with dental gas. As the sequence ends, RB is encouraging a young boy out from under a stand with his box of raisins. (In Season 2 we learn that 'RB' stands for 'Raisin Boy', his childhood nickname). 'Don't put the gas away yet', he tells his colleague.

If the ultraviolence of this sequence is reminiscent of *A Clockwork Orange* (Stanley Kubrick, 1971), this is, in large part, down to Tapia de Veer's music acting in consort with the brilliantly poised performances of Maskell as RB and Paul Ready as Lee, who manage to generate laughs near the end of the sequence and even, in RB's case, the first hints of sympathy towards his character (even as he plans to kill a child!). Taking a different tack to Wendy Carlos, but achieving the same kind of 'so wrong it's right' ends as her Rossini and Beethoven arrangements in *A Clockwork Orange*, the music's contribution to this sequence establishes what might be called funky menace. The cue begins with one of the first season's only precise synch points (cueing a sense of cartoonish violence, perhaps, appropriate to carnage unfolding in a comic book store). A whoosh of sound acts as the anacrusis to a lead pipe cracking open the back of the first victim's skull; its whack, in turn, coincides with the first beat of the cue, which proceeds across the sound of blood gushing onto a floor. Rhythm is initially suggested by the track's harmonic filler layer, which consists of pitched computer-like 'pings' (reminiscent of the ball being struck in *Pong*), a wonky mid-range synth line, and short rising vocal samples, which punctuate the textured layers as they develop. An actual beat layer of cymbals and, a little later, occasional bass drum beats and shuffle, combine with the harmonic layer's patterns to establish a synchronized and sprightly funk rhythm. In terms of melodic movement, a stereotypically exotic/sinister I -♭II—I progression is outlined by the ping's voice-leading, and the Spanish evocations of this move might conjure up (via *Carmen* and countless other audio-visual intertexts) bullfighter connotations as RB and Lee execute their innocent victims in grisly fashion, or even *Jaws* (Steven Spielberg, 1975).

More problematically, however, at least for the non-sociopathic perceiver, the music's groove encourages mimetic participation from the audio-viewer, who can do little to resist grooving along to the scene, and thus its violence, in one way or another. Behind the upbeat foreground of the cue, electroacoustic clouds of darkness and threat form, anticipating the sounds of The Network that dominate so much of what follows: in a sense, this is heard music containing unheard music. The more noticeable and memorable aspect of the music, though, is the funk. As Lee kills the shop owner, the man, collapsing, sees the previous 'sleeping' victim, wide-eyed and dead, on the floor, and panics. At this moment, the show's leitmotif for The Network and this pair in particular is heard for the first time. The low, growling, bass synth motif in a minor mode (1-♭6-4-♭6) then accompanies RB's discovery of the child, after which (and the line about not putting the gas away) the action cuts to the outside of the shop (Doomsday Comics!) and a slow motion shot of someone dancing in a giant white rabbit costume while apparently collecting for charity. The rabbit is an in-joke, of course, relating to the identity of Mr Rabbit (Milner and, later, Wilson). Its dance, however, picks up on the grooviness of Tapia de Veer's foreground layers and emphasizes the moment *Utopia*'s main title theme drops. Scored for a high, relatively clean synth, which sounds a bit like a person chirpily whistling, the melody, locking into the rhythms and harmony of the bass progression, morphs the groove to suggest ska, or at least ska as reconceived by bands like Gorillaz. And so, like the rabbit outside, and equally bizarrely, one exits the scene feeling joy—or, rather, the astonishing sensation of horror and empathy for the murder victims switching to a joy triggered by the immaculate audio-visual choreography of the carnage.[14]

By the time Season 2 is reaching *Utopia*'s denouement, this kind of paradox has become routine. Several episodes in Season 2 open with similar combinations of grooviness and slaughter. Perhaps the most memorable is Lee's execution of Ian's former boss in S2E3—a recapitulatory retread of the opening of Season 1 at the start of the pivotal episodes in Season 2 (the ones where Wilson is turned into a murderer and member of the Network). This is equally gruesome but, by this stage of the drama, disturbingly easy to find funny. That this is the case is due, in large part, to the overall trajectory of the score, which now warps its more melodramatic sentiments with outright parody (when the frayed requiem cue recurs in Season 2, for instance, it often sounds like it is being performed by Pinky and Perky), saturating many scenes with 'unheard' electroacoustic threat, and turning perverse pleasure at the continuing slaughter into just about the only joy to be found in the increasingly dark latter stages of the serial. The audio-viewer, as such, has been expertly moved into the novel position of rooting for both The Network and the broken children in the show. This move is not innovative in terms of recent TV drama's propensity for encouraging sympathy for antiheros (which is now commonplace), but rather in terms of music's role in fashioning that trap. Season 2 closes with the plot to release the flu pandemic being foiled, but also with Wilson, the new Mr Rabbit, admiring his stock of the flu virus, having already revealed his plan to unleash it in a more controlled way. This enables the audio-viewer to feel a peculiar sense of double victory: both sides have won, and positions of empathy and anempathy have both been rewarded by this peculiarly satisfying conclusion.

Channel 4's cancellation of *Utopia* (it is to be remade by David Fincher for HBO) means that its drama, like its score, remains balanced on an ethical knife-edge. That precarious sensation has been induced and inscribed in the audio-viewer through many of the show's discursive mechanisms, from its dialectical colour schemes to music's range of melodrama and menace, conventional ends and unconventional means, heard and unheard scoring. 'Janus is inside me', Jessica reveals in Season 2. By the end of *Utopia*, thanks in no small part to Tapia de Veer, Janus is inside us too.

## Notes

1. Claudia Gorbman's keynote lecture 'Hearing Music' was presented at the Music for Audio-Visual Media conference, University of Leeds, 4–6 September 2014.
2. This character is listed in the credits as Arby, but the letters—RB—are significant (see page 316).
3. In S1E3 of *Utopia*, this kind of signification of difference is achieved rather originally, and with a cheeky wit that taps knowingly on the fourth wall. Landfill

Indy is playing on a stolen car that Jessica is driving with Grant as her passenger. Grant notes the 'shit' pop music. Jessica, oblivious to the music's generic nature due to her many years on the run (i.e., 'generic' both as commercial rock-pop but also as a scoring trope suitable to a shot of a car racing across the frame in a TV drama), switches it off. *Utopia*, the moment reinforces, has an alternative musical agenda.

4. Shorter and somewhat developed versions of this cue underscore each of the 'previously on' segments, providing coherence and encouraging a sense of the familiar with the return to the show's world.
5. Click on 'Enter the Utopia experience now' at the Channel 4's website for the programme: http://www.channel4.com/programmes/utopia (accessed 22 February 2015). See also Th_nk's online video about the Inquiry: https://vimeo.com/67388712 (accessed 22 February 2015).
6. In this context an 'Easter egg is an intentional inside joke, hidden message, or feature in a work such as a computer programme, video game, movie, book, or crossword'. Wikipedia.org (accessed 22 February 2015).
7. For more information visit http://www.channel4.com/programmes/utopia (accessed 20 February 2015).
8. The first episode of *Utopia* managed only 1.14 m, an audience share of 6.98 %, though this was a little higher than the channel's slot average of 1 m in previous months. By the third episode this had fallen to less than half a million viewers (Kanter, 2013). The fans and the critics thought differently, however. In the same slot, Channel 5 achieved more than double the number of viewers for its annual Big Brother show (Plunkett, 2013).
9. Our thanks to Miguel Mera for this point.
10. However, the composer continues 'But what I'm saying here makes it all seem like a "plan", see? I'm just re-writing it backwards to make it seem like it wasn't improvised'.
11. 'God knows how he got it through customs'.
12. Timings taken from 2014 Region 2 PAL format boxset *Utopia 1 & 2* issued by Channel 4 DVD (C4DVD10541).
13. In his commentary on the final moments of S1E1 of *Utopia* (0:53:23), the director Marc Munden draws attention to a vocal provided by Tapia de Veer's wife: 'It's got a very, very immediate quality to [it]. Normally things are mixed with a bit of reverb, but it sounds like someone singing right in your ear'.
14. The coincidence of the rabbit with the punctuating vocal samples seems also to connect sonically with the voices of animal characters heard in animated cartoons of the mid-twentieth century, such as the Warner Bros. Looney Tunes series. Clearly, extreme violence (albeit animated fantasy violence in the cartoons) is another correspondence here, but potentially emphasizes the 'wrongness' even further.

CHAPTER 22

# Interview 4: Building Bridges: Sound Design as Collaboration, as Style and as Music in *The Bridge*—An Interview with Carl Edström

*Annette Davison and Martin Parker*

With over 30 years' experience, Carl Edström is one of Sweden's most well-respected sound designers. Edström has worked as sound designer and/or sound editor on a great many films and television shows. This interview concentrates specifically on his work as sound designer between 2010 and 2013 on the Swedish/Danish TV serial *The Bridge* (Rosenfeldt, 2011–). This interview focused on Edström's sound design approach, the relationship between producers, directors, sound designer and composer and specifically the integration between sound and music on a conceptual and practical level. The interview took place at the University of Edinburgh in February 2013, where it formed part of a class for a course in Sound and Fixed Media. Edström was visiting speaker, and the discussion was chaired by Martin Parker and Annette Davison (and continued over dinner the same evening).

Q: How did your involvement with *The Bridge* begin and what was the nature of your early discussions with the director, writer and producer?
CE: I got a call from a post-production supervisor called Peter Bengtsson. We go back at least 25 years and have worked together on many large and small productions, so he has a pretty good knowledge of my specialities, I think. He set up a meeting with the first director of the series, Charlotte Sieling, and I think we had a good start in understanding each other's ideas. At this point, I had read versions of the script that were still in progress. Early discussions of the aesthetics began with the

---

A. Davison • M. Parker
University of Edinburgh, UK

director in Spring 2010. Sieling directed the first four episodes and the tone and style of the sound design was set in collaboration with her. Thanks to those first four episodes, other directors and members of the production team who became involved later were obliged to follow the style that we'd managed to 'bake-in' at the outset. Together with the cinematographer and production designer, Charlotte had set the look of the series before the shooting started. I got to see stills and sketches of what the world of *The Bridge* would look like. In the first discussions there were ideas that the different locations in the series should feel isolated from each other. I got an idea that we would try to isolate the scenes/locations from each other by using hard transitions between scenes so they would not be too smooth.

Q: Please tell us more about the kinds of discussions you had in 2010. How much work was shown/heard in draft form before agreements were made? What were the responses from different members of the production team? Did you meet any resistance?

CE: Actually I didn't show anything at all beforehand! This was both very nice, in that they trusted my ideas, but also a bit scary. I must say that many of the sound design ideas were taken care of very well by Charlotte and her picture editor. Because without these occasionally quite long and slow-paced shots, some of the sound design would not have worked so well. The collaboration with Charlotte Sieling was very constructive and fun. She was fearless to try different approaches, but also unafraid to tell us what she did not like. This made the work on the important first episodes dynamic but also hard. Over the first two seasons (20 episodes) I went on to work with, I think, six editors and material from a further five directors. On the second season, one of the directors, Henrik Georgsson, who also did the last episodes of Season 1, was responsible for the post-production as director even for the episodes that he had not directed himself. This was a very good decision from the production company, I think. This way we could develop the aesthetics for the sound even further, together with the composer and also keep the production as a whole more coherent across episodes.

Q: How do you maintain design consistency across multiple episodes and series?

NB *Along with Carl Edström, the composer Johan Söderqvist and the re-recording mixer Erik Guldager are the only members of the creative team to have worked continuously through the show's (to date) two seasons.*

CE: Directors want to put their footprint in their work but this is not always so good in a concept series. My role as sound designer has been to keep them on a line. That's quite a fun part actually. There are a lot of discussions—what's good, what's less good. How much creativity you should put into something that's already set. There should be creativity, but within the borders of the established style of the series. Many times you have to show examples of what a scene would be like if you do something radical with the sound design. This is often difficult to explain in words, so it is usually better to show some kind of rough draft.

Q: The sound design of *The Bridge* is highly stylized. There are moments where, if we were to listen closely, incongruous sounds appear or suddenly disappear from the mix. There is a lurching distortion of reality that speaks to the unconscious mind. To what extent is this style something that was a deliberate fit with Rosenfeldt's script, or a more general 'opening up' of the potential for this kind of sound design in Scandinavian television in general?

CE: The style of the sound design is really a bit comparable to the visual style of a cartoon magazine. Everything is a bit stylized, and the focus is sometimes on a small detail of the picture. Also scene changes are similar to this style, I think. *Twin Peaks* (Lynch and Frost, 1990–91) came up frequently in our early discussions. The sound in *Twin Peaks* is maybe not so spectacular because there is so much music throughout the whole series. But much of the sound design was very good—in the Foley, for example, with footsteps, you'd sometimes hear the first couple and the last couple, but in your mind you'd hear all of them. It was these kinds of aesthetics I wanted to bring into *The Bridge*. I read the script a lot in the beginning of the work, and maybe the ideas for this stylized sound is in it somewhere, but I must say I think it is difficult to find the source of the inspiration this came from… I think it is probably everything from the script to the actors, grading, editing etc. I think it is the sum of it that makes it interesting.

One technique I used a lot was taking away the sounds that are there or should be there naturally. This puts attention where I want the listeners to focus, sonically. This way of moving the sonic focus was used a lot in the series. When you take away sounds that would normally be heard in a scene I find that many times the mind creates them anyway unconsciously. But the sounds that you *do* put there become even more important and get more attention from the listener. Many times we also mixed the sound of things happening further away from the camera louder than the things closer. This was also a way of pulling the sonic focus. However, you have to be very careful with these techniques because if you use them too often or too much it becomes more distracting than enhanced.

Q: This spacing and silencing generates a kind of rhythm for the sounds to bounce off one another.

CE: Silence is very important in *The Bridge*, with the music and the sound we tried to make the soundtrack a bit awkward. This was often something not very noticeable, but somehow adding extra depth. We don't have lots of layers of ambiences: some, but not lots. We don't want it to be super-realistic. We often tried to make deliberate decisions about what should be most important in a scene: the score or the sound? We did this by discussing it with the composer and we have had a lot of interesting arguments about how to interpret a scene. But I feel like we have both been very open minded, so many times he argued for sound and I argued for the score.

Q: The treatment of dialogue across the first series especially is unusual. Certain parts are just cut away, we have to imagine what's being said, use our knowledge of what's come already, to guess.

CE: We tried not to have dialogue on exteriors when cutting in: it emphasizes the cut. And also emphasizes that you are seeing/hearing but without dialogue. We often move dialogue into scenes, a lot of nudging. This was made by moving dialogue which was off-screen (not lip-synched), to keep all the dialogue that belonged to a scene within the scenes' boundaries. This is also a way of keeping the transitions from being too smooth. We move or take away lots of dialogue. This is done with the same idea that your mind can fill in missing information—and sometimes does it better! And if the mind can create the missing information, then maybe it isn´t missing?

*NB Carl then used a scene from the first episode of Season 1 to illustrate his point. EP1, (0:08:30) The focus is a conversation with a surgeon at the hospital. Here the sound design was faded out after the scene setting—to focus onto dialogue—then sound re-intrudes. In another scene in the same episode, people are talking outside a hospital room. Here Carl removed the dialogue. Instead, the first sound from this exchange we hear is a kiss: this emphasized the kiss. The kiss was not in the script until the end of the scene. EP1, (0:24:15) another example of this is in where we don´t hear the dialogue until the close-up. EP2, (0:50:30).*

Q: The series is set in two countries with two languages and presumably two different sound-worlds. What did you need to do in order to make it clear which side of the bridge we were on?

CE: The idea was to look at Sweden and Denmark as two 'islands' with no connection between them except for the bridge. How do you make this into sound? One way is to think about how the people view each other. Swedes expect Danes to behave in certain ways. Swedes think Danes are happy, drink beer and eat unhealthy food, but also that they are easy to get along with. Danes think Swedes are stiff but efficient, etc. There are also historical reasons I think. The south of Sweden belonged to the Danes a long time ago, but Denmark has also belonged to Sweden, so this gives it a very interesting background. Sound-wise there is more noise in the Danish scenes—more talk. The Swedish office is quieter. As for the two languages, some Danish dialects are easy while some southern Swedish dialects are very difficult to understand. But in reality it's not that easy to understand each other! That also makes it quite strange. In reality Swedes and Danes often have to ask each other to repeat questions, etc. But this doesn't happen in *The Bridge* other than if it is supposed to be as a joke.

If we know a scene is to be subtitled it can give us more creativity with sound. You can have a little more freedom. In Denmark/Sweden it has been a hard decision to decide where to put subtitles. Though we're very used to them. Some scenes where the dialogue goes back and forth between Swedish and Danish at a faster pace, the decision was made to subtitle the whole scene, even the Swedish lines when broadcast in Sweden. This made the scene more fluent.

I ask sound recordists to record voices everywhere. Machines, cars, etc. can be fixed in post-production but voices are more difficult. For example, the riot in the last episode of Season 2 was meant to be in Denmark but we had to bring in groups of people and loop them in, because the riot they had was recorded in Sweden. So we brought groups of people into the studio to record chants and screams and also some distinct sentences that could be heard through the shouts.

Q: Do you impose any technical restrictions? Or is there any document of the ideas that can be passed along?

CE: As mentioned before, in *The Bridge* the emphasis is on hard cuts. Long cross fades are banned. If one scene is loud, the next should be quiet. This helps to create and sustain a sense of motion.

The first pass I often watch with NO sound (whether dialog, music or temp-effects from the editor), to see what it feels like. Production sound can colour how the material is viewed. This is because you often see what you hear, and I want to have a 'clean slate' when I get the first impressions. Sometimes I will watch the whole thing without sound. And sometimes I will then listen to production sound from the edited episode without image—that helps to add fullness for both. Many times you don't have time for that. But it's a fast way to get fresh ideas.

I always write down my notes in a notebook that I keep throughout the production and that I can go back to and look at my initial thoughts. Some things which seemed a bit odd and strange at the time of writing, but maybe worth trying, have become 'naturalized' by the end of Season 2.

Q: How much production and location sound do you use?

CE: Most of the detailed sound design is Foley and sound effects. Locations are often just too noisy to use and have really nothing to do with what you want a scene to sound like. But we do use a lot of production sound. This involved a lot of cleaning, de-noising and de-reverberation tools. But this is mainly for dialogue. We keep very few other sounds in *The Bridge*.

Q: ADR [Automatic Dialogue Replacement] can be a time consuming and expensive process. Do you have any special techniques you use to help actors feel comfortable and give convincing performances?

CE: I do have some tricks for ADR—for example, I put traffic noise into headphones to generate a similar scenario for exterior dialogue, to get a slightly raised voice. Also when I do ADR for scenes where the acting is right but there are technical issues, I prefer to play the lines to the actor and have them simply repeat them without looking at the picture.

**Q:** The cars have a character in the bridge, in particular the Porsche driven by Sofia Helin's character, Saga Norén. What did you do there?

**CE:** We have some recordings of the Porsche, but we have also used other sounds. It is an old car—it doesn't always sound as we want it to and the actress is also actually quite a careful driver. So the fast driving is all added in. I ask the recordists to record car sounds that will be needed, and also get sound effects. When you need extra sounds, this can be done in the evenings (which is possible on a long production). I can give them a list of sounds that we want from the set, as we know that the actors will be back there. This is one of the advantages of starting the post-production while they are still filming the series.

**Q:** The music and sound design work extremely closely in *The Bridge*. Can you tell us more about your working process with the series' composer Johan Söderqvist?

**CE:** I read the script early but Johan didn't read it at all! He gets the final cut [of the episode] then looks. This way he gets a very good opinion on how the viewers will see it for the first time. But this also makes him very late with the final score, and there is a very tight schedule on *The Bridge*. The picture editors have had a lot of music from Johan to use while editing so some of it can actually be used in the final mix with some tweaks. Importantly, the final cut doesn't include very much of my sound design except for maybe some specific scenes. However, we decide early on where music or sound will lead and it means we have very few collisions. When he delivers the final music stems to the mix there are usually just some small adjustments that have to be made. We also spend a day or so just before the end of the final mix to make these final decisions. On this day the mixer, composer, director and I watch the episode together and make all the final creative changes.

**Q:** Can you describe what happens if there is a 'collision'?

**CE:** It's my view that the composer and sound designer should talk to each other a lot and post-production is fraught in the cases where they don't. In our case collisions between sound and music are opportunities to question our original impulse that one or the other should lead at this point or what the scene should say to us. Of course this is not always the case in all productions, but the more the composer is involved in what is happening with the sound editing, the risk of negative collisions is less I think.

Because I worked so closely with Johan it forced the editors to use music from that composer, even if not the right pieces, because we do want the sound of the music to be right. But as I said earlier, the editors had a lot of music to play with and this also helped a lot to get the right touch from the editors. I think even if you take some old stuff [music] from the right composer, this is often better than fresh stuff from the wrong composer. Or even worse, from a different film!

*NB To illustrate his point regarding the argument for collaboration between the sound and music departments Edström used an example as the car pulls into a parking space, the score contains a sound very much like the engine of a car. Season 2, Ep10, (0:25:57) This masks the entry of diegetic sound, effectively bridging the two worlds. The previous music cue dissipates just before the car is parked and with this the focus shifts to the activity of the car's driver in the car park.*

Q: What about the title music?

CE: The title music for *The Bridge* is a different story. I think this was a piece that Charlotte Sieling found, and we wanted the last phrase of the lyrics to end specially in relation to the image. On some episodes we have made editors do re-cuts for the timing of the right line. The same is true of the end of the episode and how the music should enter there.

Q: How about the mixing of the music for the title sequences? Is this in surround like everything else?

CE: We mixed the title music differently to all our music. The music is usually mixed with 5.1 with left and right as the main sources to give room for dialogue. By contrast, the title music is just behind the screen, right in front: three channels with almost equal loudness. The title music will in this case stand out from the rest of the episode also by placement. This is of course especially noticeable when listening to the surround mix, but actually it's also noticeable in the stereo mix for some strange reason. So it sounds very different. The composer Johan especially thought that it gives the title song a different character, and I think he is right. Also we have pushed the levels of the song at the end of the episodes to make an audible impact. We have had some complaints that it is too loud, but this is what we wanted.

Q: Diegetic music is used sparingly throughout the series, why?

CE: We used more in the first season. Mainly in the Danish scenes, even music at a police station. All the television in the background—we make the sound for it. Even though we seldom see what's *on* the TV. *The Bridge* has been shown in 163 countries. We have avoided music from labels. Where we do have 'source' music, it's stock music, or composed for the show. We also make our own 'TV show' sound. I find myself writing scripts for Danish television gameshows, nature programmes about elephants and so on. That's quite fun. When you listen to it, it's kind of nonsense. The reason for not using so much diegetic music is to keep the scenes 'clean' and trust the dialogue/script enough not to have anything that might disturb it. We often tried some background music, but most of the times we thought that it 'coloured' the scene in an unwanted way so we ended up without it.

Q: [At the time of our interview] *The Bridge* spans two series and 20 episodes. How have you and Johan maintained consistency and avoided clichés over this time?

CE: Like me, Johan Söderqvist believes he has to be loyal with this series' ideas and concepts. To be involved with the whole but not the details so it can be thought about with fresh ears. For me this is done by having ideas of how a scene should sound, and together with Johan (and of course the director) decide exactly where the turning points or climaxes of a scene are. Once this is done I try to explain this to the sound editors, and let them do their job. Then I will come back a few times to watch and listen to the whole episode and give feedback. If I think the sound of a scene doesn't work properly I will ask them to give it another try with some extra feedback from me. What I like with this way of working is that I can judge the results without having to think about all the work that is done to a scene. It doesn't matter if it has taken one hour or one day. Also it is sometimes easier to listen to the soundscape as a whole without knowing all the details. But once this is done I usually take the whole episode with all the tracks where I add and tweak stuff before the final mix.

So there should be a layer before the final mix—this is the sound designer or supervising editor's role. I think it is important to keep a freshness to what I do. I go in, listen and leave—but I shouldn't sit through all the trial and errors. Occasionally in certain scenes, especially late in the process, I may re-cut the sound totally. It is my job to keep the sound design true to the concept.

Q: *The Bridge* has now been franchised out and an American version has been produced as well as a British version (*The Tunnel*). In relation to the sound design, what's different, has anything of your style remained and is there a difference between what Swedish producers are able to tolerate by comparison with US producers?

CE: I don't think that much of the sound design has made it to the other versions other than when the picture cuts happen to be very similar. Even if the stories are basically the same there are so many details that are different, so perhaps the same kind of sound design simply would not work so well.

As many of the screenings with the co-producers here are done early without the designed soundtrack (due to both schedule and budget reasons) they don't have the opportunity to have much input on the sound design. This has the benefit that what they are finally presented with is a mix that has been done as perfectly as possible and with the final music score in place. This way some of the odd scene transitions that would not work in a rough mix are not a problem. On the other hand with more time and money, it would be nice to have some screenings with the final mix before it is mastered and delivered.

PART VI

# The Sound of Machines and Non-Humans

CHAPTER 23

# The Sound of an Android's Soul: Music, MIDI and Muzak in *Time Of Eve*

*Philip Brophy*

## ANIME AND FILM MUSIC

In Japan's bottomless crater of societal masks and personal simulation, *anime* perfectly mirrors the state not of what is, but of what is represented. As a representational art form dedicated to the poetics of this cleft mode of signification, *anime* is unrivalled in its propensity to never be but always appear. Developed within the Japanese cultural context where representation (the surface of things) and ontology (the nature of things) are fluidly interchangeable, *anime* depicts, narrates and projects notions and images of 'the human' as a complexly variable set of unpredictable parameters—not as an aspirational drive towards definitive statements of 'humanism'. Thus in *anime*, humans often 'unbecome' themselves through transformative moments of consciousness, while post-humans (robots and their ilk) often become human through applying a lateral logic of behaviour learnt from analysing humans.

*Anime* draws and renders its humans in precise demonstration of this contra-humanist schema of the psyche. Every detail, element, layer of *anime* is a calligraphic event of signage, wherein signification is accepted as a parallel stream of narration to all that is concurrently simulated. It is therefore not by chance that its chosen visual idiom runs counter to the enlightened progression of visual sophistication which grounds western Eurocentric Judea-Christian evaluations of cinematic art. Under such rhetoric, *anime* can appear 'flat', 'iconic', 'infantile', 'artificial', even 'soulless'.[1] But this is because *anime*—not cinema—tersely investigates the fault line between humanism and post-humanism. Its preponderance with cyborgs, androids, replicants, robots,

---

Sections of this article first appeared in *Cinefile*, Vol. 7, No. 1, 9–13.

P. Brophy
Film Director and Writer, Australia

humanoids and clones (as technological, industrial, mystical and spiritual forces) ably keys us to the primary psychological and ideological concerns of this indigenous mode of cultural address.

Yasuhiro Yoshiura's *Time of Eve* (*Evu no jikan*)—a 6-part Original Video Animation (OVA) from 2008–9, compiled into a feature film in 2010—is a recent exemplar of this, centred around a café where robots and humans can intermingle without androids having to (as required by law) declare their android status in the presence of a human. A consideration of the audiovisual construction of this film—with particular attention paid to its composer Tohru Okada's (a) musical score and (b) digital/MIDI music production—can reveal the wonderful power of 'the soulless' in a properly post-human society. For as humans have persisted in attributing a para-mystical 'soulfulness' to music deemed to move them, divisions forged by harshly exclusive ideologies have across centuries segregated 'innately human' music from music deigned void of human value. *Time of Eve* affords a rare opportunity to consider how certain reviled traits in music—discernible in purportedly innocuous, anaemic, clinical, digital, programmed Muzak-like, instrumental synthesizer compositions—symbolize and express within the compacted audiovisual simulacra of *anime*.

But to register this, we need to confront orthodox notions of 'film music'—a realm of composition which fascinates due to its contradictory and confounding quiddity. On one hand, film music collides notions of technological heterogeneity (how the medium of film determines musical effects) with ideals of formalist homogeneity (how the art of music is limited by those effects). On the other, it derives its consensual definitions from separatist discourses which hierarchically deconstruct the soundtrack for analytical purposes (choosing to highlight one element or layer over another). Reading the film score like a novel or listening to it like a concerto achieves discursive aims only by excluding a raft of signifying modes not enabled by narrational models in film or music. The matricular networking between filmic effects, musical effects, sonic effects and audiovisual effects is flattened into an undynamic planar linear chart, drafted in ways akin to either novel writing or manuscript composing.

For example, when we hear a piano in a film, are we registering it as sound or image? Is the piano object, event, effect? How precisely can we tie it to either temporal or spatial locations, and how do we parse its representational occupancy from its phenomenal apparition? What of its function as icon, symbol, sign, signifier or signified? And the next time the same piano appears in the film, does it perform identically or does its reappearance recontextualize everything deduced from its prior appearance? Finally, what if the piano is not acoustic and actual, but synthesized, sampled, simulated or approximated by electronic or digital means entirely divorced from piano mechanics? Our consideration of music in *Time of Eve* will consider these oft excluded problems from the extant taxonomy of 'film music'. Fortunately, *Time of Eve*—set in a world where androids and humans have become indistinguishable—highlights these issues of definition and separation by outrightly considering the limits of human perception in an expressive form deemed intrinsic to human endeavour: music.

## Music and Metaphor

At a crucial reveal one full hour from the start of *Time of Eve*, teen Rikuo remembers a past conversation with his best friend, Masaki. Unbeknownst to them at the time, they innocently stand at crossroads. Masaki will continue his studies in law; Rikuo is uncertain, having given up his aspirations to be a concert pianist. Masaki ridicules his decision, for Rikuo has quelled his aspirations after seeing a robot perfectly perform a piece of music on the piano. Rikuo doesn't detail to Masaki what was most disturbing about the performance: only at this point in *Time of Eve*'s back-story do we realize that Rikuo was truly moved by the robot's performance.

This is not your usual existential dilemma—a field in which teen-oriented *anime* excels, more than most western photo-cine attempts at the same. Here in this near future (sardonically tagged as 'probably Japan' in a pre-title card), the teen Rikuo has his world inverted because a robot achieved not a technically perfect actualization of classical pianoforte music, but because to Rikuo's advanced listening sensibilities (dedicated to encountering and hopefully generating such moments of actualized perfection) this robot's performance emotionally moved him. Japanese cinema and *anime* has consistently told stories in manifold genres that evidence this inversion, wherein everyday life is accepted to be 'existential' until one day a 'humanist' moment occurs and transforms things. *Anime*'s preponderance of 'androids with souls' is thus less likely to be formally motivated by generic machinations of science fiction, and more likely to be culturally determined by philosophical enquiries of dramatic fiction. *Time of Eve*—like so many speculative sci-fi/mystical *anime*—utilizes the figure of the android to investigate not how one programmes such beings, but how one constructs an idea of 'the human' as a model for such a programme.

In *Time of Eve*, we never get to hear that robot's performance, yet it weighs heavily in Rikuo's head, softly ringing with emotional gravitas. Its silence—as an absence on the soundtrack and as something unspoken by Rikuo—is crucial to the sound world of *Time of Eve*. With acumen and sensitivity, *Time of Eve*'s acute meld of sound effects design, spatial environment mixing, musical arrangement, phonographic reproduction and compositional performance aggregate a 'meta-score' moulded by concave and convex undulations of the inner surface of Rikuo's head-space. Belying an aptly Japanese sense of how dramaturgy and psychology are represented in and expressed by narrative moments, arcs and formations, *Time of Eve*'s conduction of sound and music maps the story's key themes of consciousness (a boy realizing androids have feelings, while a 'girl' android realizes her feelings to her 'master' boy) and in the process gives rise to a bounty for musicological signification.

While sound and music are easily foregrounded in *Time of Eve* due to Rikuo's character as a failed pianist, the aural issues raised are effectively showcased in the *anime* world. Therein, considerations of the minutiae of post-human behaviour (as both social interaction and personal motivation) have been staple memes ever since Osamu Tezuka's ground-breaking *manga*, *Astro Boy* (*Tetsuwan Atomu*), serialized between 1947 and 1963, then made as an animated TV series in 1963, 1980 and 2003. Astro Boy is the definitive 'android with a soul', not only questioning his own existence, but also interrogating Isaac Asimov's famous 'Three Laws of Robotics' from a robot's point-of-view.[2] (Not by coincidence is Asimov's logic similarly interrogated throughout *Time of Eve*.) More so, *anime* graphically renders humans and androids identically, positing them in a fictional realm where they are indistinguishable from each other—yet to us they appear equally 'unreal' due to their shared status as drawings. As the *anime* image gives rise to considering how appearance and simulation constitute this self-reflexivity, so too does its soundtrack give rise to how we perceive differences between 'real' and 'artificial' renderings and performances of music.

Representative of contemporary futurist speculative *anime*, *Time of Eve* defines a world within which characters are populated in situations designed to illustrate the formation of that world. Here, we have a time when androids have become so 'visibly realistic' that whenever in the presence of humans, they are required by law to activate a spinning holographic data-band which rotates above their head like a horizontal halo. The seamless fanciful technology which enables this vision of a well-designed world is undercut by its terse anthropological decline, as we witness the prejudices these 'near-perfect' human machines endure once they have been thoroughly integrated into the industry and exchange of everyday life. A nebulous Orwellian organization—the wonderfully monikered Ethics Committee—is a ubiquitous media presence with messages like 'Would you eat a tomato created by machines?', while tabloid TV features confessional exposes on 'android-holics' (in Japanese, *dorikei*, suggesting something slightly sexual)—people who harbour affections for their 'houseroid' robots.

An oasis in this troubled world is the Time of Eve café, which stipulates only one rule: ' there is to be no discrimination between humans and robots. Customers, please co-operate. Obey the rule and have a fun time '. Specifically, this covert café sends a cryptic Japlish message ('Are you enjoying the time of Eve?') to androids who make their way to the café in order to—of their own volition—experience an absence of prejudice. In a way, the café is a stage within a stage of the story's drama; a space for its characters—android and human alike—to query, reflect upon and ultimately come to terms with how they as individuals relate to the social complexion of their emotional contracts with each other. As such, the café space is also a figurative auditorium which metaphorically and materially audits and 'sounds out' those same relationships. While *Time of Eve*'s speculative themes and visual design deservedly invite sophisticated analysis, its soundtrack warrants special attention as it is directed, organized and realized in ways profoundly different from photo-cine films oppositely concerned with reductivist emoting and human-centric motivation in its characters. For if these androids have somehow mobilized themselves to behave in ways beyond their programmed parameters, the music in *Time of Eve* might be aligned not with how we as humans interpret the score, but how androids read its composition and comprehend its purpose.

## CUES AND CROSS-TALK

The afore-mentioned flashback where Rikuo and his friend Masaki discuss the android piano concert occurs shortly before Rikuo decides to perform a composition he had practised for competition prior to giving up the piano when he was 14. It's the most dramatic scene in the film, for it marks his consciousness of the debt he owes that android pianist: rather than halt Rikuo from being a pianist, the android led him to comprehend the value of post-human behaviour and sentiment. When Rikuo performs the short piece at the café, we hear a real piano being played: 'In Tender Times' (Yasashii jikan no naka de, CD track 27).[3] It's 'real' for numerous reasons: it follows 26 other cues played mostly on synthesizers and samplers, some wildly artificial and electronic, others approximating acoustic and electric keyboards; it's wholly diegetic, capturing Rikuo's uninterrupted on-screen performance; the mix levels determine a present and fulsome sound; and the recording is brimming with room acoustics, spatial reflections and the weight of the piano's body. In essence, the phenomenal aspects of the music poetically encapsulate the weight of this event upon Rikuo, exploiting *anime* (and animation's) core audiovisuality: melding real-world acoustic audio with unreal-world drawn image.

Now if this were a western Eurocentric arthouse cine-photo film with living human actors, the message would be a testament to the human spirit symbolized by the transformative power of music (as in, e.g. Roman Polanski's *The Pianist*, 2002[4]). But in *Time of Eve*, Rikuo performs in the café to six of the other main characters in the film, five of whom we and Rikuo have come to realize are androids and not humans. This arena inverts the site of his originating trauma: a human listening to an android is now a human performing to androids; where the android performance traumatized the human listener of Rikuo, the human performer of Rikuo now shares with his android listeners how he has overcome his robot resentment. Crucially, a 'real' piano is employed to facilitate empathy not with humanity but with androids.

The link between human and android is sonically thematized through *Time of Eve* by its deployment of various keyboards—but this does not mean we can interpret those keyboards' production of film music through assumptive readings. The core problem with the language of 'film music' lies in treating it as language. Mostly, one proceeds to analyse film music within narrative cinema as if it is constructively 'saying something'. It's a limiting paradigm inherited from graduate literature courses the world over ('what is the author saying in this book?'). But what if film music is not saying something: what if it's *sounding* something? *becoming* something? *appearing* to be something? *echoing* something? Furthermore, film music 'cues' are treated as saying something at the moment that they occur, as if their primary significance resides in their instantaneous prompting of immediate effect, and not elsewhere, either near to or far from that moment. A regressive rhetorical model inherited from literary analysis has thus evolved, querying 'what is the composer saying with this cue?' Contentiously, Rikuo's performance ('In Tender Times') says nothing per se, due to how it audits and interpolates what was said through previous cues. Specifically, six interludes of keyboard music precede Rikuo's piano recital at the café (Table 23.1):

Heard in isolation as music alone, these tracks will not appease those seeking music with clear authorial purpose or distinctive melodic character. In many respects, they seem slight, detached, impersonal. Yet the presumption that any music required to 'say something' should bear humanist orientation is a liability when considering music divorced of such concerns. *Time of Eve* is not a story about human enlightenment; it's a parable of how humans can face what they have produced in their guise. This means that the cues' appearances are not to be read at positivist face value, but best considered as deliberated negative signage within musical language. To wit, 'Population Two Hundred Million' (Jinkou nisenman, CD track 3) is a rootless harmonic cloud that sounds like an iPod shuffling between Erik Satie sound-bites. Its harmonic fracturing—never atonal, though in a sense hyper-tonal by appearing to be in multiple ambiguous keys—is sonically sutured by excessive 'unnatural' reverberation. Too rich for an actual space and too uniform to seem acoustic, its digital simulation is as flat as the *anime* image to which it is joined. This is the second time the cue has occurred, and each time it accompanies

**Table 23.1** Music cues in *Time of Eve*

| | | |
|---|---|---|
| CD 3 | 'Population Two Hundred Million' | *piano w/excess digital reverb* |
| | Rikuo walks through the city full of androids, tired and dejected. | |
| CD 12 | 'Time of Bewilderment' | *piano w/minimal digital reverb* |
| | Rikuo arrives at the café; he stops and stares at the piano. Without Masaki, he is lonely and depressed, though denies this when pushed by Nagi, the proprietress. | |
| CD 16 | 'Rina' | *digital synthesizer—synthetic sounds* |
| | Setoro talks to Rikuo about hurting and being hurt, and how androids can feel and express things similarly. | |
| CD 11 | 'Article One Song' | *sampler keyboard—music box sounds* |
| | Rikuo daydreams a flashback: Masaki mocks Rikuo using the android's piano performance as reason to give up the piano. | |
| – | | *digital piano* |
| CD 26 | Sammy trying to play the piano at the café. | *digital keyboard—electric piano and koto hybrid, violin, flutes, clarinet* |
| | Rikuo awakes from his daydream and sees Sammy performing for everyone at the café. | |
| CD 24 | 'Rain On The Way Back Home' | *acoustic piano* |
| | Rikuo realizes the android pianist's perfection is no reason for him to stop playing the piano. | |
| CD 27 | 'Premonition' (Yokan) | *acoustic piano* |
| | Rikuo resolves to perform right now. | |
| | 'In Tender Times' (Yasashii jikan no naka de) | |
| | Rikuo performs in the café. | |

images of the bustling city of Tokyo, with humans and robots alike moving through its streets like guided automatons, lost in their purpose yet controlled by their obligation. The hollow spatialization and disconnected harmonies poetically convey a distinctive emptiness in near-future utopian Japanese society of which Rikuo is emblematic. In other words, the cue's recorded sound marks its compositional procedures as much as its written score states its grammatical melodiousness. It's symbolic emptiness is parlayed into the next cue, 'Time Of Bewilderment' (Tomadoi no jikan, CD track 12), a sparse and delicate passage with slight reverb, heard as Rikuo enters the café and stops to stare at the baby grand piano near the entrance. Each time Rikuo has had to pass by its dead sculptural weight, actively suppressing his memories of a failed career. Then when the proprietress Nagi notes he's alone because he's without Masaki, Rikuo is irritated by the presumption that they are that close. The continuing sombre piano music is a mini-matrix of loneliness here: Rikuo's estrangement from best friend Masaki; Rikuo's feeling lost from not feeding his passion for piano playing; and his emotional dislocation from not confronting his full feelings for houseroid Sammy. Having appeared twice before in differing situations (each of which equate the tension of an android not expressing themselves with the tension caused by the film's Tokyoites not expressing themselves and bowing in too much to social and obligatory pressures), this cue hovers around Rikuo like the circling neon labels rotating around androids.

The following cues similarly articulate a sono-musical node within a network of musical signification, generating musical cross-talk not in a pure harmonic idiom but via a catalogue of aural references and effects across the spectrum of natural and unnatural musical statement. 'Rina' (CD track 16) is mannered chordal fingering on a digital synthesizer; it sounds like the intro to a Michael Bolton ballad from the late 1980s. This glistening digi-pianoforte nonetheless maintains a mannered distance from emotive accompaniment through its inexpressive, metronomic arpeggiation. In this scene (its second appearance following a scene where Rina reveals to Rikuo the complex background to her life as an android), it underscores Setoro (actually a human) pointing out to Rikuo the human fallibility of androids evident through their capacity to be hurt and hurt others despite their supposedly perfect programming—which, after all, is human. Setoro here shares his consciousness of android consciousness with Rikuo. The penny finally drops soon after as Rikuo holds a scarf embroided with 'Are you enjoying the time of EVE?' and realizes how androids can exhibit caring of their own volition and not necessarily through coded directives. We hear 'Rain On The Way Back Home' (Ame no kaeri michi, CD track 26), possibly the most faux-musical cue in *Time of Eve*'s score. More digital synthesizer arpeggios (imagine a molecular melding of koto and nylon guitar plucks with a Fender Rhodes put through a slight chorus effect) combined with near-vapid sample instruments of violin, flutes and clarinet. It's heavily quantized and noticeably devoid of any change in keyboard velocity—so much so, it feels deliberate. Accepting its self-determination to be inauthentically musical, one can read it as symbolizing how Rikuo is now finally accepting androids on their own terms. As an audience to this, we are being asked to consider this cue on android terms, not on humanist terms. It's a hard ask considering the music's uncompromising sterility. But that's precisely what Rikuo has achieved: an ability to listen carefully to androids.

## Silence and Listening

On reflection, Rikuo's breakthrough has been subtly engineered by Rikuo's houseroid, Sammy. In numerous earlier scenes of discomforting quietness, we see Rikuo at home (his parents are always out working late) undertaking mundane activities like drinking coffee, eating dinner, reading the newspaper, with Sammy standing silently nearby. She speaks only when spoken to, and Rikuo addresses her in clipped phrases intoned as questions. Yet he remains noticeably uncomfortable in treating her not as a human—a problem intensified when he discovers that she has been acting of her own volition to frequent the *Time of Eve* café, leading him to trace her there early in the film.

As Sammy has been a proto-nanny to Rikuo for many years in a household devoid of parental care and attention, Rikuo's listless state following his decision to quit a potential career as a concert pianist has fostered his confused and conflicting relation with androids in general and Sammy in particular. When Rikuo exposes Sammy's attendance at the café, her consequent dual behaviour—an affable 'human' within the café and a taciturn slave back home—further disorients him. Yet it is eventually revealed that Sammy has been as traumatized by Rikuo giving up on his concert pianist dream as he has. In a key scene after playing back her 'memory data' of various episodes at the café, she herself attains a level of consciousness of human empathy, and realizes that Rikuo was better within himself when he was playing the piano. She retrieves the original manuscript he practised (titled on the cover sheet 'A Time Of Tenderness') and attempts to play it late at night. At this point, Rikuo half-hears her halted performance. If Rikuo's head was full of the silence of his piano, the distant tinkling of Sammy's piano nocturnes slowly impregnates his unconsciousness, attempting to fill that empty space inside him. Importantly, this is not a thematic literary device: the sounds of pianos are literally and physically entering his mind, leading him to his eventual performance in the café.

When we hear the occasional notes of Sammy playing in the distance, the sound is not only stilted and amateur, but played on a digital piano (the type of which Japan has excelled in producing since the mid-1980s).[5] This perversely answers the hypothetical question 'do androids play digital pianos?'. Yes, they do in *anime*. Any piano teacher will inform you that one only plays as well as one listens, and Sammy's playing—as event (her performance) and object (its digital sound)—demonstrates not how she plays, but how she hears the sound of a better past when her and Rikuo functioned prior to his trauma. Indeed, it is possible that she could play it perfectly, but is deliberately playing it like how Rikuo first tackled the piece at a younger age. For Sammy is playing the music as an attempt to understand Rikuo (an aim expressed earlier by another android frequenting the café, the irrepressible Akiko, who wants to learn from observing others). Her private actions counter an earlier cynical assertion by Masaki: 'affection is not something they have'.

In fact Sammy represents androids as listening beings, in that androids not only speak when spoken to, but anything they say is the direct result of listening and decoding whatever a human says, either in the moment or at some previous moment, now stored in the android's inexhaustible memory data. This reinforces an android's ability to wholly inhabit simultaneous time frames, because all of Sammy's experiences constitute data unfiltered by nostalgic memory fogging or giddy sensations of being in the moment. Here is where we find an apt corollary with film music's behaviour on the soundtrack. Humans mostly think film music exists solely to trigger their own emotional gratification. Androids provide a rhetorical alternative by acknowledging film music not as emotional accompaniment but as consequential data, positioned to atemporally relate to a moment, its past, and its potential future.

## MIDI AND MATRIXES

As a giant screen simulates the tracing of an illegal data transmission from an unknown source to a random network of androids in the opening of *Time of Eve*, background music plays—or to use the Japanese acronym, BGM. It sounds electronic, computerized, current (glitched ambient techno of a Japanese melodic bent, recalling The Art of Noise's 'Moments In Love', 1982). It's a wash of digital percussion with soft fuzz-wah effects, with mannered, isolated 'stabs' of pseudo-orchestral timbral bursts. To musicologists who proffer rationalist qualitative views of how 'great' film scores heroically operate, this would likely appear to be 'non-signifying' music: something simply 'playing in the background', devoid of dramatic purpose or thematic function, lacking in the craft of composition. How sad a reading that would be here in *anime*. How perfect a place to demonstrate why music in any audiovisual form is inescapably 'signifying': there will always be effects generated from the production, generation, rendering and placement of music regardless of any qualitative criteria forced upon it.

The music in question here—'Eve Net' (Eve no ami, CD track 1)—is born of a techno ethos, wherein MIDI (Musical Instrument Digital Interface) sequencing and multi-tracking, analogue/digital synthesis, timbral simulation, and anacoustic post-production effecting and mixing, all combine to confer a deliberately alienating computerized patina. Within a Japanese cultural context, the hi-tech veneer of *Time of Eve*'s music here is a given: a non-divisive, non-polemic application of music as it contemporaneously exists in the broader social world (from night club immersion to TV jingle broadcast to download consumption). *Time of Eve*'s introductory proposition of how music exists today serves to orient a forthcoming series of more real or less real forms of music composition, production and performance in the film's story.

The 'glitched ambient techno' of 'Eve Net' also figures music can be an entirely non-human enterprise—birthing itself from an anacoustic realm where melodic occurrences are inherited not from actual instruments, human playing and real-time recording, but from MIDI's ability to position temporal events and harmonic nodes on a neural grid, *matrixing* music rather than composing it. While this is a standard reading of the pleasure drive of techno since

Kraftwerk's pioneering work in the late 1970s, such a matrixing of events here is synchronized to the large screen's display of a network of androids separately attaining a moment of consciousness (activated by receiving the mysterious Eve message). Profoundly, this 'non-human' and 'non-signifying' BGM represents not how humans bellow their humanism, but how androids quietly attain consciousness. Diverging from Kraftwerk's (and in a sense, Asimov's) celebration of programmed mechanics and automated robotics, this music is not 'machine-like' (an oft-bandied criticism of techno in general) but suggestive of how machines can animisticly 'self-generate' their own musical language.

One might interpret this reading of 'Eve Net' as disproportionate to its effect and purpose in the film. But Japanese cinema has long employed 'butterfly wing effect' dramaturgical inversions to weight the incidental with intimidating gravitas. Its consequent placement of music is governed by these obtuse arcs of dramatic significance, quite oppositely to western cinema's embrace of Wagnerian models of operatic synchronism. *Time of Eve*'s opening music requires scrutiny precisely because it seems inconsequential, offhand, insubstantial. Just as emotional tenor in *anime* is transmitted through the most subtle of line work in the characters' faces (a central aspect of characterization inherited from traditional theatre forms like *Kabuki* and *Noh*), so too is psychological symbolism conveyed within the music's minutiae, operating not at a nominal linguistic level, but at the threshold of micro-material occurrences. The act of listening to the music of *Time of Eve* is predicated on a contemplative awareness of this operational threshold—one decidedly more complex and subtle than the faux-European orchestral scores which have assailed the listener in western CGI animation movies over the last decade.

*Time of Eve*'s next musical moment—'CODE: LIFE' (CD track 2) occurs shortly after we are introduced to Rikuo and his 'houseroid' Sammy. They sit side-by-side in the lounge room, a haze of afternoon sunlight bleaching their quiet space. Both are motionless; Sammy has her abdominal cavity exposed, showing us cables connected to Rikuo's *keitai* as he reads a log of her neural activity in the preceding month. We see the scrolling data on the *keitai* screen: it's all computer code except for an English line 'Are you enjoying the time of Eve?' A bit later, Rikuo steals a second look at the log and the music cue commences, a sparkling web of sweet simulated harp and marimba embellished with one-note fuzz guitar riffing. Simultaneously, another chordal passage sweeps across this, inducing a multiplied polyphony from the passages' conflicting keys. The excerpt totals only about 20 seconds, but its combination of brevity and compaction follows Japanese hierarchical distribution, wherein the most important points are delivered with the silent slicing of a precision blade rather than the explosive boom of a cannon blast. As we hear this musical moment and register its euphoric, uplifting, transcending tone, we see Rikuo's eyes widen slightly. But it remains unclear what he is thinking or feeling, despite the clarity of its impact. 'CODE: LIFE' is repeated twice more in *Time of Eve*, and only at those later moments can we deduce the aggregated implications and syncretized effect of the music.

One of these moments involves Akiko—a girl Rikuo meets at the café whom he later discovers to be an android, but who like all the undisclosed androids there behaves devoid of their difference to humans. One day at home Rikuo notices that Sammy has been making coffee of the same blend as that served at Time of Eve—without him directing her to do so. Angered, Rikuo yells at her: 'Are you imitating humans too?' She denies this: 'I am an android. I'm not a human, master.' Rikuo suddenly remembers what Akiko said at the café: 'We look similar but we're totally different, aren't we?' Rikuo now replays that thought as voiced from an *android*, not a human, and thus realizes that androids are capable of feeling difference between themselves and humans—in contradistinction to Asimov's robots who could not achieve this sort of consciousness. The music's multiplied polyphony (conflicting harmonic keys cohabiting a single passage) then represents the bilateral consequences of human-android co-existence. Furthermore, its formidably irresolvable harmony is itself a symbol of accord and 'harmony'. We as humans would presume the concept of harmony to be unilateral and melodious (the province of conventional musical scoring), while android logic—as it functions post-Asimov in *Time of Eve*—renders it a comforting noise of contrasting voices and interfering tones. The result is a type of 'polyphonic dissonance', where harmony is employed to impassively corrupt its own data, rather than decimate it in an explosive destructive gesture. The root of *Time of Eve*'s radicalism lies in its subversion of musical language as it has developed along Eurocentric channels of thematicism, wherein the binary of consonance/dissonance has contextualized both Romantic and Modernist notions of musical progressiveness. Despite their heroic ventures beyond melodic stricture, their orthodox taxonomies of music's humanist values equate those held by Baroque and Classical composers, leaving them all dismissive of music regarded as lacking in those values. Ultimately, the consonance/dissonance binary of each side's commenting on and against its Other has thwarted the possibility of what they might signify through their dissolution. 'CODE: LIFE' provides an audible answer.

## MIDI and Non-Space

The anacoustic real of MIDI production—its absence of actual audible spatial occurrence (such as a piano playing in a room)—would seem a perfect modus operandi for the matrixed simulacra of *anime*. Just as nothing pre-exists in *anime* due to its world being engineered and actualized rather than photographed and captured, MIDI generates music that in a sense never happened. Most of *Time of Eve*'s score is MIDI generated, yet this is so because the 'spaces' in *Time of Eve* constitute a topography of non-existing zones: from the Ethics Committee's insistent regulations about how androids co-inhabit human space, to the de-sanctioning of those rules within the walls of the Eve café, to the piano practice room which Rikuo no longer frequents, to his own interior head space wherein he harbours unmentionable feelings towards the houseroid Sammy. *Time of Eve* is a dense cartography of no-go zones, and the unactual nature of MIDI aptly reflects *Eve*'s dramaturgy.[6]

Postmodern theoretical precepts would hold simulated and virtual instrumentation in line with the notion of the simulacrum, presuming that the instruments' affected sound and audible mimicry (such as the sampled marimba or bongos in *Eve*'s score previously mentioned) are meant to reference, replace or replicate their originating instruments. But that would presume that there is neither depth, density nor congestion between the original and its simulation, as if the dynamic flux of history, technology, musicology and culture somehow freezes between two binary states of musical occurrence and existence (the oft used 'real' and 'fake' dichotomy). The MIDI construction of music (a notion entirely unaddressed by the scopic and linguistic parameters of postmodern theory) has for half a century not been concerned with naturalist or realist binaries. When the sampled marimba sounds sampled, *that* is its identity. When the bongos are stridently quantized and devoid of pressure-modulated tone, they are accepted as *not* being played by a human.

Of course, since the late 1940s, *musique concrète* and its development through a range of electro-acoustic practices across the 1950s and 1960s initially articulated and explored alternatives to the 'abstract music' born of written manuscripts requiring authorial imprimatur prior to their realization by orchestral means. MIDI's implementation in the early 1980s—in a perverse conflation of the *concrète* and abstract—formed a closed Moebius loop of musical production and compositional strategy by wholly accepting that no sound should occur in an acoustic space, and that the means of composing, arranging, conducting and realizing could be done by electronic and digital modules 'talking' to each other through a protocol understood by said modules synchronized to a chosen tempo. In a sense, this fuses 'writing' with 'performing' in ways entirely unforeseen by the original *musique concrète* composers who grappled with 'real world' sounds and sought to wrangle them into compositions. In keeping with *Time of Eve*'s integrated self-reflexivity, Rikuo's directives to Sammy are analogous to the MIDI composer sending MIDI 'commands' (the protocol's terminology) to connected modules, in the same way the networking of androids via the *Time of Eve* café is analogous to how MIDI can synchronize a set of modules via a software application for notating, tracking and sequencing.

While MIDI music is viewed by musical conservatories as a ubiquitous anti-body rampantly generating 'compositions' with no understanding of the subtleties of real world instruments and their human performance—an argument hard to discount when listening to 'hold music' on a telephone—there are other ways in which it has developed. The same 'physical modelling synthesis'[7] used in early digital pianos has also been employed in tone synthesis modules integrated into a MIDI work environment. These types of synthesizers generate sounds rich in virtual timbre (woody, glassy, metallic, string-like sounds—either individually or fused into compound textures) which evoke strong 'sonic images' of material surfaces without referencing the mechanics of extant instrument design. In one of *Time of Eve*'s most unsettling moments, Rina uncontrollably shows Rikuo her damaged leg, caused by her getting in the line of fire to protect her master from an assassin. During this scene, we hear 'Her Interior' (Kanojo no nakami, CD track 15): a series of tonal sheets of hyperreal effect yet confounding identity. The cue suggests a peeling back—literally—as Rina's interior thigh wiring is exposed. MIDI and synthesis is utilized here to venture into a 'post-music' realm, acknowledging that the Romantic legacy of vicariously aping an audience's emotional response to such an incident does not well service the narrative task of showing how an android reveals their inner scars to a human. Humanist composers informed of the grand European legacy of music would presume there is no emotional content to such a scene, as Rina is just a machine. 'Her Interior' counters with 'post-music' for a post-human.

## Muzak and Environment

The world depicted in *Time of Eve*—that is, the ways in which private/public, personal/communal, domestic/official spaces are arranged—is one common to *anime* irrespective of where and when its story occurs. Everything looks clean, refined, distilled and essentialized. While *anime* can make both the urban hub or the suburban domicile look like how their architects imagine their ideal designs (photo-cinema would necessitate 'cleaning-up' reality to be so pristine), this buffed sheen of interior and exterior design is typical of Japan in reality. Foreigners are sometimes uncomfortable with the way things can appear clinical and sterile in Japan, especially if their home turf looks used and abused in comparison. But this near-perfection in the Japanese appearance of public spaces is an aesthetic based on affording the individual the feeling of being in a space by themselves rather than with others. Like the Japanese body cleansed in pure hot water only after soaping up and washing down the skin, the Japanese citizen moves through public space in a similarly isolated and ionized way. The reason for outlining this aspect of inhabiting cleansed space is to qualify the importance and relevance of 'Muzak' in Japan.

Again, we encounter another topic which in the west is treated with derision. Few musicologists have historically bothered with the signifying wealth of Muzak,[8] and when it appears to be happening in a film score, there is the assumption that the score is vapid, empty, pale, thin, 'soulless'. Muzak of all sorts plays in many public spaces in contemporary Japan (as it has ever since the post-war period) and especially so in spaces designed for rest, respite and relaxation. *Time of Eve*'s choice of a café for the stage of its themes is a pointed choice, as cafés—or the *kissaten* as it developed in Japan in the 1970s—is a place where one can feel especially relaxed by enjoying a momentary detachment from society. The *kissaten* is an infamous site for Muzak: to many a westerner it's like a nightmarishly numbing internment straight out of a Kurt Vonnegut novel. Much of the score in *Time of Eve* deftly assumes a Muzak guise in varying degrees of diegetic presence, never straying far from the type of light instrumental music which one might hear at a *kissaten*, café or *kouhii* chain like Doutor or Excelsior.

When Rikuo and Masaki make their way down the secluded stairwell to the café, the music mimes their excitement as they nervously approach the place for the first time. It starts with vamped chords played on simulated mellotron (a digital version of an archaic analogue tape instrument designed to emulate the sounds of strings, flutes and/or voices). Once they open the door to the café and see the sign of its 'rule', the music blossoms into a bouquet of wordless female voice, electronic keyboards, bongos, shakers and acoustic guitars. This arrangement is typical of the 'retro-bossa-nova' high-style pop of Omotesando and its hip designer cafés, so its musicological referencing is quite precise within the Japanese context. If one were to 'read' or evaluate the music here outside of its context, one would miss how it deliberates Muzak as a vernacular mode of music tied to the environs depicted in *Time of Eve*. But most importantly, the 'soulless' aspects of Muzak—its wilful emptying of human presence in stark contrast to the highly emotional human presence encoded within Japanese *enka* ballads and tunes—reflect not only how androids might find pleasure in listening to music which absents humanism, but also how humans—Rikuo especially, but also Masaki as we discover later—can become capable of registering emotional depth in such music precisely *because* it displays no human presence.

While we might mostly regard Muzak—and MIDI music—as an aberration of or deviation from music, *Time of Eve* gives pause to re-evaluate such categorization. Throughout its story, music, MIDI and Muzak are treated *as each other*. Rather than defined by their difference, they are registered by their sameness, thereby constituting an inclusive approach to musical definition. Just as Muzak is generated by spatial purpose ('scoring' the ambience of a physical environment), so is film music essentially designed to occupy the imaginary space evoked by a film's scenography. This accounts for the slippery positioning of film music between diegetic and non-diegetic occurrence, between subjective and objective viewpoint, and between interior and exterior description. Yet film music's nominal status as art and language tends to favour analyses which solidify these sliding scales of reference in the name of signification. *Time of Eve* nominates categories of music—(a) background Muzak played in the café, (b) diegetic music performed in the café, and (c) interior mind-state music conveyed by the score—for the express purpose of disqualifying their semantic rigidity. Not only are its cues recontextualized through repetition (not variation as per traditional compositional craft), they are also presented from both a human and an android point of view. The dramaturgical device of androids attaining consciousness in *Time of Eve* thus fortifies a non-binary arena—symbolized by the therapeutic auditorium of Eve's café—to enable new and alternative ways of considering human pleasure principles. *Time of Eve*'s androids and humans—plus its composer and its audience—can momentarily inhabit the unactual space of its musical drama, to vicariously experience how androids hear music.

## Notes

1. Historically, serious film appreciation has generally side-lined animation. Aside from acknowledging its artistry in drawing life and engineering movement, animation has rarely been treated as bearing the emotional depth or persuasive realism of photo-cine works; been granted sectarian festivals away from 'real' film festivals; and often garnered special cause for consideration because its hand-drawn fantasia manages to perform as well as photographed films. Despite the success of Hayao Miyazaki and Studio Ghibli (winning the 2001 Academy Award for *Spirited Away*), *anime* remains further ostracized in the west. The bulk of it is not theatrically released aimed at children or young adults, and shaped by seemingly unfounded lurches and surges in narrative exposition and stylistic tenor. Viewed against the Eurocentric progressive model of visual language, where archaic/iconic pictograms eventually become realistic (through Renaissance mathematics) then evocative (through Impressionist painterliness), *anime* appears retarded in its reliance on flat surfaces, child-like fixation, and unrealistic characterization of people. It's a persistent and flawed rhetoric that ultimately brands *anime* as disconnected from the enlightened arts, thereby qualifying it as lacking in essential humanist traits. And while the last decade has witnessed a refreshing rise in critical writing on *anime*, negative and dismissive terms abound when dealing with (or avoiding) popular children's titles like *Dragon Ball Z* (1989), *Sailor Moon* (1992), *Pokémon* (1997), *Yu-Gi-Oh!* (1998) and *Naruto* (2002).
2. 'The Three Laws of Robotics' are a set of rules outlined by Isaac Asimov's in his 1942 short story 'Runaround'. The three rules are as following:

    1. A robot may not injure a human being or, through inaction, allow a human being to come to harm.
    2. A robot must obey the orders given to it by human beings, except where such orders would conflict with the First Law.
    3. A robot must protect its own existence as long as such protection does not conflict with the First or Second Laws.

3. All cue titles are taken from the Aniplex Inc. CD soundtrack release (2010). The English translation is followed by the Japanese phonetic title.
4. The words 'piano' and 'pianist' appear in a sizeable number of films, nearly all of which are dedicated to the triumph of the human spirit. A notable exception is John Brahm's *Hangover Square* (1945) with a richly atonal score by Bernard Herrmann, played by the character of George Harvey Bone—a late Victoriana composer suppressing his dark side as a psychotic strangler.
5. Roland's RD100 digital piano debuted in 1986 with Structured Adaptive synthesis—its trademarked application of 'physical modelling synthesis' dedicated to emulating the physical characteristics of a sound-producing source, such as the steel piano wire, felt hammers and wooden body of the piano.
6. While not within the parameters of this article's focus on music, MIDI and Muzak, it can be noted that the general sound design for *Time of Eve* accords with the clinical attributes of urban planning, architectural form and interior dressing. Empty domestic environs, cleansed public spaces and composed media zones are represented equally by *anime*'s selective distilling of sonic elements and layers, and *Time of Eve*'s socio-techno utopia where dirt, grime, noise and dissonance are erased.

7. Physical modelling synthesis is based on employing computational mathematical formulae derived from analysing characteristic transformations and excitations in the physical properties of sound-making materials. Preceding simulations of keyboard instruments were to be found in: (a) tape loops physically encased in a mechanically constructed keyboard; (b) electronic 'additive synthesis' approximations of an instrument's characteristics through passing voltage current through oscillators and filters; (c) electronic 'reductive synthesis' reconstructions of an instrument's characteristics through timbral modulation of sine waves; and (d) digital samples of actual instrument recordings stored in the RAM of a CPU coupled to a keyboard.
8. Exceptions here would be J. Lanza (1995) *Elevator Music* (Picador) and John Zorn's long-standing appreciation of American exotica, lounge and easy listening, audible on his Tzadik albums *The Dreamers* (2008) and *O'o* (2009).

CHAPTER 24

# The Sounds in the Machine: Hirokazu Tanaka's Cybernetic Soundscape for *Metroid*

### William Gibbons

Few video games sounds are as iconic as the blip and bloops of *Pong* (1972). Like its memorable, minimal visual style and gameplay—two players control table-tennis 'paddles', sending a pixelated 'ball' back and forth until one player misses it—*Pong*'s sound effects remain instantly recognizable to generations of players (many of whom have never actually played the game). Al Alcorn, *Pong*'s designer, recollected in an interview that executives at Atari initially wanted the game's sound to include 'realistic' sounds, including cheers and boos from a large crowd. Finding the hardware entirely incapable of creating the desired effect, he opted for another solution: 'I poked around the sync generator to find an appropriate frequency or a tone. So those sounds were done in half a day. They were the sounds that were already in the machine' (Collins, 2008, p. 9). The sound was always there, in other words, lying dormant amid the circuits, patiently awaiting discovery. But perhaps it was music, and not only sound, that was 'already in the machine'. Although *Pong* ostensibly contained no music, its sound effects in actuality consisted of three musical tones, indicating when the ball hit a paddle, bounced off the edge of the screen, or exited the screen (meaning a lost point).

These musical tones—the first ever heard in games—often feature in the aural histories of game music presented in game music concerts, such as the 'classic' medleys in the immensely popular *Video Games Live* touring show, or in the increasingly common marching-band arrangements of game music. Likewise, in an insightful study of early game music, Neil Lerner suggests reading *Pong*'s sound effects as—among other things—a musical score:

---

I am grateful to William Cheng and Dana Plank, as well as this volume's editors, for their insightful comments and helpful suggestions on this chapter.

W. Gibbons
Texas Christian University, USA

> Even *Pong* ... would create in its soundtrack a minimalistic accompaniment that utilized only three notes ...; its rhythmic unpredictability, together with the aleatoricism of its severely limited pitch collection, should remind us of the contemporaneous minimalistic works of composers such as La Monte Young and Terry Riley. (2014a, p. 1)

But here is the problem: if the tones are music, they are (one assumes) non-diegetic; if they are (diegetic) sound effects, they hardly seem to belong on a game-music concert or in a comparison with works by Young and Riley. The limited technology at play—the sounds in the machine, as it were—led to a fundamental ambiguity in how we understand the game's soundscape. We might easily make a similar case for other early games. The first game to feature a continuous musical score (meaning that the music plays constantly during gameplay), for example, was the iconic arcade staple *Space Invaders* (1978), in which the player must fend off the eponymous aliens as they descend towards the bottom of the screen. The entire gameplay session is accompanied by a low, incessantly repeating descending tetrachord; as the player destroys more invaders, the aliens—and the sound—increase dramatically in speed. As with *Pong*, the nature of the sound is unclear.[1] Is this tetrachord the sound of the aliens' inexorable march, is it a musical underscore, or is it both? The game designers of *Pong* and *Space Invaders* had little choice in the matter; by necessity they used whatever tools were at hand to create effective audio. Yet this sonic ambiguity—the liminal existence of game sound between musical score and sound effect—has persisted as a feature of game audio long after technology has overcome these limitations. Karen Collins, for example, notes that

> the overall sonic texture of games can often create an interesting interplay between music and sound effects that blurs the distinction between the two. In many examples of games, we might question whether we are hearing sound effects, voice, ambience, or music .... [And] Some sound effects in games are also worth considering as music rather than as nonmusical sound. (2013, p. 3)

Games do not, of course, have a monopoly on this kind of ambiguity; indeed, as Rick Altman has compellingly argued, we can trace it back as far as silent film, when the same musicians were often responsible for both musical accompaniment and sound effects (2000, pp. 339–59). Although games are clearly a unique medium, they nonetheless borrow heavily from semiotic codes, narrative strategies, and audiovisual styles drawn from film and television—and have since the earliest days of gaming.[2] I am interested here in further exploring the relationship between cinema and gaming by delving into one particular case study of integrated sound design: Hirokazu 'Hip' Tanaka's groundbreaking audio for the science-fiction game *Metroid* (1986), one of the most iconic titles released on the Nintendo Entertainment System (or NES). By consistently—and for avowedly aesthetic reasons—blurring boundaries between diegesis and non-diegesis, and between sound and music, Tanaka raised questions about the prevailing design of 1980s game music. In particular, *Metroid*'s sound design flouts conventional understandings of the functions of game audio and applies the NES's sound hardware in unexpected ways to create unusual (and somewhat uncanny) timbres.

Tanaka's willingness to experiment with integrated sound design likely emerged from his educational and musical background. Although he studied piano at a young age, Tanaka's musical interests lay predominantly in popular music of the 1960s—he cites rock and reggae as particular influences.[3] After studying electronic engineering at university—while still performing regularly in bands—he began working for Nintendo in Japan, designing circuitry for sound effects in arcade cabinets including *Donkey Kong* (1981), *Donkey Kong, Jr.* (1982), and *Mario Bros.* (1983).[4] Although he worked on sound effects rather than music in these titles, shortly thereafter Tanaka began contributing music to some games on the newly released Nintendo Entertainment System (NES, known as the Famicom in Japan), and eventually the Game Boy and Super Nintendo in the later 1980s and early 1990s, respectively.[5]

Many of video games' most iconic musical scores emerged in this period: we might think of Koji Kondo's well-known scores for *Super Mario Bros.* (1985) or *The Legend of Zelda* (1986) as archetypical examples of this style. Yet while some of Tanaka's game scores are fairly typical of the looped, tuneful melodies common on home console games after about 1984—for example, most of *Kid Icarus* (1986) and *Dr. Mario* (1990), both for the NES—in others he deliberately bucked this trend for aesthetic reasons. As Tanaka himself puts it, in the mid 1980s

> sound designers in many studios started to compete with each other by creating upbeat melodies for game music. The pop-like, lilting tunes were everywhere.
>
> The industry was delighted, but on the contrary, I wasn't happy with the trend, because those melodies weren't necessarily matched with the tastes and atmospheres that the games originally had. (Brandon, 2002, np)

The first game in which Tanaka set out to subvert these trends was the NES action-platformer *Metroid* (1986). 'My feeling', Tanaka later revealed, 'was that audio should be more in line with the sound effects that you had control over as the player, so that there was a more unified sound to the game. I was kind of in love with the idea of a game whose audio was composed of sound effects. This concept was on my mind while making *Metroid*' (Jeriaska, 2009, np). In the following sections, I turn first to an investigation of how these concepts play out in *Metroid*, experimenting with the functions and capabilities of game audio, and then to an exploration of how this sound design echoes the main themes of the game itself.

## The Sounds of *Metroid* (1986)

Despite its now-iconic status, *Metroid* was a major departure for Nintendo in terms of tone. In contrast to the bright colours and almost obsessive focus on 'fun' for which Nintendo was (and remains) known, *Metroid* presented a dark, nerve-wracking experience focused on exploration and experimentation.

The plot of *Metroid* is (like many games of the era) sparse and more than a bit clichéd, mostly conveyed through a text introduction before the game begins. Players assume the role of Samus Aran, a spacefaring bounty hunter sent to defeat a group of Space Pirates based in a large complex on the planet Zebes, which is controlled by the malevolent Mother Brain. As Jeff Ryan notes in his book *Super Mario: How Nintendo Conquered America*, the game was 'an outstanding achievement that merged multiple play styles, horizontal and vertical action, and a tense, gripping, science-fiction atmosphere' (2011, p. 102).

Tanaka's soundscape is a central part of creating that atmosphere, constantly blurring musical and diegetic boundaries and employing avant-garde musical techniques designed to enhance (rather than obscure) the 'electronic' qualities of the NES's music hardware. In fact Tanaka's expertise allowed him to manipulate the NES's sound hardware (a five-channel Programmable Sound Generator, or PSG, chip) to create unique effects.[6] At every turn, Tanaka avoided typical norms of 1980s game music, for a clear reason. In his words:

> I had a concept that the music for *Metroid* should be created not as game music, but as music the players feel as if they were encountering a living creature. I wanted to create the sound without any distinctions between music and sound effects. The image I had was, 'Anything that comes out from the game is the sound that [the] game makes'. (Brandon, 2002, np)

This last idea—'the sound that [the] game makes'—clearly echoes Alcorn's notion of 'the sounds that were already in the machine' in *Pong*. Both invoke the spectre of technology as the origin of the musical sound, a pre-existing musical ghost in the machine that careful manipulation could release. After the title screen, there are comparably few moments of clear melody, and the approximately 30-second loops frequently verge on atonality.[7] Moreover, the pointillist, pulsing nature of some of the game's loops erodes the boundaries between an electronic musical score and the soundscape of computerized bloops and burbles that players might reasonably expect from its futuristic sci-fi setting.

In its disregard for conventional music design, its intentional blurring of diegetic boundaries—along with additional respects I will discuss below—I find that Tanaka's audio design for *Metroid* resonates strongly with the conception and execution of Louis and Bebe Barron's famous 'electronic tonalities' for *Forbidden Planet* (Fred M. Wilcox, 1956), the first entirely electronic film score. As Stephan Prock has argued in a recent study of the unique sounds of *Forbidden Planet*:

> the ambiguous nature of these sounds, divorced from familiar sources, made it possible for the Barrons to exploit the soundtrack both diegetically (sounds within the fictional film world), nondiegetically (music/sound emanating from outside the fictional world), and, more fantastically, simultaneously as music and sound, in and out of the diegesis, as if in a sonic quantum state. (2014, p. 375)

The key to this 'quantum state' in *Forbidden Planet* is the use of the same electronics to produce both sound and music: 'oscillators ... vacuum tubes, resistors, capacitors, inductors, and semiconductors' (Wierzbicki, 2005, p. 32). The same is true in *Metroid*: like all NES games, the same sound hardware created all the sounds, musical or otherwise. What differentiates *Metroid*, however, is that while most NES titles exaggerated the differences between music and sound (for both aesthetic and practical gameplay reasons), Tanaka obscures that distinction by compositing music that acts like sounds, and sounds that act like music.

I do not mean to suggest that *Metroid* contains no identifiable 'music'; indeed, it has much more than Tanaka's comments would suggest. There are, all told, 13 'musical tracks' included in the game, comprising fewer than 15 minutes of original music. Two of the cues are five- or six-second melodic signifiers (or 'earcons') that play when Samus emerges for the first time from her ship, or when the player either receives a new item. In terms of musical style and placement, either of those earcons could easily have been composed for another NES game, and the same is true of several of the longer cues. The driving rhythms and clear tonality of 'Brinstar', for example—an approximately 45-second loop that plays during Samus's time in the eponymous region of the Zebes base—would not be out of place in *The Legend of Zelda* or many other adventure games.[8] Even considering the entire soundscape of the game, including sound effects and music (the *mise-en-bande*, in Altman's words), the music would be easily separated out from sound, and would have been comfortably within players' horizons of expectations for game music of the 1980s.

In fact, there are relatively few instances in which there is a major blurring of sound/music boundaries—yet these moments of rupture stand out, both by virtue of their sheer oddity for 1980s game music and because they tend to occur at structurally significant moments in the game. Perhaps the most obviously blurred is the cue somewhat confusingly titled 'Silence', a ten-second loop which occurs in transitional moments in the game—mostly rooms leading from a central area to a power-up for Samus, or in boss rooms after the enemy is vanquished. 'Silence' consists of two elements: an atonal melody (see Fig. 24.1) and a 'burbling', quasi-pitched pattern in the bass. The two elements seem (but are not actually) random, and their offset metric patterns and tempo never lining up in any way that would suggest that they are part of a unified musical whole.[9] In a similar vein, the melody itself seems to eschew any kind of predictability. The motion of the first four pitches, which are also metrically equal, seem to establish a pattern—and one strikingly reminiscent of the opening pitches of the original *Star Trek* theme—but then the final five notes diverge sharply, leaving

**Fig. 24.1** *Metroid* (Satoru Okada, 1986), 'Silence' (transcription by author)

players in the lurch. This design is clever: the sound seems almost random even over a fairly long stretch of time (which the game does not require in these spaces), although in fact the player hears the same loop.

'Silence' serves an important structural function in *Metroid*, providing a sonic buffer between areas of the game (and thus mostly preventing jarring cuts in the music) and as a moment of relative repose in the midst of a chaotic game. These moments also, however, raise a number of significant questions of diegesis. If, as the title suggests, there is silence here, what type of silence is it? If it means there is no music, then what is producing the obviously melodic tones, so similar to what we have been hearing the entire game? And what is the source of the mysterious 'burbling' sounds in the bass? Can we only now, in 'silence', hear sounds that have been produced by the Zebes base—or its inhabitants—all along? On the other hand, if the title 'silence' means there is no diegetic sound in the room (perhaps some kind of vacuum chamber?), is all we can hear by default music?

**Fig. 24.2** *Metroid*, 'Tourian' (transcription by author)

In that case, have the noises we have attributed to the enemies all along been, in fact, musical earcons rather than diegetically produced sound?

The soundscape for Tourian—the final large area of the game—shares many of these blurry boundaries. Tourian leads directly to Mother Brain's main base of operations, and is among the more difficult points in the game—a series of rooms filled with dangerous enemies and environmental hazards. The sound that accompanies this harrowing journey (entitled 'Tourian') consists of three parts: (1) a bass melody; (2) an obsessively arpeggiated diminished-seventh chord in the treble; and (3) another 'burbling' motif in the lowest register, the diegetic status of which, as in 'Silence', is entirely unclear. Figure 24.2 illustrates the first two elements: although there is certainly pitch centricity around A, the melody's avoidance of triadic motion in favour of semitones, tritones, and perfect fourths—often quite dissonant with the treble arpeggio—obscures a clear sense of tonality. Moreover, the metrical patterns do not align—the ominous, plodding bass line is at odds with the six-note treble patterns.[10] (Note that the loop is not seamless; the arpeggio pattern is disrupted by returning to the first measure.)

Again, players are presented with multiple possible attributions for these sounds. The unmetrical burbling sounds are similar to what we experienced in 'Silence', but more prominent; an aspect of the music that seemed sedate, if mysterious, now seems agitated. These sounds could reasonably emerge from the enemies in this region of the base—particularly from the transparent, jellyfish-like Metroids that players encounter for the first time here. Or perhaps, as I will explore more in the following section, we might assume the sounds come from Mother Brain's control room, which would explain their sudden increase in volume and desperation. The arpeggios offer players a similar set of choices: we can interpret them as music, certainly. But given their rapidity and the already blurry diegetic boundaries, we might also read them as some kind of alarm motif, a warning that an intruder has reached this inner sanctum (Fig. 24.2).

At this point, it seems clear how Tanaka's sound design creates the uneasy atmosphere that permeates *Metroid*. His careful manipulation of both NES hardware and player expectations defied game sound conventions in intriguing and influential ways—but I am interested in another level of meaning to the sound-design choices in *Metroid*, as well. Let us return for a moment to Tanaka's conception of his sound design: that 'the music for *Metroid* should be created not as game music, but as music the players feel as if they were encountering a living creature'. In the following section, I would like to explore further this idea of music as 'living creature', and how such a conception might express not just *Metroid*'s atmosphere, but also serve as a sonic expression of its central themes.

## Living Circuits, Cybernetic Sounds

Although it may seem like an odd juxtaposition, the notion of electronic music as living creature is not without precedent: indeed, we may turn again to *Forbidden Planet* as an obvious parallel. During the work on the film, Louis and Bebe Barron drew heavily on the pioneering cybernetics work of Norbert

Weiner, which led them to begin conceiving of the circuits used in *Forbidden Planet*'s score as living organisms (Wierzbicki, 2005).[11] During an interview published in the early 1990s, Bebe Barron explained that many of the sounds produced from the circuits were made by emulating 'experiments done to animals to put them into a state of stress', which resulted in the circuits '*literally* shrieking'. 'It was like they were alive', she continued, 'and with a lifespan of their own' (quoted in Wierzbicki, 2005, p. 33). Louis espoused similar ideas: 'these circuits are as if a living thing were crying out, expressing itself. There's an organic type of behavior going on' (Greenwald, 1986, p. 59). For the Barrons, these electronic circuits, vacuum tubes, and transistors were merely the shell, their inner life exposed through the vitalizing powers of electricity.

Organic sounds wrapped in an electronic shell—it is difficult to think of a core concept that more deeply resonates with *Metroid*. To broaden out to a larger perspective, I believe we can read Tanaka's integrated soundtrack as a metaphor for the game's central duality between human and machine. In this, too, he follows a time-worn tradition in science fiction cinema. *Forbidden Planet*'s antagonist is the well-intentioned (?) Morbius, whose interaction with an alien supercomputer results in his unconscious thoughts manifesting as a monster composed (it seems) of pure energy. Rebecca Leydon suggests that the film's music becomes symbolic of his dual existence: 'the permeability of the diegetic/non-diegetic sound boundary acts as a kind of metaphor for the monster/Morbius situation, where the boundary between mind and matter is similarly porous' (2004, p. 71). This kind of reading is of course not limited to the Barrons's score. Michael Hannan and Melissa Carey, for example, have argued that Vangelis's electronic score for *Blade Runner* (Ridley Scott, 1982) functions similarly, with 'electronic simulation of musical sounds and the blurring of the distinction between music and effects' standing in for the central conflict between humans and their synthetic counterparts, who are simultaneously organic and artificially produced (2004, p. 160).

As I have already suggested, in *Metroid* protagonist and antagonist are mirror images. Samus spends the game wrapped in a technological power suit that provides superhuman abilities but obscures her humanity; in fact, the revelation that Samus was a 'her' at all was a 'twist ending' to the game. The game's instruction manual (which contains a lengthy set up of the plot), identifies Samus as 'a cyborg: his entire body has been surgically strengthened with robotics, giving him superpowers' (*Metroid Instruction Manual*, 1986, p. 7).[12] Mother Brain (see Fig. 24.3), on the other hand, is a large, female-gendered cybernetic brain—an organic entity surrounded by electronics, encased in an inorganic shell (in this case a glass tube). And, like the Barrons' circuits, the game manual informs us that Mother Brain makes 'a shrieking noise' when hit (*Metroid Instruction Manual*, p. 42). Protagonist and antagonist, like the Barron's circuits, are both somehow machine and more.

To an extent, Mother Brain does not simply control the Zebes complex; she *is* the complex. The base is the body, and she is the mind—the ghost in the machine. As such she seems able to control every aspect of the environment

**Fig. 24.3** Mother Brain in *Metroid* (Satoru Okada, 1986)

**Fig. 24.4** *Metroid*, 'Zebetite' (transcription by author)

in which the player has spent the entire game. This duality echoes the malevolent-haunted-house trope found in horror media, stretching from the Overlook Hotel in *The Shining* to the entire town of Silent Hill in the video game series of the same title. Tellingly, when Mother Brain is destroyed, the entire underground complex collapses, unable to function without its core in place. There is something unsettlingly grotesque about Mother Brain—she is an aberration in the manner of Frankenstein's monster, an uncanny amalgamation of nature and science. In science-fiction film, music is often a way to express that uncanny 'Otherness' (or perhaps 'alien-ness'). As Leydon notes in her study of *Forbidden Planet*'s music, in midcentury (and later) sci-fi 'electronic timbres emerged as a monolithic class of sound objects anchored to images of the aberrant' (2004, p. 64).

Not surprisingly, then, the soundscape during Samus's final confrontation with Mother Brain is perhaps the most overtly 'electronic' and ambiguously diegetic in the game. The explosions of Samus's weapons (controlled directly by the player) aside, the audio consists of two elements: a four-measure pattern of undulating sixteenth notes in the bass (see Fig. 24.4) and a metrically unrelated, vaguely organic 'burbling' sound. We may read this is an avant-garde musical composition, or we may understand it as ambient noise: the sixteenth notes as an alarm, or the workings of Mother Brain's computers, plus the 'burbling' as the grotesque sound of Mother Brain herself. At this point, we might reinterpret that mysterious 'burbling' as having been produced by Mother Brain all along—barely audible during 'Silence' throughout the base, and increasingly present as the player gets closer to the complex's centre. Tellingly, when Mother Brain is defeated all the non-tonal or diegetically ambiguous sounds disappear from the soundscape, replaced by much more traditional game music (Fig. 24.3). With the monstrosity destroyed, the game seems to imply, we can return to 'normal'.

## Conclusion: Samus' Wave

The soundscape for *Metroid* acts not just as a 'living creature', like the sound designer intended, but also as a specifically cybernetic one—the product of Tanaka's human mind and the NES's electronic circuits. Its existence in the liminal space between music and sound echoes Mother Brain's and Samus's existence between the human and the machine. And perhaps, in doing so, it echoes our own experience as well. There are several possible endings to *Metroid*, depending on how quickly players are able to complete the game. In the two best endings, Samus's cybernetic suit disappears, leaving her in various states of undress (the 'best' ending features her in a pink bikini). Looking directly into the 'camera', she then gives an energetic wave clearly directed towards the player. Despite its clearly friendly intention, this odd gesture always unnerves me. Hovering between a 'goodbye' and a 'thank you', it seems to recognize the player's agency, our direct role in 'controlling' her actions throughout the game. The wave thus takes on an uncanny aspect, not unlike a wooden dummy suddenly thanking the ventriloquist for giving it the illusion of life. We are perhaps reminded that the actions we have undertaken for the past hours are the result of a human/machine cooperation, not unlike Samus or Mother Brain—we provide the organic brain (and fingers), and the mechanical NES provides the rest.

Although this visual breaking of the fourth wall is unexpected, the soundscape has been preparing us for it the entire game. By placing us in what Prock eloquently described as a 'sonic quantum state', *Metroid*'s sound design highlights the simultaneously diegetic and non-diegetic nature of game music. Players often depend on sound to alert them to specific on-screen events or actions; a sound might indicate, say, the presence of a certain type of enemy or the need to avoid a particular environmental threat (laser beams, missiles, and so on).[13] Thus, whereas in film or television, the blurring between sound effect and music can be affecting or even alienating, in games the stakes are significantly higher. Because players make choices directly based on sound cues, any confusion about what is essential, diegetic aural information and what is background music is likely to result in some tense, disorienting moments. William Cheng, for example, notes that one of the most disturbing aspects of the survival horror game *Silent Hill* is not just 'how its noises straddle the diegetic and non-diegetic divide' but also 'how these sounds cross from the game's virtual world into the real world inhabited by the player' (2014, pp. 98–9).[14] In short, because we do not know what is sound and what is music—and thus do not know what is diegetic and what is non-diegetic—we are not able to separate what Samus hears from what we hear. We are simultaneously hearing things as she does and, because we may change her in-game actions based on sounds, vice versa. Tanaka's soundscape thus becomes an experimental reflection of how we interact with games—the fine line between human and machine, or between player and avatar.

*Metroid* emerged during a crucial era in the history of game audio, when many of the industry's prevailing trends were established, and its innovative sound design has gone on to influence decades of games since the 1980s. Although Tanaka was no longer involved with the series, we can find many of the same techniques employed in the Super Nintendo Entertainment System's *Super Metroid* (1994), including significant stretches of ambiguous musical silence. In the later 1980s and 1990s, Tanaka went on to work on the quirky *Mother* series of games for the NES and SNES, in which he and his co-audio-designer continued to push the boundaries of what music in video games could, and should, be. Narratives of game audio in the NES era often view the sound capabilities of early games purely as a technological hurdle to be overcome. Tanaka's cybernetic soundscapes for *Metroid*, however, illustrate the range of expressive possibilities inherent in this new electronic medium—through his work, designers and listeners alike learned to embrace the sounds in the machine.

## Notes

1. In Lerner's words, 'If the four-tone loop [of *Space Invaders*] is heard as the 'marching alien feet', their representation of something from the world of the game's story would enable the loop to be understood as a diegetic sound, but the short motivic loop is constructed in such a way that it functions at least equally well as a nondiegetic sound, four notes that form what can be seen as the most musically complete video game score up to its time' (2014b, p. 328).
2. Lerner, for example, has compellingly argued that such classic games as *Donkey Kong* (1981) and *Super Mario Bros.* (1984) pay homage to early cinematic models in their musical and narrative choices (2014a, p. 1). On the increasingly complex relationship between film and video games, see, for example, Brookey, 2010 and the essays in Papazian and Sommers, 2013.
3. Given the paucity of biographical research on game-music composers, I am relying for information on Tanaka on published interviews with the composer, particularly a lengthy 2014 interview conducted as part of the Red Bull Music Academy (RBMA) series. See also Greening, 2014.
4. As Tanaka points out in a 2012 interview: 'When I first entered the company, I was in the arcade division. They were creating arcade games. I was creating sound effects for arcade games, so I was in charge of making things like the boom-boom-boom sounds in *Donkey Kong*, or Mario's walking sound and jumping sound. I created specific electricity circuits for those specific sounds' (Parish, 2012).

5. Tanaka left Nintendo in 1999, focusing on creating music for the *Pokémon* anime and related games. He is currently the President of Creatures (now a subsidiary of Nintendo), which produces all Pokémon media.
6. Collins, for example, notes that 'By altering the volume and adjusting the timing of the [NES's] two pulse channels, phasing, echo effects, and vibrato could be simulated, as in *Metroid*'s 'Mother Brain' ['Zebetite'] and 'Kraid'.... *Metroid* also made other uncommon applications of the channels, such as the use of pulse wave for bass with triangle lead, in the 'hideout' music for the game' (2008, p. 23).
7. Music for the NES (and other consoles of the era) was frequently composed in infinitely repeatable loops both to conserve scarce memory resources and to allow for the indeterminacy of player action (e.g., how long an individual player would take to complete any given section of the game).
8. Here I am drawing track titles from the Game Sound Museum release of the *Metroid* soundtrack, released in 2004 by Scitron Digital Contents.
9. Although I believe 'Silence' is likely to be perceived by listeners as unmetered, it is possible to map the melody onto a 21-beat repeating pattern at approximately 150 BPM, and the bass 'burbling' onto a two-beat pattern (with the 'burbles' at approximately 60 BPM). Many thanks to Dana Plank for sharing her transcriptions and analysis of this music with me.
10. Perhaps coincidentally, the bass melody in 'Tourian' begins with the same intervals as the 'Castle' theme from *Super Mario Bros.*, released the previous year on the NES. It is possible that Tanaka was subtly nodding to the extreme popularity of the other game, suggesting to players that Tourian is the 'boss area' of *Metroid*, or both.
11. On the influence of cybernetics on the Barrons, and their concepts of 'living circuits', see Wierzbicki, 2005, especially Chapter 2.
12. The manual consistently uses masculine pronouns to describe Samus, presumably to ensure that the 'reveal' of her feminine form at the conclusion of the game would be a shock to players.
13. As Steven Reale and other scholars have begun to explore, this ambiguity has even been cultivated in games to an extent that in some games the sound/music ambiguity becomes an element of gameplay, example of which would include *Rez* (2001), *BIT.TRIP RUNNER* (2010), *Dyad* (2012), and *140* (2013). For an insightful analysis of game design as compositional process, see Reale, 2014, pp. 77–103.
14. The *Silent Hill* series, and survival horror games writ large, has attracted considerable scholarly attention for sound design, particularly for this frequent blurring of diegetic (and meta-diegetic) boundaries. See, for example: Whalen, 2004; Van Elferen, 2011, pp. 30–9; Roux-Giraux, 2010, pp. 192–212; and Roberts, 2014, pp. 138–150.

## References

Altman, R., J. McGraw and S. Tatroe (2000) 'Inventing the Cinema Soundtrack: Hollywood's Multiplane Sound System' in J. Buhler, C. Flinn, and D. Neumeyer (eds) *Music and Cinema* (Hanover, NH: Wesleyan University Press): 339–59.

Brandon, A. (2002) 'Shooting from the Hip: An Interview with Hip Tanaka'. *Gamasutra*, 25 September, http://www.gamasutra.com/view/feature/2947/shooting_from_the_hip_an_.php, date accessed 5 August 2015.

Brookey, R.A. (2010) *Hollywood Gamers: Digital Convergence in the Film and Video Game Industries* (Bloomington: Indiana University Press).

Cheng, W. (2014) *Sound Play: Video Games and the Musical Imagination* (Oxford and New York: Oxford University Press, 2014).

Collins, K. (2008) *Game Sound: An Introduction to the History, Theory, and Practice of Video Game Music and Sound Design* (Cambridge, MA and London: MIT Press, 2008).

Collins, K. (2013) *Playing with Sound: A Theory of Interacting with Sound and Music in Video Games* (Cambridge, MA and London: MIT Press).

Greening, C. (2014) 'Hirokazu Tanaka Profile', *Game Music Online*, http://www.vgmonline.net/hirokazutanaka/, date accessed 5 August 2015.

Greenwald, T. (1986) 'The Self-Destructing Modules Behind the Revolutionary 1956 Soundtrack of *Forbidden Planet*', *Keyboard* (February), 59.

Hannan, M. and M. Carey (2004) 'Ambient Soundscapes in *Blade Runner*' in P. Hayward (ed.) *Off the Planet: Music, Sound and Science-Fiction Cinema* (Eastleigh, UK: John Libbey), 149–164.

Jeriaska (2009) 'GameSetBaiyon: 'An Audience with Hirokazu Hip Tanaka', *GameSetWatch*, 10 December, http://www.gamesetwatch.com/2009/12/gamesetbaiyon_hirokazu_hip_tanaka.php, date accessed 5 August 2015.

Lerner, N. (2014a) 'Mario's Dynamic Leaps: Musical Innovations (and the Specter of Early Cinema) in *Donkey Kong* and *Super Mario Bros.*' in K.J. Donnelly, W. Gibbons and N. Lerner (eds) *Music in Video Games: Studying Play* (New York and London: Routledge), 1–29.

Lerner, N. (2014b) 'Musical Style in Video Games, 1977–1983' in D. Neumeyer (ed.) *The Oxford Handbook of Film Music Studies* (Oxford and New York: Oxford University Press), 319–347.

Leydon, R. (2004) '*Forbidden Planet*: Effects and Affects in the Electro Avant-garde' in P. Hayward (ed.) *Off the Planet: Music, Sound and Science Fiction Cinema* (Eastleigh, UK: John Libbey), 61–76.

*Metroid Instruction Manual* (1986), 7.

Papazian, G. and J. M. Sommers (eds) (2013) *Game On, Hollywood: Essays on the Intersection of Video Games and Cinema* (Jefferson, NC: McFarland).

Parish, J. (2012) 'A Conversation with Hip Tanaka', *1up.com* (August), http://www.1up.com/features/conversation-hip-tanaka, date accessed 5 August 2015.

Prock, S. (2014) 'Strange Voices: Subjectivity and Gender in *Forbidden Planet's* Soundscape of Tomorrow', *The Journal of the Society for American Music*, Vol. 8, 371–400.

Reale, S.B. (2014) 'Transcribing Musical Worlds; or, Is *L.A. Noire* a Music Game?' in K.J. Donnelly, W. Gibbons and N. Lerner (eds) *Music in Video Games: Studying Play* (London and New York: Routledge), 77–103.

Red Bull Music Academy (RBMA) series, https://www.youtube.com/watch?v=F7J5GlE3YLQ, date accessed 5 August 2015.

Roberts, R. (2014) 'Fear of the Unknown: Music and Sound Design in Psychological Horror Games', in K.J. Donnelly, W. Gibbons and N. Lerner (eds) *Music in Video Games: Studying Play* (London and New York: Routledge), 138–150.

Roux-Giraux, G. (2010) 'Listening to Fear: A Study of Sound in Horror Computer Games' in M. Grimshaw (ed.) *Game Sound Technology and Player Interaction: Concepts and Developments* (Hershey, PA: IGI Global), 192–212.

Ryan, J. (2011) *Super Mario: How Nintendo Conquered America* (New York: Penguin).

Wierzbicki, J. (2005) *Louis and Bebe Barron's Forbidden Planet: A Film Score Guide* (Lanham, MD, Toronto, and Oxford: Scarecrow).

Van Elferen, I. (2011) '¡Un Forastero! Issues of Virtuality and Diegesis in Videogame Music', *Music and the Moving Image*, Vol. 4, No. 2, 30–39.

Whalen, Z. (2004) 'Play Along: An Approach to Video Game Music', *Game Studies* Vol. 4, No., http://www.gamestudies.org/0401/whalen/, date accessed 5 August 2015.

CHAPTER 25

# Redundancy and Information in Explanatory Voice-Ins and Voice-Offs

*Cormac Deane*

Science fiction narratives commonly open with an explanatory voiceover, as in the 1981 film *Escape from New York* (John Carpenter): 'In 1988, the crime rate in the United States rises four hundred percent. The once great city of New York becomes the one maximum security prison for the entire country. ...'. As a genre, science fiction suffers from a heavy expository burden in establishing the norms of its alternative universe, and this helps to explain its prominent use of voiceovers. On television, a show's central premise may be reiterated at the start of every episode, as in *Star Trek* (1966–1969): 'Space: the final frontier. These are the voyages of the starship Enterprise. Its five-year mission: to explore strange new worlds, to seek out new life and new civilizations, to boldly go where no man has gone before'. In this chapter, I would like to draw attention to spoken information-bearing statements such as these and to suggest that their capacity to bear information to the viewer-listener may not in fact be their main function. By comparing how these voice-ins and voice-offs do or do not correlate with what is simultaneously seen, I suggest some reasons to account for the great deal of redundancy and repetition to be found in contemporary mainstream film and television. In particular, I examine industry norms in automated dialogue replacement (ADR), the noises of computers and war-machines in the technoscientific genre (as well as the speech of their operators), and infant speech for evidence of how communicational acts are not necessarily primarily motivated by the need to convey narrative information.

In screen narratives, detailed information that is essential for narrative development is conveyed primarily by the voice. The key term is *information*, especially if we understand it in the terms of information theory, where information is what is conveyed in a communications system, as opposed to the code that

C. Deane
Institute of Art, Design and Technology, Dublin, Ireland

is used (e.g., language), the technology that is used (e.g., screen and speakers), or the circumstances and identities of the sender and receiver. Of course, these elements are not separable from one another; rather, they exist in a hierarchical relation, which we will return to later. For the time being, I would like to consider the informational characteristics of explanatory voice-ins (i.e., when a character is visible and speaking) and explanatory voice-offs (i.e., when a character is invisible and speaking), especially as they are heard in markedly 'technoscientific' genres in film and television, such as forensic drama (*CSI*, 2000– present; *NCIS*, 2003– present; *Investigator Mariko*, 1999–2014), action/spy drama (*24*, 2001–2014; *Spooks*, 2002–2011; *Déjà Vu*, Tony Scott, 2006; the *Bourne* and *Mission Impossible* franchises, 2002–2012 and 1996–2015), military drama (*WarGames*, John Badham, 1983) and submarine narratives (*The Hunt for Red October*, John McTiernan, 1990; *The Abyss*, James Cameron, 1989), as well as science fiction, the ultimate machinic genre (the *Alien*, *Star Wars* and *Terminator* franchises/1979–2012, 1977–2015, and 1984–2015/). What all of these have in common is that their narratives centre on, or even consist solely of, the manipulation of technology.

Christian Metz observes that 'cinema draws all machines into itself because it is itself one' (2016, p. 115). So not only is the theme of the human struggle with and against implacable industrial technology a long established one, but the brutal logic of mechanization and the inhuman speed of the cinematic apparatus animate that very technology—consider Buster Keaton's *The General* (1926), Fritz Lang's *Metropolis* (1927), Charlie Chaplin's *Modern Times* (1936), Henri Clouzot's *The Wages of Fear* (1953), Louis Malle's *Lift to the Scaffold* (1958), Steven Spielberg's *Duel* (1971), Wolfgang Petersen's *Das Boot* (1981), and James Cameron's *Terminator* (1984). But it is the industrial temporal object (Stiegler, 2011, pp. 8–78) of the screen itself that in the past 20 years or so has become the key location/mise-en-scène in the technoscientific genres. More specifically, we find ourselves repeatedly in the control room, a place where a system is operated remotely by people seated at consoles and facing a bank of screens in a microcosmic refiguring of the cinematic *dispositif* itself. In control room scenes, we commonly watch the screens of computers that are being analysed inside the narrative and it is the explanatory voice-ins and voice-offs that accompany these that are of interest here because the 'problem' that immediately arises is that of redundancy.

In terms of information theory, redundancy refers to the parts of a message that are not informational, but that may not be removed from the message if it is to remain comprehensible (Shannon, 1948, pp. 398–9). In other words, it is a measurement of relative wastage. It seems appropriate to apply this kind of understanding of information and wastage here because these narratives are themselves about the management of the world by means of cybernetic communications systems, which are constructed on a substrate of information theory. And the penetration of informatic thinking goes deeper still—this is at the heart of Stiegler's concept of technics (Stiegler, 1994, pp. 13–18), after all, which is concerned with the industrialization of memory (Stiegler,

2008, pp. 97–187) and the proletarization of perception (Lemmens, 2011, pp. 33–41), both directly implemented by the culture industries of the twentieth century, cinema chief among them.

The great redundancy of dialogue in the technoscientific screen narrative seems at first glance to be at variance with the narrational complex that is the Hollywood system, with its extremely high levels of efficiency and its much-touted abhorrence of 'telling' in favour of 'showing'. And yet, redundancy is very evident in a television series such as *24*, which features heavily the Fantasy User Interfaces (FUIs) of control room screens at the headquarters of the secret government agency, the Counter-Terrorism Unit (CTU). The FUIs feature reams of numbers to indicate vast data sets that refer to concepts such as geographical location and vital life signs, and which are somehow derived from or applied to photographic or video images. Grids, coordinates, and other indicators of measurement are also prominent features. Their meaningfulness varies enormously from on-screen text that informs us that the computer is 'analysing data' to incomprehensibly complex lines of code. At 11.55 AM in Season 5 of *24*, two CTU agents in separate locations watch a satellite image of a car. At first, the FUI displays the information clearly, and the dialogue, which is heard in voice-in and voice-off, mirrors this: 'Valerie, the feed should be coming through to your laptop now'. But then the image quality deteriorates: 'Something's wrong. The feed's breaking up'. The same thing happens on the other screen: 'We're experiencing the same problem with our signal'. Finally, one CTU operator finds the source of the problem: 'I'm tracing the corruption [keyboard is tapped for 3 seconds] … it's the server'. The map/satellite images in this sequence (and often in others) are always accompanied by a smaller screen window where the same information in computer 'code' is displayed, that is, incomprehensible alphanumeric 'content' that scrolls down like an over-fast credit sequence. The repetition of the same information as screen text, as screen image, and as dialogue arises from the challenge of ensuring that the viewer does not get lost in the complications of plot development and from the pleasure afforded by a kind of computational aesthetic.

An associated phenomenon is the array of sounds that accompany the movement of icons, text, frames, and images on the embedded screens of computers within technoscientific screen narratives. Why should it be that these screens play effectively like animated sound films, given that computers do not generally make any noises at all in reality? In the constant security crisis of the narrative universes of *24*, *Spooks* and *Homeland* (2011– present), for instance, the panoply of screen sounds might be justified as necessary for alerting the screen operator to what is important. For example, in the 10–11 PM episode of Season 6 of *24*, a blurry image of a vehicle is processed on-screen to reveal its registration plate. The activity of processing is indicated visually by a blue bar that staggers across the image, resolving and recognizing every digit with every shift to the right. In synch with this moving bar, we and the computer operator hear staccato bleeps, ending with a trill of completion. But we know from the literature on sociotechnical systems that for maximum efficiency, the amount of data, whether visual or aural, that is directed at control room operators ought to be kept to a minimum (Nigawara et al., 1994; Woods et al., 2002), and we know from critics of hyper-capitalism that human attention has become even more scarce than physical resources (Rifkin, 2000, p. 94). And yet, fictional computer interfaces are very noisy.

Clearly, these sounds are both unrealistic and redundant, but this does not prevent their being added here and throughout the genre. It may help to think of them in terms of what Michel Chion calls the acousmetre (1999, pp. 18–19), which is a sound whose source is unseen. If they are indeed acousmetres, then the implication is that the work of computation that we can hear is taking place somewhere else, that is, not on the computer monitor. This being the case, then we can regard this noise of computation as a sound effect (or possibly even a Foley effect, if we grant a degree of embodiment to the computer), because it is a non-vocal representation of an off-screen activity. However, the millisecond-perfect synchronization of sound and moving screen image and their suggestively semantic melodies tempt us to believe that the sounds are being made by the objects on the screen itself, even though we know that this makes little sense; we do not think that we can hear the voice of the object on screen, but we may attribute some kind of cognition to it. It seems to be uttering something, enunciating something, so we ought not to think of its sounds as Foley effects. What we are confronted with here is the very paradox of viewership that is at the heart of all film-watching, which is that we simultaneously know and deny that what is on screen is not real, and that the images on screen are not actually making the sounds that we can hear. No satisfactory moment of de-acousmatization, that is, revealing of a sound's unseen source, is offered in instances of computer screen sounds. But this should not surprise us because, as Chion and Mladen Dolar both observe, de-acousmatization always opens up a gap of doubts about the never-quite-matching materiality and immateriality of sound and image (Chion, 1999, pp. 33–47; Dolar, 2006, p. 65); Chion's term for this potentially monstrous conjunction of voice and body, in Hitchcock's *Psycho* in particular, is the *anacousmetre* (pp. 140–51). So when we remember that the sounds of computers are, phenomenologically speaking, unnecessary and unmotivated, the insight that they are, psychoanalytically speaking, necessary and motivated, reveals the extent to which desire (for wholeness, for simultaneity, for presence) is at work when sound is added to screen effects. Added sound, therefore, operates as a supplement to the image, which is to say that in the same movement it covers over and reveals a gap between what we really know about the reality of what is on screen and what we really want to believe about it. And that movement, like a symptom, must be repeated.

## Information and Repetition

The mere act of repetition itself provides a kind of desirable affect for the viewer. Repetition is also central to many film music scores. Although a detailed discussion of this area of research falls outside of the scope of this chapter, listening to film music is key to understanding how repetition is used to create leitmotifs, evoke and transform genre, interpret images, and (attempt to) establish and unify mood and cultural context (for more on these, see Flinn (1992), Paulin (2000) and Scheurer (2008)). The repetition of speech, to return to our central topic, is readily apparent in the submarine movie, a great proportion of which involves the operation of machines by men at control panels as well as, crucially, spoken commands and spoken acknowledgments of commands concerning the operation of machines and concerning the relay and interpretation of data in a very information-heavy genre. Witness a typical submarine dialogue scenario early in the 1957 movie *The Enemy Below* (Dick Powell), where the German U-boat captain and his sonar officer try to interpret the sonic ping that is echoing back towards them from an American destroyer. The ping is visualized as a kink in a straight line on a monitor, which metronomically refreshes every couple of seconds with a sonic pulse. Engrossed in this machinic logic, the captain finally reaches a decision and the following dialogue is heard:

> Captain von Stolberg: Port twenty degrees, Schwaffel.
> Lieutenant Commander Schwaffel [raised voice into adjoining room]: Port twenty degrees.
> German Officer on Deck: Port twenty degrees.
> German Rudder Operator: Port twenty.
> [Dissolve from the German monitor to the American monitor]
> American Sonar Operator: Target's course changing to port.
> American Navigator: [plotting movements on a map-chart] Target's turning left, Captain. Twenty-five ... [corrects himself] Twenty degrees.

The information that is transmitted to the viewer is contained not only in its datum, but also in its performative aspects. The sequence above enacts a chain of command, transforms a command into an action, informs us that the German captain's command has been effected, demonstrates how the two sides are engaged in a shared, simultaneous, real-time technological imaginary, and in doing all of these provides informational, machinic affect. The submarine and the destroyer, it is clear, are cybernetic machines that are operated according to cybernetic cycles of command and control, information loops and feedback, input and output, protocol and execution, screen and voice.

And still there is more to what is achieved by redundancy and repetition. The more redundant a statement is, the more we become aware of it as an act of communication, as enunciation and, as such, a source of something other than mere information. In *The Princess Bride* (Rob Reiner, 1987), we hear the following dialogue as a swordfight rages between the speakers:

> Inigo Montoya:
> Hello. My name is Inigo Montoya. You killed my father. Prepare to die.
> Hello. My name is Inigo Montoya. You killed my father. Prepare to die.
> Hello. My name is Inigo Montoya. You killed my father. Prepare to die.

Count Rugen:
Stop saying that!
Inigo Montoya:
Hello. My name is Inigo Montoya. You killed my father. Prepare to die.

We have moved away from the technoscientific genre, but the point to be made here is indeed a broad one about which aspects of a message are more prominent than others. In any act of communication, the emphasis may be on the channel of communication (as in the examples from *24*), it may be on the speaker's emotional state (as in *The Princess Bride*), it may be on the desired effect upon the hearer (as in the commands in *The Enemy Below*), or on a combination of these or other emphases. As Roman Jakobson says, the general point is: 'If we analyze language from the standpoint of the information it carries, we cannot restrict the notion of information to the cognitive aspect of language' (1985, p. 153).

It is clear in *The Princess Bride* that the information that is conveyed in the statement is cognitively significant only on its first iteration (in fact, he delivers it for the first time some minutes before this sequence). The dogged repetition by Inigo Montoya transforms the statement into a ritualized threat, a personal code, a mantra, a perverse death rite, a culmination of a revenge subplot, and a justification for killing. It is also comical, idiosyncratic, playful, quotable, and highly memorable. These characteristics in turn remind us of the non-rational properties of repetitive speech in poetry, religious rite and music. The stock epithet in Homer, for instance, is a phrase with a fixed metrical pattern that is repeatedly used throughout an epic poem. Thus, in the *Iliad*, the phrase 'swift-footed Achilles' comes up again and again at least in part because it (*pódas ōkús Akhilleús*) is metrically convenient for ending a line in dactylic hexameter. The *Iliad* comes from an oral tradition and so epithets are a desirable form of redundancy because they have a mnemonic purpose, and their repetition performs a kind of emphatic, honorific purpose.

## ADR and Infant Speech

In the postproduction phase of many films and television shows, actors are brought in to a recording studio to re-voice dialogue that has been poorly captured or delivered and sometimes to record entirely new lines. This process is known as automated (or automatic) dialogue replacement (ADR) or looping. ADR is a method of adding sound at points where it may be perceived to be inadequate or missing; as such, it reveals a lot about normative attitudes to how sound and image ought to form a coherent whole (i.e., to integrate) and how they ought to be yoked meaningfully (i.e., to be integrated).

ADR is a successful method of maximizing efficiency in the filmmaking process. Because a live sound recording may be 'polluted' by an accidental or unforeseen noise, such as an overflying helicopter, the problem can often be easily tidied up at the ADR stage, at a lesser expense than reshooting the scene. But the very efficiency of ADR brings its own problems, as new material can be captured to fill in any perceived or imagined blanks in plotting and exposition, potentially resulting in a bloated, inefficient dialogue track replete with unnecessary content.

The difficulty that ADR presents for analysis points precisely to its salient aspects. 'Good' ADR, where the viewer does not detect a piece of dialogue as having been added in at a later stage, is no good for analysis because it is by definition impossible to identify. Several factors have to be in play for this to happen: the actor must succeed in re-creating the vocal energy achieved possibly months before in an entirely different context; the recordist must convincingly mix the new material, occasionally going so far as to source the microphones used during shooting; the spoken sound must synch exactly with filmed mouth movement, or timed in a plausible way to be heard when the actor's mouth is not visible. In addition, the director and/or producer must avoid the temptation provided by ADR to have the actor commit the Hollywood sin of 'telling not showing' by inserting too much expository dialogue in voice-off. ADR is a process dedicated to recording voice-ins, so adding voice-off exposition is not strictly an affordance of ADR per se, but the 'We'll fix it in post' attitude means that the possibility of adding (or taking away) dialogue in the post-production phase is difficult to ignore.

'Bad' ADR, by contrast, is good for the purposes of analysis because we notice it as ADR. The most egregious problem occurs when an actor seems to speak mouthlessly. For example, in *Thunderball* (Terence Young, 1965), the gadget-master Q (Desmond Llewelyn) impatiently commands 007, 'Now pay attention', without opening his mouth, displaying a technical sleight of mouth worthy of the mechanical toys that he specializes in while also issuing an instruction that would be best not carried out, at least not by the viewer. *Super Mario Bros* (Annabel Jankel and Rocky Morton, 1993), reputed to be one of whose post-production supervisor declared was the most heavily looped film ever (see Hoss and Applebaum, 2014a, 2014b for a full set of ADR notes), commits all kinds of ADR sins, so that actors speak without opening their mouths on perhaps a dozen identifiable occasions, while there are many instances where we cannot see a character's mouth properly as they speak in long shot, and several dozen instances of clunky exposition being delivered in voice-off. Such overuse is often an indicator of deeper problems in a production, and these are indeed apparent in the narrative development, tone, mood, set, costume design, and actors' performances of *Super Mario Bros*.

The sounds made by infants on screen is a revealing type of 'bad' ADR, in the sense that baby sounds quite frequently accompany on-screen babies whose mouths are closed. Although we must classify infant speech as non-semantic, certainly from the point of view of information, we find that it is sufficiently meaningful to be added to the image, however badly. The poor match of infant speech and image may be an unavoidable side-effect of the technical challenge that the situation poses, but that poor matching may be acceptable and possibly even desirable, as we shall see.

In *The Godfather* (Francis Ford Coppola, 1972), when Vito Corleone is brought home from hospital, all the grandchildren are there to welcome him back. The sound of the crying baby amid the hustle and bustle of the crowded hallway, as the don, still on a stretcher, is carried up the stairs, brings a strong sense of domesticity, of a multi-generational, traditional household and, above all, of family, so important to the film and its genre. But the on-screen baby is patently not producing the crying sound that we hear. In Max Ophüls's *The Earrings of Madame de …* (1953), a similarly busy scene of an extended family gathered in one room to celebrate the arrival of a new infant is accompanied throughout by the sound of its wailing. But when we finally see the placid baby at the end of the scene, it is obvious that this child has not been making any noise.

These instances may not be too surprising, given that the baby in each case is as much a cipher as a character. However, in the comedy *Three Men and a Baby* (Leonard Nimoy, 1987), the baby's intense crying is the central concern of her first scene, when the ham-fisted bachelor played by Steve Guttenberg struggles to find a way to make her stop. In general, the sounds of the baby are quite well matched to her movements, but it is clear as the scene goes on that she is not crying as violently as the soundtrack suggests, and Guttenberg increasingly holds her at an angle that prevents us from seeing her face. Another baby-dominated narrative, *Raising Arizona* (Joel and Ethan Coen, 1987), tries to avoid the problem by nearly always having its babies make noises in *off*, but is often unsuccessful when babies make noises while on screen. Most striking of all, *Look Who's Talking* (Amy Heckerling, 1989) and *Look Who's Talking Too* (Amy Heckerling, 1990), where adult actors speak for toddler actors, rudimentary attempts are made to match mouth movement with speech. If no attempt at all had been made, we could regard the adult voices as the internal thoughts of the children in question, but the fact that there is occasional matching blurs the issue and suggests that the spoken words are in fact being spoken by the children in the worldview of the children, if not in the worldview of the viewer.

Apparently, different rules seem to apply for matching baby sounds to baby images, and even high-budget movies are somehow immune from criticism, despite demanding quite a lot of license from viewers whose suspension of disbelief is conventionally total. If a sense of babyness is conveyed, that is enough. A baby is not a screen or a voice actor, so it may be more appropriate to think of the matching process as Foley sound, rather than ADR. That is, ADR is concerned with supplying a plausible recorded voice to fit an actor who is seen to be speaking, while Foley supplies other sound effects. An imperfectly matched baby sound is not intended to be understood as emanating from the baby's mouth, so we can regard it as simply a sound effect. On the other hand, as we watch *Look Who's Talking* and *Look Who's Talking Too* we are acutely aware of the adult voice-actors (Bruce Willis, Roseanne Barr) as people in the ADR studio trying and failing to achieve impossible lip-synchs. We know from Chion that lip-synching is crucial in order for the spectator to trust in the unity of body and voice on screen (1999, pp. 127, 129), and from Mary-Anne

Doane, that strict marrying of sound and vision in classical editing is a way of suppressing the heterogeneity of captured sound and image in order to provide an illusory presence to the shadows and sounds that are the cinematic experience (1980, p. 47). Given these, the implication seems to be that an on-screen baby is not to be regarded as fully human because it cannot act, it cannot match its image to its sounds.

At play here are the very mechanisms by which meaning is produced in sound film. Metz observed some years ago that 'because the theatre is too real, theatrical fictions yield only a weak impression of reality' (1974, p. 10), whereas cinema achieves its reality-effect by the patent irrealism of its technology, which serves as a kind of lightning conductor for our scepticism and enables us to suspend our disbelief in relation to the supposedly true reality within the film. Babies are an anomaly because their status as actors who do not act (i.e., real people) means they are neither part of the illusion nor separate from it. In cinema and television, an entity to which no sound can be securely assigned belongs to an uncanny category. Infants cannot speak (that is what *infant* means), which explains why babies rarely appear prominently in film or television, why a certain leeway is given by the usually demanding average viewer to mismatches of baby sounds and movements, and why highly artificial devices are employed to compensate for their inability to be part of the illusion, such as adult-voicing in the *Look Who's Talking* films. But it is clear that the background assumption throughout is that infant speech is regarded as non-linguistic, non-communicational, in the classical matrix, in a similar manner to how Martin Heidegger speaks of animals: deprived of speech, they are limited to and by their instinctual drives (1995, pp. 305–9). We will come back to this later.

## Waves of Redundancy

A lack of spoken language is not the same as a lack of communication. This is known by everyone who has met a baby and by everyone who has watched a silent film. Part of the problem we face in talking about redundancy is the word itself, with its connotations of uselessness, unemployability, and obtuseness. When we are struck by redundant speech on screen, it is useful to recognize its roots in Latin *re-* (again) and *unda* (wave). Redundant means overflowing, abundant, bounteous, loaded, as well as excessive, overdetermined, and overloaded (see Altman, 1980, p. 67 and p. 76 on sound/image redundancy).

When surfeit is present on a communication channel, we are in the realm of symbolic exchange, where the thing being exchanged is exchange itself, as a performative relationship-forming act. The Lacanian symbolic order is based on the exchange of gifts that in themselves are useless, akin to descriptions by Lévi-Strauss and Marcel Mauss of how the exchange of gifts is a formal procedure that helps establish a social order. As Slavoj Žižek describes it, 'The symbolic order emerges from a gift, an offering, which neutralizes its content in order to declare itself as a gift: when a gift is offered, what matters is not its content but the link between the giver and the receiver established when the other accepts the gift' (2006, p. 12). In this respect, the accumulation of explanatory voice-ins or voice-offs in, say, *Spooks* tips us off that the information that is being transmitted may not in fact be the primary function of what we hear. Instead, what we are witnessing is communication per se, the medium per se. Tom Gunning's powerful concept of the cinema of attractions (1986) helps us understand that when the technological medium of display itself becomes an object for our eyes and ears to enjoy, we can be lifted free of the demands of narrative and delivered into a kind of technological jouissance. When the explanatory voice-in or voice-off intervenes, it is forming a bond with us by directing its address towards us without addressing us directly.

As Žižek points out, the common sense notion of language as an instrument for communication, a set of signs for transmitting meanings (2006, p. 12), has a sociopathic dimension as it does not consider the affective qualities of communicative acts. We could also characterize information theory and the entire cybernetic apparatus that is based on it as having sociopathic tendencies, in the sense that the transfer of messages is a function of protocol, not social relation. In the presence of this kind of logic, symbolic exchange irrupts by overloading the communication channel with 'noise', making it impossible to ignore the act of communication as act.

## Communication as Communication

Michel Serres's idea of the parasite (1982) is a useful tool in this respect, as the French *parasite* means not only 'parasite' in English but also 'noise' in the sense of interference or static on a communication channel. Serres finds parasitism at work in all communicational situations, crucially noting its potential yet often effaced bidirectionality. A parasite and a host cast each other into their respective roles, to the point that the parasite introduces a new set of relations into the ecology of the host that makes it possible for the host to be itself and to be other. Viewed this way, a host can be regarded as parasitizing the environment that the parasite has helped to create. If we recall the back and forth between the possible designation of baby sounds as ADR or as Foley, we can see a similar binary start to come loose at the seams. The range of what soundtypes is covered by Foley or ADR, respectively, maps on to definitions of noise and sound, non-human and human, irrelevance and importance.

It becomes possible to ask the question: why do we find certain sounds to be redundant, but not certain images? What would redundant moving images look like? Perhaps a music video is more disposable than the song it 'illustrates' or 'explains'? Other candidates: *Little Big Man* (Arthur Penn, 1970), where the aged hero commands the historian-interviewer to switch on the tape recorder so that he can recount his life, which then appears to us via dissolve as an extended flashback; *Thunderball*, once again, where James Bond (Sean Connery), listening to a tape recording of footsteps, follows with his eyes (in point of view shot) the imaginary path that an intruder has just taken through his hotel room; *Letter from Siberia* (Chris Marker, 1958), where the same piece of film is shown several times in succession with vastly different reportage-voiceovers, each adjusting our interpretation of what we are seeing; *Train* and other cinema advertisements (1994–2003) that accompany the capacities of Dolby sound systems with image tracks, as analysed by Vivian Sobchack (2005); *Citizen Kane* (Orson Welles, 1941), where Leland's narration is bookended by the elderly version of himself being interviewed by the faceless reporter; *Double Indemnity* (Billy Wilder, 1944), where the narrative plays out as a simultaneous re-enactment of the spoken confession made by the anti-hero on the voice-recording device in his office. To different degrees, all of these (but particularly the final two) are influenced by what Fredric Jameson calls the radio aesthetic of the 1930s and 1940s, where 'the visual is always presumably incomplete' and the '"talkie" [is] a kind of radio film' (1993, p. 36).

Clearly, it makes only a limited amount of sense to regard all of these imagetracks as redundant, no matter how defined. We cannot lose sight of the fact that, while a film without sound is still a film, sound without film is 'only' sound. One of the aims here, however, is to indicate the extent to which contemporary technoscientific narratives in particular depart quite radically from the classical Hollywood system of seamlessness and coherence (if in fact this system was ever thoroughly consistent, or merely a set of general tendencies). The computational aesthetic in particular determines and is determined by a set of behaviours that are much more interactive than has traditionally been the case. To be sure, devices such as direct address, text on screen, explanatory voiceover, and so on are not exactly new, especially when we include television in our survey, but it is worth noting that the return that they yield is to a large degree far more than informational, and this explains the great investment of time and energy that is made in the screen environments that are sutured into shows such as *CSI*, *24*, and *Homeland* and films such as those in the *Bourne* franchise.

## Dead Ahead

In an air or space battle scene, such as in the *Star Wars* films, it is convenient that the pilots speak to one another by radio about what they can see and what they are about to do. Convenient because it allows for multiple explanatory voice-ins and voice-offs that strike the viewer as what the pilots might 'really' say to one another. So in *Episode III—Revenge of the Sith* (George Lucas, 2005), we share Anakin's (Hayden Christensen) point of view shot as he informs Obi-Wan (Ewan McGregor), who is flying next to him: 'General Grievous's ship is directly ahead. The one crawling with vulture droids'. Obi Wan acknowledges, 'Ah, I see it'. A minute or two later, Anakin re-identifies the target, just as we also see it: 'The General's command ship is dead ahead'. The information that is relayed among pilots, ground crew, control room operators, and others in the technoscientific genres consists of status updates, countdowns, acknowledgements of orders, and so on; but the intrinsic function of this communication is naming the thing that is in our sight. During flight scenes in *Top Gun* (Tony Scott, 1986), voice does not correlate to lip movement due to the pilots' oxygen masks, so the characters are distinguished by vividly different helmets, each emblazoned in full capitals with their nicknames. When Tom Cruise's character takes off in his jet from an aircraft carrier in a dizzyingly dynamic shot, he straightaway announces, referring to himself in the third person, 'Maverick is airborne'. This announcement is partly addressed to the control tower operators, partly to the awestruck viewer, and partly to the self-regarding ego of Cruise-Maverick. Naming what we can see undoubtedly amounts to uttering the glaringly obvious, it is true, though showing what we have been informed of by the sound track is not considered a sin when it is committed by the image track (in this vein, for a critique of the conventional priority of image over sound, see Altman, 1980, pp. 67–8).

The technoscientific genre is especially rewarding for analysis because it repeatedly enacts the key act of enunciation that is at the heart of all cinema's meaning-making activity. Metz makes it clear in 'The Cinema: Language or Language System?' that the cinema does not relay meaning to us in discrete parcels in the way that language does:

> A close-up of a revolver does not mean 'revolver' (a purely virtual lexical unit), but at the very least, and without speaking of connotations, it signifies 'Here is a revolver!' It carries with it a kind of *here* ... (1974, p. 67)

The cinematic shot is equivalent to an utterance, just as much as the explanatory voice-in or voice-off. What seems at first sight to be some kind of contaminant of the screen's capacity to 'show not tell' in fact merely brings to the fore the image's status as utterance, something which the whole system of seamlessness works to conceal. That very classical system is arguably in the process of dismantling itself from within by its growing consciousness of the screen's enunciative aspects, as has been identified in critiques of computer logic and aesthetics (Manovich, 2001, 2013; Fuller, 2005; Kittler, 1999), of neobaroque style (Cubitt, 2004, pp. 217–44), of reflexive and self-referential framing and plotting (Metz, 2016; Buckland, 2009), of the fungible temporality of screen technologies (Mulvey, 2006; Cubitt, 2004, pp. 207–12), and of the cinema-machine's capacity to mould time and space (Stiegler, 2011; Shaviro, 2010; Deleuze, 1989). To this list we might add non-scholarly explorations of hyperactive screen enunciation, such as *A Family Finds Entertainment* (2004) by video artist Ryan Trecartin, to name just one example. Finally, we ought also to consider regional screen traditions where acts of enunciation are not so hysterically suppressed; for instance, the vague mouth movements of Spaghetti westerns, whose international casts simply spoke in their own languages, and Japanese and Chinese *tokusatsu* drama, such as *Super Sentai* (1975– present), where directly recorded sound is rarely used and almost everything is synched afterwards, with considerable tolerance for 'imperfect' matches. Indeed, *Super Sentai* frequently obviates the challenge of lip-synching entirely by using helmets that include face masks with moulded, unmoving lips, which has a similar effect to that described in *Top Gun* above.

The thing that is disintegrating as we contemplate the screen in the era of its digital proliferation is not so much classical style, Hollywood or otherwise, but nothing less than humanistic metaphysics itself. Thinking about ADR in terms of enunciation forces us to face issues such as the status of speech, its meaningfulness, its relation to what is known and unknown, and who is or is not allowed, or supposed, to speak. These are all metaphysical issues, as Heidegger makes clear when he says that animals' lack of language condemns them to existing in the environment but not in the world. The implication of this is that mouthed sounds combined with coherent movement, that is, cognition, can only be attached to a conscious being; put inversely, if the mouth and its sounds do not match, the very capacity to be human is withdrawn. The screen's enormous overdetermination of speech has its correlate in Heidegger, when he says that 'the leap from living animals to humans that speak is as large if not larger than that from the lifeless stone to the living being' (Heidegger, 1980, p. 75; Aho, 2009, p. 18). Given this kind of logic, it is no wonder that the third instalment of the *Look Who's Talking* franchise, *Look Who's Talking Now* (Tom Ropelewski, 1993), has dogs instead of children being voiced by adult actors.

The efflorescence of enunciation in the digital era makes it possible to think differently about voice-in and voice-off speech. In the (globally dominant) English-speaking world, where dubbing is very rare, the match of mouth and sound has traditionally been highly prized. Evidence of enunciative alterity at work is either down to 'bad' technique or to naive viewing practices, as displayed in the *Calvin and Hobbes* comic strip when the young boy Calvin watches a dubbed Japanese programme and then comments 'I wonder why Japanese people keep moving their mouths after they're through talking' (Bill Watterson, 1986). But redundancy levels seem to be on the increase, due not only to the hegemony of technoscientific genres, but also to the infiltration of technoscientific gestures into all other genres—consider the simultaneous typing-and-voicing of the journalist Carrie in many episodes of *Sex and the City* (1998–2004). Redundant sounds and images show us that there is no clear distinction between information that is *about* the narrative and information which *is* the narrative. Attention to ADR practice reveals that screen-watching and screen-listening are dedicated only partly to the content of a sound or an image, that is, how it correlates or not to the external world, and in fact are just as dedicated to appreciation of acts of enunciation simply as acts of enunciation.

## References

Aho, K.A. (2009) *Heidegger's Neglect of the Body* (Albany: SUNY Press).
Altman, R. (1980) 'Moving Lips: Cinema as Ventriloquism', *Yale French Studies*, 60, 67–79.
Buckland W. (ed.) (2009), *Puzzle Films: Complex Storytelling in Contemporary Cinema* (Oxford: Blackwell).
Chion M. (1999) *The Voice in Cinema*, trans. by C. Gorbman (New York: Columbia University Press).

Cubitt, S. (2004) *The Cinema Effect* (Cambridge, MA: MIT Press).
Deleuze, G. (1989) *Cinema 2: The Time-Image*, trans. by H. Tomlinson (London: Athlone).
Doane, M.A. (1980) 'The Voice in the Cinema: The Articulation of Body and Space', *Yale French Studies*, 60, 33–50.
Dolar, M. (2006) *A Voice and Nothing More* (Cambridge, MA: MIT Press).
Flinn, C. (1992) *Strains of Utopia: Gender, Nostalgia, and Hollywood Film Music* (Princeton: Princeton University Press).
Fuller, M. (2005) *Media Ecologies: Materialist Energies in Art and Technoculture* (Cambridge, MA: MIT Press).
Gunning, T. (1986) 'The Cinema of Attraction: Early Film, Its Spectator, and the Avant-Garde', *Wide Angle*, Vol. 8, Nos. 3–4 (Fall), 1–14.
Heidegger, M. (1980) 'Hölderlin's "Germanium und Der Rhein"', ed. by S. Ziegler (Frankfurt am Main: Klostermann).
———. (1995) *The Fundamental Concepts of Metaphysics: World, Finitude, Solitude* (Bloomington, IN: Indiana University Press).
Hoss, R. and S. Applebaum (2014a) 'Post-Production Documents', *Super Mario Bros. The Movie Archive* http://www.smbmovie.com/SMBArchive/postproduction/postprod.htm#adr, 16 June 2015.
Hoss, R. and S. Applebaum (2014b) 'ADR Notes', *Super Mario Bros. The Movie Archive* http://www.smbmovie.com/SMBArchive/postproduction/docs/04-SMB_R&B_ADR_Notes_1-4-93.pdf, 16 June 2015.
Jakobson, R. (1985) 'Closing Statement: Linguistics and Poetics' in R. E. Innis (ed.) *Semiotics: An Introductory Reader* (London: Hutchinson), 150–6.
Jameson, F. (1993) 'The Synoptic Chandler' in J. Copjec (ed.) *Shades of Noir* (London: Verso), 33–56.
Kittler, F. (1999) *Gramophone, Film, Typewriter*, trans. by G. Winthrop-Young and M. Wutz (Stanford: Stanford University Press).
Lemmens, P. (2011) '"This System Does Not Produce Pleasure Anymore": An Interview with Bernard Stiegler', *Krisis* 1, 33–41 (www.krisis.eu).
Manovich, L. (2001) *The Language of New Media* (Cambridge, MA: MIT Press).
———. (2013) *Software Takes Command* (London: Bloomsbury Academic).
Metz, C. (1974) *Film Language: A Semiotics of the Cinema*, trans. by M. Taylor (New York: Oxford University Press).
———. (2016) *Impersonal Enunciation, or the Site of Film*, trans. by Cormac Deane (New York: Columbia University Press).
Mulvey, L. (2006) *Death 24x a Second: Stillness and the Moving Image* (London: Reaktion).
Nigawara, S., M. Fukai, M. Sugihara, K. Furudate and H. Nagai (1994) *Control System for an Industrial Plant, a Display System for such a Control System, and a Method of Controlling an Industrial Plant*, United States Patent no. 5,353,400.
Paulin, S.D. (2000) 'Richard Wagner and the Fantasy of Cinematic Unity: The Idea of the *Gesamtkunstwerk* in the History and Theory of Film Music' in J. Buhler, C. Flinn and D. Neumeyer (eds) (2000) *Music and Cinema* (Hanover, NH: University Press of New England), 58–84.
Rifkin, J. (2000) *The Age of Access: The New Culture of Hypercapitalism, where All of Life is a Paid-for Experience* (New York: J. P. Tarcher/Putnam).
Scheurer, T.E. (2008) *Music and Mythmaking in Film: Genre and the Role of the Composer* (Jefferson, NC: McFarland).

Serres, M. (1982) *The Parasite*, trans. by L. C. Shehr, (Baltimore: Johns Hopkins).
Shannon, C.E. (1948) 'A Mathematical Theory of Communication', *The Bell System Technical Journal*, 27 (July and October), 379–423; 623–656.
Shaviro, S. (2010) *Postcinematic Affect* (London: Zero).
Sobchack, V. (2005) 'When the Ear Dreams: Dolby Digital and the Imagination of Sound', *Film Quarterly*, Vol. 58, No. 4 (Summer), 2–15.
Stiegler, B. (1994) *Technics and Time 1: The Fault of Epimetheus* (Stanford: Stanford University Press).
———. (2011) *Technics and Time 3: Cinematic Time and the Question of Malaise* (Stanford: Stanford University Press).
Watterson B. (1986) *Calvin and Hobbes* (21 December). Syndicated in multiple publications.
Woods, D.D., E. S. Patterson and E. M. Roth (2002) 'Can We Ever Escape from Data Overload? A Cognitive Systems Diagnosis', *Cognition, Technology, and Work*, Vol. 4, No. 1, 22–36.
Žižek, S. (2006) *How to Read Lacan* (London: Granta).

CHAPTER 26

# Interview 5: Under the Skin of Film Sound—An Interview with Johnnie Burn

*John Hough*

Johnnie Burn is a supervising sound editor, re-recording mixer and sound designer whose work includes commercials, music videos, sonic branding and feature film. He is the recipient of the only D&AD Black Pencil ever awarded in sound and of a lifetime achievement Fellowship Award at the British Arrows. One of the results of his long-term collaboration with director Jonathan Glazer is the critically acclaimed film *Under the Skin* (2013), which earned Burn a nomination for Outstanding Technical Achievement at the British Independent Film Awards. He was interviewed by John Hough in July of 2014 at his Wave Studio in London.

JH: How did you start working with Jonathan Glazer?
JB: I had been Jonathan Glazer's 'go to' man for sound for nearly twenty years, starting with some pop promos in the 1990s followed by many commercials. I didn't work on *Sexy Beast*, his first film, but I did work on *Birth*, his second feature, for many months, and on *Under the Skin* for about a year and a half. Jon is very particular about the way he likes to work and with whom he works, and we got to the point where there is so much short-cutting in communication. He trusts me to try to experiment within the remit.
JH: How did you get into seeing/hearing things in 'his way'?
JB: It certainly does come with experience. Over a long period you benefit from common references, but there is still a stage where he is surprising me with his ideas, his take on things.
JH: When was *Under the Skin* first conceived as a film project?
JB: I think Jim Wilson gave him the book [by Michel Faber] in 2004. I know in 2008 he was hoping to do it as a 30-million feature with

---

J. Hough
University College Cork, Ireland

Brad Pitt, which was a script I read, but then the world banking crisis happened that readjusted a lot of things and it was very difficult for anyone to get a film funded. He and Walter Campbell then rewrote the script around a sole character, and that was Scarlett [Johansson], and the film is probably a hell of a lot better for it, and only cost 8 million.

JH: Could you describe your working process?

JB: I work alongside the picture edit trying out ideas. Jon absolutely explores sound. On *Under the Skin* I would go into the cutting room to listen to what they [Jon and editor Paul Watts] had been doing, react, suggest ideas, and try and understand what the hell to do with 90 minutes of no dialog. Each week I would give Paul and Jon some files that might help out with scenes they had played me the week before. Beyond the picture edit Jon's attention would move to spending much time with me and re-exploring those ideas and looking for opportunities to use the sound we had not just to enhance the images but actually tell the story. Once Jon had got the picture edit in a good place he spent about a month with me listening to all my sound rushes from my teams' various trips to Scotland recording characterful sound. Following that we had cut down thousands of hours of sound into 80 hours or so and had it all catalogued on the computer and in our heads ready to call upon to help tell the story. Next we spent a few months putting this sound to picture whilst creating a load more unique sound effects. Jon is not the type of guy to shoot a storyboard and have an assembly four weeks after the set wraps. There is the storyboard but the creative door is still wide open right up to the last day of the mix.

JH: I feel an important part of the story in *Under the Skin* is charting the shift of Scarlett's character from anempathetic to empathic. She desires to know more about humanity. Was sound used to do this?

JB: Not consciously. We were all taking chips away at the block to see what would be left at the end of it. Certainly we made a lot of effort to put ourselves in her shoes, and for the first half of the film we were trying to see how you would experience the world when hearing it for the first time. That took the form of things like not filtering out the crappy sounds that you tend to ignore, like background conversations or airplanes, and to make a point of that. We used a lot of synch sound but we didn't use it in sync with where it was recorded. Every part of it were little lattices of sound we took from other places—the scene in the shopping centre for example—we made efforts to put sound on for every single person that walked past her but what's important is the sound we chose isn't particularly like a language as you know it. We definitely aimed to present the world honestly and to allow that rich tapestry of honesty, and the fact is, that was almost an alien culture within the film genre, to not use ADR crowds, or Foley footsteps that sound nice and clean; to allow that honesty in itself sounds alien. And that representation of the real sound world would allow Scarlett's performance to bring about that sense of being alien. Her performance would be set apart from the realism of the sound world. So to answer your question, yes I guess the route we took was a decision to use sound to chart the lid lifting on her warmth. This did present challenges. There's a lot of mush, a lot of noises as there is in real life, and in typical movies that's removed. The challenge was to take real sound and make it representative and documentary but also somehow cinematic. We went to great lengths to do that, any Foley we needed to do, we went and did it in situ. Whatever noise that came with that, we just took it on the chin. A lot of the atmospheres of the city were myself and the sound team going around with microphones hidden in umbrellas and wearing lapel mics. We hired Steve Single to mix the film—at that point I had no experience of mixing a feature film and the producers were keen to have someone experienced involved.

JH: Was Steve a fresh pair of ears?

JB: Steve came at such a good time too as Jon and I had spent a year honing the sound, and a shot of energy and new thought was very useful. When Jon and I worked we were setup in a decent room with big monitors, and as we do in commercials, we were adjusting volume, reverbs, etc. The ideas were so subtle that things like volume, reverb and so on were crucial to whether an idea worked or not. So we were kind of mixing it as we went. When Steve got involved he helped us clean a lot of things up and take it to a much more traditional filmic place which felt good at first but oddly we eventually realised we missed the honesty of where we had been and we dialled a fair bit of that back. But it took that to know it, if you know what I mean!

JH: The aesthetic of 'un-adornment'—beauty would come from the truth—can you comment on this?

JB: Definitely not hearing the hand of the fader is part of that. Resisting the temptation to embellish—we were fighting it all the way. Slickness wasn't what we were going for. I didn't want anyone to feel manipulated by the sound, just to experience it like she did, and felt this would resonate with the whole premise of the film and method of shooting.

JH: Why did you decide not to use a general ambience or a production track in the shopping mall scene?

JB: That level of realism and detail—there would not be any ambience that would get that, that would have so many sounds coming at you in quick succession. Plus there wasn't any recording of what we wanted. When she enters the shopping mall, it's supposed to be: bang! Here is the world! It's her first confrontation with people and it should be in some way daunting and overwhelming, although not to her—at that stage she's quite steely—but it should certainly present to the audience the world as she's experiencing it, and I don't think anything off the shelf would do that. About seven seconds before the start of the shopping mall scene I deliberately started dropping the level of the van sound, so you start leaning in and wondering where is that going.

JH: Was there an intention to portray the ugliness of city life, with the various sounds of people partying/drinking etc.?

JB: They are certainly not pretty, but they are real. Those sounds are quite male, so there are reasons for using them in that they are sounds she might be focusing on. If you hear debauchery, maybe it's there to change the mood and not to represent Glasgow as a debauched place, or because that's 'what Glasgow should sound like'. Everything is there to steer the narrative and is drawing upon honest sounds recorded in Glasgow.

JH: What about the use of trains and planes to foreshadow threat?

JB: Yes, the train sound where the 'hoodies' attack the van. Originally we didn't want her to be somewhere completely remote when she pulls up. We wanted distant sound or in the middle distance. We started playing with trains, and the enormity of that sound just developed because the guy who comes to the window—we weren't keen on hearing his voice so we needed something to obscure it. Then we realised just how fantastic it was to 'throw the world at her', the impact of the train [sound] when the hoodies are attacking her. There's also the airplane at the end, just before she gets burned, it's in amongst the music. That was more about the idea of, 'there she is, and the world's carrying on'. Foreign sound can grow a scene.

JH: What about the sound of the airplane in the nightclub scene?

JB: I put that in because you have to believe that she hasn't heard the group of people until she actually turns the corner and sees them. I think they do signal danger in some way. But again, it's about the honesty of the world, and not being restricted in feeling like you only [have to] place sounds for things you see. I think also just leaving things ambiguous is not a bad thing. There are sounds in there that [I put] there for a reason, which might be different than the reasons why Jonathan likes them. I think with a film like *Under the Skin*, where the audience is having to think about the sound they are hearing, because there's little else, and also [because] you have taught them that it is important, then you do have license to try stuff out.

JH: What about the archetypal sounds of the wind and the sea?

JB: Years ago, when we were originally talking about how to fill the sound, 'cause we knew it wasn't going to be particularly dialog heavy, [Jon] said: 'Johnnie, make me a symphony out of wind!' So what I came up with was how to coax frequency out of wind, which is white noise really. So just really tight, chromatic EQ basically. I [re-]created the chord structure for Santana's *Black Magic Woman*, but using wind, and there were some parts of it that sounded extraordinary. So that sound which initiates the promo is the same wind we hear when she takes a nap in the bothy as the music begins. And in all the temp dubs and the rough screenings we had, that wind was one of the parts that always remained.

JH: How did you create the atmospheres in the black lair?

JB: The modulating tones in the lair in some ways mimic the neon light in the warehouse. The point of that sound was to contrast with her, because you don't hear her. Once the victim was under the surface, the void no longer needed to make any sound. To have it mute would have been a mistake and bit upsetting for audiences. As we discover, when you go below the void, all you hear is the screening room next door, so you pop the audience out of the film a bit. That tone is also at the head of the film, in the white void. Its purpose is to hold, and to make the point of the absence of other sounds more than anything else.

JH: How did you collaborate with the composer Mica Levi? Did she send you early drafts of her work?

JB: Yes, all the time. It was a tight weave. Mica worked on it for nine months and during that time any time a new track got made it would be sent to me via Dropbox and I would chuck it in to the relevant scene. Jon would see me in the morning and her in the afternoon and we would keep each other updated. The bulk of it was Jon, the composer and music supervisor, Peter Raeburn, working a way forward with the music, and passing music cues to me to make suggestions about how to bring out 'the Alien' more, particularly in the first half of the film. So [the process] was highly collaborative in terms of reacting to each other's work rather than all of us sitting down together. Jon was cool with people not knowing what might be music and what might be sound effect/design. Much of what I did was tonally adjusting my sound to Mica's eventual score. I reviewed the pitch and rhythm of every wave, car pass, drone, shout, you name it!

JH: Where was the line drawn between sound design and music composition?

JB: It's an interesting one, there is a fair bit of crossover. All the sounds in the voids are my sound design creations. I would have pitched [them] sympathetically to incoming or outgoing music. A lot of things would appear to have tone in them because I have EQ'd at very specific musical frequencies, like when she drives through the football fans, very tight EQs give a musical effect. Again that's the technique used on the wind in the bothy, where the wind is sounding a chord, which is actually used in the music which comes in 10 seconds later. Also, the atmosphere at the beginning of the film, when the 'bad man' is recovering the body to put it in the van, there's tonality there which was again heavily EQ'd, but the bulk of the drone there is coming from the music. What tended to happen was, like with the wind in the bothy, that sound stayed on from the rough cut and Mica's music fitted that. We basically worked for a year before even reaching the mix stage to make sure that every single thing was in some way sympathetic to the music around it. In many ways that was about bringing out tonality in the various sounds like the waves, etc.

JH: Where did you look for inspiration when trying to come up with sounds, for example those tones in the alien lair?

JB: Well, one thing you can't do when working with Jon is to pull something off the shelf. All the recordings we did for the white void were done in an anechoic chamber in Birmingham, part of a science lab. We did recordings from thirty feet away, to get a strange sense of perspective. It all had quite an interesting feel to it. We actually tried three different Foley companies and all of it just sounded like film Foley, which wasn't what we were looking for. So we played with different ideas. For example, in the first scene where she is driving around I had 16 outputs going to 16 radio transmitters, and ended up with 16 tracks of sync sound from everything including the engine, and we ended up scanning through them and imagining her as an alien scanning through them, but that didn't work because it was too 'sound design-y'. But off the back of that we found things like static, which we really liked. A lot of it would have come from conversations with Jon and just going and trying things, recording things in order to find a way through. We certainly didn't look outside to any other film work for inspiration. Jon did say that he liked the way sound was used in *Persona* [Ingmar Bergman, 1966]. There are some very subtle continuous ambiences in that.

JH: One of the most unsettling scenes is the one where a baby is left alone on a beach with the tide coming in. The sound of the baby crying bleeds into the next shot of Scarlett in the van and is mixed in a rhythmical way with the sound of the windscreen wipers.

JB: A very important part of the sound in the whole film is the collaboration of Jonathan Glazer and Walter Campbell on the writing. When I originally read the script, it was so descriptive of sound, I was doing backflips! That scene you mention, the sound was written into the script. With every part of the film I have spent days reviewing how the pieces fit together best.

JH: Not all directors are that much into sound?

JB: Some don't even turn up to the mix! Because the visuals might cost 30 million to get in the can, they think that's the important bit, and the sounds are chicken feed on top of that, and yet the sound is so crucial.

JH: What is you're general approach for building ambiences and atmospheres?

JB: I suppose piecemeal, the last thing I would do would be stick something general on there and say 'there you go'. Selectively, frame by frame—annoyingly! Beyond that it's about being a storyteller first, sound designer second.

JH: When you were selectively narrowing down the vast library of recording, how did you go about it? What were you listening for?

JB: We had a three metre-wide projector screen setup and this part of Nuendo called Media Bay. Every day Simon [Carroll, First assistant sound editor] would chuck a load of files in there from stuff we had recorded with keyword descriptors attached. There could be over a 100 files, and clicking on each one would bring up the waveform which we then skimmed through. We were looking for things that were characterful, unusual but correct and honest in terms of what we were looking to achieve, things that made you say 'Oh, that's really cool!', but not cool in a Hollywood slick way, not 'sound design-y'.

JH: What process did you apply to the sounds to sculpt them?

JB: Mainly EQ, duration, rhythm, and a little reverb, there were very little in the way of plug-ins. With Jonathan, if you suggest doing what Walter Murch did with the atmosphere in the white room in *THX*, he would go 'No'. Because it's been done, and done so well, what's the point in that?

JH: You mentioned playing chords with the wind sound, how did you achieve that?

JB: It wasn't like we used a sampler, which everyone thinks. I had 12 tracks in Nuendo, one tightly EQ'd for each note and it was literally using massive amounts of EQ—completely cutting off the top and bottom, just focusing on four or five prongs of a particular frequency. The result is really unusual and what's interesting is the pitch only activates when something naturally happens in the recording at that pitch; this develops the natural rhythms that occur in a sound. In sounds which are undulating, like a gusty wind or a wave—a note will turn on and off, and then it becomes much more richly textured thing. EQ is a very powerful tool when used for the right reasons. I predominately used Nuendo's EQ and created pre-sets for each note at various octaves.

JH: Vocal inflection can really change the meaning of something....

JB: Yes, in the black void when she's talking with a lonely character he says 'It's cold' and she replies 'I won't let that stop us'—that was flattened out to make it neutral. Also the line 'Come to me'. Jon would be going through the dialog in the script and say: 'Flatten that all off' to make it monotone. Which hopefully adds an innate alien-ness to it.

JH: Were the room tones from production sound?

JB: Yes, some of them were, others we recorded. We went to lots of warehouse-type places. We recorded so much that 95 % of it didn't make the cut. I even took an early version of Mica's score and set up a big sound system in the woods in Scotland and recorded it back [worldizing], and it sounded great. But there was so much that didn't get used. Jon doesn't like stock sound effects and I wouldn't want to hear anything else I had heard before, because libraries aren't that diverse and people tend to use the first thing that comes up on a search.

JH: In terms of workflow, did you create pre-mixes for the various ADR, Foley and sound effects, or was is all kept virtual?

JB: No, we didn't do that, we kept everything live. We spent much time putting everything carefully in place—the way we work on commercials together. The final mix was just using my laptop on the desk, and I had a USB/MADI cable going out to the monitor pot on a big desk, a Euphonix 5 MC with a centre section and a fader section and we did it all on that—with all the elements live, 'cause you never know with Jon. The day before the final mix we completely overhauled one of the music cues, and did a big edit—so definitely keeping things live was the way we did it.

JH: Did you use any convolution reverbs?

JB: We went to every location and took impulse responses. All ADRs were shot in the actual van. A friend of mine, Rodger Patel, has a Foley room at Elstree Studios, and we got the van and had wires running into his studio, so we did ADR with actors—who were members of the public—inside the van. The only bit we didn't do in the van was Scarlett's ADR, because she was in New York and logistically it didn't work. So in those cases we used convolution on her voice.

JH: Did you use any quad or 5.1 recordings?

JB: No, it was all mono or stereo recordings. In terms of mixing it was 5.1. Jon wasn't keen on any surround sound whatsoever. With music he's more accepting of it. We did come to use surround sound as a tool but generally the atmospheres were coming from the screen in front of you and anything else would have been an adornment. All the sound we were recording, all the covert stuff were done with tiny microphones (DPA 4060s). I also had a long umbrella with a Sennheiser 416 hidden in it. I spent over a week going around Glasgow with a recorder in my pocket and a wire going up my arm. If I saw someone coming towards me and they were having a conversation or being quite loud—a high signal to noise ratio—I would try and point the umbrella towards them. So there wasn't really room for surround recording setups, and anyway, Jon would be querying why to use it.

Jon didn't like the first mix, he thought it was too 'big' and it wasn't 'his' film. So me and him went back and did another 5–6 weeks, taking it back to the more simple thing it is now, stripping things back and removing anything too 'sound design-y', slick or 'jazzy'.

JH: Was that hard to swallow? Did it go against your creative instincts?

JB: No, I was delighted! I love how it sounds now. It was just part of the mix process. There was something really weird about the Stockholm syndrome of it all, that I missed it when it finished, despite the fact I was unhealthily tired!

PART VII

# The Musicality of Soundtrack

CHAPTER 27

# Electroacoustic Composition and the British Documentary Tradition

*Andy Birtwistle*

One of the observations that might reasonably be made of the contemporary soundtrack is that the boundaries between sound design and music are becoming increasingly blurred. This observation clearly has its merits, providing a way of thinking through how the recent technological and structural changes that have taken place within the film industry have impacted on the aesthetic dimensions of film sound practice. However, one of the things that a focus on the contemporary neglects is the fact that the erosion of boundaries between music and what is now known as sound design can also be heard in earlier forms of cinematic expression. It is perhaps also useful to remember that cinema does not have a singular identity, but is instead constituted by a multiplicity of traditions, forms and practices—a multiple identity that challenges the often tacit acceptance of narrative fiction as the paradigmatic model of cinematic form. So when Jay Beck makes the provocative statement that 'there is no sound designer' (Beck, 2008, p. 75), suggesting that the practice of sound design proposed by Walter Murch has not, in fact, impacted significantly on sound production in the Hollywood film industry, it is important to remember that his insightful comments apply only to one specific model of filmmaking. Outside of this context—for example in experimental cinema—there has been a long tradition of authorial and creative control that has often extended to the design of an integrated soundtrack, in which sound effects and speech are deployed in ways that sometimes align them closely with the forms and functions of music.

In what follows my aim is to listen outside the field of narrative cinema to consider some historical precursors of the contemporary integrated soundtrack. My analysis begins by considering points of connection and interchange between early experiments with film sound and developments in modern music, before

---

A. Birtwistle
Canterbury Christ Church University, UK

focusing on the integration of speech, sound effects and music in the work of three remarkable artists active within the British documentary tradition[1]. Examining work by the director Basil Wright, and composers Daphne Oram and Tristram Cary, my aims are to consider the ways in which the documentary soundtrack might be seen to have drawn upon, contributed to, and prefigured developments in electroacoustic music, and how some of the electroacoustic practices developed within British documentary cinema problematize the traditional tripartite division of the soundtrack into dialogue, music and effects.

During the last century, the soundscape of western art music changed radically as a result of the introduction of sounds produced by electrical means. With the widening availability of sound recording technology, and the development of electronic instruments such as the theremin and the ondes Martenot, composers were able to call upon both recorded and electronically generated sounds as new musical resources. The two key forms of electroacoustic practice that emerged from these developments—*musique concrète* and electronic synthesis—feature on a range of documentary film soundtracks in ways that set in motion the normal distinctions made between music, sound effects and speech within a cinesonic context. This blurring of boundaries was observed by Oram, who commenting on the use of her own electronic music within a cinematic context stated, 'I think our sort of sound can do things that an orchestra really can't do. I think it's somewhere between sound effect and a musical sound' (*Wee Have Also Sound-Houses*, 2008).

Before revisiting Basil Wright's celebrated 1934 film *Song of Ceylon*, I would like first to consider the international context of early experimentation in film sound practice, and how this might be understood to relate both to developments in electroacoustic music and to the evolution of electroacoustic practice within the British documentary tradition.

## Electroacoustic Composition and Cinema

Although rarely explored in histories of twentieth century art music, the relationship between cinema and the development of electroacoustic composition is one of mutual influence and interconnection. Not only did composers working in film, such as Oram and Cary, draw upon and contribute to the developments in modern music that took place after World War II, but also, prior to this, cinema had served to inspire radical composers interested in new forms of musical expression. Furthermore, innovative forms of electroacoustic practice, which prefigured and paralleled the developments that were to take place within the field of art music during the 1940s and 1950s, had already begun to take shape in cinema during the 1930s. Since the introduction of optical sound recording and playback in the late 1920s, a number of filmmakers and composers had experimented with ways of synthesizing electronic sound by painting, drawing or printing directly on the optical soundtrack. Early pioneers in this field included: Jack Ellitt in the UK; Oskar Fischinger, Rudolph Pfenninger and László Moholy-Nagy in Germany; Arthur Hoérée in France; and Arsenii Avraamov, Nikolai Voinov and Nikolai Zhelinski in the USSR.[2]

In addition to its potential to synthesize sound through direct inscription, the optical soundtrack also provided a means by which recorded sound could be edited with a high degree of precision—something that had not been possible with disc recording technology. During the 1930s and 1940s film's capacity to capture and organize sound fired the imaginations of composers interested in developing new forms of music that would employ non-instrumental, real-world, or 'concrete' sounds. For the young John Cage, film technology presented a means by which the range of sounds available to the composer could be extended to include concrete sounds, both man-made and natural. In his 1937 talk entitled *The Future of Music: Credo* Cage stated:

> We want to capture and control these sounds, to use them not as sound effects but as musical instruments. Every film studio has a library of 'sound effects' recorded on film. With a film phonograph it is now possible to control the amplitude and frequency of any one of these sounds and to give it rhythms within or beyond the reach of the imagination. Given four film phonographs, we can compose and perform a quartet for explosive motor, wind, heartbeat, and landslide. (1999, p. 3)

These comments, evidencing Cage's desire to employ concrete sounds within a musical context, also signal the fact that film technology offered new forms of sonic manipulation, as well as a degree of control over sound that had hitherto been unknown in music.

Cage's appreciation of the creative potential of film sound technology was also shared by the composer Edgard Varèse, who enthused in his 1940 article 'Organized Sound for the Sound Film':

> Any possible sound we can imagine can be produced with perfect control of its quality, intensity and pitch, opening up entirely new auditory perspectives. And these sounds must not be speculated upon as entities for sporadic, atmospheric effects, but taken as thematic material and organized into a score standing on its own merit. (1940, p. 205)

What both of these avant-garde composers heard in film was the potential for new forms of musical expression, with Cage's manifesto pointing the way towards *musique concrète* and Varèse's article proposing a sculpting of sound suggestive of electronic synthesis. These ideas, then, seemed to prefigure the developments in electroacoustic music that were to take place after World War II: most notably in Pierre Schaeffer's experiments in *musique concrète*, undertaken at the RTF studios in Paris in the late 1940s, and in the electronic music that came out of the Cologne studio of German broadcaster NWDR during the 1950s.

Outside the world of art music, however, similar ideas had already been formulated and realized by filmmakers a decade earlier. Some of these filmmakers, including Walter Ruttmann, Dziga Vertov and Jack Ellitt, had received training in music prior to working in film, or, like Sergei Eisenstein, possessed a musical sensibility that was to inform their particular approach to the use of sound. The year 1930 witnessed the production of a number of ground-breaking experiments in cinema sound, some of which were to have an important influence on the evolution of the British documentary soundtrack.

## THE INTERNATIONAL CONTEXT OF EARLY FILM SOUND EXPERIMENTATION

Although the influence of Soviet cinema on the British documentary movement has been widely discussed, relatively little attention has been paid to the ways in which it may have impacted upon the use of sound. Certainly 'The Sound Film: A Statement from USSR' (often referred to as the 'Statement on Sound'), written by Sergei Eisenstein, Vsevelod Pudovkin and Grigori Alexandrov in 1928, was hugely influential in shaping debates about the adoption of film sound technology in the early 1930s. Famously proposing a contrapuntal use of sound, in which the relationship between sound and image would be governed by strategies of montage rather than forms of naturalism, the 'Statement on Sound' was acknowledged by documentary filmmaker Basil Wright as an influence on his early thinking about the uses of film sound technology:

> ...as late as 1933 I was still shooting without access to sound. Not that this meant we were not interested. Certainly when I went on a film-making tour to the West Indies in 1933 I had in mind various possibilities for soundtracks to be added to what I was shooting, and was of course acutely aware of the Russian Manifesto. (1976, p. 114)

However, while the 'Statement on Sound' undoubtedly had an important impact on filmmakers concerned with the creative potential of sound, comments made by John Grierson, the leading figure in British documentary in 1930s, suggest another somewhat overlooked and perhaps more surprising source of Soviet influence on the soundscape of British documentary. Interviewed by the BBC in 1970 Grierson commented 'If you want to know where the courage of poetry in *Song of Ceylon* came from, or the courage of poetry in *Night Mail*, then you must go for your answer to *Old and New* or to *Romance Sentimentale*' (quoted in Wright, 1976, p. 695). Although Eisenstein had plans to retro-fit sound to the silent *Old and New* (1929), these were never realized[3]. Thus if Grierson's comments have any validity regarding the influence of Soviet cinema on the use of sound in British documentary in the 1930s, then these must necessarily relate to Alexandrov and Eisenstein's sound short *Romance Sentimentale* (1930).

Grierson's reference to the film may at first seem puzzling, since it was poorly received when first screened in 1930; indeed, as Douglas Kahn has suggested, 'the film was greeted widely as a debacle' (1999, p. 152). *Romance Sentimentale* was commissioned by the wealthy merchant Léonard Rosenthal to feature a musical performance by his lover, Mara Griy. Thus, much of the film features Griy on a studio set singing and accompanying herself on the piano. While there is nothing particularly remarkable about the musical content of the film, which explores the themes of autumn, sadness and dead love, the project offered Eisenstein and Alexandrov their first opportunity to experiment with film sound, some two years after the publication of the joint statement. The film opens with a radically innovative montage sequence that draws on a range of experimental sound manipulation techniques, including sound reversal, the generation of synthetic sound by direct inscription on the optical soundtrack and various other effects created by the cutting and splicing of optical sound recordings. Unfortunately, the energy and invention of this highly dynamic opening sequence is soon lost as the film turns its attention to Griy's somewhat melodramatic musical performance, and thus it is easy to see why the film was not the subject of critical praise.

While distancing himself from the project, Eisenstein nevertheless felt that *Romance Sentimentale* had value as an experiment, suggesting that it demonstrated the fact that, 'with the coming of sound, montage does not die but develops, amplifying and multiplying its possibilities and its method' (1988, p. 218). These comments, made in September 1930 in a lecture delivered to the Academy of Motion Picture Arts and Sciences in Hollywood, clearly locate the creative dynamic of the film in relation to montage, but give no sense of the actual outcome of the experiment that was undertaken. However, returning to the film over eighty years after it was produced, what one hears in the brief opening sequence is an emergent form of *musique concrète*, in which manipulated optical sound recordings and synthesized electronica are combined to form what was an entirely new sonic vocabulary for the film soundtrack. And it is perhaps this radical spirit of experimentation to which Grierson referred when identifying *Romance Sentimentale* as an influence on the 'poetry' of the British documentary films of the 1930s.

While Eisenstein and Alexandrov's first venture into film sound production clearly caught Grierson's attention, two other sound film projects produced in 1930 offered more sustained examples of sound experimentation, both of which proposed a 'musical' approach to the use of documentary sound. The first of these, Dizga Vertov's *Enthusiasm: Symphony of the Donbass* (1930), employs montage and various forms of manipulation to transform sound recorded on location in steelworks, mines and farms into musical form—as signalled by the film's subtitle. Vertov screened *Enthusiasm* in London in November 1931 to a select audience that included Grierson, Wright and Charlie Chaplin. The film earned the enthusiastic praise of Chaplin, who clearly understood Vertov's cinematic articulation of real-world, concrete sounds to constitute a form of music, commenting, 'Never had I known that these mechanical sounds could be arranged to sound so beautiful. I regard it as one of the most exhilarating symphonies I have heard. Mr Dziga Vertov is a musician' (Chaplin quoted in Michelson, 1984, p. 170).

The other radical film sound project made in 1930, also employing a musical approach to the use of documentary material, was Ruttmann's *Weekend*.

Strictly speaking, *Weekend* was a radio programme, but was produced using Tri-Ergon optical film sound technology, and has thus been variously described by Ruttmann and others as a 'photographic radio play', 'photographic sound art' and an 'imageless film'. The originality of Ruttmann's approach to the organization of recorded sound is most evident, perhaps, in the two 'Jazz der Arbeit' sequences that open and close the programme. Here recordings of typewriters, telephones, cash registers, hammers, saws, files, forges, office dictation, verbal commands and various machines are edited in what Ruttmann described as 'strong rhythmic counterpoint' (1930, n.p.). Rhythm invests the montages with an explicit musical quality, not only through the selection of sounds that possess a clear internal rhythm—such as the those of hammering, sawing and filing—but also by the metrical organization of the recordings achieved through editing.

What we hear in *Romance Sentimentale, Enthusiasm* and *Weekend* are early forms of electroacoustic composition in which the concrete sounds cinema usually refers to as 'effects' or 'noises' are articulated in musical form. Furthermore, in each of the three productions, these sounds are integrated with more traditional instrumental sounds or recordings of musical performances. Some of the former are subjected to various types of electroacoustic modification; for example, *Weekend* opens with the sounds of gong and cymbal, played first forwards and then reversed, while *Romance Sentimentale* features the sound of a piano chord edited to alter its sonic profile or 'envelope'. These techniques, and others which prefigure those developed independently within the field of art music over a decade later, serve to strip instrumental sounds of their familiar musical identities, thereby blurring the distinction made between music and effects.

These three projects, the discourses that surrounded them, and the development of advanced musical thinking around an art of recorded sound, provide the international context within which British documentary cinema's contribution to early electroacoustic practice might be understood and valued. While the influence of artists such as Eisenstein and Vertov on the British documentary movement is undeniable, the development of early electroacoustic practices in the UK should not be thought of, however, as simply a response to what was happening elsewhere. Ideas regarding an art of organized sound, similar to those later proposed by John Cage, were also being formulated in the UK by the composer and filmmaker Jack Ellitt. In a 1935 article entitled 'On Sound' Ellitt proposed a new form of sonic art based on recorded sounds, stating that with access to recording technology, 'all world sounds of interest now come within a sphere of creative control which may be termed Sound-Construction' (1935, p. 182). For Ellitt it was important that this new sound-based art form would depart from existing musical paradigms, evidenced by his comment that, 'Beauty in terms of sound-colours is not necessarily confined to orchestras, pianos, etc., and musical forms are only the chrysales [sic] from which more beautifully conceived forms will eventually burst forth in complete freedom and independence' (p. 185). Although the article makes no direct reference to cinema, it is likely that Ellitt's theoretical propositions on sound would have drawn on his knowledge and experience of filmmaking, gained from his involvement with the London Film Society and collaborative projects undertaken with animator Len Lye in the early 1930s. Thus, the early electroacoustic practices that emerged within British documentary cinema in the 1930s, to which I now turn, should not be thought of as mere echoes of developments that were already taking place in Germany, the USSR and elsewhere. Rather, the sound practice developed within the British documentary tradition forms an important part of a broader international context, in which filmmakers were using the resources of the soundtrack in ways that challenged the strict standardization of sound practice that was beginning to take hold within the commercial film industry.

## SONG OF CEYLON (1934)

The place of Wright's *Song of Ceylon* within an international context is evidenced by the fact that the film received both first place in the documentary group and the Pris du Gouvernement for the best film in all classes at the 1935 International Film Festival held in Brussels. The film features a highly innovative soundtrack that combines music by the composer Walter Leigh, extracts from a seventeenth century text written by the English sea captain Robert Knox, various forms of speech and a range of sound effects. Wright spent five months in Sri Lanka—then named Ceylon—researching and shooting the project, but all sound for the film was recorded during post-production at the GPO Film Unit's Blackheath studio in London. Authenticity was added to the soundtrack by two Sinhalese performers—a drummer and a dancer—brought over from Sri Lanka to record percussion and dialogue. These various elements are woven together into an integrated soundtrack that was the product of close collaboration between Wright and Leigh. Additional input was provided by Alberto Cavalcanti, who had been appointed by Grierson in 1934 to facilitate the GPO Film Unit's transition to sound, and to stimulate innovative and experimental uses of the soundtrack (Hardy, 1990, p. 5).

Wright's choice of title for the film not only indicates the centrality of sound within it, but also proposes an audiovisual poetics that aspires to more than simple experimentation. In terms of electroacoustic practice, the most innovative part of the film is located in the section entitled 'The Voices of Commerce'. This opens with shots of the Sri Lankan landscape filmed from a moving train, accompanied on the soundtrack by an appropriate rhythmic sound effect complete with train whistle and clanking bell. The film then cuts to shots of an elephant, controlled by a mahout, felling trees. As the elephant pushes against the trunk of a tree we hear a creaking, splintering sound, which like the train effect is a studio recording rather than recorded actuality. While these sound effects may not be entirely realistic, until this point in the sequence, the relationship between sound and image is nevertheless intended to be naturalistic. However, as the tree begins to fall, the sound we might expect to hear is replaced by the crash of a gong, the sound extending in duration so that it becomes a pure tone. This particular effect was produced by moving the microphone towards the gong after it had been struck (Leigh, 1935, p. 74). This technique had been devised by Cavalcanti, who later described 'advancing the microphone while the vibrations were dying so that, instead of dying, they were deformed' (Sussex, 1975, p. 56). A similar technique was developed independently over a decade later within the field of art music by Schaeffer—the leading figure in early *musique concrète*—in which the decay of a sound is compensated for by an increase in recording volume (Schaeffer, 2012, p. 7). Through this reshaping of the sound's envelope, Wright produces new sonic material that is no longer a simple instrumental sound. Over this extended tone a voice-over then announces, 'New clearings. New roads. New buildings. New communications. New developments of natural resources'.

This short sequence introduces two key elements that underpin and shape 'The Voices of Commerce' section. The first of these is a thematic concern with modernity, which contrasts with the poetic reflection on history and tradition that has dominated the film until this point. The latter is articulated on the soundtrack, in part, through the hypnotic intonation of Lionel Wendt's voice-over narration in which he reads extracts from Knox's 1681 text. Second, this introductory sequence employs electroacoustic manipulation to create an appropriate soundscape of modernity. The thematic concern with modernity and accompanying soundscape are then further developed as Wright sketches the changes taking place in modern Sri Lanka, and the ways in which the colonial exploitation of its resources locate the island and its people within global economic and communication networks. Over shots of the elephant and mahout, whose destruction of trees signifies modern development, we hear a resonant low frequency tone that is suggestive of the trumpeting of an elephant, and which was described by Wright as 'raspberry-like' (n.d.). This particular sound, reworked at various points in 'The Voices of Commerce' section, was created with a serpent: a bass wind instrument considered to be a forerunner of the tuba. Wright's own notes on this sound effect state, 'Trumpeting is not the real elephant noise—it is a sort of archetypal primeval noise ... The track was then used backwards' (Wright, n.d.). The reversal of the sound gives it an unnatural quality that foregrounds the materiality of the recording, thereby reducing its capacity to function as a naturalistic sound effect. According to composer Tristram Cary, playing a recording backwards—or 'retrograding' as it is referred to in electroacoustic musical practice—produces a radical change in sounds with percussive attacks. Cary explains that the reversed exponential decay that results from retrograding does not occur in natural sounds (1992, p. 471), and it is for this reason perhaps that the film's simulated elephant noises are not convincing as naturalistic effects.

The sequence continues with the sounds of a typewriter—itself a sonic index of modernity—and a montage of voices reading extracts from business correspondence: 'Dear Sir/In reply/Dear Sirs, with reference to our conversa ... /Twenty-two pounds seventeen and sixpence/Seven pounds nine and a penny/To acknowledge receipt'. The use of different voices, coupled with the speed and rhythm of the cutting, foreground the montage construction of the sequence, articulating its mundane speech content in a musical and poetic fashion. In addition to this use of sound montage, Wright's soundtrack also makes itself audible through a number of abrupt sound transitions. A sequence dealing with the harvesting of coconuts is initially accompanied on the soundtrack by exotica composed by Leigh, until Wright suddenly cuts to a mid-frequency tone reminiscent of the one heard previously over shots of the elephant. At the point of transition between the two recordings, the tonal sound has no obvious representational value. However, a second voice-over montage, announcing ports of call on a ship's itinerary, and subsequent shots of a ship's bow cutting through the ocean, anchor the identity of the sound as that of a ship's siren. Until this point, however, the tone is neither located as a sound effect, nor as a traditional musical device, but exists as a somewhat disturbing sonic presence over shots of a young Sinhalese man climbing a coconut palm.

As this section of the film progresses, Wright's montage of sounds becomes increasingly complex, bringing in material from commodity market reports, stock exchange listings, a telephone conversation about blueprints for a new factory, radio broadcasts in French and German, and orders given from the bridge of a ship. Interspersed with these snippets of speech are the electronic sounds of radio transmissions and Morse code, serving as powerful sonic signifiers of modernity. In the final sequence of 'The Sounds of Commerce', which revolves around the harvesting, production and sale of tea, a combination of music and Morse code is suddenly interrupted by the highly rhythmic sound of machinery, matched to shots of tea processing equipment. Here Wright is not only attempting to sound modernity, but is also listening to the music of concrete sound. In this sense, his electroacoustic practice both demonstrates some of the forms of sonic manipulation that were to emerge as key resources in electroacoustic music (including retrograding, cutting and splicing), and also serves as a practical articulation of Ellitt's proposal that, 'Beauty in terms of sound-colours is not necessarily confined to orchestras, pianos, etc'. (1935, p. 185). Thus in a small way, Wright's film signals an approach to the use of concrete sounds that problematizes their status as sound effects, and instead begins to treat them as musical material.

## Snow (1963)

Although the manipulation and reworking of pre-existing music is often seen as a feature of postmodern culture, the practice also occupied a key place in the modernist soundscape, featuring in Schaeffer's early experiments in *musique concrète*; for example, in the pieces that comprise his *Suite 14* from 1949. However, where Schaeffer had written music to be first recorded and then manipulated, later generations of electroacoustic composers simply turned to existing recordings as source material for their compositions. Thus, James Tenney's 1961 *Collage #1 (Blue Suede)* reworks the famous Elvis Presley recording, while Elaine Radigue's *Etude* and *Maquette*, both from 1970, draw on recordings of music by Frédéric Chopin and Richard Wagner. Similar techniques are also heard on a number soundtracks produced by the British composer Oram for the documentary filmmaker Geoffrey Jones. A pioneer of electronic music, and founder of the BBC Radiophonic Workshop, Oram collaborated with Jones on a total of four films produced between 1963 and 1970. The first of these, *Snow*, was commissioned by British Transport Films and documents the effects of the weather on railway workers, train services, and passengers during the winter of 1962–1963. The eight-minute film, described by the Monthly Film Bulletin as 'impressionistic' (1967, p. 50), and by *The Times* as 'expressionistic' (1963, p. 16), opens with shots of railway workers armed with shovels clearing snow-bound tracks, and ends with trains filled with warm, comfortable passengers being sped to their destinations. The film proved to be a popular success, and in addition to picking up a string of awards at major international film festivals also received an Oscar nomination for best Live Action Short.

The soundtrack for *Snow* is based on a version of Sandy Nelson's 1959 pop instrumental 'Teen Beat', which due to copyright clearance issues was re-recorded for the film by the musician and composer Johnny Hawksworth. Nelson's original hit, which is mirrored very closely in Hawksworth's arrangement, foregrounds the rhythmic drive and instrumental virtuosity of rock and roll drumming, accompanied by surf-style bass-line and guitar riffs. Hawksworth's recording was then reworked by Oram, who later described the film as, 'One of the earliest uses of electronic techniques and pop' (n.d.). The major modifications that Oram applies to the original recording are manipulation of playback speed, the application of variable filtering (in which particular frequencies of sound are amplified or reduced) and the addition of reverb and echo effects.

At the beginning of the film Hawksworth's rendition of 'Teen Beat' is heard at half speed, but as the film progresses Oram increases the rate of playback so that it reaches twice the original speed by the film's end. The music thus takes on a sluggish quality at the start of the film, where we see trains stuck in the snow, but becomes increasingly hyperactive towards its close, where images of speeding trains show that the railway network is able to maintain its efficiency even in the most challenging meteorological conditions. In addition to speed changing, variable filtering is also applied to the original recording, such that the music's timbral qualities are constantly shifting. These changes simulate spatial effects, such as Doppler shifts, which are in turn closely matched to the film's rapid montage of images. The result is a sustained, dynamic fusion of sound and image, described aptly in a press release issued for the Kraków International Festival of Short Films: 'Individual scenes are composed in a kind of choreography so as to form a unity with an electronically edited and arranged jazz composition' (International Festival of Short Films, 1964, n.p.).

The use of pre-exiting music problematizes any straightforward attribution of authorship with regard to the film's soundtrack. Thus, the film credits Hawksworth for 'music arrangement', and Oram for 'music effects'.

However, while the soundtrack never loses touch with Nelson's original tune, Oram's electronic manipulation creates some significant changes in the music. Commenting on pianist Glenn Gould's radical departures from the standardized ways of playing the baroque and classical repertoires, Gilles Deleuze and Felix Guattari propose that, 'When Glenn Gould speeds up the performance of a piece, he is not just displaying virtuosity, he is transforming the musical points into lines, he is making the whole piece proliferate' (Deleuze and Guattari, 1988, p. 8). The same is true of Oram: when she slows down 'Teen Beat' a new soundscape emerges from a piece of genre music that sounds familiar even though we may not know the original. As Timothy S. Murphy has observed, 'deceleration of a sound lowers its pitch and thus alters its tone quality, but it also alters all its other relationships and reveals qualitatively new features in them' (2004, p. 163). In this way, the treatment of the original recording in the first part of the film not only creates a feeling of things grinding to a halt, or struggling to overcome the inertia imposed by heavy snowfall, but it also produces a qualitative change whereby musical sounds are rendered as sound effects. For example, the original recording begins with a simple rhythmic drum solo, combining bass drum, snare and cymbals. When Oram slows these instrumental sounds down, they become suggestive of the noises that are made by the steam trains we see on screen: the speed-changed cymbal crashes hint at the release of steam from pistons, while the slowed-down snare and bass drum sounds suggest the rattling movement of a train over the tracks.

The sound created by a steam train in movement is, of course, a rhythmic one. This is perhaps why it features so prominently in Schaeffer's first experiment in *musique concrète*, the *Etude aux Chemins de Fer* (1947), where it brings an inherently musical quality to the composition. However, Oram's application of reverb, echo and filtering ensure that the qualities of this rhythmic sound are in constant change, such that it never becomes a simple, steady, musical riff. Furthermore, Oram's use of electronics gives these sounds an impressionistic feel, further distancing them from the territory of non-diegetic musical accompaniment. As stated above, electronic filtering is used by Oram to create spatial effects that are closely matched to movement within shots, as well as with the progression of Jones's visual edit. Thus with one particular shot of a train entering a tunnel, the sound is filtered so that it assumes a 'muffled' quality. Changes in shot perspective are also matched by changes in timbre. For example, as a camera filming a snow-covered landscape from a moving train zooms out to a wide shot, the soundtrack is mixed to remove some of the lower frequencies in the music. A few shots later in the same sequence we see the track ahead, filmed from the side of the train. The film then jump-cuts to a shot of the same tracks taken from the front of the train, at which point there is a sudden reintroduction of lower frequency sound. This use of filtering, sometimes simulating Doppler-type effects, and the addition and removal of reverb and echo, serve to give the soundtrack a synthesized spatial relationship with the images, thereby breaking with the traditions of film music, whose non-diegetic status is announced in the de-spatialized and stable sonic signature of the studio recording. Oram's spatialization of the film's soundtrack does not, however, suggest that the sounds we hear are actually meant to emerge from profilmic space—the technique Walter Murch terms 'worldizing' (2003, p. 89). Rather, the soundtrack positions the listener in the space of the moving train by substituting ambient diegetic sound with electronically treated music that simulates the dynamic spatial cues embedded in location sound recordings. In this way, the modified recording of 'Teen Beat' becomes a non-diegetic analogue of the sonic environment one would experience on a moving train. Thus, while still maintaining its identity as music, Oram's reworking of 'Teen Beat' transforms music into an effect, radically blurring the boundaries between the two categories of sound, and setting in motion the distinction between diegetic and non-diegetic sound.

## *Guinness For You* (1971)

Although the development of British documentary tradition owed much to state sponsorship, corporate sponsors had always played an important role in supporting documentary filmmaking in Britain. In some instances, promotional films made for commercial sponsors offered documentary filmmakers a significant degree of creative freedom, motivated by the hope that a prestige production would reflect positively on the funder. Thus in 1971, the Guinness brewery sponsored the production of a short film that took a radically experimental approach to the promotion of its iconic Extra Stout bottled beer. The music for the film was composed and produced by Tristram Cary who, like Oram, had been a pioneer and an early champion of electroacoustic composition in Britain. From the mid-1950s until the 1970s, Cary earned a living writing music for film, radio and television, and while some of this commercial work necessitated the production of conventional orchestral scores—such as those for the Ealing comedy *The Ladykillers* (1955), or Hammer's *Blood from the Mummy's Tomb* (1971)—other projects, like as the Guinness commission, allowed more scope for experimentation.

In addition to writing orchestral works, Cary's compositional practice embraced both of the two main strands of electroacoustic music that had developed in the post-war period: electronic synthesis and *musique concrète*. Within the context of the film, electroacoustic sound tends to be associated with the representation of modernity, used primarily in scenes that illustrate the industrial processes by which both bottles and beer are manufactured. This contrasts with those parts of the film that deal with the cultivation and harvesting of barley and hops, and which feature rural landscapes and images of nature accompanied by the more traditional instrumental sounds of harp (a play on the sponsor's famous logo), flute and percussion.

The film opens with a short pre-title sequence of images of the sun, accompanied by flute, harp and cymbal, along with a single high frequency electronic tone. The film then rapidly transports us into the interior of a pub, the camera dollying in to a close-up of a friendly barman drying beer glasses.

No naturalistic sync sound is used in the film, and thus we do not hear the welcome that the barman gives direct to camera, which is communicated only by the mute movement of his lips. Rather than using traditional location sound here, Cary takes a recording of a group of people talking—suggesting the buzz of conversation in the bar—and filters it to create a strong distancing effect. This, coupled with the barman's silent salutation, creates a soundscape for the film that is anchored in the image, but at the same time is divorced from it. This unconventional approach to sound-image relations creates an audiovisuality that is located somewhere between the naturalism of ordinary sync sound and the 'abstraction' of contrapuntal sound; and it is this relationship that underpins the radical dynamism of Cary's electroacoustic score throughout the film.

Cary structures the relationship between sound and image through the repeated use of two key devices. First, the film employs a range of sounds that have some ontological connection with the space being represented on screen. Thus, in a sequence showing the automated movement of beer bottles around a manufacturing plant, Cary samples the sound of a bottle being struck. He then transposes this single sound into a short series of discrete pitches, each one of which is matched to the moment when an individual bottle is picked up by automated machinery. In the following sequence, a similar percussive 'glass' sound is repeated to create a rapid, rhythmic, tonal texture that accompanies shots of the bottles en masse. At other times, ||||Cary uses sounds that appear to have a much more direct connection with the specific action shown on screen, and which thus possess a more naturalistic relationship with the image—for example, the scraping of coins being picked up from a bar top, or the sound created by a glass blower rolling a blowpipe across a metal support. The first iteration of each of these sounds follows the conventions of normal sync sound practice, but Cary then loops the sound to create a rhythmic texture that extends in duration beyond the initial action or event. In this way he transposes the techniques and philosophy of *musique concrète* to an audiovisual context, creating a form of music from the manipulation of what would normally be considered sound effects or location recordings.

The second key device employed by Cary in structuring sound-image relations is to synchronize sounds to the film's visuals with great precision, so that they appear to be created by whatever is presented on screen. For example, during the film's credit sequence, we see a printing press producing labels for bottles of Extra Stout. As each sheet is printed, a shadow cast by the press moves across the frame in precise synchronization with the movement of paper. On the soundtrack we hear what appears to be an appropriate mechanical noise—repetitive and rhythmic like the action it accompanies and synced exactly with the movement on screen. The sound has an electronic quality that suggests it is entirely synthetic: produced by oscillators rather than derived from concrete sounds. Yet through the power of what Michel Chion terms synchresis—'the spontaneous and irresistible weld produced between a particular auditory phenomenon and visual phenomenon when they occur at the same time' (1994, p. 63)—the electronica is rendered as a naturalistic effect, appearing to mimic the sounds we might reasonably expect a printing press to make. Similarly, in a short montage of bottles of beer being opened, Cary accompanies each shot with an electronic sound that suggests the rush of gas as the bottle cap is loosened. The fact that this is synthesized rather than concrete sound is evidenced by the fact that, later in the film, the same action is accompanied by an altogether different sound: in this case a rhythmic thud, which nevertheless serves as an appropriate match for the image. Thus it is the precise alignment of sound and image, as well as the specific qualities of the sound itself, that render these synthesized electronic sounds believable as sound effects. In this way, Cary produces a soundtrack that functions both as music and effects, in which sounds drift between the two categories depending on how they are organized in relation to one another and to the image. This soundtrack does not follow a rigid musical logic, nor does it slavishly illustrate the film's visuals. Rather, sound and image are organized to mirror and echo one another, whereby sounds are inspired and shaped by images, and images are edited according to the musical forms that emerge from the material.

## Conclusion

While the erosion of boundaries between sound design and music may be considered a characteristic of contemporary filmmaking, what the films examined here demonstrate is that the integrated soundtrack has been a feature of British documentary cinema since the introduction of film sound technology in the 1930s. What we witness in creative documentary practice, as characterized by *Song of Ceylon*, *Snow* and *Guinness for You*, is a form of cinesonic transmigration, in which sound effects, real-world sounds, and speech occupy some of the creative territory that has often been considered the exclusive preserve of music. At the same time, films such as *Snow* and *Guinness For You* demonstrate that electroacoustic techniques have been employed in documentary cinema to produce musical forms that gravitate towards the territory of sound effects.

That documentary provided a space for this creative blurring of boundaries is perhaps not so surprising. If documentary has been formulated as the creative treatment of actuality, to use Grierson's famous phrase, then its practise raises the question of how concrete sounds—the actuality of the soundtrack—might be articulated creatively. The technologies of sound recording and film editing produced one set of responses to this question, providing a means by which filmmakers and composers could manipulate and organize concrete sounds in new ways, resulting in forms of electroacoustic practice that prefigured and paralleled the radical developments that were to take place in art music after World War II. In this sense, documentary cinema can be seen not simply to have drawn on the resources of modern music, but rather to have made its own radical contribution to the soundscape of the twentieth century.

## Notes

1. I refer here primarily to commissioned films produced by and for British governmental agencies such as the Empire Marketing Board, General Post Office, Ministry of Information, Central Office of Information, National Coal Board and commercial sponsors such as Shell, BP, ICI and others. In some instances, these documentaries were produced by film units located within the agencies or companies concerned (e.g., the EMB, GPO, Crown and Shell Film Units), while others were made by independent production companies such as Strand, Realist and DATA. In using the term 'tradition', I propose a continuity of creative practice that links work produced before, during and after World War II.
2. Accounts of these experiments can be found in James (1986), McLaren (1952) and Smirnov (2013).
3. Eisenstein's notes for the sound version of *Old and New* are published in Leyda, J. and Voynow, Z. (1985) *Eisenstein at Work*. London: Methuen, pp.38–40.

## References

Beck, J. (2008) 'The Sounds of "Silence": Dolby Stereo, Sound Design, and *The Silence of the Lambs*' in J. Beck and T. Grajeda (eds) *Lowering the Boom: Critical Studies in Film Sound* (Urbana and Chicago: University of Illinois Press), 68–83.

Cage, J. (1999) *Silence: Lectures and Writings*. London: Marion Boyars.

Cary, T. (1992) *Illustrated Compendium of Music Technology* (London: Faber and Faber).

Chion, M. (1994) *Audio-Vision: Sound on Screen* (New York: Columbia University Press).

Deleuze, G. and F. Guattari (1988) *A Thousand Plateaus: Capitalism and Schizophrenia* (London: Athlone Press).

Eisenstein, S. (1988) 'The Dynamic Square' [1930] in R. Taylor (ed.) *S. M. Eisenstein Selected Works Vol. 1, Writings, 1922–34* (London: BFI and Bloomington: Indiana University Press), 206–218.

Eisenstein, S.M., W. I. Pudowkin [Pudovkin] and G. V. Alexandroff [Alexandrov] (1928) 'The Sound Film: A Statement From U.S.S.R', *Close Up*, No. 3/4 October, 10–13.

Ellitt, J. (1935) 'On Sound', *Life and Letters Today*, December, 182–4.

Hardy, F. (1990) *The G.P.O. Film Unit 1933–1940*. POST Collection Post 108/91, The Royal Mail Archive, London.

International Festival of Short Films, Kraków (1964) *Snow* [Press bulletin] n.d. Cuttings Collection, BFI Reuben Library, London.

James, R. S. (1986) 'Avant-Garde Sound-on-Film Techniques and Their Relationship to Electro-Acoustic Music', *The Musical Quarterly*, Vol. 72, No. 1, 74–89.

Kahn, D. (1999) *Noise, Water, Meat: A History of Sound in the Arts* (Cambridge, Massachusetts: MIT Press).

Leigh, W. (1935) 'The Musician and the Film', *Cinema Quarterly*, Vol. 3, No. 2 Winter, 70–4.

Leyda, J. and Z. Voynow (1985) *Eisenstein at Work* (London: Methuen).

McLaren, N. (1952) *A Brief Summary of the Early History of Animated Sound on Film* [Manuscript]. Norman McLaren Archives. National Film Board of Canada http://www3.nfb.ca/archives_mclaren/items/01.pdf, date accessed 29 August 2014.

Michelson, A. (ed.) (1984) *Kino-Eye: The Writings of Dziga Vertov* (Berkeley and Los Angeles: University of California Press).

*Monthly Film Bulletin* (1967) 'Snow, Great Britain, 1963', Vol 34 (396), 49–50.

Murch, W. (2003) 'Touch of Silence' in L. Sider, D. Freeman and J. Sider (eds) *Soundscape: The School of Sound Lectures 1998–2001* (London: Wallflower Press), 83–102.

Murphy, T. S. (2004) 'What I Hear is Thinking Too: The Deleuze Tribute Recordings' in I. Buchanan and M. Swiboda (eds) *Deleuze and Music* (Edinburgh: Edinburg University Press), 163.

Oram, D. (n.d.) *Christmad Card with notes on the back regarding 'Snow'*, Daphne Oram Collection, 8/36/001, Goldsmiths University of London, London.

Ruttmann, W. (1930) 'Ruttmanns photographiesches Horspiel', *Film-Kurier*, No. 41, 15th February, http://www.medienkunstnetz.de/source-text/96/, date accessed 1 March 2015.

Schaeffer, P. (2012) *In Search of a Concrete Music* (Berkeley: University of California Press).

Smirnov, A. (2013) *Sound in Z: Experiments in Sound and Electronic Music in Early 20th Century Russia* (London: Sound and Music & Koenig Books).

Sussex, E. (1975) *The Rise and Fall of British Documentary: The Story of the Film Movement Founded by John Grierson* (Berkeley: University of California Press).

*The Times* (1963) 'Film Documentary About Railways Last Winter', 1st November, 16.

Varèse, E. (1940) 'Organized Sound for the Sound Film', *The Commonweal*, Vol. 13, No. 8, 13th December, 204–5.

*Wee Have Also Sound-Houses*. Sunday Feature (2008) BBC Radio 3. 3rd August.

Wright, B. (1976) *The Long View: An International History of Cinema* (St. Albans: Paladin).

Wright, B. (n.d.) *Song of Ceylon*, Basil Wright Collection BCW 1/1/3, BFI Special Collections, London.

CHAPTER 28

# Renegotiating the Overture: The Use of Sound and Music in the Opening Sequences of *A Single Man* and *Shame*

*Adam Melvin*

INTRODUCTION

In *A Single Man* (2009) and *Shame* (2011), directors Tom Ford and Steve McQueen offer two contrasting yet equally arresting portrayals of a male protagonist struggling to cope with an overwhelming affliction (grief and addiction, respectively). Occupying a somewhat peripheral place in relation to the Hollywood mainstream, both films have garnered attention for their striking, if slightly derivative visual styles: the attention to the beauty of image and colour in *A Single Man* evokes a magazine-like quality that is as revealing of Ford's extensive work in fashion design and advertising as McQueen's more measured style, 'airtight construction' (Tracy, 2011) and penchant for poetic visual set-pieces are of his own background in video installation. Yet, in addition to similar plot lines (fate intervening to change the two men's lives, suicide) and recapitulatory structures, both films employ an equally extensive use of music that does not quite seem in keeping with the intimacy of their shared subject matter. The presence of a lengthy montage sequence accompanied by rather 'overblown' (Ford, 2010) scored music at the beginning of each film adopts an almost retrogressive sensibility that prompts notions of the overture and its connotations in both cinema and composed music. In both cases, the way the overture-like quality is manifest in each sequence's visual, musical and indeed sonic language makes for an interesting comparison with the more discernible employment of the overture in films both recent and past, offering possible solutions to the establishment of a more integrated audio–visual language within mainstream cinematic models today.

A. Melvin
Ulster University, UK

## Defining the Overture

Although open to a degree of interpretation, the most fundamental reading of the overture within a filmic context is still perhaps best understood in relation to the shared attributes that broadly defined its various incarnations in opera and musical theatre. Like the art music overture, its cinematic equivalent is essentially 'an orchestral number played before ... [a work's] ... action begins' (Gallo, 2006, p. 14). Its temporal frame may offer a substantial enough canvas to make a suitably developed musical statement(s); on an aesthetic level, it might even aspire to the condition of 'a significant piece, a poetic conception, the essence of the drama to which it was prefixed' (Niecks, 1906, p. 389).[1]

The overture most readily identified with film is a similarly distinct, self-contained, introductory musical entity (in this case, pre-titles). A fundamentally classical concept, it is often associated with 'classical' cinema (Bordwell, Staiger, & Thompson, 1985), in particular the musical set-pieces[2] that partitioned the two-act roadshow presentation of the early to mid-twentieth century. A form of limited release preview, the roadshow sought to expand the film screening into a cinematic event or 'performance' essentially by appropriating the formal properties of musical theatre and grand opera. It is this inflated sense of grandeur and spectacle that prompted some directors to adopt the roadshow format for more general release, particularly where the film in question was somewhat epic in nature: 'over time the roadshow became a *type* of movie ... Presentation and content became one' (Holston, 2013, p. 260).[3] In both instances, the role of the overture can be seen as fundamentally performative. As a structural entity, it serves to expand the film beyond its existing temporal frame with an autonomous auditory statement that recreates the rituals of theatre. Thanks to the absence of any visual content,[4] the overture shuns the conventional 'dual discourse' within which film music normally operates (Kalinak, 1992, p. 14), spotlighting the music itself, so as to 'indicate the mood of the ensuing narrative and to lead the spectator into the musical universe of the film' (Larsen, 2005, p. 128). Traditionally, it has tended to be characterized by (often bold) symphonic scoring, thus igniting the performative connotations of concert music, while its musical content has largely been motivated by the presentation of themes associated with what Kalinak terms the 'classical' leitmotivic Hollywood score (1992).

These same attributes tend to inform broader interpretations of the overture beyond its more conventional/historical guise. For example, in the absence of a clear musical, prefatory statement, it is not uncommon for a film's title sequence to be referred to as an overture, where the musical component shares similar stylistic and/or functional attributes to the conventional, pre-titles model. The opening titles to *Star Wars* have been labelled an overture on account of the epic quality of John Williams's orchestral score in particular, its dual, contrasting heroic and romantic themes identified by Peter Larsen as traits reminiscent of overtures in older Hollywood melodramas (2005, p. 169). Here, the presence of a visual parameter—the titles themselves—actually serves to affirm the sequence's status as an overture rather than negate it, the famous scrolling text invoking associations with classical adventure film models (Heldt, 2013, p. 28) as well as a sense of scale (Long, 2008, p. 66) that reinforce notions of the epic established in the score. Indeed, it is perhaps worth noting that outside of typical convention, the title sequence in film most frequently described as an overture is referred to as such on the basis of its musical *and* visual elements. The title sequence created by Bernard Hermann and Saul Bass for Hitchcock's *Vertigo* presents an 'overture' (Cooke, 2008, p. 207; Kirkham, 1997, p. 18)[5] whose 'unsettling' (Kalinak, 1992, p. 7) musical content establishes a springboard for an elaborate use of leitmotivic cues across the film as a whole (see Cooper, 2003) while interplaying with a variety of related visual gestures in the form of abstract images, flushes of colour and the titles themselves. The end result encapsulates the aesthetic function of an overture, albeit in an audio–visual rather than conventional sense, in a manner that is less concerned with scale and more about 'condens(ing) the complex film to its essential ideas' (Kirkham, 1997, p. 18). The abstract quality of Bass's visual language not only references Hermann's score—spiral graphics mimic a similar circling effect in the arpeggio ostinato of the music (Kalinak, 1992, p. 15)—but is organized in a way that is not dissimilar to the presentation and development of musical leitmotifs; it, effectively, provides a second (quasi-)musical layer that works in counterpoint with what takes place aurally, thus affirming the sequence's essentially musical status.

Despite this somewhat expanded interpretation, the word 'overture' is rarely applied to cinematic models that stray from the neat structural partitions on which conventional interpretations of the term are based. The presence of a 'cozy musical cushion between … [the audience's] … world and that of the diegesis' (Long, 2008, p. 67), along with the absence of narrative action and in particular diegetic sound, remain prescripts. Where the term is used beyond its conventional cinematic associations, it is often employed in a rather more generic way to refer to introductory filmic sequences, including diegetic expositions that too function to establish cinematic relationships, albeit narrative rather than necessarily musical ones. Negar Mottahedeh offers a useful definition, calling the overture a 'self-reflexive sequence in which films reflect on the process of their own coming into being' (2008, p. 214).[6] In many ways, this more liberal reading is better suited to the contemporary vernacular of cinema today where the boundaries between titles and diegesis are seldom distinct (Long, 2008, p. 66). Nevertheless, the cinematic 'heritage' of the overture would seem to warrant a slightly more conventional use of the term than one which relinquishes its established historical musical links altogether.

What is proposed here is a more holistic interpretation of the overture that engages with its long-standing cinematic conventions but reconciles these attributes beyond the sphere of historical codes of presentation. The implications of audio and visual material—diegetic and non-diegetic—are considered within both a given introductory sequence and the broader narrative frame and aesthetic language of the film it precedes. Lars von Trier's *Melancholia* (2011) offers a useful, if somewhat retrogressive, example in this respect. Here, an opening montage of slow-motion sequences depicting various scenes from the film proper is organized in a way that evokes the kind of disrupted linear narrative that Wendy Everett argues is representative of music's own ability 'to fragment, extend or reverse time through its rhythmic patterning' (2008, p. 11).[7] Set to Wagner's prelude from *Tristan und Isolde* (in its entirety), the resulting audio–visual counterpoint serves to establish preconceptions of the overture in two complimentary ways: Wagner's piece provides a self-contained concert artefact that musically emphasizes the film's sense of melodrama and tragedy. This is, in turn, reinforced by the poetic grandeur of the sequence's images—complete with a depiction of an interplanetary collision[8]—which function rather like a medley of musical motifs, affording the director the opportunity to 'strike some themes' (von Trier in Thorsen, 2011) thus establishing the film's oneiric quality 'in one full blow' (von Trier in Thorsen, 2011).[9]

Elsewhere, the use of similarly substantial musical set-pieces has enabled filmic introductions to encroach further onto diegetic content. In Gus Van Sant's *Gerry* (2002), the serenity of the two protagonists' journey through the remote, unchanging landscape of the American wilderness, serves to establish the ethereal aesthetic of the film rather than any clear narrative as such. The five-minute-long opening driving sequence represents a suitably ample and musically motivated exposition to be considered an overture. This is emphasized by the quiescent simplicity of Arvo Pärt's *Spiegel Im Spiegel* (1978) to which the sequence is set, a choice of music that transfers 'a strange sense of timelessness to the images of two figures caught in a temporal and spatial limbo', as Danijela Kulezic-Wilson argues (2012, p. 84).[10]

## SHAME AND *A SINGLE MAN*: OVERBLOWN OVERTURES

Neither *Shame* nor *A Single Man* incorporate a distinct, 'conventional' musical overture in the same way that, say, *Melancholia* does. However, both films contain substantial introductory sequences that, although absorbed within each film's narrative, remain heavily musical in both content and identity. The integration of musical and visual material along with the somewhat alien parameter of sound (in terms of the overture at least) results in an audio–visual dynamic that, in both instances, invokes and indeed advances the overture's conventional role as a vehicle for establishing themes, while also adopting the sense of performative grandeur associated with more 'classical' incarnations of the term.

Based on the Christopher Isherwood novel of the same name, *A Single Man* is a glossy and often tender day-in-the-life or 'day-in-the-mind' (Stevens, 2013, p. 99) portrayal of George (Colin Firth), a middle-aged, gay, expat college professor struggling to come to terms with the sudden death of his partner, Jim, in a car accident. Here, the opening sequence pre-empts what is an extensive use of music across the film as a whole, the nature of which is unashamedly retrogressive in both the musical language employed and the frequency of its cues. The lush lyricism of Abel Korzeniowski's substantial orchestral score coupled with the occasional use of diegetic music—soul, jazz and a somewhat clichéd[11] use of Alfredo Catalani's *La Wally* which George listens to while making the final preparations for his suicide—reflects Ford's aforementioned preoccupation with visual beauty while affirming the film's setting in early 1960s Southern California. In addition, the inclusion of scored music by Japanese composer Shigeru Umebayashi reinforces the film's 'classical' aesthetic by consciously spotlighting the filmic references that have influenced Ford. A reworking of Hermann's Wagnerian lament 'Scotty Trails Madeline' from *Vertigo* accompanies the little girl who lives next door to George wearing the same shade of green that Kim Novak's character famously adorns in the film; the same cue later introduces a shot of a giant billboard of Janet Leigh's eyes advertising Hitchcock's *Psycho*. Elsewhere, music strongly reminiscent of the composer's theme employed by Wong Kar-Wai's *In the Mood for Love* (2000), the stylistic aesthetic of which *A Single Man* has been compared to (Stevens, 2013, p. 112), accompanies a dreamy slow-motion sequence of George driving to work for what will be the last time.

While *Shame* employs relatively few scored cues, its musical content can be viewed as equally extensive. The film itself offers a stark and austere depiction of Brandon (Michael Fassbender), a thirty-something professional and compulsive sex addict whose life threatens to implode when his sister, Cissy, intrudes on his delicately balanced existence. Although rather more diffuse in terms of the range of music employed—jazz, pop and even Bach—*Shame*'s use of predominantly diegetic music in many ways reinforces McQueen's more observational directorial style serving to firmly locate the film in what seems to be present-day New York and specifically its nightlife, while subliminally hinting—through the titles and lyrics of the club tracks employed—at the predatory nature of Brandon's sexual pursuits (Pride, 2011).[12] In turn, Harry Escott's sombre score is confined to the two set-piece montage sequences that frame the film (three if one includes the piano version of the score that features in the film's end credits).

Arguably, the most significant aspect of both 'overtures' is the overblown quality of their music. In each case, music serves to install a heightened sense of melodrama from the outset, presenting each male protagonist as a fundamentally tragic (in the dramatic and more generic sense of the word) figure. Central to this dynamic is the fact that while both sequences feature original scores, the style of music is derivative of somewhat grander Hollywood scoring conventions and associations of film genre than one might expect from what are, in essence, two films about 'human beings…trying to get through a day'(McQueen in Chernick, 2011).[13] Escott's opening string score for *Shame*—a repeated Dies Irae-like ten-chord cycle that gradually grows in volume and texture over a steady clock-like tick—bears a striking resemblance to Hans Zimmer's scores for Christopher Nolan's sci-fi action film *Inception* (2010) and more notably, Terrence Malick's ethereal World War II drama, *The Thin Red Line* (1998). While neither of these scores is particularly representative of any specific film genre as such, they do constitute generic examples of dark, foreboding Hollywood film music that, in terms of the guise in which it features in *Shame*, seems overtly epic, particularly given its early place in the film's chronology (in the two Zimmer examples, the music is heard further into the dark heart of each film). Here, the overture in question takes the form of a montage sequence that gradually reveals the events of Brandon's previous night and morning after. The oppressive severity of the score (over)emphasizes the destructive nature of Brandon's life in a way that isolates him as a character; like his addiction, the music effectively 'consumes' (the montage sequence of) his day to the extent that he is—at least aurally—immersed in his own world.[14]

In *A Single Man*, both the opening score and the titles themselves adopt a more classically lavish, Hitchcockian sensibility that, while less perspicuous than the Hermann-esque interpretations elsewhere in the film, initially seems to introduce the film as a psychological thriller. Opening with a classic 'Hollywood Rocket' (Long, 2008, p. 47) in the form of an ascending harp glissando, Korzeniowski's score puts a dark twist on the more conventional musical typology of the waltz suggesting love (Brown, 1994, p. 10). Here, a somewhat turbulent two-note (short–long) descending theme forms the basis of a musical accompaniment to a full titles sequence set against the backdrop of a naked man—eventually revealed to be the film's protagonist—floating (drowning?) underwater, recalling the marriage of similarly 'tumbling' musical and visual gestures in the aforementioned titles of *Vertigo*.[15] Like *Shame*, the immersive quality of the thick orchestral texture serves to introduce the protagonist as isolated in his own lonely turmoil, although here in a far more literal way if one considers the titles' visual content.

## *A Single Man*: Dissolving Overture—Evolving Diegesis

In many ways, it is the intrinsic link between each film's musical component and its lead protagonist, specifically the unreality of each man's existence, rather than simply the grandeur of these opening statements, that is fundamental to their interpretation as overtures. In *A Single Man*, the opening titles represent only the first part of what can be seen as a continuous overture sequence that dovetails with the gradually unfolding diegesis of the film's introduction. Here, the repeated, monochrome image of the submerged man and titles establishes a visual stasis that foregrounds the music allowing Korzeniowski's two-note theme to develop organically into more fluid, undulating melodic shapes that establish the passage as a fundamentally musical entity. Like the shots of Kim Novak's face in *Vertigo*, we only get to glimpse parts of the individual onscreen. The diegetic context of what we are witnessing is unclear; it could be real but seems imagined.

Once the titles conclude and the floating man's face becomes recognizable as George's (Firth), the sequence flickers back and forth twice before settling on footage of what we later learn to be the aftermath of Jim's car accident; the car is lying overturned in the snow with Jim's body adjacent. At this point, the music shifts to a quicker, duple-time tempo. The two-note descending theme is retained in the form of both an accompanying ostinato and an isolated cuckoo-like gesture that supports a sustained solo violin melody reminiscent of the 'Scotty Trails Madeline' figure from *Vertigo* and in particular its source, Wagner's prelude to *Tristan und Isolde*.[16] While this sequence does represent a shift into the diegetic language of the film of sorts, it is in the form of a liminal space rather than the diegesis proper. As George enters the visual frame, dressed impeccably in a dark suit that seems incongruous with the surroundings, the processional manner in which he steadily walks over to Jim's body, before lying down next to him in the snow and leaning over to kiss him, confirms the sequence to be a dream. While the steadier harmonic movement of the score provides enough stasis for the events on screen to unfold, the continuity formed with the previous title sequence and the presence of a clear melodic statement enables the sequence to remain fundamentally musical. The scene comes to an abrupt halt as it cuts to an overhead close-up of George gasping—the film's first 'diegetic' sound—as he is suddenly woken from his sleep.

As it stands, this introduction forms a rather neat bipartite structure that can be seen to embody several overture-like attributes. The dual musical statements recall the sense of exposition and development (Kalinak, 1992, p. 98) and use of contrasting motifs (Larsen, 2005, p. 169) associated with classical models of the overture, while musically and visually it presents themes that are developed elsewhere in the film. The falling two-note motif evolves into a repeated cascading four-note pattern for many of the encounters with Kenny (Nicholas Hoult), the student George gradually befriends over the course of the film, notably the sequence where he and George go skinny dipping. A similar two-note figure (albeit with a weak-to-strong rhythmic emphasis) characterizes Umebayashi's score in the aforementioned driving sequence. We even have a reoccurrence of the drowning sequence towards the end of the film as Kenny watches George doze off in front of the fire in his living room; the water is now tinted red/orange, indicating that George has found warmth both mentally and physically but is still dying, while the musical figure has reversed to a long–short based, waltz-like violin melody, essentially George's final theme.

However, if we consider the sequence that follows in the same context, the language and functionality of its material make-up suggest that it too should be deemed a part of this overture. Essentially a montage of George's morning routine before he leaves for work, this passage, while certainly of an expository disposition, does not quite firmly place us within the film's narrative proper either; it is more a case of a diegetic layer having been peeled back. For one thing, the voice that communicates to us is not the George we witness getting washed and dressed on screen, but George as a voice-over, or as Ford suggests, George's soul (Ford, 2010; Stevens, 2013, p. 109). From its first utterance, 'waking up begins with saying *am* and *now*'[17]—a line that recalls Mottahedeh's earlier definition of overture—the voice-over immediately reinforces the ambiguity and unreality of George's existence (Stevens, 2013, p. 108), offering what Stevens suggests is a 'supernatural perspective' that he argues is ultimately melancholic (2013, p. 109).

Visually, the sequence is initially rather unstable, consisting of several abruptly cut close-ups of George's body (feet, hands, face) and images with a heavily metaphorical content (the ink on George's sheets, the clock on his bedside cabinet) that, while emphasizing the painful agitation of George's awakening (Stevens, 2013, p. 110), evoke a rhythmic quality that provides a degree of aesthetic continuity with the previous musically orientated sequence. These images eventually settle to steady panning and tracking shots employing more distance; like George, they 'take time to become'.[18]

The music that follows also retains a sense of continuity with the preceding scenes, introducing a calm, repeated piano figure that forms a less obtrusive take on the Wagnerian melody heard during the car accident sequence (both are defined by an ascending three-note figure). More significant, however, is the role of sound. Although overshadowed by the music, sound is actually present throughout the overture; both opening dream sequences are accompanied by a diegetic sonic backdrop of bubbling water and icy wind, respectively. While the presence of sound, at least from a conventional perspective, would seem to undermine the overture-like quality of the sequence established by Korzeniowksi's 'classical' score, here it binds the three parts of the overture, dispelling any sense of Long's 'cozy cushion'. In addition, a crescendo of white noise, initially materializing into the clearly recognizable sound of (Jim's) car crashing (which we never see), accompanied by the sound of a frantically quickening heartbeat, provides a second 'Hollywood Rocket' of sorts that marks each transition in the unfolding narrative. The fact that this sonic gesture is also heard before the opening titles commence—it announces the logo for Ford's film company *Fade to Black*—only emphasizes its structural role.

In the transition into this final third of the overture, George's startled gasp replaces the sound of the car crash while the sound of his raised heartbeat is succeeded by an invasively monotonous tapping sound, the timbre and measured regularity of which suggest a dripping tap but is actually confirmed later in the film to be the sound of the young girl, who lives next door to George, hammering on a set of bathroom scales in her garden. The voice-over utters its aforementioned first line, we hear a mother scolding her child in the distance and the tapping gives way to the already present, softer and slower tick of a clock.

In a narrative sense, the tapping and ticking serve to confirm the diegetic reality of George's waking life establishing an aural reference point that locates him in his house/neighbourhood while providing a more conventional sonic symbol of emptiness, associated with his unwanted singledom; the ticking emphasizes the lack of any other sounds in his home. Meanwhile, the rhythmic regularity of both sounds enables the sequence to sustain a musical sensibility during the initial absence of scored music; the ticking even synchronizes with some of the early quick-fire camera shots, reinforcing the images' aforementioned rhythmic quality. The fact that these sonic gestures precede their visual confirmation, in the first instance by some (temporal) distance, and immediately succeed George's fluctuating pulse, also ties them to the notion of

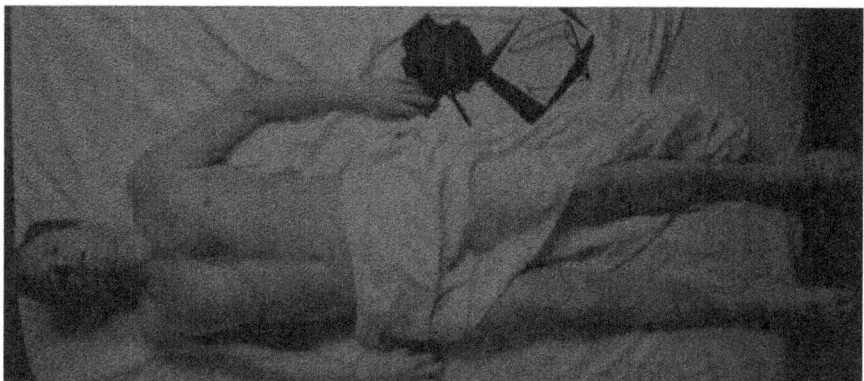

**Fig. 28.1** George (Colin Firth) in *A Single Man* (Tom Ford, 2009)

George's corporeal existence, albeit in a way that, like the voice-over, further undermines it. While George is dreaming, the sense of anxiety suggested by the sound of his raised heartbeat[19] confirms his corporeality. When he awakens, the fact that the rhythm of a steady pulse is retained but expressed with a 'synthetic' sonority seems to reflect the mechanical nature of George's existence; he is alive but only in the functional sense of maintaining the pretence of his daily routine. Indeed, his presentation here is not unlike a corpse—he lies flat on his back with his bed sheets arranged around his person like a loincloth (see Fig. 28.1) (Stevens, 2013, p. 108).[20] He is of course on borrowed time. In the film's final scene, George returns to his bedroom only to suddenly clutch his chest and collapse knocking his clock to the floor in the process. Although the sound of smashing seems to suggest the clock is broken, only now does it begin to tick, growing in volume before stopping abruptly just as George dies (Stevens, 2013, p. 110; Wallace, 2014, p. 29).

With the inclusion of the ticking clock, the overture introduces one of the film's most important sonic and visual symbols, one that is itself replete with its own long-established cinematic connotations surrounding suspense (temporal and dramatic) and, in this instance, is fundamental to the way in which the soundtrack playfully navigates the film's diegesis. The repeated image of the clock in *A Single Man* has a symbolic function that seems to locate itself somewhere between the 'icons ... of passing moments' (Front, 2011, p. 147) in the aforementioned *In the Mood for Love* and a more conventional association of 'fear and dread' as epitomized in, for example, *High Noon* (Fred Zinnemann, 1952) (Lerner, 2005, p. 158); George himself is counting down the hours until his imminent, intended suicide. As a sonic motif, the ticking of the clock continually repositions itself within the film's diegesis, beyond its initial association with George's 'duration of life' (Stevens, 2013, p. 110) as a means of emphasizing his liminal existence. In the Umebayashi-scored driving sequence, it appears in diegetic form (the clock in George's car) but at first seems divorced from the camera, marking real time against the sequence's slow-motion movement. As the scene unfolds, the sound is treated with a delay effect that gradually connects it to the pace of the visual, reinforcing the ethereal quality of the sequence but also perhaps George's slowed perception of time as he nears death (Ford argues that this sequence depicts George 'taking things in for the last time'/2010/); the same sound also marks the earlier, equally dream-like flashbacks featuring Jim. For much of this final part of the overture, the ticking undergoes a musical transformation as it is absorbed into the non-diegetic score in the form of a repeated rhythmic figure which retains the same clock-like timbre and pulse-per-second tempo underneath the aforementioned piano cue. To paraphrase Henri Lefebvre, here, 'Musical time resembles ... but reassembles [the rhythms of the body]' (2004, p. 64). As the voice-over informs us that the day we are about to witness 'is going to be different', another sonic sleight of hand—a telephone ringing in the present that triggers a flashback to the telephone call George receives informing him of Jim's death—brings the music, and overture, to a close.

## *Shame*: Audio–Visual Music

An equally musical, yet ultimately more pronounced employment of sound supports the interpretation of the opening sequence of *Shame* as constituting an overture. If Ford's film presents a linear, more cumulative deployment of filmic structures and musical materials, then *Shame* offers a more contrapuntal audio–visual dynamic within a more self-contained entity. In many ways, *Shame*'s overture revisits similar notions of repetition and ritual explored in McQueen's debut film, *Hunger* (see Melvin, 2011). Although *Shame* tends to spotlight sonic material far less than its predecessor, it adopts a similarly motivic use of sound, the treatment of which—in the case of the overture—forms an audio–visual counterpoint that arguably establishes even more of a composed, 'musical sensibility' than its predecessor (Melvin, 2011, p. 28).

Employing no formal titles sequence, *Shame* begins rather suddenly with an almost identical (bar the colour of the bed linen) 'corpselike' (Quandt, 2011, p. 51) image of its principal character to that of *A Single Man* (see Fig. 28.2). In this instance, the evocation is far more obtrusive: Brandon (Fassbender) lies entirely motionless, staring vacantly at the ceiling, his eyes almost rolled back. After a few moments, the regular electronic pulse of an alarm is heard, serving as the anacrusis for another metrical ticking sound that eventually forms the rhythmic backdrop for the sequence's scored music. Neither sound stirs him; he only reacts after hearing muffled noises from the adjacent apartment. Brandon gets out of bed and (offscreen) opens his blinds, the sound of which—a fluttering sweep of white noise—presents another Hollywood Rocket-like anacrusis that reveals the film's title onscreen against his now sunbathed sheets.

While the presence of a clock-like tick is in itself similar to *A Single Man*, its guise and connotations are very different here. The quicker tempo (four ticks per second) insinuates not the monotonous, empty passing of time but urgency and

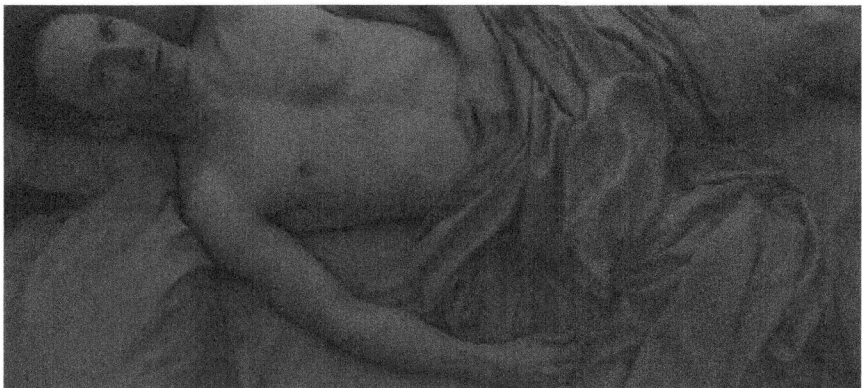

**Fig. 28.2** Brandon (Michael Fassbender) in *Shame* (Steve McQueen, 2011)

tension, perhaps the agitation of Brandon sourcing his next fix, or indeed the implication that Brandon himself is a ticking time bomb. Furthermore, because the sound forms part of the score, it is, for all intents and purposes, non-diegetic. The ambiguity of its sonority and subtle timbral shifts mean the audience never firmly associates the sound with a diegetic clock (which never appears). The closest thing we get to a visual confirmation of its source is a scene early in the movie of Brandon vigorously tapping his foot while watching pornography on his laptop in his apartment (a similar foot-tapping moment occurs in *Hunger* just before an agitated Bobby Sands—also played by Fassbender—riots in his prison cell/see Melvin, 2011, p. 29/). This prompts a further association of the ticking sound, that of the regulated rhythms of intercourse and masturbation, as Sandhu notes (2012), the sex act is mechanical for Brandon. It is perhaps also worth noting that whenever the tapping/ticking does resurface in *Shame*, it is often attached to diegetic classical music. The sequence above occurs directly after we have witnessed Brandon listening to Glenn Gould's recording of Bach's *Goldberg Variations* in his apartment. Later, Bach is heard again, also diegetically (Brandon's iPod or equivalent) during a lengthy set-piece of Brandon jogging through the streets of New York at night. Here, Brandon's footsteps provide the metrical tick, often fading in and out of audibility as the initial tick in the overture does, while the left hand ostinato of the Prelude in question, characterized by a three-quaver ascending scale figure preceded by a downbeat, recalls a similarly rising scalic motif that emerges as the countermelody in Escott's opening scored cue.[21] Whether intended or not, the musical similarity serves to integrate what have been two somewhat derided uses of music in the film.[22]

The tick is one of a number of sonic gestures presented in *Shame*'s overture—others include the sound of breathing and running water (a tap, Brandon showering and urinating)—that seem to acquire their own motivic relevance over the course of the film. Their positioning in various guises both within and outside of the film's diegesis reflects the similar crossing of diegetic planes in the overture of *A Single Man*. Furthermore, the fact that these sounds are handled with what appears to be a conscious regard for their musical properties results in a convergence of musical and sonic gestures that at times becomes uncanny, and ultimately reinforces the implied sense of unreality surrounding Brandon's existence. The most significant of these is a falling two-'note' figure that rather coincidentally resembles the opening musical motif of *A Single Man*. This first appears a little way into the non-diegetic score in the form of an ostinato—slower, yet similar to Korzeniowski's aforementioned ostinato—that emerges as a decorative figure to the music's repeated chord sequence.[23] Moments later, this motif features as the diegetic double-click of Brandon pushing the message playback button on his answering machine and more discernibly, the sound of a doorbell that signals the arrival of a prostitute to Brandon's apartment. What makes the latter unusual is that not only are the pitches of the doorbell diatonically consonant with the harmony of Escott's score but also the entry of the gesture is accurately 'in time' with the music; it is heard both as a diegetic signal *and* as part of the musical text (emphasized by the fact that it temporally pre-empts the cut to the shot of the apartment door that visually confirms its source). Indeed, the doorbell (its timbre and pitch) actually becomes a significant motif in its own right later in the film, particularly with regard to the use of diegetic pop music such as Chic's 'I want your love' and Blondie's 'Rapture', both of which feature similar doorbell-like gestures in their instrumental arrangements.

As the overture sequence progresses, the falling two-note motif is articulated once more by the disembodied female voice on Brandon's answer machine half-singing his name (Bran-don), whom we later learn to be his sister, Cissy (Carey Mulligan). This voice is intriguing, not least because we initially assume it belongs to one of Brandon's 'conquests'. The fact that the message is almost performed in what seem to be steady musical measures creates further obscurity to its entry:

'Hey' ... (beat) ... 'it's me' ... (beat) ... 'pick up' ... (beat) ... 'pick up'.

The rhythmic two-beat quality of the utterances even seems to pre-empt the motif mentioned above. The presentation of Cissy often reverts to this steadily repetitive rhythmical delivery, including her desperate phone call to whom we assume is her boyfriend ('I love you' ... (beat) ... 'I love you' ... (beat) .... 'I'll do anything') as well as her languid, dirge-like performance of 'New York, New York', which she 'slows ... down to a breaking point ... and transforms ... into a plaintive ballad of American liminality' (Sandhu, 2012, p. 77), further emphasizing her ambiguity.

More significant in the context of the overture, however, is that the voice first belongs to a visual sequence that is itself treated motivically. Interspersed between temporally displaced fragments of footage from two other narrative sequences (the prostitute's visit and Brandon's journey on the subway), the footage of Brandon exiting his bedroom and walking naked to his kitchen for a glass of water, switching on his answer machine en route, is actually repeated and extended the second time around, recalling Everett's musical analogy. If 'repetitive sound necessarily evokes music' (Chion, 2009, p. 112), then similarly, this sequence is rather like a musical theme, akin to the Bach examples mentioned earlier; it is presented and extended before being developed by other motifs (Escott's accompanying score follows a similar trajectory, of course). Recalling several of McQueen's video installation works whose similar focus on the 'repetitiveness of ... actions ... liberates them from the structure of narrative development' (Demos, 2005, p. 72), notably the looping footage of his Turner Prize-winning piece *Deadpan* (1999), the sequence further reinforces the ritualistic mundanity of Brandon's life—each day is essentially the same—as well as the unreal nature of his existence. Indeed, the totality of this opening overture can be seen to embody precisely 'the *uncertainty* between the real and the virtual' (Demos, 2005, p. 66) stressed in many of the director's artworks arguably to a greater extent than any other passage in his three film releases to date. This particular sequence is given further emphasis by the fact that each repetition is announced by an additional sweep of Brandon's blinds (offscreen). Although comparable to the similarly structural white noise gesture in *A Single Man*, here the sonic marker functions not to partition the overture but to anchor its multiple narrative strands and motivic gestures. All this serves to spotlight the arrival point on which the sequence settles, a powerfully drawn-out silent flirtation (fruitless in the end) between Brandon and a woman sat opposite him on the subway, the melodramatic intensity of which is magnified by what is arguably the most effective employment of Escott's score.

## Concluding Comments

Aside from Ford's acknowledged allusion to *Vertigo* in *A Single Man*, neither director has referred to either opening sequence as an overture or indeed expressed any intent to capture an overture-like dynamic in their respective films. In a sense, the use of music in both, particularly their lavish scores, can be dismissed simply as an over-exuberant attempt on the part of each director to position his film more strategically within the mainstream either by establishing a sense of cinematic heritage with a more 'classical' bygone era (Ford) or simply by employing music more typical of generic contemporary Hollywood models (Hans Zimmer scored McQueen's third film, *12 Years a Slave*/2013/).

While the later moments of both films can be accused of overcooking the marriage of music and film, particularly the 'bathetic Barber-like' (Quandt, 2012) reprise of Escott's score[24] in the much derided conclusion of *Shame*, it should perhaps not detract from the way in which both directors have managed to integrate the audio–visual language of these surprisingly similar opening salvos in a manner that, while 'a bit melodramatic',[25] is balanced by a functionality that is both deftly handled and relevant to the narrative progression of each film. Both sequences succeed in renegotiating conventional film scoring practices surrounding the stating and developing of themes within an audio–visual rather than purely musical canvas. The pivotal role of sound and focus on the musical potential of repeated gestures within the larger diegetic complex that frames and indeed epitomizes their lead protagonists in each case presents a somewhat richer and less retrogressive variant on the overture than its more rudimentary use in, say, the von Trier example mentioned earlier, one that embodies and indeed advances the cohesion and musical sensibility of the *Vertigo* exemplar. Despite Ford's obvious stylistic homage to Hitchcock, it is the interwoven construction of *Shame*'s exposition that emerges as an equally, if not more relevant comparison in this respect. The fact that both films could conceivably begin from the moment both overtures cease, and still remain intact in the narrative sense (albeit with their aesthetic lessened somewhat), reinforces the existence of each sequence as both distinct musical entity and diegetic exposition. Returning to Niecks's definition, both are significant, certainly poetic and the very essence of the dramas they prefix.

## Notes

1. Niecks's quote is in direct reference to Gluck's landmark overture to *Iphigénie en Aulide* (1774) which he identifies as the template for the 'modern' overture.
2. Commonly an overture, entr'acte and exit music.
3. The same practice is still occasionally used today: the Director's Cut to Ridley Scott's *Kingdom of Heaven* (2005) incorporates the roadshow format along with some 45 minutes of additional footage and seems to have received more favourable reviews than the original theatrical version.
4. Hollywood has been keen to preserve the overture's musical autonomy if one considers the often perfunctory use of text (the word 'overture'), images in stasis or indeed the blank screen as a substitute for the roadshow's closed curtains.
5. Inverted commas are used by both writers in reference to the sequence and in Kirkham's case, to Bass's contribution. One assumes that the sequence is an 'overture' because of its visual content and would need to be purely musical in order to constitute an overture (no inverted commas).
6. There is still a musical undercurrent here. The quote refers to the opening credits sequence of *DelShodegan* (Ali Hatami, 1992) which is accompanied by music and depicts a craftsman making musical instruments.
7. Besides the use of an existing operatic overture, one wonders if it is because of this fundamentally musical sensibility that von Trier himself refers to *Melancholia*'s opening as an overture. His 2009 film, *Antichrist,* features a similar opening slow-motion montage sequence accompanied by Handel's Aria, 'Lasciach'iopianga'. However, the director titles the passage (onscreen) a Prologue. The difference here is that *Antichrist* presents a clear, linear narrative exposition (it depicts the death of a couple's baby son) rather than a more abstract visual statement.
8. There are obvious parallels here with Kubrick's *2001: A Space Odyssey* (1968), a film that employs one of the most celebrated uses of an overture in recent film history.
9. The precise quote is 'that gets rid of the aesthetic side in one full blow', although presumably von Trier means 'establishes the aesthetic side'.

10. Kulezic-Wilson also draws comparisons between the two lead characters' homonymous presentation and the title of Pärt's piece (translated as 'Mirror(s) in the Mirror') as well as its musical make-up; both the violin and piano articulate what is fundamentally the same musical line at different rates (2012, p. 84).
11. The scene recalls what Susan McClary calls 'the standard catharsis Hollywood had conditioned us to expect' in reference to a scene incorporating an operatic aria in *Philadelphia* (Jonathan Demme, 1993) (2007, p. 61).
12. Pride's rather negative review of *Shame* calls this 'gleeful contrivance'.
13. Although in reference to *Shame*, McQueen's sound bite echoes George's first utterance onscreen in *A Single Man*: 'Just get through the goddamn day'.
14. There are parallels with similar purgatorial states in which the Zimmer example features in the two films cited.
15. Although Ford does not implicitly state that *Vertigo* influenced this title sequence, he does mention Hitchcock's film in his audio commentary during the opening titles.
16. One might draw parallels with a similar appearance of the spectre of a lost love at the conclusion of *Vertigo*, featuring Hermann's Wagnerian score.
17. Also the first line of Isherwood's novel (Ford, 2010).
18. The voice-over line is 'it takes time in the morning for me to become George'.
19. For a thorough discussion on the relationship between fear and heartbeats, see Winters (2008).
20. I disagree with Stevens's otherwise excellent paper when he says 'at first, the sleeping George looks dead'. While the image of him might be interpreted that way, we never actually see George asleep and his first appearance in situ is marked by the sound of his gasping confirming him as anything but dead.
21. The similarity is made more apparent once Escott's score is transferred to piano for the end credits.
22. While Sukhdev calls the use of Bach 'heavyhanded' (2012), McQueen has justified its inclusion as providing a sense of order—'a mathematical equation in music'—for Brandon within his chaotic world (Huppert, 2011).
23. This too is more pronounced in the piano version of Escott's score.
24. Almost all the criticism of Escott's score has been directed at this sequence. See Tracy (2011) and Quandt (2011).
25. George as voice-over says this immediately after the line mentioned in note 13.

## References

Bordwell, D., J., Staiger and K. Thompson (1985) *The Classical Hollywood Cinema: Film, Style and Mode of Production to 1960* (London: Routledge).

Brown, R. S. (1994) *Overtones and Undertones: Reading Film Music* (London and Berkley: University of California Press).

Chernick, A. (2011) 'The Confessions of Steve McQueen', *Nowness*, 11 October http://www.nowness.com/day/2011/10/11/1670/the-confessions-of-steve-mcqueen?utm_source=YOUT&utm_medium=SM&utm_campaign=YT1001, date accessed 14 July 2014.

Chion, M. (2009) *Film, A Sound Art*, trans. C. Gorbman, (New York: Columbia University Press).

Cooke, M. (2008) *A History of Film Music* (Cambridge: Cambridge University Press).

Cooper, D. (2003) 'Film Form and Musical Form in Bernard Hermann's Score to *Vertigo*', *The Journal of Film Music*, Vol. 1, No. 2–3, 239–248.

Demos, T.J. (2005) 'The art of darkness: On Steve McQueen', *October* 114 (Fall), 61–89, http://www.ucl.ac.uk/art-history/about_us/academic_staff/dr_tj_demos/further?publications, date accessed 4 April 2011.

Everett, W. (2008) 'Image, Music, Film', *Studies in European Cinema* Vol. 5, No. 1, 7–16.

Front, S. (2011) 'Labyrinth of Time in Wong Kar-Wai's *In the Mood for Love* and *2046*', *Asian Journal of Literature, Culture and Society*, Vol. 5, No. 1 (April), 144–155.

Ford, T. ([2009] 2010) 'DVD Extras: Director's Audio Commentary', *A Single Man*, DVD, Icon.

Gallo, D. (2006) *Opera: The Basics* (New York and London: Routledge).

Heldt, G. (2013) *Music and Levels of Narration in Film: Steps Across the Border* (Bristol: Intellect).

Holston, K. R. (2013) *Movie Roadshows: A History and Filmography of Reserved-Seat Limited Showings, 1911–1973* (Jefferson, North Carolina: McFarland Publishings).

Huppert, C. (2011) 'Steve McQueen's Sense of Release', *Interview Magazine* http://www.interviewmagazine.com/film/steve-mcqueen-shame/, date accessed 25 June 2014.

Kalinak, K. (1992) *Settling the Score: Music and the Classical Hollywood Film* (Madison, Wisconsin: University of Wisconsin Press).

Kirkham, P. (1997) 'The Jeweller's Eye', *Sight and Sound* (April), 18–19.

Kulezic-Wilson, D. (2012) 'Gus Van Sant's Soundwalks and Audio-visual *Musique Concrète*' in J. Wierzbicki (ed.) *Music, Sound and Filmmakers: Sonic Style in Cinema* (New York and London: Routledge), 76–88.

Larsen, P. (2005) *Film Music* (London: Reaktion Books).

Lefebvre, H. (2004) *Rhythmanalysis: Space, Time and Everyday Life*. trans. E. Stuart and G. Moore (London: Continuum).

Lerner, N. (2005) '"Look at that big hand move along": Clocks, Containment, and Music in *High Noon*', *South Atlantic Quarterly*, Vol. 104, No. 1 (Winter), 151–173.

Long, M. (2008) *Beautiful Monsters: Imagining the Classic in Musical Media* (Berkeley, Los Angeles: University of California Press).

McClary, S. (2007) 'Minima Romantica' in D. Goldmark, L. Kramer and R. Leppert (eds) *Beyond the Soundtrack: Representing Music in Cinema* (Berkley and London: University of California Press), 48–65.

Melvin, A. (2011) 'Sonic motifs, structure and identity in Steve McQueen's *Hunger*', *The Soundtrack*, Vol. 4, No. 1, 23–32.

Mottahedeh, N. (2008) *Representing the Unpresentable: Historical Images of National Reform from the Qajars to the Islamic Republic of Iran* (New York: Syracuse University Press).

Niecks, F. (1906) 'Historical Sketch of the Overture', *Sammelbände der Internationalen Musikgesellschaft*, Vol. 7, No. 3, 386–390.

Pride, R. (2011) 'The Blame of "Shame": Steve McQueen's Sex and the City', *NewCityFilm* (Chicago), http://newcityfilm.com/2011/11/30/the-blame-of-shame-steve-mcqueens-sex-and-the-city/, date accessed 25 June 2014.

Quandt, J. (2012) 'Cock and Bull Story: James Quandt on Steve McQueen's *Shame*', *Artforum International*, Vol. 50, No. 5, 51.

Sandhu, S. (2012) 'Shame', *Sight & Sound* (February), 77.

Stevens, K. (2013) 'Dying to Love: Gay Identity, Suicide, and Aesthetics in *A Single Man*', *Cinema Journal*, Vol. 52, No. 4 (Summer), 99–120.

Tracy, A. (2011) 'Shame', *Cinemascope*, 49 (December), http://cinema-scope.com/currency/shame-steve-mcqueen-uk/, date accessed 14 July 2014.

Thorsen, N. (2011) 'Longing for the end of all: Interview', *Melancholia* Presskit. http://www.melancholiathemovie.com/#_interview, date accessed 14 July 2014.

Wallace, L. (2014) 'Tom Ford and his Kind', *Criticism*, Vol. 56, No. 1, 21–44.

Winters, B. (2008) 'Corporeality, Musical Heartbeats, and Cinematic Emotion', *Music, Sound and the Moving Image*, Vol. 2, No. 1 (Spring), 3–25.

CHAPTER 29

# Interview 6: Orchestration, Collaboration, and the Integrated Soundtrack—An Interview with Matt Dunkley

*Ian Sapiro*

Orchestrator and conductor Matt Dunkley has been working in the film-music industry since the mid-1990s. A graduate of London College of Music, Dunkley initially worked as a trumpet player before becoming an assistant under the guidance of legendary Hollywood orchestrator Christopher Palmer. Dunkley created arrangements in the pop world before assisting Craig Armstrong on his first film score, *Romeo + Juliet* (1996). He has orchestrated for him ever since and has also established long-time working partnerships with top film composers A.R. Rahman, Clint Mansell, Tuomas Kantelinen, and Marco Beltrami.

**IS:** Given the individuality of composer/orchestrator partnerships, what is the nature of your working practices and relationships with some of your regular collaborators?

**MD:** I've known Craig (Armstrong) for twenty-five years and we're friends as well as colleagues. When we first worked together, we would spend intensive weeks working side by side on the orchestrations at his studio in Glasgow. Now, when I'm working on a film with him, because we understand each other so well, we'll watch the film through, listen to the score cues, and Craig will discuss the general thrust of the score. I'll say 'very good Craig', he'll say 'you know what to do', and we'll go and have a nice meal. Tuomas (Kantelinen) is a little more hands-on with the orchestration. He usually gives me some manuscript as a sketch, which is unusual these days, and then we'll talk through the orchestration. His demos are not very advanced, so there's a lot more for me to do because he's not working so much in the MIDI domain. He'll give me a basic notation sketch, which will

I. Sapiro
University of Leeds, UK

just have some strings and then he'll put little notes all over it saying 'more loveliness here, less loveliness here, ugly here', which gives me great creative latitude. For film, Craig always writes in his sequencer programme, Logic, and there will be quite an advanced orchestrated demo, whereas Tuomas finds that boring so he tends to just write down from the piano and then we talk endlessly about what he wants for each cue. It's more like when I first started out in the industry, a lot more old school. A.R. Rahman also writes in Logic and does quite involved demos, but if we're working on an Indian movie there's a lot more latitude; not so much on Hollywood pictures, because it's all prescribed and the directors want to hear the demo on the scoring stage. A.R. is very quick and intuitive when he composes. He's taught himself to write cue by cue when he's doing a Hollywood movie, but he much prefers doing broad sweeps and long pieces that can then be cut into a film, which often happens in Indian filmmaking.

IS: Those composers, certainly Armstrong and Kantelinen, are Academy-trained musicians, whereas another of your regular collaborators, Clint Mansell, comes from the pop-music world.

MD: Very true, certainly Tuomas and Craig. Craig studied at the Royal Academy in London and Tuomas studied at the Sibelius Academy in Helsinki, so they are very 'legit', classically trained guys. Clint obviously came from a completely different background, as the lead singer in Pop Will Eat Itself, so he relies more on me to be his interface with the orchestra. He's got a narrower bandwidth of what he likes and what he doesn't like and also what he can write and what he can't write, and he's very honest about it. Some composers are more flexible or chameleon-like in the movie world and that's certainly not somebody like Clint who very much has his style and his sound, and if it goes outside of that then he's very true to his own inner voice and won't go beyond that. There is a real integrity to that. He's very respectful of the team around him, myself and his recording/mix engineer Geoff Foster, whom I work with a lot. We did a big film this year, *Noah*, which we recorded in New York, and Clint said to me at the end of scoring that 'the first question I ask when I get asked to do a film is "are Matt and Geoff free?"', which is a wonderful complement to have from somebody of his stature in the industry. He's just very different. You have to be very careful arranging his music that you don't get too sweet or too clichéd, and certainly not look down your nose at him just because he's not familiar necessarily with the orchestral vocabulary. He's got a really strong voice, increasingly so, and he picks up a lot of big movies with interesting directors because he has that voice and he has that kind of purity of thought. He really agonises and he's not one to just bash something out. He really takes a lot out of himself after every film.

IS: Do you have a direct working relationship with Geoff Foster as orchestrator and engineer, or is it more that you are both conduits for the composer?

MD: I really like working with an engineer I know well, and Geoff is the engineer for virtually all of the composers I work with. He recommended me to Clint and I recommended him to A.R., so although I do work with other engineers—and there are some great engineers out there—if I have a choice I'll work with Geoff just because I know we have a really good relationship, we're very good friends, and I respect his opinions. He won't try and orchestrate over the talk back system at recording sessions, so if I'm conducting and he's in the booth with the composer he won't try and tell me how to fix something, he'll just say 'that's not coming through for us', or 'we're finding that too loud against the dialogue', and then I'll fix it. He's very clear—'too loud, too quiet, too high, too low'—there's nothing fancy in what he's telling me. He's telling me what I need to know and then with my technical experience I can fix the problem. Some recording engineers, who have come from the classical tradition, basically try to tell you how to orchestrate, and you almost end up having to justify yourself to them, and I don't really want to have this conversation. I wouldn't tell them where to put the mics! In the classical world, the engineer is almost like the producer as well, but in the film world, it is really a collaboration and if you have a really good relationship between the composer, the orchestrator and the engineer then that works very well as a scoring team.

IS: What sort of involvement do you have with the other streams of sound in a film?

MD: In an ideal world I get the movie, so when I play the composer's demo I have the movie along with it and I can see how he's ducked in and out of the dialogue track and things like that. I prefer to have it because otherwise you are working in the dark to a certain extent. Musically, there might be things that are suggested by the music—perhaps places where a melody might be doubled or chords thickened—but you have to refrain from doing them when you hear the music in context. And I think if you don't have that context then you often find that you go to the scoring stage and you're stripping away the stuff that you've added, so it's effectively a waste of time. It makes more sense to have the picture, but it's just not always possible; production companies are incredibly tight on security these days and sometimes you just don't quite get to the right person to get the picture in time.

IS: Presumably the composer has already accounted for this to a large extent, but if you have some orchestrational licence to vary from the demo, it enables you to keep everything in balance?

MD: I find it rather dull if all I'm doing is replicating the demo, and the composers I have as my regular clients give me some flexibility, but obviously you have to understand the context. Nothing is ever set in movie scoring until it's actually on the film, so quite often we're working to the wrong picture cut because you just have to draw a line somewhere. So we might be two versions of the film behind and we'll get to the scoring stage and suddenly have to quieten everything down and massage it. That's why you have music editors to help. The music is never really completely set, and a lot of detail still gets changed on the scoring stage. Part of the reason why most composers like their orchestrators to conduct is that you can make quick fixes over the stand.

IS: Do you discuss things and meet with music editors, directors, and other members of the film-production team?

MD: Music editors more so, because a good music editor can be invaluable on a project. Directors are usually so busy during post-production, with digital effects, automatic dialogue replacement, and all sorts of other things, so their time is very precious and you don't normally get to meet them unless you are in the composer's studio all the time. You certainly meet them at recording sessions and you discuss things with them there, but their relationship is with the composer. Unless it's somebody like Baz Luhrmann, who seems to have a relationship with every single person on the crew!

IS: You were heavily involved in the manipulation of Tchaikovsky's *Swan Lake* ballet music for Darren Aronofsky's *Black Swan* (2010), which was scored by Clint Mansell. Who was involved in the decision-making process on that score, given that the *Swan Lake* material plays a key role in the narrative construction of the story?

MD: It was a really interesting one. The ballet material was shot first and they used recordings from the Mariinsky Theatre, big blocks of action that, for various financial and copyright reasons, we had to recreate. This meant that I spent a lot of time putting a click track to a Russian conductor's tempos, and they were really quite extreme some of them. I spent a lot of time doing that just so we could recreate these performances, but I didn't change the original orchestration. So we had a full Tchaikovsky orchestra in the studio. We recorded at AIR studios and the Tchaikovsky just played itself once we'd negotiated our way round the tempos. So that was one aspect of it, these big blocks of action that were unchangeable. And then the real challenge was to come in and out of the Tchaikovsky without ever feeling the transitions, so the idea was to bleed in between the ballet music and the original score. Clint set some things up using a mocked-up MIDI version of the whole ballet score, and then he put his own spin on it; so quite often we would record and then he would twist it acoustically, reverse it, put some strange filters on, and things like that. In terms of the orchestration, the real thing was to meld the two orchestras together so you didn't feel like one was stopping and the other starting. It was quite a technical challenge. Darren always wanted the score to be in the sonic world of the film, because sometimes you are in the theatre and sometimes you are in Nina's (Natalie Portman) head, but gradually, the whole world is taken over. We had many long nights working it out and sketching it out and thinking about how to move from ballet to score and vice versa but somehow keep the same orchestration. Clint was very sweet because he gave me an adaptation and arranging credit as well as orchestrating and conducting, because quite often I'd add elements of the ballet score over the top of his music just so that we kept the thematic ideas going. There would be little snippets of Tchaikovsky's motifs while Clint was doing his dark, brooding material, which was representing Nina's mental breakdown. So it was a real collaboration and very satisfying.

**IS:** Did you have to work at all with any of the sound team, or did that stay separate?

**MD:** We had some early sound discussions, and we always say at the beginning of a project that it would be great to work with the sound team, but they're chasing their deadlines, we're chasing our deadlines, and it never happens. Clint's score used some soundscape ideas alongside the ballet music, and I think the sound design was basically layered on top. Darren was across both areas, but there just wasn't time for us to work more directly. The whole idea was that the score was almost like a Salvador Dali painting—the two musics kind of dripping into each other.

**IS:** By contrast, you have worked with Craig Armstrong on a few pictures that have combined original scoring with pre-existing pop songs—*Moulin Rouge!* (2001), *Love, Actually* (2003), and *The Great Gatsby* (2013) for instance. How does the inclusion of this additional musical element in the soundtrack alter or otherwise affect your work?

**MD:** The songs were present in the original script for *Moulin Rouge!*, so we had to create big, lush orchestrations for the songs and Craig wrote the score around them. I remember the 'Elephant Love Medley' scene, the duet for Satine (Nicole Kidman) and Christian (Ewan McGregor), was particularly complicated. We went through thirteen different songs and the editing was very tight and didn't really give us much flexibility for tempo changes.

Something like *Gatsby* was challenging because the picture was not locked down, so we didn't really know what was going to be in a scene. I think we did three versions of every scene, so we scored the movie three times, which was a colossal amount of work. We weren't quite sure what was going to go in because Luhrmann was talking to Prince about using some of his music, and he had The Xx, Gotye, Florence and the Machine, and Jay Z all submitting tracks, and stuff was coming in constantly. In the end, there was a track by Gotye ('Heart's a Mess') that was really simple but really pretty, and it became one of the big themes in the movie so we quickly had to create some strings supporting the song and rescore some cues to incorporate this theme into the score, because it suddenly became one of the themes alongside Craig's lovely 'Gatsby' theme. So that was quite a challenge just because we didn't know what song was coming in and what key it was in, so we were recording cues in different keys, recording different 'beds' (backing, intros and outros) for the different possible songs, and that's how Baz likes to work. It's always organised chaos! You're going from one scene and then you're not quite sure what it's going into because he's said that there will be a song there, but you don't know what song. He'll give you three possibilities, but then they'll all be in different keys so you've got to approach those and record your orchestra in a key that doesn't cause a semitone clash that you can't fix. You normally have to have different approaches for each potential song. And then you've got to get out of that song, that you don't know which one it's going to be, into your next specific bit of score, so again you have to have different links for that as well. For instance, in the party scene, we used Gershwin's *Rhapsody in Blue*, but then we jumped out of that and into a Jay Z track in the middle of it, and then we jumped back again, but we weren't quite sure where we were going out and where we were coming back, so we had all these different musical buffer zones. It means you have to do everything two or three times to cover yourselves, and then at the mix Baz will make his final choices. He's a real auteur and he doesn't like making choices until he has to, so he'll leave it to the very last minute. He had options, he loves options, so he had options for everything just like when he films; he shoots quite a lot and he has 'coverage', and in the same sense in the score, he has coverage. He'll have all these different pop acts do something for the scene but he'll also have Craig compose something for the scene in three versions, meaning there are three different versions of the score, and three different songs, and like a chef Baz will mix the elements that he wants. He knows what he's doing, but it's not easy to work with, it's exhausting because—and I've heard he does this with other departments in the film as well—he wrings out your very last ounce of energy.

IS: You might imagine that when a score includes pre-existing pop material that your role is somewhat marginalised, but it sounds like it could be the opposite on some pictures.

MD: It depends. Baz integrates pop and original score in a lot of his movies, using the two together, whereas a film like *Love, Actually* was much more straightforward. The pop songs we used were more for montage scenes and things like that, used more conventionally, so *Love, Actually* was a straight-ahead scoring film with pop songs that were dropped in, but we knew which ones they were and we knew which keys they were in. With someone like Baz, who uses the pop tracks integrated into the score and the two bleed into each other, it's a very different way of doing it and that makes it a bit more challenging.

IS: Are you usually involved in the creation of new rearrangements for or additions to existing pop songs for a film project?

MD: It varies. Sometimes a composer might ask you to add some strings to a track. For instance, we had a song in *Noah*, a Patti Smith song ('Mercy Is'), and in the film they'd used snippets of it as a lullaby theme, but for the end titles Darren decided he wanted a full song version of it. So Patti did a demo with just her voice and a guitar, and then Clint said to me 'can you do a string arrangement around it'. I did an arrangement and then he made a few suggestions and we finally recorded it live in the studio with Patti and the Kronos Quartet. Sometimes a song will be rerecorded, but it will be the music supervisor who deals with that, and they will talk directly to the artist and the artist's producer and come up with something. Normally—unless it's someone like Baz—you don't get involved too much with pop tracks; that just comes out of the box and it may well be that it's something to do with a package deal that the production company has done with a label, who are actually putting money into the production to get their artist promoted.

IS: You've mentioned technology a few times, and I was wondering how that impacts on the collaborative working that you do?

MD: It's made a huge difference from when I first started out working as an assistant for an orchestrator. It was pencil-and-paper composer sketches, pencil-orchestrated full scores and hand-copied orchestral parts. Digital demos were very, very limited, and quite often composers would demo a score on the piano alone. This was fine until the director got to the scoring stage and heard that little tinkly piano theme suddenly fully scored for a symphony orchestra, and they'd have a breakdown and you'd have all sorts of rewrites. So it was quite a risky business back then. With modern technology, samples, and MIDI mock-ups, you can get demos of such high quality that some directors don't even bother turning up to the scoring stage because they've signed off on it and it's only going to sound better. And technology-wise, it's just quicker too, especially if a composer is using one of the sequencers. You can have MIDI alongside live audio alongside picture as a writing tool, and from that the composer can generate demos to send as mp3 files to the director. When I receive a cue, I get the sequencer file and a balance of the mix, so I have all the MIDI data and the demo, and the picture as well normally, and then I manipulate that data into my notation software programme for scoring. I use Finale, the other main one is Sibelius, and I can send my completed orchestrated score to the copyist. So all the time, it's only been one input of the data from the composer. I'm manipulating that data, adding material and texture and working with it, but all the raw data is already there; it's not like I'm starting from scratch as we used to in pencil-and-paper times. Then the copyists extract the parts from the score—there's slightly more to it than just pressing a button, but it's still data manipulation. It speeds up the whole process hugely.

I have colleagues in Los Angeles who will work on a movie with me. We can send a file by email, whereas back in the day it was couriers and sending boxes of parts or scores or trying to fax them, and it was very clunky and slow and fraught with problems. So it makes everything much quicker. The downside is that because everything is much quicker it means everything can go much later, and with digital editing now, everything is edited much later because they can edit right up to the wire. Digital editing means the picture changes constantly, and that means the music has to change constantly to fit, so it has its downsides and it has its upsides. But I do think that for filmmakers today, there are fewer nasty surprises when it gets to the scoring stage and that's a good thing for everyone. They've already heard a fairly good representation of the composer's orchestrated music in the demo and understand the sonic landscape in which it sits.

**IS:** Do you think contemporary technology has made the process more or less collaborative?

**MD:** I think it's about the same really. There are some composers who write in their sequencers and think they don't need an orchestrator because it's already orchestrated, and they give it to the copyists and it never sounds quite right, because they don't quite understand what we do in terms of voicing and assimilation of tracks. Orchestration is a very skilled process and if you just replicate exactly what's in a demo, it's never going to sound the same as something that's been properly orchestrated. So there is that kind of element of ignorance at times, but most people who actually know their business and are not arrogant about it understand that you still need the same team around you and you still collaborate in the same way. It's just using the latest technology available and I think composers have always done that; it makes your life easier and enhances what you do. It's a great privilege for a composer to hear almost a full symphonic mock-up of what he or she is doing, so I don't think people should be scared of technology. The best people with the best technology available at their hands in Hollywood still collaborate with the same people that they worked with fifty years ago when it was pencil and paper, so they must still be getting something out of that relationship.

**IS:** Finally, how do you see your role with regard to the overall film soundtrack?

**MD:** My role is to best serve the composer's wishes and vision. The composer is my main concern and focus, and my job is to make what his vision was when he wrote it as successful as possible. So I make the orchestra sound as close to that vision as possible, and direct the orchestra to give him the performances that he wants to make his vision for the soundtrack artistically satisfying for him but also achieving what the director wants from that composer. If I start getting in the way of the director–composer relationship, then I'm not doing my job because I'm putting my voice in the way of his voice. Inevitably there are ways that I voice things and orchestrate things, but I'd like to think the reason I have long relationships with my composers is because they can hear themselves and not me in what I deliver to the studio.

CHAPTER 30

# Musically Conceived Sound Design, Musicalization of Speech and the Breakdown of Film Soundtrack Hierarchy

*Danijela Kulezic-Wilson*

Although Christopher Nolan's *Interstellar* was a great box-office success, its release in the autumn of 2014 was nevertheless accompanied by a minor controversy as many viewers complained that some key moments of the dialogue were unintelligible. The complaint received enough publicity to prompt one cinema in Rochester, New York, to post a notice confirming that its equipment was 'in full working order' while a poster at the Cinemark Tinseltown read: 'Christopher Nolan mixed the soundtrack with an emphasis on the music. This is how it is intended to sound' (Child, 2014). Meanwhile, Nolan himself responded by admitting that his 'impressionistic approach to sound' was maybe 'unusual for a mainstream blockbuster' but was the 'right approach for this experiential film':

> Many of the film-makers I've admired over the years have used sound in bold and adventurous ways. I don't agree with the idea that you can only achieve clarity through dialogue. Clarity of story, clarity of emotions—I try to achieve that in a very layered way using all the different things at my disposal—picture and sound. (Quoted in Child, 2014)

This anecdote highlights a couple of issues concerning the aesthetics and functional hierarchy of the contemporary cinema soundtrack that I intend to examine in this chapter. On one hand, it confirms audiences' habitual reliance on language and speech as the main sources of relevant narrative information obtained through sound. As Michel Chion pointed out, cinema is, like human listening, naturally vococentrist (1999, pp. 5–6). Attempts to relativize

D. Kulezic-Wilson
University College Cork, Ireland

speech are rare because they not only undermine the ideological and aesthetic premises of classical narration but—as this case confirms—are potentially disorienting, confusing and even frustrating for audiences. On the other hand, the example of *Interstellar* brings to light the fact that these firmly established pillars of soundtrack hierarchy are slowly shifting to give space to new practices. Chion was, as usual, ahead of the curve when he wrote at the beginning of the 1990s in *Audio-Vision* that the 'pursuit of sensations' and the improvement in Dolby technology gave more prominence to noise in cinema, 'reintroducing an acute feeling of the materiality of things and beings'. According to him, this was already a sign that 'with the new place that noises occupy, speech is no longer central to film' (1994, p. 155). His pronouncement might have heralded the breakdown of film soundtrack hierarchy a couple of decades too early but it did identify two crucial protagonists in the changes to come: advancements in technology and the quest for the sensuous aspect of the cinema experience.

The importance of the 'sensory experience' of cinema is also discussed by Anahid Kassabian in her book *Ubiquitous Listening* (2013). While acknowledging the influence of 'boom aesthetics' on the contemporary experience of cinema, like Chion, Kassabian observes that some films 'focus more centrally on the sensory experience rather than the traditional features of narrative, such as plot structure and character development' (p. 36), a point which is also applicable to the case studies discussed in this chapter. My choice of the word 'sensuous' instead of 'sensory', however, emphasizes the pleasurable aspect of the audio–visual experience which is more aesthetic than purely physical. I refer to the engagement with film which takes pleasure in the sensuousness of the form itself (its rhythm, flow, melodic/harmonic content, texture, visual composition and so on) rather than 'the pursuit of sensations' that is generally associated with advanced projection technology. This relates to my notion of film as an inherently musical form which can produce the sense of fluency and immediacy generally associated with music (see Kulezic-Wilson, 2015). In this chapter, I will argue that this idea of film musicality is often an essential component in the broader trend of films challenging the structure of classical soundtrack hierarchy, a trend which manifests itself through a number of strategies including undermining the denotative function of dialogue, the increasingly asynchronous use of language, emphasizing musical and dramaturgical properties of sound effects and the sensuous properties of music.

Of course, the challenge to traditional soundtrack hierarchy is not a recent invention; the musical approach to sound effects can be traced back to the early years of recorded sound in cinema. As early as 1930 Dziga Vertov created a symphony of banging, rattling and hammering in his *Enthusiasm: Symphony of the Donbass*, demonstrating the musical impact of repetitive quotidian sounds, an approach which would later be embraced by directors as different as Andrei Tarkovsky and Sergio Leone. The process of eroding the line between score and sound effects became particularly notable with the introduction of synthesizers into film scoring in the late 1970s and greatly accelerated during the late 1990s with the employment of digital software—originally designed for the production of music—for processing both dialogue and sound effects (Donnelly, 2014, pp. 124–5). Again, the influence of music should not be forgotten here, because if we consider some of the most famous examples of a musicalized use of sound effects such as in Darren Aronofsky's first two films *Pi* (1998) and *Requiem for a Dream* (2000) and Joe Wright's *Atonement* (2007) and *Anna Karenina* (2012), we'll see that what allows us to perceive these sound effects as musical is not so much related to technology as to the fact that they are given a distinctly percussive function in both musical and non-musical contexts (see Kulezic-Wilson, 2008, 2015).

While the musicalization of sound effects has been a 'hot' topic among film music scholars in recent years,[1] challenges to the traditional narrative role of spoken language have not been given the same attention. This chapter will demonstrate that musical and sensuous uses of speech have been significant factors in the ongoing breakdown of soundtrack hierarchy. By using examples from several recent films with strong musical underpinnings—Drake Doremus' *Breathe In* (2013), Harmony Korine's *Spring Breakers* (2012) and Shane Carruth's *Upstream Color* (2013)—I will identify the main strategies involved in the musicalization of soundtrack in general and spoken word in particular. I will argue that undermining the narrative sovereignty of the spoken word and endorsing the interchangeability of speech and music promote modes of perception which can change our expectations of narrative film and emphasize its musical and sensuous qualities.

## *Breathe In*: Musicalization of Soundtrack and 'Verbal Chiaroscuro'

In all the films that are examined in this chapter, music plays a number of different roles beyond its conventional functions. In *Breathe In*, a story about a middle-age high school teacher who falls for a much younger foreign exchange student staying in his house, music is from the beginning established as the primary means of communication in both narrative and narrating terms. The two main characters are both musicians: Keith Reynolds (Guy Pearce), a former rock musician tired of his teaching job with the ambition of becoming a chair cellist in a symphony orchestra and Sophie Williams (Felicity Jones), a precocious music student whose passionate and virtuosic musicianship stirs deep-seated desires in Keith. In addition to diegetic performances of music by Chopin and Schumann, the film is submerged in Dustin O'Halloran's warm, atmospheric score which is given the same attention as the dialogue, sometimes simmering in the background like the characters' suppressed desires, sometimes dominating the sonic field.

Language, on the other hand, is approached with less reverence than is typical of narrative film and is treated almost with distrust. According to the director, the actors were encouraged to improvise their lines around certain plot points and those scenes were then rigorously workshopped until they had been 'distilled into the essence of the mood/emotion. The goal [was] to say as little as possible' (Doremus, 2013). Most of the time spoken words are intelligible, but they are usually combined with music in such a way that their denotative importance becomes less significant than the characters' body language, glances and silences.

This ongoing dialogue between speech and music is introduced from the very beginning. The opening credits on a black screen are at first accompanied only by gentle arpeggios in piano; before the blackness is replaced by the first image, a tranquil melody in middle register is introduced, followed by sounds of chatter which are soon identified as coming from Keith and his family. The musical intro and a slight delay in matching the voices with their visual source not only allow us to become attuned to the film's tone with our hearing first but also encourage us to perceive the voices as part of the music. The first shot is interior, showing a big window looking out at a garden in which Keith poses for a family photo with his wife and daughter, their figures reduced to a single corner of a symmetrically framed shot, their voices equally indistinct. Although the next shot moves outside to the garden, showing the characters in wide and then medium shots, their chatter does not become more distinct nor does the volume of their speech significantly change, even though our point of view/hearing does. If anything, the music becomes slightly more prominent, enveloping the chatter of the characters. The effect produced by this approach is best described by Chion's expression *verbal chiaroscuro*[2] because the mix of words and music 'inscribe[s] speech in a visual, rhythmic, gestural, and sensory totality where it would not have to be the central and determining element' (Chion, 1994, p. 178).

One could argue that this approach is not that unusual in scenes in which the purpose is to paint the everyday atmosphere of family life—chatting at the dinner table, visiting friends—rather than present information relevant to the plot.[3] Doremus, however, applies it even in intimate situations, most memorably in the scene in which Keith and Sophie meet at the river after realizing that their feelings for each other are mutual (1:02:11–1:05:50).[4] They talk about escaping the constraints of their lives and what it means to be free but instead of the conventional framing usually applied in dialogue scenes, the protagonists here are often shot from a distance or from behind while they are speaking, or the camera rests on the face of the person not speaking, on details of the couple touching each other, holding hands, Keith playing with Sophie's hair and so on. The only moment which employs a variation on shot-reverse shot editing in dialogue and synchronous sound is when Sophie asks Keith what makes him happy and he replies that there is only one thing at the moment which makes him happy, his unfinished sentence the closest their conversation gets to acknowledging their feelings verbally. After that point their speech becomes even more fragmented and is again mostly presented asynchronously, their whispered words (Sophie: 'What do you think?' and Keith's 'I want you to steal me away') barely audible and only comprehensible after multiple viewings. Music, however, is present throughout the scene, the sounds of piano and string quartet enveloping the characters, filling the spaces between their words and replacing their words completely towards the end of the scene.

The process of mixing is, obviously, crucial here in striking a well-judged balance between music and spoken word that ensures the audibility of both. What really enables this type of aesthetics, however, is the director's working style which involves the composer in every stage of the filmmaking process and considers music 'as the fifth character of the ensemble of characters' (Doremus, 2013). That both Keith and Sophie are musicians is an important detail because the way they respond to each other's musical performances is crucial to the plot development. It could be argued that Keith starts thinking about Sophie only after hearing her highly accomplished performance of Chopin's Ballad No. 2 in F, op. 38 in class. The other turning point is when Sophie, after revealing that her reluctance to perform is connected with the fact that her uncle who taught her piano recently died, decides to play for Keith. The soft, yearning melody Sophie plays (O'Halloran's 'Opus 20') communicates her feelings more eloquently than any words could and Keith responds by touching her for the first time. The choice of style, texture and instrumentation in the original score is also relevant here as it enables an easy sonic interaction between music and spoken words. O'Halloran's score in the tradition of Romantic piano literature spins a web-like texture, its gentle arpeggios and delicate melodies centred around the middle register, like the characters' voices. The result is a soundtrack in which the familiar hierarchy between its elements is replaced by a more fluid relationship in which music and speech alternately come in and out of focus, an approach which supports the film's visual emphasis on mise-en-scène and the protagonists' non-verbal communication conveyed through close-ups of their faces, touching hands and stolen glances.

The attention given to music in the soundtrack, its narrative significance and the way it gently interacts with the characters and their spoken words create an audio–visual field which invites the audience to loosen its vococentrist stance and absorb language as one of its constitutive elements, as relevant to the story as music and mise-en-scène. In that sense Doremus' film supports Nolan's assertion that clarity of dialogue is not essential for achieving 'clarity of story and emotions'. That *Breathe In* is more effective in this approach than *Interstellar* is partly due to the fact that it is much easier for the audience to accept an 'impressionistic' mix of dialogue and music in a context which deals with basic human emotions and where there are no plot twists involving a journey through time and different dimensions, as in Nolan's film. Instances of successful verbal chiaroscuro are still relatively rare, though; in most cases, the musicalization of speech relies on other devices, including the use of repetition, rhythmic editing and asynchronous sound, examples of which will be examined in the following sections.

### *Spring Breakers*: Repetition and Asynchronous Sound

Despite the general perception that narrative forms based on linear storytelling avoid repetition and focus instead on establishing forward, goal-oriented movement, all forms that aim for some kind of rhythm in their structure, including film, employ repetition to create patterns, 'rhyming effects' (Bellour, 1981, p. 103) and networks of associations (Cohen, 2002, p. 227). As one of the essential compositional devices, repetition is also integral to most musical scores, not least those in the classical Hollywood tradition with their elaborate networks of leitmotifs and themes.

The situation with repetition in speech in a narrative context is somewhat different, though. Repetition in dialogue, for instance, not only clashes with the goal of making the narration as fast and forward moving as possible but also poses a threat to the carefully constructed illusion of the 'invisibility' of means cultivated by classical cinema. However, repetition in speech can be utilized for the purpose of creating a musical effect, as can be heard in Harmony Korine's *Spring Breakers*, where it is usually paired with an asynchronous use of speech.

*Spring Breakers* is the story of four childhood friends, Faith (Selena Gomez), Candy (Vanessa Hudgens), Brit (Ashley Benson) and Cotty (Rachel Korine), whose spring break in Florida takes a violent turn after they get involved with local rapper and drug-dealer Alien (James Franco). Inspired by contradictions in a youth culture in which 'sexualised and violent imagery' is juxtaposed with 'childlike pop-culture indicators, the fluorescent bathing suits and Hello Kitty bags' (Korine quoted in Taubin, 2013, p. 29), Korine's film walks a fine line between exploitation and a critical take on the excesses of youth culture. Simon Reynolds compares the film's phantasmagorical and hyperbolical representation of spring break and the girls' descent into crime and murder to Bakhtin's definition of carnival as 'an event in which all rules, inhibitions and regulations which determine the course of everyday life are suspended', adding: 'the world is turned upside down in a potlatch of pleasure, profanity and insubordination' (2013, p. 28). Although very different from Doremus' film in terms of narrative style and content, Korine's film is nevertheless, like *Breathe In*, also deeply steeped in music, combining Cliff Martinez's mellow, deep-pulsating techno evocative of his score for Steven Soderbergh's *Traffic* (2000) with more aggressive, penetrating tracks by Skrillex. The film's musical spirit is not confined to the score, though, but permeates the whole film, affecting editing patterns, the use of sound effects and speech.

Although the film's general narrative arc is linear, a very small part of it is presented using conventional means of continuity editing and synchronized speech. The story is mostly told through montage sequences immersed in music and bathed in day-glo colours, showing the girls in their everyday habitat at the beginning—sitting in class, in the library, smoking, taking drugs, driving in a car—and later partying, getting arrested, making out with Alien and so on. These sequences are assembled non-chronologically, many of them using already seen shots just in a different order. According to the director, this structure which 'recirculates' micro-scenes was inspired by loop-based and trance-like electronic music (Taubin, 2013, p. 29) which is also the basis of Martinez's original score soundtrack. Its ambient textures and soft harmonies provide the montage sequences with a sense of continuous flow, creating a 'floaty', dreamy feel and a suitable background for music-like repetitions of spoken words.

The theme of violence dominates the narrative, both visually and aurally. Allusions to guns permeate the story from the beginning, with characters using squirt guns or miming the gestures of firing guns. The sounds of cocking a gun and actual gun shots are employed throughout the film as punctuation marks between scenes, becoming more frequent as the story moves towards its violent ending. They sonically 'contaminate' the film's core to the point that even 'innocent' foley sounds like Faith's friends opening the shutters in her room when they come to wake her up (0:09:20)[5] or flicking a lighter (0:11:45) are given a harsh, metallic quality, evocative of the sound of a cocking gun. In one of the later scenes the same sound is synchronized with the gesture of Alien miming taking a photo—a foreboding substitute for the sound of a camera shutter (0:49:43). Not long after the girls meet Alien this pervasive sound finally becomes synchronized with its actual source—real guns being cocked.

One of the crucial devices aiding the repetitions, 'loopy' editing and score to supply a 'dreamy' feel to the film is a fairly consistent asynchronous use of language. As Mary Ann Doane (1985a, 1985b) pointed out, matching audio and visual perception is at the heart of cinematic illusion, even more so, Kevin Donnelly argues (2014, p. 202), than the illusion of continuity. The fact that words in *Spring Breakers* are often divorced from their visual source undermines our usual expectations of realistic representation of characters and events. This somewhat 'detaching' impact of asynchronous speech and non-chronological editing becomes particularly obvious when compared to one of the rare moments in which dialogue is presented synchronously, the scene in which Alien tries to persuade Faith not to return home (0:44:16–0:47:20). Bar one editing intervention which interrupts this scene with an image of Faith surrounded by her friends, crying and pleading that they all return home, the exchange between Alien and Faith is mostly presented synchronously and in real time. As a consequence, Alien's predatory body language and Faith's fear and discomfort come across as more real and unsettling than the later scenes of violence.[6]

The asynchronous image/sound editing also facilitates the use of repetition in speech. The first explicit appearance of repetition coincides with the initial turning point in the narrative, when Candy, Brit and Cotty decide to rob a diner with toy guns to get cash for their spring break trip. Their lines 'Just pretend it's a fucking video game', 'Act like you're in a movie, or something', 'You can't be scared of shit, you have to be hard' and similar, are initially paired with images of the girls talking themselves into carrying out the robbery, interspersed with images of them taking drugs (0:13:13–0:13:45). These lines are then repeated verbatim asynchronously over shots of the road, details of the car in motion and the girls standing in the rain (0:13:52–0:14:14). After Faith and then Cotty go home, leaving Brit and Candy with Alien, the story edges further towards fantasy, encouraging the impression that the characters are indeed becoming part of a video game, the connection between image and speech becomes even looser and words are more subject to repetition. Alien's speech patterns are particularly musicalized, including the often cited scene in which he lists his possessions, punctuating his monologue with the boastful 'Look at my shit!'. His monologues are sung like nursery rhymes ('Four little chickies...'; 'Four little girls...') while his sing-song repetitions of the films' title ('spring breaaak, spring breaaak, spring break fo-rever') punctuate the second half of the film like chants. According to Korine, these repetitions stem from his original idea of conceiving the film as a 'liquid' narrative with 'things that would repeat like mantras or choruses in pop songs' (quoted in Taubin, 2013, p. 29).

The extensive repetitions are not only applied to monologues and fragments of dialogue but also to actual dialogue exchanges, as in the montage sequences showing the characters kissing, having sex and playing with guns. A few lines of dialogue (Alien: 'So you wanna do this or what?' Brit: 'You're scared, aren't you?' Candy: 'Scaredy Pants' ... Candy: 'Are you scared?' Alien: 'I'm real scared') are first heard at 1:14:00 following a montage sequence of Alien, Candy and Brit making love in a pool after Cotty's departure. Following the film's familiar editing pattern the scene is then interrupted by the insertion of a montage sequence showing previously seen images of the girls partying, here accompanied by Alien reciting his 'Four little girls ...' rhyme. As the rhyme finishes with him chanting 'spring breaak, spring breaak, spring break fo-rever', we are transported back to the scene in the pool and the lines 'Y'all wanna do this or what?', 'You're scared, aren't you', 'Scaredy pants' and 'I'm a big ol' fuckin' scaredy pants' are repeated three more times consecutively, punctuated by lazy, erotic laughter.

Repetitions of spoken lines also resonate on the level of the macro-form, combined with a traditional use of asynchronous speech to expose the underlying contradictions in the characters or even their hypocrisy.[7] In *Spring Breakers* this type of juxtaposition is first heard in the scene in which Faith's phone message to her grandmother is matched with images of wild partying ('This place is special. I'm starting to think this is the most spiritual place I've been ... I think we found ourselves here ... I can't believe how many new friends we made' ...) (0:18:20–0:19:35). Her words are echoed at the very end by Candy, accompanying the scene in which she and Brit take out all Big Arch's people during the final (and particularly unrealistic) shoot-out: 'I think we found ourselves here ... we saw some beautiful things here ... I know we made friends that will last us a lifetime...'.

Apart from this formal closure using repetition and asynchrony to hammer home its message about unsettling aspects of youth culture, in all other cases repetitions are redundant from the narrative point of view. Instead of being used for a denotative or even connotative function, language is employed here for its rhyming and rhythmic properties. Its asynchronous use is an important part of this because by divorcing the spoken word from its source the filmmaker draws our attention to its purely sonic aspects, emphasizing its musical qualities. We find a similar situation in *Breathe In*: even though the musical approach to language in this film does not rely on repetition, the most musical instances of verbal *chiaroscuro* in it all involve asynchrony, as if its free-floating deployment divorced from the image 'liberates' the language from its visual anchor and allows the filmmaker to use it in a more musical way, almost as a score.

The musicalization of language in *Spring Breakers* is a significant departure from the conventions of classical narrative that still dominate mainstream cinema. Considering Korine's penchant for the controversial, innovative and downright subversive, as demonstrated in his previous films such as *Gummo* (1997), *Julien Donkey-Boy* (1999) and *Trash Humpers* (2009), his use of non-conventional strategies in *Spring Breakers* is not a surprise. However, despite the film's provocative content and representation of female characters about which critics couldn't agree if it was sexist and exploitative or feminist, Korine's film also features audience-friendly names such as James Franco and Disney princesses Selena Gomez and Vanessa Hudgens, and it infiltrated the mainstream to earn considerable critical attention and box-office success. The film's excessive use of asynchronous speech and repetition thus implies audiences' increasing tolerance of strategies typical of non-mainstream cinema. One should not forget, though, that in the case of *Spring Breakers* this tolerance was greatly facilitated by the film's musical 'feel' and audio–visual style which its target audience raised on MTV would have been accustomed to.

The final film I intend to discuss uses all the devices addressed so far—non-chronological editing, asynchronous use of speech, verbal and visual repetition and verbal *chiaroscuro*. Although they are incorporated into a unique narrative style which cannot be easily compared or categorized, I will argue in the next section that its innovative features are, as in the previous two case studies, informed by a distinctly musical logic.

## Upstream Color: Musically Conceived Soundtrack and Editing

Shane Carruth's *Upstream Color*, like his first feature *Primer* (2004), breaks some new ground by seemingly operating from a space not accountable to any narrative conventions and, as Jonathan Romney says, 'may even mark the emergence of a new strain of narrative film language ... which requires us to engage with [Carruth's] singular mind-set, on his terms' (2013, p. 51). In that sense, the breakdown of soundtrack hierarchy discussed in this chapter comes hand in hand with the breakdown of storytelling and editing conventions, resulting not only in an immersive but also in many ways enigmatic story with a strong musical undercurrent. Carruth's DIY approach, also applied in his debut, includes writing, directing, acting, producing, co-editing and cinematography. The fact that he also composed the score for the film—while still working on the script—indicates the extent to which music was from the beginning considered an integral part of the film's expressive language. Even more interesting in this context is Carruth's comment that he was 'hoping people would watch this film repeatedly, as they might listen to a favourite album' (Romney, 2013, p. 52), which suggests the existence of a more comprehensive idea of musicality extending beyond the score, as in the previous two case studies. This approach, which foregrounds the sensuous aspect of cinema, seems inseparable, or possibly stems, from Carruth's distinctive storytelling methods which do not shy away from the bizarre and confusing.

The narrative of the film is organized in three distinct sections, each representing a particular part of the journey experienced by the protagonist Kris (Amy Seimetz) either externally or internally. The first part shows Kris being kidnapped by the Thief (Thiago Martins) and contaminated with a worm that keeps her in a trance-like state during which she is made to perform a number of meaningless tasks, including copying Thoreau's *Walden*. After signing over all her possessions to the Thief, Kris wakes up with the worm crawling under her skin and is dewormed by the Sampler (Andrew Sensenig) who transfers the parasite into a pig that maintains a physical and/or metaphorical connection to Kris. Kris later meets and falls in love with Jeff (Shane Carruth) who, we later discover, has been a victim of the same ordeal. The last third sees Kris searching for the cause of her trauma. After tracking down and killing the Sampler and finding evidence of his collaboration with the Thief, Kris contacts all the previous victims and together they take over the maintenance of the pigs that they became connected to in the process of de-worming.

Carruth makes it clear that the third section is not a 'classical' resolution of the plot and should not be taken at face value because it is 'nothing but subtext' (Carruth, 2013). He says that the plot is veiled for a reason as the film 'is really trying to change the form that it exists in ... It's trying to adopt the language that we've come to understand—and then, proving that it understands that language, it's trying to push it as far as it will go' (Carruth quoted in Romney, 2013, p. 51). As a consequence, the two main themes of the film—being influenced by unknown forces and the invisible connection between people who share a similar trauma—are conveyed through audio–visual devices that actively destabilize the audiences' passive position. Their purpose is to conjure a sense of the protagonists' brokenness and the connection between them, rather than simplify our understanding of the plot. In addition, hardly any information that could be considered vital is communicated through language. The outer parts of the film barely feature any speech at all, while elsewhere some lines, like Kris reciting passages from *Walden*, are employed as much for 'musical' as for narrative effect reminding us of the protagonists' deep-buried trauma.

One of the most eloquent tools in Carruth's unconventional approach to storytelling is editing, for which he shares the credit with fellow indie director David Lowery (*Ain't Them Bodies Saints*, 2013). On the one hand, editing is responsible for confusing the timelines of a number of events involving the protagonists or for mixing their storylines with those of people who don't seem to have any relevance to their story; on the other hand, it emphasizes the link between the two main characters and the Sampler and his pigs. Editing also undercuts the significance of speech across the film. When we hear conversations, they are fragmented and often appear as asynchronous, matched with temporally displaced visual segments of the characters not speaking. As in *Breathe In*, we're encouraged to focus on body language or mise-en-scène rather than trying to discern every spoken word. For instance, the sequence depicting Kris and Jeff repeatedly meeting on a train does not contain any speech at all. However, a handful of shots showing Jeff stealing looks at Kris indicate the passing of time and Jeff's increasing interest in and attraction to her.

Repetition is embedded in every aspect of the non-chronological ellipses that dominate many sequences, creating syncopated audio–visual rhymes. This approach is particularly obvious in the montage sequence in which Kris and Jeff argue over the ownership of their memories, whose similarities suggest that they were implanted during the characters' kidnappings (0:59:05–1:02:02).[8] Here, both the passing of time and the recurrence of the characters' argument is conveyed through the repetition of images that become visual refrains: Kris and Jeff lying on the floor, walking, watching birds flying above trees, Kris putting her make-up on, the couple touching each other. Their conversations are also fragmented and rhythmicized through repetition, but are presented 'in syncopation' with the visual repetitions. For instance, the opening lines—Jeff saying 'we should go on a trip', Kris asking 'where should we go?' and him responding 'somewhere bright'—are at first heard in synch with the image of the couple lying on the floor. The following few shots accompanied only by music symbolize the 'honeymoon' phase of their relationship, the couple kissing or holding hands. The rest of the dialogue consists of snippets of their conversations about different childhood memories, some of them heard in sync with their source—Kris and Jeff in different interior and exterior locations—some of them appearing as voice-overs over images of the protagonists not speaking. A shift in mood, pointing towards the dark mystery behind the uncanny overlap in their memories, is marked by a repetition of the same dialogue heard at the beginning of the sequence starting with Jeff saying 'we should go on a trip', but this time played asynchronously over the shot of him and Kris moving into their own place. The rest of the conversation, which increasingly sounds like an argument, is created from non-chronologically assembled snippets of similar conversations in which Kris accuses Jeff of taking her childhood memories and making them his own. The only repeated sentence which is always matched with similar images is 'They could be starlings'. Uttered by Jeff and then repeated by Kris, this sentence is paired with an image of the couple looking at birds. This audio–visual 'sample' is repeated twice more, the call-and-response exchange between the couple emphasizing the underlying strength of their connection and anchoring the scene in a more positive light.

Mary Ann Doane argues that the use of asynchronous speech threatens to expose 'the material heterogeneity of cinema' by drawing our attention to the space beyond what is represented by the image and the hidden artifice (1985b, p. 167).[9] She adds, though (paraphrasing Pascal Bonitzer), that narrative film exploits this marginal anxiety 'by incorporating its disturbing effects within the dramatic framework' (p. 167). This use of asynchrony is typical of *Upstream Color*: the spatio-temporal fragmentation and the scarcity of synch points reflect a sense of displacement in the characters and a lack of grounded identity. This is particularly apparent in the middle third of the film which presents the characters trying to understand their place in the world: '... Kris and Jeff are dealing and reacting to things that they don't understand ... the characters are being affected at a distance in the way that they can't speak to, so all cinema tools are being used to convey that subjective experience' (Carruth, 2013).

Matching the characters' loss of a stable sense of self and their place in the world is the loss of a privileged and centralized point of view or point of audition: viewers are thrown into an audio–visual space without clear temporal or spatial coordinates; one day merges into another which could be a week or a month later; some events happen in two places at once! Temporal displacement of the image and dialogue here is evocative of Carruth's use of sound in his debut *Primer* where it appears as the result of overlapping several temporalities and an unknown number of protagonists' doppelgangers produced by time travel.[10] In *Upstream Color*, time-/space-bending is reserved not only for the idea that the protagonists' lives are affected from a distance by the Sampler, but also for Kris and Jeff in the scene where they are shown lying in bed and also in the middle of the pig farm, which emphasizes the connection between the pigs and the main characters. Significantly, the spatio-temporal overlap in the scene in which Kris kills the Sampler, which happens simultaneously in an empty apartment and at the pig farm, is one of the clues suggesting that this 'killing' should be understood in metaphorical terms, possibly as Kris' breakthrough in facing and confronting the source of her brokenness, anxiety and paranoia.

It should be noted, though, that despite this flexibility in the representation of the unity of time and space and the extensive use of non-chronological ellipses that reinforces the idea of living with a shattered sense of identity, the film maintains fluency in purely sensuous terms. This is mostly thanks to Carruth's score which, with its soft ambient colours and sustained chords, provides a feeling of continuous flow. Its unobtrusive but reassuring presence brings to mind the idea of running water, which is one of the key narrative motifs. For one thing, it is implied in the title which is related to Conrad's *Heart of Darkness* and the idea of 'going upriver to solve the problem in some way' (Carruth quoted in Romney, 2013, p. 52). The film is also punctuated with images of the stream into which the Sampler throws piglets or pages of his score, repeated shots of the taps in Jeff's and Kris' apartments, and the leitmotif of Kris diving into a swimming pool to collect stones. It is appropriate then that the main association produced by the presence of the prolonged electronic sounds that feature in most of the scenes without dialogue is that of being submerged: events and spoken words lying under the layer of sustained chords in the same way the characters' memories and sense of identity are buried deep in the subconscious following the drug-induced trauma and loss of memory.

While the score is embedded in the film's foundations but remains unobtrusive, and speech is often relativized through fragmentation, sound effects have a prominent narrative role, sound being the Sampler's main means of communication with the kidnapping victims. When Kris wakes up from her trance-like state with the worm crawling under her skin, the Sampler 'calls' her to the site for de-worming by broadcasting a repetitive whooshing sound from speakers face down on the ground, creating vibrations in the soil (0:19:30). Another striking montage sequence (0:36:00–0:39:12) shows the Sampler recording outdoor sounds and composing. His recordings of water gurgling, bricks falling, stones sliding down an iron pipe and similar, merge with sounds that Kris and Jeff make at home and at work—photocopier buzzing, bathroom tap running, sewing machine humming—and then fuse again with the Sampler's recordings, eloquently pointing to the communication between the three of them.

In one sense this scene acts as an exposure of cinematic means of construction, a reflexive glimpse into usually hidden processes of production. Like the theme of filmmaking in David Lynch's films, recording sound in *Upstream Color* can be seen as a symbol of the multi-layered nature of reality. Even more importantly, it is a look 'behind the scenes' of Kris' and Jeff's lives and how they are influenced by the Sampler's actions. It eloquently illuminates some of the main themes of the film, the questions of what we are made of, what determines our behaviour and the sense of who we are. In the context of the narrative, the Sampler's role, actions and his relationship to all the characters can be interpreted as a metaphor for subconscious 'programming'—all the familial, social and cultural influences that we are exposed to from an early age. On another level, presenting the Sampler as a composer and sound artist whose actions affect the protagonists' lives symbolically portrays him as a Creator and simultaneously establishes sound-making and musicality as the film's primary creative principles. The dominance of sound in both scenes amplifies the power of the senses and our affective response to sound, music and the sensuous aspects of film, the director luring us into his world like the Sampler with his speakers sending vibrations deep into the ground.

## Conclusion

The privileged position of speech and dialogue in soundtrack has been one of the constants of the cinema tradition, rarely challenged outside the confines of modernist and experimental cinema. In that sense, we can draw some parallels between the strategies applied in the three films discussed here and the modernist experiments with form and soundtrack conducted by Alain Resnais and Jean-Luc-Godard in the 1960s, for instance, but we'll also find significant differences between them. One might be particularly tempted to compare the editing rhymes of *Upstream Color* to the looped conversational patterns in *Last Year in Marienbad* (Alain Resnais, 1961), not least because both films address processes of the mind through cinematic devices (even though Carruth admitted in one interview that he had never heard of Resnais—see Romney, 2013, p. 53). The sense of deliberate artifice that permeates Resnais' film, however, or Godard's Brechtian deconstructions of classical form (see Davison, 2004; Williams, 1985) differ significantly from Carruth's attempt to create an engaging story with a strong emphasis on the tactile and sensuous aspects of cinema.

At the same time, all the examined films are permeated with a musical logic which goes beyond the soundtrack alone, affecting different aspects of film form.

Korine's idea of a 'liquid narrative' inspired by electronic music can be applied to Carruth's film as well, both films utilizing non-chronological editing rhythmicized through repetitions to convey a sense of 'morphing' and the protagonists' distance from reality. In each film the actual music is not only crucial for supplying the flow of continuity to the jagged narrative but is elevated to the role of an actual character, to paraphrase Doremus. Both *Breathe In* and *Upstream Color* feature protagonists who are musicians while Carruth's film is even scored by the director himself. And in each film music provides a suitable background, or is a partner for the musical use of words, lending itself to the musical use of language.

Each example also demonstrates that the asynchronous use of language is an inherent part of its musicalization. On one hand, it encourages us to focus on the sonic properties of the spoken word; on the other, it facilities the emancipation of speech. Divorced from the image, speech is then able to establish its own flow, becoming yet another line in the sonic counterpoint of the soundtrack in which there are no previously assigned roles and no pre-established hierarchy.

All three films emphasize sensuous aspects of cinema sometimes even at the expense of comprehensible storytelling and intelligibility of speech. *Upstream Color* in particular is one of those films that demands more than one viewing in order to satisfy one's intellectual desire to grasp the principles of its storytelling, but even on first encounter it does not fail to provide a sense of aesthetic fulfilment through the combination of intellectual, emotional and sensory stimulation. It is worth emphasizing here, though, that the sensory stimulation I refer to is not that usually associated with the immersive projection experience—large screens, Dolby and Surround Sound system, elaborate sound and visual effects. Rather, it is the result of utilizing the film's audio–visual devices in a manner which foregrounds the sensuous aspect of the medium itself—its sonic and visual textures, composition, movement and flow.

Although this chapter focuses on elucidating the significance of aural stimuli in accentuating the musical qualities of film, it is the combination of the tightly interwoven strands of music, speech and sound effects with narrative and visual elements that activate the aesthetic dimension of film's sensuousness. Each of the examined films suspends the classical rules of narration to different degrees, foregrounding music and the language of mise-en-scène and, in two cases, non-chronological editing rather than relying on dialogue or continuity editing to tell their stories. All three films also stimulate 'haptic visuality' (Marks, 2000) not only by highlighting the narrative and visual importance of tactile actions such as musical performances, erotic encounters or, as in *Upstream Color*, repeated images of hands touching surfaces or the protagonists touching each other, but also through other visual and sonic means, whether the assault of day-glo colours in *Spring Breakers* or the whooshes and rumbles emanating from big speakers, pipes and machines in *Upstream Color*. Owing to these combined stimuli and the musical logic behind many of the decisions determining the films' structures and flow, all three possess a quality which allows repeated viewings in a manner similar to what Carruth alluded to when he compared recurring encounters with his film to listening to one's favourite album.

## Notes

1. See, for instance, the programmes of the 2014 and 2015 *Music and the Moving Image* conferences at NYU Steinhardt.
2. *Chiaroscuro* is a term used in painting which refers to the use of strong contrast between light and dark or the 'quality of being veiled or partly in shadow' (Merriam-Webster Dictionary online). Chion here refers to the latter meaning.
3. Consider, for instance, the films of Robert Altman, in which an improvisatory style of acting conveys everyday situations in which people interrupt each other, speak at the same time, shout over the noise of traffic and so on.
4. This is the timing of the scene in the DVD release of *Breathe In*, Curzon Film World, 2013.
5. This is the timing of the scene in the DVD release of *Spring Breakers*, Universal, 2013.
6. For a detailed study on image/sound synchronization and the asynchronous use of sound, see Donnelly (2014).
7. A memorable example is the iconic baptism scene in *The Godfather* (Francis Ford Coppola, 1974) in which Michael Corleone's (Al Pacino) vows to accept God and denounces the devil are paired with images of his opponents being slaughtered on his orders; or more recently, in *Killing Them Softly* (Andrew Dominik, 2012) speeches by George W. Bush, Barack Obama and other politicians commenting on the American financial crisis on the eve of the 2008 presidential election are juxtaposed with a story about small-time crooks trying to get away with a big robbery.
8. This is the timing of the scene in the DVD release of *Upstream Color*, New Video, 2013.
9. 'The use of the voice-off always entails a risk—that of exposing the material heterogeneity of the cinema. Synchronous sound masks the problem and this at least partially explains its dominance' (Doane, 1985b, p. 167).
10. See Johnston (2012) for a detailed analysis of the sound in *Primer*.

## References

Bellour, R. (1981) 'Segmenting/Analysing' in Rick Altman (ed.) *Genre: The Musical* (London, Boston and Henley: Routledge and Kegan Paul), 102–133.

Carruth, S. (2013) 'New Directors/New Films Film Q&A: *Upstream Color*, Shane Carruth', Film Society of Lincoln Center, https://www.youtube.com/watch?v=5cjq_Lb2F2I, date accessed 15 March 2014.

Child, B. (2014) 'Interstellar's sound 'right for an experimental film', says Nolan', *The Guardian*, 17th November, http://www.theguardian.com/film/2014/nov/17/interstellar-sound-christopher-nolan, date accessed 17 November 2014.

Chion, M. (1994) *Audio-Vision: Sound on Screen*, ed/trans. C. Gorbman (New York: Columbia University Press).

Chion, M. (1999) *The Voice in Cinema*, trans. C. Gorbman (New York: Columbia University Press).

Cohen, A. J. (2002) 'Music Cognition and the Cognitive Psychology of Film Structure', *Canadian Psychology* Vol. 43, No. 4, 215–232.

Davison, A. (2004) *Hollywood Theory, Non-Hollywood Practice: Cinema Soundtracks in the 1980s and 1990s* (Aldershot: Ashgate).

Doane, M. A. (1985a) 'Ideology and the Practice of Sound Editing and Mixing' in E. Weis and J. Belton (eds) *Film Sound: Theory and Practice* (New York: Columbia University Press), 54–62.

Doane, M. A. (1985b) 'The Voice in the Cinema: The Articulation of Body and Space' in E. Weis and J. Belton (eds) *Film Sound: Theory and Practice* (New York: Columbia University Press), 162–176.

Donnelly, K. J. (2014) *Occult Aesthetics: Synchronization in Sound Film* (New York: Oxford University Press).

Doremus, D. (2013) 'Special Features: Interview with Drake Doremus', *Breathe In* DVD, Curzon Film World.

Johnston, N. (2012) 'Beneath Sci-fi Sound: Primer, Science Fiction Sound Design, and American Independent Cinema', *Alphaville: Journal of Film and Screen Media* 3 (Summer), http://www.alphavillejournal.com/Issue%203/HTML/ArticleJohnston.html, date accessed 22 February 2015.

Kassabian, A. (2013) *Ubiquitous Listening: Affect, Attention, and Distributed Subjectivity* (Berkeley/Los Angeles/London: University of California).

Kulezic-Wilson, D. (2008) 'Sound Design is the New Score', *Music, Sound and the Moving Image*, Vol. 2, Issue 2, 127–131.

Kulezic-Wilson, D. (2015) *The Musicality of Narrative Film* (Basingstoke: Palgrave Macmillan).

Marks, L. (2000) *The Skin of the Film: Intercultural Cinema, Embodiment and the Senses* (Durham and London: Duke University Press).

Reynolds, S. (2013) 'You Only Live Once', *Sight & Sound* (May), 26–31.

Romney, J. (2013) 'Enigma Variations', *Sight & Sound* (September), 50–53.

Taubin, A. (2013) 'Cultural Mash-up', *Sight & Sound* (May) 29.

Williams, A. (1985) 'Godard's Use of Sound' in E. Weis and J. Belton (eds), *Film Sound: Theory and Practice* (New York: Columbia University Press), 332–345.

# Filmography

*À bout de souffle* (*Breathless*, Jean-Luc Godard, France, 1960).
*The Abyss* (James Cameron, USA, 1989).
*The Adventures of Priscilla, Queen of the Desert* (Stephan Elliott, Australia, 1994).
*Alien* (Ridley Scott, USA, 1979).
*Aliens* (James Cameron, USA, 1986).
*Alien 3* (David Fincher, USA, 1992).
*All Quiet on the Western Front* (Lewis Milestone, USA, 1930).
*American Graffiti* (Francis Ford Coppola, USA, 1973).
*L'Amour fou* (Jacques Rivette, France, 1969).
*Andrei Rublev* (Andrei Tarkovsky, Soviet Union, 1966).
*Anna Karenina* (Joe Wright, UK, 2012).
*Antichrist* (Lars von Trier, Denmark/France/Italy/Germany/Poland/Sweden, 2009).
*Apocalypse Now* (Francis Ford Coppola, USA, 1979).
*Apollo 13* (Ron Howard, USA, 1995).
*Armageddon* (Michael Bay, UA, 1998).
*Art History* (Joe Swanberg, USA, 2011).
*Atonement* (Joe Wright, UK, 2007).
*Babel* (Alejandro González Iñárritu, USA, 2006).
*Barton Fink* (Joel Coen and Ethan Cohen, USA, 1991).
*Battleship Potemkin* (Sergei Eisenstein, Soviet Union, 1925).
*Le beau Serge* (Claude Chabrol, France, 1958).
*A Beautiful Mind* (Ron Howard, USA, 2001).
*Birth* (Jonathan Glazer, USA, 2004).
*The Black Stallion* (Carroll Ballard, USA, 1979).
*Black Swan* (Darren Aronofsky, USA, 2010).
*Blade Runner* (Ridley Scott, USA, 1982).
*The Bling Ring* (Sofia Coppola, USA, 2013).
*Blood from the Mummy's Tomb* (Seth Holt and Michael Carreras/uncredited/, UK, 1971).
*Blue Velvet* (David Lynch, USA, 1986).
*Das Boot* (Wolfgang Petersen, West Germany, 1981).
*The Bourne Identity* (Doug Liman, USA, 2002).

*The Bourne Supremacy* (Paul Greengrass, USA, 2012).
*The Bourne Ultimatum* (Paul Greengrass, USA, 2007).
*Boyhood* (Richard Linklater, USA, 2014).
*Breathe In* (Drake Doremus, USA, 2013).
*The Burning Plain* (Guillermo Arriaga, USA/Argentina, 2008).
*Cat People* (Jacques Tourneur, USA, 1942).
*Un Chien Andalou* (Luis Buñuel, France, 1929).
*Children of Men* (Alfonso Cuarón, UK/USA, 2006).
*Citizen Kane* (Orson Welles, USA, 1941).
*A Clockwork Orange* (Stanley Kubrick, UK, 1971).
*La collectionneuse* (*The Collector*, Éric Rohmer, France, 1967).
*Cop Land* (James Mangold, USA, 1997).
*Dans ma peau* (*In My Skin*, Marina de Van, France, 2002).
*Days of Heaven* (Terrence Malick, USA, 1978).
*The Day the Earth Stood Still* (Robert Wise, USA, 1951).
*Deadpan* (Steve McQueen, UK, 1997).
*Dead Poets Society* (Peter Weir, USA, 1989).
*The Deer Hunter* (Michael Cimino, USA, 1978).
*Déjà Vu* (Tony Scott, USA, 2006).
*Destination Moon* (Irving Pichel, USA, 1950).
*Don Juan* (Alan Crosland, USA, 1926).
*Donny Darko* (Richard Kelly, USA, 2001).
*Don't Look Now* (Nicolas Roeg, UK/Italy, 1973).
*Double Indemnity* (Billy Wilder, USA, 1944).
*Drinking Buddies* (Joe Swanberg, USA, 2013).
*Drive* (Nicolas Winding Refn. USA, 2011).
*Duel* (Steven Spielberg, USA, 1971).
*Duma* (Carroll Ballard, USA, 2005).
*Dune* (David Lynch, USA, 1984).
*The Earrings of Madame de …* (Max Ophüls, France, 1953).
*The Elephant Man* (David Lynch, USA, 1980).
*The Empire Strikes Back* (Irvin Kershner, USA, 1980).
*The Enemy Below* (Dick Powell, USA, 1957).
*The English Patient* (Anthony Minghella, USA, 1996).
*Enthusiasm: Symphony of the Donbass* (Dziga Vertov, Soviet Union, 1930).
*Eraserhead* (David Lynch, USA, 1977).
*Escape from New York* (John Carpenter, USA, 1981).
*A Family Finds Entertainment* (Ryan Trecartin, USA, 2004).
*Fight Club* (David Fincher, USA/Germany, 1999).
*Forbidden Planet* (Fred M. Wilcox, USA, 1956).
*Full Metal Jacket* (Stanley Kubrick, UK/USA, 1987).
*The General* (Buster Keaton, USA, 1926).
*Gerry* (Gus Van Sant, USA, 2002).
*Ghost World* (Terry Zwigoff, US, 2001).
*Gladiator* (Ridley Scott, USA/UK, 2000).
*The Godfather* (Francis Ford Coppola, USA, 1972).
*Goya's Ghosts* (Miloš Forman, USA/Spain, 2006).
*The Grandmother* (David Lynch, USA, 1970).
*Gravity* (Alfonso Cuarón, UK/USA, 2013).

*The Great Gatsby* (Baz Luhrmann, Australia/USA, 2013).
*Guinness for You* (Anthony Short, UK, 1971).
*Gummo* (Harmony Korine, USA, 1997).
*Happy Christmas* (Joe Swanberg, USA, 2014).
*The Healer* (a.k.a. *Julie Walking Home*, Agnieszka Holland, USA/Germany/Canada, 2002).
*Henry And June* (Philip Kaufman, USA, 1990).
*High Noon* (Fred Zinnemann, USA, 1952).
*Hilary and Jackie*, (Anand Tucker, UK, 1998).
*The House of the Devil* (Ti West, USA, 2009).
*Hunger* (Steve McQueen, UK, 2008).
*The Hunt for Red October* (John McTiernan, USA, 1990).
*Idealisten* (Christina Rosendahl, Denmark, 2015).
*Inception* (Christopher Nolan, USA/UK, 2010).
*Interstellar* (Christopher Nolan, USA/UK, 2014).
*In the Mood for Love* (Wong Kar-wai, Hong Kong, 2000).
*Jackie Brown* (Quentin Tarantino, USA, 1998).
*Jaws* (Steven Spielberg, USA, 1975).
*The Jazz Singer* (Alan Crosland, USA, 1927).
*Julien Donkey-Boy* (Harmony Korine, USA, 1999).
*Killing Them Softly* (Andrew Dominik, USA, 2012).
*Kingdom of Heaven: Director's Cut* (Ridley Scott, UK/Germany/USA, 2005).
*The Ladykillers* (Alexander MacKendrick, UK, 1955).
*Last Days* (Gus Van Sant, USA, 2005).
*Last Year in Marienbad* (*L'Année dernière à Marienbad*, Alain Resnais, France, 1961).
*Letter from Siberia* (Chris Marker, France, 1957).
*Lift to the Scaffold* (Louis Malle, France, 1958).
*Lisztomania* (Ken Russell, UK, 1975).
*Little Big Man* (Arthur Penn, USA, 1970).
*Logan's Run* (Michael Anderson, USA, 1976).
*Look Who's Talking* (Amy Heckerling, USA, 1989).
*Look Who's Talking Now* (Tom Ropelewski, USA, 1993).
*Look Who's Talking Too* (Amy Heckerling, USA, 1990).
*Lost Highway* (David Lynch, USA, 1997).
*Lost in Translation* (Sofia Coppola, USA, 2003).
*Love Actually* (Richard Curtis, UK, 2003).
*A Man Escaped* (Robert Bresson, France, 1956).
*The Man of Steel* (Zack Snyder, USA, 2013).
*Marie Antoinette* (Sofia Coppola, USA/France/Japan, 2006).
*Melancholia* (Lars von Trier, Denmark/Sweden/France/Italy/Germany, 2011).
*Metropolis* (Fritz Lang, Germany, 1927).
*Mirages d'un Eldorado* (Martin Frigon, Canada, 2008).
*Mission: Impossible* (Brian de Palma, USA, 1996).
*Mission: Impossible II* (John Woo, USA, 2000).
*Mission: Impossible III* (J. J. Abrams, USA, 2006).
*Mission: Impossible—Ghost Protocol* (Brad Bird, USA, 2011).
*Mission: Impossible—Rogue Nation* (Christopher McQuarrie, USA, 2015).
*Modern Times* (Charlie Chaplin, USA, 1936).
*Mr. Jones* (Mike Figgis, USA, 1993).

*The Mosquito Coast* (Peter Weir, USA, 1986).
*Moulin Rouge!* (Baz Luhrmann, Australia/USA, 2001).
*Nashville* (Robert Altman, USA, 1975).
*Never Cry Wolf* (Carroll Ballard, USA, 1983).
*Old and New* (Grigori Aleksandrov and Sergei Eisenstein, Soviet Union, 1929).
*Paris nous appartient* (*Paris Belongs to Us*, Jacques Rivette, France, 1961).
*Persona* (Ingmar Bergman, Sweden, 1966).
*Pi* (Darren Aronofsky, USA, 1998).
*The Pianist* (Roman Polanski, France/Germany/Poland/UK, 2002).
*Philadelphia* (Jonathan Demme, USA, 1993).
*Pirates of the Caribbean: Dead Man's Chest* (Gore Verbinski, USA, 2006).
*Platform* (*Zhantai*, Jia Zhangke, China, 2000).
*Platoon* (Oliver Stone, USA, 1986).
*Pride and Prejudice* (Joe Wright, UK, 2005).
*The Princess Bride* (Rob Reiner, USA, 1987).
*Prometheus* (Ridley Scott, USA, 2012).
*Psycho* (Alfred Hitchcock, USA, 1960).
*Pulp Fiction* (Quentin Tarantino, USA, 1994).
*Punch-Drunk Love* (Paul Thomas Anderson, USA, 2002).
*Quatermass and the Pit* (US title: *Five Million Years to Earth*, Roy Ward Baker, UK, 1967).
*Quatermass 2* (US title: *Enemy from Space*, Val Guest, UK, 1957).
*The Quatermass Xperiment* (US title: *The Creeping Unknown*, Val Guest, UK, 1955).
*Les quatre cents coups* (*The 400 Blows*, François Truffaut, France, 1959).
*Raiders of the Lost Ark* (Stephen Spielberg, USA, 1981).
*Raising Arizona* (Joel and Ethan Coen, USA, 1987).
*Requiem for a Dream* (Darren Aronofsky, USA, 2000).
*Reservoir Dogs* (Quentin Tarantino, USA, 1991).
*Return of the Jedi* (Richard Marquand, USA, 1983).
*Revanche* (Götz Spielmann, Austria, 2008).
*Rising Sun* (Philip Kaufman, USA, 1993).
*Rocketship X-M* (Kurt Neumann, USA, 1950).
*Romance Sentimentale* (Grigori Aleksandrov and Sergei Eisenstein, France, 1930).
*The Royal Tenenbaums* (Wes Anderson, USA, 2001).
*The Sacrament* (Ti West, USA, 2014).
*Salmon Fishing in the Yemen* (Lasse Hallström, UK, 2011).
*Saving Private Ryan* (Steven Spielberg, USA, 1998).
*Scanners* (David Cronenberg, Canada, 1981).
*Shame* (Steve McQueen, UK, 2011).
*Silent Hill* (Christophe Gans, Canada/France, 2006).
*Silent Hill: Revelation* (Michael J.Bassett, Canada/France/USA, 2012).
*Silver Bullets* (Joe Swanberg, USA, 2011).
*A Single Man* (Tom Ford, USA, 2009).
*The Skin* (*La Pelle*, Liliana Cavani, Italy, 1981).
*Snow* (Geoffrey Jones. UK, 1963).
*The Social Network* (David Fincher, USA, 2010).
*Solaris* (Andrei Tarkovsky, Soviet Union, 1972).
*The Soloist* (Joe Wright, UK/USA/France, 2009).
*Somewhere* (Sofia Coppola, USA, 2010).

*Song of Ceylon* (Basil Wright, UK, 1934).
*Spirited Away* (Hayao Miyazaki, Japan, 2010).
*Spring Breakers* (Harmony Korine, USA, 2012).
*A Star Is Born* (Frank Pierson, USA, 1976).
*Star Trek* (J.J. Abrams, USA, 2009).
*Star Wars* (George Lucas, USA, 1977).
*Star Wars Episode I: The Phantom Menace* (George Lucas, USA, 1999).
*Star Wars Episode II: Attack of the Clones* (George Lucas, USA, 2002).
*Star Wars: Episode III—Revenge of the Sith* (George Lucas, USA, 2005).
*Star Wars Episode VII: The Force Awakens* (J. J. Abrams, USA, 2015).
*Stoker* (Park Chan-Wook, UK/USA, 2013).
*Superman* (Richard Donner, USA, 1978).
*Super Mario Bros* (Annabel Jankel and Rocky Morton, USA, 1993).
*Suzanne Simonin, la Religieuse de Denis Diderot* (*The Nun*, Jacques Rivette, France, 1966).
*Terminator* (James Cameron, USA, 1984).
*Terminator Genisys* (Alan Taylor, USA, 2015).
*Terminator 2: Judgment Day* (James Cameron, USA, 1991).
*Terminator 3: Rise of the Machines* (Jonathan Mostow, USA, 2003).
*Terminator Salvation* (McG, USA, 2009).
*There Will Be Blood* (Paul Thomas Anderson, USA, 2007).
*Things to Come* (William Cameron Menzies, UK, 1936).
*The Thin Red Line* (Terrence Malick, USA, 1998).
*The 39 Steps* (Alfred Hitchcock, UK, 1935).
*Three Kings* (David O. Russell, USA, 1999).
*Three Men and a Baby* (Leonard Nimoy, USA, 1987).
*Thunderball* (Terence Young, UK, 1965).
*Time Of Eve* (Yasuhiro Yoshiura, Japan, 2010).
*Top Gun* (Ridley Scott, USA, 1986).
*Trainspotting* (Danny Boyle, UK, 1996).
*Traffic* (Steven Soderbergh, USA, 2000)
*Trash Humpers* (Harmony Korine, USA, 2009).
*Tron* (Steven Lisberger, USA, 1982).
*Trouble Every Day* (Claire Denis, France/Germany/Japan, 2001).
*Tommy* (Ken Russell, UK, 1975).
*24 Exposures* (Joe Swanberg, USA, 2013).
*2001: A Space Odyssey* (Stanley Kubrick, UK/USA, 1968).
*The Unbearable Lightness of Being* (Philip Kaufman, USA, 1988).
*Uncle Kent* (Joe Swanberg, USA, 2011).
*Under the Skin* (Jonathan Glazer, UK/USA/Switzerland, 2013).
*Unknown Pleasures* (*Ren xiaoyao*, Jia Zhangke, China, 2002).
*Upstream Color* (Shane Carruth, USA, 2013).
*V for Vendetta* (James McTeigue, UK/USA/Germany, 2006).
*Vertigo* (Alfred Hitchcock, USA, 1958).
*V/H/S* (Matt Bettinelli-Olpin, David Bruckner, Tyler Gillett, Justin Martinez, Glenn McQuaid, Radio Silence, Joe Swanberg, Chad Villella, Ti West, Adam Wingard, USA, 2012).
*The Virgin Suicides* (Sofia Coppola, USA, 1999).
*Vivre sa vie* (Jean-Luc Godard, France, 1962).

*The Wages of Fear* (*Le salaire de la peur*, Henri Clouzot, France, 1953).
*Wall:E* (Andrew Stanton, USA, 2008).
*WarGames* (John Badham, USA, 1983).
*Wild at Heart* (David Lynch, USA, 1990).
*Xiao Wu* (Jia Zhangke, China, 1997).
*Young and Innocent* (Alfred Hitchcock, UK, 1937).
*Young Frankenstein* (Mel Brooks, USA, 1974).
*You're Next* (Adam Wingard, USA, 2011).
*The Zone* (Joe Swanberg, USA, 2011).

## Television and Radio

*Arrow* (The CW, 2012–).
*Astro Boy* (*Tetsuwan Atomu*, Fuji TV, 1963–1966; NTV, 1980–1981; Fuji TV, 2003–2004).
*Battlestar Galactica* (ABC, 1978–9).
*Battlestar Galactica* (Sci-Fi, 2004–9).
*Boardwalk Empire* (HBO, 2010–2014)
*The Bridge* (SVT1, DR1, 2011–).
*Buck Rogers* (Ford Beebe and Saul A. Goodkind, Universal serial, 1939).
*Captain Video and His Space Rangers* (Dumont, 1949–1955).
*The Crimson Petal and the White* (BBC, 2011).
*CSI: Crime Scene Investigation* (CBS, 2000–2015).
*Dimension X* (NBC Radio, 1950–1).
*Dragon Ball Z*, (Fuji TV, Animax, Tokyo MX, 1996–2003).
*Everwood* (The WB, 2002–6).
*Flash Gordon* (Frederick Stephani, Universal serial, 1936).
*Flash Gordon* (Dumont/syndicated in the US, 1954).
*Flash Gordon Conquers the Universe* (Ray Taylor and Ford Beebe, Universal serial, 1940).
*Flash Gordon's Trip to Mars* (Frederick Stephani, Universal serial, 1938).
*Forbrydelsen* (DR1, 2007–2012).
*Friday Night Lights* (NBC, 2006–2011).
*Homeland* (Showtime, 2011–).
*Investigator Mariko* (KIKU TV, 1999–2014).
*The Mentalist* (CBS, 2008–2015).
*Naruto* (TXN, 2002–7).
*NCIS: Naval Criminal Investigative Service* (CBS, 2003–).
*The Outer Limits* (ABC, 1963–5).
*Pokémon* (TV Tokyo, 1997–).
*Quantum Leap* (NBC, 1989–93).
*Quatermass* (Thames/ITV, 1979).
*Quatermass and the Pit* (BBC, 1958–9).
*The Quatermass Experiment* (BBC, 1953).
*The Quatermass Experiment* (Channel 4, 2005).
*Quatermass II* (BBC, 1955).
*Sailor Moon* (TV Asahi, 1992–7).
*Sex and the City* (HBO, 1998–2004).
*The Sopranos* (HBO, 1999–2007).
*Spooks* (BBC, 2002–2011).

*Star Trek* (NBC, 1966–9).
*Stranger from Space* (BBC, 1951–2).
*Super Sentai* (TV Asahi, 1975–).
*The Time Machine* (BBC, 1949).
*Tom Corbett, Space Cadet* (ABC, CBS, NBC, and Dumont at various times during 1950–5 run).
*24* (Fox, 2001–2010).
*The Twilight Zone* (CBS, 1959–64).
*2000 Plus* (Mutual Radio, 1950).
*Utopia* (Channel 4, 2013–2014).
'War of the Worlds', *Mercury Theatre on the Air* (CBS Radio, 1938).
*The Wire* (HBO, 2002–8).
*X-Minus One* (NBC Radio, 1955–8).
*Yu-Gi-Oh!* (TV Asahi, 1998; TV Tokyo, 2000–8).

## GAMES

*BIT.TRIP RUNNER* (Designer Alex Neuse, 2010).
*Donkey Kong* (Creator Shigeru Miyamoto, 1981).
*Donkey Kong, Jr.* (Creator Shigeru Miyamoto, 1982).
*Dyad* (Designer Shawn McGrath, 2012).
*The Legend of Zelda* (Creators Shigeru Miyamoto, Takashi Tezuka, 1986).
*Mario Bros.* (Designers Shigeru Miyamoto, Gunpei Yokoi, 1983).
*Metroid* (Satoru Okada, 1986).
*140* (Developer Jeppe Carlsen, 2013).
*Pong* (Designer Allan Alcorn, 1972).
*Rez* (Designers Hiroyuki Abe, Katsuhiko Yamada, 2001).
*Silent Hill* games (Creator Keiichiro Toyama).
*Silent Hill* (1999) [for Playstation, later versions ported for PC].
*Silent Hill 2* (2001) [Play Station 2, PC, Xbox].
*Silent Hill 3* (2003) [PS2, PC].
*Silent Hill 4: The Room* (2004) [PS2, PC, Xbox].
*Silent Hill Origins* (2007) [PSP handheld].
*Silent Hill: Homecoming* (2008) [PS3, XboX, PC].
*Silent Hill: The Escape* (2008) [iOS].
*Silent Hill: Shattered Memories* (2009) [Wii, PS2, PSP].
*Silent Hill: Downpour* (2012) [PS3, XboX].
*Silent Hill: Book of Memories* (2012) [PSVita].
*Space Invaders* (Designer Tomohiro Nishikado, 1978).
*Super Mario Bros.* (Director Shigeru Miyamoto, 1985).
*Super Metroid* (Director Yoshio Sakamoto, 1994).

# Index[1]

**A**
À bout de souffle (Breathless), 197
Academy Award, 19, 33, 34, 64, 100, 139, 345n1
acousmatic
  effect, 76
  sound, 76, 83
  voice, 240
acoustic disgust, 7, 183–92. *See also* violence
acoustic space, 8, 230, 231, 234, 239–43, 342
Adorno, Theodor, 180
ADR, 10, 11, 278, 293, 295, 301, 325, 326, 361, 366–70, 373, 378, 384
  bad ADR, 367
*Adventures of Priscilla, Queen of the Desert, The*, 43
aesthetics
  character, 73
  choices, 11, 18
  cinematic, 92, 302
  classical, 407
  computational, 363, 371
  direct sound, 204
  film, 10, 108
  of a given culture, 62
  lo-fi indie-sound, 10
  lucidity, 102
  of the music, 70

Muzak, 10
nineteenth-century aesthetics, 61
political, 239
radio, 8, 371
raw, 300
of spatialization, 103
affect, 4, 7, 12, 18, 68, 153–67, 173, 183–92, 220, 228n4, 364, 365, 425
AFM, 44, 46–54, 282, 286n15
Albrechtsen, Peter, 40
Alcorn, Al, 347
Alexandrov, Grigori, 390, 391
*Alien*, 11, 91, 101, 165, 188, 216, 218, 227, 228, 308, 348, 354, 362, 378, 381, 382, 406, 434–6
Alliance of Theatrical Stage Employees (IATSE also known as IA). *See* IA
*All Quiet on the Western Front*, 51
*Almost Famous*, 264
Altman, Rick, 2, 17, 18, 55n10, 170, 171, 348, 369, 372
Altman, Robert, 160, 280
*Ambient 4: On Land*, 75
*American Cinematographer* (magazine), 281
American Federation of Musicians. *See* AFM
*American Graffiti*, 269, 285n2
American Indie films, 8

[1] Note: Locators followed by 'n' refers to notes

American Society of Composers, Authors and Publishers. See ASCAP
*anacousmetre*, 364
analogue
  analogue to digital (analogue/digital), 273–86, 339
  synthesizers, 275, 276
Anderson, Paul Thomas, 7, 171, 264, 305
Anderson, Wes, 9, 246–8, 269
*Andrei Rublev*, 188
android, 10, 331–46. *See also* sound, of machines
  android-holics, 334
anempathetic/empathetic, 10, 23, 97, 99, 184, 305–19, 378
Anglophone cinema, 4
animal recordings, 5, 277. *See also Duma*
  animal vocalization, 5
anime, 331–41, 343, 345n1, 358n5
*Anna Karenina*, 7, 139, 146, 148, 150, 431
Ant, Adam, 270
*Antichrist*, 190, 416n7
antiphony, 234
*Apocalypse Now*, 3, 163, 269, 273, 285n2
*Apollo 13*, 100, 101, 104
arbitrary noise, 156
*Armageddon*, 100
Armstrong, Craig, 12, 421, 422, 425
Aronofsky, Darren, 12, 166, 424, 431
*Arrow*, 64, 377
*Art History*, 10, 291, 293, 296–300, 302
art house cinema/films, 3, 4, 10, 29, 335
articulate utterances, 24, 25
*Art of Noises, The*, 21, 128, 339
ASCAP, 47, 54
Asimov, Isaac, 214, 334, 345n2
*2001: A Space Odyssey*, 86n11, 92, 96, 98, 109n6, 416n8
*Astro Boy (Tetsuwan Atomu)*, 333, 334
asynchronous
  image/sound, 435
  sound, 22, 297, 430, 433–7, 443n6
  speech, 434–7, 439
Atalli, Jacques, 23, 24
*Atonement*, 6, 7, 123–7, 132, 134, 139–42, 431
audible mimicry, 342

audience
  as an internal auditor, 171, 173
  audio-viewer, 93–9, 104, 106–8, 305–10, 312, 314–18
  first-person perspective, 98, 125, 130–2, 134
  listening position of the audience, 6, 7
  of the sound film, 98, 104, 154
  as spectator-auditors, 172, 173, 175–80, 181n3
audio close-up, 7, 187, 188, 191
audiovisual
  choreography, 97, 318
  close-up, 188, 189
  construction, 332
  dynamic, 12, 406, 412
  effects, 332
  field, 433
  language, 403, 415
  marriage, 415
  music, 412–15
  simulacra, 332
  space, 178, 180, 440
auditorium space, 104, 106
aural fantasy, 254
auteur, 3, 426
  music, 9
authorship, 228n4, 298–302, 396
automated dialogue replacement. *See* ADR
Auto Music, 261
avant-garde
  composers, 389
  electronica, 313
  music, 11, 76, 197
  musical composition, 356
  musical techniques, 350
  soundscapes, 308
Avraamov, Arsenii, 389

B
*Babel*, 169, 170, 172
Badalamenti, Angelo, 39
BAFTA, 269
Ballard, Carroll, 5, 19, 28, 33–5, 38
Barron, Louis and Bebe, 350, 353, 354
Barthes, Roland, 126–30, 134
*Barton Fink*, 166

Bass, Saul, 405
*Battlestar Galactica*, 215, 307
Baudrillard, Jean, 58
*beau Serge, Le*, 197
*Beautiful Mind, A*, 166
Beethoven, Ludwig van, 139, 143–5, 147, 317
Beggs, Richard, 34, 262, 266, 268
Bellour, Raymond, 156, 434
Beltrami, Marco, 421
Bender, Lon, 186
Benstead, Chris, 103, 104, 106, 107
Bernard, James, 217
BGM, 339, 340
*Billboard* (magazine), 274, 283
*Black Stallion, The*, 19, 28, 33, 34
*Black Swan*, 12, 424
*Blade Runner*, 354
*Bling Ring, The*, 9, 261, 266–8
blockbuster, 3, 29, 30, 161, 163, 429
*Blood from the Mummy's Tomb*, 398
*Blue Velvet*, 5, 19, 20, 22, 23, 25, 28, 29, 33, 37, 39, 40
*Boardwalk Empire*, 307
Bollywood, 8, 231
*Boogie Nights*, 262, 264
Boulez, Pierre, 198, 202
*Boxtrolls, The*, 139
*Boyhood*, 245
*Breathe In*, 12, 431–4, 436, 438, 442, 443n4
Bresson, Robert, 119
*Bridge, The*, 10, 321–8
British documentary, 11, 387–401
  influence of Soviet cinema on, 390
Brody, Richard, 290, 298
*Broken*, 75, 76, 189, 202, 314–16, 318, 411
Bujalski, Andrew, 289
*Burning Plain, The*, 164
Burns, Johnnie, 11
Burtt, Ben, 29, 277, 278
butterfly wing effect, 340

C
Cage, John, 26, 126, 128, 129, 262, 389, 392
Campan, Véronique, 130

Carlos, Wendy, 281, 317
*Carnival of the Animals*, 159
Carruth, Shane, 12, 431, 437, 438, 440–2
Cary, Tristram, 388, 394, 398–400
*Cat People*, 158, 164, 167n6
Cavalcanti, Alberto, 393, 394
CD format, 8
cellular film, 198
*chien andalou, Un*, 187
*Children of Men*, 7, 171, 174, 177, 178
China
  Chinese cinema, 239
  Chinese instruments, 229
  Cultural Revolution, 8, 229–31, 235, 241
  Open Door era, 241
  post-socialist project, 237
Chion, Michel, 2, 6, 7, 20, 76, 83, 92, 96, 97, 99, 115, 125, 126, 135n4, 135n5, 155, 167n5, 170, 173, 185, 188, 240, 293, 364, 368, 399, 415, 429, 430, 432, 443n2
cinematic *dispositif*, 362
cinematic realism, 249
cinematic sound, 154, 157, 158, 160, 161, 184, 191, 302
cinesonic transmigration, 11, 400
*Citizen Kane*, 371
classical music logo, 216
*Clockwork Orange, A*, 317
close-up
  auditory close-up, 186, 188, 190, 191
  corporeal close-up, 188
CMI, 277, 280
Coen brothers, 26, 166, 247
*Collage #1 (Blue Suede)*, 395
*collectionneuse, La (The Collector)*, 197
communism, 235, 236
Computer Music Instrument. *See* CMI
conventions, 4, 61, 67, 80, 81, 85, 155, 170, 173, 185, 208, 305–19, 353, 399, 405, 407, 437
Cook, Nicholas, 61
*Cop Land*, 7, 171, 178, 180
Coppola, Carmine, 34
Coppola, Francis Ford, 3, 18, 34, 160, 163, 273, 285n2, 368, 443n7
Coppola, Sofia, 9, 247, 261

*Crimson Petal and the White, The,* 307–9, 311
crystal-image, 8, 197–212. *See also* Deleuze, Gilles
*CSI,* 362, 371
Cuarón, Alfonso, 3, 7, 40, 92, 102, 103, 105, 113, 119, 165, 171

## D

D&AD Black Pencil, 377
Danna, Jeff, 78
*Dans ma peau,* 190
Davis, Paul, 40
DAW, 26, 59, 64, 82, 86n17, 274, 277–9, 284
*Days of Heaven,* 159, 161–3, 167n7
*Day the Earth Stood Still, The,* 214
3-D cinema, 92
*Dead Poets Society,* 26, 28
deafness, 165, 176
Debussy, Claude, 128, 129
Deleuze, Gilles, 210, 211, 211n2, 212n2, 372, 397
*Destination Moon,* 214
Devil Got My Woman, 246, 256–8
DGA, 26, 269
diegesis
  diegetic ambience, 79
  diegetic audible elements, 179
  diegetic clock, 413
  diegetic documentary, 200
  diegetic language, 409
  diegetic listening, 250
  diegetic music, 99, 100, 237, 327, 344, 407
  diegetic pop music, 236, 237, 414
  diegetic presence, 343
  diegetic sound, 11, 79–83, 159, 169, 172–4, 176, 177, 184, 236, 237, 253, 327, 352, 357n1, 398, 405, 409
  diegetic sound effects, 81–3, 273, 274, 348
  diegetic soundscape, 20, 230
  diegetic sounds of electricity, 80
  diegetic source, 224, 253
  diegetic space, 69, 85, 124, 126, 203, 230, 253
  diegetic world, 6, 81, 92, 100, 102, 208, 252
  extra-diegetic music, 156, 163
  non-diegetic film music, 273
  non-diegetic incidental music, 83
  non-diegetic music, 81, 82, 100, 103, 174, 176, 202, 209, 274, 306
  non-diegetic musical accompaniment, 397
  non-diegetic sound, 179, 180, 354, 357n1, 398
  non-diegetic status, 397
  non-diegetic voiceover, 253
  supra-diegetic mixing, 248, 249
Digital Audio Workstation. *See* DAW
digital instruments, 273–7, 282–5, 285n6. *See also* instruments
digital music file, 259
Digital Surround Sound, 99
digital synthesizers, 9, 273–86, 336, 337
digital technology, 5, 9, 29, 82, 245, 259, 273, 275, 284, 289
8Dio, 64
director-*mélomanes*. *See mélomanes*
Directors Guild of America. *See* DGA
direct sound, 198, 203, 204, 208, 210, 230, 239, 293, 294
Di, Zhang, 236
Doane, Mary Ann, 199, 368–9, 435, 439, 443n9
docudrama, 100. *See also* realism
documentary
  film, 239, 388, 391
  method, 230, 239
  soundtrack, 388, 390
  tradition, 387–401
Dolby
  Atmos, 6, 40, 93, 102, 108n2
  matrix, 43
  noise-reduction, 7, 160, 162
  non-Dolby film, 163
  pre-Dolby noises, 164
  Stereo, 98, 99
  stereophonic playback, 162
  surround sound, 93, 94, 99, 108, 161, 163, 442
  three-dimensional sounds, 163
*Don Juan,* 47, 206
*Donkey Kong,* 349, 357n2

*Donkey Kong, Jr*, 349
*Donnie Darko*, 166
*Don't Look Now*, 164
*Doors of Perception*, 124, 129, 130, 132, 133
Doppler effect, 172
Doremus, Drake, 12, 431–4, 442
double entendre, 158, 159, 166
*Double Indemnity*, 371
dramatic fiction, 333
dream states, 6, 114, 116–19
*Drinking Buddies*, 10, 291, 300–2
*Drive*, 51, 173, 185, 186, 188–90, 204, 211, 218, 267, 277, 278, 297, 309, 331, 339, 369, 381, 396
*Dr. Mario*, 349
*Duma*, 5, 33, 35, 36
*Dune*, 19, 26
Dunkley, Matt, 12, 421–8
dynamic control, 65
dynamic variation, 59

E
early sound films, 50, 390–3
*Earrings of Madame de, The*, 368
Edström, Carl, 10, 321–8
Eisenstein, Sergei, 83, 87n21, 187, 390–2
electroacoustic
  composers, 395
  music, 11, 388, 389, 395, 398
electronic synthesis, 388, 389, 398
electronic tonalities, 83, 350
*Elephant Man, The*, 19, 20, 23, 24
Ellitt, Jack, 388, 389, 392, 395
Eloy, Jean-Claude, 198, 199
embodied resonating listening, 125, 130–4
empathy/anempathy, 10, 24, 305–19, 335, 338
*Enemy Below, The*, 365, 366
Engber, Daniel, 185, 188
*English Patient, The*, 40
Eno, Brian, 75, 87n23
*Enthusiasm: Symphony of the Donbass*, 391, 430
*Epic Taiko Ensemble*, 64
equalization (EQ), 65, 115, 255

*Eraserhead*, 19, 20, 22, 29, 83
*Escape from New York*, 276, 281, 361
*Etude aux Chemins de Fer*, 397
*Everwood*, 64
experimental
  cinema, 387, 441
  music, 129
  sound, 391
*EXS24*, 63, 86n18

F
fake sound, 154, 156
*Family Finds Entertainment, A*, 372
Fantasy User Interfaces (FUIs), 363
*Farben*, 128
felt sound, 125, 131–4
fiction films, 7, 10, 101, 293, 355
fidelity paradigm, 292, 302
*Fight Club*, 166
film
  composers, 43, 70n2, 139, 143, 147, 263, 274, 281, 282, 421
  effects, 81, 332
  music, 1–3, 18, 45, 54, 68, 70n2, 79–81, 144, 150, 258, 261–70, 273, 285n3, 331–2, 335, 339, 344, 355, 364, 365, 397, 404, 408, 421, 431, 442
  musicality, 430
  phonograph, 389
  sound, 1–3, 6, 9, 17–21, 30, 45, 46, 49, 50, 54, 77–81, 108, 113, 120, 131, 154, 156, 165, 170, 171, 178, 179, 192n4, 203, 273–86, 293–5, 302, 363, 369, 377–84, 387–93, 400
Fincher, David, 57, 166, 318
first-person perspective, 98, 125, 130–2, 134
Fischinger, Oskar, 388
flashback, 203, 208, 224, 314, 335, 336, 370, 412
fluctuation range, 116
Foley artist, 155, 167n2, 186, 280, 296
*Forbidden Planet*, 10, 83, 350, 351, 353–5
Ford, Tom, 11, 403, 407, 409, 411, 412, 415, 417n17

Forman, Miloš, 160, 165
*forte*, 59
Foster, Geoff, 64, 422
Fremer, Michael, 280, 281
*Friday Night Lights*, 307
*Full Metal Jacket*, 163
*Full Moon*, 291, 298–300, 302
futzing, 115

### G

Gans, Christophe, 74
genre
   analogue, 245
   horror, 227, 290, 299
   machinic, 362
   music, 397
   science fiction, 361
   technoscientific, 361, 362, 366, 371–3
   thrillers, 120, 158, 216, 408
*Gerry*, 406
*Ghost World*, 8, 246, 248, 255–9
*Gladiator*, 63
Glazer, Jonathan, 11, 377, 382
Godard, Jean-Luc, 197, 294, 441
*Godfather, The*, 18, 368, 443n7
González Iñárritu, Alejandro, 169
Gorbman, Claudia, 2, 9, 86n8, 96, 305, 318n1
Gould, Glenn, 397, 413
*Goya's Ghosts*, 165
*Grandmother, The*, 19, 37
gravitational pull, 102–8
*Gravity*, 3, 6, 40, 92, 93, 102–8, 113–21
Great Depression, 46, 53
*Great Gatsby, The*, 12, 166, 425
Grierson, John, 390, 391, 393, 400
Griffith, D. W., 48
*Guardian, The* (newspaper), 310
Guattari, Felix, 397
*Guinness for You*, 398–400
Guldager, Erik, 322

### H

Hammer film, 8, 214, 217, 218, 224, 225
*Hannibal*, 261
*Hans Zimmer percussion*, 63, 64

*Happy Christmas*, 301
harmony, 12, 25n1, 26, 69, 146, 232, 234, 241, 315, 317, 341, 414, 431, 434
Hawksworth, Johnny, 396
HBO, 181n2, 294, 306, 307, 318
*Healer, The*, 164
hearing loss, 7, 175
Heidegger, Martin, 369, 373
*Henry and June*, 27, 31n6
Hermann, Bernard, 405
*Hilary and Jackie*, 165
hip-hop, 268, 308
Hitchcock, Alfred, 157, 158, 167n4
Hoérée, Arthur, 389
Hoffman, Eilam, 40
Holland, Agnieszka, 164
Hollywood
   and live screen performances, 5
   melodramas, 404
   pre-Hollywood, 157
   sound workers in, 53
   studios, 75, 109n4, 167n2, 286n8
Holowicki, E.J., 35
Holst, Gustav, 216
*Homeland*, 363, 371
Hometown Trilogy. *See Platform*; *Unknown Pleasures*; *Xiao Wu*
horror films. *See* genre
Howarth, Alan, 281
humanism
   humanistic metaphysics, 373
   post-humanism, 331
*Hunger*, 412, 413
Husserl, Edmund, 125, 127, 131, 134, 135n3, 135n6
Hykes, David, 26, 27
hyper-capitalism, 364
hyperinstruments, 5, 6, 64–70. *See also* instruments
hyperorchestra. *See also* digital technology
   hyper-drums, 66, 67
   hyperinstrument, 5, 6, 64–70
   hyperorchestration tools, 57–71
hyperreality, 58, 281, 282, 312
hyper-tonal, 336
hypnagogic, 118, 119
hypnopompic, 118, 119
*HZ01: Hans Zimmer Percussion London Ensembles*, 63

## I

IA, 45, 46, 53
*Idealisten*, 40
Ihde, Don, 125, 180
images/ideas, 85
image-sound, 200, 202, 369, 399, 435, 443n6
immersion, 4, 6, 74, 77, 84, 91–4, 102, 108, 188, 190, 257, 339
*Inception*, 47, 407
*Indiana Jones*, 68
Indiewood, 9, 245–59
innovations, 4, 5, 9, 93, 99, 100, 102, 160, 185, 274, 275, 284, 286n8, 306, 307
instruments
  acoustic piano, 336
  digital piano, 336, 338, 342, 345n5
  instrumental synthesizer, 332
  musical instrument industry, 275
  percussion, 198, 307
intensity, 23, 67, 129, 158, 185, 187, 189, 198, 217, 224, 226, 255, 259, 313, 389, 415
*Interstellar*, 66, 429, 430, 433
interstellar space, 91, 95, 106, 108
inter-subjective, 24, 113, 180, 234
*In the Mood for Love*, 407, 411
*intonarumori*, 128

## J

*Jackie Brown*, 255
Jameson, Fredric, 371
Janus Project, 305–19
Japan
  Japanese animé, 10
  Japanese cinema, 4, 333, 340
  Japanese culture, 10
Jarre, Maurice, 36, 37
*Jazz Singer, The*, 48
*Jin ju* (Jin opera), 230
*Mr. Jones*, 166
Jones, Geoffrey, 11, 396
Joyce, James, 21

## K

*Kabuki*, 340
Kahn, Douglas, 21, 390

Kaleta, Kenneth C., 20
Kantelinen, Tuomas, 421, 422
karaoke, 238, 242, 265
Katz, Aaron, 289
Kaufman, Philip, 19, 27, 31n6, 160
Kerins, Mark, 92, 99, 167n8, 192n4
*Keyboard* (magazine), 273, 274, 283, 285n1
*Kid Icarus*, 349
*Kill Bill: Volume 1*, 252
kinaesthetic, 93, 131, 135n6
*Kinectimals*, 36
kinescope, 213, 217
Kojima, Hideo, 74
Kolnai, Aurel, 184, 190
Konami, 73–5
Kondo, Koji, 349
*Kontakt*, 63
Korg's PS-3000, 275
Korine, Harmony, 12, 431, 434
Korzeniowski, Abel, 406, 408, 414
Kroeber, Ann, 5, 19, 25, 33–42
Kubrick, Stanley, 86n11, 92, 96, 98, 160, 163, 317
Kurtz, David, 282, 283

## L

Labarthe, André S., 200, 205
labour, 4, 5, 43–55, 274, 284, 291–6, 302
*Ladykillers, The*, 398
*L'amour fou*, 8, 197–212
*Last Days*, 6, 9, 123–5, 130, 132, 133
*Last Year in Marienbad*, 441
Lefebvre, Henri, 412
*Legend of Zelda, The*, 349, 351
Leigh, Walter, 11, 393–5
Leone, Sergio, 120, 430
*Letter from Siberia*, 370
Levi, Mica, 11, 381
Lewton, Val, 158, 162, 165
LFE, 101, 104, 107
Lievsay, Skip, 26
Ligeti, György, 128
Linklater, Richard, 245, 247

listening
  alert, 126
  filmic, 130
  listening from within, 132–4, 173
  mode, 126, 127, 130, 133, 134, 167n5, 235–9
  new, 127, 129
  open, 127–9, 132
  panic, 126–8, 130, 134
  vinyl, 246
*Lisztomania*, 160
*Little Big Man*, 370
lo-fi sound, 294, 295, 298, 300, 302
*Logan's Run*, 160
Logic X, 59, 62
*Look Who's Talking*, 368, 369, 373
*Look Who's Talking Now*, 373
*Look Who's Talking Too*, 368
loss of hearing, 7, 171, 175, 180
*Lost Highway*, 38
*Lost in Translation*, 9, 261, 263, 265–7, 269, 270
*Love, Actually*, 12, 425, 426
*Love on the Ground*, 208
Low Frequency Effects. *See* LFE
Lucas, George, 98, 115, 160, 161, 278, 285n2, 371
Luhrmann, Baz, 12, 166, 424, 425
Lynch, David, 5, 19–22, 27, 33, 37, 38, 42, 83, 192n2, 247, 323, 441
Lynne, Jeff, 262

M
Macar, Rich, 279
Malick, Terrence, 159–62, 407
*Man Escaped, A*, 119
manga, 333
*Man of Steel, The*, 66–8
Mansell, Clint, 12, 421, 422, 424
Maoism
  egalitarian socialism, 240
  Mao Zedong, 231, 232
  post-Mao period, 8, 231, 242
  reform-era, 8, 230, 231, 235, 237, 238
*Maquette*, 395
Marianelli, Dario, 6, 7, 124, 127, 139–50
*Marie Antoinette*, 9, 261, 266–8, 270

*Mario Bros.*, 349, 357n2, 358n10, 367
Mars, 216–18, 220, 227
Martinez, Cliff, 434
masking method, 126
McLuhan, Marshall, 58, 59
McQueen, Steve, 11, 403, 407, 413
MDL, 48, 50–4
mechanical trades, 52
med-lab, 224–5
*Melancholia*, 405, 406, 416n7
*mélomanes*, 9
memory, 4, 8, 27, 75, 78, 84, 144, 203, 229–43, 248, 277, 338, 339, 358n7, 362, 440
*Mentalist, The*, 64
mental representations, 94, 95, 97. *See also* spatial situation
Mercury Theatre, 215
metacompositional principle, 198
*Metal Gear Solid*, 74
meta-score, 333
metonymy, 23
metric rhythm, 128
*Metroid (Jeriaska)*, 349
micro-budget, 9, 30
microphone placement, 47, 66, 67, 292
MIDI, 10, 59, 62, 275–9, 283, 331–46, 421, 427. *See also* synthesizer
Minghella, Anthony, 40
*Mirages d'un Eldorado*, 308
mirror-image, 8, 354
mise-en-abyme, 231
*mise-en-bande*, 351
*mise-en-scène*, 167, 213, 214, 362, 433, 438, 442
misophonia, 188
  non-misophonic listener, 188
*Mix* (magazine), 274, 283
mixing, 6, 39, 57–71, 76, 77, 81, 99, 107, 179, 248, 249, 261–70, 278, 285n4, 293, 294, 327, 333, 339, 379, 384, 433, 438
Moholy-Nagy, László, 389
*Mojo* (magazine), 312
monophony, 276. *See also* synthesizer
montage, 251, 267, 285n2, 390–2, 394–6, 400, 403, 406–9, 413n7, 426, 434, 436, 439, 441
  voice-over montage, 395

Moog Music's Polymoog, 275. *See also* synthesizers
*Mosquito Coast, The*, 36
Motion Picture Editors Guild, 54, 55n16
Motion Picture Producers and Distributors of America (MPPDA), 46
motivated noise, 156
*Moulin Rouge!*, 12
Movietone, 47
mumblecore, 9, 289, 290, 293, 296, 300
  post-mumblecore, 289–91
Murch, Walter, 3, 18, 40, 113, 123, 130, 131, 161, 273, 285n2, 383, 387, 398
music
  abstract, 342
  canned, 45, 47, 49, 51, 52
  editing, 29, 34
  film music composers, 54
  game, 74, 75, 77, 78, 80, 81, 347–51, 353, 356, 357n3
  incidental, 75–8, 83
  keyboard, 336
  live, 44, 45, 47, 48, 50, 51, 53
  musical cushion, 12, 405
  musical object, 125, 127, 129, 134, 135n2, 216
  musical silence, 226, 357
  musical wallpaper, 69
  music as a collage, 261
  nationalist music, 234
  non-musical sources, 129
  non-signifying music, 339
  pop, 8, 236, 237, 246, 319n3, 414, 422
  popular, 9, 11, 230, 235, 236, 242, 295, 307, 349
  pre-existing popular, 307
  source, 238, 265, 327
  as a subset of sound, 61, 62, 69, 70
  technology, 82, 252, 253
  written, 26, 78, 276, 395
musical analysis, 61
Musical Instrument Digital Interface. *See* MIDI
musicality, 4, 5, 12, 26, 35, 36, 87n21, 106, 149, 430, 437, 441

musicalization
  of language, 437
  of sound effects, 431
  of soundtrack, 431–3
  of speech, 12, 429–43
musical object, 125, 127, 129, 134, 135n2, 216
musical sound, 76, 106, 128, 248, 279, 350, 351, 354, 388, 397
Music Defense League. *See* MDL
*musicianly listening*, 125, 132–4
musicology, 342
  traditional musicology, 61
*musique concrète*, 2, 26, 120, 125, 129–30, 134, 167n5, 273, 285n2, 342, 388, 389, 391, 394, 395, 397–9
Muzak, 10, 331–46

N

narrative
  classical, 167n3, 173, 437
  commentary, 9, 248
  film, 12, 431, 437, 439
  linear, 167n9, 406, 416n7
  multiple, 169, 415
  musico-narrative, 307
  present-day, 248
  screen, 361, 363
  submarine, 362
  time-line, 8
  tropes, 213
  unfolding, 410
  visual/narrative, 257
*Nashville*, 160
National Industrial Recovery Act (NIRA), 46
needle-drop, 249–51, 254–6
Neely, Blake, 64
neo-Victorianism, 308
NES, 348–51, 353, 356, 357, 358n7, 358n10
*Never Cry Wolf*, 28, 29, 38
New Documentary Film Movement, 239
New England Digital (NED), 277, 278, 283
New Wave, 197, 263
*New Yorker, The* (magazine), 290

*Night Mail*, 390
Nintendo Entertainment System. *See* NES
*Noah*, 12, 208, 422, 426
*Noh*, 340
noise
  absence of, 20
  list of, 21
  meaningful, 7, 153–67
  pollution, 20, 294
  speech-like, 24
  surface, 8, 248, 255–9
Nolan, Christopher, 64, 66, 407, 429
non-verbal utterances, 115, 116, 120
non-verbal vocalizations, 117–18
Nordic Noir, 10
nostalgia, 4, 86n7, 230, 237, 246
*nouvelle vague*, 197

O
*objets trouvés*, 128
Okada, Tohru, 332
*Old and New*, 390
optical sound recordings, 388, 391
Oram, Daphne, 11, 388, 396–8
orchestral
  faux-European, 340
  film, 80
  instruments, 62, 67
  music, 61, 106
  soundtrack, 120
  vocabulary, 422
Original Video Animation (OVA), 332
Oscar. *See* Academy Award
Otherness, 83, 355
Otherworld, 73, 76, 77, 85
*Outer Limits, The*, 215
overture, 11, 308, 309, 311, 403–17
  cinematic heritage of the overture, 405

P
Palmer, Christopher, 421
Palmer, Shelton Leigh, 283
panic listening, 126–8, 130, 134. *See also* listening
  as a non-referential listening, 127
*Parade*, 49, 128

parasitism, 370
*Paris nous appartient (Paris Belongs to Us)*, 197, 198
Penderecki, Krzysztof, 262, 263
*Persona*, 203, 313, 382
phenomenology, 123, 125–7, 131, 134, 135n3
phonetic language, 58, 59
phonographic reproduction, 333
*Pi*, 431
pianissimo, 162, 224
*Pianist, The*, 7, 170, 174, 175, 178, 333, 335, 336, 338, 345n4, 397
Piano Roll, 59, 60
*Pirates of the Caribbean: Dead Man's Chest*, 63
pitch, 59, 61, 69, 101, 114, 120, 128, 129, 135n4, 159, 176, 217, 225, 226, 234, 276, 277, 284, 315, 316, 348, 351, 353, 381, 383, 389, 397, 399, 414
*Platform (Zhantai)*, 229, 231, 234, 236, 237, 241
*Platoon*, 163
playback, 162, 189, 226, 246, 259, 274, 275, 277, 281, 388, 396, 414
POA
  point-of-audition events, 170, 174, 176
  point-of-audition sound, 169–81
*Poème electronique*, 129
point of audition. *See* POA
point of view. *See* POV
Polanski, Roman, 7, 171, 335
political propaganda, 230
polyphonic dissonance, 341
*Pong*, 317, 347, 348, 350
postproduction, 3, 9, 12, 18, 19, 29, 46, 51, 70, 107, 274, 275, 277, 278, 280, 283, 285, 285n4, 293, 294, 299–302, 321, 322, 325, 326, 339, 366, 367, 393, 424
*Potemkin*, 187
POV, 165, 217
*Prélude à l'après-midi d'un faune*, 128
Price, Steven, 103
*Pride and Prejudice*, 139, 141, 148
Primary Egocentric Reference Frame (PERF), 94, 95, 97, 104, 107

*Primer*, 437, 440
*Princess Bride, The*, 365, 366
*Priscilla, Queen of the Desert* (musical), 43, 44, 53
Programmable Sound Generator (PSG), 350
Prophet 5, 87n18, 275, 276, 280. *See also* synthesizers
Pro Tools, 23, 26, 27, 284, 82274
pseudo-orchestra, 339
pseudo-silence, 99–102, 107, 108
*Psycho*, 364, 407
psychological abnormality, 166
psychological beats, 203
*Pulp Fiction*, 8, 241, 246, 248, 251–5
*Punch-Drunk Love*, 305
punk, 9, 251, 261–70
pure music, 123, 198, 199. *See also* sound

## Q

*Quatermass* (1979, miniserie), 214
*Quatermass and the Pit* (1958-59) (US title: *Million Years to Earth*), 214
*Quatermass Experiment* (tv series, 1953), 8, 213, 214, 221
*Quatermass Experiment* (tv series, 2005), 8
*Quatermass II* (US title: *Enemy from Space*), 214
*Quatermass Xperiment, The* (film, 1955), 8, 214
*Quatermass Xperiment, The* (US title: *The Creeping Unknown*), 214
*quatre cents coups, Les* (*The 400 Blows*), 197

## R

racism, 256
Radigue, Elaine, 395
radio. *See also War of the Worlds*
radio with pictures, 216
Raeburn, Peter, 381
Rahman, A.R., 421, 422
*Raiders of the Lost Ark*, 163
Rainbow Voice, 26, 27
*Raising Arizona*, 368

realism, 97, 100, 104, 156, 160, 184, 185, 188, 249, 298, 305, 345n1, 378, 379
  sonic realism, 185
real-time sound synthesis, 274
rebirth, 119
reduced listening, 125, 127, 129, 134, 135n4
redundancy, 10, 11, 361–73
Reitzell, Brian, 9, 261–70
Renoir, Jean, 211
repetition, 10, 78, 344, 361, 363–6, 412, 415, 433–7, 439, 442
*Requiem for a Dream*, 166, 431
Resnais, Alain, 441
*Return of the Jedi*, 68
*Revanche*, 164
re-voice dialogue, 366
Reznor, Trent, 57, 86n5
rhythm, 61, 66, 69, 76, 79, 106, 124, 126–9, 135n4, 149, 205, 216–18, 232–5, 263, 309, 312, 317, 323, 351, 381, 383, 389, 392, 395, 411–13, 430, 433
  asymmetrical rhythm, 216, 218
Riley, Terry, 348
*Rising Sun*, 27, 28, 31n6
Rivette, Jacques, 8, 197–212
robotic humanoid, 51. *See also* sound
robots, 51, 52, 331–6, 341, 345n2
*Romance Sentimentale*, 390-2
*Romeo + Juliet*, 421
Rona, Jeff, 279
Ross, Atticus, 57
*Royal Tenenbaums, The*, 8, 246, 248–51, 254, 255
Russolo, Luigi, 21, 128, 129
Ruttmann, Walter, 389–92

## S

Saint-Saëns, Camille, 159
*Salmon Fishing in the Yemen*, 139
sample libraries, 5, 62–4, 66, 67, 71n6. *See also* hyperorchestra
Satie, Erik, 128, 129, 336
*Saving Private Ryan*, 7, 170, 171, 173, 174, 178, 181n3

464　INDEX

*Scanners*, 276
Schaeffer, Pierre, 76, 125, 127–9, 132, 134, 135n2, 135n4, 167n5, 285n2, 389, 394, 395
sci-fi/mystical anime, 333
score, 2, 3, 5–7, 9–12, 26, 34, 43, 58–64, 67, 69, 70, 75–9, 81–4, 116, 120, 128, 139–41, 143, 144, 147–9, 159, 161, 176, 179, 198, 207, 217, 224, 227, 256, 263–5, 269, 273, 276, 281, 282, 299, 306–8, 311–13, 318, 324, 326–8, 332, 334, 337, 339–44, 347–50, 354, 364, 381, 383, 389, 398, 399, 404–10, 412–15, 421, 424–7, 430, 431, 433–5, 437, 440
Scott, Ridley, 46, 63, 86n10, 91, 109n3, 188, 354, 416n3
screen media, xiii, 1, 3, 5–7, 12, 18, 27–9
self-reflexivity, 334, 342
semiotics, 113, 114, 120, 121, 153, 156, 165, 312, 348
sensuousness, 430, 442
Serafine, Frank, 273, 276, 279–84, 286n12
*Sex and the City*, 373
*Sexy Beast*, 377
*Shame*, 11, 12, 43, 403–17
Shenkerian reduction, 61
Shields, Kevin, 265, 268, 269
Sieling, Charlotte, 321, 322, 327
silence. *See also* vacuum
　fear of, 28
　musical, 226, 357
　pseudo-silence, 99–102, 107, 108
　witnessed, 108
silent films, 17, 154, 167n2, 348, 369
　silent actors, 47
*Silent Hill 2*, 74, 75, 78, 80
*Silent Hill 3*, 74, 75
*Silent Hill* (film), 6, 73–87
*Silent Hill* (franchise, video game), 6, 73–87
*Silent Hill: Revelation*, 74, 79, 80
*Silver Bullets*, 10, 290, 291, 296, 299
*Single Man, A*, 11, 12, 403–17
Single, Steve, 379
*Skin, The*, 21, 128, 185, 188–90, 209, 343, 377–84, 438, 440

slapback, 84
slow sinusoidal wave (LFO), 66
SMPTE, 275–9, 281
*Snow*, 11, 395–8, 400, 408, 409
*Social Network, The*, 57, 58, 64, 67, 68
Society for Motion Picture Technicians and Engineers. *See* SMPTE
Söderqvist, Johan, 10, 322, 326, 328
softstudios, 82
*Solaris*, 120
*Soloist, The*, 7, 141, 143, 144, 166
*Somewhere*, 36, 130, 140, 266, 292, 296, 313, 315, 323, 364, 380, 388, 399, 411, 423, 439
*Song of Ceylon*, 11, 388, 390, 393–5, 400
sonic
　ambience, 85
　hapticity, 7, 188
　space, 43, 223, 227–8, 235
Sonnenschein, David, 2, 6, 28, 100, 113–21
*Sopranos, The*, 306
soulfulness, 332
sound
　absence of, 27, 170
　affective, 7, 156, 157, 163, 167n6
　alteration, 65, 66
　ambiguous, 83, 356
　arrival of synchronized, 47, 55n10
　baby, 367–70
　bad, 9, 289
　breathing, 24, 189
　cacophony of, 172
　close-up, 175, 179
　created by words, 25
　direct sound, 198, 203, 204, 208, 210, 230, 239, 293, 294
　electronic, 115, 116, 225–8, 282, 339, 388, 395, 400, 440
　electrostatic, 79
　embodied, 130
　encoded, 130
　hyper-real, 165, 166, 167n9
　hyper-synchronous, 22
　infrasound, 185
　lack of, 5, 97
　of machines, 10
　materials, 100
　moist sounds, 7, 186, 190, 191

monophonic, 160, 179
naturalistic, 120, 394
non-human, 4, 10, 11, 370
on-the-air, 114, 120
playback, 226
from the real world, 165
recorded, 6, 11, 44, 45, 47–54, 58, 63, 67, 82, 123–5, 129, 134, 160, 162, 208, 273, 285n2, 337, 372, 380, 389, 391, 392, 430
recording, 5, 25, 33–42, 58, 65, 66, 82, 155, 203, 239, 273, 277, 292, 294, 300, 302, 366, 388, 391, 398, 400, 441
sound/image, 200, 202, 369, 399
spectra, 62
stereophonic, 160
stylized, 323
typewriter, 124–8, 134, 140, 392, 394
underwater, 172
urban, 11
wind, 383
sound design
composition as, 69–70
holistic approach, 3
sound designer, 3, 10, 11, 19, 22, 26–9, 33, 35, 38, 40, 41, 43, 69, 70, 75, 82, 104, 130, 145, 146, 239, 273, 277, 280–3, 285n4, 286n13, 290, 291, 299, 300, 321, 322, 326, 328, 349, 356, 377, 382, 387
SoundDroid, 278, 279. *See also* synthesizers, sound editing
sound effects
musicalization of, 431
real sounds, 198, 378, 379
sound experienced as, 124
*Sound Mountain* (sound effects library), 5, 19, 23, 33 (*see also* sound effects)
sound object (*objet sonore*), 125, 127, 129, 130, 134, 158, 191, 355
soundscape
heterogeneous, 238
of modernity, 394
of western art music, 388
Sound Spheres model, 116, 118, 121
soundtrack. *See also* musicalization, of soundtrack

evolution of, 3
hierarchy, 12, 429–43, 437
integrated, 2, 3, 9, 12, 30, 92, 108, 354, 387, 393, 400, 421–8
non-diegetic musical, 251
non-musical, 252
optical, 160, 388, 389, 391
pop, 246
satirical, 237
*Sound Waves* (magazine), 49, 50
*Space Invaders*, 348, 357n1 (*see also* vacuum, in space)
space vacuum, 91–109. *See also* vacuum, in space
spatial
placement, 65, 66
presence, 91–109
situation, 94, 97
spatial situation model (SSM), 94, 97
speech, 2, 6, 11, 12, 23, 25, 27, 28, 30, 48, 113–15, 117, 120, 126, 130, 169, 205, 227, 292, 361, 365–9, 373, 387, 388, 393, 395, 400, 429–43. *See also* musicalization, of speech
*Spiegel Im Spiegel*, 406
Spielberg, Steven, 7, 170, 317, 362
Spielmann, Götz, 164
Splet, Alan, 5, 19–24, 26–9, 30n4, 33, 83
*Spring Breakers*, 12, 431, 433–7, 442, 443n5
Springsteen, Bruce, 178
*Star Is Born, A*, 160
*Star Trek*, 101, 104, 109n3, 215, 281, 351, 361
*Star Trek: The Motion Picture*, 276, 280, 281, 286n12
*Star Wars*, 42, 98, 99, 101, 115, 160, 161, 163, 277, 362, 371, 404
Statement on Sound, 390
*39 Steps, The*, 157–9, 164
Stockhausen, Karlheinz, 198, 199, 313
*Stoker*, 166
*StormDrum 3*, 64
Strauss, Richard, 96, 128
superfield, 92, 99, 100
*Superman*, 163
*Super Mario Bros.*, 349, 357n2, 358, 367

*Super Metroid*, 357
*Super Sentai*, 372
surreal sound, 165, 166, 167n6
*Suzanne Simonin, Religieuse de Denis Diderot, LA (The Nun)*, 197
Swanberg, Joe, 9, 289–302
*Swan Lake*, 424
synchronicity, 234
synchronous and asynchronous sound, 22
syncopated audio-visual rhymes, 439
synthesized sounds, 5, 9, 64, 66, 224, 274, 277, 281
synthesizers
  analogue, 275, 276
  digital, 9, 273–86, 336, 337
  DX-7, 276
  polyphonic, 275
  sound editing, 278, 281
  Synclavier, 277, 278, 282, 283, 286n9–11

T
tactile elements, 140
taiko drum, 64
Taiwanese pop music, 8
Takemitsu, Toru, 28, 262
Tanaka, Hirokazu (hip), 10, 347–58
Tapia de Veer, Cristobal, 10, 305–19
Tarkovsky, Andrei, 120, 188, 430
technoscientific, 11, 361–3, 366, 371–3
Teen Beat, 396–8
teen-oriented, 333. *See also* anime
*Telegraph, The* (newspaper), 311
*Telemusik*, 199
tempered scale, 61
terror, 106, 114–16, 119, 172, 187, 242
Tezuka, Osamu, 333
theatre, 40, 43–5, 47–52, 55n11, 99, 102, 109n6, 109n8, 146, 148, 154, 159–62, 184, 201, 213, 215, 230, 231, 340, 369, 404, 424
theatrical crystal, 211
Thèberge, Paul, 9, 274–6, 283, 285n6
*There Will Be Blood*, 7, 171, 174, 175, 177, 178, 305
*Thin Red Line, The*, 407
3-D sound, 91–109
*Three Kings*, 7, 170, 173–5, 178, 181n4
*Three Men and a Baby*, 368

*Thunderball*, 367, 370
timbre, 61, 128, 129, 227, 234, 262, 276, 308, 313–15, 342, 349, 355, 397, 410, 412, 414
time, 1, 2, 4, 8, 18–22, 28, 29, 34, 37–9, 41, 42, 44–52, 54, 57, 59, 61, 62, 64, 66, 69, 70, 71n6, 75, 76, 79–81, 98, 103, 114, 115, 123, 133, 139–46, 148, 150, 153–5, 158, 161, 164, 166, 170, 173, 174, 176, 177, 180, 189, 201, 203–5, 208, 209, 214–16, 220, 221, 223–7, 229, 230, 232–6, 238, 240, 241, 243, 245, 246, 250, 252–4, 256, 257, 261–4, 266–8, 274–6, 280–2, 285n4, 300, 308, 311, 316–18, 323–8, 331–46, 351–4, 357n1, 362, 366, 371, 372, 378, 379, 381, 384, 396, 399, 400, 404, 406, 407, 410–15, 417n18, 423–8, 431–3, 435, 436, 439–41, 443n3
*Time Machine, The*, 214
*Time of Eve (Evu no jikan)*, 10, 331–46
tinnitus, 175, 177–9
*Tommy*, 160
tonality, 83, 128, 189, 224, 350, 351, 353, 381
*Top Gun*, 371, 372
Tourneur, Jacques, 158
*Traffic*, 434
*Trainspotting*, 166
*Train to Shaoshan (Huoche xiangzhe Shaoshan pao)*, 231
transectorial innovation, 9, 274, 275
transitional music, 220
trauma, 7, 116, 171, 179, 181n2, 316, 335, 338, 438, 440
*Travelling in Suzhou (Gusu xing)*, 231, 234
Trecartin, Ryan, 372
Tri-Ergon, 392
*Trois nocturnes: Nuages*, 128
*Tron*, 279–81
*Trouble Every Day*, 189, 190
Tryon, Chuck, 289, 290
*24*, 307, 362, 363, 366, 371
*24 Exposures*, 290, 299
*12 Years a Slave*, 415
*Twilight Zone, The*, 215
*Twin Peaks*, 323

## U

ultrafield, 92, 99–103, 106
ultra-low-budget, 291, 293, 298, 300–2
*Ulysses*, 21
Umebayashi, Shigeru, 407
*Unbearable Lightness of Being, The*, 27, 28, 31n6
*Uncle Kent*, 293, 298
*Under the Skin*, 11, 377–84
*Unknown Pleasures (Ren xiaoyao)*, 229, 240–2
unwatchable, 183
*Upstream Color*, 12, 431, 437–42
*Utopia*, 10, 305–19

## V

vacuum. *See also* space vacuum
  cinematic space, 95, 108
  objective-internal sound, 96, 97, 100, 107
  silent, 98
  in space, 91, 103
Van Leeuwen, Theo, 6, 113, 116
Van Sant, Gus, 6, 9, 123, 124, 133, 406
Varèse, Edgar, 129, 389
verbal *chiaroscuro*, 431–3, 436, 437
*Vertigo*, 405, 407–9, 415, 416, 417n15, 417n16
Vertov, Dziga, 389, 391, 392, 430
*V for Vendetta*, 139
*V/H/S*, 299
video games, 3, 5, 6, 10, 33, 36, 40, 64, 73–7, 80, 81, 84, 85, 86n5, 87n22, 91, 98, 191n1, 227, 269, 280, 311, 319n6, 347, 349, 355, 357, 435
*Video Games Live*, 347
video game sound, 5, 80, 81, 280, 347
vinyl records
  vinyl aficionado, 247
  vinyl-centricity, 250, 252
  vinylphiles, 247
  vinylphilic, 247
  vinyl sound, 247, 249, 251, 255, 258, 259
violence
  listening to violence, 7, 169–81
  sonic, 185, 186

*Virgin Suicides, The*, 9, 261–4, 266–8
visual darkness, 219
visuocentrism, 125
Vitaphone, 47
*Vivre sa vie*, 294
vococentrism, 114
voice
  voice-in, 114, 155, 239, 240, 253, 361–73, 428
  voice-off, 361–73, 443n9
Voinov, Nikolai, 389
von Trier, Lars, 190, 405, 406, 416, 416n7, 416n9

## W

*Wall:E*, 30
*War of the Worlds*, 215, 216, 220, 222, 226
*Weekend*, 391, 392
Weir, Peter, 19, 26, 27, 36–8
Welles, Orson, 215, 216, 222, 371
Wells, H.G., 214–16, 222
Westerkamp, Hildegard, 6, 123, 124, 129, 132–4
Western music, 58, 61, 67, 127
Western orchestra, 58
West, Ti, 290, 299
Wilcox, Fred M., 10, 83, 350
Williams, John, 161, 404
*Wire, The*, 294, 302, 306, 307
Wishart, Trevor, 313
Wood, Robin, 200–2, 211
World War I, 45
World War II, 11, 158, 167n5, 174, 214, 220, 285n2, 388, 389, 400, 401n1, 407
  post-war, 214
Wright, Basil, 11, 296, 388, 390, 391, 393–5
Wright, Joe, 6, 7, 123, 139, 166, 431

## X

Xiaoping, Deng, 237, 241
*Xiao Wu*, 229, 231, 237–41

## Y

Yamaoka, Akira, 74, 75, 78, 84, 86n3, 86n4, 86n6
Yoshiura, Yasuhiro, 10, 332
*Young and Innocent*, 157–9
Young, La Monte, 348

## Z

Zhangke, Jia, 8, 229–43
Zhelinski, Nikolai, 389
Zimmer, Hans, 63, 64, 66, 407, 408, 415, 417n14
*Zone, The*, 10, 291, 293, 298–300, 302

The manufacturer's authorised representative in the EU is Springer Nature Customer Service Centre GmbH, Europaplatz 3, 69115 Heidelberg, Germany. If you have any concerns regarding our products, please contact ProductSafety@springernature.com

Printed and bound by CPI Group (UK) Ltd, Croydon, CR0 4YY

25/03/2026

02078225-0012